**Biographical Dictionary of
American Sports**

BASEBALL,
REVISED AND EXPANDED EDITION

Biographical Dictionary of American Sports

BASEBALL, REVISED AND EXPANDED EDITION
A–F

Edited by David L. Porter

GREENWOOD PRESS
Westport, Connecticut • London

Library of Congress Cataloging-in-Publication Data

Biographical dictionary of American sports. Baseball / edited by
  David L. Porter.—Rev. and expanded ed.
     p. cm.
   Includes bibliographical references (p.) and index.
   Contents: [1] A–F — [2] G–P — [3] Q–Z.
   ISBN 0–313–29884–X (set : alk. paper). — ISBN 0–313–31174–9 (A–F
: alk. paper). — ISBN 0–313–31175–7 (G–P : alk. paper). — ISBN
0–313–31176–5 (Q–Z : alk. paper)
   1. Baseball—United States Biography Dictionaries. 2. Baseball—
United States—History. I. Porter, David L., 1941– .
II. Title: Baseball.
GV865.A1B55   2000
796.357'092'273—dc21   99–14840
  [B]

British Library Cataloguing in Publication Data is available.

Copyright © 2000 by David L. Porter

Library of Congress Catalog Card Number: 99–14840
ISBN: 0–313–29884–X (set)
      0–313–31174–9 (A–F)
      0–313–31175–7 (G–P)
      0–313–31176–5 (Q–Z)

First published in 2000

Greenwood Press, 88 Post Road West, Westport, CT 06881
An imprint of Greenwood Publishing Group, Inc.
www.greenwood.com

Printed in the United States of America

The paper used in this book complies with the
Permanent Paper Standard issued by the National
Information Standards Organization (Z39.48–1984).

10 9 8 7 6 5 4 3 2 1

Cover photographs: National Baseball Hall of Fame Library, Cooperstown, NY.

Unless otherwise credited, all photographs appearing in this volume are courtesy of the National
Baseball Hall of Fame Library, Cooperstown, NY.

Every reasonable effort has been made to trace the owners of copyright materials in this book,
but in some instances this has proven impossible. The editor and publisher will be glad to
receive information leading to more complete acknowledgments in subsequent printings of the
book and in the meantime extend their apologies for any omissions.

Contents

Illustrations

VOLUME 3

Photos for Volume 3 follow page 1509.

Preface

The *Biographical Dictionary of American Sports (BDAS)* series began because of a need for a scholarly, comprehensive biographical dictionary of notable American athletic figures. Sports encyclopedias typically had concentrated on statistical achievements of notable American athletic figures and contained comparatively little biographical background data. Sports biographies, meanwhile, usually featured just the greatest or most prominent athletic figures.

The *BDAS* series, consisting of six volumes published between 1987 and 1995, has profiled 3,383 notable American sports figures. To date, 973 entries have featured major league baseball players, managers, umpires, and/or executives. A majority appeared in a 1987 volume devoted exclusively to baseball, while the remainder were included in either the 1992 or 1995 supplemental volumes.

This three-volume book, arranged alphabetically, features 1,450 baseball entries. It contains revised and updated entries for all 973 figures included in the earlier volumes. These figures typically compiled impressive career statistical records as players, managers, coaches, umpires, and/or executives. One quarter are members of the National Baseball Hall of Fame in Cooperstown, New York. The position players often batted above .300 lifetime with at least 2,000 career hits and/or 300 career home runs. In some instances, they demonstrated remarkable fielding and/or running abilities. Starting pitchers typically compiled at least 175 major league victories with outstanding win–loss percentages and excellent earned run averages, while relief pitchers ranked among career save leaders.

An additional 477 baseball luminaries who have helped shape the development of the national pastime from the mid–nineteenth century to the present are also profiled. Roberto Alomar, Jeff Bagwell, Albert Belle, Dante Bichette, Craig Biggio, Kevin Brown, Ken Caminiti, David Cone, Andres

Galarraga, Tom Glavine, Juan Gonzalez, Ken Griffey, Jr., Randy Johnson, David Justice, Chuck Knoblauch, Barry Larkin, Kenny Lofton, Greg Maddux, Edgar Martinez, Pedro Martinez, Tino Martinez, Mike Mussina, Mike Piazza, Ivan Rodriguez, Garry Sheffield, John Smoltz, Sammy Sosa, Frank Thomas, Jr., Mo Vaughn, Larry Walker, Matt Williams, and other current stars with several years of major league experience are featured for the first time.[1] A vast majority of the new entries are former major league players, managers, umpires, and executives. New baseball entries also include 31 Negro League and 33 All-American Girls Professional Baseball League (AAGPBL) stars. The AAGPBL operated from 1943 to 1954. Jean Faut Eastman, Betty Weaver Foss, Dottie Kamenshek, Sophie Kurys, Dottie Schroeder, Joanne Weaver, Connie Wisniewski, and other AAGPBL players are profiled.

The selection of the new baseball entries proved very challenging. Before making final choices, the editor thoroughly researched several baseball encyclopedias and histories.[2] Frederick Ivor-Campbell assisted in the selection of nineteenth-century personalities, while Rick Center suggested many AAGPBL entries. Other contributors also suggested subjects worthy of inclusion. Of course, the editor assumes ultimate responsibility for any significant baseball figures inadvertently excluded from this volume.

The additional baseball entries met three general criteria. First, they either were born in or spent their childhood years in the United States. Foreigners who made exceptional impacts on the national pastime are also covered. Second, they typically compiled impressive statistical records. Major leaguers, for example, batted above .275 with at least 1,000 hits and/or 100 home runs, recorded at least 100 major league victories with fine win–loss percentages and/or earned run averages, demonstrated fine fielding and/or running abilities, or excelled as managers, coaches, umpires, or executives. Third, they made a major impact on professional baseball, earning significant awards or performing for championship teams.

Biographies usually indicate the subject's full given name at birth; date and place of birth and, when applicable, date and place of death; parental background; formal education; spouse and children, when applicable; and major personal characteristics. Entries feature the subject's baseball career through December 1999 and typically include information about his or her entrance into professional baseball; positions played; teams played for with respective leagues;[3] lifetime batting, fielding, and/or pitching records and achievements; individual records set, awards won, and All-Star and World Series appearances; and impact on baseball. Biographical and statistical data frequently proved elusive for Negro Leaguers and early major leaguers. Entries on managers usually cover their teams guided, with inclusive dates; major statistical achievements; career win–loss records with percentages; premier players piloted; and managerial philosophy, strategy, and innovations.

Biographies of club executives, league officials, umpires, sportswriters, and sportscasters describe their various positions held, notable accomplishments, and impact on baseball.

Brief bibliographies list pertinent sources for each biographical entry. Authors benefited from interviews or correspondence with biographical subjects, relatives, or acquaintances. Former major leaguers and AAGPBL players proved especially cooperative in furnishing information. The National Baseball Library in Cooperstown, New York, *The Sporting News* in St. Louis, MO, the Northern Indiana Historical Society in South Bend, IN, college, university, and public libraries, radio and television networks, newspapers, and magazines also provided invaluable assistance. When an entry cites a subject covered elsewhere in this book, an asterisk follows the person's name. Appendices list biographical entries by place of birth and players alphabetically by main position played. Other Appendices list major league managers, executives, and/or umpires, National Baseball Hall of Fame members, Negro Leaguers, and AAGPBL players.

One hundred fifty-two contributors, mostly members of the Society for American Baseball Research or North American Society for Sport History, contributed baseball entries for this revised and expanded volume. Sixty-seven people contributed new baseball entries for this volume. Most authors are university or college professors with baseball expertise. School teachers, administrators, writers, publishers, editors, journalists, librarians, businessmen, government employees, clergymen, consultants, and others also participated. Contributors are cited alphabetically with occupational affiliation following the index.

The editor deeply appreciates the enormous amount of time, energy, and effort expended by contributors in searching for biographical information. I am especially grateful to William E. Akin, Dennis S. Clark, Scott A.G.M. Crawford, John L. Evers, John R. Hillman, Frederick Ivor-Campbell, William J. Miller, Frank J. Olmsted, Frank V. Phelps, James A. Riley, Duane A. Smith, Luther W. Spoehr, Robert E. Weir, and Jerry J. Wright, each of whom wrote at least 10 new baseball entries. Akin, Evers, David Fitzsimmons, James N. Giglio, Hillman, George W. Hilton, Miller, Scot E. Mondore, Olmsted, Riley, Victor Rosenberg, William M. Simons, Edward J. Tassinari, Sarah L. Ulerick, and Weir kindly agreed to write additional entries when contributor Stan W. Carlson died in December 1996 and when other last-minute cancellations occurred. Mondore, Bill Deane, and Richard Topp supplied family information on numerous players. Biographical subjects, relatives, or acquaintances often furnished data. Richard H. Gentile and Thomas C. Eakin sent biographical material on Massachusetts and Ohio entries, respectively. William Penn University librarians again provided considerable assistance. Cynthia Harris gave adept guidance and helped in the planning and writing of this volume, while Elizabeth Meagher furnished valuable assistance in the production stage. As always, my wife, Marilyn, demonstrated considerable patience, understanding, and support throughout the project.

NOTES

1. Several other promising stars are not included because they are still in the early phases of their major league careers.

2. The principal baseball reference sources examined for major league baseball players included *The Baseball Encyclopedia*, 10th ed. (New York, 1996); John Thorn et al., eds., *Total Baseball*, 5th ed. (New York, 1997); David Nemec, *The Great Encyclopedia of 19th Century Major League Baseball* (New York, 1997); David Neft et al., eds., *The Sports Encyclopedia: Baseball* (New York, 1997); Charles F. Faber, *Baseball Ratings: The All-Time Best Players at Each Position*, 2d ed. (Jefferson, NC, 1995); *The Complete 1998 Baseball Record Book* (St. Louis, MO, 1998); *The Sporting News Official Baseball Register, 1998* (St. Louis, MO, 1998); *The Sporting News Official Baseball Guide, 1998* (St. Louis, MO, 1998); and Mike Shatzkin, ed., *The Ballplayers* (New York, 1990). James A. Riley, *The Biographical Encyclopedia for the Negro Baseball Leagues* (New York, 1994) and W. C. Madden, *The Women of the All-American Girls Professional Baseball League: A Biographical Dictionary* (Jefferson, NC, 1997) proved invaluable sources for Negro League and AAGPBL players, respectively.

3. Professional major leagues represented include the National Association (1871–1875), National League (1876–), American Association (1882–1891), Union Association (1884), Players League (1890), American League (1901–), Federal League (1914–1915), Negro National League (1920–1931, 1933–1948), Eastern Colored League (1923–1928), East-West League (1932), Negro Southern League (1932), Negro American League (1933–1950), and All-American Girls Professional Baseball League (1943–1954).

Abbreviations

The abbreviations, listed alphabetically, include associations, baseball terms, conferences, journals, leagues, organizations, and reference sources mentioned in the text and bibliographies.

AA	American Association
AAGPBL	All-American Girls Professional Baseball League
AAGPBLPA	All-American Girls Professional Baseball League Players Association
AAU	Amateur Athletic Union
ABA	American Basketball Association
ABC	American Broadcasting Company
ABCA	American Baseball Coaches Association
ABL	American Basketball League
AC	Athletic Club
ACAB	*Appleton's Cyclopaedia of American Biography*
ACBC	American College Baseball Coaches
ACC	Atlantic Coast Conference
ACFL	Atlantic Coast Football League
AFL	American Football League
AH	*American Heritage*
AHI	*American History Illustrated*
AIL	Arizona Instructional League
AL	American League
AlFL	Alabama-Florida League
AlL	Alaskan League

AlSL   Alaska Summer League
AM   *American Mercury*
AmBC   American Bowling Congress
AMeL   Arizona-Mexico League
AML   Arkansas-Missouri League
AmLit   *American Literature*
AmM   *American Magazine*
ANL   American Negro League
AOA   American Olympic Association
AP   Associated Press
ApL   Appalachian League
ArSL   Arizona State League
ArTL   Arizona-Texas League
AS   *American Scholar*
ASL   Alabama State League
AtA   Atlantic Association
AtL   Atlantic League
AtM   *Atlantic Monthly*
AV   *American Visions*
BA   *Baseball America*
BAA   Basketball Association of America
BBM   *Beckett's Baseball Monthly*
BBWAA   Baseball Writers Association of America
BC   Business College
BD   *Baseball Digest*
BDAC   *Biographical Dictionary of the American Congress*
BEaC   Big East Conference
BEC   Big Eight Conference
BeL   Bethlehem Steel League
BGL   Blue Grass League
BH   *Baseball History*
BHR   *Baseball Historical Review*
BL   Border League
BL   *Boy's Life*
BM   *Baseball Magazine*
BNC   Big Nine Conference
BoM   *Boston Magazine*

BPBP	Brotherhood of Professional Baseball Players
BPRA	Bowling Proprietory Association of America
BPY	Baseball Players of Yesterday
BQ	*Baseball Quarterly*
BR	*Boston Referee*
BRJ	*Baseball Research Journal*
BRL	Blue Ridge League
BRQ	*Baseball Research Quarterly*
BRS	Bottomley Ruffing Schalk
BRuL	Babe Ruth League
BS	*Black Sports*
BSC	Big Six Conference
BSL	Bi-State League
BStL	Big State League
BT	*Biography Today*
BTC	Big Ten Conference
BUDS	Baseball Umpire Development School
BVL	Blackstone Valley League
BW	*Baseball Weekly*
CA	Central Association
CA	*Contemporary Authors*
CAB	*Cyclopedia of American Biography*
CAD	*Coach and Athletic Director*
CaL	California League
CAL	Canadian-American League
CaPL	Canadian Provincial League
CarA	Carolina Association
CaSL	California State League
CB	*Current Biography Yearbook*
CBCA	College Baseball Coaches of America
CbL	Cumberland League
CBS	Columbia Broadcasting System
CC	Community College
CCNY	City College of New York
CCo	*Cooperstown Corner*
CCSL	Copper Country Soo League
CdL	Colorado League

CH	*Chicago History*
ChNL	Chicago National League
CIF	California Interscholastic Federation
CIL	Central Interstate League
CKAL	Central Kentucky Amateur League
CL	Central League
ClL	Colonial League
CmA	Commercial Association
CML	Connie Mack League
CnL	Canadian League
CNL	Cuban National League
CNN	Cable News Network
CntL	Continental League
CoC	Country Club
CoPL	Coastal Plain League
CPL	Central Pennsylvania League
CPrL	Canadian Provincial League
CQR	*Congressional Quarterly Researcher*
CrA	Carolina Association
CrL	Carolina League
CRL	Cocoa Rookie League
CSC	*Canadian Sports Collector*
CSL	Cotton States League
CSSL	California State Semipro League
CtL	Connecticut League
CtSL	Connecticut State League
CUL	Cuban League
CUSL	Cuban Summer League
CUWL	Cuban Winter League
CWL	California Winter League
DAB	*Dictionary of American Biography*
DaM	*Dawn Magazine*
DH	designated hitter
DIB	*Dictionary of International Biography*
DL	Dakota League
DM	*Dodgers Magazine*
DRWL	Dominican Republic Winter League

DSM	*Diamond Sports Memorabilia*
DT	*Delaware Today*
EA	Eastern Association
EaIL	Eastern Intercollegiate Athletic League
ECA	Eastern Championship Association
ECAC	Eastern Collegiate Athletic Association
ECaL	Eastern Carolina League
ECL	Eastern Colored League
EDL	Eastern Dixie League
EIL	Eastern Interstate League
EL	Eastern League
EPL	East Penn League
ERA	earned run average
ESL	Eastern Shore League
ESPN	Eastern Sports Network
ESUTS	Eastern States Umpire Training School
ETL	East Texas League
EvL	Evangeline League
EWL	East-West League
FBC	Fox Broadcasting Network
FCA	Fellowship of Christian Athletes
FECL	Florida East Coast League
FIL	Florida International League
FInL	Florida Instructional League
FL	Federal League
FlL	Florida League
FSL	Florida State League
FWL	Far West League
GAL	Georgia-Alabama League
GC	Golf Club
GCL	Gulf Coast League
GCRL	Gulf Coast Rookie League
GFL	Georgia-Florida League
GML	Green Mountain League
GQ	*Gentlemen's Quarterly*
GSL	Georgia State League
HAF	Helms Athletic Foundation

HB	*Harper's Bazaar*
HR	home run(s)
HRL	Hudson River League
IA	International Association
IAD	*Italian-American Digest*
IAL	Inter-American League
IaL	Iowa League
IBA	International Baseball Association
ID	*In Dixieland*
IdSL	Idaho State League
IIAC	Illinois Intercollegiate Athletic Conference
IIL	Illinois-Iowa League
IInL	Illinois-Indiana League
IlML	Illinois-Missouri League
IlSL	Illinois State League
IL	International League
Ind	Independent
InL	Instructional League
IOBL	Idaho-Oregon Baseball League
IOL	Iron and Oil League
IoSL	Iowa State League
IS	*Inside Sports*
ISA	Interstate Association
ISDL	Iowa and South Dakota League
ISL	Interstate League
IVL	Imperial Valley League
IvL	Ivy League
JAC	*Journal of American Culture*
JC	Junior College
JCL	Japan Central League
JEE	*Journal of Economic Education*
JeSH	*Jewish Sports History*
JPC	*Journal of Popular Culture*
JPL	Japanese Pacific League
JSH	*Journal of Sport History*
JSS	*Jewish Social Studies*
JW	*Journal of the West*

KL	Kitty League
KOML	Kansas-Oklahoma-Missouri League
KSL	Kansas State League
LCS	League Championship Series
LD	*Literary Digest*
LL	Longhorn League
LM	*Lippincott's Magazine*
LPGA	Ladies Professional Golfers Association
LSL	Lone Star League
LSU	Louisiana State University
MAC	Mid-American Conference
MAL	Middle Atlantic League
MasL	Massachusetts League
MD	*Magazine Digest*
MEL	Mexican League
MEWL	Mexican Winter League
MH	*Men's Health*
MISL	Michigan State League
MiVL	Mississippi Valley League
MkL	Mandak League
ML	Midwest League
MLPA	Major League Players Association
MLPAA	Major League Players Alumni Association
MLUA	Major League Umpires Association
MM	*Mariners Magazine*
MnL	Manila League
MOL	Michigan-Ontario League
MOVL	Mississippi-Ohio Valley League
mph	miles per hour
MSA	Massachusetts State Association
MSL	Middle States League
MtL	Montana League
MtnSL	Mountain State League
MtSL	Montana State League
MUL	Muny League
MVC	Missouri Valley Conference
MVL	Missouri Valley League

MVP	Most Valuable Player
MWL	Minnesota-Wisconsin League
NA	National Association
NaBC	National Baseball Congress
NAIA	National Association of Intercollegiate Athletics
NAL	Negro American League
NAML	National Association of Minor Leagues
NAPBL	National Association of Professional Baseball Leagues
NASSH	North American Association for Sport History
NAtL	North Atlantic League
NBA	National Basketball Association
NBBC	National Baseball Congress
NBC	National Broadcasting Company
NCAA	National Collegiate Athletic Association
NCAB	*National Cyclopedia of American Biography*
NCBWA	National Collegiate Baseball Writers Association
NCC	North Central Conference
NCL	North Carolina League
NCSL	North Carolina State League
NEA	Newspaper Enterprise Association
NEAL	Northeast Arkansas League
NECSL	Northeastern Connecticut State League
NEL	New England League
NeL	Northeastern League
NEQ	*New England Quarterly*
NeSL	Nebraska State League
NFL	National Football League
NGBL	National Girls Baseball League
NHL	National Hockey League
NIFL	Negro Independent Football League
NL	National League
NLe	*New Leader*
NNL	Negro National League
NoA	Northern Association
NoL	Northern League
NR	*New Republic*
NSD	*National Sports Daily*

NSL	Negro Southern League
NTL	North Texas League
NWL	Northwestern League
NY	*New York*
NYJ	*New York Journal*
NYNJL	New York-New Jersey League
NYPL	New York-Pennsylvania League
NYSBC	New York State Boxing Commission
NYSL	New York State League
NYT	*New York Times*
NYU	New York University
NYWT	*New York World Telegram*
OAB	*Oberlin Alumni Bulletin*
OHQ	*Ohio Historical Quarterly*
OIL	Ohio-Indiana League
OKSL	Oklahoma State League
OL	Ohio League
OPL	Ohio-Pennsylvania League
OrL	Oregon League
OSL	Ohio State League
OTBA	Old Timers Baseball Association
OTBN	*Oldtyme Baseball News*
PAPBP	Protective Association of Professional Baseball Players
PCC	Pacific Coast Conference
PCL	Pacific Coast League
PEC	Pacific Eight Conference
PIL	Pacific International League
PiL	Piedmont League
PL	Players' League
PNL	Pacific Northwest League
PoL	Pony League
POML	Pennsylvania-Ohio-Maryland League
PPAA	Pittsburgh Pirates Alumni Association
PPVL	Panhandle-Pecos Valley League
PrL	Pioneer League
PRL	Puerto Rican League
ProL	Provincial League

PRWL	Puerto Rican Winter League
PSA	Pennsylvania State Association
PSL	Pennsylvania State League
PT	*Psychology Today*
PTC	Pac-Ten Conference
PW	*People Weekly*
RAL	Rookie Appalachian League
RB	*Ragtyme Baseball*
RBI	runs batted in
RD	*Readers Digest*
RR	*Reds Report*
RRVL	Red River Valley League
RS	*Ragtyme Sports*
SA	Southern Association
SABR	Society for American Baseball Research
SAL	South Atlantic League
SBC	Sun Belt Conference
SC	Southern Conference
SCD	*Sports Collectors Digest*
SCQ	*Southern California Quarterly*
SDL	South Dakota League
SEAL	*The Scribner Encyclopedia of American Lives*
SEC	Southeastern Conference
SEL	Southeastern League
SEP	*Saturday Evening Post*
SeS	*Senior Scholastic*
SH	*Sports Heritage*
SI	*Sports Illustrated*
SIAA	Southern Intercollegiate Athletic Association
SIC	*Sports Illustrated Canada*
SIL	Southwest International League
SL	Southern League
SL	*Sport Life*
SML	Southern Michigan League
SMU	Southern Methodist University
SN	*Saturday Night*
SNEL	South New England League

SPBA	Senior Professional Baseball Association
SpL	Sophomore League
SpL	*Sporting Life*
SR	*Saturday Review*
SS	*Sports Scoop*
SSBM	*Street & Smith Baseball Magazine*
SSL	Sooner State League
ST	*Sporting Times*
STL	South Texas League
SuL	Sunset League
SW	*Sport World*
SWaL	Southwestern Washington League
SWC	Southwest Conference
SWL	Southwestern League
TAC	*The American Chronicle*
TAI	*The Annals of Iowa*
TBA	*The Berean Alumnus*
TBR	*The Baseball Review*
TCU	Texas Christian University
TD	*The Diamond*
TF	*The Fan*
3IL	Three I League
TL	Texas League
TM	*Texas Monthly*
TNP	*The National Pastime*
TNY	*The New Yorker*
TOL	Texas-Oklahoma League
TP	*This People*
TPI	Total Pitcher Index
TrM	*Trenton Magazine*
TSL	Tri-State League
TSN	*The Sporting News*
UA	Union Association
UCLA	University of California at Los Angeles
UIL	Utah-Idaho League
UL	Union League
UP	United Press

UPI	United Press International
USAT	*USA Today*
USC	University of Southern California
USL	United States League
USOC	U.S. Olympic Committee
UtA	Utah Association
VaL	Valley League
VL	Virginia League
VSL	Virginia State League
VVL	Virginia Valley League
VWL	Venezuelan Winter League
WA	Western Association
WAC	Western Athletic Conference
WC	Western Conference
WCAC	West Coast Athletic Conference
WCaL	Western Canadian League
WCL	West Carolinas League
WeIL	Western International League
WIBC	Women's International Bowling Congress
WIL	Wisconsin-Illinois League
WL	Western League
WM	*World Monitor*
WNABA	Women's National Adult Baseball Association
WPL	Western Pennsylvania League
WSC	Western State Conference
WSJ	*Wall Street Journal*
WSL	Wisconsin State League
WTL	Western Tri-State League
WTNML	West Texas-New Mexico League
WTxL	West Texas League
WWA	*Who's Who in America*
WWE	*Who's Who in the East*
WWIB	*Who's Who in Baseball*
WWM	*Who's Who in the Midwest*
WWWA	*Who Was Who in America*
YM	*Yankee Magazine*
YMCA	Young Men's Christian Association

CROSS-REFERENCE TO BIOGRAPHICAL DICTIONARY VOLUMES

*	Current Volume
FB	Football Volume
IS	Basketball and Other Indoor Sports Volume
OS	Outside Sports Volume

A

AARON, Henry Louis "Hank" (b. February 5, 1934, Mobile, AL), player and executive, is the son of Herbert Aaron and Estelle (Pritchett) Aaron. His father worked as a rivet bucker in a shipbuilding company. His brother, Tommy, played major league baseball with him for three years in Milwaukee and four years in Atlanta and then coached with the Braves until his death. Other siblings include Sarah, Herbert, Jr., Gloria, Alfred, and Alfreda.

Aaron attended Central High School and graduated from Josephine Allen Institute in 1951. He played end and halfback with the football team, but the institute fielded no baseball team. At age 16, he began playing semiprofessional baseball with the Mobile Black Bears. He performed one year with the Indianapolis Clowns (NNL) before signing with the Boston Braves in 1952. After playing in Eau Claire, WI, and Jacksonville, FL (SAL) as a shortstop, he joined the Milwaukee Braves (NL) in 1954 and was converted to an outfielder.

During his 23-year major league career, he established 12 major league career records. His best known, the home run record of 755, surpassed Babe Ruth's* 714. His 715th HR came on April 8, 1974, against Al Downing of the Los Angeles Dodgers at Fulton County Stadium. Other career records included most games played (3,298), most times at bat (12,364), most total bases (6,856), most extra-base hits (1,477), and most RBI (2,297). His career records for games played and most at bats have been broken. He ranks second in runs scored (2,174) and eighth in doubles and sixth in putouts and chances among outfielders. Aaron, who had a major league lifetime .305 batting average and .555 slugging percentage, set more major league career records than any other player.

As a major leaguer, Aaron played first, second, and third base, gained recognition as a great outfielder, and won a Gold Glove for defensive excellence in 1958. Besides playing in 24 All-Star games, he appeared in the

World Series against the New York Yankees in 1957 and 1958 and batted .364 in these Series (fourth highest). He was selected as the Major League MVP in 1957 and *TSN* Player of the Year in 1956 and 1963.

Aaron led the NL four times in HR (1957, 1963, 1966, 1967), RBI (1957, 1960, 1963, 1966) and slugging percentage (1957, 1959, 1962, 1971), twice in hits (1956, 1959), twice in batting average (.328, 1956; .355, 1959), and three times in runs scored (1957, 1963, 1967). He slugged 30 HR and scored 100 runs on 15 occasions, both major league records.

In 1969, Atlanta Braves fans named Aaron the Greatest Player Ever. He played his final two years with the Milwaukee Brewers (AL) in 1975 and 1976 and returned to the Braves as corporate vice-president in charge of player development in 1976. In January 1982, Aaron was elected to the National Baseball Hall of Fame and missed unanimous selection by only nine votes (406 of 415 votes). Willie Mays* alone received more votes, while only Ty Cobb* gained a higher percentage of the total vote.

Aaron married Barbara Lucas on October 3, 1953, and had five children, Gail, Hank Jr., Larry, Dorinda, and Ceci. After a 1971 divorce, Aaron married Billy Suber Williams on November 12, 1973. As director of player development until 1989, he built the Atlanta Braves farm system into one of the most productive in baseball. Since 1990, Aaron has served as senior vice-president and assistant to the president. He also serves as corporate vice-president for community relations for TBS and vice-president of business development for The Airport Channel, and operates a company producing apparel. He owns 13 Arby's and Church's Fried Chicken restaurant franchises and six airport gift shops. Aaron protests injustices in baseball and believes the game has lagged behind in hiring minorities for decision-making positions. He sponsors the Hank Aaron Scholarship Program and is involved with the Cystic Fibrosis Foundation, Sickle Cell Anemia Research Program, Salvation Army, and Boy Scouts. Aaron made Major League Baseball's All-Century Team and ranked 13th among ESPN's top century athletes.

BIBLIOGRAPHY: Hank Aaron, "How I Broke Babe Ruth's Home Run Record," *Ebony* 46 (July 1991), pp. 68ff; Henry Aaron and Furman Bisher, *Aaron* (New York, 1974); Atlanta Braves publications and media files, Atlanta, GA; Stanley Baldwin, *Bad Henry* (Radnor, PA, 1974); John Benson et al., *Baseball's Top 100* (Wilton, CT, 1997); Robert T. Bowen, interview with Henry Aaron, January 17, 1985; Donald Honig, *The Power Hitters* (St. Louis, MO, 1989); Larry Moffi and Jonathan Kronstadt, *Crossing the Line* (Jefferson, NC, 1994); David Porter, ed., *African-American Sports Greats* (Westport, CT, 1995); John Thom, *Champion Batsman of the 20th Century* (Los Angeles, CA, 1992); Milton Shapiro, *The Henry Aaron Story* (New York, 1961); H. Stein, "Henry Aaron," *Sport* 77 (December 1986), pp. 95ff; Bob Buege, *The Milwaukee Braves: A Baseball Eulogy* (Milwaukee, WI, 1988); Gary Caruso, *The Braves Encyclopedia* (Philadelphia, PA, 1995); Hank Aaron with Lonnie Wheeler, *I Had a Hammer: The Hank Aaron Story* (New York, 1991); Chuck Johnson, "Aaron Paid a Price for Beating Ruth," *USAT*, April 8, 1994, pp. 1A–2A; John Thorn et al., eds., *Total Braves* (New York, 1996); Barbara Carlisle Bigelow, ed., *Contemporary Black Biography*, vol. 5 (Detroit, MI, 1994), pp. 1–4; W. Ladson, "Hank Aaron," *Sport* 84 (February 1993), pp. 70–75; Dan Valenti, *Clout! The Top Home Runs in Baseball History* (Lexington, MA, 1989); Tom Meany, *Milwaukee's Miracle Braves* (New York, 1957).

Robert T. Bowen, Jr.

ABERNATHY, Theodore Wade "Ted" (b. March 6, 1933, Stanley, NC), player, is the son of Wade Abernathy and Gena Abernathy. A late-blooming, well-traveled pitcher, Abernathy graduated from Stanley High School in 1951. The 6-foot 4-inch, 215-pound, right-hander played high school, semi-professional, and American Legion baseball in the Gastonia, NC, area. After signing with the Washington Senators (AL) organization, he pitched for Roanoke Rapids, NC (CoPL) in 1952 and Chattanooga, TN (SL) and then served in the United States Army. Abernathy started for Washington from 1955 to 1957 with a stint in Louisville, KY (AA) in 1956, but produced undistinguished results. He pitched for Chattanooga in 1958, Miami, FL (IL) and Charlotte, NC (SAL) in 1959, Austin, TX (TL), Washington, and Louisville in 1960, Vancouver, Canada (PCL) in 1961, and Jacksonville, FL (IL) in 1962 and 1963.

After injuring his arm and undergoing surgery in 1959, Abernathy learned a submarine style from Washington teammate Dick Hyde and refined his motion in the minor leagues. By 1963, he returned to the major leagues permanently. He ranked among the top relievers in the game for the Cleveland Indians (AL) in 1963 and 1964, Chicago Cubs (NL) in 1965 and 1966, Atlanta Braves (NL) in 1966, Cincinnati Reds (NL) in 1967 and 1968, Chicago Cubs (NL) in 1969 and 1970, St. Louis Cardinals (NL) in 1970, and Kansas City Royals (AL) from 1970 to 1972. Abernathy led the NL in saves in 1965 with 31 and in 1967 with 28, earning NL Fireman of the Year honors. He pitched in 681 major league games, including all but 34 in relief, compiling a 63–69 win-loss record, a 3.46 ERA, and 148 saves.

Abernathy subsequently worked for a fuel oil company in Gastonia. He and his wife, Margie (Clemmer) Abernathy, have two sons, Ted and Todd.

BIBLIOGRAPHY: Ted Abernathy file, National Baseball Library, Cooperstown, NY; Bob Addie, "A Submarine in Washington," *BD* 15 (May 1956), pp. 69–71; Martin Appel, *Yesterday's Heroes* (New York, 1988); Eddie Gold and Art Ahrens, *The New Era Cubs, 1941–1985* (Chicago, IL, 1985); Bob Cairns, *Pen Men* (New York, 1993); Jerry Holtzman, "Elated Cubs Hail Abby as Flag Factor," *TSN*, January 25, 1969, p. 34; Jerry Holtzman, "Hurler Abernathy Proves Lifesaver as Ace Rescuer," *TSN*, June 12, 1965; Terry Pluto, *The Curse of Rocky Colavito* (New York, 1994); Floyd Connor and John Snyder, *Day-by-Day in Cincinnati Reds History* (West Point, NY, 1984); Bob Rathgeber, *Cincinnati Reds Scrapbook* (Virginia Beach, VA, 1982).

Jim L. Sumner

ADAMS, Charles Benjamin "Babe" (b. May 18, 1882, Tipton, IN; d. July 27, 1968, Silver Spring, MD), player and sportswriter, was the son of a poor farmer of English descent. After moving to Mt. Moriah, MO, he attended school there for eight years. Since his family was poor, he was "adopted" by a local farmer, Lee Sarver, who encouraged his baseball ambitions. In 1905, he won around 15 games as a pitcher for Parsons, KS (MVL). He pitched the first half of the 1906 season with the St. Louis Cardinals (NL) and then hurled for Denver, CO (WL) in late 1906 and 1907. After a brief stay with the Pittsburgh Pirates (NL) in late 1907, he pitched for Louisville, KY (AA) the next year.

Adams performed for the Pittsburgh Pirates from 1909 through 1926, but spent 1917 with St. Joseph, MO and Hutchinson, KS (WL) and most of 1918 with Kansas City (AA). The highlight of his major league career came in 1909, when he won 12 of 15 decisions in the regular season and triumphed in all three complete-game starts for the Pittsburgh Pirates against the Detroit Tigers in the World Series. Besides hurling a shutout in the decisive seventh game, he allowed only five runs and 18 hits in the three games. The right-hander won 22 decisions in 1911, 21 in 1913, 18 in 1910, and 17 in 1919 and 1920. After the 1926 season, he left the Pittsburgh Pirates, allegedly because Fred Clarke* shared the management with William McKechnie.* Adams spent the 1927 season with Johnstown, PA (MAL) and Springfield, MO (WA) before retiring from baseball.

Control proved crucial to his success. During 19 major league seasons, he walked only 430 batters and struck out 1,036 in 2,995.1 innings. In 1920, he walked only 18 batters in 263 innings. Adams averaged less than one walk a game in 1909, 1919, 1920, and 1922 and holds the major league record for the longest game pitched without surrendering a base on balls (21 innings against the New York Giants on July 17, 1914). He 12 times compiled ERAs under 3.00, highlighted by a sparkling 1.98 ERA in 1919. Forty-four of his 194 wins were shutouts, including an NL-leading eight in 1920. He completed 206 of his 354 starts, losing 140 games and posting a 2.76 ERA. The 5-foot 11½-inch, 185 pounder possessed a good fastball, but depended on his curveball as his most intimidating pitch.

After leaving baseball, Adams farmed at Mt. Moriah, became a sportswriter, and went overseas as a correspondent during World War II and the Korean War. He married Blanch Wright Adams on March 2, 1909 and moved with her to Silver Spring, MD in 1958. Although remembered mainly for his 1909 World Series heroics and overshadowed by great contemporaries like Christy Mathewson,* Adams enjoyed a long, noteworthy career that embraced both the dead and live ball eras.

BIBLIOGRAPHY: Charles Adams file, National Baseball Library, Cooperstown, NY; Harry Grayson, *They Played the Game* (New York, 1945); Frederick G. Lieb, *The Pittsburgh Pirates* (New York, 1948); Bill James, *The Baseball Book 1990* (New York, 1990); Bill Madden, *The Hoosiers of Summer* (Indianapolis, IN, 1994); Richard L. Burtt, *The Pittsburgh Pirates: A Pictorial History* (Virginia Beach, VA, 1977); Bob Smizik, *The Pittsburgh Pirates: An Illustrated History* (New York, 1990).

Luther W. Spoehr

ADAMS, Daniel Lucius (b. November 1, 1814, Mount Vernon, NH; d. January 3, 1899, New Haven, CT), player, umpire, and organizer, performed the central role in the development of baseball's first club, the Knickerbocker Base Ball Club of New York, as well as the game's first at-large organization, the NABBP.

The son of Daniel Adams, a physician, and Nancy (Mulliken) Adams, he graduated with a Bachelor's degree from Yale University in 1835 and received his M.D. from Harvard University in 1838. After establishing a medical practice in New York City, he joined the fledgling Knickerbocker Base Ball Club about a month after its September 23, 1845 organization. Adams provided leadership for the club and the organized game as both developed over the next two decades. He was elected vice-president of the club the next spring and president in 1847. During this formative period, the Knicks comprised the game's only club. Adams led twice a week intra-club matches in spite of often poor attendance, made all the balls, and supervised the turning of the bats.

As the number of clubs grew, Adams always was involved in cooperative efforts. At baseball's first convention of clubs in 1857, he was made Presiding Officer. Adams later chaired the body's rules committee. During his tenure or through his proposals, bases were set 30 yards apart, the bound out was abolished, and definitions for games of nine innings and teams of nine players were made.

Adams played every baseball position except pitcher and proved noteworthy at shortstop, a position he may have created. He often umpired important matches.

The Knickerbockers honored Adams upon his retirement from the club by proclaiming him "Nestor of Ball Players." He had served the club 16 years, including 12 as officer.

Adams married Cornelia A. Cook in 1861 and retired from his medical practice in 1865, moving to Connecticut to bring up his family of four children. He called his marriage "the crowning achievement of my life."

His autobiographical sketches curiously do not mention baseball. The game may not have been the most important aspect of his life, but Adams played a crucial role in the development of the game and was called by one historian "The Nurturing Father of Baseball."

BIBLIOGRAPHY: Daniel Adams file, National Baseball Library, Cooperstown, NY; Roger C. Adams, *Nestor of Ball Players* (Buffalo, NY, 1939); Frederick Ivor-Campbell et al., eds., *Baseball's First Stars* (Cleveland, OH, 1996); Frederick Ivor-Campbell, *Two "Fathers of Baseball"* (Warren, RI, 1995); *Obituary Record of Graduates of Yale University*, June 1899 and *Biographical and Historical Record of the Class of 1835*, 1881, Yale University Library, New Haven, CT; Charles A. Peverelly, *Book of American Pastimes* (1866), reprinted in *The Vintage & Classic Baseball Collector*, Issue 2 (Tacoma, WA, 1995), pp. 22–29; Dean A. Sullivan, *Early Innings* (Lincoln, NE, 1995); John Thorn et al., eds., *Total Baseball*, 5th ed. (New York, 1997); Richard L. Wolfe, Harvard Medical Library, Letter to John R. Husman, October 25, 1995; Seymour R. Church, *Base Ball* (Princeton, NJ, 1902); Robert W. Henderson, *Ball, Bat, and Bishop* (New York, 1947); Harold Peterson, *The Man Who Invented Baseball* (New York, 1969).

John R. Husman

ADAMS, Earl John "Sparky" (b. August 26, 1894, Zerbe, PA; d. February 24, 1989, Pottsville, PA), player, was the son of John Adams and Elizabeth (Jones) Adams; of German-Welsh descent. After playing shortstop for Tremont, PA High School, he performed for the Cressona Tigers railroad team. Adams worked in a machine shop for four years, declining minor league baseball offers because they paid less. He entered organized baseball in 1919 with Reading, PA (IL) and played infield for Danville, VA (PiL) in 1920 and Syracuse, NY (IL) in 1921. His .340 batting average for Wichita Falls, TX (TL) in 1922 earned him promotion to the major leagues. Adams performed 13 major league seasons with the Chicago Cubs (NL, 1922–1927), Pittsburgh Pirates (NL, 1928–1929), St. Louis Cardinals (NL, 1930–1933), and Cincinnati Reds (NL, 1933–1934). In November 1927, he was traded with Pete Scott to Pittsburgh for Kiki Cuyler.*

Adams, originally dubbed "Rabbit" for his speed and small size, was nicknamed "Sparky" by Cubs teammate Rabbit Maranville.* Maranville wanted to be the only "Rabbit" on the team. The era's smallest player, the 5-foot 5 1/2-inch, 150-pound Adams was mistaken for a bat boy by Philadelphia manager Connie Mack* before the 1930 World Series. He led the NL in fielding average at second base with .983 in 1925 and at third base with .966 in 1930 and .963 in 1931. Adams also paced the NL in double plays and doubles (46) in 1931 and in at bats from 1925 through 1927. An outfielder and a shortstop also, he finished with a .286 lifetime average, nine HR, 249 doubles, and 394 RBI. Adams reached career highs with a .314 batting average in 1930 and 100 runs scored in 1927. In the 1930 and 1931 World Series for the Cardinals, he batted just .160 with one RBI against the Philadelphia Athletics. His biggest baseball thrill, a spectacular defensive stop, began a 10th-inning double play in September 1930. St. Louis defeated the Brooklyn Dodgers and moved into first place for the rest of the season.

After retiring from major league baseball, Adams served as a semiprofessional player–manager in Pennsylvania. He bought a farm and later opened a garage, which included repair and storage services and a Ford dealership. He married Bertha Frew of Newtown, PA on August 26, 1918, their mutual twenty-fourth birthday. They had two children, Earl, Jr. and Doris (Enders). In 1990, he was posthumously inducted into the Pennsylvania State Hall of Fame.

BIBLIOGRAPHY: Earl Adams file, National Baseball Library, Cooperstown, NY; Bill James, *The Baseball Book 1990* (New York, 1990); Eddie Gold and Art Ahrens, *The Golden Era Cubs, 1876–1940* (Chicago, IL, 1985); Warren Brown, *The Chicago Cubs*

(New York, 1946); Frederick G. Lieb, *The Pittsburgh Pirates* (New York, 1948); Frederick G. Lieb, *The St. Louis Cardinals* (New York, 1945); John Thorn et al., eds., *Total Baseball*, 5th ed. (New York, 1997); Bob Broeg and Jerry Vickery, *St. Louis Cardinals Encyclopedia* (Grand Rapids, MI, 1998); Lee Allen, *The Cincinnati Reds* (New York, 1948); Mike Shatzkin, ed., *The Ballplayers* (New York, 1990); John J. Ward, "Spark Plug Adams and His Sensational Plays," *BM* 39 (June 1927), pp. 302–303.

Victor Rosenberg

ADCOCK, Joseph Wilber "Joe" (b. October 30, 1927, Coushatta, LA; d. May 3, 1999, Coushatta, LA), player and manager, grew up in rural northwest Louisiana and was the son of Ray Adcock, a farmer and sheriff of Red River Parish. An All-State basketball star in high school, Adcock began playing baseball seriously upon entering Louisiana State University in 1944. After attending LSU from 1944 to 1947, he left school to play professional baseball. He played first base for Columbia, SC (SL) in 1947–1948 and Tulsa, OK (TL) in 1949 and joined the Cincinnati Reds (NL) in 1950.

Adcock, traded to the Boston Braves (NL) in February 1953, played on the original Milwaukee Braves when the franchise moved in 1953. Milwaukee's regular first baseman from 1953 through 1962, he developed into one of baseball's hardest hitters. On July 31, 1954, he hit four HR and a double against the Brooklyn Dodgers, setting a major league record with 18 total bases in one game. With his HR the previous day, Adcock tied the record for most HR (5) in two consecutive games. The 6-foot 4-inch, 210-pound slugger became the first player to hit a ball into the center field bleachers at the Polo Grounds and the only one to slug a ball over the left field grandstands at Ebbets Field.

At Milwaukee, Adcock teamed with Henry Aaron* and Eddie Mathews* to form one of the NL's most dangerous trios. Adcock considered the Milwaukee Braves' pennant and World Series victory over the New York Yankees in 1957 his greatest baseball thrill. Although repeating as pennant winners in 1958, the Braves lost the World Series to the Yankees. Adcock's best seasons included 1954 (.308 batting average), 1956 (38 HR, 103 RBI), and 1961 (35 HR, 108 RBI). In 1960 he played in both All-Star games.

Adcock spent four mediocre AL seasons with the Cleveland Indians (1963) and California (Los Angeles) Angels (1964–1966). In 1,959 career games, Adcock slugged 336 HR, knocked in 1,122 runs, batted .277, and compiled a .485 slugging average. After managing Cleveland (AL) to eighth place in 1967 and Seattle (PCL) in 1968, he left baseball. He married Joan James in November 1956 and lived on a 288-acre thoroughbred horse farm in Coushatta, LA.

BIBLIOGRAPHY: Joseph Adcock file, National Baseball Library, Cooperstown, NY; Atlanta *Journal Constitution*, December 18, 1983; Bob Buege, *The Milwaukee Braves: A Baseball Eulogy* (Milwaukee, WI, 1988); Gary Caruso, *The Braves Encyclopedia* (Philadelphia, PA, 1995); Henry Aaron with Furman Bisher, *Aaron* (New York, 1974);

Allison Danzig and Joe Reichler, *The History of Baseball* (Englewood Cliffs, NJ, 1959); Gene Karst and Martin J. Jones, Jr., *Who's Who in Professional Baseball* (New Rochelle, NY, 1973); Craig Carter, ed., *Daguerreotypes*, 8th ed. (St. Louis, 1990); Bill James, *The Baseball Book 1990* (New York, 1990); John Thorn et al., eds., *Total Braves* (New York, 1996); Tom Meany, *Milwaukee's Miracle Braves* (New York, 1957); Mark Onigman, *This Date in Braves History* (New York, 1982).

Clark Nardinelli

AGUILERA, Richard Warren "Rick" (b. December 31, 1961, San Gabriel, CA), player, is a 6-foot 5-inch, 210-pound pitcher who throws and bats right-handed. He graduated in 1980 from Edgewood, CA High School, where he made All-League as an infielder. He majored in architectural design at Brigham Young University and began pitching his sophomore season. He and his wife, Sherry (Snider), have one daughter, Rachel, and one son, Austin.

The St. Louis Cardinals (NL) selected Aguilera in the 1980 free-agent draft, but he did not sign. The New York Mets (NL) signed him following the 1983 draft and assigned him to Little Falls, NY (NYPL). Aguilera split the 1984 season with Lynchburg, VA (CrL) and Jackson, TX (TL) and started the 1985 campaign with Tidewater, VA (IL). On June 12, 1985, Aguilera debuted with the Mets and earned his first major league victory. With the exception of rehabilitation assignments at Tidewater in 1987 and 1988 and at St. Lucie, FL (FSL) in 1988, he started five seasons for the New York Mets with a 37–27 won–lost record and produced a career-best 11–3 mark in 1987.

In July 1989, the New York Mets traded Aguilera to the Minnesota Twins (AL). He relieved exclusively for Minnesota, recording 184 saves between 1990 and 1995 and a career-high 42 saves in 1991. Aguilera holds the Minnesota Twins' all-time record for most saves and was named the Twins' Pitcher of the Year in 1990 and 1993. In July 1995, he was traded to the Boston Red Sox (AL) and posted 20 saves the remainder of the season. Declared a free-agent after the 1995 season, Aguilera rejoined the Twins. He pitched two games for Fort Myers, FL (FSL) on rehabilitation assignment before joining the starting rotation for Minnesota, where he finished 8–6 in 1996. He compiled a 5–4 record with 26 saves in 1997 and a 4–9 mark with 38 saves in 1998. In May 1999, the Chicago Cubs acquired him in a trade.

Aguilera played on World Championship teams in 1986 and 1991, winning twice, losing once, and earning two saves. He hurled in eight League Championship Series games with three saves and appeared in one Division Series contest. Aguilera made three consecutive All-Star Game relief appearances from 1991 to 1993, allowing five hits and striking out five batters in three innings pitched.

In 14 major league seasons through 1999, Aguilera has compiled a 85–79 won–lost record with a 3.52 ERA. He has appeared in 678 games, completing 10 of 89 starts and recording 289 saves. Aguilera has surrendered 1,186 base hits and 333 walks in 1,243.2 innings pitched while striking out 1,159 batters.

BIBLIOGRAPHY: Richard Aguilera file, National Baseball Library, Cooperstown, NY; *Minnesota Twins Media Guide*, 1998; *TSN Official Baseball Guide*, 1998.

John L. Evers

ALEXANDER, David Dale "Moose" (b. April 26, 1903, Greeneville, TN; d. March 2, 1979, Greeneville, TN), player, manager, and scout, was born on a tobacco farm. Nicknamed "Moose" because of his 6-foot 3-inch, 210-pound size and the enormous distance he could hit a baseball, he began his professional baseball career in 1924 with Greeneville, TN (ApL) and played two years each with Charlotte, NC (SA) and Toronto, Canada (IL) before joining the Detroit Tigers (AL) in 1929 as a regular first baseman. Always an outstanding hitter, Alexander debuted in spectacular fashion. He set a record that year for batting average by a rookie with a .343 mark, recording 215 hits, making 43 doubles, 15 triples, and 25 HR, and driving in 137 runs. In 1930, he achieved a 29-game hitting streak. His best year came in 1932, when he batted .367 to edge out Jimmie Foxx* for the AL batting title.

In an unprecedented move partway through June 1932, Detroit traded Alexander to the Boston Red Sox (AL). Only one other player in major league history was traded during a season in which he won the batting title. Although slow afoot, Alexander seemed destined for a long major league career when he injured a knee on May 30, 1933 against the Philadelphia Athletics. A mistake made by the team trainer with a diathermy treatment resulted in third-degree burns. Gangrene set in, nearly costing Alexander his leg. In five major league seasons, he batted .331 with 811 hits, 61 HR, and 459 RBI. Unable to play at the major league level thereafter, he moved to the minor leagues. He performed for numerous minor league teams from 1934 through 1942 and managed Sanford, FL (FSL) in 1939. Despite his physical problems, Alexander consistently hit over .300 except the year of his accident. Subsequently, he continued in professional baseball as a part-time scout and then retired to his Greeneville, TN farm.

BIBLIOGRAPHY: David Dale Alexander file, National Baseball Library, Cooperstown, NY; Robert Redmount, *The Red Sox Encyclopedia* (Champaign, IL, 1998); William M. Anderson, *The Detroit Tigers* (South Bend, IN, 1996); Richard Bak, *A Place for Summer* (Detroit, MI, 1998); Joe Falls, *Detroit Tigers* (New York, 1975); *The Baseball Encyclopedia*, 10th ed. (New York, 1996); Frederick G. Lieb, *The Boston Red Sox* (New York, 1947); Frederick G. Lieb, *The Detroit Tigers* (New York, 1946); Joseph L. Reichler, ed., *The Great All-Time Baseball Record Book* (New York, 1981); Michael Santa Maria and James Costello, "The Sad Tale of Dale Alexander," *BRJ* 20 (1991), pp. 61–62; Fred Smith, *995 Tigers* (Detroit, MI, 1981); John Thom, *Champion Batsman of the 20th Century* (Los Angeles, CA, 1992).

Horace R. Givens

ALEXANDER, Doyle Lafayette (b. September 4, 1950, Cordova, AL), player, was a much-traveled right-handed pitcher. He defeated every major league team and recorded 194 major league victories during an impressive career spanning 19 years. After starring in basketball and baseball at Woodlawn High School in Cordova and attending Jefferson State JC, Alexander was drafted by the Los Angeles Dodgers (NL) in the 44th round of the June 1968 draft and was signed by Leon Hamilton. After stints at Tri-City (NWL), Daytona Beach, FL (FSL), Albuquerque, NM (TL), and Spokane, WA (PCL), the wiry, 6-foot 3-inch, 200-pound Alexander joined the Los Angeles Dodgers in midseason of 1971 and compiled a 6–6 record. In December 1971, Los Angeles sent him to the Baltimore Orioles (AL) as part of a trade that included National Baseball Hall-of-Famer Frank Robinson.* This marked the first of seven deals in which he was to be involved. Thereafter, he played with the New York Yankees (AL, 1976, 1982–1983), Texas Rangers (AL, 1977–1979), Atlanta Braves (NL, 1980, 1986–1987), San Francisco Giants (NL, 1981), Toronto Blue Jays (AL, 1983–1986), and Detroit Tigers (AL, 1987–1989).

Not an overpowering pitcher, Alexander never won 20 games in a season. He recorded 17 victories on three separate occasions, leading the AL in winning percentage (.739) with a 17–6 mark in 1984. Alexander never played in an All-Star game, despite being selected to the AL team in 1988. He did not triumph in six post-season starts with Baltimore (1973), New York (1976), Toronto (1985), and Detroit (1987). Although known as a "loner," Alexander proved a tough survivor who knew how to pitch and earned $1.5 million per year in his prime. In 1989, he took his regular turn on the mound despite a broken jaw and developed a knuckleball to extend his career.

The highlight of Alexander's long career perhaps came when he was traded to the Detroit Tigers in August 1987 just before his 37th birthday. He sparked the Tigers to their dramatic come-from-behind victory in the AL Eastern Division race by winning all nine decisions with a 1.53 ERA in that stretch drive. During his major league career, Alexander won 194 games and lost 174 with a 3.76 ERA, 1,528 strikeouts, and 978 bases on balls.

Alexander, who is of Irish and Indian descent, and his wife, Pat, have two children, Lisa and Christopher.

BIBLIOGRAPHY: Doyle Alexander file, National Baseball Library, Cooperstown, NY; Richard Bak, *A Place for Summer* (Detroit, MI, 1998); Ted Patterson, *The Baltimore Orioles* (Dallas, TX, 1995); Mark Gallagher, *The Yankee Encyclopedia*, vol. 3 (Champaign, IL, 1997); Peter Bjarkman, *The Toronto Blue Jays* (New York, 1990); Alison Gordon, *Foul Balls* (Toronto, Canada, 1986); William M. Anderson, *The Detroit Tigers* (South Bend, IN, 1996); Sparky Anderson and Dan Ewald, *Sparky* (New York, 1990); Detroit Tigers, *The Press Guide, 1989*; John Thorn et al., eds., *Total Baseball*, 5th ed. (New York, 1997).

Sheldon L. Appleton

ALEXANDER, Grover Cleveland "Pete," "Old Pete," "Old Low-and-Away" (b. February 26, 1887, Elba, NE; d. November 4, 1950, St. Paul, NE), player, was the sixth of eight surviving children of farmer William Alexander and Margaret (Cootey) Alexander. After completing St. Paul High School, he became a telephone lineman and entered professional baseball as a pitcher in 1909 with Galesburg, IL (IlML). The following year he won 29 games, including 15 shutouts, for Syracuse, NY (NYSL), and was acquired by the Philadelphia Phillies (NL) for less than $1,000.

During his spectacular rookie season (1911), he recorded 28 wins, 7 shutouts (4 consecutive), 31 complete games, 367 innings pitched, 227 strikeouts, and a 2.57 ERA. His victories included a twelve-inning, one-hit, 1–0 shutout over the legendary Cy Young.* Until he left the Phillies in 1918, Alexander peformed better each year. In 1915 he won 31 games, 9 of them consecutively. His 12 shutouts included 4 one-hitters (3 within 31 days) and 3 two-hitters. Besides pitching a league-leading 36 complete games, he hurled 376 innings and struck out 241 batters. Only eight pitchers in baseball history have surpassed his 1.22 ERA.

In 1916, Alexander established career highs for victories (33), innings pitched (389), complete games (38), and shutouts (16). He shut out the Cincinnati Reds five times and all other opposing clubs at least once, allowed only 50 walks, and compiled a 1.55 ERA. In 1917, he won at least 30 games for the third straight year.

Fearing that Alexander would soon be lost to the U.S. Army, the Phillies traded him to the Chicago Cubs (NL) with his longtime battery mate, "Reindeer Bill" Killefer, in December 1917. In seven years, Alexander had won 32 percent of Philadelphia's victories.

After pitching three games for the Cubs in the spring of 1918 and marrying Aimee Marie Arrants on May 31, he was shipped to France with a field artillery unit, the 342nd Battalion of the 89th Division. He returned from the war with sergeant's stripes and a hearing loss from gunfire and began suffering from epileptic seizures. His longtime dependency on alcohol was aggravated.

In eight years with the Cubs, Alexander pitched impressively, but not at the phenomenal level he achieved in Philadelphia. Although increasingly eccentric from alcohol and epilepsy, he still won 128 games, or a quarter of Chicago's total, before being waived at age 39 to the St. Louis Cardinals (NL) in June 1926.

"Old Pete," as he now was known, contributed 200 innings and nine victories to the Cardinals' pennant drive and easily won the second and sixth games of the World Series against the New York Yankees. Perhaps the best-remembered event of his splendid baseball career, however, came when he relieved Jesse Haines* in the seventh inning of the seventh game with two out and the bases full. Debate continues whether Alexander was sober or hung over when summoned from the bullpen. Nevertheless, he struck out Tony Lazzeri* on four knee-high curves to end the inning and set down the Yankees in the eighth and ninth inning to assure the Cardinals' championship.

"Old Low-and-Away" won 21 games in 1927 (thereby earning his peak contract of $17,500) and 16 in 1928, but his skills began fading. Traded back to the Philadelphia Phillies, he was released in 1930 without earning the 374th victory that would have moved him ahead of Christy Mathewson.* He finished the 1930 season with Dallas, TX (TL).

Alexander's superb major league statistics rank him among baseball's best pitchers: 373 wins and 208 losses (.642), 5,190 innings pitched, 2,198 strikeouts, and an average of only 1.65 bases on balls per nine-inning game. Aside from victories, he also tied Mathewson in complete games (437) and consecutive 30-win seasons (3). He holds the NL record for season shutouts (16), ranks second in lifetime shutouts (90), and twice won two games in one day. In three World Series, he won three games and lost two. An excellent fielder, he ranks third on the lifetime list for assists (1,419), fifth for total chances (1,633), and eighth for fielding average (.985).

Alexander's later life proved sad and humiliating. He pitched until age 51 for semipro and independent clubs, notably the bearded House of David. He was divorced by Aimee, remarried her, and was divorced again without having children.

Although 6-feet 1-inch and a well-built 185 pounds, Alexander appeared unathletic. His manner seemed lackadaisical and his gait shambling, and his uniform never seemed to fit. Yet on the mound he performed with grace, economy, and perfect coordination. The right-hander's motion was easy, with barely a windup and scarcely a stride. He pitched quickly, his games often lasting only ninety minutes.

In a tough era, he treated rookies generously and bore his uncontrollable physical torments quietly. He was elected to the National Baseball Hall of Fame in 1938 and saw his Phillies in the 1950 World Series a month before he died.

BIBLIOGRAPHY: Grover Cleveland Alexander file, National Baseball Library, Cooperstown, NY; Lee Allen and Tom Meany, *Kings of the Diamond* (New York, 1965); Bob Broeg, "Incredible Alex—The Mound Master," *TSN*, June 14, 1969, pp. 28–29; Jerry E. Clark and Martha Ellen Webb, *Alexander the Great* (Omaha, NE, 1993); Jerry E. Clark, *Nebraska Diamonds* (Omaha, NE, 1991); Joe Dittmar, "Alexander the Great," *TNP* 11 (1991), pp. 14–17; Paul F. Doherty, "Cy Young's Final Fling," *BRJ* 8 (1979), pp. 6–9; Stanley Fleming, "Complete Games by Pitchers," *BRJ* 6 (1976), pp. 96–98; Leonard Gettelson, "Iron Man Pitching Performances," *BRJ* 7 (1977), pp. 19–23; Grand Island (NE) *Daily Independent*, November 4, 1950; Donald Honig, *October Heroes* (New York, 1979); Gordon Hurlburt, "Alexander's Shutout Record in 1916," *BRJ* 11 (1982), pp. 13–15; Eddie Gold and Art Ahrens, *The Golden Era Cubs, 1876–1940* (Chicago, IL, 1985); Jack Kavanagh, *Ol' Pete: The Grover Cleveland Al-*

exander Story (South Bend, IN, 1996); Frederick G. Lieb and Stan Baumgartner, *The Philadelphia Phillies* (New York, 1953); Warren Brown, *The Chicago Cubs* (New York, 1946); Jim Enright, *Chicago Cubs* (New York, 1975); Frederick G. Lieb, *The St. Louis Cardinals* (New York, 1945); Allen Lewis, *The Philadelphia Phillies* (Virginia Beach, VA, 1981); Frederick G. Lieb, *Baseball as I Have Known It* (New York, 1977); John P. McCarthy, *Baseball's All-Time Dream Team* (Cincinnati, OH, 1994); Tom Meany, *Baseball's Greatest Players* (New York, 1953); Lawrence S. Ritter, *The Glory of Their Times* (New York, 1966); Harold Seymour, *Baseball: The Golden Age* (New York, 1971); *Spalding's Official Base Ball Record, 1910* (New York, 1910); A. D. Suehsdorf, telephone interview with Mrs. Ruby Alexander, November 1983; Rich Westcott and Frank Bilovsky, *The New Phillies Encyclopedia* (Philadelphia, PA, 1993); Warren Wilbert and William Hageman, *Chicago Cubs: Seasons at the Summit* (Champaign, IL, 1997).

A. D. Suehsdorf

ALLEN, Ethan Nathan (b. January 1, 1904, Cincinnati, OH; d. September 15, 1993, Brookings, OR), player, executive, author, broadcaster, and coach, starred in several sports at Withrow High School in Cincinnati. He earned a B.S. degree from the University of Cincinnati in 1926 and an M.A. degree in Physical Education at Columbia University in 1932. The 6-foot 1-inch, 180-pound Allen, who batted and threw right-handed, signed as an outfielder with the Cincinnati Reds (NL) directly from the University of Cincinnati in 1926. Cincinnati traded him to the New York Giants (NL) in May 1930. He was shipped to the St. Louis Cardinals (NL) in October 1932, sold to the Philadelphia Phillies (NL) in January 1934, traded to the Chicago Cubs (NL) in May 1936, and sold to the St. Louis Browns (AL) in December 1936. Allen batted .300 lifetime with 1,325 hits and 501 RBI, hitting a career-best .330 and leading the NL in doubles with 42 in 1934.

Allen retired at the end of the 1938 season and became NL Director of Film Bureau. From 1946 to 1968, he served as head baseball coach at Yale University. His teams won five EIL championships and finished second in the 1947 and 1948 College World Series. His Yale players included future President of the United States George Bush. The prolific author wrote numerous baseball instructional books, including *Winning Baseball, Major League Baseball* (1938), and *Baseball: Major League Techniques and Tactics*. Allen also made numerous instructional films and took many photographs of players for use in his books. He developed many baseball board games, the most notable being All Star Baseball (1941) from the Cadeco Company. He married Doris Wetzel in 1928 and had a son and daughter.

BIBLIOGRAPHY: Ethan Allen file, National Baseball Library, Cooperstown, NY; Lee Allen, *The Cincinnati Reds* (New York, 1948); Frank Graham, *The New York Giants* (New York, 1952); Bill James, *The Baseball Book 1990* (New York, 1990); *NYT*, September 19, 1993, p. 54; Joseph L. Reichler, ed., *The Great All-Time Baseball Record Book* (New York, 1981); Rich Westcott, *Masters of the Diamond* (Jefferson, NC, 1994);

Rich Westcott and Frank Bilovsky, *The New Phillies Encyclopedia* (Philadelphia, PA, 1993); *The Baseball Encyclopedia*, 10th ed. (New York, 1996).

Horace R. Givens

ALLEN, John Thomas "Johnny" (b. September 30, 1905, Lenoir, NC; d. March 29, 1959, St. Petersburg, FL), player, manager, and umpire, was one of four children of Robert L. Allen, an unskilled laborer, and Alymra Allen. When Robert died in 1913, his wife could not support her children and went to live with a sister. She sent her children to Baptist Orphanage in Thomasville, NC, about 100 miles east of Lenoir.

After graduating from the orphanage high school, Allen worked as a hotel clerk in several North Carolina cities and pitched semiprofessional baseball. Fayetteville, NC (ECaL) signed him in 1927. Allen won 20 games for Asheville, NC (SAL) in 1928. The New York Yankees (AL) purchased his contract and assigned him to Jersey City, NJ (IL) in 1930 and Toronto, Canada (IL) in 1931. The 6-foot, 180-pound right-hander was promoted to the New York Yankees in 1932 and enjoyed a spectacular rookie season with a 17–4 mark, 3.70 ERA, and league-leading .810 winning percentage. Allen followed with 15–7, 5–2, and 13–6 records from 1933 to 1935, but alienated teammates with his violent temper.

Allen was traded to the Cleveland Indians (AL) for Monte Pearson* in December 1935 following an altercation with New York Yankee manager Joe McCarthy* and compiled a 20–10 mark and 3.44 ERA in 1936. Allen's best season came in 1937, when he won his first 15 decisions and then lost to the Detroit Tigers on the final day, 1–0, to finish 15–1 with a 2.55 ERA. *TSN* named him Player of the Year. He won 12 straight in 1938, but hurt his arm in the All-Star game and ended 14–8. Allen never recovered from this sore arm. He continued in the major leagues until 1944, pitching for the St. Louis Browns (AL) in 1941, Brooklyn Dodgers (NL) from 1941 to 1943, and the New York Yankees again in 1943 and 1944. He served as player–manager for Greensboro, NC (CrL) in 1945 and umpired in the CrL in the late 1940s. After compiling a career 142–75 major league mark and 3.75 ERA, Allen worked in real estate. Allen, who married Mary Leta Shields in October 1931, had one son, John Allen, Jr. He was inducted into the North Carolina Sports Hall of Fame in 1977.

BIBLIOGRAPHY: John Allen file, National Baseball Library, Cooperstown, NY; Clifford Bloodgood, "Cleveland's Ace in the Hole," *BM* 57 (July 1936), pp. 355–356; Mark Gallagher, *The Yankee Encyclopedia*, vol. 3 (Champaign, IL, 1997); Bill James, *The Baseball Book 1990* (New York, 1990); Frank Graham, *The New York Yankees* (New York, 1943); Dave Anderson et al., *The Yankees* (New York, 1979); Franklin Lewis, *The Cleveland Indians* (New York, 1949); Bob Feller with Bill Gilbert, *Now Pitching Bob Feller* (New York, 1990); Frank Graham, *The Brooklyn Dodgers* (New York, 1945); John F. Steadman, "Johnny Allen Had a Temper and a Talent," *BD* 38 (November 1969), pp. 41–43; Jim L. Sumner, "Almost Perfect: Johnny Allen's

1937 Season," *TNP* 14 (1994), pp. 51–54; John Thorn et al., eds., *Total Indians* (New York, 1996).

Jim L. Sumner

ALLEN, Newton Henry "Newt" (b. May 19, 1903, Austin, TX; d. June 11, 1988, Cincinnati, OH), player, proved a slick fielding, switch-hitting second baseman from 1922 through 1944. The 5-foot 8-inch, 170 pounder attended Western Baptist College for two and one-half years and had two sons from a marriage that terminated when he still played baseball. Aside from playing in 1931 with the St. Louis Stars (NNL), Allen spent his entire career with the Kansas City Monarchs (NNL, NAL). During winters, he played baseball in California, Cuba, Mexico, Puerto Rico, and Venezuela and toured the Far East in 1935–1936 with the Monarchs.

Noted for his pivot ability on double plays, he keystoned some outstanding infields on ten championship teams (NNL: 1923–1925, 1929, 1931; and NAL: 1937, 1939–1942). The 1924–1925 unit included Lemuel Hawkins (1B), Allen (2B), Newt Joseph (3B), and Dobie Moore* (SS). The 1924 team won the first interleague Black World Series, while the 1925 team lost the repeat match. The 1929 Monarchs touted Dink Mothel (1B), Allen (2B), Joseph (3B), and Hallie Harding (SS), whereas the 1931 Stars featured George Giles* (1B), Allen (2B), Dewey Creacy (3B), and Willie Wells* (SS). Kansas City infields of the late 1930s and early 1940s boasted John "Buck" O'Neil* (1B), Allen and later Bonnie Serrell* (2B), Rainey Bibbs and Allen (3B), and Ted Strong* and then Jessie Williams (SS). The 1942 team won the revived Black World Series by sweeping the Washington Grays.

Allen's World Series appearances produced batting averages of .282 in 1924, .259 in 1925, and .267 in 1942 for an aggregate .270 mark, with 22 hits and 9 doubles in 81 at bats. He appeared in four East-West (Negro League) All-Star games, starting the 1936 through 1938 and 1941 contests.

Ranked among the top second basemen from the old Negro leagues, Allen usually held down the number two spot in the batting order. He hit .301 against white major league pitching in the off-season. Scanty Negro league figures place his lifetime batting average at .298. He proved an aggressive and intimidating performer whether defending or running the bases. After retiring from baseball, Allen participated in Kansas City politics for the Democratic party and worked as a foreman at the Kansas City County courthouse.

BIBLIOGRAPHY: Janet Bruce, *The Kansas City Monarchs* (Lawrence, KS, 1985), Chicago *Defender*, October 1924, October 1925; John B. Holway, *Voices from the Great Black Baseball Leagues* (New York, 1975); Robert W. Peterson, *Only the Ball Was White* (Englewood Cliffs, NJ, 1970); Philadelphia *Afro-American* and *Independent Tribune*, September, October 1942; Pittsburgh *Courier*, October 1924; James A. Riley, *The All-Time All-Stars of Black Baseball* (Cocoa, FL, 1983); James A. Riley, *The Biographical Encyclopedia of the Negro Baseball Leagues* (New York, 1994).

Merl F. Kleinknecht

ALLEN, Richard Anthony "Richie," "Dick" (b. March 8, 1942, Wampum, PA), player and coach, became a leading power hitter of the 1960s and 1970s. Allen's father abandoned his wife, Eva, a domestic, leaving her with nine children. Allen starred in basketball at Wampum High School and was offered over 100 college athletic scholarships. Allen entered professional baseball as an infielder at Elmira, NY (NYPL) in 1960. He played for Twin Falls (PrL) in 1961, Williamsport, PA (EL) in 1962, and Arkansas (IL) in 1963 before joining the Philadelphia Phillies (NL) in late 1963. The NL Rookie of the Year in 1964, he hit .318, made 201 hits, scored 125 runs, and batted in 91 runs. Adversely, he struck out 138 times, a then NL record, and was considered a defensive liability at third base. Through 1967, he hit over .300 each season. Allen's team proved quite dependent on his batting and suffered badly during his slumps and frequent injuries. After Allen played first base during the 1969 season, the Phillies grew tired of him and his personality conflicts and traded him. He spent single seasons with the St. Louis Cardinals (NL) and Los Angeles Dodgers (NL) without achieving his earlier distinction.

In December 1971, Allen was traded to the Chicago White Sox (AL). In spacious Comiskey Park a power hitter of Allen's character seemed unlikely to flourish. But Allen enjoyed his finest seasons there, hitting over .300 for three consecutive years. Remarkably, he led the AL in HR with 37 in 1972 and 32 in 1974. In 1972 he drove in 113 runs and was chosen AL MVP. By this time, he had become a competent fielder at first base and had pioneered wearing a batting helmet in the field.

In May 1975, Allen returned to the Phillies (NL). After hitting .233 and .268 the next two seasons, he signed as a free agent with the Oakland Athletics (AL) in March 1977. In 1977, he hit only .240 in 54 games and retired from baseball. Allen alienated managements by avoiding spring training, which he found unnecessary because of his strong physique, and by leaving teams before the end of seasons. During 15 seasons, he batted .292 in 1,749 games, hit 351 HR, and batted in 1,119 runs. Although never on a pennant winner, he played on the Phillies' 1976 divisional champions. He made two hits in nine times at bat as the Reds swept the series in three games.

Allen married Barbara Moore on February 18, 1962. They had three children before their 1981 divorce. Following his baseball career, he became a gentleman farmer and an owner of racehorses. He worked as a hitting coach for the Texas Rangers (AL) in 1982 and as a roving minor league hitting instructor for the Chicago White Sox in 1985 and the Philadelphia Phillies in 1994 and 1995.

BIBLIOGRAPHY: Richard Allen file, National Baseball Library, Cooperstown, NY; *TSN Baseball Register, 1966*; *TSN Official Baseball Guide, 1961–1978*; Richard Lindberg, *Who's on Third?* (South Bend, IN, 1983); Bob Vanderberg, *Sox: From Lane and Fain to Zisk and Fisk* (Chicago, IL, 1982); Frank Dolson, *The Philadelphia Story* (South Bend, IN, 1981), Allen Lewis, *The Philadelphia Phillies: A Pictorial History* (Virginia

Beach, VA, 1981); *WWIB, 1977*, 62nd ed.; Richard Allen with Tim Whitaker, *Crash* (New York, 1989); Rich Westcott, *Diamond Greats* (Westport, CT, 1988); John Benson et al., *Baseball's Top 100* (Wilton, CT, 1997); Mark Lazarus, "Dick Allen's 1972: A Year to Remember," *TNP* 4 (Spring 1985), pp. 42–44; David Halberstam, *October 1964* (New York, 1997); Rich Westcott and Frank Bilovsky, *The New Phillies Encyclopedia* (Philadelphia, PA, 1993).

George W. Hilton

ALLEY, Leonard Eugene "Gene" (b. July 10, 1940, Richmond, VA), player, is of Irish-German descent and the son of a railroad worker who pitched semiprofessional baseball. His father died in an automobile accident when Gene was only two. Alley, whose mother reared two boys and two girls, played PoL and American Legion baseball in Richmond. At Hermitage High School, he made the All-City and All-District baseball teams for two years. As a senior, Alley hit .429, captained the team, and was voted the District's MVP. He also played high school basketball for three years, making the All-City team as a senior co-captain.

Upon graduating from high school in 1959, Alley was offered athletic scholarships by the University of Richmond and Randolph-Macon College. The Pittsburgh Pirates (NL), however, signed him for a $2,000 bonus. In his first year of professional baseball, he batted .287 and hit 15 HR for Dubuque, IA (ML), showing great range and a strong arm at shortstop. Although only 5-feet 11-inches and 160 pounds, Alley exhibited surprising power. In 1960 he played at Burlington, IA (3IL); Grand Forks, ND (NoL), where he was named the League's MVP; and Columbus, OH (IL). An arm injury caused the Pittsburgh organization to shift him briefly to third base and second base in 1959 and 1960, but he returned to shortstop by 1961. He spent 1961 and most of 1962 at Asheville, NC (SAL), finishing the campaign at Columbus. In 1963 Alley hit 19 HR in 146 games at Columbus and was called up briefly by the Pittsburgh Pirates. After leading the AIL in batting at .364 that fall, he played with the Pittsburgh Pirates for the next decade.

Alley batted only .211 in 81 games for the Pittsburgh Pirates in 1964. The team continued to search for a successor to Dick Groat,* who had been traded after the 1962 season. Alley's great arm and fielding range won him the shortstop job in 1965, as he hit .252 in 153 games. He and second baseman Bill Mazeroski* combined for an NL-record 215 double plays in 1966. Alley won Gold Gloves in 1966 and 1967 and was voted to start the 1966 All-Star game as the NL shortstop, but an injury kept him from playing.

Despite a 1966 beaning and a 1967 shoulder injury, those campaigns marked Alley's finest seasons. He complemented his fielding by hitting .299 in 1966 and .287 in 1967. Although he played 133 games in 1968, his batting average slid to .245. Hand, shoulder, and knee injuries forced him to retire in November 1973. In his 11-year major league career, the quiet competitor hit .254 in 1,195 games with 999 hits and 55 HR. In 10 NL Championship Series and World Series games, he managed only one hit in 27 at-bats. His most memorable play came in the field, as he glided smoothly and efficiently into the hole or up the middle to turn apparent hits into outs. He and Mazeroski comprised what Hall-of-Famer Pie Traynor* called "the best double play combination in my time." Traynor added that, for all-around play, Alley was "one of the finest shortstops I ever saw."

Alley married Elizabeth Ann Tilley on September 29, 1962 and has two daughters, Lori and Debbie. Since retiring from baseball, he has worked for a company that manufactures printing plates for various types of printing jobs near Richmond, VA.

BIBLIOGRAPHY: Gene Alley file, National Baseball Library, Cooperstown, NY; Richard L. Burtt, *The Pittsburgh Pirates, A Pictorial History* (Virginia Beach, VA, 1977); Chuck Greenwood, "Cards Were Right Up Gene's Alley," *SCD* 23 (December 6, 1996), p. 182; *The Baseball Encyclopedia*, 10th ed. (New York, 1996); Bob Smizik, *The Pittsburgh Pirates: An Illustrated History* (New York, 1990); Greg Spalding, *Sailing the Three Rivers to the Title* (Pittsburgh, PA, 1994).

                                                                          Luther W. Spoehr

ALLISON, William Robert "Bob" (b. July 11, 1934, Raytown, MO; d. April 9, 1995, Rio Verde, AZ), player, was one of three children born to William Allison. At Raytown High School, he excelled in football. Since the school did not have a baseball program, he learned his early diamond skills in city youth recreational programs. Following graduation from Raytown High School in 1951, Allison played in 1951 and 1952 for the Raytown Cubs of the American Legion and in 1953 and 1954 for the Milgrams of the semi-professional Ban Johnson League of Kansas City, MO. He captained the Milgrams in 1954. Allison played football at the University of Kansas. He signed a minor league contract with the Washington Senators (AL) organization in 1955 and spent 1955 at Hagerstown, MD (PiL), 1956 at Charlotte, NC (SAL), and 1957 and 1958 at Chattanooga, TN (SL).

The 6-foot 3-inch, 205-pound Allison joined the Washington Senators in September 1958. In his first full major league season, the right-handed fielder and slugger in 1959 batted .261, hit 30 HR, compiled 85 RBI, scored 83 runs, led the AL in triples with 9, and was named the AL's Rookie of the Year. His best statistical year came in 1963, when he led the AL in runs scored (99), placed second in slugging average (.533), finished third in HR (35), HR percentage (6.6), and base on balls (90), tied for fourth with Rocky Colavito* in RBI (91), and garnered fifth in total bases (281). He participated in two AL Championship Series (1969, 1970) against the Baltimore Orioles and in one World Series (1965) against the Los Angeles Dodgers.

Allison appeared in 1,541 major league games, playing 1,320 in the outfield and 145 at first base. He compiled a lifetime .255 batting average and

.471 slugging average, hit 256 HR, and drove in 796 runs. Allison belted 20–29 HR five times (1961, 1962, 1965, 1967, 1968) and hit over 30 HR three times (1959, 1963, 1964). On two occasions, Allison drove in over 100 runs (1961, 1962). He and Harmon Killebrew* combined for 70 or more HR in six seasons (1959, 1961–1964, 1967). Allison spent 13 major league seasons in the same organization, playing for the Washington Senators (1958–1960) and the Minnesota Twins (1961–1970). He served as general manager for Coca-Cola Bottling Midwest of St. Paul, MN and on the board of directors of the Major League Baseball Players Alumni Association. He died from complications due to ataxia. Allison married Elizabeth Shearer in February 1956 and had three children Mark, Kirk, and Kyle, before their divorce.

BIBLIOGRAPHY: William Allison file, National Baseball Library, Cooperstown, NY; *The Baseball Encyclopedia*, 10th ed. (New York, 1996); *Facts on File Year 1959* 21 (New York, 1960); Dave Moina and Dave Jarzyna, *Twenty-five Seasons* (Minneapolis, MN, (1986); Tom Ibarra, sports reporter for the Kansas City *Star*, phone conversation with James Welch, November 1989; Tom Mee, vice-president of Public Relations, Minnesota Twins, phone conversation with James Welch, November 1989; *NYT Biographical Service*, April 1995, p. 539.

James E. Welch

ALOMAR, Roberto Velazquez "Robbie" (b. February 5, 1968, Ponce, PR), player, is the son of Santos "Sandy" Alomar, Sr. and Maria Angelita (Velazquez) Alomar and attended Luis Munoz Rivera High School in Salinas, PR. His father played infield for six major league teams, while his brother, Sandy Jr., catches for the Cleveland Indians (AL). In February 1985, the San Diego Padres (NL) signed Alomar for $80,000.

The 6-foot, 185-pound second baseman, who switch hits and throws right-handed, progressed rapidly through the Padre farm system with Charleston, SC (SAL) in 1985, Reno, NV (CaL) in 1986, Wichita, KS (TL) in 1987, and Las Vegas, NV (PCL) briefly in 1988 before joining the San Diego Padres as a 20-year-old regular second baseman. Although the NL's youngest player, he batted .266 and was named San Diego Rookie of the Year. Teammate Tony Gwynn* honed Alomar's batting skills. In 1989, Alomar hit .295 with 42 stolen bases.

A blockbuster December 1990 trade sent Alomar and Joe Carter* to the Toronto Blue Jays (AL) for Tony Fernandez* and Fred McGriff.* Alomar batted .295 with 41 doubles and a career-high 11 triples in 1991, helping Toronto capture the AL East. The Oakland A's won the 1991 AL Championship Series, but Alomar batted .474 with four RBI. In 1992, he hit .310 and set the AL record for fewest errors (5) by a second baseman. His .423 batting average, two HR, and four RBI in the 1992 AL Championship Series earned him MVP honors and helped the Blue Jays vanquish Oakland. Toronto triumphed over the Atlanta Braves in the 1992 World Series.

In 1993, Alomar batted .326 with 17 HR and 93 RBI and hit .292 in the AL Championship Series against the Chicago White Sox. His .480 batting average with 12 safeties and six RBI helped Toronto defeat the Philadelphia Phillies in the World Series. A broken ankle sidelined Alomar the first part of 1994, but he batted at least .300 the next two seasons.

The Baltimore Orioles (AL) signed him as a free agent in December 1995. His best season came in 1996, when he batted .328 and set career highs with 193 hits and 43 doubles and hit .294 with four RBI in the Division Series against the Cleveland Indians. AL President Gene Budig* suspended him five games for spitting in the face of umpire John Hirschbeck after a called third strike at Toronto on September 27, 1996. Alomar batted a career-high .333 in 1997, helping Baltimore capture the AL East. He doubled twice with two RBI in the AL Division Series against the Seattle Mariners and homered once with two RBI in the AL Championship Series against the Cleveland Indians. He signed a $32 million, four-year contract with the Cleveland Indians (AL) in 1998. He set career highs with 138 runs, 24 HR, and 120 RBI in 1999 and batted .368 in the 1999 AL Division Series.

Through 1999, Alomar has batted .304 with 372 doubles, 151 HR, 829 RBI, and 377 stolen bases. He has appeared in 10 All-Star games (1990–1999), earned eight Gold Gloves (1991–1996, 1998, 1999), and made the 1992, 1996, and 1999 *TSN* AL All-Star and Silver-Slugger Teams and the AP All-Star Team. Alomar has batted .316 with 36 hits, three HR, and 15 RBI in five AL Championship Series and .347 with 17 hits and six RBI in two World Series. He combines consistency and power at the plate with speed on the base paths and exceptional range defensively. Alomar resides in Salinas, PR.

BIBLIOGRAPHY: Roberto Alomar file, National Baseball Library, Cooperstown, NY; John Benson et al., *Baseball's Top 100* (Wilton, CT, 1997); Barry Bloom, "Alomar, As in All-Star," *Sport* 82 (March 1991), pp. 46–48, 50–51; Barry Bloom, "Roberto Alomar," *Sport* 88 (January 1997), pp. 12ff; Tim Kurkjian, "Public Enemy No. 1," *SI* 85 (October 14, 1996), pp. 28–30; Barry Newman, "Home Suite Home," *SI* 76 (June 8, 1992), pp. 36–39; *San Diego Padres 1991 Media Guide*; *TSN Official Baseball Register*, 1998.

David L. Porter

ALOU, Felipe (Rojas) (b. May 12, 1935, Haina, DR), player, coach, and manager, is the son of Jose Rojas and Virginia (Alou) Rojas and grew up with five siblings in the poverty-stricken environs of Haina. Two of his younger brothers, Mateo* and Jesus, joined Felipe later as major league baseball players. In his youth, Felipe excelled as an all-around athlete and during his senior year of high school set the Dominican record in throwing the javelin. At the University of Santo Domingo, he played on the Dominican baseball squad in the 1955 Pan-American contests. That same year, Horatio Martinez, a university baseball coach and a scout for the New York Giants (NL), signed Alou to a professional baseball contract.

The 6-foot, 195-pound Dominican slugger spent the next two years as a minor league outfielder before his debut with the San Francisco Giants (NL) in June 1958. His best year with the San Francisco Giants came in 1962, when he hit 25 HR, drove in 98 tallies, and batted .316. His best year overall, however, took place in 1966 during his tenure with the Atlanta Braves (NL). That year, he belted 31 HR, batted in 74 runs, led the NL with 218 hits and 122 runs scored, and finished second in the batting race with a career-high .327 average. In 1968, he again paced the NL with 210 hits. Between 1970 and 1974, Alou performed for the Oakland Athletics (AL), New York Yankees (AL), and Montreal Expos (NL) and concluded his major league career with the Milwaukee Brewers (AL). He finished his playing days with 206 HR, 852 RBI, 985 runs scored, and a .286 career batting average.

Alou joined the Montreal Expos organization as a minor league manager for the 1975 season and compiled an 844–751 win–loss record in 12 seasons, finishing first three times and winning two minor league championships. He coached for the Montreal Expos in 1979, 1980, 1984, and 1992. On May 22, 1992, he took over the Montreal Expos after manager Tom Runnells was fired. At that point, the Montreal Expos were struggling with a 17–20 mark. The crafty rookie manager guided the Montreal Expos to an 87–75 second-place finish in the NL Eastern Division. In his second year as manager, the Montreal Expos again contended for the title and repeated in second place with a 94–68 record. During the strike-shortened 1994 season, Alou managed the Montreal Expos to first place with a 74–40 mark and won AP Major League and BBWAA NL Manager of the Year honors. The financially strapped Montreal Expos traded most of their premier players, including Alou's youngest son, Moises, but he continued to perform reasonably well with mediocre talent. The Montreal Expos finished second in the NL East with an 88–74 record in 1996, 78–84 in 1997, 65–97 in 1998, and 68–94 in 1999. In eight seasons through 1999, Alou has compiled a 603–590 win–loss record and .505 winning percentage.

Alou, currently married to Lucie Gagdon from Canada, has nine children through three previous marriages.

BIBLIOGRAPHY: Felipe Alou file, National Baseball Library, Cooperstown, NY; Felipe Alou with Arnold Hano, "Latin-American Ballplayers Need a Bill of Rights," *Sport* 37 (November 1963), pp. 21, 76–79; Felipe Alou with Herm Weiskopf, *Felipe Alou: My Life and Baseball* (Waco, TX, 1967); Steve Bitker, *The Original San Francisco Giants* (Champaign, IL, 1998); Michael Farber, "Diamond Heirs," *SI* 82 (June 19, 1995), pp. 88–92; Gary Caruso, *The Braves Encyclopedia* (Philadelphia, PA, 1995); David Plaut, *Chasing October* (South Bend, IN, 1994); Tim Kurkjian, "Northern Exposure," *SI* 77 (July 27, 1992), pp. 54–55; W. Leavy, "Baseball's Minority Managers, Taking Charge on the Field," *Ebony* 48 (May 1993), pp. 10–12; Steve Marantz, "The Father and the Son," *TSN*, June 21, 1993, pp. 10–13; Larry Moffi and Jonathan Kronstadt, *Crossing the Line* (Jefferson, NC, 1994); Nick Peters, *Giants Almanac* (Berkeley, CA, 1988).

Samuel O. Regalado

ALOU, Mateo (Rojas) "Matty" (b. December 22, 1938, Haina, DR), player and scout, is the son of Jose Rojas and Virginia (Alou) Rojas and was the middle of the three Alou brothers who played in the major leagues. Smaller but faster than either Felipe* or Jesus, the 5-foot 9-inch, 160-pound left-handed batting outfielder hit the ball to all fields and also beat out innumerable infield hits.

The San Francisco Giants' (NL) legendary Latin American scout Horacio Martinez initially signed Alou. Alou began his professional baseball career in 1957 at Michigan City, IN (ML). His other minor league stops included St. Cloud, MN (NoL), Springfield, MA (EL), and Tacoma, WA (PCL) before he debuted with the San Francisco Giants in 1960. Alou remained with the San Francisco Giants as a part-time player through the 1965 season and only once batted more than 250 times. Alou, however, made four hits in 12 at bats with one RBI in the 1962 World Series when the New York Yankees defeated the San Francisco Giants in seven games.

The San Francisco Giants traded Alou to the Pittsburgh Pirates (NL) in October 1965. Alou came into his own as the Pirates' leadoff hitter and center fielder. Pirates manager Harry Walker* convinced Alou to switch to a heavier bat and hit to left field. The diminutive Dominican averaged .327 at the plate and scored 434 runs during his five years from 1966 to 1970 with the Pittsburgh Pirates. In 1966, Alou won the NL batting title with a .342 average. Alou finished second with a .332 batting average in 1968, third behind teammate Roberto Clemente* with a .338 batting average in 1967, and fourth with a .331 batting average in 1969. During 1969, the speedy Alou led the NL with 231 hits and 41 doubles and also set a major league record for most at bats in one season with 698. Alou's hitting exploits secured him positions on the NL All-Star team in 1968 and 1969 and *TSN* All-Star team in 1969.

In January 1971, the Pittsburgh Pirates traded Alou to the St. Louis Cardinals (NL) for pitcher Nelson Briles* and outfielder Vic Davalillo. After hitting .315 for the St. Louis Cardinals, he was sent in August 1972 to the Oakland Athletics (AL). As a late season addition to the A's roster, Alou hit .381 in the 1972 AL Championship Series. He faltered, however, in the World Series against the Cincinnati Reds. The Oakland A's won the World Series for their first championship, but Alou made only one hit in 24 at bats.

In November 1972, the Oakland A's traded Alou to the New York Yankees (AL). He played for the St. Louis Cardinals in 1973 and finished his 15 years in the major leagues with the San Diego Padres (NL) in 1974. During his major league career, Alou appeared in 1,667 games and batted .307 with 1,777 hits. He hit over .300 seven times and made 200 or more hits on two occasions.

The Santo Domingo, DR resident married Theresa Vasquez on October 24, 1962. In January 1999, he joined the San Francisco Giants (NL) as a scout.

BIBLIOGRAPHY: Mateo Alou file, National Baseball Library, Cooperstown, NY; Richard L. Burtt, *The Pittsburgh Pirates: A Pictorial History* (Virginia Beach, VA,

1977); Felipe Alou with Herm Weiskopf, *Felipe Alou: My Life and Baseball* (Waco, TX, 1967); Larry Moffi and Jonathan Kronstadt, *Crossing the Line* (Jefferson, NC, 1994); Nick Peters, *Giants Almanac* (Berkeley, CA, 1988); *The Baseball Encyclopedia*, 10th ed. (New York, 1996); David Plaut, *Chasing October* (South Bend, IN, 1994); Mike Shatzkin, ed., *The Ballplayers* (New York, 1990); Bob Smizik, *The Pittsburgh Pirates: An Illustrated History* (New York, 1990).

Frank W. Thackeray

ALSTON, Walter Emmons "Smoky" (b. December 1, 1911, Venice, OH; d. October 1, 1984, Oxford, OH), player and manager, was the son of farmer and automobile worker Emmons Alston and Lenora (Neanover) Alston. He graduated in 1929 from Milford Township High School, Darrtown, OH and in 1935 from nearby Miami University, Oxford, OH, where his all-around athletic abilities qualified him for its Hall of Fame. Alston, who immediately joined the St. Louis Cardinals (NL) farm system, married Lela Alexander of Darrtown on May 10, 1930 and had one child.

As a slugging first baseman, Alston spent 13 years in the minors from 1935 to 1947. His clubs included Greenwood, SC (EDL), Huntington, WV (MAL), Rochester, NY (IL), Houston, TX (TL), Columbus, GA (SAL), Springfield, OH (MAL), Trenton, NJ (ISL), Nashua, NH (NEL), and Pueblo, CO (WL). He won various league HR crowns four times, RBI titles twice, hit above .300 seven times, and once hit .350. Despite these impressive statistics, he batted only once in the major leagues because stars Rip Collins,* Jim Bottomley,* and Johnny Mize* played first base for the Cardinals. During the off-seasons, he taught and coached football and basketball at New Madison, OH and Lewistown, OH high schools. Branch Rickey,* who established the Cardinals' farm chain, regarded Alston as a fine managerial prospect and in 1940 made him a playing manager. Alston managed in the minor leagues for twelve seasons at Portsmouth, OH and Springfield, OH (MAL), Trenton, NJ (ISL), Nashua, NH (NEL), Pueblo, CO (WL), St. Paul, MN (AA), and Montreal, Canada (IL), winning three pennants and finishing second three times. Rickey took over the Brooklyn Dodgers (NL) and in 1946 brought Alston into their system.

When Brooklyn fired Chuck Dressen* after the 1953 season, Alston became the Dodgers' manager. The Dodgers had refused to give Dressen, who had won two consecutive NL championships, a multiyear contract. Alston managed the Dodgers for 23 seasons through 1976 and never asked for a multiyear contract. Alston's Dodgers won seven NL pennants (1955, 1956, 1959, 1963, 1965, 1966, 1974). In 1959 the Dodgers tied the Milwaukee Braves for first place, winning the playoff series in two straight games. In 1962 the Dodgers tied the San Francisco Giants and lost the playoff, two games to one. Alston was noted for quiet leadership and for meeting problems directly. During his tenure, the Dodgers won four world championships (1955, 1959, 1963, 1965). His outstanding players included Jim Gilliam,* Maury Wills,* Sandy Koufax,* Roy Campanella,* Don Newcombe,* Duke Snider,* Sal Maglie,* Pee Wee Reese,* Don Drysdale,* Steve Garvey,* Carl

Furillo,* and Jackie Robinson,* while his coaching staff included Leo Durocher,* Chuck Dressen,* and Tommy Lasorda.* Alston was named *TSN* Major League Manager of the Year in 1955, 1959, and 1963 and was elected to the National Baseball Hall of Fame in 1983.

After retiring, Alston resided in Darrtown, served as an adviser and coach for the Dodgers, hunted avidly, rode horseback and trail bikes, and pursued furniture building and woodworking.

BIBLIOGRAPHY: Walter Alston file, National Baseball Library, Cooperstown, NY; Tommy Holmes, *The Dodgers* (New York, 1975); Richard Goldstein, *Superstars and Screwballs* (New York, 1991); Walter Alston with Si Burick, *Alston and the Dodgers* (New York, 1966); Walter Alston with Jack Tobin, *A Year at a Time* (Waco, TX, 1976); Thomas Aylesworth and Benton Minks, *The Encyclopedia of Baseball Managers* (New York, 1990); Peter Golenbock, *Bums* (New York, 1984); Donald Honig, *The Man in the Dugout* (Lincoln, NE, 1995); Leonard Koppett, *The Man in the Dugout* (New York, 1993); William F. McNeil, *The Dodgers Encyclopedia* (Champaign, IL, 1997); *The Baseball Encyclopedia*, 10th ed. (New York, 1996); Bill James, *The Baseball Book 1990* (New York, 1990).

John E. DiMeglio

ALTOBELLI, Joseph Salvatore "Joe" (b. May 26, 1932, Detroit, MI), player, coach, manager, and executive, grew up in Detroit and graduated in 1950 from Eastern High School, where he made the All-City baseball, basketball, and football teams. The Cleveland Indians (AL) signed the 6-foot, 185-pound left-handed hitting first baseman in 1950. He also played in the Los Angeles Dodgers (NL), Minnesota Twins (AL), and Baltimore Orioles (AL) organizations. During his first professional season with Daytona Beach, FL (FSL) in 1951, Altobelli set a record hitting safely in 36 consecutive games.

His minor league playing career included stints at Reading, PA (EL) in 1952 and 1953, Indianapolis, IN (AA) from 1954 to 1956 and in 1958, Columbus, OH (IL) in 1957, Toronto, Canada (IL) in 1959, Montreal, Canada (IL) in 1960, Syracuse, NY (IL) in 1961, Omaha, NE (AA) in 1962, and Rochester, NY (IL) from 1963 to 1966. The slick-fielding Altobelli led AA first basemen in double plays in 1954 and 1955, fielding percentage in 1958, and putouts, assists, and double plays in 1962. He topped the IL with 30 HR and 105 RBI in 1960. His minor league career featured a .275 batting average, 178 HR, and 945 RBI. He spent parts of major league seasons with the Cleveland Indians in 1955 and 1957 and the Minnesota Twins in 1961, batting .210 with five HR and 28 RBI in 166 games.

During 1965 and early 1966, Altobelli combined player-coach duties at Rochester. In 1966, his managerial career began at Bluefield, WV (ApL). He piloted Bluefield in 1967, Stockton, CA (CaL) in 1968, Dallas-Fort Worth, TX (TL) in 1969 and 1970, Rochester from 1971 to 1976, and Columbus in 1980, capturing pennants at Bluefield in 1967, Rochester in 1971, 1974, and 1976, and Columbus in 1980. His 1971 Rochester club won the Junior World Series over the Denver Bears in seven games. He was named Manager of the Year at Bluefield in 1967, Rochester in 1971 and 1976, and Columbus in 1980 and *TSN* Minor League Manager of the Year in 1974.

Altobelli managed the San Francisco Giants (NL) from October 1976 to September 1979, garnering AP 1978 NL Manager of the Year accolades. After being third base coach for the New York Yankees (AL) in 1981 and 1982, he was named Baltimore Orioles manager in November 1982. The Orioles won the 1983 AL pennant and defeated the Philadelphia Phillies, four games to one, in the World Series. Altobelli became just the seventh manager to capture both Junior World Series and World Series titles and only the ninth pilot to win the World Series in his first year, earning UPI AL Manager of the Year honors. After being removed as Baltimore manager in June 1985, he served as bench coach for the New York Yankees in 1986 and as the New York Yankees minor league coordinator in 1987. After a stint as hitting and dugout coach for the Chicago Cubs (NL) from 1988 to 1991, Altobelli held the general manager position for the Rochester Red Wings from November 1991 to early 1995. The Rochester, NY resident married Pat Wooten in 1952 and has six children, Mike, Mark, Judy, Jackie, Jerry, and Joe.

BIBLIOGRAPHY: Joseph Altobelli file, National Baseball Library, Cooperstown, NY; *Baltimore Orioles 1983 Media Guide*; James H. Bready, *Baseball in Baltimore* (Baltimore, MD, 1998); Thomas Aylesworth and Benton Minks, *The Encyclopedia of Baseball Managers* (New York, 1990); *Chicago Cubs 1990 Media Guide; International League 1997 Record Book*; Bill James, *The Baseball Book 1990* (New York, 1990); Jim Mandelaro and Scott Pitoniak, *Silver Seasons* (Syracuse, NY, 1996); Ted Patterson, *The Baltimore Orioles* (Dallas, TX, 1995); Nick Peters, *Giants Almanac* (Berkeley, CA, 1988); *Rochester Red Wings 1994 Media Guide; San Francisco Giants 1979 Media Guide.*

Robert J. Brown

AMES, Leon Kessling "Red" (b. August 2, 1882, Warren, OH; d. October 8, 1936, Warren, OH), player and manager, entered professional baseball with Zanesville, OH (OPL) in 1901 and pitched for Ilion, NY (NYSL) in 1902–1903. He joined the New York Giants (NL) in September 1903 and won both his starts. His best season came in 1905, when he compiled a 22–8 record for the World Champion New York Giants. Ames flirted with baseball immortality on April 15, 1909, holding the Brooklyn Superbas (NL) hitless for nine innings. He gave up a hit in the tenth inning and lost, 3–0, in 13 innings. In 1911, he lost his only World Series start to the Philadelphia Athletics (AL). Ames won consistently for the Giants, having a solid 108–77 record over 11 years from 1903 to 1913.

The New York Giants traded Ames, pitcher Art Fromme, and infielder Eddie Grant to the Cincinnati Reds (NL) in May 1913 for infielder Heinie Groh* and outfielder Josh Devore. With weaker NL teams during the 1913–

1919 period, the 5-foot 10 1/2-inch, 185-pound right-hander struggled to a 75–90 win–loss record. Two difficult years with the Cincinnati Reds included Ames leading all NL pitchers with 23 losses in 1914. The Reds sold him to the St. Louis Cardinals (NL) in July 1915. The redheaded Ohioan remained with the Cardinals until being sent to the Philadelphia Phillies (NL) in September 1919. Almost immediately an automobile accident reduced his effectiveness. His major league career ended after the 1919 season. Ames pitched for Kansas City, MO (AA) from 1920 to 1922 and managed Dayton, OH (OSL) in 1923.

A cold-weather pitcher even as a veteran, Ames compiled a career 183–167 win–loss record and a 2.63 ERA in 3,198 innings. His only child, Leon K., Jr., pitched minor league baseball for several years, but did not come close to reaching the major leagues.

BIBLIOGRAPHY: Leon Ames file, National Baseball Library, Cooperstown, NY; Noel Hynd, *The Giants of the Polo Grounds* (New York, 1988); Frank Graham, *The New York Giants* (New York, 1952); Lee Allen, *The Cincinnati Reds* (New York, 1948); Ray Robinson, *Matty: An American Hero* (New York, 1993); Frank Graham, *McGraw of the Giants* (New York, 1944); Frederick G. Lieb, *The St. Louis Cardinals* (New York, 1945); Bob Broeg and Jerry Vickery, *St. Louis Cardinals Encyclopedia* (Grand Rapids, MI, 1998); *The Baseball Encyclopedia*, 10th ed. (New York, 1996); John Thorn et al., eds., *Total Baseball*, 5th ed. (New York, 1997); *TSN*, October 10, 1936, p. 45.

Fred Stein

ANDERSON, Brady Kevin (b. January 18, 1964, Silver Spring, MD), player, graduated from Carlsbad, CA High School and majored in economics at the University of California, Irvine. After being drafted by the Boston Red Sox (AL) in June 1985, he was traded with pitcher Curt Schilling to the Baltimore Orioles (AL) for hurler Mike Boddicker* in July 1988. The left-handed Anderson, who is single, possessed a keen eye at the plate and superb speed, making him an ideal leadoff batter. In 1992, he batted .271, stole 53 bases, and hit 21 HR. He developed determination, setting definite personal goals before each season. The 6-foot 1-inch, 190-pound Anderson pursued rigorous physical conditioning, including weight lifting, and resembled a well-conditioned heavyweight boxer. He participated in other sports, especially basketball, boxing, surfing, and tennis.

The 1996 campaign demonstrated Anderson's dedication, for he batted .297 with 110 RBI and 172 hits. He clouted an astounding 50 HR, second only to 52 by Oakland's Mark McGwire.* Anderson's total established an Oriole team HR record, surpassing Frank Robinson's* 49 in 1966. In 1996, Anderson belted 12 leadoff HR. Four came in successive games. His last regular season game witnessed his landmark HR off Pat Hentgen* of the Toronto Blue Jays. Manager Davey Johnson* saw that Anderson thrived on the challenge of the leadoff position and getting the Orioles "on the board real quick." He climaxed 1996 by slugging three more HR in post-season competition. Anderson amazingly played all season with an acute appendix, postponing surgery until afterward. Anderson could have batted either third or cleanup, but Johnson rebutted, "There's no rule that says your leadoff hitter can't have power."

Anderson played in the 1992, 1996, and 1997 All-Star Games and developed a friendship with teammate Cal Ripken, Jr.,* accepting him as a model in studying pitchers, batting form, and the treatment of fans. The Poway, CA resident admired Ripken's dedication to the game, a trait he likewise possessed. Through the 1999 season, he batted .261 with 182 HR and 661 RBI.

BIBLIOGRAPHY: Brady Anderson file, National Baseball Library, Cooperstown, NY; Michael Bamberger, "Brady Hits 'Em in Bunches," *SI* 86 (April 14, 1997), pp. 50–52ff; John Thorn et al., eds., *Total Baseball*, 5th ed. (New York, 1997); Tim Kurkjian, "Going Batty for Brady," *SI* 76 (June 22, 1992), pp. 52–55; Ted Patterson, *The Baltimore Orioles* (Dallas, TX, 1995); James H. Bready, *Baseball in Baltimore* (Baltimore, MD, 1998); David S. Neft and Richard M. Cohen, eds., *The Sports Encyclopedia: Baseball*, 17th ed. (New York, 1997); *TSN Official Baseball Register*, 1998; Peter Schmuck, "Brady Anderson," *Sport* 84 (March 1993), pp. 20–21; David Srinvasan and Doug Myers, eds., *The Scouting Report, 1997*; Zander Hollander, ed., *1997 The Complete Handbook of Baseball* (New York, 1997); *WWIB, 1997*, 87th ed.; *Street and Smith's Guide to Baseball, 1997*.

William J. Miller

ANDERSON, George Lee "Sparky" (b. February 22, 1934, Bridgewater, SD), player, manager, and sportscaster, is one of five children of Leroy Anderson and Shirley Anderson of Riverside, CA. Leroy, a house painter, moved his family to Los Angeles in 1942 to seek employment in the emerging defense industry. Anderson learned to love baseball by playing with his father, a pitcher, and an uncle, a former minor league catcher. Rod Dedeaux,* the enormously successful baseball coach at the nearby University of Southern California, nurtured Anderson's interest by making him team batboy. Anderson played baseball at Dorsey High School, from which he graduated in 1953, and spent his first professional season at Santa Barbara, CA (CaL). On October 3, 1953, Anderson married Carol Valle, his high school sweetheart, whom he had known since fifth grade. The couple has three children, George Jr., Shirley, and Albert, and resides in Thousand Oaks, CA.

Anderson, one of the most successful major league managers ever, proved a fiery if marginally talented player for one major league and ten minor league seasons from 1953 to 1963. His early clubs included Pueblo, CO (WL) in 1954, Fort Worth, TX (TL) in 1955, Montreal, Canada (IL) in 1956 and 1958, and Los Angeles, CA (PCL) in 1957. After being named MVP of the Montreal Royals (IL), the 5-foot 9-inch, 168-pound Anderson earned his only big league job with the 1959 Philadelphia Phillies (NL). In 152 games as the Phillies' second baseman, he batted only .218 with 34 RBI and was assigned to Toronto, Canada (IL) the next season. He played with Toronto through the 1963 season. Anderson realized that his limited physical skills would not take him back to the majors and consequently concentrated on learning managerial skills. Former major league manager Charley Dressen,* who valued Anderson's competitiveness, fighting spirit, and alertness, encouraged him. "Little Man," he told him, "you ain't never missed a sign. Someday you'll be a manager."

He spent five years as a minor league manager at Toronto in 1964, Rock Hill, SC (WCL) in 1965, St. Petersburg, FL (FSL) in 1966, Modesto, CA (CaL) in 1967, and Asheville, NC (SL) in 1968 and served as a coach for the San Diego Padres (NL) in 1969. In 1970 Anderson was named manager of the Cincinnati Reds (NL). From 1970 to 1978 he guided the decade's most dominant team, winning NL pennants in 1970, 1972, and 1973 and World Series titles in 1975 over the Boston Red Sox and in 1976 over the New York Yankees. The 1976 team, led by Pete Rose,* Joe Morgan,* and Johnny Bench,* ranks with the 1927 and 1961 Yankees among the three greatest teams of all time. No NL team since the 1921–1922 New York Giants had won two successive World Series. Anderson twice was named NL Manager of the Year and piloted the Reds longer than any other manager.

Despite his great success at Cincinnati, Anderson was released following the 1978 season. After being hired in 1979 by the Detroit Tigers (AL), Anderson through 1984 guided his talented young club to better records each year. In 1983, the Tigers won 92 games to finish in second place. After making Anderson the only manager to win 100 games in a season in both leagues, the Tigers in 1984 defeated San Diego in the World Series. Detroit won 35 of their first 40 games that season. Anderson guided the Tigers to first place in the AL East in 1987 with a 98–64 record and to second place finishes in 1988 and 1991 and retired following the 1995 season. The AL Manager of the Year in 1984 and 1987, he compiled the third most victories in major league history with a 2,194–1,834 (.545) mark. Anderson remains the winningest pilot in Tigers history and the first manager to garner at least 800 victories with two different teams.

Anderson, respected for his hard work, honesty, and loyalty, has never forgotten his humble beginnings. His autobiography, *The Main Spark*, gratefully acknowledges the people who helped him attain prominence. He broadcast for the Anaheim Angels (AL) in 1997.

BIBLIOGRAPHY: Sparky Anderson file, National Baseball Library, Cooperstown, NY; Sparky Anderson and Si Burick, *The Main Spark: Sparky Anderson and the Cincinnati Reds* (Garden City, NY, 1978); Anthony Cotton, "Platoon, For-r-r-d Harch!" *SI* 52 (July 21, 1980), pp. 44ff; *CB* (1977), pp. 23–26; Ron Fimrite, "Sparky and George," *SI* 60 (June 11, 1984), pp. 70–74ff; Bill James, *The Baseball Book 1990* (New York, 1990); Mike Lupica, "The People's Manager," *Esquire* 110 (July 1988), pp. 33–34;

Leonard Koppett, *The Man in the Dugout* (New York, 1993); Roger Kahn, "The Cincinnati Kid," *Time* 109 (April 11, 1977), p. 78; Fred T. Smith, *Tiger Tales and Trivia* (Lathrup Village, MI, 1988); Joe Falls, *The Detroit Tigers: An Illustrated History* (New York, 1989); Sparky Anderson and Dan Ewald, *Sparky* (New York, 1990); William M. Anderson, *The Detroit Tigers* (South Bend, IN, 1996); Richard Bak, *A Place for Summer* (Detroit, MI, 1998); Robert H. Walker, *Cincinnati and the Big Red Machine* (Bloomington, IN, 1988); Thomas Aylesworth and Benton Minks, *The Encyclopedia of Baseball Managers* (New York, 1990); Sparky Anderson with Dan Ewald, *They Call Me Sparky* (Chelsea, MI, 1998); Greg Rhodes and John Erardi, *Big Red Dynasty* (Cincinnati, OH, 1997); *NYT Biographical Service* 26 (February 1995), pp. 87–88; Steve Rushin, "The New Perfesser," *SI* 78 (June 28, 1993), pp. 54–58.

Allen E. Hye

ANDERSON, John Joseph "Honest John," "Long John," "Terrible Swede" (b. December 14, 1873, Sarpsborg, Norway; d. July 23, 1949, Worcester, MA), player, was one of four Norwegians to perform in the major leagues and the finest hitter from a Scandinavian nation.

His family immigrated to Worcester, MA when he was a boy, and that city remained his home until his death. He dropped out of school after the eighth grade and later married a local girl, Emma Christina Juhlin. The 6-foot 2-inch, 180-pound, handsome, clean-cut youth possessed a reputation for honesty and thriftiness, but also for mental errors and a "peculiar disposition."

In August 1894, the Brooklyn Bridegrooms (NL) purchased his contract from Haverhill, MA (NEL). Anderson had started his professional career earlier that season. After enjoying three strong seasons in Brooklyn with .286, .314, and .325 batting averages, he was shipped to the Washington Senators (NL) during the 1898 season. That year, he led the NL in triples (22) and slugging average (.494), and established himself as a crowd favorite. Adoring Senators fans presented him with a silver tea service and years later remembered him as "one of the most colorful characters in Washington history."

After Washington sold him back to Brooklyn, Anderson contributed to manager Ned Hanlon's* 1899 championship Brooklyn, NY Superbas club. National Baseball Hall-of-Famers Joe Kelley* and Wee Willie Keeler* combined with Anderson to provide Hanlon an explosive offensive outfield.

Between 1900 and 1908, he played for five AL clubs: the Milwaukee Brewers (1901), St. Louis Browns (1902–1903), New York Highlanders (1904–1905), Washington Nationals (1905–1907), and Chicago White Sox (1908). In 1901 with Milwaukee, he batted a career high .330 and 99 RBI. After his career season, his playing skills and concentration declined. He led the AL with 39 stolen bases in 1906, but sportswriter Frank Graham noted that, as late as the 1940s, a mental mistake on the base path was referred to as a "John Anderson."

After batting a career low .262 in 1908, Anderson quit the game. In 14 major league seasons, he batted .290 with 1,841 hits, 976 RBI, and 338 stolen bases. He served as a policeman in Worcester until hardening of the arteries forced his retirement.

BIBLIOGRAPHY: John Anderson file, National Baseball Library, Cooperstown, NY; Morris Bealle, *The Washington Senators* (Washington, DC, 1947); Richard Goldstein, *Superstars and Screwballs* (New York, 1991); Frank Graham, *The New York Yankees* (New York, 1943); Bill James, *The Baseball Book 1990* (New York, 1990); Shirley Povich, *The Washington Senators* (New York, 1954); Bill Borst, ed., *Ables to Zoldak*, vol. 1 (St. Louis, MO, 1988).

William E. Akin

ANSON, Adrian Constantine "Cap," "Pop" (b. April 17, 1852, Marshalltown, IA; d. April 18, 1922, Chicago, IL), player and manager, was the son of Henry Anson and Jeannette Rice Anson, both of English descent. His father, a transplanted New Yorker who founded Marshalltown, IA, homesteaded and operated a hotel there. Anson, a mediocre student, attended Marshall-town public schools, Notre Dame University, and the University of Iowa. In 1867, he played second base on the state championship Marshalltown baseball team.

From 1871 to 1875, Anson played professional baseball in the NA and received a salary of $800 to $1,800. In 1871, he played third base for Rock-ford Forest City, IL (NA) and led his club with a .325 batting average. Because Rockford disbanded, he joined the Philadelphia Athletics (NA) in 1872 and hit a composite .364 average the next four seasons. When the NL was formed, the Chicago White Stockings secretly signed him for $2,000. When the Athletics offered him $2,500, Anson unsuccessfully sought to be released from the Chicago contract. In 1876, Anson married Virginia Fiegal of Philadelphia. They had seven children, Grace, Adrian H., Adele, Adrian, Jr., Dorothy, John, and Virginia.

Anson played with Chicago (NL) from 1876 to 1897, setting a major league longevity record. The 6-foot 1-inch, 220-pound Anson compiled a .334 lifetime batting average and was the first NL player to surpass 3,000 hits. Anson hit .399 in 1881, exceeded the .300 mark in 20 of 22 seasons, and won batting titles in 1879, 1881, 1887, and 1888. A power hitter in a dead ball era, he drove in 1,879 runs, hit 97 HR, and led the NL in RBI 8 times and in doubles three times. Anson, an inconsistent fielder, led first basemen in fielding five times and in errors three times, making 725 miscues.

The premier nineteenth-century manager, Anson piloted the White Stockings from 1879 to 1897. Ranked high among all-time managers, he won 1,296 games for a .578 career win-loss percentage. In his first eight years at the helm, Anson directed Chicago to five NL pennants (1880–1882, 1885–1886). Chicago played St. Louis (AA) in the 1885–1886 post-season championships. In 1888, he signed a ten-year contract giving him control over field operations and 130 shares of club stock.

Anson, who popularized baseball, managed many exceptional players, including Larry Corcoran,* Jim McCormick,* Clark Griffith,* Michael Kelly,* Ed Williamson,* and Bill Lange.* A strong disciplinarian, he did not allow his players to drink alcoholic beverages, smoke cigarettes or cigars, or use drugs. He was a strict taskmaster, expecting aggressive, team-oriented behavior. The innovative Anson utilized spring training, invented signals, devised the hit-and-run play, encouraged base stealing, developed coaching boxes, and rotated pitchers. He participated on American All-Star teams visiting England in 1874 and touring the world in 1888–1889.

Anson played an instrumental role in barring black players from organized baseball. He nearly cancelled games with Toledo and Newark because those clubs had black players and persuaded the New York Giants not to promote outstanding Negro pitcher George Stovey.* From 1891 to 1897, Anson feuded with Chicago president James Hart over club policies and saw his team experience several losing seasons. Dismissed as manager in early 1898, he briefly piloted the New York Giants (NL) and returned to Chicago.

In *A Ball Player's Career* (1900), he described his professional baseball days and goodwill tours. Anson established billiard and bowling businesses in Chicago and organized a semiprofessional baseball team, but these enterprises foundered financially. From 1905 to 1907, he served as city clerk of Chicago. Despite touring the vaudeville circuit to earn additional income, he went bankrupt and saw his home foreclosed. The NL attempted to establish a pension fund for Anson, but he rejected any assistance. Anson, who had hoped to become baseball's first commissioner in 1920, managed Chicago's Dixmoor Club at the time of his death. In 1939 he was elected to the National Baseball Hall of Fame. Anson's hitting and managerial skills, innovative leadership, and aggressive style helped transform a sandlot sport into the national pastime.

BIBLIOGRAPHY: Adrian Anson file, National Baseball Library, Cooperstown, NY; Chicago Historical Society, Chicago IL; Adrian C. Anson, *A Ball Player's Career* (Chicago, IL, 1900); Arthur Bartlett, *Baseball and Mr. Spalding* (New York, 1951); "Baseball's Grand Old Man," *LD* 73 (May 6, 1922), pp. 62–65; Chicago *Tribune*, 1876–1898, April 18, 1922; Jerry E. Clark, *Anson to Zuber: Iowa Boys in the Major Leagues* (Omaha, NE, 1992); Robert Creamer, *The Baseball Hall of Fame 50th Anniversary Book* (New York, 1988); Warren Brown, *The Chicago Cubs* (New York, 1946); *DAB* 1 (1928), pp. 311–312; Frederick Ivor-Campbell et al., eds., *Baseball's First Stars* (Cleveland, OH, 1996); S. Jantz, "Hall of Famer Cap Anson Was Baseball's Best Player and Most Strident Racist," *Sport* 70 (May 1993), p. 70; Bill James, *The Baseball Book 1990* (New York, 1990); Eddie Gold and Art Ahrens, *The Golden Era Cubs, 1876–1940* (Chicago, IL, 1985); Jim Enright, *Chicago Cubs* (New York, 1975); Peter Levine, *A. G. Spalding and the Rise of Baseball* (New York, 1985); George S. May, "Major League Baseball Players from Iowa," *The Palimpsest 36* (April 1955), pp. 133–165; *NYT*, 1876–1898, April 18, 1922; Tom Nawroki, "Captain Anson's Platoon,"

TNP 15 (1995), pp. 34–37; David L. Porter, "Cap Anson of Marshalltown: Baseball's First Superstar," *The Palimpsest 61* (July/August 1980), pp. 98–107; Albert G. Spalding, *America's National Game* (New York, 1911); Roger H. Van Bolt, " 'Cap' Anson's First Contract," *TAI* 31 (April 1953), pp. 617–625; Warren Wilbert and William Hageman, *Chicago Cubs: Seasons at the Summit* (Champaign, IL, 1997); Brad Herzog, *The Sports 100* (New York, 1995); Noel Hynd, *The Giants of the Polo Grounds* (New York, 1988).

David L. Porter

ANTONELLI, John August (b. April 12, 1930, Rochester, NY), player and executive, is the son of August Antonelli, an Italian immigrant railroad contractor, and Josephine (Messore) Antonelli and batted and threw left-handed. The 6-foot 1½-inch, 185-pound Antonelli starred as a baseball pitcher at Jefferson High School in Rochester in 1947 and 1948 and was signed in 1948 out of semiprofessional baseball by the Boston Braves (NL) as one of the first "bonus babies," receiving a reported $75,000. Bonus rules required Antonelli to stay on the major league roster, as the Boston Braves played him sporadically over the next three years. From 1951 through 1952, he was engaged in military service. He joined the Milwaukee Braves (NL) in 1953 and enjoyed his first successful season, winning 12 games with a 3.18 ERA.

In February 1954, Antonelli figured prominently in a multiplayer trade with the New York Giants (NL). With New York that season, Antonelli enjoyed his greatest success by winning 21 games while losing only seven. He led NL pitchers in winning percentage (.750), shutouts (6), and ERA (2.30). Antonelli added a complete game win and save in the World Series, as the New York Giants swept the heavily favored Cleveland Indians in four games. His performance earned him third place in the 1954 MVP voting. Antonelli won 20 games and hurled five shutouts in 1956, finishing the season with 11 victories in his last 12 games and triumphs in the final seven contests. In 1959, with the Giants now in San Francisco, Antonelli won 19 games and hurled four shutouts to pace the NL for the second time. The San Francisco Giants in December 1960 traded Antonelli to the Cleveland Indians (AL). Cleveland sent him to the Milwaukee Braves (NL) in July 1961. After winning only one decision with the Milwaukee Braves that year, he was traded in October 1961 to the New York Mets (NL). Antonelli, instead retired from baseball. He pitched in the 1954 and 1956 All-Star Games, gaining a save in the latter, and was selected to the major league BBWAA All-Star team in 1954 and 1959. After retiring from baseball, he entered the tire business in Rochester and served as a director of the Rochester Red Wings (IL). Antonelli married Rosemarie Carbone in October 1951 and has three daughters, Lisa, Donna, and Regina, and one son, John, Jr.

BIBLIOGRAPHY: John August Antonelli file, National Baseball Library, Cooperstown, NY; *The Baseball Encyclopedia*, 10th ed. (New York, 1996); Steve Bitker, *The Original San Francisco Giants* (Champaign, IL, 1998); Noel Hynd, *The Giants of the Polo*

Grounds (New York, 1988); Bill James, *The Baseball Book 1991* (New York, 1991); Rich Marazzi, "The Giants Swept the Indians in a Classic World Series," *SCD* 21 (October 28, 1994), pp. 150–151; Fred Stein and Nick Peters, *Giants Diary* (Berkeley, CA, 1987); Jack Orr, "Johnny Antonelli's War with San Francisco," *Sport* 28 (December 1959), pp. 18–19, 78–80; Joseph L. Reichler, ed., *The Great All-Time Baseball Record Book* (New York, 1981).

Horace R. Givens

APARICIO, Luis Ernesto, Jr. "Little Looie" (b. April 29, 1934, Maracaibo, Venezuela), player, manager, and executive, is the son of Luis E. Aparicio, Sr. and attended Maracaibo public schools. His father, an oil company tractor driver and an outstanding professional baseball player, was the first Venezuelan ever offered a major league contract and taught young Luis diamond skills. The good-natured 5-foot 9-inch, 155-pound son left high school after his sophomore year to join a Caracas amateur baseball team. After batting .350 for Venezuela in the Latin American World Series, he played shortstop for the Barquisimeto Cardenales. In 1953, Aparicio began his pro career by replacing his father as shortstop with the Maracaibo Gavilanes. Chicago White Sox (AL) scout Luman Harris soon signed the excellent fielder for $6,000.

Aparicio played shortstop in 1954 with Waterloo, IA (3IL) and in 1955 with Memphis, TN (SA), leading the SA in stolen bases and fielding. The right-handed throwing Aparicio, who married Sonia Llorente on October 1, 1956, and has five children, replaced Venezuelan Chico Carrasquel as starting Chicago White Sox shortstop in 1956. Besides thrilling fans with his fielding and base running, he batted .266 and stole 21 bases as AL Rookie of the Year. From 1956 to 1964, he established a major league record by leading the AL nine straight seasons in stolen bases. In 1959, his career-high 56 stolen bases helped the White Sox dethrone the New York Yankees as AL champions. He pilfered 160 bases from 1959 to 1961 to become the first major leaguer since Ty Cobb* to record at least 50 for three consecutive campaigns.

Aparicio tied a major league record by leading AL shortstops eight consecutive seasons in fielding (1959–1966) and broke one by pacing AL shortstops six straight years in assists (1956–1961). His AL records included most years (5) leading shortstops in games played (1956–1960) and highest fielding percentage by a shortstop in a season (.9826) in 1963. In tandem with second baseman Nelson Fox,* he topped AL shortstops in double plays (117) in 1960. Chicago president Bill Veeck* commented, "Luis always makes plays that can't be made." The Gold Glove was awarded to Aparicio as the best AL fielding shortstop from 1958 to 1962 and in 1964, 1966, 1968, and 1970. *TSN* made him its All-Star team shortstop in 1964, 1966, 1968, 1970, and 1972.

In January 1963, the White Sox traded the right-handed batter to the

Baltimore Orioles (AL). Aparicio hit .276 to help the Orioles win the 1966 AL pennant and sweep the Los Angeles Dodgers in the World Series. He returned in November 1967 to the White Sox, where he enjoyed his best hitting seasons with .280 in 1969 and a career-high .313 in 1970. He was traded in December 1970 to the Boston Red Sox (AL) and finished his career there in 1973. The Maracaibo resident also co-owned a baseball club and managed several winters in Venezuela. During his 18-year major league career, he appeared in 2,599 games (AL record for shortstops), made 2,677 hits, scored 1,335 runs, stole 506 bases (10th best), and batted .262 lifetime. The eight-time AL All-Star was selected from 1958 through 1962 and in 1969 and 1970. In World Series competition, he batted .308 in 1959 and .250 in 1966 against the Los Angeles Dodgers. Besides reviving base stealing, he demonstrated what smaller players could accomplish and that base running and fielding could rival home runs for excitement among fans. In 1984, he was elected to the National Baseball Hall of Fame.

BIBLIOGRAPHY: Luis Aparicio file, National Baseball Library, Cooperstown, NY; James H. Bready, *Baseball in Baltimore* (Baltimore, MD, 1998); Ed Linn, "How Luis Aparicio Steals the Limelight," *Sport 33* (June 1962), pp. 62–70; "Luis Aparicio," *The Lincoln Library of Sports Champions*, vol. 1 (Columbus, OH, 1974); Tom Mortensen, " 'Little Looie' Put the Go in 'Go-Go' White Sox," *SCD 25* (August 21, 1998), p. 10; Ted Patterson, *The Baltimore Orioles* (Dallas, TX, 1995); Richard Lindberg, *Sox* (New York, 1984); Bob Vanderberg, *Sox: From Lane and Fain to Fisk and Zisk* (Chicago, IL, 1982); Richard Lindberg, *Who's on Third?* (South Bend, IN, 1983); Bill James, *The Baseball Book 1991* (New York, 1991); Lowell Reidenbaugh, *Baseball's Hall of Fame-Cooperstown* (New York, 1993); Harold Rosenthal, "Luis Aparicio, SS," *Sport 28* (November 1959), pp. 20–21, 64–65; "Sharpest Shortstop," *Newsweek 53* (June 29, 1959), pp. 86–87; Leonard Shecter, "The Case Against Aparicio," *Sport 35* (June 1963), pp. 42–44, 78–79; *TSN Baseball Register, 1967, 1973*; George Vecsey, "Luis Aparicio: New Life at 36," *Sport 50* (December 1970), pp. 42–45, 84–85; *WWIB*, 59th ed. (1974), p. 4; *WWA*, 38th ed. (1974–1975), p. 81.

David L. Porter

APPIER, Robert Kevin (b. December 6, 1967, Lancaster, CA), player, is the son of Betty Appier, an accountant, and lettered in baseball at Lancaster's Antelope Valley High School, where he was later inducted into the school's Hall of Fame. Appier played baseball at Antelope Valley JC and Fresno State University before the Kansas City Royals (AL) selected the pitcher in the first round of the 1987 June free agent draft as the ninth pick overall.

Appier debuted in the major leagues on June 4, 1989, but compiled a lackluster 1–4 record over the next month and was optioned to Triple-A Omaha, NE (AA) in July. Kansas City recalled him early the next season. Appier responded with a solid rookie campaign, starting 24 games, finishing 12–8 with a 2.76 ERA, and earning *TSN* Rookie Pitcher of the Year honors. *BD* named him to their All-Rookie team, and he finished third in the AL's Rookie of the Year balloting behind Sandy Alomar, Jr. and Kevin Maas.

Although struggling early in the 1991 season, Appier rebounded by posting a 9–3 record after June. He continued this momentum into 1992, compiling a 15–8 record with a 2.46 ERA. He was named the AL Pitcher of the Month for July. Appier fared even better in 1993, winning 18 of 26 decisions with an AL best 2.56 ERA. These numbers earned him a spot on *BA*'s postseason All-Star team and a third place finish in the Cy Young Award balloting behind Jack McDowell* and Randy Johnson.* After a disappointing strike-shortened 1994 season, Appier started strong in 1995 and earned his first appearance in an All-Star Game. He finished with a 15–10 record with a 3.89 ERA, going on to a 14–11 mark with a 3.62 ERA in 1996.

The 6-foot 1-inch, 195-pound Appier throws a 90-plus-miles per hour fastball, a tight slider, and a nasty forkball. These pitches, combined with an unorthodox pitching motion that often confuses opposing batters, has made him one of the AL's top right-handed starting pitchers in the 1990s. In July 1999, the Oakland A's acquired Appier. Through 1999, Appier has compiled a 121–94 career record and a 3.54 ERA with 1,373 strikeouts. The Overland Park, KS resident and his wife, Laurie, have two children, Britney and Garrett.

BIBLIOGRAPHY: Kevin Appier file, National Baseball Library, Cooperstown, NY; *Kansas City Royals 1998 Media Guide*; Tim Kurkjian, "A Royal Start," *SI* 82 (May 15, 1995), p. 81; "Kevin Appier," *Microsoft Complete Baseball* CD-ROM (Redmond, WA, 1994).

Kent M. Krause

APPLING, Lucius Benjamin "Luke," "Old Aches and Pains" (b. April 2, 1907, High Point, NC; d. January 3, 1991, Cumming, GA), player, coach, and manager, grew up in a family of seven children in High Point and attended Fulton High School in Atlanta, GA. Active in all sports, he played football and baseball for Fulton and was selected All-City shortstop. Appling participated in the same sports for Oglethorpe College, once hitting four HR in a single game. At the end of his sophomore year in 1930, he signed professionally with Atlanta, GA (SA). Although making 42 errors that year, the 5-foot 10-inch, 180-pound Appling was called the SA's best shortstop and batted .326. Following that season, the Chicago White Sox (AL) paid Atlanta $20,000 for his contract. Appling substituted for two years and from 1933 to 1949 held the regular shortstop position there. He hit over .300 his first nine of ten full seasons and achieved that level 16 times. A weak fielder initially, he improved greatly under instruction from Lew Fonseça* and Jimmy Dykes.* The right-handed Appling led the AL three times in chances and seven times in assists.

Appling's hitting made him famous. His lifetime record includes 2,749 hits, 1,302 walks, only 528 strikeouts, and a .310 batting average. Although remembered for his homer off Warren Spahn* in a 1983 Old-timers game at age 75, he hit only 45 HR in his career. But he proved a superb contact hitter, whom Dykes called the league's most dangerous batter with two strikes. Allegedly, he once hit 14 consecutive foul balls into the stands to get even with an owner who would not give him two extra game passes. He led the AL in hitting twice, batting .388 in 1936 and .328 in 1943. His 1936 mark, a personal high, led both leagues. Appling also made 204 hits in 1936, the only time he reached that level. Although the White Sox did not reach the World Series during Appling's active career, he made the All-Star team eight times and in 1964 was elected to the National Baseball Hall of Fame.

Appling often complained of having bad ankles, pink eye, the flu, and a perpetual sore back and suffered a broken finger and a broken leg. Nevertheless, Appling usually led the White Sox in games played and, at age 42, still batted .301. For many years, he held the AL record for total games played at shortstop. Even military service failed to hurt Appling's game. He missed all 1944 games and all but 17 contests in 1945, yet still hit .362.

Appling, one of the most popular players, subsequently was offered many coaching jobs. He managed Memphis, TN (SA) from 1951 to 1953 and was chosen 1952 minor league Manager of the Year. Appling also piloted Richmond, VA (IL) in 1954–1955, Memphis (SA) in 1959, and Indianapolis, IN (AA) in 1962. He coached for the Detroit Tigers (AL) in 1960, Cleveland Indians (AL) in 1960 and 1961, Baltimore Orioles (AL) in 1963, and Kansas City Athletics (AL) from 1964 to 1967. In 1967, he managed Kansas City to a 10–30 record. Appling scouted for the Oakland Athletics (AL) in 1968 and 1969 and coached for the White Sox in 1970 and 1971 and Minnesota Twins (AL) in 1973. He served part-time as a minor league hitting instructor for the Atlanta Braves (NL) from the 1970s to 1990. He married Faye Dodd in February 1932 and had two daughters and one son.

BIBLIOGRAPHY: Luke Appling file, National Baseball Library, Cooperstown, NY; Lee Allen, *The American League Story* (New York, 1962); Martin Appel and Burt Goldblatt, *Baseball's Best: The Hall of Fame Gallery* (New York, 1977); Warren Brown, *The Chicago White Sox* (New York, 1952); Richard Lindberg, *Who's on Third?* (South Bend, IN, 1983); Bill James, *The Baseball Book 1991* (New York, 1991); David Neft et al., *The Sports Encyclopedia: Baseball*, 9th ed. (New York, 1989); *Newsweek* 30 (September 22, 1947), pp. 79–80; *NYT*, 1933–1974, December 28, 1936, March 29, 1938, November 28, 1943, January 4, 1991, p. A-18; Lowell Reidenbaugh, *Baseball's Hall of Fame-Cooperstown* (New York, 1993); Rich Westcott, *Diamond Greats* (Westport, CT, 1988); John Thorn, *Champion Batsman of the 20th Century* (Los Angeles, CA, 1992); Richard Lindberg, *Sox* (New York, 1984).

Thomas L. Karnes

ARLETT, Russell Loris "Buzz" (b. January 3, 1899, Oakland, CA; d. May 16, 1964, Minneapolis, MN), player and scout, won acclaim as the greatest switch-hitting slugger in minor league history. The youngest of four sons born to railroad inspector Harry Arlett and Lillian (Klepfer) Arlett, he played baseball at Fremont High School in Melrose, CA. A factory and shipyard worker, Arlett debuted professionally as a pitcher in 1918 with Oakland, CA (PCL) and played with the Oaks through 1930. After rookie struggles, he excelled as a pitcher with a 95–71 win–loss record from 1919 to 1922 and compiled a 29–17 mark in 1920. Arlett's switch from a spitball to a dominant curveball, however, caused him to develop a sore arm. The determined right-hander learned to switch-hit, moved to the outfield, and earned the title "the human buzz saw." With the Oaks from 1923 to 1930, the 6-foot 3-inch, 225 pounder batted between .328 and .374 and averaged 30 HR and almost 140 RBI per season (including 189 in 1929). Arlett holds the PCL career records for HR (251) and RBI (1,135). Despite such heroics, his price tag, inconsistent fielding, periodic injuries, increasing age, and frustration prevented him from receiving a major league trial until 1931.

Upon suing the PCL for injury inflicted by a mask-wielding umpire, Arlett was sold in 1931 to the Philadelphia Phillies (NL). In his sole major league season, he batted .313 with 18 HR, 72 RBI, and a .538 slugging mark. Fielding lapses, however, prompted his sale to Baltimore, MD (IL). With the 1932 Orioles, he led the IL with 54 HR and twice (July 1, July 4) registered 4 HR in one game. With Minneapolis, MN, he led the AA with 41 HR in 1934 and earned a .360 batting average the following season. In 1936, the aging Arlett batted .316 as a part-timer for Minneapolis. He married Vivian Johnson in October 1938 and had two children, Michael and Judy. Four hitless appearances for Syracuse, NY (IL) ended his great minor league career. His minor league career statistics included a .341 batting average, 1,610 runs scored, 432 HR, and 1,786 RBI. Like "Ike" Boone and Smead Jolley, Arlett demonstrated great hitting at all levels and was handicapped by weak defensive skills. After retiring as a player, he operated a popular Minneapolis, MN tavern, enjoyed hunting and fishing, and spent three years scouting for the New York Giants (NL).

BIBLIOGRAPHY: Russell Arlett file, National Baseball Library, Cooperstown, NY; Harry T. Brundidge, "Buzz Arlett—The Game's Big Mystery Man," *TSN*, December 17, 1931, p. 6; Frederick G. Lieb and Stan Baumgartner, *The Philadelphia Phillies* (New York, 1953); John Thorn et al., eds., *Total Baseball*, 5th ed. (New York, 1997); SABR, *Minor League Baseball Stars* (Cooperstown, NY, 1978); Gerald Tomlinson, "A Minor League Legend: Buzz Arlett, the 'Mightiest Oak,'" *BRJ* 17 (1988), pp. 13–16; Rich Westcott and Frank Bilovsky, *The New Phillies Encyclopedia* (Philadelphia, PA, 1993).

James D. Smith III

ARMAS, Antonio Rafael (Machado) "Tony" (b. July 2, 1953, Puerto Piritu, Anzoategui, Venezuela), player and executive, is the son of Jose Rafael Armas and Julieta Machado Armas and grew up in the cattle-grazing state of Anzoategui in northeastern Venezuela. Armas, one of 10 boys in a family of 14 children, dropped out of school in the sixth grade to play baseball. Despite an unorthodox batting style of lifting his front foot and "stepping in the bucket" on every pitch, he starred in Venezuela in the late 1960s. The 6-foot 1-inch, 200-pound, right-handed hitting and throwing outfielder signed with the Pittsburgh Pirates (NL) as a free agent in 1971 and broke into professional baseball that season with Monroe, NC (WCL) and Bradenton, FL (GCL). Although his batting averages were only .227 and .231, Armas looked impressive defensively at Bradenton and led the GCL in chances and putouts. He hit .266 at Gastonia, NC (WCL) in 1972 and raised his batting average above .300 (.301) for the first time at Sherbrooke, Canada (EL) in 1973. He became a consistent run producer at Thetford Mines, Canada (EL) in 1974 and Charleston, WV (IL) in 1975 and 1976. In 1974, Armas belted 15 HR, drove in 81 runs, and hit a respectable .277. The following year, he collected 135 hits, batted .300 with 12 HR and 72 RBI in 128 games, and shared the IL lead in outfield assists. His batting average slipped to .235 in 1976, but he clouted 21 HR and knocked in 67 runs. Following a brief stint with the Pittsburgh Pirates in September 1976, Armas the next March was traded, along with pitchers Dave Giusti, Doc Medich, Doug Bair, and Rick Langford and outfielder Mitchell Page, to the Oakland Athletics (AL) for infielders Phil Garner* and Tommy Helms and pitcher Chris Batton.

Injuries from crashing into walls sidelined Armas for substantial parts of the 1977–1979 seasons at Oakland. He then combined with Rickey Henderson* and Dwayne Murphy to form one of the best all-around outfields in baseball. Following the advice of his hitting mentor Felipe Alou,* Armas became a bona fide big league slugger in 1980 with 35 HR, 109 RBI, and a solid .279 batting average. In the split 1981 season, he helped the A's win the AL pennant, shared the AL lead in HR (22), and finished second in total bases (211) and RBI (76). He also led the AL in strikeouts with 115. He had 28 HR and 89 RBI in 1982, but hit only .233 and struck out 128 times. In December 1982, the Oakland Athletics traded the free-swinging Armas to the Boston Red Sox (AL) with catcher Jeff Newman for third baseman Carney Lansford,* the AL batting champion, outfielder Garry Hancock, and pitcher Jerome King.

In Boston, centerfielder Armas played in another hardhitting outfield between Jim Rice* and Dwight Evans.* Armas, finding Fenway Park's left-field wall to his liking, hit 36 HR and drove home 107 runs in 1983. At the same time, he fanned 131 times, walked only 29 times, and batted just .218. A year later, he led the AL in HR (43), RBI (123), and strikeouts (156) and hit .268. Arm and leg injuries in 1985 and 1986 caused his power numbers to drop precipitously. Those two seasons brought 44 HR and 122 RBI. Armas spent his last three major league seasons from 1987 to 1989 with the California Angels (AL) mostly as a part-time player. In a 14-year major league career, he collected 1,302 hits with 204 doubles, 251 HR, and 815 RBI, compiled a .252 lifetime batting average, and made the 1981 and 1984 AL All-Star teams. A national hero in Venezuela, Armas still lives in Puerto Piritu and serves as general manager of a winter league team. He and his wife, Luisa Antonio, have four children, Griselda, Maria Luisa, Antonio, and Antoinnette. Antonio pitches in the Montreal Expos (NL) organization.

BIBLIOGRAPHY: Tony Armas file, National Baseball Library, Cooperstown, NY; *The Baseball Encyclopedia*, 10th ed. (New York, 1996); *Boston Red Sox 1986 Media Guide*; Gerald Astor, "Baseball's Best Outfield," *IS* 3 (June 1981), pp. 65–70; Phil Elderkin, "Tony Armas: The Hitter Who Lifts His Foot and Average," *BD* 40 (August 1981), pp. 35–37; Bill James, *The Baseball Book 1991* (New York, 1991); Robert Redmount, *The Red Sox Encyclopedia* (Champaign, IL, 1998); Peter Golenbock, *Fenway* (New York, 1992); Peter Gammons, *Beyond the Sixth Game* (Boston, MA, 1985); John Thorn et al., eds., *Total Baseball*, 5th ed. (New York, 1997); Dan Shaughnessy, *One Strike Away: The Story of the 1986 Red Sox* (New York, 1986); Dan Shaughnessy, *The Curse of the Bambino* (New York, 1990).

Richard H. Gentile

ASHBURN, Don Richard "Richie," "Whitey," "Put-Put" (b. March 19, 1927, Tilden, NE; d. September 9, 1997, New York, NY), player and broadcaster, was the son of blacksmith Neil Ashburn and Genevieve Ashburn. Nicknamed "Whitey" and "Put-Put," he attended Norfolk JC in Nebraska. On November 6, 1949, he married Nebraskan Herberta Cox; they had four daughters and two sons.

In 1945 Ashburn began his career as a catcher with Utica, NY (EL), but manager Eddie Sawyer shifted him to the outfield. After a year in military service and another year at Utica, he excelled from 1948 to 1959 as center fielder for the Philadelphia Phillies (NL). An alert player and a clutch performer, he made a perfect throw to nail the Brooklyn Dodgers' Cal Abrams at home plate to enable the 1950 Phillies to win the NL pennant on the season's final day. After being traded to the Chicago Cubs (NL) in January 1960, Ashburn was sold to the New York Mets (NY) in December 1961. He joined the Phillies' television-radio broadcasting team in 1963 and combined perceptive commentary with a wry sense of humor until his death.

With a career .308 batting average and 2,574 hits, Ashburn won NL batting titles in 1955 and 1958 and four times led the NL in singles to tie the league record. Ashburn also led the NL in walks three times and tied for the lead once and paced the league three times in hits, twice in triples, and once in stolen bases. In 1948, he hit safely in 23 consecutive games to set an NL rookie record. Defensively, he established records by leading the NL in outfield putouts and total chances accepted nine years, in most years with 500 or more putouts by an outfielder (4), and in most years with 400 or more putouts by an outfielder (9). He paced the NL in outfield assists three times and once led and twice tied for the lead in double plays involving an outfielder. A durable player, he appeared in 731 consecutive games and averaged 146 games his 15 seasons. In three All-Star games, he batted an extraordinary .556.

A serious, hustling player with a superb knowledge of the strike zone,

Ashburn excelled as a defensive outfielder and an intelligent hitter and was elected to the National Baseball Hall of Fame in 1997. Besides his television career, Ashburn wrote the introduction to Allen Lewis' *The Philadelphia Phillies: A Pictorial History* (1981) and compiled the *Phillies Trivia Book*. He served as a columnist for the Philadelphia *Bulletin and Daily News* from 1974 to 1991. The humble, happy-go-lucky Ashburn died suddenly of a heart attack at a Manhattan hotel, where the Phillies were staying.

BIBLIOGRAPHY: Richie Ashburn file, National Baseball Library, Cooperstown, NY; Jerry E. Clark, *Nebraska Diamonds* (Omaha, NE, 1991); Robin Roberts and C. Paul Rogers III, *The Whiz Kids and the 1950 Pennant* (Philadelphia, PA, 1996); Joe Archibald, *The Richie Ashburn Story* (New York, 1960); Rich Westcott and Frank Bilovsky, *The New Phillies Encyclopedia* (Philadelphia, PA, 1993); Mary G. Bonner, *Baseball Rookies Who Made Good* (New York, 1964); Brent P. Kelley, *The Case for: Those Overlooked by the Baseball Hall of Fame* (Jefferson, NC, 1992); Allen Lewis, *The Philadelphia Phillies: A Pictorial History* (Virginia Beach, VA, 1981); Allen Lewis and Larry Shenk, *This Date in Philadelphia Phillies History* (Briarcliff Manor, NY, 1979); Frederick G. Lieb and Stan Baumgartner, *The Philadelphia Phillies* (New York, 1953); Bill James, *The Baseball Book 1991* (New York, 1991); Jerry Mathers, "Richie Ashburn," *TNP* 15 (1995), pp. 43–44; Harry Paxton, *The Whiz Kids* (New York, 1950); T. S. O'Connell, "Richie Ashburn," *SCD* 25 (June 5, 1998), pp. 90–91; John Thom, *Champion Batsman of the 20th Century* (Los Angeles, CA, 1992).

Ralph S. Graber

ASHFORD, Emmett Littleton (b. November 23, 1914, Los Angeles, CA; d. March 1, 1980, Marina Del Ray, CA), umpire, became the first black major league umpire and a racial pioneer in sports officiating. Abandoned at an early age by their father, Ashford and an older brother grew up with their mother, an ambitious, achievement-oriented woman who worked as a secretary for the *California Eagle*, a black newspaper. He attended Los Angeles public schools and served as the first black student body president and newspaper editor at Jefferson High School. An excellent student, he matriculated at Los Angeles City College. Ashford received a Bachelor of Science degree from Chapman College, where he played baseball and was sports editor of the college newspaper.

Ashford began umpiring sandlot and recreation league games during a brief career as a semipro player. After serving in the U.S. Navy (1944–1947), he took a civil service job with the U.S. Post Office in Los Angeles. Ashford devoted an increasing amount of time to umpiring high school, junior college, and college games. In 1951, he became the first black umpire in professional baseball on the recommendation of major league scout Rosey Gilhousen. During 15 years in the minor leagues, he umpired in the SIL (Class C), 1951–1952; ArTL (Class C), 1952; WeIL (Class A), 1953; and PCL (Class AAA), 1954–1965; and served as PCL umpire-in-chief, 1963–1965. In the off-season, Ashford became the first black to referee high school, junior college, and small college football and basketball in California. He also umpired during the winter in the Dominican Republic (1958–1959, 1964).

In 1966 Ashford reached the major leagues as a member of the AL staff. He umpired the 1967 All-Star Game and the 1970 World Series and conducted umpiring clinics in Canada, Europe, and Korea. After retiring in 1970, Ashford umpired PTC Conference college games, served as commissioner and umpire-in-chief of the pro-amateur AIL, and worked until his death as the West Coast public relations representative for Commissioner Bowie Kuhn.*

Ashford's major league career proved controversial apart from the racial slurs and hostilities directed toward the first black umpire. Some umpires resented his popularity with the fans and the press. He was criticized for his flamboyance, symbolized by wearing cufflinks and using exaggerated motions to make calls. He was also charged with being a "clown" who sacrificed accuracy for attention. Others believed that he was promoted to the majors only because of pressures from civil rights groups and government officials.

The criticisms were misplaced. Although his skills had deteriorated by the time he reached the majors at age 51, he proved a thoroughly competent arbiter. His style and popularity violated the traditionally conservative demeanor of umpires but helped initiate the modern era of sports officials with personality and recognition. Political pressures aided his promotion, but his long overdue elevation to the majors had been delayed by racist attitudes.

A pioneer of racial integration in sport, the courageous, determined Ashford used wit and charm to overcome the obstacles of racism on and off the field. Ashford may be of greater historical importance than Jackie Robinson* because he represents the advancement of blacks in baseball to a role other than that of hired performer.

BIBLIOGRAPHY: Emmett Ashford file, National Baseball Library, Cooperstown, NY; "Ashford Arrives," *Ebony* 21 (June 1966), pp. 65–70; "Emmett Ashford: Ultra Ump," *Look* 30 (October 4, 1966), pp. 92–95; Larry R. Gerlach, *The Men in Blue: Conversations with Umpires* (New York, 1980); Bill James, *The Baseball Book 1991* (New York, 1991); Brent P. Kelley, *The Case for: Those Overlooked by the Baseball Hall of Fame* (Jefferson, NC, 1992); Los Angeles *Sentinel*, March 6, 1980; Los Angeles *Times*, March 2, 4, and 7, 1980; *NYT*, June 13, 1954, September 16, 1965, December 4, 1970, and March 4, 1980; Art Rust, Jr., *Get That Nigger Off the Field!* (New York, 1976).

Larry R. Gerlach

AUKER, Elden LeRoy (b. September 21, 1910, Norcatur, KS), player, is the son of a rural mail carrier and graduated from Kansas State University with a B.S. degree in Medicine in 1932. Besides lettering in baseball, football, and basketball, Auker made BSC All-Star teams and All-America teams in all three sports. A broken shoulder, incurred playing football, forced him to develop a unique successful underhand pitching style. The Detroit Tigers (AL) signed the 6-foot 2-inch, 194-pound Auker, who batted and threw right-handed, in 1932 and optioned him to Decatur, IL (3IL). After being promoted that year to Moline, AL (MVL) and beginning 1933 with Beaumont, TX (TL), he pitched for the Detroit Tigers from 1933 through 1938. Auker was traded in December 1938 to the Boston Red Sox (AL) and sold in February 1940 to the St. Louis Browns (AL). After winning 14 games in 1942, he retired to work full-time during World War II in the industry.

During 10 major league seasons, Auker compiled a 130–101 win-loss record with a 4.42 ERA in 1,963.1 innings. He led the AL in winning percentage (.720) in 1935 with 18 wins and seven losses. He started 261 major league games, completing 126. Auker won the fourth game of the 1934 World Series against the St. Louis Cardinals, but lost the pivotal seventh game. He also hurled six innings without a decision in Game 3 of the 1935 World Series against the Chicago Cubs. Auker later became president and chief executive officer of the Bay State Abrasives Company in Westboro, MA and held several board memberships and trade association offices. The Vero Beach, FL resident married Mildred Purcell in February 1933 and has one son.

BIBLIOGRAPHY: Elden Auker file, National Baseball Library, Cooperstown, NY; Bill James, *The Baseball Book 1992* (New York, 1992); Richard Bak, *A Place for Summer* (Detroit, MI, 1998); William M. Anderson, *The Detroit Tigers* (South Bend, IN, 1996); Brent P. Kelley, *In the Shadow of the Babe* (Jefferson, NC, 1995); Bill Borst, ed., *Ables to Zoldak*, vol. 1 (St. Louis, MO, 1988); Bill Borst, *Still Last in the American League* (West Bloomfield, MI, 1992); Fred Smith, *995 Tigers* (Detroit, MI, 1981); Joe Falls, *Detroit Tigers* (New York, 1975); Frederick G. Lieb, *The Baltimore Orioles* (New York, 1955); Robert Redmount, *The Red Sox Encyclopedia* (Champaign, IL, 1998); Joseph L. Reichler, ed., *The Great All-Time Baseball Record Book* (New York, 1981); *The Baseball Encyclopedia*, 10th ed. (New York, 1996).

                                                                                    Horace R. Givens

AUSTIN, Thomas. *See* Thomas Austin Yawkey.

AVERILL, Howard Earl "Rock," "The Earl of Snohomish" (b. May 21, 1902, Snohomish, WA; d. August 16, 1983, Everett, WA), player, was the son of logger Joseph Averill and area pioneer Annie (Maddox) Averill. After attending Snohomish public schools, Averill played with the Snohomish Pilchuckers town team and then semiprofessionally with teams in Bellingham, WA, and Butte, MT. In 1926, he began his professional career with the San Francisco Seals (PCL). He married Gladys Loette Hyatt on May 15, 1922, and had four sons, Howard, Bernard, Earl, and Lester. Young Earl played major league baseball from 1956 through 1963.

Nicknamed "Rock," Averill excelled for San Francisco three seasons before the Cleveland Indians (AL) purchased him. The first National Baseball

Hall-of-Famer to homer his first time at bat, the left-handed slugger hit 238 HR over 13 seasons. After playing for Cleveland from 1929 to 1939, he was traded in June 1939 to the Detroit Tigers (AL). He spent 1940 with the Tigers, participating in his only World Series. He concluded his major league career in 1941 with the Boston Braves (NL), retiring prematurely because of a back injury suffered in 1937.

One of the game's great outfielders, Averill compiled a lifetime .318 batting average and achieved a career high of .378 in 1936. At various times the center fielder led the AL in games (1934), hits (1936), at bats (1931), triples (1936), and putouts (1929, 1934). During his ten peak years, "Rock" averaged 189 hits, 37 doubles, 12 triples, 23 HR, 115 runs scored, 108 RBI, and a .534 slugging percentage. He played in 673 straight games from 1931 through 1935, one of the longest such records.

The batter who broke Dizzy Dean's* toe with a line drive in the 1937 All-Star Game, Averill became the only outfielder selected for the first six All-Star games. He made *TSN* Major League All-Star team in 1931, 1932, 1934, and 1936. Averill toured in 1931 with the Babe Ruth All-Stars and in 1934 played on the All-Star team visiting the Orient. In a 1930 doubleheader against Washington, "The Earl of Snohomish" hit four HR, nearly missed on two other long flies, and drove in 11 runs.

Averill, who stood 5-feet 9-inches and weighed 172 pounds, saw his number 3 uniform retired by the Indians. In 1975 Averill belatedly was elected to the National Baseball Hall of Fame.

BIBLIOGRAPHY: Earl Averill file, National Baseball Library, Cooperstown, NY; *SEAL*, vol. 1 (1981–1985), pp. 26–27; Martin Appel and Burt Goldblatt, *Baseball's Best: The Hall of Fame Gallery* (New York, 1997); Bill James, *The Baseball Book 1992* (New York, 1992); Bob Feller with Bill Gilbert, *Now Pitching Bob Feller* (New York, 1990); Frederick G. Lieb, *The Detroit Tigers* (New York, 1946); Russ Dille, "I Remember Earl Averill," *SCD* 10 (October 14, 1983), pp. 144, 146; John Eichmann, "Perennial American League Centerfielder," *SS* 1 (March–July 1973); Joe Falls, *Detroit Tigers* (New York, 1975); Franklin Lewis, *The Cleveland Indians* (New York, 1979); Steve Mitchell, "DeWitt Nominates Earl Averill," *SS* 2 (March 1974), p. 35; Lowell Reidenbaugh, *Baseball's Hall of Fame-Cooperstown* (New York, 1993); Doug Simpson, "The Earl of Snohomish," *BRJ* 11 (1982), pp. 151–161; Seattle, WA *Times*, August 17, 1983; John Thorn et al., eds., *Total Indians* (New York, 1996).

Douglas G. Simpson

AVILA, Roberto Francisco "Bobby" (b. April 2, 1924, Veracruz, Mexico), player and executive, is the ninth child and fourth son of Jose Avila, a lawyer, and Andrea Avila. He attended Preparatoria School in Veracruz and completed three years at the University of Mexico. After concentrating on soccer, he turned to baseball at age 16. He soon progressed to the MEL, where he played for five years. In 1947, he hit a league-leading .347. That year, super-scout Cyril C. Slapnicka signed him to a Cleveland Indians (AL) contract. Avila debuted with Class AAA Baltimore, MD (IL) in 1948 before joining the Cleveland Indians the following season. He batted only 14 times in 1949, but hit .299 the next year in 80 games. He married Elsa Diaz Miron in 1951 and resides in Veracruz, Mexico with their children, Roberto, Elsa, Patricia, and Jose Alberto.

Avila, the first Mexican to experience real major league success, enjoyed his most productive seasons from 1951 through 1954, hitting .300 or better three times, batting no lower than .286, and leading the AL in triples with 11 in 1952. On June 20, 1951, he belted three HR, a single, and a double against the Boston Red Sox. On July 1, 1952, he tied an AL record by making 13 assists in a 19-inning game. Twice, he scored more than 100 runs. His best season came in 1954, the year the Cleveland Indians set a then record with 111 victories and won the AL pennant. Despite a broken thumb, the right-hander led the AL with a career-best .341 batting average, hit career-best 15 HR and 27 doubles, and scored 112 runs. Defensively, although having a mediocre throwing arm, the 5-foot 10-inch, 175-pound second baseman led the AL in assists. At the 1954 All-Star Game in Cleveland, he made hits in all three at bats. Avila's Cleveland Indians lost the 1954 World Series to the New York Giants in four consecutive games, as he managed only two singles for a .133 batting average.

Despite vowing to hit .400, Avila never came close to the preceding four-year statistics. His batting average slumped to .272 in 1955, but he hit 13 HR and scored 83 runs. The next season, his batting average plummeted to .224 with only 10 HR and 74 runs scored. Salary disputes had caused dissatisfaction and delayed his spring training appearances. He purchased the Mexico City Reds (MEL) in late 1954, managing and playing second base there. Conceivably, Avila might have overextended himself. Moreover, he suffered an eye infection in the summer of 1955, which probably impaired his vision. Avila, an adept bunter and daring base runner, continued his mediocre play with the Cleveland Indians through the 1959 season. In 1957, he led starting AL second basemen in fielding. He made the All-Star team in 1952 and 1955. In 1959, he closed out his career with the Baltimore Orioles (AL), Boston Red Sox (AL), and Milwaukee Braves (NL). His baseball idol, Ted Williams* of the Red Sox, retired that same year. Avila's major league career statistics include a .281 batting average, 725 runs scored, 1,296 hits, and 185 doubles in 1,300 games. He returned to Mexico, serving as president of the MEL, a member of the Mexican Congress during the 1960s and 1970s, and mayor of Veracruz from 1976 to 1979.

BIBLIOGRAPHY: Roberto Avila file, National Baseball Library, Cooperstown, NY; Roberto Avila, letter to James N. Giglio, July 2, 1993; Cleveland (OH) *News*, March 20, 1953; April 30, 1953; January 7, 1955; February 3, 1955; July 22, 1955; March 8, 1956; February 28, 1957; April 9, 1958; Cleveland (OH) *Plain Dealer*, October 2, 1954; Gordon Cobbledick, "Viva Avila!," *Sport* 15 (September 1953), pp. 26–27, 83–

85; Bruce Dudley, *Bittersweet Season* (Annapolis, MD, 1995); John Phillips, *Winners* (Cabin John, MD, 1987); Bill James, *The Baseball Book 1992* (New York, 1992); John Thorn et al., eds., *Total Indians* (New York, 1996); Jack Torry, *Endless Summers* (South Bend, IN, 1995).

James N. Giglio

B

BAERGA, Carlos Obed (b. November 4, 1968, San Turce, PR), player, is the son of Jose Baerga, a newspaper employee, and Baldry Baerga. After playing in Puerto Rico's top amateur league while attending Barbara Ann Rooshart High School in Rio Piedra, Baerga on his seventeenth birthday received a $60,000 bonus for signing with the San Diego Padres (NL) in 1985. The next season, the infielder hit .270 for Charleston, SC (WCL). After batting .275 with 10 HR at Las Vegas, NV (PCL) in 1989, Baerga was traded that December to the Cleveland Indians (AL) with catcher Sandy Alomar, Jr. and outfielder Chris James for All-Star outfielder Joe Carter.* Baerga soon became a significant part of the Tribe's resurgence.

Although initially slated for third base, the switch-hitting Baerga became the Cleveland Indians' regular second baseman in 1991. In his six seasons with the Indians, he exceeded all expectations. He hit .312 in 1992 and .321 in 1993, accumulating at least 200 hits, 20 HR, and 100 RBI each season. No other major league second baseman had reached those standards except Hall-of-Famer Rogers Hornsby.* His 205 hits in 1992 marked the highest total for any Indians player since Earl Averill* attained 232 in 1936. In April 1993 against the New York Yankees, he became the first major leaguer to hit a HR from both sides of the plate in the same inning. In the strike-shortened 1994 and 1995 seasons, Baerga batted .314 both times, drove in and scored at least 80 runs, and belted 19 and 15 HR, respectively. In the 1995 postseason play, he hit .286 in the AL Division three-game sweep of the Boston Red Sox. In the AL Championship Series six-game series with the Seattle Mariners, Baerga batted .400, second to teammate Kenny Lofton,* and led the Cleveland Indians with four RBI. In the World Series against the victorious Atlanta Braves, he batted only .192 with five hits, two doubles, and a team-tieing four RBI.

The 5-foot 11-inch, 200-pound Baerga rarely strikes out or walks, the latter contributing to his large number of official at-bats. Defensively, he possesses a strong arm and has improved his fielding appreciably. In 1994, he led the AL second basemen in total chances and ranked second in total putouts and assists. The three-time All Star (1992, 1993, and 1995) and inspirational player exerts a positive influence on teammates. Baerga participated in Esparanza, an hispanic scholarship program. In the off-season, he plays baseball for the San Juan Metros to remain in contact with Puerto Rican fans.

In July 1996, Cleveland traded Baerga to the New York Mets (NL). Baerga spent the 1997 and 1998 seasons with the New York Mets, being released in October 1998. After having tryouts with the St. Louis Cardinals (NL) and Cincinnati Reds (NL), he joined the San Diego Padres (NL) in June 1999 and in August rejoined the Cleveland Indians. He became a free agent in December 1999. Baerga's ten-year major league statistics include a .291 batting average with 1,400 hits, 659 runs scored, 124 HR, and 686 RBI. Baerga married Miriam Laboy Cruz and has a daughter, Karla, and a son, Carlos.

BIBLIOGRAPHY: Carlos Baerga file, National Baseball Library, Cooperstown, NY; Franz Lidz, "Slick with the Stick," *SI* 80 (April 4, 1994), pp. 62–64, 66; Terry Pluto, *The Curse of Rocky Colavito* (New York, 1994); Jack Torry, *Endless Summers* (South Bend, IN, 1995); David S. Neft et al., eds., *The Sports Encyclopedia: Baseball*, 16th ed. (New York, 1996); Bill Deane to James N. Giglio, letter, April 24, 1996; John Thorn et al., eds., *Total Indians* (New York, 1996); Russell Schneider, *The Glorious Indian Summer of 1995* (Cleveland, OH, 1995).

                                                                                                James N. Giglio

BAGBY, James Charles Jacob, Sr. "Sarge" (b. October 5, 1889, Barnett, GA; d. July 28, 1954, Marietta, GA), player and umpire, was major league baseball's best pitcher in 1920. He led the Cleveland Indians (AL) to their first AL pennant while topping the AL with 31 wins, a .721 winning percentage, 339.2 innings pitched, 48 mound appearances, 30 complete games, and 6 relief victories. His 2.89 ERA, however, remains the highest for a 30-game winner in the twentieth century. In the World Series against the Brooklyn Robins (NL), Bagby lost the second game and rebounded to win the strange Game 5. With two teammates on base, he hit the first-ever World Series HR by a pitcher. Elmer Smith* preceded him with the first-ever World Series grand-slam HR and Bill Wambsganss* followed with his unique, unassisted triple play.

The son of W. H. Bagby and Minnie (Rocker) Bagby, the Georgia native completed high school at Richmond Academy and earned his nickname there. In 1910, he entered professional baseball with Augusta, GA (SAL) and Hattiesburg, MS (CSL). Montgomery, AL (SA) sold him to the Cincinnati Reds (NL) in 1912 and reacquired him after he compiled a 2–1 record with the Reds. Over the next two years, he became an established pitcher and a respected hitter with New Orleans, LA (SA). In 1915, he hurled 293 innings and batted .270 in 58 games before being sold to the Cleveland Indians.

Aside from his superb 1920 campaign, Bagby enjoyed only one other 20-win season with a 23–13 slate in 1917. He achieved a 17–11 mark in 1919 and finished around .500 in three other years. After sagging to 4–5 in 1922, he was waived in November to the Pittsburgh Pirates (NL) and won three of five decisions in his final major league season. Overall, his major league career record included 127 victories, 88 defeats, and a 3.11 ERA. The sturdy six-footer, who threw right-handed and was nicknamed "Sarge," allowed many hits but few walks. Twenty-one of his wins came in relief. He was credited with 29 career saves, although primarily a starting pitcher. A switch-hitter, he batted .218 lifetime. Not surprisingly, his best offensive year occurred in 1920, when he made 33 hits and belted one of his two regular-season HR.

Bagby finished the 1923 campaign with Seattle, WA (PCL) and played in the minor leagues until 1930. His final stop came at York, PA (NYPL). He umpired until suffering a stroke during a 1942 PiL game. After his baseball career, he owned a cleaning and dyeing establishment in Atlanta, GA. He married Mabel Margaret Smith on February 10, 1913. Their son, Jim, Jr., another right-hander, won 97 games and lost 96 contests between 1938 and 1947 with the Boston Red Sox (AL), Cleveland Indians (AL), and Pittsburgh Pirates (NL).

BIBLIOGRAPHY: James Bagby file, National Baseball Library, Cooperstown, NY; *The Baseball Encyclopedia*, 10th ed. (New York, 1996); Richard M. Cohen et al., eds., *The World Series* (New York, 1979); Bill James, *The Baseball Book 1992* (New York, 1992); Franklin Lewis, *The Cleveland Indians* (New York, 1949); John Thorn et al., eds., *Total Baseball*, 5th ed. (New York, 1997); John Thorn et al., eds., *Total Indians* (New York, 1996).

A. D. Suehsdorf

BAGWELL, Jeffrey Robert "Jeff" (b. May 27, 1968, Boston, MA), player, is a 6-foot, 195-pound infielder who throws and bats right-handed. He graduated from Xavier High School in Middletown, CT and attended the University of Hartford, where he compiled a .413 career batting average. Bagwell batted safely in 87 of 112 collegiate games over three seasons, being twice named ECAC Player of the Year.

The Boston Red Sox (AL) selected Bagwell in the fourth round of the June 1989 free agent draft and assigned him to their GCL rookie team and Winter Haven, FL (FSL) during the 1989 season. In 1990 Bagwell played for New Britain, CT (EL), where he batted .333, led the circuit in hits and total bases, and was named EL MVP. The Boston Red Sox traded Bagwell to the Houston Astros (NL) in August 1990 for pitcher Larry Anderson.

The Houston Astros in 1991 moved Bagwell from third base to first base, as he became the first Astro to win the BBWAA NL Rookie of the Year award. With a .294 batting average, he also was named Houston's MVP and led the Astros in HR, RBI, walks, slugging, and on-base percentage. Bagwell, who compiled a .273 batting average in 1992, ranked among NL leaders in RBI, walks, runs, sacrifice flies, intentional walks, and being hit by pitches, and finished third best in fielding percentage among NL first basemen. He placed sixth in the NL with a .320 batting average in 1993 despite missing the first 20 games with a broken hand. Bagwell the same season compiled 171 hits and repeated as MVP for the Astros.

The BBWAA unanimously chose him as NL MVP in 1994. Only two other NL players have been selected unanimously. The same year Bagwell earned *TSN, USAT Baseball Weekly, BD*, and AP Player of the Year honors. No player had finished first or second in the NL in batting average, runs, RBI, and HR since Willie Mays* in 1955, while no player had led the NL in runs scored (104) and RBI (116) since Mike Schmidt* in 1981. Bagwell ranked among NL leaders in batting average (.368) and hits (147) and set club records with 39 HR, 116 RBI, and 73 extra base hits. He also led the NL with a .461 on-base percentage and .750 slugging percentage. He became just the fifth NL batter to play in over 100 games and average more than one RBI per contest and the first player in 14 years to record more RBI than games played. Bagwell, named to the NL All-Star squad for the first time, earned his initial Rawlings Gold Glove award and was named team MVP for the third time. He again suffered a broken hand in 1995, missing 30 games. His batting average dropped to .290, but he recorded 130 base hits and 21 HR. Bagwell batted .315 with 31 HR and 120 RBI in 1996, pacing the NL with 48 doubles. In 1997, his league-leading 135 RBI and career-high 43 HR and 31 stolen bases helped Houston capture the NL Central Division. He made only one hit, however, as the Atlanta Braves swept the NL Division Series. Bagwell participated in the 1996, 1997, 1998, and 1999 All-Star games. His .304 batting average, 34 HR, and 111 RBI helped the Astros capture the NL Central Division in 1998. San Diego Padre pitchers limited him to .143 and .154 batting averages in the 1998 and 1999 NL Division Series. His .304 batting average, 42 HR, 126 RBI, NL-best 143 runs scored, and 149 walks helped Houston take another NL Central Division Crown in 1999. Bagwell made *TSN* Silver Slugger and All-Star Teams and AP All-Star Team in 1999.

In nine seasons with the Astros, Bagwell has played in 1,267 games, made 1,447 hits, scored 878 runs, driven in 961 runs, and batted .304. He has notched 314 doubles, 21 triples, 263 HR, 885 walks, 158 stolen bases, and 906 strikeouts.

Bagwell and his wife, Shaune, reside in Sugarland, TX.

BIBLIOGRAPHY: Jeff Bagwell file, National Baseball Library, Cooperstown, NY; *Houston Astros Media Guide*, 1998; Leigh Montville, "Trade Deficit," *SI* 79 (July 26, 1993), pp. 44–48; *TSN Official Baseball Register*, 1998; *USAT Baseball Weekly*, October 4–10, 1995, pp. 44, 47; Rick Weinberg, "One on One Interview," *Sport* 86 (May 1995), pp. 18–20.

John L. Evers

BAILEY, Lonas Edgar "Ed," "Gar" (b. April 15, 1931, Strawberry Plains, TN), player, is the son of Lonas Edgar Bailey, Sr., a grocery business owner, and

Edna (Cox) Bailey. Bailey won All-State honors in basketball and baseball at Rush Strong High School in Strawberry Plains and earned an athletic scholarship to the University of Tennessee, where he played freshman basketball and baseball. Cincinnati Reds (NL) scout Paul Florence offered the 6-foot 2-inch, 205-pound, left-handed hitting catcher a $12,000 signing bonus in November 1949. Bailey accepted the offer and withdrew from Tennessee.

Bailey, who rejected the offers of 12 other clubs, was sent to Ogden, UT (PrL), where he caught in 124 games and compiled a .313 batting average. After being drafted into the U.S. Army in March 1951, he played baseball for two seasons at Ft. Jackson, SC. In 1953 he returned to the Cincinnati Reds but was ignored at spring training by manager Rogers Hornsby* and relegated to catching batting practice. After the frustrated Bailey announced plans to leave camp to receive his Army discharge, Hornsby challenged him by playing him that very day. Bailey responded with six RBI on two HR, two doubles, and a single. In his first major league at bat, he doubled off Bob Buhl.*

A broad, looping all-out swing and some defensive deficiencies delayed his development during the next three seasons. Bailey alternated between being a back-up catcher with the Cincinnati Reds, playing with Tulsa, OK (TL) and San Diego, CA (PCL), and performing winter ball in Venezuela. In 1956, new Cincinnati Reds manager Birdie Tebbetts* advised Bailey to use a new batting stance and controlled swing. Bailey responded with his finest year in 1956. Although appearing in only 118 games counting pinch hitting duty, he hit 28 HR to set a new club record for catchers. Two HR were grand slams; two came as a pinch-hitter; and three were hit in the same game on June 24. As a team, the Cincinnati Reds hit 221 HR to tie the major league record. His .300 batting average and career-high 75 RBI enabled him to be named "Sophomore of the Year" and catcher on the UPI NL All-Star team.

After several other productive years with the Reds, Bailey played with the San Francisco Giants (NL) from 1961 to 1963, the Milwaukee Braves (NL) in 1964, and the San Francisco Giants and Chicago Cubs (NL) in 1965. Following five games with the California Angels (AL) in 1966, he retired with a .256 major league batting average, 155 HR, and 540 RBI. Bailey twice made unassisted double plays and briefly caught his brother, Jim, in 1959. He was selected for five NL All-Star teams (1956–1957, 1960–1961, 1963) and appeared in six games of the 1962 World Series against the New York Yankees.

Bailey married Betty Lou Carr on May 16, 1953 and has four sons, Jeff, Joe, Jack, and Jim. Following his major league career, the Knoxville, TN resident worked in public relations and sales with Peterbilt and as marketing director for Browning-Ferris Industries.

BIBLIOGRAPHY: Edgar Bailey file, National Baseball Library, Cooperstown, NY; Bill James, *The Baseball Book 1992* (New York, 1992); Bob Pille, "Bailey—Next Catching Great?," *BD* 15 (August 1956), pp 49–54; Milton Richmond, "Bailey's the Best," *Sport* 24 (September 1957), pp 18–19; Bruce Jacobs, *Baseball Stars of 1957* (New York, 1957).

Richard D. Miller

BAILEY, Robert Sherwood "Bob," "Beetle" (b. October 13, 1942, Long Beach, CA), player, of Irish-German descent, is the son of Paul "Buck" Bailey, who played briefly for the St. Louis Cardinals (NL) organization. Bailey played shortstop and never batted below .450 for three seasons at Woodrow Wilson High School in Long Beach. A teammate of Tommie Sisk, he was named Conference Player of the Year and to the All-State team. He also played football for three years and was named an All-Conference quarterback. He performed in American Legion baseball for four years and played in 1957 and 1958 for the Dodger Rookies. After Bailey graduated from high school, the Pittsburgh Pirates (NL) in 1961 used profits from their 1960 World Series victory to outbid several teams, including the Los Angeles Dodgers (NL) and New York Yankees (AL). Bailey signed for a record bonus, reportedly between $135,000 and $200,000.

Bailey hit only .220 in 75 games with Asheville, NC (SAL) in 1961, but the following season hit .299 with 28 HR and 108 RBI at Columbus, OH (IL), was named Minor League Player of the Year, and was called up to the Pittsburgh Pirates. In 1963, although still only 20 years old, he replaced Don Hoak at third base. Bailey did not meet Pittsburgh's expectations, batting only .228. By season's end, the press criticized him as an "expensive fizzle." The best of his five seasons with the Pirates came in 1964, when he hit .281.

In December 1966, the Pittsburgh Pirates traded Bailey and Gene Michael to the Los Angeles Dodgers (NL) for Maury Wills.* He remained enthusiastic, but hit only .227 in each of his two seasons there. In 1969, he became a charter member of the Montreal Expos (NL). Despite suffering a broken leg in his first season at Montreal, Bailey enjoyed his best seasons there. Three times in six seasons, he hit over 20 HR and produced over 80 RBI. He recorded career highs of 28 HR in 1970 and 86 RBI in 1973. A streak hitter, he drove in seven runs in one game against the New York Mets and six tallies in another contest against the Chicago Cubs. As with Pittsburgh and Los Angeles, however, he did not hit particularly well in his home ballpark and was booed frequently for not excelling consistently. From 1969 through 1971, he served as the Expos' player representative. In December 1975, he became the last original Expo to leave the team when he was traded to the Cincinnati Reds (NL).

Bailey performed part-time on the Cincinnati Reds' 1976 World Champions at third base, first base, and the outfield and as a pinch-hitter. Cincinnati traded him to the Boston Red Sox (AL) in September 1978. He gained dubious fame when fastballer Goose Gossage* struck him out looking at a crucial moment in the seventh inning of the famous playoff game against the New York Yankees. He retired after the 1978 season.

In 17 major league seasons, the black-haired, blue-eyed Bailey batted .257, belted 189 HR among his 1,564 hits, and drove in 773 runs. The 6-foot, 175 pounder threw right-handed and possessed offensive power. Montreal manager Gene Mauch* remarked, "Bailey means wood; Bailey doesn't mean leather." Despite his reputation as an erratic fielder, however, he won the 1971 Gold Glove at third base and led NL third basemen with a .960 fielding percentage. Subsequently, he played in the outfield and first base.

Bailey married Karen Crozier, whom he has known since childhood, on November 18, 1961, and has three children. He used his signing bonus to pursue business with his father. After leaving baseball, he engaged in real estate, equipment leasing, and other businesses.

Despite playing competently in the major leagues for nearly two decades and enjoying streaks of brilliance during that time, the congenial, outgoing, accommodating Bailey never lived up to the exceptionally high expectations and demands that accompanied being the most expensive "bonus baby" of his era. Anything short of a National Baseball Hall of Fame career was destined to be considered inadequate. Resentment of "overpaid" ballplayers did not begin in 1975 with the advent of high-priced free agents.

BIBLIOGRAPHY: Bob Bailey file, National Baseball Library, Cooperstown, NY; Richard L. Burtt, *The Pittsburgh Pirates, A Pictorial History* (Virginia Beach, VA, 1977); Bill James, *The Baseball Book 1992* (New York, 1992); Ed Linn, *The Great Rivalry* (Boston, MA, 1991); *The Baseball Encyclopedia*, 10th ed. (New York, 1996); Dan Shaughnessy, *The Curse of the Bambino* (New York, 1991); Bob Smizik, *The Pittsburgh Pirates: An Illustrated History* (New York, 1990).

Luther W. Spoehr

BAINES, Harold Douglass (b. March 15, 1959, Easton, MD), player, starred as a hard-hitting outfielder and the leading Chicago White Sox (AL) player in the 1980s. Baines attracted attention at a younger age than virtually any other major league baseball player. Bill Veeck,* who resided on the Eastern Shore of Maryland during a hiatus in his ownership of major league clubs, spotted Baines playing in local youth baseball at age 12. On resuming ownership of the Chicago White Sox, Veeck made young Baines the first choice in the entire 1977 major league baseball draft. After performing with White Sox farm teams at Appleton, WI (MWL), Knoxville, TN (SL), and Des Moines–based Iowa (AA), he reached the parent club in 1980 and immediately became the team's regular right fielder. He hit .255 in 1980 and increased his batting average to .304 in 1984 and .309 in 1985. In 1984, he led the AL with a .541 slugging percentage. Besides driving in a career-high 113 runs in 1985, he was named to *TSN* and UPI All-League teams. He represented the White Sox in the 1985, 1986, 1987, and 1989 All-Star games. He enjoyed several excellent individual performances, hitting three HR on July 17, 1982 and September 17, 1984. In a marathon game of May 8–9, 1984 against the Milwaukee Brewers, he tied a major league record by batting 12 times and won the game with a HR in the 25th inning. His bat was sent to the museum of the National Baseball Hall of Fame at Cooperstown, NY. In 1983 he set a major league record with 22 game-winning RBI, including a sacrifice fly against the Seattle Mariners (AL) on September 17 to clinch the western divisional championship for the White Sox.

Baines suffered several knee injuries beginning in 1986, interfering with his mobility and reducing him mainly to a DH. He enjoyed an excellent season in 1989, hitting .309. In July 1989, the Chicago White Sox traded Baines to the Texas Rangers (AL). Baines held the team record for HR (186) and saw the White Sox retire his numeral 3. In need of a left-handed batter, the Oakland Athletics (AL) acquired Baines from the Texas Rangers in August 1990. Baines compiled a .364 batting average with 3 RBI as a DH in the 1990 AL Championship Series against the Boston Red Sox and belted a 2-run HR in the 1990 World Series against the Cincinnati Reds. In 1991, he was named to the AL All-Star team for the fifth time. Baines led the Athletics in 1991 with a .295 batting average, 19 points higher than any teammates. Baines batted .440 with 11 hits, one HR, and four RBI in the 1992 AL Championship Series against the Toronto Blue Jays. In January 1993, the Oakland Athletics traded him to the Baltimore Orioles (AL). He batted .313 with 78 RBI for Baltimore in 1993 and remained there through the 1995 season. He rejoined the Chicago White Sox as a free agent in December 1995 and hit over .300 the next 1.5 seasons there. The Baltimore Orioles reacquired him in July 1997. After helping Baltimore capture the AL East, Baines batted .400 with one HR in the AL Division Series against the Seattle Mariners and .353 with one HR and two RBI in the AL Championship Series against the Cleveland Indians. In 1999, he batted .312 in limited action and made the AL All-Star Team. The Indians acquired him in August 1999. He batted .357 in the AL Division Series. Through the 1999 season, he has batted .292 with 2,783 hits, 474 doubles, 373 HR, and 1,583 RBI. The Orioles reacquired him in December 1999.

Baines possesses a quiet manner and remains a consummate professional in the best tradition of Lou Gehrig* and Henry Aaron.* He married Marla Henry Baines and has two daughters, Antoinette and Britni.

BIBLIOGRAPHY: Harold Baines file, National Baseball Library, Cooperstown, NY; Peter C. Bjarkman, ed., *Encyclopedia of Major League Baseball Team Histories American League* (Westport, CT, 1991); *Baltimore Orioles Media Guide, 1998*; Bill James, *The Baseball Book 1992* (New York, 1992); Richard Lindberg, *Who's on Third?* (South Bend, IN, 1983); Richard Lindberg, *Sox* (New York, 1984); Bob Vanderberg, *Sox: From Lane and Fain to Zisk and Fisk* (Chicago, IL, 1982); William L. Mobray, *The Eastern Shore Baseball League* (Centreville, MD, 1989); *TSN Official Baseball Guide, 1978–1998*; *WWIB*, 1998.

George W. Hilton

BAKER, Delmar David "Del" (b. May 3, 1893, Sherwood, OR; d. September 11, 1973, San Antonio, TX), player, manager, and coach, was the fifth of seven children of Thomas M. Baker, a farmer, and Mary E. Baker. After graduating in 1909 from Behmke-Walker BC in Portland, OR with an accounting degree, Baker worked as a bookkeeper in Wasco, OR. He and four of his brothers played semiprofessional baseball with the Sherwood, OR White Sox until 1911, when he entered organized baseball as a catcher with Helena, MT (UA). He caught for Helena in 1912 and Lincoln, NE (WL) in 1913. After being purchased by the Detroit Tigers (AL), Baker appeared in only 173 major league games as a third-string catcher from 1914 through 1916 with a .209 batting average and a .948 fielding average. He was optioned to San Francisco, CA (PCL), where he hit .266 in 1917. He enlisted in the U.S. Navy in 1917 and served eight months in the European theater. Upon his discharge in 1919, Baker joined Portland, OR (PCL). He was sold to Mobile, AL (SA) in 1922 and Oakland, CA (PCL) in 1923. Statistically, the 5-foot 11½-inch, 176-pound catcher's best season came in 1924 with a career high .301 batting average and a league-leading .989 fielding percentage. He remained with Oakland for the next three seasons.

In 1927, Oakland appointed Baker manager of the Ogden, UT club (UIL). He piloted Ogden in 1928, but returned to Oakland in 1929. He was sold in 1929 to Ft. Worth, TX (TL), serving as a catcher and interim manager. In 1930, Baker became player–manager of the Beaumont, TX Exporters (TL), a Detroit Tigers farm club. In his last season as an active player, he led Beaumont to its first championship in 1932.

With Beaumont, Baker fostered the development of future stars Hank Greenberg,* Pete Fox,* Elden Auker,* Schoolboy Rowe,* and Jo Jo White. The Tigers promoted Baker to head coach under manager Bucky Harris* in 1933 and made him temporary manager for two games at the end of the season. Mickey Cochrane* became the next manager, while Baker remained as the third base coach. Baker served as interim manager in place of the ill, injured Cochrane for 98 games in 1936 and 1937. He continued as coach and sometime-manager in 1938 until replacing Cochrane in August. The Tigers rallied under Baker's direction to finish fourth in 1938 and fifth in 1939. After capturing the AL pennant and losing the World Series to the Cincinnati Reds in 1940, Detroit finished fourth in 1941 and fifth in 1942.

Baker coached with the Cleveland Indians (AL) in 1943 and 1944 and with the Boston Red Sox (AL) for three seasons, briefly serving as interim manager in 1947. He managed the Sacramento, CA Solons (PCL) in 1949 and San Diego, CA (PCL) in 1950 and 1951. The soft-spoken Baker returned to the major leagues, coaching with the Boston Red Sox from 1953 through 1960. He served as interim manager with the Red Sox in mid-1960. Baker compiled a .538 winning percentage as a major league manager with 419 wins and 360 losses. He helped coach the Trinity University baseball team in San Antonio, TX until illness forced him out in 1972.

Baker was recognized as one of the most adroit sign stealers in baseball history. In 1956, the Gillette Safety Razor Company asked 484 sportswriters and broadcasters to choose the top signal stealers since World War I. Baker, Charley Dressen,* and Art Fletcher* were deemed the best. Baker married Mamie Turner on October 27, 1937. They had two sons, Del, Jr. and Walter.

BIBLIOGRAPHY: Thomas Aylesworth and Benton Minks, *The Encyclopedia of Baseball Managers* (New York, 1990); Delmar Baker file, National Baseball Library, Cooperstown, NY; *The Baseball Encyclopedia*, 10th ed. (New York, 1996); Bill James, *The Baseball Book 1992* (New York, 1992); William M. Anderson, *The Detroit Tigers* (South Bend, IN, 1996); Richard Bak, *A Place for Summer* (Detroit, MI, 1998); Frederick G. Lieb, *The Detroit Tigers* (New York, 1946); Joe Falls, *Detroit Tigers* (New York, 1975); John Thorn et al., eds., *Total Baseball*, 5th ed. (New York, 1997).

Jack C. Braun

BAKER, John Franklin "Home Run" (b. March 13, 1886, Trappe, MD; d. June 28, 1963, Trappe, MD), player, manager, and executive, was the son of Franklin Adams Baker, a farmer, and Mary Catherine (Rust) Baker. After grade school, Baker began playing baseball in local leagues and later failed in a tryout with the Baltimore Orioles. In 1908 he signed professionally with Reading, PA (TSL).

In late 1908, the Philadelphia Athletics (AL) acquired his contract. The 5-foot 11-inch, 175-pound Baker quickly became a regular third baseman. In his 1909 debut, Baker hit a HR in the first inning with the bases loaded. In the dead ball era, he led the AL in HR from 1911 through 1914. Nicknamed "Home Run," he hit two HR in the 1911 World Series against the New York Giants. Despite his nickname, Baker never hit more than 12 HR in a single season and slugged only 96 lifetime, ranking behind scores of later HR sluggers.

With the Athletics for seven years, Baker played under renowned manager Connie Mack.* The Philadelphia club made the World Series four times during the span (1910, 1911, 1913, and 1914), winning the world championship twice. In 1914 Baker played with Stuffy McInnis,* Eddie Collins,* and Jack Barry in the Athletics' famous "$100,000 infield." Baker was sold to the New York Yankees (AL) for $37,500 in February 1916, when Mack trimmed his team's budget by selling his high-paid stars. After playing semipro ball in Upland, PA in 1915, Baker played for the New York Yankees (AL) until 1922. In 1920 he temporarily retired following the death of his first wife, Ottilie Rosa Tschantre, whom he had married in 1909. They had two daughters. He rejoined the Yankees for the 1921 and 1922 seasons, participating in World Series both times. In 1919 Baker hit 10 HR, placing second in the AL behind Boston Red Sox pitcher Babe Ruth.* A year later, Ruth hit 54 HR and rewrote all previous power standards.

A left-handed batter who threw right-handed, Baker holds the sixth highest career batting average in World Series history. Using a 52 ounce bat, he compiled a .307 career batting average. Baker's speed declined, causing him to retire after the 1922 season. That year he married Margaret E. Mitchell and subsequently had two children.

After retiring as a player, Baker served in 1924 and 1925 as a manager of Easton, MD (ESL), and later was president of that club for a year. During retirement he managed several Maryland farms, raised and trained hunting dogs, fished, and hunted. In 1955, he was chosen for the National Baseball Hall of Fame. Baker's power focused attention on the HR, preparing the baseball world for later sluggers who revolutionized the national sport. One must speculate what Baker might have done with a lighter bat and a livelier ball.

BIBLIOGRAPHY: *DAB*, Suppl. 7 (1961–1965), pp. 27–28; *NYT*, June 29, 1963; *The Baseball Encyclopedia*, 10th ed. (New York, 1996); Mark Gallagher, *The Yankee Encyclopedia*, vol. 3 (Champaign, IL, 1997); Lowell Reidenbaugh, *Baseball's Hall of Fame-Cooperstown* (New York, 1993); Connie Mack, *My 66 Years in the Big Leagues* (Philadelphia, PA, 1950); Frederick G. Lieb, *Connie Mack* (New York, 1945); Frank Graham, *The New York Yankees* (New York, 1943); Lawrence S. Ritter, *The Glory of Their Times* (New York, 1966).

Stephen D. Bodayla

BAKER, Johnnie B., Jr. "Dusty" (b. June 15, 1949, Riverside, CA), player, coach, and manager, is the son of Johnnie Baker, Sr. and Christine (Russell) Baker. The 6-foot 2-inch, 190-pound outfielder excelled as an all-around athlete in baseball, football, basketball, and track and field at Del Campo High School in Carmichael, a suburb of Sacramento, CA. Baker chose professional baseball over Santa Clara University when the Atlanta Braves (NL) drafted him in the 26th round in 1967 and offered him a $15,000 bonus. He saw action with four minor league teams before being promoted to Richmond, VA (IL) in 1969.

Baker, who threw and batted right-handed, filled in for injured Orlando Cepeda* as the Atlanta Braves' center fielder in 1972, his first full major league season. He finished the 1972 season with a .321 batting average, third best in the NL. In 1973 he led NL outfielders in total chances (407) and putouts (390), hit 21 HR, and drove in 99 runs. Baker's accomplishments, however, were overshadowed by Hank Aaron,* Davey Johnson,* and Darrell Evans,* who each hit 40 or more HR that season. Never before had three players on a team accomplished such a feat.

The Los Angeles Dodgers (NL) secured Baker as a left fielder in November 1975. Baker and teammates Steve Garvey,* Reggie Smith,* and Ron Cey* all hit at least 30 HR in 1977 to establish another major league record. Baker signed a five-year, $4 million contract with the Los Angeles Dodgers after an outstanding 1980 season, in which he belted 29 HR and knocked in 97 runs. After being granted free agency in February 1984, he played one year with the San Francisco Giants (NL) and ended his major league career with the Oakland Athletics (AL) in 1985 and 1986.

The broad-shouldered, slender Baker, a graceful fielder, only twice compiled a fielding average below .980. He never made more than seven errors in one season and committed only one miscue in 1976. An intelligent batter and base runner, he seldom struck out and tied a major league record at age 35 by stealing three bases in one inning against the Cincinnati Reds on June 27, 1984.

Baker was selected to the NL All-Star team in 1980 and 1981 and appeared in the NL Championship Series with the Los Angeles Dodgers in 1977, 1978, 1981, and 1983. He tied NL Championship Series records for most grand-slam HR in a game (1) and most RBI in an inning (4) on October 5, 1977, most RBI in a four-game series (8) in 1977, and highest batting average in a four-game series (.467) in 1978. He played in the World Series against the New York Yankees in 1977, 1978, and 1981.

Baker finished his 19-year major league career with a .278 batting average, 320 doubles, 242 HR, and 1,013 RBI. He served as batting coach for the San Francisco Giants from 1988 through 1992 and piloted the Scottsdale, AZ Scorpions (AzFL) in 1992. He has managed the San Francisco Giants since 1993 to a 558–512 win-loss record. His best record came in 1993, when he guided San Francisco to second place in the NL West with a 103–59 mark and was named BBWAA NL Manager of the Year. The San Francisco Giants finished first in the NL West in 1997 with a 90–72 mark, but lost to the Florida Marlins in the NL Division Series. Baker guided the San Francisco Giants to an 89–74 mark in 1998, losing a one-game playoff, 5–3, to the Chicago Cubs to determine the NL Wild Card. He and his ex-wife, Harriet, have one daughter, Natosha.

BIBLIOGRAPHY: *The Baseball Encyclopedia*, 10th ed. (New York, 1996); Ron Fimrite, "Icing on His Cake," *SI* 55 (August 31, 1981), pp. 70, 72; Gene Karst and Martin J. Jones, Jr., *Who's Who in Professional Baseball* (New Rochelle, NY, 1973); W. Leavy, "Baseball's Minority Managers: Taking Charge on the Field," *Ebony* 48 (May 1993), pp. 10–12; William F. McNeil, *The Dodgers Encyclopedia* (Champaign, IL, 1997); L. Mpho Mabunda, ed., *Contemporary Black Biography*, vol. 8 (Detroit, MI, 1995); William C. Matney, ed., *Who's Who among Black Americans*, 4th ed. (Lake Forest, IL, 1985); Lawrence S. Ritter and Donald Honig, *The Image of Their Greatness* (New York, 1979); John Thorn et al., eds., *Total Baseball*, 5th ed. (New York, 1997); TSN *Official Baseball Register, 1998*; Clint Wilson, Jr., "The Dusty Baker Revival," *Sepia* 28 (August 1978), pp. 20–26.

                                                                    Gaymon L. Bennett

BALDWIN, Marcus Elmore "Mark," "Fido" (b. October 29, 1863, Pittsburgh, PA; d. November 10, 1929, Pittsburgh, PA), player, pitched baseball professionally for 10 years and spent seven seasons in three major leagues. In 1886, the 6-foot, 190-pound right-handed fastballer pitched Duluth, MN to the NWL pennant. The Chicago White Stockings, NL pennant winners, signed him that October and hoped to use him in the World Series, but the opposing St. Louis Browns objected. Baldwin, thus, began his major league career with Chicago in 1887, compiling an 18–17 record in 40 games. In 1888, a leg injury limited him to 30 games and a 13–15 record. He hurled for the Chicago White Stockings on their world tour that winter, but was released before the 1889 season.

After being signed by Columbus, OH (AA), he compiled a 27–34 record in 1889 and led the AA in games (63), innings pitched (513.2), and strikeouts (368). The following season, he jumped to the Chicago Pirates (PL) club and again led his league in games (58), complete games (53), innings pitched (492), and strikeouts (206). He also topped PL pitchers in wins with a 33–24 mark.

When the PL dissolved after one season, Baldwin signed with the Pittsburgh Pirates (NL) and enticed pitcher Charles "Silver" King* of St. Louis (AA) to join his club. Pittsburgh soon became known as the "Pirates." Irate St. Louis owner Christian Von der Ahe* had Baldwin jailed briefly. Baldwin sued him for false arrest and eventually received several thousand dollars in damages and court costs after Von der Ahe was forcibly brought to court in 1898.

Baldwin won 22 games for the Pittsburgh Pirates in 1891 and 26 contests in 1892. But he lost 28 and 27 games those two seasons and was released after pitching just 2.1 innings in 1893. He signed with the New York Giants (NL), but was again released after a 16–20 campaign.

After spending two minor league seasons in the PSL and EL, the unmarried Baldwin retired from baseball to study medicine. He received his M.D. degree from Baltimore Medical College in 1900 and practiced surgery in New York, Pittsburgh, and Rochester, MN.

In his seven major league seasons, Baldwin won 155 games and lost 165 contests for a .484 winning percentage. He started 328 of his 346 games, completing 295 of them and compiling a 3.37 ERA.

BIBLIOGRAPHY: Mark Baldwin file, National Baseball Library, Cooperstown, NY; Cappy Gagnon, "Major Leaguers Who Attended College," *Nineteenth Century Notes* (July 1992), p. 5; Frederick Ivor-Campbell et al., eds., *Baseball's First Stars* (Cleveland, OH, 1996); *NYT*, September 6, 1898, p. 5; Daniel Pearson, *Baseball in 1889* (Bowling Green, OH, 1993); John Thorn et al., eds., *Total Baseball*, 5th ed. (New York, 1997).

Frederick Ivor-Campbell

BALL, George Walter "Georgia Rabbit," "Black Diamond" (b. September 13, 1877, Detroit, MI; d. December 16, 1945, Chicago, IL), player, was the son of John Ball and Ella (Swift) Ball and starred in all-black baseball. Ball played white semipro baseball in the upper midwest from 1893 to 1902. He pitched for various Minnesota and North Dakota teams, beginning with the St. Paul Young Cyclones in 1893. Ball was credited with 25 victories for the 1899

North Dakota champion Grand Forks (RRVC) club and captained the 1901 York, ND team. He helped pitch St. Cloud, MN to the championship of eastern Minnesota in 1902 and entered black professional baseball with Frank Leland's Chicago Union Giants. Ball remained active professionally through 1923.

Ball's diamond talent kept him in high demand among the independent all-black teams of the early twentieth century. Since player contracts were meaningless or non-existent, Ball switched teams often and even during the season. In 1905, he reportedly pitched for the Chicago Union Giants, Chicago Leland Giants, Brooklyn Royal Giants, and Cuban X-Giants, all premier teams bidding for his services. He also hurled for the 1904 Cuban X-Giants, 1906 Quaker Giants, 1907 St. Paul Gophers, 1908 Minneapolis Keystones, 1912 St. Louis Giants and Chicago American Giants, 1913 Brooklyn Royal Giants and Mohawk Giants, 1914 Lincoln Giants and Lincoln Stars (both of New York), and 1915 Chicago American Giants.

Despite frequently switching teams, Ball rejoined the Leland Chicago Giants from 1905 through 1910 and from 1917 until 1923. He reportedly also pitched for an Augusta, GA team and the Milwaukee Giants. Limited statistical data exists on Ball's career. In 1909, he compiled a 12–1 record, hit .238, and fielded .926 in 25 games in helping the Leland Giants claim the Chicago city pennant. He batted .302 with a 1.000 fielding mark for the 1914 Lincoln Stars. His 1921 NNL appearance produce a 0–3 slate. Ball also played for the Fe (CUWL) club. He pitched 26 games during three winters in Cuba from 1908 through 1911, completing 20 starts, winning 9 of 23 decisions, and hitting .261.

Ball also played the outfield and made a phenomenal catch in right field that won a 1908 title for the Leland Giants. He dueled Chicago Cubs (NL) ace Mordecai "Three Finger" Brown* in a hard-fought post-season exhibition 4–2 loss in 1909. Ball's black professional baseball career typified the era and its conditions. The better black performers often switched teams during the season for monetary reasons. These teams were forced to carry a minimum number of players on their rosters because of cost and regular traveling. Late in Ball's career, the black ball scene stabilized with the formation of the NNL in 1920. The Chicago Giants became a charter member of this circuit, enabling Ball to spend the twilight of his career in the first viable Negro League.

Ball worked as a custodian until his death and left a 38-year-old widow, Jeanette, who believed him to be in his mid-fifties.

BIBLIOGRAPHY: Dick Clark and Larry Lester, *The Negro Leagues Book* (Cleveland, OH, 1994); *Frank Leland's Chicago Giants Base Ball Club* (Chicago, IL, 1910); James A. Riley, *The Biographical Encyclopedia of the Negro Baseball Leagues* (New York, 1994).
                                                                          Merl F. Kleinknecht

BANCROFT, David James "Dave," "Beauty" (b. April 20, 1891, Sioux City, IA; d. October 9, 1972, Superior, WI), player, coach, and manager, was the son of Milwaukee Railroad news vendor and truck farmer Frank Bancroft and Ella (Gearhart) Bancroft. The youngest of three children, he had a brother, Robert, and a sister, Annis Jane (Garretson). Bancroft attended Hopkins Grade School and Sioux City Central High School (1908–1910), playing baseball there and on community sandlots. After moving to Superior, WI, he married Edna H. Gisin in November 1910; they had no children. In 1909, he began his professional baseball career with a brief stint at Duluth, MN (MWL). After being released, he joined Superior, WI (MWL) as the regular shortstop the same season. The light-hitting Bancroft starred defensively there through 1911 and at Portland, OR (PCL) from 1912 to 1914.

In the NL, he played shortstop with the Philadelphia Phillies (1915–1920), New York Giants (1920–1923, 1930), Boston Braves (1924–1927), and Brooklyn Dodgers (1928–1929). The scrappy 5-foot 9½-inch, 160-pound Bancroft made 2,004 hits, including 320 doubles, and compiled a career .279 batting average. A leadoff batter, the switch-hitting Bancroft crowded the plate and walked 827 times. Nicknamed "Beauty," he batted over .300 five seasons, stretched many singles into extra-base hits, scored 1,048 runs, and knocked in 591 runs. Defensively, Bancroft possessed quick hands, moved gracefully in either direction, and excelled at fielding bad-hop ground balls, cutting off outfield throws, and picking runners off base. He made only 666 errors in 12,000 fielding chances for a lifetime .944 mark. Sportswriter Frank Graham called Bancroft "the greatest shortstop the Giants ever had and one of the greatest that ever lived," while the Philadelphia Sports Writers Association in 1954 named him the Phillies' "all-time outstanding shortstop."

As a rookie in 1915, Bancroft hit .254 for Philadelphia and sparked the Phillies to their first NL pennant. Although he batted .294 in the World Series, the Phillies lost to the Boston Red Sox. New York Giants manager John McGraw,* who considered Bancroft baseball's best shortstop, acquired him in a June 1920, trade and made him team captain. Later that month, Bancroft made six singles in a game against Philadelphia. An energetic, competitive, inspirational, intuitive leader, he helped the Giants win the 1921–1923 NL pennants and two World Series titles. Bancroft threw out three New York Yankee runners attempting to take extra bases in the 1921 World Series. In 1922, he handled 984 chances defensively and led shortstops in double plays.

From 1924 to 1927, Bancroft piloted the Boston Braves (NL). Although batting over .300 twice, he lacked talented players and managed the club to four second division finishes. Bancroft coached with the New York Giants (1930–1932) and had hoped to pilot the club when McGraw retired. He managed the Minneapolis, MN Millers (AA) in 1933, Sioux City, IA Cowboys (WL) in 1936, and St. Cloud, MN Rox (NoL) in 1947. Bancroft worked as warehouse supervisor for Lakehead Pipe Line Company until his 1956 retirement. His honors included election to the National Baseball Hall of Fame (1971), Iowa Sports Hall of Fame (1954), Superior Athletic Hall of Fame (1964), Sioux City Athletic Hall of Fame (1965), and Duluth Sports Hall of Fame (1971).

BIBLIOGRAPHY: Martin Appel and Burt Goldblatt, *Baseball's Best: The Hall of Fame Gallery* (New York, 1977); Dave Bancroft file, National Baseball Library, Cooperstown, NY; Thomas Aylesworth and Benton Minks, *The Encyclopedia of Baseball Managers* (New York, 1990); Jerry E. Clark, *Anson to Zuber: Iowa Boys in the Major Leagues* (Omaha, NE, 1992); Robert S. Fuchs and Wayne Soini, *Judge Fuchs and the Boston Braves* (Jefferson, NC, 1997); Charles C. Alexander, *John McGraw* (New York, 1988); Gary Caruso, *The Braves Encyclopedia* (Philadelphia, PA, 1995); Des Moines *Register*, March 28, 1954, October 11, 1972; Frank Graham, *The New York Giants* (New York, 1952); Harold Kaese, *The Boston Braves* (New York, 1948); Al Hirshberg, *Braves, the Pick and the Shovel* (Boston, MA, 1948); Noel Hynd, *The Giants of the Polo Grounds* (New York, 1988); Frederick G. Lieb and Stan Baumgartner, *The Philadelphia Phillies* (New York, 1953); George S. May, "Major League Baseball Players from Iowa," *The Palimpsest* 36 (April 1955), pp. 133–165; *NYT*, November 13, 1923, October 15, 1927, October 10, 1972; David L. Porter, correspondence with Frank Garretson, July 13, 1984, David L. Porter Collection, Oskaloosa, IA; David L. Porter, correspondence with David Mook, July 11, 1984; *The Baseball Encyclopedia*, 10th ed. (New York, 1996); Lowell Reidenbaugh, *Baseball's Hall of Fame-Cooperstown* (New York, 1993); Sioux City *Journal*, November 26, 1926; Robert Smith, *Baseball's Hall of Fame* (New York, 1973); Superior *Evening Telegram*, July 30, 1927, January 23, 1954, October 10, 1972; Rich Westcott and Frank Bilovsky, *The New Phillies Encyclopedia* (Philadelphia, PA, 1993).

David L. Porter

BANCROFT, Francis Carter "Banny" (b. May 9, 1846, Lancaster, MA; d. March 30, 1921, Cincinnati, OH), manager and executive, was associated with professional baseball for over 40 years. The son of Lorey F. Bancroft and Ann (Carter) Bancroft, he enlisted with the Union Army, 8th New Hampshire Volunteers and served four years during the Civil War. Bancroft drew upon his amateur playing experience to organize baseball matches among Union regiments. After the war, he settled in New Bedford, MA and founded a prosperous hotel. Bancroft pursued many business ventures, including theater, opera, ice hockey, and baseball.

In 1878 New Bedford entered a team in the IA, baseball's first minor league. Bancroft served as manager, but his duties encompassed all aspects of business and field management. He demonstrated an excellent ability to handle athletes and an innovative business style. He pulled his team from the IA and embarked on a barnstorming tour, playing a record 130 games. Over the winter, he took a team to Cuba and introduced the game there. The next year, he moved to Worcester, MA and formed a baseball team so good that the Ruby Legs was admitted to the NL in 1880.

He managed a still-record seven major league clubs during his nine seasons at the helm. His clubs included the Worcester Ruby Legs (NL) in 1880, Detroit Wolverines (NL) in 1881–1882, Cleveland Blues (NL) in 1883, Providence, RI Grays (NL) in 1884–1885, Philadelphia Athletics (AA) in 1887, Indianapolis Hoosiers (AA) in 1889, and Cincinnati Reds (NL) in 1902. The 1884 season marked the pinnacle of his managerial career. His Providence Grays won the NL pennant by 10½ games with an 84–28 record and swept the first World Series from the New York Metropolitans (AA). His lifetime managerial record stands at 375–333–10 for a .530 winning percentage. Bancroft, an independent, strong-willed sort, often resented ownership involvement in the running of the team. His dissatisfaction with front office interference caused his frequent team changes.

Bancroft joined the front office with which he was so often at odds when he became business manager for the Cincinnati Reds (NL) in 1890. He returned to Cuba with the Reds and also took them to Hawaii. He remained in his post until his death, ranking among the most popular and well-liked executives in the game.

The twice-married Bancroft had at least four children and left his second wife financially well-off.

BIBLIOGRAPHY: Francis Bancroft file, National Baseball Library, Cooperstown, NY; Thomas Aylesworth and Benton Minks, *The Encyclopedia of Baseball Managers* (New York, 1990); Lee Allen, *The Cincinnati Reds* (New York, 1948); Bill Ballou, "Mighty Bancroft Struck Nothing But Goldmines," Worcester (MA) *Sunday Telegram*, October 13, 1985; Frank C. Bancroft, letter to Town Clerk, Lancaster, MA, January 21, 1913; *The Baseball Encyclopedia*, 10th ed. (New York, 1996); Cincinnati (OH) *Commercial Tribune*, March 31, 1921; April 21, 1921; Frederick Ivor-Campbell, "1884: Old Hoss Radbourn and the Providence Grays," *TNP* 4 (Spring 1985), pp. 33–38; Lew Lipset, *New York Clipper Woodcuts, 1879–1880* (Manhattan, KS, 1984); Robert L. Tiemann and Mark Rucker, eds., *Nineteenth Century Stars* (Kansas City, MO, 1989).

John R. Husman

BANDO, Salvatore Leonard "Sal" (b. February 13, 1944, Cleveland, OH), player and executive, is the son of Ben Bando, a self-employed contractor, and Angela Bando. His brother, Chris, played with the Cleveland Indians (AL). A graduate of Warrensville Heights (OH) High School, Bando was named All-State in football and baseball. Bando attended Arizona State University, where he earned a Bachelor's degree in Business Administration in 1966. On February 8, 1969, he married Sandra Fortunato. Bando's outstanding college baseball career featured him batting .480 in the 1965 College World Series while leading his team to the national title and being voted the World Series' Outstanding Player. In 1965, Bando was signed by the Kansas City Athletics (AL). A 6-foot, 200-pound, right-handed third baseman, he played in the ML and PCL and made the All-Star team in both leagues. He was brought up to the major leagues for part of the 1967 season after batting .291 for Vancouver, Canada (PCL).

After the Athletics moved to Oakland for the 1968 season, Bando established himself as a premier major league third baseman. He hit with power and played outstanding defense, having a powerful arm. His career high of 31 HR and 113 RBI came in 1969. Two years later, he finished as runner-up to Vida Blue* in the AL MVP voting with 24 HR and 94 RBI. Bando captained the Oakland A's to five Western Division titles (1971–1975) and three World Series crowns (1972–1974). A four-time All-Star (1969, 1972–1974), Bando played his best in clutch situations and either tied or set several AL Championship Series records. The Milwaukee Brewers (AL) signed Bando in November 1976. He played there until retiring in 1981 and still ranks in the top ten on some Brewers' all-time hitting lists. His career batting average was .254, with 1,790 hits, 242 HR, and 1,039 RBI. Bando resides in Mequon, WI with his wife and sons, Sal, Jr., Sonny, and Stefano. Bando worked for the Milwaukee Brewers as a special assistant to the general manager until October 1991 and as senior vice president of baseball operations until August 1999, when he was named special assistant to the president. Milwaukee shifted to the NL in 1998. He also holds a partnership in the Bando-McGlocklin Capital Corporation with former Milwaukee Bucks (NBA) star Jon McGlocklin and is involved in many community service projects.

BIBLIOGRAPHY: Salvatore Bando file, National Baseball Library, Cooperstown, NY; Salvatore Bando, interview with Al Figone, September 25, 1989; *Milwaukee Brewers Media Guide, 1981*; *The Baseball Encyclopedia*, 10th ed. (New York, 1996); Bruce Markusen, *Baseball's Last Dynasty* (New York, 1998); *TSN*, September 24, 1966, p. 16, May 27, 1967, p. 8; Washington (DC) *Daily News*, July 22, 1969.

                                                                          Albert J. Figone

BANKHEAD, Samuel Howard "Sam" (b. September 18, 1905, Empire, AL; d. July 24, 1976, Pittsburgh, PA), player and manager, was the son of Garnet Bankhead and Gina (Armstrong) Bankhead and starred in the NNL and throughout Latin America and Canada from 1929 through 1951. Bankhead's professional baseball career began with the Birmingham Black Barons (NNL) in 1929 and continued with a brief stint for the black Louisville Black Caps in 1932. He then joined the Nashville Elite Giants (NNL) from 1932 through 1934. Aside from a 1937 trip to the Dominican Republic with Satchel Paige's* All-Star team, Bankhead played with the Pittsburgh Crawfords (NNL) from 1935 through 1938. In 1939 and from 1942 through 1950, Bankhead spent 10 seasons with the Homestead Grays (NNL). The 1940 and 1941 campaigns saw him with Monterrey, Mexico (MEL). In 1951 he became the manager of Farnham, Canada (ProL), making him organized baseball's first black manager. Farnham finished in seventh place with 52 wins and 71 losses.

Bankhead batted .318 lifetime in the Negro League and .351 in 1940 and 1941. Bankhead hit .371 in the 1932–1933 CWL, .297 in four CWL seasons, .318 in the MEL, .350 in the 1944 Black World Series against the Birmingham Black Barons, .287 and .282 in the 1944 and 1945 NNL seasons, and .274 with Farnham in 1951. He led the MEL with 32 stolen bases in 1940. Although not noted for his power, he tied Monte Irvin* and Fernando Pedroso for the 1945–1946 PRWL HR leadership with three. Bankhead hit white major league pitching for a .342 average in 21 exhibition contests.

Bankhead performed on seven NNL pennant winners, including the 1935 Pittsburgh Crawfords and the 1939, 1942, 1943, 1944, 1945, and 1948 Homestead Grays. He participated in five Black World Series from 1942 through 1948, helping his teams win titles in 1943, 1944, and 1948. The strong-armed, 5-foot 8-inch, 175-pound right-hander proved a versatile performer, receiving All-Star recognition as a second baseman, shortstop, and outfielder. Bankhead started four East-West All-Star Games, each at a different position: in 1934 at right field, in 1936 at left field, in 1938 at center field, and in 1943 at second base. Bankhead also appeared in the 1933, 1942, and 1944 East-West matchups and collected 9 hits, 2 doubles, 5 runs, 4 RBI, and a .346 batting average in that competition. Four of Bankhead's younger brothers also played professional baseball. His brother, Dan, became the white major league's first black pitcher with the Brooklyn Dodgers (NL) in 1947.

Bankhead worked for the sanitation department for Pittsburgh, PA in 1949–1950. After retiring from baseball in 1951, he worked as a hotel porter and fell victim to a homicide while on duty at Pittsburgh's William Penn Hotel. His death resulted from a gunshot wound inflicted by a friend after Bankhead had provoked an argument that escalated into a drunken fight. His wife, Helen, survived him. In 1952, the Pittsburgh *Courier* named Bankhead to its All-Time Black All-Star Team as a first team utility player.

BIBLIOGRAPHY: John B. Holway, *Blackball Stars* (Westport, CT, 1988); Merl F. Kleinknecht personal files, Galion, OH; Robert W. Peterson, *Only the Ball Was White* (Englewood Cliffs, NJ, 1970); James A. Riley, *The All-Time All-Stars of Black Baseball* (Cocoa, FL, 1983); James A. Riley, *The Biographical Encyclopedia of the Negro Baseball Leagues* (New York, 1994); Pepe Seda, *Don Q Base Ball Cues* (Ponce, PR, 1970); *TSN Baseball Guide, 1952*.

                                                                    Merl F. Kleinknecht

BANKS, Ernest "Ernie," "Mr. Cub" (b. January 31, 1931, Dallas, TX), player and coach, is the son of laborer Eddie Banks and Essie Banks and had seven brothers and four sisters. At Booker T. Washington High School in Dallas, Banks starred in football, basketball, track, and baseball. During the summer, he played for the Detroit Colts, a Negro baseball team. Following graduation in 1950, Banks joined the Kansas City Monarchs (NAL). After serving in the U.S. Army (1951–1952), Banks rejoined the Monarchs until the Chicago Cubs (NL) purchased him in 1953.

Banks, a shortstop–first baseman, played for the Cubs from 1953 to 1971. Although the Cubs finished pennantless, Banks starred in contrast. In 2,528 games, he batted 9,421 times, scored 1,305 runs, made 2,583 hits, 407 doubles, 90 triples, 512 HR (twelfth place on the all-time list), knocked in 1,636 runs, and compiled .274 batting and .986 fielding averages. Banks, who leads the Cubs in many modern all-time offensive departments, holds the NL record with five grand-slam HR in 1955. He slugged 12 career grand slams.

Besides establishing a major league season record for HR by a shortstop (47), Banks hit over 40 HR in five different seasons and led the NL in 1958 and 1960. He hit at least two HR in one game 42 times and three in one game four times. In 1958 and 1959, he led the NL in RBI with 129 and 143, respectively.

An outstanding defensive player, Banks in 1969 led NL first basemen with a .997 fielding mark. Ten years earlier, he had set the single season major league record for fielding percentage as a shortstop (.985), making the fewest errors (12) at that position. A team player and an inspirational leader, Banks in 1969 was voted the "Greatest Cub Ever" and "Chicagoan of the Year" and later was the first black enshrined in the Texas Hall of Fame. Banks, the NL's MVP two consecutive seasons (1958–1959), made several All-Star teams (1955–1962, 1965, 1967, and 1969).

Married to Eloyce Johnson in 1958, Banks has three children, twin sons, Joey and Jerry, and daughter Jan Elizabeth. Since retirement, Banks has served as a coach and director of group sales and community relations for the Cubs. In 1982 he became vice-president of Associated Film Promotions in Los Angeles. The co-author of the book "*Mr. Cub,*" Banks in 1977 was elected to the National Baseball Hall of Fame and became the eighth player so honored in the first year of eligibility. Banks made Major League Baseball's All-Century Team.

BIBLIOGRAPHY: Ernie Banks and Jim Enright, "*Mr. Cub*" (Chicago IL, 1971); John Benson et al., *Baseball's Top 100* (Wilton, CT, 1997); Jim Enright, *Chicago Cubs* (New York, 1975); Donald Honig, *The Power Hitters* (St. Louis, MO, 1989); Larry Moffi and Jonathan Kronstadt, *Crossing the Line* (Jefferson, NC, 1994); *TSN Official Baseball Register 1973*; Eddie Gold and Art Ahrens, *The New Era Cubs 1941–1985* (Chicago, IL, 1985); David L. Porter, ed., *African-American Sports Greats* (Westport, CT, 1995); Warren Wilbert and William Hageman, *Chicago Cubs: Seasons at the Summit* (Champaign, IL, 1997); Jim Langford, *The Game Is Never Over* (South Bend, IN, 1980); Lowell Reidenbaugh, *Baseball's Hall of Fame-Cooperstown* (New York, 1993).

John L. Evers

BARFIELD, Jesse Lee (b. October 29, 1959, Joliet, IL), player and coach, is the son of Jesse Hester Barfield and Annie Barfield and graduated from Joliet Central High School in 1977. The Toronto Blue Jays (AL) selected the 6-foot 1-inch, 200-pound, right-hander hitter in the ninth round of the 1977 free agent draft. Barfield chose professional baseball over an academic scholarship to study architecture at Bradley University.

The outfielder struggled at the plate in the minor leagues from 1977 to 1981 with Utica, NY (NYPL), Dunedin, FL (FSL), Kinston, NC (CrL), and Knoxville, TN (SL). The Toronto Blue Jays placed him on their major league roster on September 3, 1981. He started immediately due to an injury to Barry Bonnell and singled in his debut.

Barfield remained with the Toronto Blue Jays, sharing right field duties with Dave Collins from 1982 to 1984. Toronto traded Collins in December 1984 and installed Barfield as their full-time right fielder. An excellent defensive player, Barfield spent the 1985 through 1988 seasons as a fixture in right field. He combined with Lloyd Moseby* in center field and George Bell* in left field to form one of the finest major league outfields. Barfield hit a league-leading 40 HR in 1986 and led the AL in assists four times. In both 1985 and 1986, the Toronto right fielder posted his career high batting average with .289. Barfield made one post-season appearance, playing in all seven games of the 1985 AL Championship Series. He hit .280 with one HR against the Kansas City Royals.

The Toronto Blue Jays traded Barfield to the New York Yankees (AL) for pitcher Al Leiter in April 1989. He signed a three-year contract on October 12 to remain a Yankee. Foot and wrist injuries limited Barfield to 84 games in 1991 and only 30 contests in 1992. He played two games in 1992 at Albany-Colonie, NY (EL) on rehabilitation assignment.

The New York Yankees released Barfield after the 1992 season. The Yomiuri, Japan Giants (JCL) signed Barfield in December. Barfield hit 26 HR in 1993, but batted only .215 due to a nagging wrist injury. The Houston Astros (NL) acquired him in February 1994, but released him one month later.

Barfield finished his major league career with 1,219 hits, 241 HR, 162 assists, and a .256 batting average. He received Gold Glove awards in 1986 and 1987 and played in the 1986 All-Star game. *TSN* named him to their 1986 AL Silver Slugger team. He received the 1985 Toronto Player of the Year Award from Labatt and the Toronto chapter of the BBWAA.

The Houston Astros hired Barfield as an outfield coach for the 1995 season. He served on the minor league coaching staff of the Texas Rangers (AL) in 1996 and on the Seattle Mariners (AL) from December 1997 to October 1999 as a hitting instructor. The Houston resident and his wife, Marla, have three children, Joshua, Jessica, and Jeremy.

BIBLIOGRAPHY: Jesse Barfield file, National Baseball Library, Cooperstown, NY; *TSN Baseball Register*, 1993; Peter C. Bjarkman, *The Toronto Blue Jays* (New York, 1990).

John Hillman

BARLICK, Albert Joseph "Al" (b. April 2, 1915, Springfield, IL; d. December 27, 1995, Springfield, IL), umpire, was the son of coal miner John Barlick and Louise (Gorence) Barlick. His attendance at Converse High School, Springfield, was cut short by financial necessity. He worked as a loader (helping his father) at bituminous coal mine Peabody No. 59 in Springfield until a labor strike shut it down. Barlick began umpiring in 1935 in a local municipal league. In August 1936, he entered organized baseball as umpire in the Class D NEAL. Barlick's ability, efficiency, and hard work earned him rapid promotion to the PiL in 1937 and 1938, the EL in 1939, and the IL in 1939 and 1940.

During September 1940, Barlick joined the NL umpires as a replacement for the ailing Bill Klem.* With a strong performance and Klem's endorsement, Barlick become a regular NL umpire in 1941 and remained one until retirement after the 1971 season. Interruptions included World War II service in the U.S. Coast Guard from October 1943 to November 1945; medical leave during the 1956 and 1957 seasons because of heart strain; and "resignation" for five days in 1960 due to a misunderstanding with NL officials. During his active career, he umpired in seven World Series and seven All-Star games. He served as an NL consultant from 1972 to 1994.

The burly 5-foot 11-inch, 185-pound Barlick frequently was called the loudest, most colorful, and best umpire in baseball. Unique vigorous "out" gestures and booming "stee-ruck-huh" calls identified him unmistakably. Barlick's total commitment, unerring accuracy, and complete control of the game made him a truly great arbiter. When *TSN* writers' poll in 1961 voted Barlick the best NL umpire, he protested his displeasure of the results as a slur on his peers by persons not competent to judge the arbiters' professionalism. He accepted an Umpire of the Year award in 1970, however, because the balloting had been conducted among umpires. A lifetime Springfield, IL resident, Barlick married Jennie Marie Leffel of Springfield in February 1941 and had two daughters, Marlene and Kathleen. He was elected to the National Baseball Hall of Fame in 1989, the sixth umpire so honored.

BIBLIOGRAPHY: Albert Barlick file, National Baseball Library, Cooperstown, NY; Albert J. Barlick, "Voice of the Umpires," *TSN*, October 26, 1974; Harold Parrott, "Al Barlick, 25, Youngest Umpire ...," *TSN*, October 17, 1940; Frank V. Phelps, correspondence with Albert J. Barlick, October 19, 1985, Frank V. Phelps Collection, King of Prussia, PA; Lowell Reidenbaugh, *Baseball's Hall of Fame-Cooperstown* (New York, 1993); *TSN Baseball Register, 1958*; *TSN*, November 6, 1957, August 2, 1961, October 15, 1966, December 25, 1971; Brad Wilson, "Veteran Al Barlick Honored as Umpire of Year," *TSN*, February 20, 1971; Herbert Warren Wind, "How an Umpire Gets That Way," *SEP* 226 (August 8, 1953), pp. 25, 119–122.

Frank V. Phelps

BARNARD, Ernest Sargent "Barny" (b. July 17, 1874, West Columbia, WV; d. March 27, 1931, Rochester, MN), executive, was the son of minister Elias Barnard, who moved his family to several West Virginia towns before settling in Delaware, OH. He attended Otterbein Academy and College, graduating in 1895, and coached the football and baseball teams there the next three years. After moving to Columbus, OH, he became secretary of that city's Builders Exchange and also coached the Ohio Medical University football team. Nicknamed "Barny," he became sports editor in 1900 of the Columbus *Dispatch*.

In 1903 Cleveland Indians owner Charles Somers* hired Barnard as the club's traveling secretary. After the 1908 season, he was elevated to vice-president and general manager and introduced uniform numbers. When James C. Dunn purchased the team in 1916, he initially took Barnard's responsibilities away. Dunn reappointed Barnard to his former position as general manager after two years. His 1920 club won Cleveland's first AL pennant and defeated Brooklyn in the World Series.

Upon Dunn's death in 1922, Barnard assumed the presidency of the Cleveland Indians. His clubs generally finished in the middle of the AL standings and challenged for the pennant only in 1926, when they finished a close second to the New York Yankees. In the mid–1920s, Barnard played an increasingly important role as mediator and peacemaker in the bitter disputes between baseball commissioner Judge Kenesaw Mountain Landis* and AL president Ban Johnson.*

The AL owners in 1927 ousted Johnson, the league's founder and president since 1900. Barnard was named AL president after satisfying Dunn's widow by selling the Indians to a group of Cleveland businessmen headed by Alva Bradley. As AL president, he acted as an administrator and left the public spotlight to the commissioner. He applied modern management principles to the AL office in Chicago, running it with an even disposition and a sense of order. In 1930, the AL owners reelected him to a five-year term.

He entered the Mayo Clinic in March 1931 and died there only a few hours before Johnson. He was survived by his widow, the former Josephine Flick of Cleveland, whom he had married in 1918. His quiet, efficient administrative approach and his concern for good public relations contributed to baseball's image of respectability in the 1920s.

BIBLIOGRAPHY: Lee Allen, *The American League Story* (New York, 1962); Ernest Barnard file, National Baseball Library, Cooperstown, NY; Franklin Lewis, *The Cleveland Indians* (New York, 1949); Eugene C. Murdock, *Ban Johnson* (Westport, CT, 1982); Harold Seymour, *Baseball: The Golden Age* (New York, 1971); J. G. Taylor Spink, *Judge Landis and Twenty-five Years of Baseball* (New York, 1947).

William E. Akin

BARNES, Jesse Lawrence (b. August 26, 1892, Perkins, OK; d. September 9, 1961, Santa Rosa, NM), player, was the son of Luther C. Barnes, a plasterer, and Sarah E. Barnes. Barnes, who was of English and Pennsylvania-Dutch ancestry, came from an athletic family. His brother, Virgil, played baseball for the New York Giants (NL) from 1922 to 1928, while another brother performed in minor league baseball. When Jesse and Virgil were teammates on the Giants, they were nicknamed "Big Knub" and "Little Knub" respectively because they wore the smallest caps in the club. Barnes' hobbies of hunting, fishing, and wood carving reflected his athletic nature.

Barnes began his professional career in organized baseball at Keokuk, IA (CA) in 1912. He pitched for Davenport, IA (3IL) in 1913 and, after a brief trial with the Chicago Cubs (NL) in early 1914, returned to Davenport for the 1914–1915 seasons. He joined the Boston Braves (NL) at the end of the 1915 season and was traded with Larry Doyle* to the New York Giants (NL) in January 1918 for Buck Herzog.* The 1918–1919 campaigns proved eventful for Barnes. After starting the 1918 season with a 6–1 record, he entered the US Army for the duration of World War I. On June 17, 1919, he married Rebecca Margaret Shaffer. Barnes remained with the New York Giants until 1923, enjoying his most productive years there. He returned to Boston in June 1923 and finished his 13-year major league career with the Brooklyn, NY Robins (NL) in 1926 and 1927.

The 6-foot, 175-pound, right-handed pitcher who batted left-handed appeared in 422 games, completing 180 of 312 starts. The lifetime .214 hitter fielded above average. His best season came in 1919, when he led the NL with 25 wins and compiled a 2.40 ERA with the New York Giants. He enjoyed a 20-victory season in 1920 and won 10 or more games for eight consecutive seasons from 1919 to 1926. He finished his major league career with 152 wins, 150 losses, and a 3.22 ERA. When pitching for weak Boston teams, he led the NL in losses with 21 in 1917 and 20 in 1924 despite compiling ERA well below the NL average.

Barnes pitched a 6–0 no-hitter against the Philadelphia Phillies on May 7, 1922, but the highlight of his major league career came in the 1921 World Series. During the the third and sixth games, Barnes relieved the New York Giants' starting pitcher Fred Toney and won both contests through his "courage and good control." He also singled to start a four-run rally in the third game. In the sixth game, he struck out 10 batters in an 8–5 victory while surrendering two runs, four hits, and four walks in 8.1 innings. In the 1921 World Series against a New York Yankees team led by Babe Ruth,* Barnes allowed only six hits in 16.1 innings in three relief appearances and struck out 18 batters. He also made four hits in nine at bats while compiling his two victories. In the 1922 World Series, Barnes pitched the 10-inning, 3–3 tie game called on account of darkness by umpire George Hildebrand. Since many observers thought it had been light enough to continue, baseball Commissioner Kenesaw Mountain Landis* ordered the gate receipts, minus the players' share, be turned over to local charities.

After concluding his major league career, Barnes pitched four minor league seasons. He appeared with Toledo, OH (AA) in 1927 and 1928 and Buffalo, NY (IL) in 1929–1930, compiling a 61–39 record. Barnes, who suffered heart trouble, died while traveling with his family.

BIBLIOGRAPHY: Jesse Barnes file, National Baseball Library, Cooperstown, NY; Noel Hynd, *The Giants of the Polo Grounds* (New York, 1988); Robert S. Fuchs and Wayne Soini, *Judge Fuchs and the Boston Braves* (Jefferson, NC, 1997); Harold Kaese, *The Boston Braves* (New York, 1948); Al Hirshberg, *Braves, the Pick and the Shovel* (Boston, MA, 1948); Frank Graham, *The New York Giants* (New York, 1952); *TSN Baseball Register*, 1945, 1952; *Spalding's Baseball Guide*, 1922, 1923.

Michael J. McBride

BARNES, Roscoe Conkling "Ross" (b. May 8, 1850, Mt. Morris, NY; d. February 5, 1915, Chicago, IL), player, was a hard-hitting infielder for five consecutive NA and NL pennant winners from 1872 to 1876. Barnes hit over .400 for the Boston Red Stockings (NA) from 1871 to 1873 and the Chicago White Stockings (NL) in 1876, won the batting championship in 1872, 1873, and 1876, and hit for power. His lifetime .390 batting average led the NA, while his NL career mark was .319. His career .359 batting average paced all infielders including Rogers Hornsby.*

The right-handed hitting Barnes exploited one of the scoring rules. Through the 1876 season, any batted ball hit in fair territory was considered fair even if it subsequently went foul. Barnes mastered this type of hitting and proved virtually impossible to defend against. Before the 1877 season, the rule was changed to the present requirement. Although NL averages increased from 1876 to 1877, Barnes found the change disastrous and hit only .269 in his last three major league seasons. He suffered a serious illness, which caused him to miss many games in 1877. When Chicago refused to pay his full salary, Barnes became the first star to go to court for redress of contractual grievances. The court ruled in favor of the owners, setting a pattern until the 1970s.

Although only 5-feet 8-inches tall and weighing 145 pounds, Barnes compensated for his small stature by being a fast runner and an above-average fielder. Primarily a second baseman, he led that position in fielding percentage in 1876. Barnes captained the Tecumsehs of London, Canada (IA) in 1878, led shortstops in chances per game for the Cincinnati Reds (NL) in 1879, skipped baseball in 1880, and ended his major league career as a shortstop for Boston (NL) in 1881. He held various white-collar jobs around Chicago and remained a bachelor until his death.

BIBLIOGRAPHY: Roscoe Barnes file, National Baseball Library, Cooperstown, NY; Warren Brown, *The Chicago Cubs* (New York, 1946); John Duxbury, "The National League's First Batting Champ," *BRJ* 5 (1976) pp. 70–72; Eddie Gold and Art Ahrens, *The Golden Era Cubs, 1876–1940* (Chicago, IL, 1985); Jim Enright, *Chicago Cubs* (New York, 1975); Warren Wilbert and William Hageman, *Chicago Cubs: Seasons at the Summit* (Champaign, IL, 1997); *The Baseball Encyclopedia*, 10th ed. (New York, 1996), Robert L. Tiemann and Mark Rucker, eds., *Nineteenth Century Stars* (Kansas City, MO, 1989); William J. Ryczek, *Blackguards and Red Stockings* (Jefferson, NC, 1992);

George Wright, *Record of the Boston Base Ball Club Since Its Organization* (Boston, MA, 1874).

Gordon B. McKinney

BARNHILL, David "Dave" "Impo" "Skinny" (b. October 30, 1914, Greenville, NC; d. January 8, 1983, Miami, FL), player, was a small, hard-throwing strikeout artist with the New York Cubans during the 1940s. Barnhill began his baseball career on the sandlots of North Carolina, where he was signed by the touring Miami Giants in 1936. The Miami team evolved into the Ethiopian Clowns in 1937. Barnhill, pitching under the "Clown name" Impo, remained their star attraction through 1940 until signing with Alejandro Pompez's New York Cubans.

The diminutive hurler also demonstrated his wizardry in Puerto Rico, with a PRWL-leading 193 strikeouts in 1940–1941. He also led the CUWL in strikeouts, wins, and complete games, while compiling a composite three-year win–loss record of 23–19.

Beginning in 1941, Barnhill pitched in three consecutive East-West All-Star games and recorded an aggregate six strikeouts in nine innings. After having been credited with the victory over Satchel Paige* in the 1942 contest, he was selected to start the next season's game against Paige. Managers often paired him opposite Paige in regular season competition. The pair split two earlier encounters that year in crowd-pleasing matchups at Yankee Stadium. He compiled sensational records of 18–3 in 1941 and 26–10 in 1943.

During his prime, Barnhill in 1942 received a telegram about a tryout with the Pittsburgh Pirates (NL) that would have made him the first black in the major leagues. Although the 5-foot 7-inch, 155-pound right-hander was rated as a "sure fire" prospect, the offer was rescinded. He helped pitch the New York Cubans to an NNL pennant in 1947 and tossed a shutout victory over the Cleveland Buckeyes in the ensuing World Series, as the New York Cubans captured the Negro Championship.

In 1949, the New York Giants (NL) organization signed Barnhill and Ray Dandridge* and assigned them to the Giants' franchise in Minneapolis, MN (AA). Barnhill registered an 11–3 record and 3.60 ERA in 1950 to help the Millers win the AA pennant. He was accused of "cutting" the ball, as opposing managers watched his every move, trying to catch him. When they couldn't find any evidence to support their claim, they accused third baseman Dandridge of doing it for him.

Barnhill's age kept him from appearing in the major leagues. Barnhill played with Miami Beach, FL (FIL), where he finished 13–8 with a 1.19 ERA in 1952 under manager Pepper Martin.* He spent the next year with Ft. Lauderdale, FL in the same league, splitting two decisions in only four games pitched. This marked his last year in baseball. After leaving the diamond, he resided in Miami with his wife and daughter and worked with the

Miami Department of Recreation and Parks for 28 years until his retirement in 1981.

BIBLIOGRAPHY: L. Robert Davids, ed., *Insider's Baseball* (New York, 1983); John B. Holway, *Black Diamonds* (Westport, CT, 1989); Robert W. Peterson, *Only the Ball Was White* (Englewood Cliffs, NJ, 1970); James A. Riley, "Dave Barnhill," *BRJ* 10 (1981), pp. 56–59; James A. Riley, *The All-Time All-Stars of Black Baseball* (Canton, GA, 1983); James A. Riley, *The Biographical Encyclopedia of the Negro Baseball Leagues* (New York, 1994); James A. Riley, interviews with former Negro League players, James A. Riley collection, Cocoa, FL; Mike Shatzkin, ed., *The Ballplayers* (New York, 1990); *The Baseball Encyclopedia*, 10th ed. (New York, 1996).

James A. Riley

BARR, George McKinley (b. July 19, 1892, Scammon, KS; d. July 26, 1974, Tulsa, OK), umpire and executive, founded the first professional umpire school. The elder of two sons born to Alexander Bundy Barr, a Scottish immigrant, and Mary Jane (Reed) Barr, he moved to Tulsa, OK in 1915 and became fascinated with umpiring while ushering at the local baseball park. The 5-foot 7-inch, 175-pound Barr umpired in the WA (Class C) in 1924 and 1925, the TL (Class A) from 1926 through 1931, and the NL from 1931 to 1949. No previous TL umpire had reached the major leagues. He worked two All-Star games (1937, 1944) and 21 games in four World Series (1937, 1942, 1948, 1949). Besides popularizing the inside chest protector, he umpired three consecutive extra-inning games in 1944. The 19-inning September 11 contest between the Cincinnati Reds and Brooklyn Dodgers was the longest scoreless game in major league history. Barr umpired behind the plate for Babe Ruth's* last game in 1935, Carl Hubbell's* 200th victory in 1938, and the Boston Braves–Cleveland Indians World Series game of October 10, 1948, which was witnessed by a record 86,288 fans.

Barr's greatest contribution came as a teacher. He opened his pioneering umpiring school in Hot Springs, AR in 1935 and soon relocated it to Florida. He also conducted umpiring clinics in Canada, Germany, Hawaii, and Puerto Rico and made three extensive trips to Japan and Korea (1951–1953) to conduct classes for military personnel and civilians. The superb administrator presided over three minor leagues, including the WA (Class C) 1949–1954; KOML (Class D) 1952–1954, and SSL (Class D) 1955–1956. Beginning in 1961, he served 14 years as a Babe Ruth League international director, was selected its first umpire-in-chief, and established the league in Europe. In 1962, the Oklahoma American Legion junior baseball program named Barr head. For his numerous contributions to umpiring and promoting baseball at all levels, Barr was inducted into the Oklahoma Hall of Fame in 1963 and the Babe Ruth League Hall of Fame in 1968.

Barr married Mary Elizabeth de Vaughn in 1925. After her death in 1958, he wed Ardis Nott in 1961. The Barrs had no children and donated their extensive collection of baseball memorabilia to the Seminole, OK JC Library.

BIBLIOGRAPHY: George Barr file, National Baseball Library, Cooperstown, NY; George Barr file, *TSN* Archives, St. Louis, MO; George Barr, "You Can't Kill the Umpire," *AM* 143 (March 1947), pp. 48–49, 94–96, condensed in *BD* 6 (May 1947), pp. 3–5, 45–49; Clifford Bloodgood, "A Rookie Umpire Who Made Good," *BM* 50 (March 1933), pp. 445–446, 475; Clifford Bloodgood, "Tulsa's Best Known Barr," *BM* 78 (January 1947), pp. 261–262; *TSN Official Baseball Register, 1943–1946*.

Larry R. Gerlach

BARROW, Edward Grant "Ed," "Cousin Ed" (b. May 10, 1868, Springfield, IL; d. December 15, 1953, Port Chester, NY), manager and executive, was the eldest of four sons of farmer and grain dealer John Barrow and Effie Ann (Vinson-Heller) Barrow. His name was synonymous with the success of the New York Yankees (AL) between 1921 and 1945. During his tenure as general manager, the Yankees won 14 AL pennants and 10 World Series and captured five fall classics without losing a game. Barrow organized and developed the farm system that established the Yankees as the all-time kings of baseball. Baseball peers respected his genius at evaluating talent and his administrative ability. The forceful, straightforward Barrow possessed an explosive temper, once challenging Babe Ruth* to a fight, and exercised strict discipline as manager and executive.

Barrow moved with his family to Des Moines, IA in 1877 and quit school at age 16 to clerk for the Des Moines *Daily News*. He soon joined the Des Moines *Blade*, became advertising manager of the Des Moines *Leader*, and managed a semipro baseball team. In 1890 he moved to Pittsburgh, where he became assistant manager of the Staley Hotel and entered into partnership with Harry Stevens. Stevens operated scorecard concessions at the Pittsburgh Pirates' Exposition Park. Four years later, he began his professional baseball career as manager, general manager, and one-third owner of the Wheeling, WV club of the newly organized ISL. When the ISL dissolved in midseason, the partners shifted the winning club to the IOL. Barrow in 1895 acquired the Paterson, NJ franchise in the newly formed AtL, discovered and developed Honus Wagner,* and served as president of the circuit between 1896 and 1900. In 1900, he purchased a part interest in Toronto, Canada (EL) and became its manager. Two years later, he piloted Toronto to the EL championship. The Detroit Tigers (AL) signed Barrow as manager in 1903, but he resigned in 1904 following a dispute with the general manager. Barrow managed Indianapolis, IN (AA) in 1905 and 1906 and guided Toronto (EL) to a pennant in 1907. He then left baseball and spent the next three years managing a Toronto hotel.

After his wife died in 1910, Barrow returned to baseball as Montreal, Canada (EL) manager. He married Frances Taylor in 1912 and had one daughter, Audrey. From 1910 to 1918, Barrow served as EL president and renamed it the IL. He fought the attempted inroads of the FL, thus gaining the respect of AL president Ban Johnson.* In 1918, the Boston Red Sox (AL) named Barrow field manager upon Johnson's recommendation. Barrow immediately led Boston to the AL pennant and World Series title over the Chicago Cubs in six games. That same season, he began converting pitcher Babe Ruth* into an outfielder. In January 1920, the powerful Ruth was sold to the New York Yankees. At the close of that season, Barrow became New York's secretary and general manager. Barrow's five seasons as a major league manager resulted in 310 victories in 630 games. At the time, he was the only front office executive ever to win a pennant and World Series title. The Yankees won their initial pennant in 1921 in Barrow's first year with the club and then repeated in 1922 and 1923. After the Yankees experienced disappointing seasons in 1924 and 1925, Barrow's rebuilding program produced successive AL pennants.

With the help of a farm system built by Barrow and his assistant, George Weiss,* New York developed the most consistent pennant-winning organization in major league history. The Yankees captured AL pennants in 1932 and from 1936 through 1939. When Yankees owner Colonel Jacob Ruppert* died in 1939, Barrow became club president. He held that position until January 1945 when a syndicate of Leland MacPhail, Sr.,* Dan Topping,* and Del Webb bought the Yankees. From 1941 through 1943, New York captured additional AL pennants. Barrow served as chairman of the board from 1945 until his retirement and was enshrined in the National Baseball Hall of Fame in September 1953.

BIBLIOGRAPHY: Ed Barrow file, National Baseball Library, Cooperstown, NY; "Ed Barrow: Founder of the Yankee Dynasty," *YM* (April 12, 1984); Edward G. Barrow with James Kahn, "My Baseball Story," *Collier's* 125 (May 20-June 24, 1950); *DAB*, Supp. 5 (1951–1955), pp. 40–41; Dan Daniel, "From Peanuts to Pennants: The Story of Edward G. Barrow," New York *World Telegram*, February 1933; Thomas Aylesworth and Benton Minks, *The Encyclopedia of Baseball Managers* (New York, 1990); Mark Gallagher, *The Yankee Encyclopedia*, vol. 3 (Champaign, IL, 1997); Frank Graham, *The New York Yankees* (New York, 1943); Edward G. Barrow with James M. Kahn, *My Fifty Years in Baseball* (New York, 1951); Frederick G. Lieb, *The Boston Red Sox* (New York, 1947); Howard Liss, *The Boston Red Sox* (New York, 1982); Craig Carter, ed., *TSN Daguerreotypes*, 8th ed. (St. Louis, MO, 1990); Tom Meany, *The Yankee Story* (New York, 1960); *NYT*, December 16, 1953, pp. 1, 54; Robert Redmount, *The Red Sox Encyclopedia* (Champaign, IL, 1998); Lowell Reidenbaugh, *Baseball's Hall of Fame-Cooperstown* (New York, 1993); Ed Walton, *Red Sox Triumphs and Tragedies* (New York, 1980).

Donald J. Proctor and John L. Evers

BARTELL, Richard William "Dick," "Rowdy Richard" (b. November 22, 1907, Chicago, IL; d. August 4, 1995, Alameda, CA), player, coach, and manager, was the only child of Harry Bartell and Emma (Greakel) Bartell. His father worked as an accountant, real estate agent, and county supervisor, and as a semipro baseman once made an unassisted triple play. The Bartells moved to California during his infancy. He graduated from Alameda High School in 1926 and was offered athletic scholarships by three colleges, but instead signed with the Pittsburgh Pirates (NL). He married Olive Loretta Jensen on October 24, 1928 and had two children. On August 1, 1981 he married Anise Walton.

In 1927, he began his pro career by batting .280 as a shortstop for Bridgeport, CT (EL). His 18-year major league career began in 1927 with one game for the Pirates. By 1929, he had replaced Glenn Wright* as regular shortstop. After hitting .320 in 1930, he was traded to the Philadelphia Phillies (NL). Four years later, after having played in the first All-Star Game, he in November 1934 was traded to the New York Giants (NL) for four players and cash. In December 1938 the Giants sent Bartell to the Chicago Cubs (NL) in a six-player deal. In December 1939, Chicago traded him to the Detroit Tigers (AL). He returned to the New York Giants (NL) in 1941 for three wartime seasons, served in the U.S. Navy in 1944–1945, and ended his career with five games for the Giants in 1946. In three World Series (1936–1937, 1940), he hit .294.

A lifetime .284 hitter, Bartell batted over .300 in seven seasons and usually hit first or second in the order. Besides being a good bunter, he hit well behind the runner and seldom struck out. He slashed 442 doubles, ranking 63rd on the all-time list. In 1933 he equalled the major league record for most doubles in one game with four. At shortstop, he frequently led the NL in double plays, putouts, assists, and total chances per game. Ironically, he once played a ten-inning game without a single fielding chance. A lively, aggressive player, he was nicknamed "Rowdy Richard."

He managed at Sacramento, CA (PCL) in 1947, Kansas City, MO (AA) in 1948, and Montgomery, AL-Knoxville TN (SAL) in 1956, and coached for the Tigers from 1949 to 1952 and Cincinnati Reds (NL) in 1954 and 1955. Between 1957 and 1972, he worked as a sales representative for a dairy products company and owned a liquor store. He remained active in the Association of Professional Baseball Players and died following a battle with Alzheimer's disease.

BIBLIOGRAPHY: Dick Bartell file, National Baseball Library, Cooperstown, NY; Dick Bartell and Norman Macht, *Rowdy Richard* (Berkeley, CA, 1987); Fred Stein, *Under Coogan's Bluff* (Glenshaw, PA, 1978); Frank Graham, *The New York Giants* (New York, 1952); Eddie Gold and Art Ahrens, *The Golden Era Cubs, 1876–1940* (Chicago, IL, 1985); Frederick G. Lieb and Stan Baumgartner, *The Philadelphia Phillies* (New York, 1953): Richard M. Cohen et al., *The World Series* (New York, 1979); Noel Hynd, *The Giants of the Polo Grounds* (New York, 1988); F. C. Lane, "A Human Dynamo at Short," *BM* 52 (January 1934), pp. 347–348; Allen Lewis, *The Philadelphia Phillies* (Virginia Beach, VA, 1981); Jim McMartin, "Two Measures of Fielding Ability," *BRJ* 12 (1983), pp. 56–61; *NYT*, August 7, 1995, p. B10; A. D. Suehsdorf, interviews with Richard Bartell, October 15, 1983, March 9, 1984; *The Baseball Encyclopedia*, 10th ed. (New York, 1996); Rich Westcott, *Diamond Greats* (Westport, CT, 1988); Rich Westcott and Frank Bilovsky, *The New Phillies Encyclopedia* (Philadelphia, PA, 1993); Peter Williams, *When the Giants Were Giants* (Chapel Hill, NC, 1994).

David L. Porter

BAUER, Henry Albert "Hank" (b. July 31, 1923, East St. Louis, IL), player, manager, and scout, was nicknamed and variously described as "Bauer the Man of the Hour" and "the man with a face like a fist." He was employed as an iron worker in 1941, when Oshkosh, WI (WSL) signed him. Bauer, a 6-foot, 200 pounder in his prime, spent four years in the minor leagues (1941, 1946–1948), the last two with Kansas City, MO (AA), and four years (1942–1946) in the U.S. Marine Corps before making his major league debut in September 1948 with the New York Yankees (AL).

Bauer spent the next 14 years in the major leagues, including 12 with the New York Yankees. In those seasons in pinstripes, Bauer batted .280 with 158 HR. These numbers nearly matched those of New York Yankee teammate Charlie Keller,* a player who Bauer had been favorably compared with by the sons of Larry MacPhail,* the New York Yankees' owners, during spring training in 1948. With the New York Yankees under platoon-happy manager Casey Stengel,* Bauer showed a steady but consistent growth as right fielder in his first six years. His batting average peaked at .320 in 1950 and reached .304 in 1953, but began to fade after 1954. By retirement, Bauer's lifetime average dropped to .277. Around 1955, his HR production began to rise. Bauer was never ranked among batting leaders—at least statistically—although sharing the AL lead in triples with nine in 1957. Teammates Harry Simpson and Gil McDougald* also hit nine triples that year. Bauer appeared in three All-Star Games from 1952 to 1954, hitting two singles in seven at bats. The New York Yankees traded Bauer in December 1959 to the Kansas City Athletics (AL), where he spent his final two major league seasons. During 14 major league seasons, Bauer made 1,424 hits, 229 doubles, and 164 HR, scored 833 runs, and knocked in 703 runs in 1,544 games.

The World Series produced Bauer's most memorable games. Although batting only .245 in 53 games spanning eight fall classics, he set a World Series record by hitting safely in 17 consecutive games. At least twice, his hitting heroics kept the New York Yankees alive or won the game. In 1955, he batted a superlative .429 against the Brooklyn Dodgers. Three years later, he tied a World Series record with four HR against the Milwaukee Braves. The strongest World Series image of Bauer came defensively in the ninth inning of the sixth game of the 1951 World Series, when he made a diving, sliding catch of a sinking line drive by the New York Giants' Sal Yvars to preserve a Yankee victory.

Bauer also made his mark in managing, guiding the Baltimore Orioles to their first World Series title in 1966 with a four-game sweep of the favored Los Angeles Dodgers. Three victories came by shutout. In eight managerial seasons, Bauer's teams finished third or higher five times and completed a 594–544 mark for a .522 winning percentage. Bauer managed the Kansas City Athletics in 1961 and 1962, Baltimore Orioles from 1964 through 1968, and Oakland Athletics (AL) in 1969. In 1966, *TSN* named him Manager of the Year. He also piloted Tidewater, VA (IL) in 1971 and 1972. He later owned a liquor store and scouted for the New York Yankees until July 1987.

Bauer, who married Charlene Friede in October 1949, lives in Overland Park, KS and has two daughters and two sons. One son, Herman, is named after Bauer's older brother, who was killed in France during World War II.

BIBLIOGRAPHY: Hank Bauer file, National Baseball Library, Cooperstown, NY; Dom Forker, *The Men of Autumn* (Dallas, TX, 1989); Rich Marazzi and Len Fiorito, *Aaron to Zuverink* (New York, 1982); Rich Marazzi, "Hank Bauer Was the Classic Hard-Nosed Ballplayer," *SCD* 24 (February 7, 1997), pp. 90–91; Rich Marazzi, "For Hank Bauer, the World Series Was His Stage," *SCD* 24 (February 14, 1997), pp. 90–91; Peter Golenbock, *Dynasty* (Englewood Cliffs, NJ, 1975); Mark Gallagher, *The Yankee Encyclopedia* (Champaign, IL, 1997); Tom Meany, ed., *The Magnificent Yankees* (New York, 1952); Thomas Aylesworth and Benton Minks, *The Encyclopedia of Baseball Managers* (New York, 1990); James M. Bready, *Baseball in Baltimore* (Baltimore, MD, 1998); Ted Patterson, *The Baltimore Orioles* (Dallas, TX, 1995); John Thorn et al., eds., *Total Baseball*, 5th ed. (New York, 1997); *TSN Baseball Register*, 1968.

Lee E. Scanlon

BAYLOR, Don Edward (b. June 28, 1949, Austin, TX), player, coach, and manager, excelled as an AL outfielder, first baseman, and DH for 19 years beginning in 1970. His father, George Baylor, worked for the railroad, while his mother, Lillian Baylor, served as a dietitian at an all-white high school near their home in the Clarkesville section of Austin. Two other blacks joined Baylor in integrating O. Henry Junior High School in Austin. Baylor lettered in football, basketball, and baseball at Stephen Austin High School. He married Aronetta J. Cash on June 3, 1970 and had one son, Don, Jr. Following their divorce, Baylor married Becky Giles.

Baylor joined the Baltimore Orioles' (AL) farm system after graduation from high school. His minor league career proved as distinguished as his long major league career. In his first year with Bluefield, VA, he was named the 1967 ApL Player of the Year. Three years later with Rochester, NY (IL), he was selected Minor League Player of the Year. His major league service included stints with six different AL teams, including the Baltimore Orioles (1970–1975), Oakland A's (1976, 1988), California Angels (1977–1982), New York Yankees (1983–1985), Boston Red Sox (1986–1987), and Minnesota Twins (1987). An original free agent, he opted for free agency following the 1976 and 1982 seasons.

Baylor provided considerable offensive skills. He combined speed and power for the first 10 years of his major league career, stealing 52 bases (1976) and hitting 36 HR (1979). The 1979 campaign marked Baylor's most productive year, as he led the AL in runs scored (120) and RBI (139), batted .296, and was named the AL's MVP and an AL All-Star. Although Baylor's speed diminished in later years, his power increased. Overall, Baylor amassed 2,135 career hits, 338 HR, 285 stolen bases, 1,276 RBI, a .260 batting average, and a .436 slugging percentage. He also holds the major league record for most times hit by pitches with 267.

Baylor also developed a reputation for team leadership, although never actually being named field captain of a team. On four occasions (1973, 1974, 1979, 1982), his team lost in the AL Championship Series. Beginning in 1986, however, Baylor played on three consecutive AL champions in three different cities (Boston, Minnesota, Oakland). The Minnesota Twins captured the World Series in 1987. In 1991, the Milwaukee Brewers (AL) hired Baylor as a batting coach. He coached for the St. Louis Cardinals (NL) in 1992.

In 1993, the expansion Colorado Rockies (NL) named Baylor manager. He piloted the Colorado Rockies to a 440–469 record and .484 winning percentage from 1993 through 1998. His best season came in 1995, when the Rockies finished second in the NL West with a 77–67 mark and lost the NL Division Series to the Atlanta Braves. In 1995, he earned *TSN* and BBWAA Manager of the Year honors. Jim Leyland* replaced Baylor as Colorado Rockies manager in October 1998. Baylor joined the Atlanta Braves (NL) as batting coach in November 1998. The Braves made the 1999 World Series and the Chicago Cubs named Baylor manager in November.

BIBLIOGRAPHY: Don Baylor file, National Baseball Library, Cooperstown, NY; Don Baylor file, Biography Committee, SABR, Cleveland, OH; Don Baylor and Claire Smith, *Nothing but the Truth* (New York, 1989); Barbara Carlisle Bigelow, ed., *Contemporary Black Biography*, vol. 6 (Detroit, MI, 1994); Craig Neff, "His Honor Don Baylor," *SI* 64 (June 16, 1986), pp. 58–62; J. Friedman, "For Don Baylor, Baseball Is a Hit or Be Hit Proposition," *PW* 28 (August 24, 1987), pp. 89–90; Mark Gallagher, *The Yankee Encyclopedia*, vol. 3 (Champaign, IL, 1997); David Falkner, *The Short Season* (New York, 1987); W. Leavy, "Baseball Minority Managers: Taking Charge on the Field," *Ebony* (May 1993), pp. 10–12; C. Pierce, "Don Baylor Carries a Big Stick," *GQ* 63 (July 1993), pp. 45–46; W. Leavy, "Don Baylor: On Top of the World in Colorado," *Ebony* 51 (August 1996), pp. 44ff; *NYT Biographical Service* 19 (October 1988), pp. 1091–1092; Ted Patterson, *The Baltimore Orioles* (Dallas, TX, 1995); Ross Newhan, *The California Angels* (New York, 1982); Roger Clemens with Peter Gammons, *Rocket Man* (Lexington, MA, 1987); Dan Shaughnessy, *One Strike Away* (New York, 1987).

Leverett T. Smith, Jr.

BEAUMONT, Clarence Howeth "Ginger" (b. July 23, 1876, Rochester, WI; d. April 10, 1956, Burlington, WI), player, was a one-time NL batting champion and star center fielder for the Pittsburgh Pirates (NL) from 1899 to 1906. The first player to bat in a World Series game (1903), he was nicknamed "Ginger" for his red hair. Older players harassed him for his "sissified" name of Clarence. The son of Thomas Beaumont and Mary (Jones) Beaumont, he attended Rochester, WI Academy and later Beloit College for one year and played semiprofessional baseball in Wausau, WI. Connie Mack,* manager of the Milwaukee, WI club (WL), signed him in 1898. After batting .354 for Milwaukee in 24 games, the hard-hitting, speedy Beaumont was purchased by the Pittsburgh Pirates (NL) for the 1899 season. He remained with the Pirates until December 1906, when he was traded to the Boston Nationals (NL) with Claude Ritchey for Ed Abbaticchio. He played with Boston from 1907 to 1909 and with the Chicago Cubs (NL) in 1910, his last major league season. Following the 1911 year with St. Paul, MN (AA), Beaumont retired from baseball. He married Norma Olive Vaughan in November 1901 and had two daughters and a son.

Beaumont joined Pittsburgh two years before manager Fred Clarke* assembled the great 1901–1903 pennant-winning Pirate clubs. Although overshadowed by National Baseball Hall-of-Famers Clarke and Honus Wagner,* he contributed substantially to his team's success. In 1902, he led the NL in batting (.357) and hits (193). The next season, he batted .341 and paced the NL in at bats (613), runs (137), and hits (209). Beaumont led the NL in hits again in 1904, the first player ever to top a major league in hits three consecutive seasons. At Boston in 1907, he also led the NL in hits. During 12 major league campaigns, he collected 1,759 hits and compiled a .311 batting average.

The stocky 5-foot 8-inch, 190-pound Beaumont possessed good speed. Besides stealing over 30 bases three times, he pilfered 254 bases in his career. Expert at punching the ball through the infield and beating out slow rollers, he on July 22, 1899 made six infield hits in six at bats and scored six times. On the fourth hit, Beaumont recalled, "The third baseman stood ten feet from the plate and I still beat out a bunt." A weak fielder initially, Beaumont improved quickly and nearly led the NL center fielders in 1902 with a .975 mark.

BIBLIOGRAPHY: Ginger Beaumont file, National Baseball Library, Cooperstown, NY; Richard L. Burtt, *The Pittsburgh Pirates, A Pictorial History* (Virginia Beach, VA, 1977); Gary Caruso, *The Braves Encyclopedia* (Philadelphia, PA, 1995); William Connelly, "The Greatest Baseball Team in All History," *BM* 12 (May 1914), pp. 33–42, 96; MacLean Kennedy, *The Great Teams of Baseball* (St. Louis, MO, 1928); Harold Kaese, *The Boston Braves* (New York, 1948); Frederick G. Lieb, *The Pittsburgh Pirates* (New York, 1948); Craig Carter, ed., *TSN Daguerreotypes*, 8th ed. (St. Louis, MO, 1990); Alfred H. Spink, *The National Game: A History of Baseball* (St. Louis, MO, 1911); *TSN*, April 18, 1956; John Thom, *Champion Batsman of the 20th Century* (Los Angeles, CA, 1992); Robert Smizik, *The Pittsburgh Pirates: An Illustrated History* (New York, 1990); Dennis De Valeria and Joanne Burke De Valeria, *Honus Wagner: A*

Biography (New York, 1996); William Hageman, *Honus: The Life and Times of a Baseball Hero* (Champaign, IL, 1996).

Eugene Murdock

BECKERT, Glenn Alfred "Bruno" (b. October 12, 1940, Pittsburgh, PA), player, was selected an all-city basketball and baseball player at Pittsburgh's Perry High School and graduated with a B.A. degree from Allegheny College in 1961. The Boston Red Sox (AL) originally signed him, but the Chicago Cubs (NL) drafted him in 1962. Following three minor league seasons at Waterloo, IA (ML), Wenatchee, WA (NWL), and Salt Lake City, UT (PCL), Beckert became the Chicago Cubs' second baseman in 1965. Don Kessinger,* his shortstop partner for the next nine years, also arrived at Chicago that season.

A career major league .283 hitter, the 6-foot 1-inch, 190-pound Beckert led the NL from 1966 through 1969 as the "toughest to strike out." In 1968, he struck out once in every 32.15 trips to the plate. His career 243 strikeouts included one every 21.3 at bats. Never a slugger, the right-hander hit only 22 HR and 196 doubles in his 11-year major league career. He enjoyed two memorable hitting games. When the Chicago Cubs defeated the Houston Astros, 9–3, on August 4, 1969, Beckert made five hits in six at bats. On July 26, 1970, he went five for five, as the Chicago Cubs edged the Atlanta Braves, 4–3. Beckert's best hitting year came in 1971, when he batted a career-high .342. He lost the batting crown, however, being sidelined for a month when he injured his right thumb in September.

A smooth-fielding second baseman, Beckert in 1968 won a Gold Glove Award and was named "Chicago Player of the Year." He was selected the All-Star second baseman for four consecutive years, from 1968 through 1971. Injuries began to take their toll on the scrappy Beckert, whose batting average and game appearances dropped steadily after the 1971 season. In November 1973, the Chicago Cubs traded him to the San Diego Padres (NL) for Jerry Morales. After playing in only 73 games during the next two seasons, Beckert retired. In 11 major league seasons, Beckert had 1,473 hits and knocked in 360 runs. Beckert had two daughters and lives in Cape Haze, FL.

BIBLIOGRAPHY: Art Ahrens and Eddie Gold, *Day by Day in Chicago Cubs History* (West Point, NY, 1982); Glenn Beckert file, National Baseball Library, Cooperstown, NY; *Chicago Cubs Official Roster Book*, 1972, 1973; Jim Enright, *Chicago Cubs* (New York, 1975); Eddie Gold and Art Ahrens, *The New Era Cubs, 1941–1985* (Chicago, IL, 1985); Jim Langford, *The Game Is Never Over* (South Bend, IN, 1980); Warren Wilbert and William Hageman, *Chicago Cubs: Seasons at the Summit* (Champaign, IL, 1997).

Duane A. Smith

BECKLEY, Jacob Peter "Jake," "Eagle Eye" (b. August 4, 1867, Hannibal, MO; d. June 25, 1918, Kansas City, MO), player, manager, and umpire, ranked among the game's most notable performers around the turn of the century. In 20 major league seasons, the 5-foot 10-inch, 200-pound Beckley batted above .300 14 times. Beckley began his professional career with Leavenworth, KS and Lincoln, NE (WL) in 1886 and 1887 and played 34 games in his third minor league season with St. Louis, MO (WA). The left-handed first baseman then joined the Pittsburgh Alleghenies (NL) as a 20-year-old in June 1888 and in 71 games batted .343, one point less than NL batting champion Cap Anson.*

After eight seasons with Pittsburgh (NL) and one with the Pittsburgh Burghers (PL) (1890), Beckley was traded to the New York Giants (NL) in 1896. Beckley then played for the Cincinnati Reds (NL) from 1897 through 1903 and for the St. Louis Cardinals (NL) from 1904 through 1907. Despite being a weak thrower, Beckley tied for the NL lead in fielding percentage (1889) and led the NL (1898–1899) in that category. He paced the circuit in putouts six seasons (1892, 1894–1895, 1900, 1902, 1904) and batted above .300 six consecutive campaigns (1899–1904). Beckley's major league records include most games played (2,386), most putouts (23,709), and most chances accepted (25,505) at first base. By leading the NL in putouts six seasons, Beckley tied Frank McCormick* for the major league record. On September 27, 1898, he made 21 putouts at first base in one game. Beckley also paced the NL with 2,265 games played, 22,438 putouts, and 23,687 chances accepted at first base. On September 26, 1897, Beckley slugged three HR in a game at St. Louis and became the last major leaguer to perform that feat until 1922. Twice he hit three triples in one game.

Beckley, credited with developing an unusual hidden-ball trick, concealed the baseball under one corner of the bag, extracted it, and then tagged out the runner. Beckley's lifetime major league statistics included 2,930 hits, 1,600 runs scored, 1,575 RBI, 473 doubles, and 243 triples. In 2,386 games, he hit 86 HR, stole 315 bases, and compiled a .308 batting average. Beckley played 2,377 games at first base, trailing only Eddie Murray.*

Beckley completed his baseball career as player–manager with Kansas City, MO (AA) in 1908 and 1909, Bartlesville, OK (WA) and Topeka, KS (WL) in 1910, and Hannibal, MO (CA) in 1911. He managed a semipro team in Kansas City (1912) and last appeared in baseball as an umpire in the FL (1913). The National Baseball Hall of Fame enshrined him in 1971.

BIBLIOGRAPHY: Jake Beckley file, National Baseball Library, Cooperstown, NY; Lee Allen, *The Cincinnati Reds* (New York, 1948); Craig Carter, ed., *TSN Daguerreotypes*, 8th ed. (St. Louis, 1990); Frederick Ivor-Campbell et al., eds., *Baseball's First Stars* (Cleveland, OH, 1996); Frederick G. Lieb, *The Pittsburgh Pirates* (New York, 1948); Richard L. Burtt, *The Pittsburgh Pirates, A Pictorial History* (Virginia Beach, VA, 1977); Frederick G. Lieb, *The St. Louis Cardinals* (New York, 1945); Bob Broeg, *Redbirds: A Century of Cardinals Baseball* (St. Louis, MO, 1981); Bob Broeg and Jerry Vickery, *St. Louis Cardinals Encyclopedia* (Grand Rapids, MI, 1998); Lowell Reidenbaugh, *Baseball's Hall of Fame-Cooperstown* (New York, 1993); *TSN Official Baseball Record Book, 1998* (St. Louis, MO, 1998).

John L. Evers

BECKWITH, John (b. 1902, Louisville, KY; d. 1956, New York, NY), player and manager, first played baseball as a child in Sunday School leagues in Chicago and began his professional career in 1919 with the Chicago Giants. Upon signing with Rube Foster's* Chicago American Giants (NNL) in 1921, the 6-foot 3-inch, 230-pound right-handed pull hitter already had become one of the game's most versatile players. He caught, played any infield or outfield position, and even pitched in a pinch, but achieved his greatest fame as one of the most intimidating power hitters in black baseball. Pitcher Willie Foster* called him one of the toughest hitters he ever faced. As a 19-year-old, he became the first player ever to hit a ball over the left field fence in Cincinnati's Redland Field. In 1921, he batted .407 for the second best mark in the NNL. He hit for both power and average. For the Baltimore, MD Black Sox (ANL), he batted .403 and clubbed 40 HR in 1924 and hit .402 and finished second in HR in 1925. With the Harrisburg, PA Giants in 1927, he batted .335 and finished second in ANL HR, reputedly hitting 72. After slugging 54 HR the next year for the Homestead, PA Grays, he batted .380 in 1929 to finish second in ANL standings. The next year he led the ANL in hitting with a remarkable .493. His .356 lifetime average in league play was supplemented by his .337 average in exhibitions with major leaguers. He left the American Giants in 1924, perhaps because of his combative personality, and spent the remainder of his career with various eastern teams, including the Baltimore Black Sox, Homestead Grays, Harrisburg Giants, Lincoln Giants, and New York Black Yankees.

BIBLIOGRAPHY: John B. Holway, "The Black Bomber Named Beckwith," *BRJ* 5 (1976), pp. 100–103; John B. Holway, *Voices from the Great Black Baseball Leagues* (New York, 1975); Robert W. Peterson, *Only the Ball Was White* (Englewood Cliffs, NJ, 1970); James A. Riley, *The Biographical Encyclopedia of the Negro Baseball Leagues* (New York, 1994).

Gerald E. Brennan

BEDROSIAN, Stephen Wayne "Steve," "Bedrock" (b. December 6, 1957, Methuen, MA), player and coach, is one of two sons of Michael Bedrosian, a Western Electric employee, and Bobby Jean (Stephens) Bedrosian. He graduated from Methuen High School, where he participated in baseball, wrestling, and soccer. He attended Northern Essex CC in Haverhill, MA and New Haven College in New Haven, CT, playing baseball at both institutions. He abandoned plans for a law enforcement or forestry career in favor of baseball.

The Atlanta Braves (NL) made the 6-foot 3-inch, 200-pound right-handed pitcher the first pick in the third round of the June 1978 draft. After pitching at Kingsport, TN (ApL) and Greenwood, SC (WCL) in 1978, he hurled for Savannah, GA (SL) in 1979 and 1980. In 1981, he compiled a 2.69 ERA in 25 starts for Richmond, VA (IL) and was promoted to the Atlanta Braves. After surviving a serious automobile accident that winter in the Dominican Republic, he started the 1982 season with the Braves.

Atlanta Braves manager Joe Torre* thought Bedrosian's intensity and imposing presence would make him a natural reliever. In 1982, he won eight games and lost six with a 2.42 ERA and struck out 123 batters in 137.2 innings to help the Braves win the NL's Eastern Division. He appeared briefly in two games of the NL Championship Series, which the St. Louis Cardinals swept from the Braves. *TSN* named him Rookie Pitcher of the Year. Throwing fastballs and sliders timed in the mid-90s, he recorded 41 saves, 27 victories, and 24 defeats as a reliever for the Braves through 1984. Atlanta reconverted him to a starter in 1985 after acquiring Bruce Sutter.* He won only seven decisions while losing 15 and was traded in December 1985 to the Philadelphia Phillies (NL).

Philadelphia used him in the bullpen, where Bedrosian enjoyed a fine year in 1986 with 29 saves. His best season came in 1987, when he won five games, led the NL with 40 saves, and lost only three with a 2.83 ERA and 74 strikeouts in 89 innings. Besides appearing in the 1987 All-Star game, he won both the NL's Cy Young Award and *TSN* Fireman of the Year Award. In 1988, Bedrosian suffered pneumonia and pleurisy and underwent rehabilitation at Portland-based Maine (IL). After rejoining the Phillies, he won six games and saved 28. In June 1989, the Philadelphia Phillies traded him to the San Francisco Giants (NL). Bedrosian saved 17 games to help them win the NL West Division and saved three more games in the San Francisco Giants' NL Championship Series victory over the Chicago Cubs. He appeared twice in the World Series without giving up an earned run, but the Giants were swept by the Oakland A's.

After Bedrosian saved 17 games for the San Francisco Giants in 1990, San Francisco traded him to the Minnesota Twins (AL) in December 1990. He compiled six saves in 56 games, appearing twice in the five-game AL Championship Series against the Toronto Blue Jays and in three World Series games to help the Twins defeat the Atlanta Braves. His rising ERA indicated his fading effectiveness. When a circulatory problem left him without feeling in two fingers of his pitching hand, he did not play in 1992.

Bedrosian signed with the Atlanta Braves in 1993 and won five and lost two with a 1.63 ERA. He did not appear in the NL Championship Series, which the Braves lost to the Philadelphia Phillies. He retired in August 1995. In 13 major league seasons, Bedrosian won 76 decisions and lost 79 games with 184 saves. He compiled a 3.38 ERA with 921 strikeouts in 1,191 innings.

Bedrosian and his wife, Tammy, have three sons, Carson, Cody, and Kyle. When his middle son contracted leukemia, Bedrosian started the Cody Bedrosian Fund to finance research into childhood cancers. He serves as a pitching instructor in the Atlanta Braves' minor league system.

The burly, bearded Bedrosian, often compared with Goose Gossage,* ranked among the most prominent "stoppers" of the mid-1980s and made the most of his ability to throw intimidatingly hard.

BIBLIOGRAPHY: Steve Bedrosian file, National Baseball Library, Cooperstown, NY; Bob Cairns, *Pen Men* (New York, 1993); Gary Caruso, *The Braves Encyclopedia* (Philadelphia, PA, 1995); Rich Westcott and Frank Bilovsky, *The New Phillies Encyclopedia* (Philadelphia, PA, 1993); *TSN Official Baseball Register; 1996*; Peter Pascarelli, "The Phils' Steve Bedrosian: Rebirth of a Reliever," *BD* 46 (November 1987), pp. 60–63; John Thorn et al., eds., *Total Braves* (New York, 1996); Ken Young, *Cy Young Award Winners* (New York, 1994).

Luther W. Spoehr

BELANGER, Mark Henry "Blade" (b. June 8, 1944, Pittsfield, MA; d. October 6, 1998, Baltimore, MD), player, attended the University of Tampa (FL) and signed with the Baltimore Orioles (AL) in 1962. The 6-foot 2-inch, 179-pound Belanger excelled as starting shortstop for the Orioles from 1967 to 1981. Luis Aparicio,* his roommate and the Orioles' regular shortstop in 1965 and 1966, instructed him in the position. Belanger took over in November 1967, when Aparicio was returned to the Chicago White Sox. Manager Earl Weaver* initially criticized Belanger for not living up to his standard set in the minor leagues at Elmira, NY (EL) and Rochester, NY (IL). Weaver admonished him for making "silly errors" and hitting only .208 in 1968, too low a figure for a regular. Belanger responded with his best season in 1969, batting .287 with a .968 fielding mark.

Belanger eventually set an AL career fielding record of .977 for shortstops with over 1,000 games and participated in the 1969, 1970, 1971, and 1979 World Series. Baltimore Oriole fans praised his poise and unfailing consistency defensively. He seemed always in control. Billy Hunter, Oriole coach and outstanding shortstop, commented, "He has incredible range as well as a tremendous, accurate arm." Belanger blended well with the remarkable Oriole infield of third baseman Brooks Robinson,* second baseman Davey Johnson,* and first baseman "Boog" Powell.* Manager Earl Weaver remarked of Belanger, "He's like a machine in the field." Reggie Jackson,* who spent just the 1976 season with Baltimore, claimed "Nobody saves any more runs than that guy." Belanger's defensive play earned considerable respect from other players. For several years, he served as the Orioles' player representative. Aficianados often compared him with the fine St. Louis Cardinals' shortstop Marty Marion.* Belanger, who played in just the 1976 All-Star Game, combined a .228 career batting average with an amazing .977 fielding percentage. Oriole fans admired him as part of an infield that provided outstanding defensive coordination. Belanger summarized his defensive success: "To me fielding is instinct." A heavy smoker, he died after battling lung cancer for around a year.

BIBLIOGRAPHY: Doug Brown, " 'Silly Errors' by Belanger Giving Weaver a Big Pain," *TSN*, September 21, 1968; Phil Jackman, "The Indispensable Man? For Orioles It's Belanger," *TSN*, April 18, 1970; Lou Hatter, "Challenger Grich Sparks Belanger to Fast Getaway," *TSN*, May 6, 1972; Jim Henneman, "Belanger Adds Torrid Bat To Go with Flashy Glove," *TSN*, June 12, 1976; Jim Henneman, "1976 Best Year Ever for Super SS Belanger," *TSN*, November 13, 1976; Ken Nigro, "Belanger, Nearing 37, Has to Fight for Job," *TSN*, March 21, 1981; John Thorn et al., eds., *Total Baseball*, 5th ed. (New York, 1997); *TSN Official Baseball Register*, 1983; *WWIB, 1982*, 67th ed.; Mike Shatzkin, ed., *The Ballplayers* (New York, 1990); Ted Patterson, *The Baltimore Orioles* (Dallas, TX, 1995); James H. Bready, *Baseball in Baltimore* (Baltimore, MD, 1998).

                                                                                    William J. Miller

BELL, David Gus "Buddy" (b. August 27, 1951, Pittsburgh, PA), player, coach, and announcer, is the son of Gus Bell,* former major leaguer with the Pittsburgh Pirates, Cincinnati Reds, New York Mets, and Milwaukee Braves (NL), and Joyce (Sutherland) Bell. Bell grew up in Cincinnati, where he graduated from Archbishop Moeller High School in 1969 and played baseball, basketball, and football. Upon his father's advice, he dropped football after two years. Bell studied during the off-seasons at Xavier University in Cincinnati and at Miami University in Oxford, OH. On February 6, 1971, Bell married his childhood sweetheart, Gloria Jean Eysoldt. The couple has four children and resides in Cincinnati. His sons, David and Mike, play major league baseball. As the son of a major leaguer, Bell grew up around baseball players and frequently visited his father's clubhouse. Although never pushed by his family to pursue baseball, he nurtured the dream of playing for the hometown Cincinnati Reds. To his disappointment, the Cincinnati Reds did not select him in the 1969 free agent draft. Bell, an infielder, was not chosen until the 16th round by the cross-state Cleveland Indians (AL).

Bell's association with the Cleveland Indians proved very rewarding. After only three minor league seasons with Sarasota, FL (GCL), Sumter, SC (WCL), and Wichita, KS (AA), he made the 1972 Cleveland Indians roster. Bell's strong spring hitting and successful conversion from third base to the outfield helped him. He made only three errors his first year and hit well enough to finish high in the balloting for AL Rookie of the Year. When an opening developed at third base, Bell returned to the infield in 1973 and remained there. In seven years with Cleveland, he batted .274 with 64 HR. Bell, an extremely popular player, exhibited hard play and selfless regard for the team.

On December 8, 1978, Bell was traded to the Texas Rangers (AL) and proved a consistent bright spot for a generally mediocre team. Besides batting .295 his seven years with the Texas Rangers, Bell led the AL in game-winning RBI (16) in 1979 and sacrifice flies (10) in 1981. Bell also excelled defensively, winning a Gold Glove every season from 1979 to 1984. At least once, he led the AL third basemen in total chances, assists, putouts, and double plays. He appeared in five All-Star games (1973, 1980–1982, and 1984). In July 1985, the Texas Rangers traded Bell to the Cincinnati Reds (NL). He was sent to the Houston Astros (NL) in June 1988 and finished his major league career with the Texas Rangers (AL) in 1989. In 18 major league seasons, he batted .279 with 2,514 hits, 425 doubles, 201 HR, and 1,106 RBI. In the winter of 1985–1986, Bell announced Xavier University basketball games.

Bell served as a minor league hitting instructor for the Cleveland Indians in 1990, director of minor league instruction for the Chicago White Sox (AL) from 1991 to 1993, and coach for the Cleveland Indians in 1994 and 1995. He managed the struggling Detroit Tigers (AL) to marks of 53–109 in 1996 and 79–83 in 1997. Larry Parrish replaced Bell as manager in September 1998 after the club posted a disappointing 52–85 mark. In three seasons as manager, Bell compiled 184 wins, 277 losses, and a .399 winning percentage. The Cincinnati Reds (NL) named him minor league field coordinator in September 1998 and director of player development in August 1999. He became manager of the Colorado Rockies in October 1999.

BIBLIOGRAPHY: Jim Kaplan, "For Whom the Bell Tolls . . . ," *SI* 58 (April 18, 1983), pp. 66ff; Buddy Bell file, National Baseball Library, Cooperstown, NY; Robert E. Kelly, *Baseball's Best* (Jefferson, NC, 1988); Terry Pluto, *The Curse of Rocky Colavito* (New York, 1994); Peter C. Bjarkman, ed., *Encyclopedia of Major League Baseball Team Histories American League* (Westport, CT, 1991); Russell Schneider, "Bell Tolls Knell of Tribe Outfield Competition," *TSN*, April 8, 1972; Russell Schneider, "Buddy's Friendly Gesture Booms Indians' Battle Cry," *TSN*, April 30, 1977, p. 15; Russell Schneider, "Pressure on Bell in '73—Shift to Tribe Hot Corner," *TSN*, January 13, 1973; *TSN Baseball Register*, 1998; John Thorn et al., eds., *Total Indians* (New York, 1996); Jack Torry, *Endless Summers* (South Bend, IN, 1995).

Allen E. Hye

BELL, David Russell "Gus" (b. November 15, 1928, Louisville, KY; d. May 7, 1995, Cincinnati, OH), player, was nicknamed "Gus" by his baseball fan parents, who admired major league catcher Gus Mancuso. The 6-foot 1½-inch, 190-pound power-hitting outfielder, who batted left-handed and threw right-handed, graduated from Flaget High School in 1946 and made his major league debut with the Pittsburgh Pirates (NL) in 1950. Joining future National Baseball Hall of Famer Ralph Kiner* in the Bucs outfield, Bell hit 12 triples in 1951 to lead the NL.

Frequent disagreements with Pittsburgh management prompted the Pirates to trade Bell to the Cincinnati Reds (NL) in October 1952. During his nine years with the Cincinnati Reds, Bell supplied both batting average and power in cozy Crosley Field. In 1953, Bell batted .300 with 30 HR and 105 RBI. This performance earned him the first of four (1953, 1954, 1956, 1957) All-Star Game appearances. In 1954, Bell produced 101 RBI. He batted a career-high .308 with 104 RBI the following year and attained a career best 115 RBI in 1959. For the power-rich but pitching-poor Cincinnati Reds, Bell hit 27 HR in 1955 and 29 HR in 1956. Bell, an accomplished outfielder, held the major league record for most consecutive errorless games by an outfielder (200) and led NL outfielders defensively in 1958 and 1959. In 1961, Bell appeared in his only World Series and went hitless in three pinch hit at bats. The Cincinnati Reds lost the World Series to a mighty New York Yankees team.

In 1957, Bell was selected to the All-Star team for the final time. Cincinnati fans stuffed the ballot box, electing Reds to seven of the eight starting positions. Baseball Commissioner Ford Frick,* incensed at this perceived injustice, ordered that Bell and teammate Wally Post* be removed from the NL starting lineup.

The New York Mets (NL) selected Bell in the 1961 expansion draft. Bell recorded the first base hit in Met history, singling on April 11, 1962 against the St. Louis Cardinals. In November 1962, the New York Mets traded Bell to the Milwaukee Braves (NL) for Frank J. Thomas.* Bell finished his major league career in 1964 with the Milwaukee Braves. During his 15 years in the major leagues, Bell hit .281 with 206 HR and 942 RBI.

Bell married Joyce Sutherland on December 4, 1949 and had five children, Becky, Randy, Timmy, Debby, and Buddy. Bell managed a temporary employment service company in Cincinnati. His son, Buddy,* played 18 major league seasons as an infielder and managed the Detroit Tigers and Colorado Rockies. His grandson, David Bell, plays for the Seattle Mariners, while another grandson, Mike Bell, performs at third base for the Arizona Diamondbacks (NL). The Bells and the Boones (Ray,* Bob,* Bret, and Aaron) are the only three-generation major league families.

BIBLIOGRAPHY: Gus Bell file, National Baseball Library, Cooperstown, NY; Peter C. Bjarkman, *Baseball's Great Dynasties: The Reds* (New York, 1991); Floyd Connor and John Snyder, *Day-by-Day in Cincinnati Reds History* (West Point, NY, 1984); *The Baseball Encyclopedia*, 10th ed. (New York, 1996); Donald Honig, *The Cincinnati Reds* (New York, 1992); *NYT*, May 10, 1995, D22; Bob Rathgeber, *Cincinnati Reds Scrapbook* (Virginia Beach, VA, 1982); Mike Shatzkin, ed., *The Ballplayers* (New York, 1990); Bob Smizik, *The Pittsburgh Pirates: An Illustrated History* (New York, 1990); Lonnie Wheeler and John Baskin, *The Cincinnati Game* (Wilmington, OH, 1988).

                                                                Frank W. Thackeray

BELL, George Antonio Mathey (b. October 21, 1959, San Pedro de Macoris, DR), player, entered professional baseball in 1978. His brothers include Juan, a major league infielder from 1989 through 1995, and Rolando, a minor league infielder from 1985 through 1987. Bell, a 6-foot 1-inch, 200-pound power hitting outfielder, possessed a strong arm and a penchant for committing errors. He increasingly was used as a DH by 1992.

Bell achieved stardom during a nine-season tour with the Toronto Blue Jays (AL, 1981, 1983–1990), winning the AL MVP award in 1987. During his MVP campaign, Bell led the major leagues in total bases (369) and the AL in RBI (134) while hitting a career-high 47 HR and batting .308. He also started in left field for the AL in the All-Star Game and was named *TSN* Major League Player of the Year. In 1,181 games for the Toronto Blue Jays, Bell compiled 202 HR, drove 740 teammates home, and hit .286. He signed as a free agent with the Chicago Cubs (NL) in December 1990 and moved across town to the Chicago White Sox (AL) in March 1992.

Bell has also starred in the DRWL, leading the circuit in slugging average, total bases, and doubles in 1983–1984. He helped the 1980–1981 and 1981–1982 Escogido entries win the DRWL title and the 1984–1985 Licey club win the DRWL and Caribbean Series crowns. Bell enjoyed a .298 career batting average and a .463 slugging average in the DRWL.

The Spanish-speaking Bell's difficulty expressing himself in English, coupled with an on-the-field confrontation after being hit by a pitch early in his career and disagreement with Toronto manager Jimy Williams over his full-time use as a DH, was exploited by the press. Newspapers sometimes portrayed Bell negatively despite his success as a player.

Bell's AL MVP award marked the first won by either a Dominican Republic native or a member of a Canadian team. His other accomplishments include hitting three HR on April 4, 1988, sharing the AL lead with 15 game-winning hits in 1986, and leading the AL with 14 sacrifice flies in 1989.

Bell helped the Toronto Blue Jays capture East Division crowns in 1985 and 1989 and Chicago White Sox (AL) take a West Division title in 1993 and owned a .271 batting average in 12 AL Championship Series contests. He compiled a .278 career batting average with 265 HR and 1,002 RBI in 12 major league seasons and retired following the 1993 campaign.

Bell married Marie Louisa Beguero on November 11, 1981.

BIBLIOGRAPHY: George Bell file, National Baseball Library, Cooperstown, NY; Peter C. Bjarkman, *The Toronto Blue Jays* (New York, 1990); Alison Gordon, *Foul Balls* (Toronto, Canada, 1986); *Baseball America's 1993 Almanac* (Durham, NC, 1992); *The Baseball Encyclopedia*, 10th ed. (New York, 1996); *Blue Jay Scorebook Magazine* (Toronto, Canada, 1985); *Dominican Baseball Guide* (Santo Domingo, DR, 1986); Ron Fimrite, "Toronto's Big Brass Bell," *SI* 67 (September 7, 1987), pp. 24–26; Peter Gammons, "Home Is Where His Heart Is," *SI* 72 (February 12, 1990), pp. 174–176; Buck Martinez, *From Worst to First—The Toronto Blue Jays in 1985* (Toronto, Canada, 1985); Rick Matsumoto, "Barfield & Bell," *SSBM* 47 (1987), pp. 96–97; Michael Oleksak and Mary Oleksak, *Beisbol* (Grand Rapids, MI, 1991); *TSN Baseball Guide*,

1993; *TSN Baseball Register*, 1993; R. A. Wetzsteon, "A Long Way from Toronto," *Sport* 79 (May 1988), pp. 34–36; Ernie Whitt with Greg Cable, *Catch—A Major League Life* (Toronto, Canada, 1989).

Merl F. Kleinknecht

BELL, James Thomas "Cool Papa" (b. May 17, 1903, Starkville, MS; d. March 7, 1991, St. Louis, MO), player and manager, was the son of a farmer and the great-grandson of an Oklahoma Indian. In 1920 he joined his older brothers in St. Louis, MO, there being no high school and few job opportunities in Starkville. He attended high school for two years, worked in a packing plant, and pitched for the semipro Compton Hill Cubs. In 1922, he signed his first professional contract for $90 per month with the St. Louis Stars (NNL). From 1922 to 1931, Bell played for the Stars and initially performed as a left-handed pitcher. His knuckler and screwball complemented his curveball, which he threw with three different motions. His calm demeanor impressed other players and manager Bill Gatewood so much that he thereafter was nicknamed "Cool Papa." Besides being an effective pitcher, Bell also proved extremely fast and a good right-handed hitter. In 1924, Gatewood installed him in the outfield and made him into a switch-hitter.

After the 1931 season, the NNL disbanded for one season. In 1932 the 6-foot, 145-pound Bell played briefly for the Detroit Wolves, the Homestead Grays' farm club. When the Wolves folded, he joined the Kansas City Monarchs. From 1933 to 1936, Bell roamed center field for the Pittsburgh Crawfords (NNL) that included manager Oscar Charleston,* Satchel Paige,* Judy Johnson,* Josh Gibson,* Jimmie Crutchfield,* and Ted Page.* In 1937 the dictator of the Dominican Republic, Rafael Trujillo, lured Bell, Paige, and other Crawfords south to play for the Trujillo All-Stars. Bell played in Mexico from 1938 to 1941, earning $450 per month and enjoying life in an integrated society. In 1940, Bell batted a career-high .437 and led the MEL in every offensive category.

Two years later, Bell returned to the United States to play for the Chicago American Giants (NAL) and briefly for the Memphis Red Sox. The 1943–1946 summer seasons were spent with the Homestead Grays (NNL) and the 1947 campaign with the Detroit Senators. Bell concluded his baseball career from 1948 to 1950 as player–manager for the Kansas City Stars, the Monarchs' farm club. After declining an offer in 1951 from the St. Louis Browns (AL), Bell worked as a custodian and then as night security officer at St. Louis City Hall until retiring in 1970. He resided with his wife, Clarabelle, near the site of old Busch Stadium.

Bell became one of the greatest hitters and outfielders and perhaps the fastest player of all time. In 1933, he stole 175 bases in about 200 games. Even during his forties, he ranked among the league leaders in stolen bases. Bell, considered faster than Ty Cobb* and even Jesse Owens (OS), once circled the bases in 12 seconds flat to easily beat the major league record. He routinely scored from second base on ground balls and scored from first on a bunt in 1948 against Bob Lemon's* All Stars. Paul Waner* and Bill Veeck* included the outstanding hitting Bell on their all-time outfield. According to available records for his 29 summer and 21 winter seasons, Bell batted over .400 twice and compiled an estimated .337 lifetime average. In 54 recorded games against white major leaguers, he batted .391. In recognition of a truly outstanding career hidden from a majority of fans by segregation, Bell in 1974 was inducted into the National Baseball Hall of Fame.

BIBLIOGRAPHY: James Bell file, National Baseball Library, Cooperstown, NY; Martin Appel and Burt Goldblatt, *Baseball's Best: The Hall of Fame Gallery* (New York, 1977); James Bankes, "How Fast Was Cool Papa Bell?" *TNP* 1 (Fall 1982), pp. 10–12; James Bankes, *The Pittsburgh Crawfords* (Dubuque, IA, 1991); James Bell and John B. Holway, "How to Score from First on a Sacrifice," *AH* 21 (August 1970), pp. 30–36; William Brashler, *Josh Gibson: A Life in the Negro Leagues* (New York, 1978); Bob Broeg, "Cobb on a Rampage," *BRJ* 20 (1991), p. 38; Anthony J. Connor, *Voices from Cooperstown* (New York, 1982); John B. Holway, *Voices from the Great Black Baseball Leagues* (New York, 1975); Donald Honig, *Baseball When the Grass Was Real* (New York, 1975); M. Kram, "No Place in the Shade," *SI* 80 (June 20, 1994), pp. 65–68; *NYT*, March 9, 1991, p. 11; Robert W. Peterson, *Only the Ball Was White* (Englewood Cliffs, NJ, 1970); David L. Porter, ed., *African-American Sports Greats* (Westport, CT, 1995); Lowell Reidenbaugh, *Baseball's Hall of Fame-Cooperstown* (New York, 1993); James A. Riley, *The Biographical Encyclopedia of the Negro Baseball Leagues* (New York, 1994).

Douglas D. Martin

BELL, Jay Stuart (b. December 11, 1965, Elgin AFB, FL), player, is the son of Ron Bell, U.S. Air Force officer, and accompanied his family on tours of duty in Germany and Italy. The Bells moved to Pensacola, FL in 1972. He graduated from Tate High School in Gonzalez, FL, where he made the Florida All-Star team his senior year and helped his team win the Florida Quad-A State championship. Bell also played football, basketball, and tennis in high school. In June 1984, the Minnesota Twins (AL) signed Bell as their first-round selection in the free agent draft and eighth player taken overall.

The 6-foot 1-inch, 185-pound, right-handed shortstop began his professional baseball career at Elizabethton, NC (ApL). In August 1985 Minnesota traded him to the Cleveland Indians (AL) organization. In September 1986, he was called up by Cleveland and became only the 11th major league player to hit the first pitch thrown to him for a HR.

After shuffling between the Cleveland Indians and the minor leagues, Bell was traded to the Pittsburgh Pirates (NL) in March 1989 and helped the Pirates win three consecutive NL East Division titles from 1990 to 1992. Bell led the major leagues with 39 sacrifice bunts in 1990 and compiled a 22 game hitting streak in 1992, the longest of the year in the NL. Bell's finest year came in 1993, when he batted .310 with 102 runs scored and led the club with 187 hits. He led NL shortstops with a .986 fielding percentage, won the Rawlings Gold Glove Award, and was named to the Hillerich and

Bradsby Silver Slugger Team. He was selected to the NL All-Star team and was chosen Dapper Dan Man of the Year, an award given annually to a Pittsburgh sports figure for outstanding national achievement. In 1994, Bell paced all NL shortstops in chances for the fifth consecutive year and led the club in hits (117). Two years later, he paced NL shortstops with a .986 fielding percentage. In December 1996, Pittsburgh traded him to the Kansas City Royals (AL). He joined the expansion Arizona Diamondbacks (NL) as a free agent in November 1997. Fans selected him starting NL shortstop in the 1999 All-Star Game. His 38 HR and 112 RBI helped Arizona win the NL West Division in 1999. Through 1999, Bell has batted .269 with 1,677 hits, 963 runs scored, 162 HR, and 732 RBI. He ranked fourth in games (1,487) and errors (169) in the 1990s.

In the 1991 NL League Championship Series against the Atlanta Braves, Bell tied the series record for most singles (9). In 20 NL League Championship Series games between 1990 and 1992, Bell batted .282 with 22 hits.

Bell and his wife, Laura, have two children, Brianna and Brantley, and reside in Valrico, FL. He participated in the players' union and received the 1993 Pittsburgh Points of Light Foundation Award for his community service work.

BIBLIOGRAPHY: Jay Bell file, National Baseball Library, Cooperstown, NY; *The Baseball Encyclopedia*, 10th ed. (New York, 1996); Jay Bell file, *TSN*, St. Louis, MO; Chuck Greenwood, "Bell Part of Happy Pittsburgh Family," *SCD* 23 (August 16, 1996), pp. 60–61; *Pittsburgh Pirates 1996 Record and Information Guide*; S. L. Price, "It Pays to Be Nice," *SI* 88 (March 2, 1998), pp. 82–83.

Frank W. Thackeray

BELLE, Albert Jojuan "Joey" (b. August 25, 1966, Shreveport, LA), player, became one of baseball's leading sluggers in the mid-1990s. The son of Albert Belle and Carrie Belle, both teachers, and the twin brother of Terry, a financial analyst, he grew up in Shreveport, LA. Belle rose to Eagle Scout and graduated in 1984 from Huntington High School near the top of his class. He attended Louisiana State University for three years, twice being named to the All-SEC baseball team.

The Cleveland Indians (AL) drafted Belle in June 1987 and assigned him to Kinston, NC (CrL). He also played at Waterloo, IA (ML) and Canton-Akron, OH (EL) before debuting with Cleveland in July 1989. After being optioned to Colorado Springs, CO (PCL) in May 1990, Belle spent two summer months in the Cleveland Clinic overcoming alcohol addiction. He renounced his childhood nickname "Joey" and finished the season at Canton-Akron.

Belle played with Cleveland in 1991, except for a brief demotion to Colorado Springs in June. After alternating between DH and the outfield through 1992, the 6-foot, 2-inch, 210-pound right-hander became the Indians' regular left fielder in 1993.

From 1992 through 1996, Belle ranked among the AL's top four in HR and RBI. He led the AL in HR in 1995 (50) and in RBI in 1993 (129), 1995 (tie, 126), and 1996 (148). In 1995, Belle paced the AL in slugging average (.690), shared the AL lead in runs (121) and doubles (52), and became the first major leaguer ever to hit 50 doubles and 50 HR in the same season. His 1995 performance helped bring the Indians their first AL pennant since 1954, with *TSN* naming him major league Player of the Year. *Total Baseball's* total player ratings rank Belle first among AL position players for 1994, second for 1995, and fourth for 1996. He made the AL All-Star team from 1993 through 1998. In 1998, he led the AL in slugging percentage (.655) and total bases (399), finished second in doubles (48), HR (49), and RBI (152), ranked third in batting average (.328), and placed fourth in hits (200).

Belle's quick temper led to numerous altercations with fans and the press and several suspensions, overshadowing his charity and community service. He earned the Cleveland club's nominations for the Roberto Clemente Award in 1993 and 1994 and Branch Rickey Award in 1994. His verbal attack on television reporter Hannah Storm during the 1995 World Series led acting baseball commissioner Allan H. "Bud" Selig* to fine him a record $50,000. As a free agent in November 1996, Belle signed a five-year $55 million contract with the Chicago White Sox (AL) and become baseball's first player to earn over $10 million per year. In December 1998, the Baltimore Orioles (AL) signed him to a $65 million, five-year contract.

In 1,237 major league games through 1999, Belle batted .296 with 352 doubles, 358 HR, 1,136 RBI, 903 runs scored, and a .573 slugging average. In 18 postseason championship games in 1995 and 1996, he batted .230 with 6 HR and 14 RBI. He made *TSN* AL All-Star team (1993–1996, 1998) and *TSN* Silver Slugger team (1993–1996, 1998). He ranked first in RBI (1,099) and fourth in HR (351) in the 1990s.

BIBLIOGRAPHY: Albert Belle file, National Baseball Library, Cooperstown, NY; Michael Bamberger, "He Thrives on Anger," *SI* 74 (May 6, 1996), pp. 72–76ff; *Chicago White Sox Media Guide*, 1997; P. M. Johnson, "Albert Belle," *Sport* 87 (November 1996), pp. 22ff; D. A. Kaplan, "Heavy Hitter," *Newsweek* 127 (March 25, 1996), pp. 62–63; Edward Kiersh, "Albert Belle: Not Another Mistake by the Lake," *IS* (June 1993), pp. 22–24, 26–27; Franz Lidz, "The Belle Jar," *SI* 74 (June 24, 1991), p. 68; B. Livingston, "Raging Belle," *Sport* 83 (February 1992), pp. 58–61; Deron Snyder, "Albert Belle Hates to Lose," *BW*, November 29, 1995, pp. 20–22; Deron Snyder, "Towers of Power," *BW*, December 4, 1996, pp. 8–10; *TSN Baseball Register*, 1997; John Thorn et al., eds., *Total Indians* (New York, 1996); John Thorn et al., eds., *Total Baseball*, 5th ed. (New York, 1997); Jack Torry, *Endless Summers* (South Bend, IN, 1995); Russell Schneider, *The Glorious Indian Summer of 1995* (Cleveland, OH, 1995); Tim Wendel, "Albert Belle Makes Most of Second Chance," *BW*, June 30, 1993, pp. 20–21.

Frederick Ivor-Campbell

BENCH, Johnny Lee (b. December 7, 1947, Oklahoma City, OK), player and announcer, grew up in Binger, OK, where his father Ted, a truck driver, had moved his family when Johnny was age five. Bench earned All-State honors in baseball and basketball at Binger High School, from which he graduated as class valedictorian in 1965. Rejecting several college scholarship offers, he signed a bonus contract with the Cincinnati Reds (NL). After three minor league seasons with Tampa, FL (FSL) in 1965, Peninsula, VA (CrL) in 1966, and Buffalo, NY (IL) in 1967, Bench joined the Reds late in the 1967 season. In 1968, the catcher batted .275 in 154 games and was named NL Rookie of the Year. Two years later, Bench led the NL with 45 HR and 148 RBI. For leading the Reds to the NL pennant, Bench was named NL MVP. He won the MVP award again in 1972, when he led the NL with 125 RBI and 40 HR.

With Bench as starting catcher throughout the 1970s, the Reds won six NL Western Division titles, four NL pennants, and world championships in 1975 and 1976. Bench was selected MVP of the 1976 World Series, which the Reds won in a four-game sweep of the New York Yankees to become the first NL team in over fifty years to win consecutive World Series. During the 1970–1979 decade, Bench led the major leagues with 1,013 RBI and the NL three times in RBI. His lifetime 389 HR surpassed that of all other major league catchers. During his career, he drove in 1,376 runs and complied a .267 batting average. In 2,158 games, he made 2,048 hits, 381 doubles, 1,091 runs, and 1,278 strikeouts. Additionally, he was recognized as an outstanding, durable defensive catcher. He caught over 120 games in each of his first ten major league seasons and won ten consecutive Gold Gloves for outstanding defense behind the plate.

Bench retired as an active player after the 1983 season to concentrate on various business and professional interests. Having once undergone minor cancer surgery, he headed the Athletes' Division of the American Cancer Society. Bench frequently competed in celebrity golf tournaments to raise money for charitable organizations. He ranks along with Hall-of-Famers Bill Dickey,* Mickey Cochrane,* Yogi Berra,* and Ivan Rodriguez* as one of the greatest offensive and defensive catchers in baseball history. In 1986 ABC hired Bench as a baseball commentator. The National Baseball Hall of Fame enshrined him in 1989. Bench made Major League Baseball's All-Century Team and rejoined the Reds in 1999 as special consultant to the general manager.

BIBLIOGRAPHY: Johnny Bench file, National Baseball Library, Cooperstown, NY; Johnny Bench and William Brashler, *Catch You Later* (New York, 1979); John Benson et al., *Baseball's Top 100* (Wilton, CT, 1997); Donald Honig, *The Cincinnati Reds* (New York, 1992); Greg Rhodes and John Erardi, *Big Red Dynasty* (Cincinnati, OH, 1997); Lowell Reidenbaugh, *Baseball's Hall of Fame-Cooperstown* (New York, 1993); George Vecsey, "Johnny Bench: The Man Behind the Mask," *Sport* 54 (October 1972), pp. 101–112; Peter C. Bjarkman, *Baseball's Great Dynasties: The Reds* (New York, 1991); Bob Rathgeber, *Cincinnati Reds Scrapbook* (Virginia Beach, VA, 1982); Bob Hertzel, *The Big Red Machine* (Englewood Cliffs, NJ, 1976); Floyd Connor and John Snyder, *Day-by-Day in Cincinnati Reds History* (West Point, NY, 1984); Ross

Foreman, "Johnny Bench Tries His Hand at Managing," *SCD* 23 (January 12, 1996), p. 146; Robert H. Walker, *Cincinnati and the Big Red Machine* (Bloomington, IN, 1988).

Fred M. Shelley

BENDER, Charles Albert "Chief" (b. May 5, 1884, Crow Wing County, MN; d. May 22, 1954, Philadelphia, PA), player, coach, manager, and scout, grew up at White Earth (Indian) Reservation, MN. He was the son of Albertus Bliss Bender, a farmer of German-American descent, and Mary Razor (Indian name: Pay shaw de o quay) of half Ojibwa (Chippewa) parentage. Bender attended Lincoln Institution, a school for Indians and whites at Philadelphia, from age eight to 12 and then returned briefly to White Earth. At Carlisle Indian School (PA) from 1898 to 1901, he played baseball and football. In 1902, he attended Dickinson College. As "Charles Albert," he pitched that summer for Harrisburg (PA) Athletic Club and was discovered there by Philadelphia Athletics (AL) scout Jesse Frisinger.

Resembling a full-blooded Indian, the swarthy, rangy Bender reported the next spring to Philadelphia and immediately was nicknamed "Chief." From 1903 through 1914, the 6-foot 2-inch, 185-pound right-hander won 191 games for the Athletics. In his best season (1910), he compiled a 23–5 won–lost record and a 1.58 ERA and hurled a no-hit game. He won six and lost four in five World Series and posted two victories each in the 1911 and 1913 fall classics. Bender, who lacked abundant stamina, was used by manager Connie Mack* principally in "must win" games and proved an effective stopper. His winning percentages led the AL in 1910 and 1914. Twice Bender won more than 20 games in a season. The cool, relaxed Bender exhibited excellent control and curves and utilized his hard fastball as his best pitch. A career .212 batter, he occasionally pinch-hit and played outfield or first base.

Bender joined the FL in 1915, compiling a 4–16 mark with the Baltimore Terrapins. He recorded 7–7 and 8–2 seasons in 1916 and 1917 with the Philadelphia Phillies (NL), giving him 210 career wins, 127 losses, 1,711 strikeouts, and a 2.45 ERA. After working in a shipyard during 1918, he managed Richmond, VA (VL) in 1919 and pitched 29 victories against only 2 defeats (which he called his finest baseball achievement).

Subsequently, Bender pitched and managed at New Haven, CT (EL) in 1920–1921, Reading, PA (IL) in 1922, and Johnstown, PA (MAL) in 1927; coached for the Chicago White Sox (AL) in 1925–1926, New York Giants (NL) in 1931, and the U.S. Naval Academy in 1928; and managed at the independent House of David during the 1930s, Erie, PA (CL) in 1932, Wilmington, DE (ISL) in 1940, Newport News, VA (VL) in 1941, and Savannah GA (SAL) in 1946. For the Athletics, he scouted in 1945 and 1947 through 1950. He then coached there through 1953, the year he was elected to the National Baseball Hall of Fame.

Bender married Marie Clements of Detroit in 1904; they had no children.

The gentle, intelligent, and versatile hurler engaged in the watchmaking, jewelry, and clothing businesses; painted landscapes in oils; and proved an excellent marksman, trapshooter, golfer, and billiard player.

BIBLIOGRAPHY: Charles A. Bender, "Record of Graduates and Returned Students, United States Indian School, Carlisle, Pennsylvania," ca. 1908–1909; Charles A. Bender file, National Baseball Library, Cooperstown, NY; Craig Carter, ed., *TSN Daguerreotypes*, 8th ed. (St. Louis, MO, 1990); Philadelphia *Press*, September 12, 1909; Frederick G. Lieb, *Connie Mack* (New York, 1945); Connie Mack, *My 66 Years in the Big Leagues* (Philadelphia PA, 1950); *The Baseball Encyclopedia*, 10th ed. (New York, 1996); Jerome C. Romanowski, *The Mackmen* (Upper Darby, PA, 1979); J. G. Taylor Spink, *TSN*, December 24, 1942, December 30, 1953; Robert Tholkes, "Chief Bender—The Early Years," *BRJ* 12 (1983), pp. 8–13; *TSN*, June 2, 1954.

Frank V. Phelps

BENNETT, Charles Wesley "Charlie" (b. November 21, 1854, New Castle, PA; d. February 24, 1927, Detroit, MI), player, was the son of parents of English and Dutch descent. Teammates and fans alike respected the very popular 5-foot 11-inch, 160-pound catcher, who batted and threw right-handed. Bennett started his professional baseball career in 1874 with Neshannock, PA and joined the major leagues with the Milwaukee Brewers (NL) in 1878.

Bennett spent 15 seasons in the major leagues as a great defensive catcher. After catching for the Worcester, MA Ruby Legs (NL) in 1880, he starred for the Detroit Wolverines (NL) from 1881 to 1888. His body and hands took a beating in the era prior to protective equipment. Receiving fastballs so deformed his hands that he would not let them be photographed. His wife, Alice, who he married in 1882, created the first breast protector in 1886. The pad worked so well in a private tryout that he wore it in public. Soon, most other catchers wore the protector, too.

Bennett led NL catchers seven times in fielding percentage and played on four pennant-winning teams. With Detroit, he batted a career-high .305 in 1883 and led NL catchers in fielding in 1881, 1883, 1886, and 1888. In 1887, the Wolverines won the NL pennant and defeated the St. Louis Browns (AA) in a 15-game traveling World Series.

Bennett completed his major league career with the Boston Beaneaters (NL) from 1889 to 1893, catching Kid Nichols,* John Clarkson,* and Hoss Radbourne.* He paced NL catchers in fielding percentage from 1889 to 1891 and helped Boston to consecutive NL pennants from 1891 to 1893. In 15 major league seasons, he batted .256 with 978 hits, 203 doubles, 533 RBI, and a .942 fielding percentage and often led the NL in putouts, total chances, and double plays.

In January 1894, Bennett lost both legs in a tragic Wellsville, KS train accident. He was disembarking from a train to speak to a friend when he was run over. Now confined to a wheelchair, Bennett returned to Detroit and opened a cigar and newspaper store. Fans and friends went out of their way to patronize his shop. In 1896, Detroit christened a new park named in his honor. The Detroit Tigers (AL) played at Bennett Park until 1911. At Charlie Bennett Day, he was presented with a wheelbarrow of silver dollars.

BIBLIOGRAPHY: Charles W. Bennett file, National Baseball Library, Cooperstown, NY; William M. Anderson, *The Detroit Tigers* (South Bend, IN, 1996); Richard Bak, *A Place for Summer* (Detroit, MI, 1998); Michael Benson, *Ballparks of North America* (Jefferson, NC, 1989); Peter Filichia, *Professional Baseball Franchises* (New York, 1993); Joe Falls, *Detroit Tigers* (New York, 1975); Frederick G. Lieb, *The Detroit Tigers* (New York, 1976); John Thorn et al., eds., *Total Baseball*, 5th ed. (New York, 1997); Robert L. Tiemann and Mark Rucker, eds., *Nineteenth Century Stars* (Kansas City, MO, 1989).

Scot E. Mondore

BERGER, Walter Antone "Wally" (b. October 10, 1905, Chicago, IL; d. November 30, 1988, Redondo Beach, CA), player and manager, learned to play baseball on San Francisco sandlots. He played third base for a Mission High School team that included Joe Cronin* at second base. Berger began organized baseball in 1927 as an outfielder at Pocatello, ID, where he led the UIL in putouts, batted .385, and hit 24 HR before moving up to the PCL. He played for Los Angeles, CA from 1927 to 1929, hitting .365 his first year, .327 in 1928, and .355 in 1929. In 1929, he belted 40 HR and produced 166 RBI. Berger remains among the all-time leading sluggers in minor league history. From 1930 to 1937, Berger starred for the Boston Braves (NL). He set the club season record with 38 HR and 169 extra bases on long hits his rookie season when he batted .310 and drove home 119 runs. Berger's HR as a rookie remained the NL standard until bested by Frank Robinson* in 1956. In his next three seasons, Berger compiled .323, .307, and .313 batting marks. He played in three consecutive major league All-Star games from 1933 through 1935 and was named to *TSN*'s Major League All-Star team in 1933. Although his batting average dropped below .300 after 1933, the 6-foot 2-inch, 205-pound outfielder remained a productive power hitter. He hit 34 HR in 1934 and 1935, leading the NL the latter year. His 130 RBI in 1935 paced the NL and set a Boston Braves record.

In June 1937 the Braves traded Berger to the New York Giants (NL). After spending one year there, he played for the Cincinnati Reds until being released in 1940. He played 20 games for the Philadelphia Phillies (NL) before being sent to Indianapolis, IN (AA). In 1941, Berger finished his playing career as a first baseman–outfielder for Los Angeles (PCL). Berger, who had married Bertha Wilson in October 1929 and then Martha Subzhak in April 1942, managed Manchester, NH (NEL) in 1949. Among his era's premier sluggers and run producers, he played in 1,350 games, amassed 1,550 hits, 299 doubles, 242 HR, and 898 RBI, compiled a .522 slugging percentage, and hit .300 in five of 11 major league seasons. Berger resided in Manhattan Beach, CA.

BIBLIOGRAPHY: Walter Berger file, National Baseball Library, Cooperstown, NY; Walter A. Berger and George M. Snyder, . . . *Freshly Remember'd* (Rondondo Beach, 1994); Robert S. Fuchs and Wayne Soini, *Judge Fuchs and the Boston Braves, 1923–1935* (Jefferson, NC, 1998); Harold Kaese, *The Boston Braves* (New York, 1948); Al Hirshberg, *Braves, the Pick and the Shovel* (Boston, MA, 1948); Gary Caruso, *The Braves Encyclopedia* (Philadelphia, PA, 1995); Lee Allen, *The Cincinnati Reds* (New York, 1948); Craig Carter, ed., *TSN Daguerreotypes*, 8th ed. (St. Louis, MO, 1990); NAPBL, *The Story of Minor League Baseball* (Columbus, OH, 1952); *NYT*, December 3, 1988, p. 33; Lowell Reidenbaugh, "Memories . . . The Fifteen Surviving Members of the First All-Star Game Remember the Big Event," *TSN 1983 All-Star Special* (St. Louis, MO, 1983), pp. 3–8; John Thorn et al., eds., *Total Braves* (New York, 1996).

                                                                                Douglas D. Martin

BERRA, Lawrence Peter "Yogi" (b. May 12, 1925, St. Louis, MO), player, manager, and coach, is the son of shoe factory worker Peter Berra and Pauline (Longsoni) Berra, both of Italian origin. In 1932 the Berra family moved to the famed Italian "Hill" section of St. Louis, where Yogi attended the Wade Grammar School. Boyhood friend Jack Maguire nicknamed him "Yogi" after seeing a movie about India. Berra, who left school at age 14, worked in a coalyard, drove a soft-drink truck, and toiled as a tack-puller in the shoe factory. At age 17, Berra tried out with Joe Garagiola (OS) for the St. Louis Cardinals (NL). Despite being the best athlete in South St. Louis and a star for the YMCA Stags, he failed to impress Cardinals executive Branch Rickey.* The Cardinals offered $500 to Garagiola, who showed more discipline at the plate. The New York Yankees (AL) eventually signed Berra for $500.

After spending 1943 with Norfolk, VA (PiL), Berra joined the U.S. Navy. He was stationed on a rocket launcher off the coast of Normandy Beach for fifteen days following the D-Day attack. After being discharged in 1946, Berra hit .314 for the Newark, NJ Bears (IL). With the New York Yankees that same year, Berra wore number 35 while alternating between left field and home plate. Yankee great Bill Dickey* helped make Berra a more accurate thrower and one of the sport's best catchers.

In 1951, 1954, and 1955, Berra was named the AL's MVP. A notorious bad-ball hitter, he hit with power (30 HR in 1952 and 1956) and batting average (.322 in 1950). Berra hit 313 HR, the most then by an AL catcher. He played with the New York Yankees from 1946 to 1964 and appeared in four games for the New York Mets (NL) in 1965, hitting .285 in 2,120 career games, slugging 358 HR, and knocking in 1,430 runs. A participant in 14 World Series, he played on 10 championship teams.

Berra holds many fielding records, including playing in 148 consecutive games without an error. During that streak from 1957 to 1959, he accepted

950 chances, also a major league mark. He made an unassisted double play against the St. Louis Browns in 1947 to tie an AL record. His World Series records include most games (75) and most hits (71). The first player to pinch-hit a HR in the World Series in 1947, he in 1956 joined a handful of players hitting grand slams in the fall classic.

In his first full season as manager of the Yankees, Berra guided the team to the 1964 pennant and a near World Series triumph. Player discontent, most notably the Phil Linz harmonica incident, prompted the Yankees to fire him. He coached the New York Mets (NL) from 1965 to 1972 and managed them to the NL pennant the next season. The 1973 Mets nearly defeated the Oakland Athletics in the World Series. From the middle of 1975 through 1983, Berra coached for the Yankees. After being named Yankees' manager in December 1983, he guided New York to an 87–75 record in 1984. The Yankees removed Berra as manager after a lackluster 6–10 start in 1985. He coached for the Houston Astros (NL) from 1986 through 1989. His career managerial record through 1985 remained 484–444 for a .522 percentage. In 1972, he was elected to the National Baseball Hall of Fame.

On January 21, 1949, he married Carmine Short, a former waitress for Musial and Biggies in St. Louis. They have three sons, including former major league shortstop Dale. A shy, affable New York man with a penchant for comic books, Berra has made many malapropisms. While giving gratitude at a benefit, Berra commented, "I want to thank all those who made this evening necessary." After experiencing difficulty playing left field in Yankee Stadium, Berra remarked, "It gets late early out there!" Montclair State University houses the Yogi Berra Museum. For many years he served as vice president of the Yoo Hoo soft drink company. Berra made Major League Baseball's All-Century Team.

BIBLIOGRAPHY: Maury Allen, *Baseball's 100* (New York, 1959); Bob Broeg, *Superstars of Baseball* (St. Louis, MO, 1971); Yogi Berra file, National Baseball Library, Cooperstown, NY; John Benson et al., *Baseball's Top 100* (Wilton, CT, 1997); Yogi Berra, *The Yogi Book* (New York, 1998); Yogi Berra and Thomas N. Horton, *Yogi: It Ain't Over* (New York, 1989); Bob Burnes, "My Favorite Yankee," *TSN Baseball Register 1958* (St. Louis, MO, 1958); Arthur Daley, *Sports of the Times* (New York, 1959); Ed Fitzgerald, *The Autobiography of a Professional Baseball Player* (New York, 1961); Dom Forker, *The Men of Autumn* (Dallas, TX, 1989); Dom Forker, *Sweet Seasons* (Dallas, TX, 1991); Joe Garagiola and Dave Anderson, "Yogi of the Yankees," *RD* 85 (July 1964), pp. 110–113; William Gleason, "Is Lollar Better Than Berra?" *SEP* 229 (June 15, 1957), pp. 36ff.; David Halberstam, *Summer of '49* (New York, 1989); Peter Golenbock, *Dynasty* (New York, 1975); Gene Karst and Martin J. Jones, Jr., *Who's Who in Professional Baseball* (New York, 1973); Craig Carter, ed., *TSN Daguerreotypes*, 8th ed. (St. Louis, MO, 1990); Tony Kubek and Terry Pluto, *Sixty-One* (New York, 1987); Richard Marazzi and Len Fiorito, *Aaron to Zuverink* (New York, 1982); Rich Marazzi, "Yogi," *SCD* 25 (October 30, 1998), pp. 122–124; Tom Meany, *Magnificent Yankees* (New York, 1957); Tom Meany and Tom Holmes, *Baseball's Best* (New York, 1964); Jim Ogle, "Why the Yankees Fired Berra," *Look* 28 (December 29, 1964), pp. 30ff; Harry T. Paxton, "Everything Happens to Me," *SEP* 272 (April 29, 1950), pp. 32–33ff; Phil Pepe, *The Wit and Wisdom of Yogi Berra* (Westport, CT, 1988); Joe Reichler, "Mr. Backstop," in *Baseball Stars of 1955* (New York, 1955); J. Rosenthal, "As Yogi Says," *NYT Magazine*, September 15, 1991, pp. 24ff; *WWA*, 41st ed. (1980–1981), p. 278; *Yogi Berra: An American Original* (Champaign, IL, 1998).

William A. Borst

BESCHER, Robert Henry "Bob" (b. February 25, 1884, London, OH; d. November 29, 1942, London, OH), player, was a son of Antone Bescher, a brick manufacturer, and Mary Bescher. After completing high school locally, he attended Notre Dame College from 1898 to 1902 and played left field three years on the baseball varsity. Bescher left college to work 14 months on a Nebraska ranch and then played semiprofessional baseball in Ohio for two years before attending Wittenberg College, where he starred as a football left halfback.

The genial, clean-living athlete entered organized baseball with Lima, OH (ISA) in 1906 and soon was traded to Dayton, OH (CL). In late 1908, the Cincinnati Reds (NL) purchased him from Dayton. Through 1913, he provided the Reds a left-handed, strong-armed left fielder. Bescher led the NL in stolen bases from 1909 through 1912 with 54, 70, 81, and 67. Allegedly, catchers caught him stealing only three times in 1911 and 10 times in 1912. His 81 thefts remained a post-1900 NL record until Maury Wills* surpassed it in 1962. Bescher's style featured quick starts, sheer speed, and long, graceful hook slides. He also led the NL in runs (120) in 1912 and bases on balls (94) in 1913.

The New York Giants (NL) traded Buck Herzog* and Grover Hartley to the Cincinnati Reds for him in December 1913. The light-hitting Ohioan experienced a disappointing 1914 season due mainly to some loss of speed. He finished his major league career with the St. Louis Cardinals (NL) from 1915 through 1917 and briefly with the Cleveland Naps (AL) in 1918. From 1917 to 1925, he played for Milwaukee, WI (AA), Columbus, OH (AA), Wichita Falls, TX (TL), Fort Worth, TX (TL), and Columbus again.

The popular Bescher worked as an Ohio state oil inspector and enjoyed hunting. The lifelong bachelor died at a railroad crossing near London when a train struck his automobile. Bescher, a burly 6-foot 1½-inch, 200-pound switch hitter, batted more effectively from the right side. During 11 major league seasons, he played in 1,228 games with a .258 batting average, 1,171 hits, and 428 stolen bases.

BIBLIOGRAPHY: Lee Allen, "Base-Stealer Bescher Early Product of Notre Dame," *TSN*, September 22, 1962; Lee Allen, *The Cincinnati Reds* (New York, 1948); Bob Bescher file, National Baseball Library, Cooperstown, NY; "Bob Bescher Killed in Crash . . . ," *Cincinnati Enquirer*, November 30, 1942; F. C. Lane, "The King of the Base Stealers," *BM* 9 (August 1912), pp. 31–37; Pat Harmon, "Bescher Drank Lemonade," *The Post & Times Star*, October 8, 1962; Donald Honig, *The Cincinnati Reds* (New York, 1992); Bob Rathgeber, *Cincinnati Reds Scrapbook* (Virginia Beach, VA,

1982); Frederick G. Lieb, *The St. Louis Cardinals* (New York, 1945); Bob Broeg and Jerry Vickery, *St. Louis Cardinals Encyclopedia* (Grand Rapids, MI, 1998); John Thorn, et al., eds., *Total Baseball*, 5th ed. (New York, 1997); *TSN*, "Robert H. Bescher," December 3, 1942.

Frank V. Phelps

BICHETTE, Alphonse Dante (b. November 18, 1963, West Palm Beach, FL), player, is a 6-foot 3-inch, 225-pound outfielder who bats and throws right handed. He is the son of Maurice Bichette, a retired swimming pool builder, and Mary Bichette. After graduating from Jupiter, FL High School in 1982, he played baseball at Palm Beach, FL JC and led his team to the state tournament. Bichette and his wife, Marianna, who married in 1993 and have a son, Dante, Jr., donate much time to community youth groups.

The California Angels (AL) selected Bichette in the June 1984 free-agent draft and assigned him to Salem, OR (NWL) in 1984 and Quad Cities (ML) in 1985. He split the 1986 season between Palm Springs, CA (CaL) and Midland, TX (TL) and spent the following two seasons with Edmonton, Canada (PCL). Bichette was promoted to the California Angels for 21 games in September 1988 before starting for the Angels on opening day in 1989. California optioned him to Edmonton after 39 games. Bichette played a full season for California in 1990 before being traded to the Milwaukee Brewers (AL) in March 1991 for Dave Parker.* For the Brewers in 1992, he batted .287 with 111 hits and 27 doubles.

On November 17, 1992, the Milwaukee Brewers traded Bichette to the Colorado Rockies (NL) for Kevin Reimer. In one swing of the bat on April 7, 1993 against the New York Mets, Bichette established three "firsts" for the Rockies by driving in and scoring the first run with the first HR in team history. The 1993 season saw him bat .310 and establish career highs in doubles (43) and triples (5). In 1994 Bichette hit .304, led the NL in games played (116) and times at bat (484), and was selected to the NL All-Star squad.

Besides being selected to the NL All-Star team in 1995, Bichette almost won the Triple Crown of batting. The Colorado outfielder led the NL with 197 hits, 40 HR, and 128 RBI and ranked third in batting at .340, helping the third-year Rockies win the wild card spot in the NL Division Series. Colorado lost to the Atlanta Braves while Bichette batted .588 with 10 hits. He paced the NL in hits (197), slugging percentage (.620), and total bases (359), ranked second in doubles (38), and placed fourth in runs scored (102). He finished second in the NL's MVP voting behind Cincinnati's Barry Larkin* and won a *TSN* Silver Slugger Award. Bichette became only the 14th player in major league history to attain a .340 batting average, 100 runs, 40 HR, 120 RBI, and 350 total bases in one season. In 1996, he batted .313 with 31 HR and established career highs in runs (114) and RBI (141). Bichette hit .308 with 26 HR and 118 RBI in 1997 and made the NL All-Star squad for the fourth consecutive season. In 1998, he again made the NL All-Star team, leading the NL with a career-best 219 hits, sharing second in doubles with a career-high 48, and ranking third in batting average with .331. Bichette batted .298 with 34 HR and 133 RBI in 1999. The Cincinnati Reds acquired him in October 1999.

In 12 major league seasons, Bichette has played in 1,442 games, scored 809 runs, and made 1,625 hits. He has compiled a .300 batting average with 339 doubles, 24 triples, 239 HR, and 1,002 RBI, recording 286 walks, 911 strikeouts, and 145 stolen bases.

BIBLIOGRAPHY: *Colorado Rockies Media Guide*, 1998; *The Carmi* (IL) *Times*, November 16, 1995, p. 8; G. Guss, "Bichette Happens," *Sport* 87 (June 1996), pp. 81–84; Tim Kurkjian, "More Child's Play," *SI* 83 (July 3, 1995), pp. 50–53; *TSN 1996 Baseball Yearbook*, pp. 28–31; *TSN Official Baseball Register*, 1998; *USAT Baseball Weekly*, October 4–10, 1995, p. 43.

John L. Evers

BIERBAUER, Louis W. "Lou" (b. September 28, 1865, Erie, PA; d. January 31, 1926, Erie, PA), player, was the son of German immigrants John Bierbauer and Barbara Bierbauer and excelled at second base in the AA, PL, and NL. Bierbauer played for his hometown Erie, PA club as a teenager and in 1885 performed for Hamilton, Canada (CL). After spending four seasons with the Philadelphia Athletics (AA), he jumped in 1890 to the Brooklyn Wonders in the renegade PL. When the PL folded after one season, Bierbauer signed with the Pittsburgh Pirates (NL). The Athletics claimed they had reserved him for 1891, but baseball's National Board disagreed and awarded him to Pittsburgh. This action precipitated a new war between the NL and AA and contributed to Pittsburgh's new nickname, the "Pirates."

Bierbauer played six seasons for the Pirates and concluded his major league career with the St. Louis Browns (NL) in 1897–1898. He performed for Grand Rapids, MI (WL) in 1899 and in the then-minor AL for Cleveland, OH, Milwaukee, WI, and Buffalo, NY in 1900. In 1901, he moved with Buffalo into the EL and finished the season with Hartford, CT. His playing career concluded in 1902 with Newark, NJ.

The 5-foot 8-inch, 140-pound Bierbauer, who batted left-handed and threw right, hit over .300 in 1889, 1890, and 1894. He ranked fourth in the AA with 105 RBI in 1889, but was better known for his defensive skills. On June 22, 1888, his 12 putouts set a nine-inning-game record unmatched for 78 years. Bierbauer led league second basemen in putouts in 1889, double plays in 1890, fielding average in 1893, and assists in 1888, 1890, 1892, 1894, and 1895. In 1889, 1890, and 1892, he ranked among the top three fielders in his league at all positions.

Bierbauer played all but 19 of his 1,383 major league games at second base, where his fielding ranks eighth all time. His 6.07 chances accepted per game rank third among major league second basemen, while his 2.74 putouts per game and 3.34 assists per game rank fourth. He batted .267 with 1,521 hits and 819 runs scored.

Bierbauer resided in Erie, where he was employed as a brass molder. He died of pneumonia and was survived by his wife, Jennie, and son, Louis.

BIBLIOGRAPHY: Louis Bierbauer file, National Baseball Library, Cooperstown, NY; Richard L. Burtt, *The Pittsburgh Pirates, A Pictorial History* (Virginia Beach, VA, 1977); James Charlton, ed., *The Baseball Chronology* (New York, 1991); Frederick G. Lieb, *The Pittsburgh Pirates*, (New York, 1948); David Nemec, *The Beer and Whisky League* (New York, 1994); *Reach's Official American Association Base Ball Guide 1891* (Philadelphia, PA, 1891); Bob Smizik, *The Pittsburgh Pirates: An Illustrated History* (New York, 1990); Dean A. Sullivan, ed., *Early Innings* (Lincoln, NE, 1995); John Thorn et al., eds., *Total Baseball*, 5th ed. (New York, 1997); Robert L. Tiemann and Mark Rucker, eds., *Nineteenth Century Stars* (Kansas City, MO, 1989).

Frederick Ivor-Campbell

BIGGIO, Craig Alan (b. December 14, 1965, Smithtown, NY), player, is the son of Gordon Biggio and Johnna Biggio. A 5-foot 11-inch, 180-pound second baseman, catcher, and outfielder, Biggio bats and throws right-handed. He graduated from Kings Point, NY High School and attended Seton Hall University, being named All-America in 1987 after batting .407 as a junior.

The Houston Astros (NL) selected Biggio in the first round of the June 1987 free agent draft and assigned him to Class A Asheville, NC (SAL), where he batted .375 as a catcher and outfielder. He opened the 1988 season at Triple A Tucson, AZ (PCL) and later appeared in 50 games for the Houston Astros. In Biggio's first full season (1989) with the Houston Astros, he earned *TSN* Silver Slugger Award as the NL top offensive catcher. He finished second among NL catchers in HR and RBI and led major league catchers with 21 stolen bases. Biggio became the first Astros catcher ever to lead the Astros in batting when he hit .276 in 1990. He also paced Houston in at-bats, hits, and doubles while stealing 25 bases. Besides being the first Astros catcher ever named to the NL All-Star team, Biggio in 1991 led the club in batting for the second straight year with a .295 average.

Houston moved Biggio in 1992 to second base, where he became the first player in major league history to make the All-Star team as a catcher and second baseman. Besides hitting .277, Biggio ranked among NL leaders in runs, walks, and stolen bases and reached career highs in games (162) and walks (94). He batted .287 in 1993, leading the club in games, at-bats, runs, hits, doubles, HR, total bases, and walks. Biggio was selected to the NL All-Star team for the third time in 1994 and paced the NL in stolen bases (39). He shared the NL lead in doubles (44) and batted .318, both career highs. His honors included his first Rawlings Gold Glove Award and being named to *TSN* Silver Slugger team. In 1995, Biggio batted .302 with 77 RBI and 22 HR. He led the NL in runs scored (123), ranked second in on-base percentage (.406), finished third in walks (80), placed fourth in base hits (167), and again was named to the NL All-Star team. He batted .286 in 1996 and .309 in 1997, making the NL All-Star team both years. His 1997 season featured career bests in runs (146) and HR (22, tied) with 191 hits, 81 RBI, and 47 stolen bases, helping Houston win the NL Central title. The Atlanta Braves limited him to just one hit in the NL Division Series. Biggio in 1998 established career highs in batting average (.325), hits (210), and RBI (88), enabling the Astros to repeat as Central Division champions. He batted only .182 in the NL Division Series loss to the San Diego Padres. Biggio made *TSN* All-Star team and Silver Slugger teams in 1995, 1997, and 1998 and won NL Gold Gloves from 1995 through 1997. In 1999, Biggio led the NL with 56 doubles but made only two hits in the NL Division Series.

In 12 seasons with the Houston Astros, Biggio has played in 1,699 games, made 1,868 hits, scored 1,120 runs, and driven in 706 runs with a .292 batting average. He has notched 389 doubles, 38 triples, 152 HR, 796 walks, and 344 stolen bases and has struck out 973 times. He ranked second in games (1,515) and third in hits (1,728) during the 1990s.

Biggio and his wife, Patty, have a son, Connor Joseph, and make their off-season home in Haskell, NJ.

BIBLIOGRAPHY: Craig Biggio file, National Baseball Library, Cooperstown, NY; Chuck Greenwood, "Biggio a Gem in Major League Baseball," *SCD* 23 (November 8, 1996), pp. 90–91; *Houston Astros Media Guide*, 1998; "On Deck," *Sport* 79 (August 1988), p. 79; *TSN Official Baseball Register*, 1998; *USAT Baseball Weekly*, October 4– 10, 1995, pp. 44, 47.

                                                              John L. Evers

BILLINGHAM, John Eugene "Jack," "Cactus Jack" (b. February 21, 1943, Orlando, FL), player and coach, was the most durable, dependable pitcher for the Cincinnati Reds (NL) during their Big Red Machine glory years from 1972 to 1977. He is the son of Jack Billingham and Dorothy (Newton) Billingham and worked in his father's gasoline station in Winter Park, FL. Billingham pitched for Winter Park High School and signed with the Los Angeles Dodgers (NL) organization in 1961. The Dodgers groomed him as a relief pitcher during seven minor league seasons and called him up in 1968. Billingham pitched in 50 games, all but one in relief, with a 3–0 record. The Montreal Expos (NL) selected the 6-foot 4-inch, 195-pound right-hander in the 1969 expansion draft, but traded him in January to the Houston Astros (NL). He spent all of 1969 in the bullpen, but started 24 games with a 13–9 record in 1970.

In November 1971, Houston traded Billingham, Joe Morgan,* and Ceasar Geronimo to the Cincinnati Reds in the multiple-player transaction that solidified the "Big Red Machine." The laid-back Billingham proved that his demeanor did not diminish his competitiveness, posting a six-year record of 87–63 with the Cincinnati Reds. In 1973, he finished 19–10 with a 3.04 ERA and led the NL with 40 starts, seven shutouts, and 293.1 innings pitched, the most innings hurled by a Red in 32 years. In the 1972, 1975, and 1976

World Series, he won two decisions and allowed only one earned run in 25.1 innings. No other pitcher in World Series history hurled at least 25 career innings with an ERA under 0.50. On Opening Day of 1974, Billingham served up Hank Aaron's* record-tying 714th career home run.

Billingham, traded to the Detroit Tigers (AL) in March 1978, posted a 25–15 record during his two-year stay there and ended his major league career in 1980 with the Boston Red Sox (AL). His final career statistics included a 145–113 won–lost record and a 3.83 ERA over 13 major league seasons. He married Jolene Suslar on October 9, 1964 and has a son, John, and daughter, Jennifer. He returned to Winter Park, FL and owned and operated a sporting goods store there from 1981 to 1987 before becoming a minor league pitching coach for the Houston Astros.

BIBLIOGRAPHY: William G. Holder, "Jack Billingham, from 'Throw-In' to Stardom," *BD* 32 (October 1973), pp. 25–29; Donald Honig, *The Cincinnati Reds* (New York, 1992); Greg Rhodes and John Erardi, *Big Red Dynasty* (Cincinnati, OH, 1997); Robert H. Walker, *Cincinnati and the Big Red Machine* (Bloomington, IN, 1988); Floyd Connor and John Snyder, *Day-by-Day in Cincinnati Reds History* (West Point, NY, 1984); Bob Hertzel, *The Big Red Machine* (Englewood Cliffs, NJ, 1976); John Erardi, " 'Cactus Jack' Still Laid Back," *Cincinnati Enquirer*, August 12, 1986, p. C-1.

Richard D. Miller

BISHOP, Max Frederick "Tilly," "Camera Eye" (b. September 5, 1899, Waynesboro, PA; d. February 24, 1962, Waynesboro, PA), player, scout, and coach, was the son of Lulu Bishop and spent 12 years in the AL as a slick-fielding second basemen and sharp-eyed leadoff man.

In 1918 the Baltimore Orioles (IL) signed Bishop out of Baltimore City College, a high school for superior students. Bishop remained the Orioles' second sacker until being sold to the Philadelphia Athletics (AL) after the 1923 season. From 1924 through 1933, he proved a mainstay for Connie Mack's* Philadelphia Athletics and teamed with shortstop Joe Boley to form an outstanding double-play combination. Faced with financial problems, Mack in December 1933 sold Bishop, Lefty Grove,* and Rube Walberg* to the Boston Red Sox (AL) for a reported $125,000 and two players. In Boston, Bishop did not provide the expected strength at second base and shared the position in 1934 and 1935. He completed his playing career with Baltimore, MD (IL) in 1936. After scouting a year for the Detroit Tigers (AL) in 1937, he served as baseball coach at the U.S. Naval Academy from 1938 to 1961. His midshipmen won 306 games and lost only 143.

In 1,338 major league games, Bishop produced 1,216 hits with 236 doubles, 35 triples, and 41 HR. His .271 career batting average included a high of .316 in 1928. He scored 966 runs, batted in 379 runs, and stole 43 bases. In three World Series, he hit only .182 in 18 games. His keen eye at the plate led to his reputation for taking a pitch a quarter inch out of the strike zone. In 1929, he led the AL in walks with 128 and twice drew eight free passes in a doubleheader. He averaged almost a walk a game, recording 1,153 for 1,338 contests. Defensively, Bishop in 1932 set a record of 53 consecutive errorless games by a second baseman, a mark that stood until 1965. He set a record fielding average for a second baseman (.987) in 1926 and then bettered it in 1932 with a .988 mark. He also led the AL second basemen in fielding percentage in 1928.

A longtime resident of Baltimore, Bishop in 1962 returned to his native town of Waynesboro, PA to attend the funeral of his mother, Lulu. While there, he died in his sleep.

BIBLIOGRAPHY: Max Bishop file, National Baseball Library, Cooperstown, NY; James H. Bready, *The Home Team: Baseball in Baltimore*, 3rd ed. (Baltimore, MD, 1979); Al Hirshberg, *The Red Sox, the Bean and the Cod* (Boston, MA, 1947); Frederick G. Lieb, *The Boston Red Sox* (New York, 1947); Frederick Lieb, *Connie Mack* (New York, 1945); Connie Mack, *My 66 Years in the Big Leagues* (Philadelphia, PA, 1950); *NYT*, February 26, 1962; Robert Redmount, *The Red Sox Encyclopedia* (Champaign, IL, 1998); Jerome C. Romanowski, *The Mackmen* (Upper Darby, PA, 1979); *TSN*, March 7, 1962.

Ralph S. Graber

BLACKWELL, Ewell "The Whip" (b. October 23, 1922, Fresno, CA; d. October 29, 1996, Hendersonville, NC), player, batted and threw right-handed with a 6-foot 6-inch, 195-pound frame. The son of Flugin Blackwell, he played baseball and basketball at Bonita High School. After attending the University of California and La Verne Teachers College, he worked at Vultee Aircraft Company in Downey, CA. He played semiprofessional baseball in Downey until the Cincinnati Reds (NL) signed him in 1942 and optioned him to Ogden, UT (PrL). The same year, Blackwell won 15 games for Syracuse, NY (IL). After being drafted in 1943, he spent three years in the U.S. Army.

Blackwell's return to the Cincinnati Reds in 1946 saw him win only nine games, but he led the NL in shutouts with five. Blackwell enjoyed an exceptional year in 1947, leading the NL in victories (22), strikeouts (193), and complete games (23). He recorded 16 consecutive victories, all complete games. The eighth triumph in the streak featured a no-hitter against the Boston Braves on June 18, 1947. In his next start, Blackwell lasted 8.1 innings before surrendering two hits to the Brooklyn Dodgers in the ninth inning. Blackwell compiled several good seasons, but several physical problems limited his effectiveness. His health problems included a sore shoulder in 1948, kidney surgery in 1949, and an emergency appendectomy in 1950, when he still won 17 games and struck out 14 Chicago Cubs in a 10-inning game.

In August 1952, the Cincinnati Reds traded Blackwell to the New York Yankees (AL). He appeared in his only World Series that year, surrendering four earned runs in five innings against the Brooklyn Dodgers. He encountered little success in New York and was voluntarily retired in 1954. He was traded in March 1955 to the Kansas City Athletics (AL), but appeared in only 2 games before permanently retiring. During his 10-year major league career, Blackwell won 82 games, lost 78 decisions, compiled a 3.30 ERA, and recorded 839 strikeouts. The intimidating pitcher used a sidearm motion and threw with exceptional speed in his early seasons. His fastball, virtually unhittable, seemed to explode at the batter from the third base side of the mound. At Syracuse, Blackwell's teammates refused to take batting practice against him. In 1960, fans elected him to the Cincinnati Baseball Hall of Fame. He was named to the NL All-Star team in 1947 and 1951. Blackwell engaged in retail sales for a large distillery in Tampa, FL and Columbia, SC and also worked as a security guard. He resided with his wife, Dottie, in Hendersonville, NC, and had two children.

BIBLIOGRAPHY: Lee Allen, *The Cincinnati Reds* (New York, 1948); Martin Appel, *Yesterday's Heroes* (New York, 1988); *The Baseball Encyclopedia*, 10th ed. (New York, 1996); Ewell Blackwell file, National Baseball Library, Cooperstown, NY; Donald Honig, *Baseball Between the Lines* (New York, 1976); Donald Honig, *The Cincinnati Reds* (New York, 1992); Tom Meany, *Baseball's Greatest Pitchers* (New York, 1951); *NYT Biographical Service* 27 (October 1996), p. 1588; Ritter Collett, *The Cincinnati Reds* (Virginia Beach, VA, 1976); Bob Rathgeber, *Cincinnati Reds Scrapbook* (Virginia Beach, VA, 1982); Joseph L. Reichler, ed., *The Great All-Time Baseball Record Book* (New York, 1981); Rich Westcott, *Diamond Greats* (Westport, CT, 1988); Lonnie Wheeler and John Baskin, *The Cincinnati Game* (Wilmington, OH, 1988).

Horace R. Givens

BLAIR, Paul L. D. (b. February 1, 1944, Cushing, OK), player, attended East Los Angeles, CA JC and signed with the New York Mets (NL) in 1962. The Baltimore Orioles (AL) drafted him November 1962. His speed and defensive abilities impressed Elmira, NY (EL) manager Earl Weaver,* who called him "a winning player." From 1964 to 1976, Blair dominated center field for the Baltimore Orioles. After batting .277 in 1966, Blair made just one hit in his first World Series against the Los Angeles Dodgers. His HR won the third game, 1–0, for pitcher Wally Bunker. Blair batted .293 and led the AL with 12 triples in 1967. Oriole manager Hank Bauer* compared Blair to Curt Flood* of the St. Louis Cardinals. Blair regularly spoke at Baltimore schools, often led the Orioles' basketball team in scoring, and averaged in the lower 80s as a golfer.

Blair performed solidly for several great Baltimore Oriole teams, playing in the 1966, 1969, 1970, and 1971 World Series. His defensive skills commanded admiration. He recalled, "I can tell by the batter's swing where the ball is going to go." But misfortune also intervened. After breaking his ankle playing winter ball in Puerto Rico, Blair batted only .211 in 1968. On May 31, 1970, a pitch from Ken Tatum of the California Angels almost crushed his left cheekbone and eye socket. Blair became timid at the plate, but the counsel of Dr. Jacob Conn, a hypnotherapist, relaxed him. He tried switch-hitting at 1971 spring training, but dropped the experiment. When Blair clouted a three-run HR off Tatum in September 1973, his recovery was assured. He made the 1969 and 1973 AL All-Star teams. The Baltimore Orioles traded him to the New York Yankees (AL) in January 1977, enabling him to play in their 1977 and 1978 World Series. Overall, he batted .288 in 28 World Series games and .250 with 620 RBI in 1,947 regular season games. Star center fielder Jimmy Piersall* called Blair "the best defensive center fielder I've ever seen."

Blair married Evelyn Cohen on April 16, 1965.

BIBLIOGRAPHY: Steve O'Neill, "Blair, Blefary—Birds' Boom-Boom Boys," *TSN*, May 8, 1965; Doug Brown, "Blair Despite Broken Ankle Would Play Winter Ball Again," *TSN*, January 20, 1968; Doug Brown, "Speedy Blair Steps Out Front in Oriole Center Field Derby," *TSN*, April 3, 1965; Phil Jackman, "Only Fences Can Hold Orioles' Flychaser Blair," *TSN*, April 4, 1970; Lou Hatter, "Blair Regains Star Route with Aid of Hypnotist," *TSN*, July 14, 1973; Phil Pepe, "Yanks' Blair Makes Martin Look Like a Genius," *TSN*, July 16, 1977; James H. Bready, *Baseball in Baltimore* (Baltimore, MD, 1998); Ted Patterson, *The Baltimore Orioles* (Dallas, TX, 1995); John Thorn et al., eds., *Total Baseball*, 5th ed. (New York, 1997); Mike Shatzkin, ed., *The Ballplayers* (New York, 1990); *TSN Official Baseball Register*, 1981; *WWIB 1979*, 64th ed.

William J. Miller

BLASS, Stephen Robert "Steve" (b. April 18, 1942, Canaan, CT), player and sportscaster, is the son of Warren J. "Bob" Blass, a Falls Village, CT plumber, and Rose Blass and has two brothers and a sister. He played Little League baseball and attended Housatonic Valley Regional High School in Falls Village, where he pitched five no-hitters.

The Pittsburgh Pirates (NL) signed Blass as a free agent in 1960 for a $4,000 bonus. In 1960, he pitched seven games with Kingsport, TN (ApL) and five contests for Dubuque, IA (ML). The following season, he won 13 and lost six for Batavia, NY (NYPL). After beginning 1962 with Asheville, NC (SAL), Blass then won 17 and lost three with a league-leading 1.97 ERA for Kinston, NC (CrL). He struck out a league-leading 209 in 178 innings and led the CrL with eight shutouts. In 1963, he won 11 and lost eight for the Pirates' top farm team in Columbus, OH (IL). He divided the 1964 season between Columbus and the Pittsburgh Pirates, spent 1965 in Columbus, and then made the Pirates to stay in 1966.

After two mediocre years with the Pittsburgh Pirates, Blass in 1968 compiled 18 wins and only six losses for a NL-leading .750 winning percentage and a 2.12 ERA. His ERA more than doubled when the mound was lowered in 1969, but he still notched 16 wins against only 10 defeats. The Pirates won the NL's Eastern Division in 1970, as he lowered his ERA to 3.52 while registering only 10 wins against 12 losses.

The 1971 and 1972 seasons marked Blass' finest campaigns. In 1971 the

6-foot 1-inch, 170-pound right-hander won 15 games and lost only eight decisions with a 2.85 ERA, leading the Pittsburgh Pirates' staff with 240 innings pitched. After two rough outings in the NL Championship Series against the San Francisco Giants, he pitched two complete-game victories in the World Series against the Baltimore Orioles. His 2–1 triumph clinched the deciding seventh game. The next season, he won 19 and lost only eight with a 2.48 ERA. The Pittsburgh Pirates again won the Eastern Division, but lost to the Cincinnati Reds in the NL Championship Series. Blass' unassuming nature and exuberant style made him a popular figure. He put so much effort into his pitches that his hat would fly off and he would end up prone beside the mound. At the end of a victorious game, he would shake hands excitedly with everybody he could reach.

Then Blass' control deserted him. In 1973 he finished just 3–9 with a 9.85 ERA, worst in the NL. In 1974 the Pirates assigned him to Charleston, WV (IL) to work on his delivery, but he struggled with a 2–8 mark and 9.74 ERA. He unsuccessfully tried wearing glasses, modifying his delivery, and even working with a hypnotist. The Pirates waived him in March 1975 after he posted an 0–2 record with a 17.51 ERA in 6.2 innings in spring training. His career major league record included 103 wins, 76 losses, and a 3.63 ERA.

Blass married Karen Louise Lamb on October 5, 1964 and has two sons. His brother-in-law, John Lamb, also pitched professionally. He subsequently worked for a jewelry company and ran baseball camps before becoming a Pirates broadcaster in 1986.

Blass exhibited unaffected joy in his success, with the image of him leaping into the arms of his catcher after getting the last out of the 1971 World Series being constantly reprinted in Pittsburgh. He also demonstrated grace when his pitching talent suddenly and inexplicably disappeared. Nobody begrudges the success he has enjoyed since retiring as a player.

BIBLIOGRAPHY: Steve Blass file, National Baseball Library, Cooperstown, NY; Roger Angell, *Five Seasons: A Baseball Companion* (New York, 1977); John T. Bird, *Twin Killing: The Bill Mazeroski Story* (Birmingham, AL, 1995); Richard L. Burtt, *The Pittsburgh Pirates, A Pictorial History* (Virginia Beach, VA, 1977); Christopher Fletcher, "Battling Bucs," *Pittsburgh* (October 1996), pp. 78–81; Pat Jordan, "Pitcher in Search of a Pitch," *SI* 40 (April 15, 1974), pp. 64–66; *The Baseball Encyclopedia*, 10th ed. (New York, 1996); Bob Smizik, *The Pittsburgh Pirates: An Illustrated History* (New York, 1990).

Luther W. Spoehr

BLUE, Luzerne Atwell "Lu" (b. March 5, 1897, Washington, DC; d. July 28, 1958, Alexandria, VA), player, was the seventh son of Charles Blue, a strict clerk in the U.S. Government Printing Office. His father, of German descent, whipped him for playing hookey from school to watch the Washington Senators (AL) play. After attending two years of high school, Blue learned to play baseball at Briarly Hall Military School in Poolsville, MD.

Blue matriculated there for three years, but left before graduating to play professional baseball in Martinsburg, WV (BRL) in 1916. Blue's parents denied him permission to play baseball, but he played anyway. Blue once hit successive grand-slam HR while switch-hitting late in a game.

The Detroit Tigers (AL) drafted Blue in 1917. Tigers manager Hugh Jennings* brought him up briefly at the end of the 1917 season, but returned him to St. Paul, MN (AA) before he appeared in a major league game. In 1918, he joined Portland, OR (PCL). Blue entered the military service and served with the U.S. Army at Camp Lee, VA until the Armistice was signed in 1919. The Detroit Tigers recalled him toward the end of the 1919 season and then returned him to Portland.

In 1921, Blue played in 153 games for Detroit Tigers manager Ty Cobb.* Blue developed a reputation for being "difficult" in Detroit, often fighting with his teammates. Cobb rode him unmercifully. His next manager, George Moriarty, accused Blue of malingering and once benched him for Johnny Neun, who had a broken hand. Although some unpleasant memories marked his days in a Tiger uniform, Blue always considered the Tigers his team.

Blue, a hustler, possessed an easy grace around first base in the style of George Sisler.* The 5-foot 10-inch, 165 pounder scrapped, possessed good speed, and hit from both sides of the plate. Blue, a scientific hitter, studied pitchers and often acted on the insights offered by Cobb. In December 1927, Blue was traded to the St. Louis Browns (AL) with future National Baseball Hall of Famer "Heinie" Manush* for Elam Vangilder and two other players.

Dan Howley of the St. Louis Browns helped Blue regain his lost confidence, but Blue's teams usually suffered losses. Blue was sold to the Chicago White Sox (AL) for $15,000 in April 1931. After one at bat with the Brooklyn Dodgers (NL) in 1933, Blue ended his 13-year major league career. His last baseball venture, a diamond school, closed in 1940. Blue married Pauline Chambers in 1924. In 1941, the childless couple retired to a chicken farm in Cloverly, VA to raise New Hampshire Reds.

Blue hit .300 or better in four of his first five major league seasons, including a career high of .311 in 1924. During his major league career, Blue wore four different major league uniforms. He played in 1,571 games at first base and just one contest in the outfield, hitting 44 career HR, batting .287, and making 1,696 hits, 319 doubles, and 109 triples. Blue scored 1,151 runs, knocked in 695 runs, walked 1,092 times, and fanned just 436 times, a fantastic ratio. His batting eye often was compared with that of the legendary Max Bishop* of the Philadelphia A's (AL). Blue also stole 151 bases.

BIBLIOGRAPHY: Lu Blue file, National Baseball Library, Cooperstown, NY; Charles C. Alexander, *Ty Cobb* (New York, 1984); *The Baseball Encyclopedia*, 10th ed. (New York, 1996); Bill Borst, ed., *Ables to Zoldak*, vol. 1 (St. Louis, MO, 1988); Bill Borst, *Still Last in the American League* (West Bloomfield, MI, 1992); Frederick G. Lieb, *The Detroit Tigers* (New York, 1946); Joe Falls, *Detroit Tigers* (New York, 1975); Fred

Smith, *995 Tigers* (Detroit, MI, 1981); Ira L. Smith, *Baseball's Famous First Basemen* (New York, 1956).

William A. Borst

BLUE, Vida Rochelle, Jr. (b. July 28, 1949, Mansfield, LA), player, is the son of Vida Rochelle Meschach Abednego Blue, Sr. and Sallie (Henderson) Blue. His father, an iron foundry worker, died during Vida's senior year at Desoto High School. Blue, who led his school to district championships in both football and baseball that year, declined many football scholarship offers to sign with the Kansas City Athletics (AL) partly to help support his family.

The A's selected Blue in the second round of the free agent draft in 1967 and signed him for a bonus reportedly between $28,000 and $50,000. He pitched for Burlington, IA (ML) in 1968 and for Birmingham, AL (SL) in 1969. Blue started the 1970 season with Iowa (AA), where he compiled the league's best winning percentage and strikeout record. He finished with the Oakland A's (AL), hurling one- and no-hitters in his two decisions. Altogether, he compiled five career one-hitters and four two-hitters.

The 6-foot, 190-pound left-handed fastballer pitched regularly for the Oakland A's from 1971 to 1977. In 1971 he compiled a 24–8 record, leading the AL in shutouts with 8 and in ERA with 1.82. He won both the Cy Young* and AL MVP awards and was named *TSN* AL Pitcher of the Year. Blue experienced a losing season in 1972, when he did not start pitching until May 24 because of a salary dispute with owner Charles O. Finley.* He posted winning records the next four years, winning 20 in 1973 and 22 in 1975. Blue appeared in five AL Championship Series from 1971 to 1975, posting a 1–2 record, and pitched in three World Series without recording a win. A six-time All-Star, he won twice and became the only pitcher to win for each league.

In 1978, Blue was traded to the San Francisco Giants (NL) for seven players and $390,000. He initially was paid $205,000, but the Giants in 1979 gave him a new pact reportedly worth $750,000 per year. With the best won–lost record on the Giants' staff, he was named *TSN* 1978 NL Pitcher of the Year. The Giants traded him in 1982 to the Kansas City Royals (AL), where he pitched until August 5, 1983.

Blue, who is single and lives in Pleasanton, CA, worked in public relations for Pakon Industries in Union City, CA in 1984. He played winter ball in 1984 for Ponce and Arecibo (PRWL) and compiled an 8–8 mark in 1985 and a 10–10 record in 1986 with the San Francisco Giants.

Blue, known primarily for his moving fastball, compiled a 209–161 record with a 3.26 ERA, 2,175 strikeouts, and 35 shutouts. During Blue's first full season in the majors, attendance at Oakland and other AL cities increased markedly for his appearances. He similarly affected Giants' attendance in 1978.

Blue made numerous speaking appearances as community representative for the San Francisco Giants from 1990 to 1996 and was inducted into the Bay Area Sports Hall of Fame in 1995.

BIBLIOGRAPHY: Vida Blue file, National Baseball Library, Cooperstown, NY; "Baseball's Amazing Vida Blue," *Ebony* 26 (September 1971), pp. 95–99; Bill Ballew, "Vida Blue," *SCD* 23 (April 26, 1996), pp. 170–172; Roy Blount, "Humming a Rhapsody in Blue," *SI 35* (July 12, 1971), pp. 22–27; Vida Blue, "Next Year Is Going to Be Different," *Ebony* 27 (October 1972), pp. 132–138; *CB* (1972), pp. 39–41; Jack Hicks, "Unwinding with Vida Blue," *Sport* 68 (June 1979), pp. 70–76; Larry Keith, "These Giants Are Jolly Blue," *SI* 48 (May 29, 1978), pp. 22–23; Robert E. Kelley, *Baseball's Best* (Jefferson, NC, 1988); Bruce Markusen, *Baseball's Last Dynasty* (New York, 1998); Nick Peters, *Giants Almanac* (Berkeley CA, 1988); *The Baseball Encyclopedia*, 10th ed. (New York, 1996); *TSN Official Baseball Register, 1984*; *TSN*, October 17, 1983, p. 24, January 21, 1985, pp. 35, 45; Wells Twombly, "How to Throw the Ultimate Fast Ball," *NYT Magazine* (July 25, 1971), pp. 22–24; *WWA*, 42nd ed. (1982–1983), p. 306; Ken Young, *Cy Young Award Winners* (New York, 1994).

Gaymon L. Bennett

BLUEGE, Oswald Louis "Ossie" (b. October 24, 1900, Chicago, IL; d. October 14, 1985, Edina, MN), player, coach, manager, and executive, spent his entire baseball life with Clark Griffith and Calvin Griffith.* No other Washington Senator (AL) played in the club's three World Series. The son of Adam Bluege and Olga (Gothe) Bluege, he completed Hammond Elementary School and then joined the accounting department at International Harvester Company. The starting shortstop for the St. Mark's Lutheran Church team at age 14, he advanced to Chicago's famous semiprofessional Logan Squares and then secured his father's consent to join the Peoria, IL Tractors (3IL) in 1920. The Washington Senators bought him two years later for $3,500 and paid him a $2,000 salary.

Shortstop Bluege (pronounced *Blu*-ghy) combined with second baseman Bucky Harris* for six double plays in his first spring exhibition game in 1922, but Roger Peckinpaugh,* newly arrived from the Boston Red Sox (AL), was slated to be the Senators' regular shortstop. After a 19-game trial at third base, Bluege was sent to Minneapolis, MN (AA) to improve his hitting. He hiked his batting average to .313 and once handled a record 27 chances during a doubleheader. Recalled in 1923, he began a string of 17 consecutive seasons as infield anchor for the Washington Senators. Consistent and reliable although lacking flash or color, Bluege performed the third base duties expertly. Teammate Luke Sewell* judged him the best third baseman ever ahead of Brooks Robinson.* In time, Bluege helped Cecil Travis* and Buddy Lewis* to learn the third base position, moved to shortstop when Joe Cronin* was traded to the Boston Red Sox (AL), and backed up Buddy Myer* at second base. From 1934 on, Bluege wore glasses.

Bluege's .272 career major league batting average covered from 1922 to

1939. In 1,867 games, he made 1,751 hits and 43 HR, scored 883 runs, and drove in 848 runs. Defensively, he led AL third basemen four times in assists, twice in double plays, and once for fielding average. He never exceeded his 1929 salary of $10,000. Bluege served as a Washington Senators coach from 1940 to 1942 and was their manager from 1943 to 1947. He produced a small miracle in his first managerial season, elevating Harris's seventh-place finishers to second place. Overall, Bluege compiled a 375–394 record as manager before Joe Kuhel* succeeded him in 1948. Clark Griffith appointed Bluege as his farm system supervisor.

Off-season, Bluege earned accounting and business administration degrees from several institutions, including LaSalle Extension University of Chicago. Clark Griffith tried to halt Bluege's academic studies, fearing that his third baseman would lose his batting eye. Calvin Griffith appointed him club comptroller, a position he held with Washington and with the Minnesota Twins (AL) from 1957 until his retirement in 1971. Bluege married Wilor Marie Maxwell in 1940 following the death of his first wife and had three daughters. His younger brother, Otto, played shortstop for the Cincinnati Reds (NL) in 1933.

BIBLIOGRAPHY: Thomas Aylesworth and Benton Minks, *The Encyclopedia of Baseball Managers* (New York, 1990); *The Baseball Encyclopedia*, 10th ed. (New York, 1996); Oswald Bluege file, National Baseball Library, Cooperstown, NY; Morris Bealle, *The Washington Senators* (Washington, DC, 1947); Paul Green, *Forgotten Fields* (Waupaca, WI, 1984); Donald Honig, *The Man in the Dugout* (Lincoln, NE, 1995); Walter M. Langford, *Legends of Baseball* (South Bend, IN, 1987); Jane Levy, "Ossie Bluege: The Quirkless Man," *TNP* 6 (Winter 1987), pp. 18–21; Henry W. Thomas, *Walter Johnson* (Washington, DC, 1995); Shirley Povich, *The Washington Senators* (New York, 1954); John Thorn et al., eds., *Total Baseball*, 5th ed. (New York, 1997).

A. D. Suehsdorf

BLYLEVEN, Rik Aalbert "Bert" (b. April 6, 1951, Zeist, The Netherlands), player, coach, and sportscaster, was one of seven children born to Joseph Blyleven. At Santiago High School in Garden Grove, CA, he excelled in cross-country, basketball, and baseball. Following graduation in 1969, Blyleven was selected as a pitcher in the third round of the June free-agent draft by the Minnesota Twins (AL). His two partial minor league seasons included seven games with Sarasota, FL (GCL) and six games with Orlando, FL (FSL) in 1969 and eight games with Evansville, IN (AA) in 1970.

The 6-foot 3-inch, 205-pound right-handed Blyleven joined the Minnesota Twins early in 1970. In 27 games, he compiled a 10–9 record and 3.18 ERA, struck out 135 batters in 164 innings, and was named *TSN* AL Rookie Pitcher of the Year. Blyleven pitched for five different teams, including the Minnesota Twins (AL, 1970–1976, 1985–1988), Texas Rangers (AL, 1976–1977), Pittsburgh Pirates (NL, 1978–1980), Cleveland Indians (AL, 1981–1985), and California Angels (AL, 1989–1992). His best statistical year came in 1973, when he led the AL in shutouts (9), placed second in strikeouts (258), ERA (2.52), and fewest walks per 9 innings (1.86), finished third in complete games (25) and strikeouts per 9 innings (1.86), and was the losing pitcher in the All-Star Game.

In 22 major league seasons, Blyleven appeared in 692 regular-season games, won 287 contests, lost 250 decisions, pitched in 4,970 innings, compiled a 3.31 ERA, struck out 3,701 batters, walked 1,293 batters, and surrendered 4,632 hits. He participated in the AL Championship Series in 1970 and 1987 and the NL Championship Series in 1979, compiling a 3–0 record. He pitched in two World Series, winning one game for the Pittsburgh Pirates against the Baltimore Orioles in 1979 and splitting two decisions for the Minnesota Twins against the St. Louis Cardinals in 1987. On September 22, 1977, Blyleven pitched a no-hitter against the California Angels. Blyleven ranks third in strikeouts (3,701), seventh in HR allowed (430), and ninth in shutouts (60) on baseball's all-time list. Blyleven underwent two shoulder operations for tears in his right rotator cuff, sidelining him for the 1991 season, and retired after a sub-par 1992 season.

Blyleven serves as a color television analyst for the Minnesota Twins and works for Midwest Sports Channel in Minneapolis, MN. He also was employed as a pitching coach for Cedar Rapids, IA (ML) in 1994 and as president of Up Front Sports and Entertainment in Anaheim, CA. Blyleven married Patricia Ann Whitehead and has four children, Todd, Tim, Tom, and Kim.

BIBLIOGRAPHY: Bert Blyleven file, National Baseball Library, Cooperstown, NY; Dave Moina and Dave Jarzyna, *Twenty-five Seasons* (Minneapolis, MN, 1986); Bob Smizik, *The Pittsburgh Pirates: An Illustrated History* (New York, 1990); Terry Pluto, *The Curse of Rocky Colavito* (New York, 1994); *The Baseball Encyclopedia*, 10th ed. (New York, 1996); Ross Forman, "Bert Blyleven," *SCD* 23 (May 31, 1996), pp. 80–82; Robert Obojski, "Blyleven Eligible for HOF Consideration," *SCD* 25 (January 2, 1998), p. 130; Robert E. Kelley, *Baseball's Best* (Jefferson, NC, 1988); Jack Torry, *Endless Summers* (South Bend, IN, 1995); Rick Weinberg, "Profile," *Sport* 81 (November 1990), p. 12; Steve Wulf, "Baseball's Dutch Treat," *SI* 62 (January 28, 1985), pp. 80–84ff.

James E. Welch

BODDICKER, Michael James "Mike" (b. August 23, 1957, Cedar Rapids, IA), player, is the son of Mary (Emanuel) Boddiker and was a 5-foot 11-inch, 172-pound pitcher who threw and batted right-handed. He grew up in Norway, IA, a farming community, and labored for a mere $4.50 daily wage at the local grain elevator. Boddiker played baseball and basketball at Norway High School. The Baltimore Orioles (AL) signed him in 1978.

Boddicker reached the major leagues in 1983, but sprained his ankle that spring and was optioned to Rochester, NY (IL). The Baltimore Orioles recalled him just weeks later. He responded with a 16–8 record and 2.77 ERA in 1983, becoming the first rookie to pace the AL in shutouts (5) in 57 years.

He won 12 of his last 16 decisions, leading Baltimore to the World Series title. Boddicker, who possessed a smoothly "efficient," effortless delivery, did not overpower hitters. He caught hitters offstride by varying his speeds, fanning 120 batters in 179 innings. His fastball, used sparingly, consequently proved that much more effective. He defeated the Chicago White Sox, 4–0, in the AL Championship Series, and the Philadelphia Phillies, 4–1, in the World Series. Appreciative manager Joe Altobelli* lauded Boddicker's performance as "a fantastic job."

After being named the AL's Rookie of the Year for 1983, Boddicker in 1984 led the AL in victories with a 20–11 mark and in ERA (2.79) and made the AL All-Star squad. Astute Oriole pitching coach Ray Miller observed, "He's such an intelligent kid. He can take what he has on any given day and win with it . . . like Jim Palmer.*" But Boddiker had achieved all except one of his AL leading marks by 1984. In July 1988, the Baltimore Orioles traded Boddicker to the Boston Red Sox (AL). He started once in each of the AL Championship Series for 1988 and 1990, losing both times. After compiling a 17–8 record and earning a Gold Glove Award in 1990, Boddiker signed with the Kansas City Royals (AL) for two years and finished his major league career with the Milwaukee Brewers (AL) in 1993. Drawing upon a work ethic from his rural American Midwest origins, he posted a major league career total of 134 wins and 116 defeats and 3.80 ERA.

BIBLIOGRAPHY: Mike Boddiker file, National Baseball Library, Cooperstown, NY; James H. Bready, *Baseball in Baltimore* (Baltimore, MD, 1998); Ted Patterson, *The Baltimore Orioles* (Dallas, TX, 1995); Peter Golenbock, *Fenway* (New York, 1992); John Thorn et al., eds., *Total Baseball*, 5th ed. (New York, 1997); *The Baseball Encyclopedia*, 10th ed. (New York, 1996); David S. Neft et al., eds., *The Sports Encyclopedia: Baseball, 1996*, 16th ed. (New York, 1996); Mike Shatzkin, ed., *The Ballplayers* (New York, 1990); *WWIB, 1993*, 78th ed.; *TSN*, November 7, 1983; *TSN*, September 24, 1984, p. 20; *TSN*, August 8, 1988; *TSN Official Baseball Register, 1994*.

William J. Miller

BOGGESS, Lynton Ross "Dusty" (b. June 7, 1904, Terrell, TX; d. July 8, 1968, Dallas, TX), umpire, player, manager, executive, and scout, was the son of Henry R. Boggess, a former minor league pitcher who operated a variety store, and Mattie Elizabeth Boggess. A multiple sports star at Waco High School, Boggess was ruled ineligible for sports competition his senior year after playing semipro baseball for Cleburne, TX (TOL) as "Dusty Bogus." After graduating in 1922, Boggess, whose nickname came from the habit of dusting his hands with dirt before going to bat and wiping them on his hair, signed with the St. Louis Cardinals (NL). Although originally a third baseman, the versatile performer frequently played every position during a game. In 1932 he became manager and part-owner of Muskogee, OK (WA), but the club went bankrupt during the season. He ended his playing career in 1934 as a catcher, leading Galveston, TX (TL) to the pennant.

A high school and college sports official, Boggess began his professional umpiring career in 1939 with Class D WL and advanced the next year to the Class A TL. He enlisted in the U.S. Navy in 1942, but soon received a medical discharge and in 1943 umpired in the Class AA IL. Boggess joined the NL in 1944, but retired because of "ill health" after the 1948 season. He soon recovered, joining the Class AAA AA in 1949 and returning to the NL that September.

Boggess, who stood 5-foot 11-inches and weighed 228 pounds, battled various health problems ranging from excessive weight to high blood pressure throughout his 18-year career. Although tough-minded and outspoken, he used a keen sense of humor and engaging personality to establish good relations with players and managers. Fred Fleig, the NL's supervisor of umpires, declared, "Dusty has to be the greatest diplomat in handling situations on the field of any umpire I have ever seen." Boggess, who umpired five All-Star games (1946, 1952, 1955, and both 1960 games) and four World Series (1940, 1952, 1956, 1960), retired after learning in January 1963 that he had been selected to receive the first annual Bill Klem* Award as the most outstanding NL umpire.

Subsequently, Boggess scouted for the Chicago White Sox (AL) and the Pittsburgh Steelers (NFL) and performed public relations for the Lone Star Brewery, which published his autobiography *Kill the Ump!* (1966). After being divorced in 1938, he married Manalee Wilmeth on October 20, 1942. He had no children. Boggess died of a lung ailment and, as stipulated in his will, was buried with a souvenir baseball autographed by every umpire he had worked with during his major league career.

BIBLIOGRAPHY: Dusty Boggess file, National Baseball Library, Cooperstown, NY; U.S. Census, 1910: Texas, Vol. 97, ED 88, Sheet 9; Dusty Boggess as told to Ernie Helm, *Kill the Ump! My Life in Baseball* (San Antonio, TX, 1966); *TSN*, March 23, 1963, pp. 3, 6; *NYT*, July 9, 1968, p. 39; *TSN*, July 20, 1968, p. 42.

Larry R. Gerlach

BOGGS, Wade Anthony (b. June 15, 1958, Omaha, NE), player, was reared in Tampa, FL by his parents Win Boggs, a U.S. Air Force master sergeant and semiprofessional softball player, and Sue Boggs. His heavy hitting at Tampa's Plant High School outshone his mediocre fielding and slowness afoot and earned him selection by the Boston Red Sox (AL) in the seventh round of the June 1976 free agent draft. The 6-foot 2-inch, 197-pound third baseman rose slowly through Boston's farm system with stops at Class A Elmira, NY (NYPL) in 1976 and Winston-Salem, NC (CrL) in 1977, Class AA Bristol, CT (EL) in 1978–1979, and Class AAA Pawtucket, RI (IL) in 1980–1981. His .335 batting average led the IL in 1981.

After being promoted to the Boston Red Sox in 1982, Boggs became the regular third baseman when Carney Lansford* was injured in late June. Although Boggs recorded too few plate appearances to qualify for the AL batting title, his .349 batting average surpassed official titlist Willie Wilson* by 17 points. Boggs shifted to first base when Lansford returned to the lineup, but returned to third base after Lansford was traded to the Oakland Athletics in December 1982.

From 1983 through 1989, Boggs, who bats left-handed and throws right-handed, led the AL five times in batting (1983, 1985–1988, with a career high of .368 in 1985); six times in on-base percentage (1983, 1985–1989); twice in doubles (1988, 1989), walks (1986, 1988), and runs scored (1988, 1989); and once in hits (240 in 1985), the most for a major leaguer since 1930). In 1985, he set an AL record with 187 singles and tied the major league record by hitting safely in 135 games. His seven consecutive 200-hit seasons (1983–1989) rank him second only to Willie Keeler's* eight. From 1986 to 1989, Boggs became the first major leaguer ever to record four consecutive seasons with both 200 hits and 100 walks. He also holds the modern major league record for most consecutive seasons (7) with at least 200 hits (1983–1989). For six years (1983–1988), Boggs ranked among the four most valuable AL players in *Total Baseball*'s ranking. His rankings included first place in 1987 and second place in 1988.

Boggs attracted the attention of the nonbaseball public in June 1988, when he was sued for breach of contract by California real estate broker Margo Adams. Boggs had broken off a romantic liaison with Adams. Her suit was unsuccessful, but Boggs's celebrity status grew when Adams detailed their affair in *Penthouse* magazine. Boggs and his wife, Deborah Bertercelli, whom he had married in 1976, appeared on network television to affirm the renewed solidity of their marriage.

Boggs's offensive production plummeted to a career low .259 batting average in 1992 partly because of eyesight problems. The Boston Red Sox consequently lost interest in him. In December 1992, the New York Yankees (AL) signed free agent Boggs. During the strike-shortened 1994 season, he batted .342 with 11 HR and 55 RBI to help the New York Yankees capture first place in the AL East Division and won his first Gold Glove award. Boggs batted .324 in 1995 and .311 in 1996 and led AL third basemen with a .970 fielding percentage in 1993 and a .981 fielding percentage in 1995. Although hitting only .292 in 1997, he batted a sizzling .429 in the AL Division Series against the Cleveland Indians. The Tampa Bay Devil Rays (AL) selected him in the November 1997 expansion draft. On August 7, 1999, Boggs homered off Chris Haney of the Cleveland Indians to become the 22nd major leaguer with 3,000 career hits and the first to reach that milestone with an HR. In November 1999, Boggs became special assistant to Tampa Bay's general manager.

In 18 major league seasons, Boggs compiled a .328 batting average with 3,010 hits, 578 doubles, 118 HR, and 1,014 RBI. He appeared in 12 All-Star games (1985–1996), three AL Division Series (1995–1997), four AL

Championship Series (1986, 1988, 1990, 1996), and two World Series, batting .290 in 1986 against the New York Mets and .273 in 1996 against the Atlanta Braves.

The Boggses have one daughter, Meagann, and one son, Brett. His literary credits include an autobiography, a batting instructional, and *Fowl Tips*, a collection of his mother's and wife's chicken recipes.

BIBLIOGRAPHY: Wade Boggs file, National Baseball Library, Cooperstown, NY; Jack Lautier, *Fenway Voices* (Camden, ME, 1990); Wade Boggs, *Boggs!* (Chicago, IL, 1986); Wade Boggs and David Brisson, *The Techniques of Modern Hitting* (New York, 1990); *CB* (1990), pp. 66–70; Peter Gammons, "Pretty Fair for a Fowl Guy," *SI* 64 (April 14, 1986), pp. 44–46; Danny Knobler, "Baseball's Best Leadoff Hitters," *Sport* 81 (July 1990), pp. 40–42; Ed Lucas and Paul Post, "3,000 Hits Is Boggs' Goal," *SCD* 25 (November 27, 1998), p. 146; *NYT Biographical Service* 17 (October 1986), pp. 1237–1238; R. Wetzsteon, "The Loneliness of the .351 Hitter," *Sport* 77 (July 1986), pp. 36–37ff; Chuck Scoggins, "Wade Boggs' Hidden .400 Season," *BRJ* 20 (1991), p. 57; Robert Redmont, *The Red Sox Encyclopedia* (Champaign, IL, 1998); Peter Golenbock, *Fenway* (New York, 1992); Dan Shaughnessy, *One Strike Away* (New York, 1987); Dan Shaughnessy, *The Curse of the Bambino* (New York, 1990); John Thom, *Champion Batsman of the 20th Century* (Los Angeles, CA, 1992); E. M. Swift, "Facing the Music," *SI* 70 (March 6, 1989), pp. 38–40, 45; John Thorn et al., eds., *Total Baseball*, 5th ed. (New York, 1997).

Frederick Ivor-Campbell

BOND, Thomas Henry "Tommy" (b. April 2, 1856, Granard, Ireland; d. January 24, 1941, Boston, MA), player and manager, became a successful right-handed pitcher in professional baseball's early years and one of the sport's first immigrant ballplayers. In 1874, Bond began his 10-year career with the Brooklyn Atlantics (NA). Pitching his team's entire 55 games, Bond led the NA with 32 losses. During his first season with Hartford, CT, Bond in 1876 blossomed into one of baseball's premier pitchers. His 31 victories represented the NL's third best, while his 1.68 ERA came out fourth best. The small 5-foot 7-inch, 160-pound Bond led the NL in strikeout average, earning his reputation as a "cannon ball" thrower.

From 1877 to 1880, Bond excelled as the chief pitcher for the highly successful Boston Red Stockings (NL). Besides hurling over 490 innings annually, Bond consistently ranked among NL leaders in strikeouts and ERA. From 1877 to 1879, he won 40 or more games and led the NL in shutouts. No other major league pitcher since 1876 has compiled at least 40 victories in three consecutive seasons. Despite using a more natural underhand motion, Bond apparently developed a sore arm. He continued pitching in 1881, 1882, and 1884, but lost most of his effectiveness. In the twilight of his career, Bond sought to remain in the game as a manager. He directed the Worcester, MA (NL) Ruby Legs during the 1882 season, but was released after his weak team won only 5 of 27 games. Unlike many contemporary players, Bond made a successful transition to a second career. After briefly working in the leather business and coaching the Harvard varsity nine, he was employed for 35 years in the Boston city tax assessor's office. He tutored aspiring Boston-area hurlers, including John Clarkson* and Timothy Keefe.*

BIBLIOGRAPHY: Thomas Bond file, National Baseball Library, Cooperstown, NY; Gary Caruso, *The Braves Encyclopedia* (Philadelphia, PA, 1995); Harold Kaese, *The Boston Braves* (New York, 1948); *The Baseball Encyclopedia*, 10th ed. (New York, 1996); Robert L. Tiemann and Mark Rucker, eds., *Nineteenth Century Stars* (Kansas City, MO, 1989); John Thorn et al., eds., *Total Braves* (New York, 1996); Al Hirshberg, *Braves, the Pick and the Shovel* (Boston, MA, 1948); *NYT*, January 26, 1941.

Gordon B. McKinney

BONDS, Barry Lamar (b. July 24, 1964, Riverside, CA), player, is the son of Bobby Bonds,* a former major league baseball player, and Pat Bonds. The 6-foot 1-inch, 190-pound left-handed outfielder graduated from Serra High School in San Mateo, CA and attended Arizona State University, where he hit .347 with 45 HR, 175 RBI, and 57 stolen bases during three seasons. In June 1985, the Pittsburgh Pirates (NL) signed Bonds as their first-round selection in the free agent draft and sixth player taken overall.

After spending only 115 games in the minor leagues, Bonds joined the Pittsburgh Pirates in May 1986. During the 1986 season, he led all rookie NL players in HR (16), RBI (48), stolen bases (36), and walks (65). Pittsburgh Pirates manager Jim Leyland* brought Bonds along slowly. Bonds hit his stride in 1990, when he moved from the leadoff position to the fifth spot in the batting order. Bonds batted .301 with 104 runs scored, 33 HR, 114 RBI, and 52 stolen bases, and led the NL with a .565 slugging percentage. His honors included being named NL Player of the Month for July, making his first All-Star appearance, and winning the first of five consecutive Gold Gloves for his play in left field. Bonds, chosen the NL MVP, was selected *TSN* Major League Player of the Year. *TSN* also named him NL Player of the Year in 1991, 1992, and 1993.

Bonds continued his superb play during the 1991 and 1992 seasons. In 1991, he registered 116 RBI and led the NL with a .419 on-base percentage while finishing second to Terry Pendleton* in the NL MVP balloting. In 1992 he garnered his second NL MVP award, hitting .311 with 34 HR and 103 RBI. He led the NL in runs scored (109), slugging percentage (.624), on-base percentage (.461), walks (127), intentional walks (32), and HR ratio (1 every 13.9 at bats). Bonds, however, did not perform well in the NL Championship Series against the Cincinnati Reds in 1990 and Atlanta Braves in 1991 and 1992. In the three NL Championship Series, he batted only .191 with just one HR and three RBI.

In December 1992, the San Francisco Giants (NL) signed free agent Bonds to a $43.75 million contract over six years. During the first half of the 1993 season, with his father serving as hitting instructor for the Giants, Bonds led the San Francisco Giants to the top of the NL West Division.

He was chosen NL Player of the Month for April and was named to the NL All-Star team for the third time. Bonds became the seventh major league player to win the MVP award three times and the first to earn it three times in four seasons. He set career highs for batting average (.336), runs scored (129), and HR (46), leading the NL in the latter category. He also paced the NL with 123 RBI, a .463 on-base percentage, and a .677 slugging percentage. The Giants set a franchise record with 103 victories in 1993, being edged on the final day by the Atlanta Braves for the NL West Division title. During the strike-shortened 1994 season, Bonds batted .312 with 37 HR and 81 RBI, led the NL with 74 walks, and repeated as an NL All-Star team member. Bonds batted .294 with 33 HR and 104 RBI in 1995 and .308 with 42 HR and a career-high 129 RBI in 1996. His .291 batting average, 40 HR, and 101 RBI helped the San Francisco Giants win the NL West in 1997, but he hit just .250 in the NL Division Series against the Florida Marlins. Bonds batted .303 with 37 HR and 122 RBI in 1998, finishing fourth in slugging percentage and on-base percentage. He has made the NL All-Star team each year since 1992 and led the NL in walks five times (1992, 1994–1997).

Through 1999, Bonds batted .288 with 423 doubles, 445 HR, 1,299 RBI, and 460 stolen bases. He shares the major league record for most consecutive seasons (6) leading the league in intentional walks. His honors include making seven *TSN* NL All-Star teams (1990–1994, 1996–1997) and eight Gold Glove Awards (1990–1994, 1996–1998). Bonds ranked third in HR (361) and RBI during the 1990s.

Bonds, who resides in Atherton, CA, is separated from his wife, Sun, and has two children, Nikolai and Shikari.

BIBLIOGRAPHY: John Benson et al., *Baseball's Top 100* (Wilton, CT, 1997); "Barry Bonds' Big Bat and $7 Million Salary Make Him the Best in Baseball," *Jet* 84 (August 9, 1993), pp. 52–55; Barry Bloom, "Barry Bonds," *Sport* 87 (October 1996), pp. 16ff; *The Baseball Encyclopedia*, 10th ed. (New York, 1996); Barbara Carlisle Bigelow, ed., *Contemporary Black Biography*, vol. 6 (Detroit, MI, 1994); *CB* (1994), pp. 55–58; Barry Bonds file, National Baseball Library, Cooperstown, NY; Kevin Cook, "Playboy Interview: Barry Bonds," *Playboy* 40 (July 1993), pp. 59–72, 148; Hank Hersch, "30/30 Vision," *SI* 72 (June 25, 1990), pp. 59–60; Richard Hoffer, "The Importance of Being Barry," *SI* 78 (May 24, 1993), pp. 13–21; David A. Kaplan, "The Rising Stock of Bonds," *Newsweek* 121 (May 31, 1993), p. 64; W. Ladson, "Barry Bonds," *Sport* 83 (March 1992), pp. 28–32; W. Leavy, "Barry Bonds: Baseball's $60 Million Man," *Ebony* 48 (September 1993), pp. 118–120; *Pittsburgh Pirates 1991 Record and Information Guide*, pp. 29–31; David L. Porter, ed., *African-American Sports Greats* (Westport, CT, 1995); P. Richmond, "Why Isn't Barry Bonds a Willie Mays?" *GQ* 64 (April 1994), pp. 174–181; B. Schoenfeld, "Unfinished Business," *Sport* 85 (April 1994), pp. 80–82; J. Weinstock, "Barry Bonds," *Sport* 84 (April 1993), pp. 60–65; Ed Lucas and Paul Post, "Bonds Showed Flashes of Brilliance in 10th Grade," *SCD* 26 (January 1, 1999), pp. 94–95; *San Francisco Giants 1993 Record and Information Guide*, pp. 52–53; Mike Shatzkin, ed., *The Ballplayers* (New York, 1990); Bob Smizik, *The Pittsburgh Pirates: An Illustrated History* (New York, 1990).

Frank W. Thackeray

BONDS, Bobby Lee (b. March 15, 1946, Riverside, CA), player and coach, is the son of a building contractor. After attending Riverside public schools and graduating from Riverside Polytechnic High School in 1964, he married Patricia Howard in May 1965. His son, Barry,* plays major league baseball with the San Francisco Giants (NL). Bonds played Little League ball at age seven and starred in baseball, football, basketball, and track at Riverside Polytechnic. Named Southern California Schoolboy Athlete of the Year in 1964, Bonds signed with the San Francisco Giants (NL) and began his 17-year playing career with Lexington, NC (WCL). He spent 1966 with Fresno, CA (CaL), 1967 with Waterbury, CT (EL), and early 1968 with the Giants' top farm club in Phoenix, AZ (PCL). On June 25, 1968, he hit a grand-slam HR in the seventh inning of his first major league game.

In his first full major league season, Bonds in 1969 shared the NL lead in runs scored with Pete Rose* at 120, became only the fourth player in baseball history to hit 30 HR and steal 30 bases in the same season, and established an NL record with 187 strikeouts. He led in strikeouts again in 1970 and 1973, including a major league record (189) in 1970. In 1973, Bonds paced in runs scored (131) and total bases (341). The much-traveled outfielder played in the AL with the New York Yankees (1975), California Angels (1976–1977), Chicago White Sox (1978), Texas Rangers (1978), and Cleveland Indians (1979) and then returned to the NL, joining the St. Louis Cardinals (1980). The Chicago Cubs (NL) purchased him in June 1981 from the Rangers' minor league system for his final major league playing season. After being released at the season's end, he played with the Columbus, OH Clippers (IL) from May through June 1982. Bonds served as a batting and base running coach for the Cleveland Indians (AL) from 1984 through 1987 and coached for the San Francisco Giants (NL) from 1993 through 1996. In 1997, he became a vice-president of the Major League Baseball Players Alumni Association.

With one of the best combinations of speed and power in baseball history, Bonds established then records for most HR by a leadoff batter lifetime (35) and single season (11 in 1973). The only player to hit 30 HR and steal 30 bases in one season in both major leagues, he accomplished this feat five times. Bonds made *TSN* All-Star teams five consecutive years (1973–1977) and appeared in three All-Star games, one of a limited number to represent both leagues. He retired with a lifetime .268 batting average, 302 doubles, 332 HR, 1,258 runs scored, 1,024 RBI, and 461 stolen bases.

BIBLIOGRAPHY: Bobby Bonds file, National Baseball Library, Cooperstown, NY; J. Dodd, "Family of Giants," *PW* 40 (October 4, 1993), pp. 101–102; Gene Karst and Martin J. Jones, Jr., *Who's Who in Professional Baseball* (New Rochelle, NY, 1973); David Klein, *Stars of the Major Leagues* (New York, 1974); Ed Lucas and Paul Post, "Bobby Bonds," *SCD* 23 (December 20, 1996), p. 140; Ross Newhan, *The California Angels* (New York, 1982); Nick Peteri, *Giants Almanac* (Berkeley, CA, 1988); *The*

Baseball Encyclopedia, 10th ed. (New York, 1996); *TSN Official Baseball Baseball Guide, 1983*; R. Wuhl, "Arliss & Bonds," *Sport* 88 (October 1997), pp. 42–45.

Alan R. Asnen

BONHAM, Ernest Edward "Ernie," "Tiny" (b. August 16, 1913, Ione, CA; d. September 15, 1949, Pittsburgh, PA), player, was the 13th of 14 children and grew up on a farm, where he proved as adept at milking cows as throwing a baseball. He pitched for Ione High School and later starred for the American Legion Junior Club. Bonham, a logger in northern California, played semiprofessional baseball in Mother Lode Valley. New York Yankee (AL) scout Joe Devine discovered Bonham in 1935. After starting with Modesto, CA (CSSL), Bonham compiled a 14–8 mark in 1936 with Akron, OH (MAL). He finished the 1936 season with Binghamton, NY (NYPL) and compiled a 17–16 mark the next season for the Oakland, CA Oaks (PCL). With Newark, NJ (IL), Bonham in 1938 won eight of 10 decisions. Later that season, he recorded a 3–4 slate with the Kansas City, MO Blues (AA). At Kansas City, former New York Yankee Frank Makosky taught Bonham the forkball, later his most effective pitch in the big leagues. The 6-foot 2-inch, 215-pound right-handed Bonham, one of the first to have success with the forkball, stayed with the Blues until the New York Yankees called him up in 1940.

Although Bonham's back still bothered him from a 1939 logging accident, his 1.90 ERA in just 12 games led the AL in 1940. Chronic back problems plagued Bonham during his 10-year major league career. His finest major league season came in 1942, when he compiled a 21–5 record and led the AL with an .808 winning percentage, 22 complete games, and six shutouts. Bonham earned a berth on the AL All-Star team in 1942. The mainstay of the New York Yankees staff, he won 79 games while losing 50 during his tenure there. Bonham won the fifth and final game of the 1941 World Series against the Brooklyn Dodgers, but lost one game to the St. Louis Cardinals in each of the 1942 and 1943 World Series.

On October 21, 1946, the New York Yankees traded the tall, quiet pitcher with a keen wit to the Pittsburgh Pirates (NL) for Arthur Cuccurullo. Bonham compiled winning records in 1947 and 1949 for Pittsburgh. He pitched his last game for the Pittsburgh Pirates on August 27, 1949, an 8–2 win over the Philadelphia Phillies (NL) at Shibe Park. On September 6, after weeks of stomach cramps, Bonham entered the hospital. Appendicitis symptoms were discovered. Bonham's wife, Ruth Munsterman, was at his bedside when he succumbed to what doctors later reported as cancer of the colon. The couple had two children, Donna Marie and Ernie, Jr. His composite major league record was 103 wins, 72 losses, a .589 winning percentage, and a 3.06 ERA.

BIBLIOGRAPHY: Ernest Bonham file, National Baseball Library, Cooperstown, NY; Mark Gallagher, *The Yankee Encyclopedia*, vol. 3 (Champaign, IL, 1997); Frank Graham, *The New York Yankees* (New York, 1943); Donald Honig, *The New York Yankees* (New York, 1987); Gene Karst and Martin Jones, Jr., *Who's Who in Professional Baseball* (New Rochelle, NY, 1973); Frederick G. Lieb, *The Pittsburgh Pirates* (New York, 1948); Richard L. Burtt, *The Pittsburgh Pirates: A Pictorial History* (Virginia Beach, VA, 1977); Mike Shatzkin, ed., *The Ballplayers* (New York, 1990); *TSN*, September 21, 1949, September 28, 1949.

William A. Borst

BONILLA, Roberto Antonio, Jr. "Bobby" "Bobby Bo" (b. February 23, 1963, New York, NY), player, is the son of Roberto Bonilla, Sr., an electrician, and Regina Bonilla. The 6-foot 3-inch, 240-pound, switch-hitting Bonilla graduated from Lehman High School in New York. The Pittsburgh Pirates (NL) signed him as a nondrafted free agent in 1981.

After Bonilla experienced an unexceptional minor league career, the Chicago White Sox (AL) drafted him in December 1985. Bonilla debuted as an outfielder for the Chicago White Sox in April 1986, but was traded back to a woeful Pittsburgh Pirates club that July. Bonilla helped lead a baseball renaissance in Pittsburgh that culminated in three consecutive NL East Division titles.

In 1987, the powerful Bonilla played third base, hit .300 for the first time in his career, and became only the fourth player to belt a fair ball into the upper deck at Three Rivers Stadium. For Bonilla, 1988 marked a banner year. He slugged 24 HR and drove in 100 runs, tying him with teammate Andy Van Slyke* for third in the NL. His honors included being named NL Player of the Month for both April and May, election to the NL All-Star team as starting third baseman, and selection for *TSN* Silver Slugger Team. In 1989, Bonilla led the Pittsburgh Pirates in HR (24) and RBI (86). He also earned his second of four consecutive spots on the NL All-Star team and was tabbed NL Player of the Month for September.

In 1990, the Pittsburgh Pirates moved Bonilla from third base, where his fielding was barely adequate, to right field. He welcomed the switch, setting career marks for hits (175), RBI (120), and runs scored (112). His 32 HR set a season record for a Pirates right fielder. Bonilla led the NL in extra base hits (78) and finished second in RBI, runs scored, doubles (39), and total bases (324).

Bonilla continued to play well in 1991, hitting .302 with 100 RBI and an NL-leading 44 doubles. Like the rest of the Pittsburgh Pirates sluggers, however, he slumped in the NL Championship Series against the Cincinnati Reds in 1990 and Atlanta Braves in 1991. In the 1990 and 1991 NL Championship Series, Bonilla produced a combined .250 with no HR and only two RBI.

Following the 1991 season, Bonilla became a free agent and signed a five-year, $29 million contract with the New York Mets (NL). New Yorkers expected Bonilla to lead the New York Mets to glory, but his production declined in 1992. Despite his career-high 34 HR in 1993, he received fan and media criticism for the failure of the grossly overrated and overpaid New York Mets. Bonilla batted .325 for the New York Mets in 1995 and tied a major league record by clouting two doubles in the eighth inning on July 21 against the Colorado Rockies, making the NL All-Star team for the sixth and final time.

On July 28, 1995, the Baltimore Orioles (AL) obtained him. Bonilla batted .333 for the Baltimore Orioles and enjoyed a 20-game hitting streak at the end of the 1995 season. In 1996, he hit .287 with 28 HR and 116 RBI and tied an AL record with 17 sacrifice flies. Bonilla clouted two HR with five RBI in the AL Championship Series against the New York Yankees. In November 1996, the Florida Marlins (NL) signed him as a free agent. His .297 batting average, 17 HR, and 96 RBI helped Florida capture a wild card playoff spot in 1997. He hit .333 with one HR and three RBI in the NL Division Series against the San Francisco Giants and .261 with four RBI in the NL Championship Series against the Atlanta Braves. His one HR and 3 RBI contributed to the Marlins's triumph over the Cleveland Indians in the World Series. In May 1998, the Florida Marlins sent him to the Los Angeles Dodgers (NL) in a blockbuster trade. The New York Mets reacquired him in November 1998. Through 1999, Bonilla has batted .281 with 388 doubles, 277 HR, and 1,124 RBI in 1,906 games.

Bonilla and his wife, Millie, live in Bradenton, FL, with their daughter, Danielle.

BIBLIOGRAPHY: *The Baseball Encyclopedia*, 10th ed. (New York, 1996); E. Levin, "Save That Ball, Boys—The Way Bobby Bonilla's Going, It'll Be Valuable," *PW* 30 (July 18, 1988), pp. 74–75; K. Kerasotis, "Bobby Bonilla," *Sport* 83 (June 1992), pp. 30–34; *New York Mets 1993 Information Guide*, pp. 29–32; Bruce Newman, "Pirate on the Plank," *SI* 175 (October 14, 1991), pp. 34–36; *NYT Biographical Service* 23 (February 1992), pp. 150–151; *The Official Major League Baseball 1992 Stat Book*, p. 29; *Pittsburgh Pirates 1991 Record and Information Guide*, pp. 31–33; Ken Rappoport, *Bobby Bonilla* (New York, 1993); Mike Shatzkin, ed., *The Ballplayers* (New York, 1990); Dave Rosenbaum, *If They Don't Win It's a Shame* (Tampa, FL, 1998); Bob Smizik, *The Pittsburgh Pirates: An Illustrated History* (New York, 1990).

Frank W. Thackeray

BONURA, Henry John "Zeke" (b. September 20, 1908, New Orleans, LA; d. March 9, 1987, New Orleans, LA), player, was the son of Sicilian immigrants Henry (b. Enrico) Bonura, a wealthy banana dealer, and Rosa (Amato) Bonura. A superb all-around athlete, Bonura graduated from St. Stanislaus College prep school in Bay St. Louis, MS in 1927 and attended Loyola University in New Orleans, LA for two years. At St. Stanislaus, he captained the football, basketball, track and field, and baseball teams. Knute Rockne (FB) scouted him to play football for the University of Notre Dame. At the 1925 AAU Championships, Bonura won the javelin throw with an American record of 213 feet, 10½ inches after only two months of training. He declined an invitation to be on the United States Olympic team in 1928, preferring to concentrate on a baseball career.

After playing semiprofessional baseball in Louisiana from 1926 to 1928, Bonura starred in the minor leagues with the New Orleans, LA Pelicans (SL) from 1929 through 1931 and Dallas, TX Steers (TL) in 1932 and 1933. The TL MVP in 1933, he moved to the major leagues with the Chicago White Sox (AL) from 1934 to 1937. Bonura also played first base for the Washington Senators (AL) in 1938, New York Giants (NL) in 1939, and Washington (AL) and the Chicago Cubs (NL) in 1940. A fine hitter, he batted .307 lifetime with 1,099 hits, 232 doubles, 119 HR, and 704 RBI. As a rookie, Bonura became the first Chicago White Sox player ever to hit 20 HR. Two years later he drove in 138 runs to set a White Sox record. Bonura hit .300 four times, including .330 in 1936 and .345 in 1937.

His fielding, however, proved more controversial. Bonura led AL first basemen in fielding average with .996 in 1934, .996 in 1936, and .993 in 1938 and fielded .992 lifetime, but his range was often questioned. Although often waving his glove at ground balls, he paced the AL in putouts and assists in 1936. Some of his managers defended his fielding ability.

Bonura also aroused controversy for his frequent spring holdouts, but he was always signed to a contract and ready to play by the start of the season. Although many sluggers were beginning to swing lighter bats, the 6-foot, 205–215-pound Bonura stuck with a 38-ounce model.

Bonura started the 1941 season with the Minneapolis, MN Millers (AA), but the draft soon intervened. He was stationed in North Africa during World War II, organizing baseball leagues and setting up 20 fields.

Bonura later managed several minor league teams, leading Fargo, ND–Moorhead, MN (NoL) to the NoL pennant in 1953 with rookie Roger Maris.* The lifetime bachelor acquired an international reputation for raising pedigreed beagles and traveled around the United States.

BIBLIOGRAPHY: Zeke Bonura file, National Baseball Library, Cooperstown, NY; John Thorn et al., eds., *Total Baseball*, 5th ed. (New York, 1997); Mike Shatzkin, ed., *The Ballplayers* (New York, 1990); Morris Bealle, The *Washington Senators* (Washington, DC, 1947); Clifford Bloodgood, "Big Zeke, Slugger of the Senators," *BM* 61 (July 1938), pp. 349–359; Clifford Bloodgood, "The Leading Socker of the Senators," *BM* 60 (March 1938), pp. 431–432; Warren Brown, *The Chicago White Sox* (New York, 1952); Evans J. Casso, "Lest We Forget! Zeke Bonura, A Legendary Hero," *IAD* (Summer 1981), pp. 7ff; Richard Lindberg, *Sox* (New York, 1984); Shirley Povich, *The Washington Senators* (New York, 1954); John J. Ward, "The Home-Run Rookie of the White Sox," *BM* 53 (September 1934), pp. 449–451.

Victor Rosenberg

BOONE, Raymond Otis "Ray," "Ike" (b. July 27, 1923, San Diego, CA), player and scout, is the son of Donald E. Boone, a lather, and Beulah Boone, a seamstress, of Irish-German ancestry. After graduating from Herbert Hoover High School in San Diego in 1942, he signed with the Cleveland Indians (AL) as a catcher. He played briefly for Wausau, WI (NoL) before beginning a three-year stint in the U.S. Navy. Upon his release, he married Patricia D. Brown, an accomplished synchronized swimmer, in October 1946. They have three children, Robert,* a renowned major league catcher, Rodney, and Theresa.

After converting to shortstop in the Indians farm system, Boone joined the Cleveland Indians in 1948 as backup for player–manager Lou Boudreau.* He requested Class AAA assignment after three weeks of inactivity. He returned from Hollywood, CA (PCL) late in the 1948 season to witness the Cleveland Indians' World Series triumph over the Boston Braves. For the next four seasons, the 6-foot, 180-pound Boone played shortstop for the Cleveland Indians. The high-strung Boone performed in the shadow of the injury-plagued Boudreau, the 1948 AL MVP who departed in 1951. Boone booted balls, which booing fans insisted were routine outs for his predecessor. The right-hander led AL shortstops in errors with 33. He batted .301 in 1950, but his batting average never exceeded .263 in his other three full seasons for Cleveland. In that span, he never clouted more than 12 HR. The Cleveland Indians traded him in June 1953 to the Detroit Tigers (AL), where he enjoyed his best seasons. The Detroit Tigers moved Boone to third base, where he performed steadily and hit .312 in June 1953 and .308 in 1956. His HR production increased to 26 in 1953 and ranged from 20 to 25 for the next three years. In 1953, he tied an AL standard by hitting four grand-slam HR during the same season. He homered in the 1954 All-Star Game and also made the 1956 AL All-Star squad. In 1955, he and Jackie Jensen* shared the AL lead in RBI with 116. From 1953 through 1956, Boone remained the Detroit Tigers' most consistent power hitter for a perennial second-division team.

Following Boone's move to first base, the Detroit Tigers traded the slumping infielder to the Chicago White Sox (AL) in June 1958. That season, he hit only 13 HR. After batting .273 as a part-time player with the Kansas City Athletics (AL) in 1959, he closed out his major league career in 1960 with the Milwaukee Braves (NL) and Boston Red Sox (AL). He scouted with the Boston Red Sox organization from 1961 through 1992. In his 13 major league seasons, Boone batted .275 with 1,260 hits, 151 HR, and 737 RBI. Defensively, he compiled a .958 fielding percentage, tied an AL record for most putouts by a third baseman with seven on April 24, 1954, and led the AL third basemen in putouts with 170 in 1954.

BIBLIOGRAPHY: Raymond Boone file, National Baseball Library, Cooperstown, NY; Richard Bak, *A Place for Summers* (Detroit, MI, 1998); Joe Falls, *Detroit Tigers* (New York, 1975); William M. Anderson, *The Detroit Tigers* (South Bend, IN, 1996); Raymond Boone, letter to James N. Giglio, January 9, 1993; Cleveland (OH) *News*, May 14, 1952; March 6, 1953; February 17, 1956; Cleveland (OH) *Plain Dealer*, May 4,

1948; March 6, 1970; February 24, 1974; James N. Giglio, telephone interview with Raymond Boone, June 10, 1993; Lee Heiman et al., *When the Cheering Stops* (New York, 1990); John Phillips, *Winners* (Cabin John, MD, 1987); Fred Smith, *995 Tigers* (Detroit, MI, 1981); Russell Schneider, *The Boys of Summer of '48* (Champaign, IL, 1998); Brent P. Kelley, *Baseball Stars of the 1950s* (Jefferson, NC, 1993).

James N. Giglio

BOONE, Robert Raymond "Bob" (b. November 19, 1947, San Diego, CA), player, coach, manager, and executive, is the son of Ray Boone,* a fine hitting major league infielder from 1948 to 1960, and Patricia (Brown) Boone. His brother, Rodney, caught in the minor leagues from 1972 to 1975, while his son Bret plays infield for the San Diego Padres (NL) and son Aaron plays infield for the Cincinnati Reds (NL). Boone graduated from Crawford High School in San Diego, CA and received a bachelor's degree in psychology from Stanford University before signing with the Philadelphia Phillies (NL) in 1969. As a third baseman with Raleigh-Durham, NC (CrL) in 1969, Boone hit .300. He played third base for Reading, PA (EL) in 1970 and 1971, but was converted to catcher at Eugene, OR (PCL) in 1972.

Boone joined the Philadelphia Phillies in September 1972. Mike Ryan, a veteran Phillies backstop, helped Boone hone his catching skills. In 1973, the right-handed Boone became the Phillies's regular catcher and appeared in 145 games behind the plate. After catching 146 games the next season, he shared duties with Johnny Oates because of weak offense in 1975. Boone regained everyday status by batting .282 over the next four seasons. After Boone's batting average plunged to .211 in 1981, the Phillies rendered the 34-year-old, 6-foot 2-inch, 205-pound Boone too old for the rigors of everyday catching and sold him that December to the California Angels (AL).

Boone averaged 138 games per season behind the plate from 1982 through 1988 for the California Angels. Angels manager Gene Mauch* said that Boone's "biggest asset is the way he handles pitchers." Boone ranked among the best at blocking balls in the dirt and throwing out would-be base stealers and frequently led his league in assists among catchers. In 1987, he caught his 1,919th game to surpass the major league mark held by National Baseball Hall-of-Famer Al Lopez.* In 1988, Boone reached a career high .295 batting average. Martial arts workouts enabled him to stay in excellent condition. Boone signed as a free agent with the Kansas City Royals (AL) in November 1988 and enjoyed another splendid season in 1989, batting .274 and winning a seventh Gold Glove.

Although known primarily for his defensive skills, Boone starred offensively in postseason play. He batted .310 in six AL Championship Series and established the AL record for highest batting average in a seven-game Championship Series with a .455 mark against the Boston Red Sox in 1986. In his only World Series appearance, Boone helped power the Philadelphia Phillies past the Kansas City Royals in 1980 by batting .412. His four All Star contests saw him produce a .400 batting average. Boone, who was voted California's Most Inspirational Player by the Angels' Booster Club in 1987 and 1988, retired after the 1991 season with 1,838 hits, 105 HR, 826 RBI, and a .254 batting average in 2,264 games.

After managing Tacoma, WA (PCL) in 1992 and 1993, Boone coached for the Cincinnati Reds (NL) in 1994. He managed the Kansas City Royals (AL) from 1995 through July 1997 to a 181–206 composite record. Boone serves as special assistant to the general manager for the Cincinnati Reds and as a vice president of the Major League Baseball Players Alumni Association.

BIBLIOGRAPHY: Bob Boone, "The Game I'll Never Forget," *BD* 46 (November 1988), pp. 55–57; Phil Elderkin, "Bob Boone, The Angels' Steadying Influence Behind the Plate," *BD* 41 (October 1982), pp. 32–34; Peter Gammons, "Baseball Is in His Blood," *SI* 69 (July 4, 1988), pp. 44–46; P. Korn, "Old Catchers Never Die," *Sport* 80 (July 1989), pp. 44–49; Howie Newman, "Bob Boone, the Majors' Most Durable Catcher," *BD* 45 (January 1987), pp. 61–64; Peter Schmuck, "Bob Boone: The Majors' New Iron Man Catcher," *BD* 46 (March 1988), pp. 74–76; Rich Westcott and Frank Bilovsky, *The New Phillies Encyclopedia* (Philadelphia, PA, 1993); *TSN Baseball* Register, *1997*; George Vass, "Major Leaguers Follow in the Footsteps of Their Fathers," *BD* 41 (February 1982), pp. 36–43; Allen Lewis, *The Philadelphia Phillies* (Virginia Beach, VA, 1981).

Frank J. Olmsted

BOTTOMLEY, James LeRoy "Jim," "Sunny Jim" (b. April 23, 1900, Oglesby, IL; d. December 11, 1959, St. Louis, MO), player, manager, and scout, was nicknamed "Sunny Jim" because of his ever-present smile and good humor. The 6-foot, 175-pound Bottomley was the son of a miner and worked in the mine after graduation from high school in Nokomos, IL. He broke into professional baseball with Sioux City, IA (WL) in 1920 and came to the St. Louis Cardinals (NL) in 1922 after minor league seasons at Mitchell, SD (SDA), Houston, TX (TL), and Syracuse, NY (IL). Bottomley played 16 seasons at first base for the Cardinals (1922–1932), NL Cincinnati Reds (1933–1935), and AL St. Louis Browns (1936–1937). On September 16, 1924, he enjoyed one of the greatest batting days in major league history against the Brooklyn Dodgers. He drove in 12 runs with 2 HR, 1 double, and 3 singles to power the Cardinals to a 17–3 victory. In 1928 he slugged 31 HR to tie Hack Wilson* for the NL lead and led the NL in triples (20) and RBI (136) to win the MVP Award.

Bottomley's lifetime .310 batting average included a career-high .371 mark for the 1923 season. He made 2,313 hits with 465 doubles, 151 triples, 219 HR, 1,177 runs scored, and 1,422 RBI. In 1931, he participated in the closest batting championship race in baseball history. Bottomley finished third with a .3482 average, placing behind teammate Chick Hafey* (3.489) and the New York Giants' Bill Terry* (.3486). With left-hander Bottomley at first base, the Cardinals won NL pennants in 1926, 1928, 1930, and 1931 and captured the World Series in 1926 and 1931. In December 1932, Bottomley was traded to the Cincinnati Reds (NL). In March 1936 he joined the St. Louis Browns (AL) and managed them to a 21–58 record from July 22, 1937 to the end of that season. After completing his major league career, Bottomley piloted Syracuse, NY (IL) in 1938. In 1957, he scouted for the Chicago Cubs (NL) and managed Pulaski, VA (ApL). Bottomley, who married Betty Brawner on February 4, 1933, had no children and resided in Borbon, MO. He was elected to the National Baseball Hall of Fame in 1974 and is honored in the BRS Museum in Nokomis, IL.

BIBLIOGRAPHY: Jim Bottomley file, National Baseball Library, Cooperstown, NY; Bill Borst, ed., *Ables to Zoldak*, vol. 1 (St. Louis, MO, 1988); Gene Karst and Martin J. Jones, Jr., *Who's Who in Professional Baseball* (New Rochelle, NY, 1973); Cindy Landage and Janna Seiz, "Museum Named after Baseball HOFers," *SCD* 25 (May 1, 1998), p. 135; *The Baseball Encyclopedia*, 10th ed. (New York, 1996); Rob Rains, *The St. Louis Cardinals* (New York, 1992); Frederick G. Lieb, *The St. Louis Cardinals* (New York, 1945); Lowell Reidenbaugh, *Baseball's Hall of Fame-Cooperstown* (New York, 1993); Bob Broeg and Jerry Vickery, *St. Louis Cardinals Encyclopedia* (Grand Rapids, MI, 1998); Bob Broeg, *Redbirds: A Century of Cardinals' Baseball* (St. Louis, MO, 1981); Lee Allen, *The Cincinnati Reds* (New York, 1948); Joseph L. Reichler, *The Great All-Time Baseball Record Book* (New York, 1981).

Horace R. Givens

BOUDREAU, Louis, Jr. "Lou" (b. July 17, 1917, Harvey, IL), baseball and basketball player, manager, and sportscaster, is the son of Louis Boudreau, Sr., a machinist and semipro baseball player, and Birdie (Henry) Boudreau. He graduated from Thornton High School in Harvey and the University of Illinois in 1939. Boudreau married Della De Ruiter in June 1938 and has four children. One son played professional baseball, while one daughter married former Detroit pitcher Dennis McLain.* Boudreau quickly demonstrated fine leadership and athletic ability. He captained his high school basketball team as a sophomore, made All-State three years, and in 1933 helped his team win the state championship. He also starred at third base for Thornton. At the University of Illinois, he played third base and captained the basketball team as a junior.

In 1938, Boudreau played 60 games for Cedar Rapids IA (3IL) and one contest with the Cleveland Indians (AL). After dividing the 1939 season between Buffalo, NY (IL) and Cleveland, he played shortstop for the Indians from 1940 through 1950. In 1942 24-year-old Boudreau became manager, making him the youngest to pilot a full season in the majors. In 1944, he led the AL in batting with a .327 mark. He managed the Indians through 1950, the Boston Red Sox (AL) from 1952 through 1954, and the Kansas City Athletics (AL) from 1955 through 1957. He became a sports broadcaster in Chicago in 1958 and in May 1960 replaced Charlie Grimm* as manager of the Chicago Cubs. Grimm took his place in the broadcasting booth, but in 1961 Boudreau returned permanently to broadcasting. As a major league manager, Boudreau compiled 1,162 wins and 1,224 losses for a .487 mark.

Boudreau proved extremely popular with the fans. In 1947, public outcry prevented Bill Veeck* from trading Boudreau to the St. Louis Browns. The next year Boudreau won the AL MVP and *TSN* Player of the Year awards. In the 1948 playoff game for the AL title, Boudreau hit two HR and two singles and walked once to spark his club to an 8–3 victory over the Boston Red Sox. In the World Series, he led the Indians with bat and glove to the championship over the Boston Braves.

Boudreau compiled a career .295 batting average and led the AL shortstops in fielding eight seasons. In 1,646 games, he made 1,779 hits, 385 doubles, 68 HR, 861 runs, 789 RBI, and 51 stolen bases. He not only recorded the best lifetime fielding percentage of any shortstop to that time, but also devised a successful shift against Boston Red Sox pull hitter Ted Williams.* All four infielders were stationed to the right of second base, with the second baseman in short right field. Two outfielders played to the right of center. Only the left fielder remained on the left side of the diamond, 20 feet back of the normal shortstop spot. Williams usually tried to overpower that defense, but in 1946 once hit to left field for an inside-the-park homer. The round tripper not only won the game, but clinched the AL pennant for Boston.

In 1941 and 1942, Boudreau coached freshman baseball and basketball at the University of Illinois. The author of *Good Infield Play* (1949), he played professional basketball with Hammond (NBL) in 1940 and 1941. Of his numerous honors, Boudreau particularly cherishes his 1970 election to the National Baseball Hall of Fame. He broadcast for the Chicago Cubs until 1989 and lives in Dalton, IL. In 1993, he co-authored *Lou Boudreau* with Russell Schneider.

BIBLIOGRAPHY: Louis Boudreau file, National Baseball Library, Cooperstown, NY; Russell Schneider, *The Boys of Summer of '48* (Champaign, IL, 1998); Lee Allen and Tom Meany, *Kings of the Diamond* (New York, 1965); Martin Appel and Burt Goldblatt, *Baseball's Best* (New York, 1977); John Phillips, *Winners* (Cabin John, MD, 1987); John Benson et al., *Baseball's Top 100* (Wilton, CT, 1997); Bill Deane, "The Best Fielders of the Century," *TNP* 2 (Fall 1982), pp. 3–4; Lou Boudreau with Ed Fitzgerald, *Player-Manager* (Boston, MA, 1949); Lou Boudreau with Russell Schneider, *Lou Boudreau: Covering All Bases* (Champaign, IL, 1993); Peter Golenbock, *Fenway* (New York, 1992); Daniel Okrent and Harris Lewine, eds., *The Ultimate Baseball Book* (Boston, MA, 1979); Jack Lautier, *Fenway Voices* (Camden, ME, 1990).

                                                                                Emil H. Rothe

BOWA, Lawrence Robert "Larry" (b. December 6, 1945, Sacramento, CA), player, coach, and manager, is the son of former minor league infielder– manager Paul Bowa and the nephew of former minor league infielder Frank Bowa. After graduating from McClatchy High School in Sacramento, he attended Sacramento City College. Bowa began his professional baseball career in 1966 in Spartanburg, SC (WCL) and San Diego, CA (PCL). He also played with Bakersfield, CA (CaL) in 1967 Reading, PA (EL) in 1967 and 1968, and Eugene, OR (PCL) in 1969. As a National Leaguer, he performed for the Philadelphia Phillies (1970–1981), Chicago Cubs (1982–1985), and New York Mets (1985). In January 1982, he was traded with infielder Ryne Sandberg* for shortstop Ivan DeJesus. After being released by the Cubs in August 1985, Bowa joined the New York Mets for the rest of that season.

The 5-foot 10-inch, 155-pound switch-hitter led NL shortstops in fielding percentage a record six times (1971–1972, 1976, 1978–1979, 1983) and set an NL record for most games by a shortstop (2,222). The winner of Gold Glove awards (1972 and 1978), he set major league records for the highest career fielding percentage by a shortstop with .980 and for a season with .991 in 1979. Bowa also established season NL records for fewest errors (6) in 1979 and for total chances (843) in 1971. As a batter, he enjoyed his finest performances with a .305 mark in 1975 and a .294 average in 1978 and made *TSN* NL All-Star teams both seasons. He led the NL in at bats (650) in 1971, triples (13) in 1972, and singles (153) in 1978. Besides playing in five All-Star games, Bowa batted .375 and stole three bases against the Kansas City Royals in the 1980 World Series. Bowa also appeared in post-season playoffs in 1976, 1977, 1978, 1981, and 1984. During his 16-year career, Bowa compiled a .260 batting average in 2,248 games, made 2,191 hits scored 987 runs, and stole 318 bases. Bowa managed the Las Vegas Stars to the PCL championship with an 80–62 record in 1986 and replaced Steve Boros as manager of the San Diego Padres (NL) in October 1986. The Padres compiled a lackluster 81–127 mark under Bowa in 1987 and 1988 before firing him. His aggressive, often combative style proved ineffective. He coached for the Philadelphia Phillies from 1988 through 1996 and for the Anaheim Angels (AL) from 1997 to 1999. In November 1999, the Seattle Mariners named him third base coach. The Seminole, FL resident is married to Sheena Gibson and has one child, Victoria.

BIBLIOGRAPHY: Larry Bowa file, National Baseball Library, Cooperstown, NY; Larry Bowa and Barry Bloom, *Bleep! Larry Bowa Manages* (Chicago, IL, 1988); *Chicago Cubs Press Guide 1984*; *TSN Baseball Register, 1984*; *San Diego Padres 1988 Media Guide*; Ron Fimirite, "Padre with a Passion," *SI* 66 (May 4, 1987), pp. 52–54; Eddie Gold and Art Ahrens, *The New Era Cubs, 1941–1985* (Chicago, IL, 1985); R. Spiritosanto and Mary Huzinec, "Bowa Manages Temper and Team," *NYT Biographical Service* 17 (August 1986), pp. 1061–1063; Allen Lewis, *The Philadelphia Phillies* (Virginia Beach, VA, 1981); *WWIB 1984*, 69th ed.; Rich Westcott and Frank Bilovsky, *The New Phillies Encyclopedia* (Philadelphia, PA, 1993).

Brian R. Kelleher

BOYER, Cletis Leroy "Clete" (b. February 9, 1937, Cassville, MO), player, coach, and manager, is one of 14 children born to Vern Boyer and Mabel

Boyer and the brother of former major leaguers Cloyd and Ken. His brothers Len and Ron played in the minor leagues. He graduated in 1955 from Alba, MO High School.

In 1955, Boyer signed with the Kansas City Athletics (AL) and spent two years there. He was optioned for most of the 1957 season before being traded to the New York Yankees (AL). The Yankees shifted Boyer from shortstop to third base, where he became a regular in 1960.

From 1960 to 1966, Boyer ranked among the AL third base leaders in fielding categories. Although admirers dubbed him a "human vacuum cleaner," he never won a Gold Glove with the Yankees as a contemporary of the Baltimore Orioles's Brooks Robinson.*

The large dimensions of Yankee Stadium mitigated against Boyer's pull hitting. His best year with the Yankees came in 1962, when he hit .272 with 18 HR and 68 RBI. Boyer hit .233 in five World Series appearances from 1960 to 1964 and collected 66 assists, second lifetime among third basemen.

The New York Yankees traded Boyer to the Atlanta Braves (NL) in November 1966. He enjoyed his finest season in 1967, clouting 26 HR, driving in 96 runs, collecting his 1,000th career hit, and earning Comeback Player of the Year honors. Boyer's hitting plummeted thereafter, but he led the NL in fielding percentage in 1967 and 1969 and finally won a Gold Glove in 1969.

Off the field, Boyer quarreled with management numerous times between 1968 and 1971. The Atlanta Braves released him in May 1971. After spending most of 1971 with Hawaii (PCL), he was traded to the Taiyo, Japan Whales in 1972 in the first direct transaction with the Japanese major leagues. He played, coached, and managed in Japan for four campaigns, retiring after the 1975 season.

Boyer spent three seasons as a minor league infield instructor and scout for the Atlanta Braves, coached at third base for the Oakland A's (AL) from 1980 to 1984, and coached and managed in the New York Yankees minor league system from 1987 through 1991. He served as the New York Yankees third base coach from 1992 to 1995, leaving because of a knee operation.

In 16 major league seasons, Boyer batted .242, with 162 HR, 654 RBI, and a .965 lifetime fielding percentage. Boyer, who married Marilyn Sue King in 1955, has four children and resides in Webb City, MO.

BIBLIOGRAPHY: Clete Boyer file, National Baseball Library, Cooperstown, NY; "Clete Returns as Braves Tutor," TSN, January 14, 1978; "Anderson: Clete's Blast 'Baloney,' " TSN, December 19, 1985; Bill Ballew, "Brothers," SCD 21 (December 9, 1994), pp. 150–152; "Clete Boyer," Complete Baseball (Redmond, WA, Microsoft CD-ROM, 1994); Tony Kubek and Terry Pluto, Sixty-one (New York, 1987); Don Forker, Sweet Seasons (Dallas, TX, 1991); Mark Gallagher, The Yankee Encyclopedia, vol. 3 (Champaign, IL, 1997); Peter Golenbock, Dynasty (New York, 1975); Ralph Houk and Robert W. Creamer, Season of Glory (New York, 1988); Gary Caruso, The Braves Encyclopedia (Philadelphia, PA, 1995); David Neft and Richard Cohen, eds.,

The Sports Encyclopedia: Baseball 1997 (New York, 1997); Robert Obojski, "Ex Yankee, Brave Clete Boyer Interviewed," *SCD* 25 (August 14, 1998), p. 58; Public Relations Office, New York Yankees Baseball Club.

Robert E. Weir

BOYER, Kenton Lloyd "Ken" (b. May 20, 1931, Liberty, MO; d. September 7, 1982, Ballwin, MO), player, coach, and manager, was the son of marble-cutter Chester Boyer and Mabel (Means) Boyer. All six Boyer brothers played professional baseball. Cloyd pitched for the St. Louis Cardinals (NL), while Cletis* enjoyed his best years as the New York Yankees (AL) third baseman. St. Louis Cardinals scout Runt Marr, who had inked Cloyd four years earlier, signed Ken in 1949 after his graduation from, Alba, MO High School. Boyer, who played for Buford Cooper's Alba Aces, agreed to the contract and a $6,000 bonus to help pay for his father's medical bills.

During his first season at Lebanon, PA (NAtL), Boyer pitched and sported a lofty .455 batting average. He moved swiftly through the St. Louis Cardinals minor league system, hitting .306 as a third baseman for Omaha, NE (WL) in 1951. Before Boyer could report to Houston, TX (TL), however, he was drafted into the U.S. Army in 1951. Discharged as a corporal in 1953, he hit .319 for Houston the following season.

The St. Louis Cardinals liked his progress so much that they traded regular third baseman Ray Jablonski to the Cincinnati Reds in December 1954. Boyer, an unabashed success his rookie season, hit .264 and fielded his position with skill. In 1956 he raised his batting average to .306, the first of five times he exceeded the .300 level in his 15-year career. Boyer slumped to .265 in 1957 partly because he feuded with general manager Frank Lane.* Lane wanted him to assert himself more defensively so the club would draw more fans.

In 1957, Boyer moved to center field in an unselfish attempt to allow the St. Louis Cardinals to use rookie Eddie Kasko at third base. The outfield gave the thick-legged, deceptively fast Boyer more room to display his fielding ability. He led the NL outfielders with a .996 fielding average.

In 1964 Boyer enjoyed his greatest year, hitting .295, knocking in 119 runs, slugging 24 HR, and winning the NL's MVP award. His grand slam off New York Yankees hurler Al Downing in the fourth game of the World Series sparked the Cardinals, who won the classic in seven games.

A bad back in 1965 hampered Boyer, whose batting average slipped to .260. The Cardinals traded him in December 1965 to the New York Mets (NL) for Al Jackson and Charley Smith. In July 1967 New York traded him to the Chicago White Sox (AL). Boyer finished his active career with the Los Angeles Dodgers (NL) in 1969.

In 2,034 career games, Boyer scored 1,104 runs, made 2,143 hits, slugged 282 HR, knocked in 1,141 runs, and compiled a .287 average. Boyer won five Gold Glove awards (1958–1961, 1963) and led the NL five consecutive years in double plays (1956–1960), tying a record. *TSN* All Star in 1956 and 1961 through 1964, Boyer hit .222 in the 1964 World Series.

After managing Little Rock–based Arkansas (TL) in 1970, Boyer coached the next two seasons for the Cardinals. A good organization man, he managed Sarasota, FL (GCL) in 1973 and Tulsa, OK (AA) in 1974. In 1977 he advanced to Rochester, NY (IL) but was not chosen to succeed Red Schoendienst* as Cardinals manager. The team instead selected Vern Rapp, a strict disciplinarian. When Rapp was fired during the 1978 season, Boyer became Cardinals manager and compiled a 166–191 record through June 8, 1980. Boyer was scheduled to manage the Cardinals franchise at Louisville, KY (AA) in 1982 when it was discovered that he had inoperable lung cancer. He married Kathleen Oliver on April 11, 1952 and had two daughters and two sons.

BIBLIOGRAPHY: Ken Boyer file, National Baseball Library, Cooperstown, NY; Bob Broeg and Jerry Vickery, *St. Louis Cardinals Encyclopedia* (Grand Rapids, MI, 1998); David Halberstam, *October 1964* (New York, 1994); David Craft, *Redbirds Revisited* (Chicago, IL, 1990); Bob Broeg, *Redbirds: A Century of Cardinals' Baseball* (St. Louis, MO, 1981); Jack Lang and Peter Simon, *The New York Mets* (New York, 1986); Richard Lindberg, *Who's on Third?* (South Bend, IN, 1983); *CB* 43 (1982), p. 44; Gene Karst and Martin J. Jones, Jr., *Who's Who in Professional Baseball* (New York, 1973); Craig Carter, ed., *TSN Daguerreotypes*, 8th ed. (St. Louis, MO, 1990); Richard Marazzi and Len Fiorito, *Aaron to Zuverink* (New York, 1982); *Newsweek* 100 (September 20, 1982), p. 86; *NYT*, September 8, 1982; *TSN*, September 20, 1982; Rob Rains, *The St. Louis Cardinals* (New York, 1992).

William A. Borst

BRADLEY, William Joseph "Bill" (b. February 13, 1877, Cleveland, OH; d. March 3, 1954, Cleveland, OH), player, manager, and scout, stood 6-foot 1-inch, weighed 190 pounds, and batted and threw right-handed. He received an eight-year parochial school education. He married Anna Kellackey in 1905 and had two daughters, Anna and Norma, and a son, Norman.

Bradley began his professional baseball career at Utica, NY (NYSL) in 1898, continuing there through most of 1899. In late 1899, the Chicago Orphans (NL) promoted him to play third base, which he did through 1900. In 1901, Bradley jumped to the Cleveland Blues in the newly founded AL and enjoyed hometown favorite status as a regular third sacker for the Cleveland Blues and the Cleveland Naps (AL) through 1910. He briefly managed the Naps to a 20–21 record in 1905. In 1906, he suffered a broken arm when hit by a pitch. This injury and a later typhoid fever attack diminished his playing skills. From 1911 through 1913, he played and managed for Toronto, Canada (EL, IL). He moved to the FL, the rival major league, as manager of the Brooklyn Tip-Tops in 1914 and piloted them to a 77–77 record. His playing career ended in 1915, when he performed intermittently for the Kansas City Packers (FL). The Cleveland Indians employed him as a scout from 1928 until his retirement in 1953. Bradley's Cleveland property enabled his family to live comfortably.

Bradley, a good fielder with a strong arm, made many errors, largely a by-product of the small gloves then used. He still shares the AL record for putouts by a third baseman in a nine-inning game with seven, accomplished on September 21, 1901 and May 13, 1909. His lifetime fielding average was .933. Prior to his arm injury and typhoid attack, he ranked among the AL's better hitters. In 1902, 1903, and 1904, his name appeared among AL leaders in doubles, triples, HR, runs scored, RBI, batting average, slugging percentage, and total bases. In 1902, he became the first batter to hit HR in four consecutive games. His 14-year major league career included a .271 batting average, 1,471 hits, 275 doubles, 84 triples, and 552 RBI.

BIBLIOGRAPHY: Bill Bradley file, National Baseball Library, Cooperstown, NY; Scott Longert, "Bill Bradley," *TNP* 16 (1996), pp. 127–128; Franklin A. Lewis, *The Cleveland Indians* (New York, 1949); John Phillips, *Who Was Who in Cleveland Baseball 1901–10* (Cabin John, MD, 1988); *NYT*, March 13, 1954; *The Baseball Encyclopedia*, 10th ed. (New York, 1996).

Lowell L. Blaisdell

BRAUN, Sanford. *See* Sanford Koufax.

BREADON, Sam (b. July 26, 1876, New York, NY; d. May 10, 1949, St. Louis, MO), owner, combined with Branch Rickey* to bring the St. Louis Cardinals to NL prominence from the 1920s through the 1940s after the franchise had struggled through the first two decades of the century. Breadon's 27 years with the Cardinals saw the development of the NL's first successful farm system, the emergence of the famed Gashouse Gang, and NL pennant wins in 1926, 1928, 1930–1931, 1934, 1942–1944, and 1946.

The son of William and Jane (Wilson) Breadon, he attended public schools in New York City (whose accent he never lost). He earned $125 a month as a bank clerk in 1902, moved west to St. Louis, and entered the newly developing automobile business. Breadon started as a $90 a month mechanic and eventually became a partner of socially prominent Marion Lambert in a successful auto sales venture. Breadon first bought into the Cardinals organization with four shares of stock at $50 a share. (He eventually controlled about 80 percent of the club's stock.) Encouraged by civic leader James Jones, he contributed about $7,000 to help buy out Cardinals owner Helene Britton in 1917. Rickey was lured away from the St. Louis Browns (AL) as club president. In 1920, the Cardinals syndicate moved Breadon into the presidency and made Rickey vice-president and general manager. Breadon's first move involved arranging with Browns owner Philip Ball for a lease on Sportsman's Park in 1921. (The Cardinals continued as tenants until they bought out the Browns in the early 1950s.) In the Cardinals' first NL pennant years in 1926 and 1928, Breadon and Rickey began their history of controversial, generally successful trades and sales. The Cardinals sent their formidable player–manager Rogers Hornsby* to the New York Giants in December 1926 for Frank Frisch,* who led the Cardinals to four NL pennants. In 1938 and 1940 Breadon and Rickey traded Dizzy Dean* and Joe Medwick* of the legendary Gashouse Gang when both stars had passed their prime. During the 1940s, Mort Cooper,* Walker Cooper,* Johnny Mize,* and less famous players were sold for very high prices with the fulfilled expectations of youthful replacements from the farm system. Before selling the franchise to Fred Saigh and Postmaster General Robert Hannegan in November 1947, Breadon witnessed the Cardinals win nine NL pennants and six World Series under his ownership.

Breadon was considered a hard, fair bargainer by his players, with whom he maintained a formal but genial relationship. With his first wife, Josephine (married in 1905), and second wife Rachael (married in 1912), he had two daughters. From 1947 until his death from cancer in 1949, he worked with Hampton Village real estate development in St. Louis.

BIBLIOGRAPHY: Sam Breadon file, National Baseball Library, Cooperstown, NY; Bob Broeg, *Redbirds: A Century of Cardinals' Baseball* (St. Louis, MO, 1981); Bob Broeg and Jerry Vickery, *St. Louis Cardinals Encyclopedia* (Grand Rapids, MI, 1998); Rob Rains, *The St. Louis Cardinals* (New York, 1992); Frederick G. Lieb, *The St. Louis Cardinals* (New York, 1945); *WWA*, 24th ed. (1950–1951), p. 310.

Leonard H. Frey

BRECHEEN, Harry David "The Cat" (b. October 14, 1914, Broken Bow, OK), player and coach, excelled as a left-handed pitcher for the St. Louis Cardinals (NL) in the 1940s and remains one of few hurlers to win three games in a single World Series. His long apprenticeship in the minor leagues started with Greenville, SC (EDL), Galveston, TX (TL), and Bartlesville, OK (WA) in 1935 and 1936 and featured 21 wins in 27 decisions for Portsmouth, VA (Pil) in 1937. With Houston, TX (TL) in 1938 and 1939, he won 31 contests and lost only 17 games. He enjoyed three outstanding seasons from 1940 to 1942 at Columbus, OH (AA), compiling marks of 16–9, 16–6, and 19–10. In 1942, his ERA, strikeouts, and shutouts paced the AA.

After joining the St. Louis Cardinals (NL) in 1943, Brecheen quickly became a starter with a 9–6 mark as a rookie and strong 16–5 and 15–4 showings in 1944 and 1945. In 1945, his .789 winning percentage paced the NL. The next three seasons marked the peak performances of Brecheen's career. Although compiling a 15–15 ledger, he boasted an outstanding 2.49 ERA with a NL-leading 5 shutouts during the 1946 regular season and pitched two complete game victories over the Boston Red Sox in the World Series. He won the seventh game in relief, as Enos Slaughter* scored from first base on a single. Brecheen's three World Series wins resulted from an astounding 0.45 ERA. His subsequent performances included a 16–11 record and 3.30 ERA in 1947, a 20–7 mark, an NL-leading 2.24 ERA, 149 strikeouts, and 7 shutouts in 1948, and a 14–11 slate and 3.35 ERA in 1949. Arm troubles subsequently slowed his production. His last active campaign came in 1953 with the St. Louis Browns (AL), where he slumped to a 5–13 record.

In 10 seasons with the St. Louis Cardinals, Brecheen won 127 games, lost 79 contests, and produced a 2.91 ERA, ranking among the top 10 Cardinals pitchers in victories and ERA. At 5-feet 10-inches and 165 pounds, Brecheen proved exceptionally agile defensively and rated among the NL's better fielding pitchers. A Warren Spahn* prototype, he succeeded through intelligence and style rather than overpowering physicality. Altogether, Brecheen won 133 games, lost 92 decisions, struck out 901 batters in 1,907.2 innings, and compiled a 2.92 ERA. From 1954 to 1967, he coached for the Baltimore Orioles (AL). Brecheen married Vera Caperton in September 1933, enjoys hunting and fishing, and lives in Ada, OK.

BIBLIOGRAPHY: Harry Brecheen file, National Baseball Library, Cooperstown, NY; *The Baseball Encyclopedia*, 10th ed. (New York, 1996); John Benson et al., *Baseball's Top 100* (Wilton, CT, 1997); Bob Broeg, *Redbirds: A Century of Cardinals' Baseball* (St. Louis, MO, 1981); Rob Rains, *The St. Louis Cardinals* (New York, 1994); Bob Broeg and Jerry Vickery, *St. Louis Cardinals Encyclopedia* (Grand Rapids, MI, 1998); *TSN Baseball Register*, 1944–1954.

Leonard H. Frey

BREITENSTEIN, Theodore P. "Ted" (b. June 1, 1869, St. Louis, MO; d. May 3, 1935, St. Louis, MO), player, was the son of Ida (Uhlmansier) Breitenstein and pitched for Green Bay, MI (WL) and Grand Rapids, MI (WL) before joining the St. Louis Browns (AA) late in 1891. In the final days of the AA, manager Charles Comiskey* gave Breitenstein his first major league start on October 4, 1891. The hometown hurler dazzled St. Louis fans by tossing an 8–0 no-hitter against the Louisville Colonels, the last AA no-hitter thrown.

In 1892, the St. Louis Browns joined the NL. Breitenstein, however, did not pitch for the same team that won four pennants in the previous seven years. Beer baron and owner Chris Von der Ahe* sold stars to pay off alimony, law suits, and poor real estate investments and let player–manager Comiskey jump to the Cincinnati Redlegs (NL). With a weak supporting cast, Breitenstein won nine and lost 19. However, he hurt his cause by walking 148 batters. Only once in 11 campaigns did his strikeout total exceed his bases on balls. The 5-foot 9-inch, 165-pound left-hander developed into a respectable hitter, baserunner, and fielder. Managers occasionally played him in the outfield.

In 1893, Von der Ahe, never short on gimmicks to draw fans and sell more beer, promoted St. Louisan Heinie Peitz to catch Breitenstein. A fan who spotted the two strikingly handsome players nibbling pretzels in a tavern nicknamed them the "Pretzel Battery." With Peitz behind the plate, Breitenstein led the NL with a 3.18 ERA and won 19 of 43 decisions for a tenth place St. Louis team. The new Sportsman Park contained outfield sections lacking fences, a scoreboard under which balls could roll for HR, and a pitching distance lengthened from 50 feet to 60 feet, 6 inches. He led the NL in 1894 and 1895 with 50 starts and 46 complete games. Breitenstein won 27 and lost 23 in 1894, but compiled a 19–30 record for an 1895 Browns team that triumphed only 39 times. He suffered 20 setbacks the next season for the fourth consecutive time.

Von der Ahe sold Breitenstein to the Cincinnati Redlegs (NL) in 1896 for a then unheard of $10,000. The transaction reunited Breitenstein with Peitz, who was traded a year earlier. Breitenstein fashioned four good years for the Redlegs, including marks of 23–12 in 1897 and 20–14 in 1898. He became the first pitcher to hurl no-hitters in two major leagues, blanking the Pittsburgh Pirates 11–0 on April 22, 1898. This also marked the first time two pitchers tossed no-hitters on the same day, as the Baltimore Orioles's (NL) Jim Hughes held the Boston Beaneaters (NL) hitless. Breitenstein finished his major league career with the St. Louis Cardinals (NL) in 1901. His career included 379 games pitched, 300 complete games, 2,964.1 innings, 160 wins, 170 losses, 889 strikeouts, and 4.04 ERA. He also played 65 games in the outfield, recording 126 RBI, 30 stolen bases, and a .216 batting average.

From 1902 to 1911, Breitenstein pitched for St. Paul, MN (WL), Memphis, TN (SL), and New Orleans, LA (SA). He umpired in the SL, SWL, and TL from 1912 to 1921.

BIBLIOGRAPHY: Theodore Breitenstein file, National Baseball Library, Cooperstown, NY; Bill Borst, *Baseball through a Knothole: A St. Louis History* (St. Louis, MO, 1980); Bob Broeg, *Redbirds: A Century of Cardinals' Baseball* (St. Louis, MO, 1981); Bob Broeg and Jerry Vickery, *St. Louis Cardinals Encyclopedia* (Grand Rapids, MI, 1998); Joe Hoppel and Craig Carter, eds., *Baseball: A Doubleheader Collection of Facts, Feats & Firsts* (New York, 1992); Gene Karst and Martin J. Jones, Jr., *Who's Who in Professional Baseball* (New Rochelle, NY, 1973); Rob Rains, *The St. Louis Cardinals* (New York, 1992); Mike Shatzkin, ed., *The Ballplayers* (New York, 1990); Robert L. Tiemann and Mark Rucker, eds., *Nineteenth Century Stars* (Kansas City, MO, 1989).

Frank J. Olmsted

BREMER, Eugene Joseph, Sr. "Gene," "Flash" (b. July 18, 1916, New Orleans, LA; d. June 19, 1971, Cleveland, OH), player, was the son of Amanda Bremer, a homemaker, and had two older sisters. He was educated at New Orlean's Valena C. Jones Elementary School.

Bremer entered professional baseball as a pitcher in 1932, moving from the Broadview Red Sox and Algiers Giants to the New Orleans Crescent Stars (NSL) for three seasons. The 5-foot 8-inch, 160-pound right-hander pitched for the Shreveport, LA Giants (NSL) in 1935 and spent the following two seasons with the Cincinnati, OH Tigers (NAL). Bremer joined the Memphis, TN Red Sox (NAL) in 1938. With the exception of a 1–2 mark and 3.12 ERA with Monterrey, Mexico (MEL) in 1939, he remained with Memphis through 1940 and started in the 1940 East-West All-Star game.

Bremer hurled for championship teams in 1933 when New Orleans captured the NSL and Negro Dixie Series crowns and in 1938 when Memphis claimed the NAL title. An outstanding football player, he starred in the backfield for the 1939 NIFL champion New Orleans Brutes. Gridiron prowess earned him monikers of "Flash" and "Snake Hips."

Bremer temporarily left baseball in 1941, but joined the newly formed Cincinnati-Cleveland, OH Buckeyes (NAL) the following year and represented the Buckeyes in the 1942, 1944, and 1945 East-West All-Star games. On June 14, 1942, Bremer outdueled Satchel Paige* of the Kansas City Monarchs 2–1 in Cleveland's League Park. In 1945, Bremer sparked the NAL champion Cleveland Buckeyes to a 3–2 victory over the Homestead, PA Grays. He also produced a ninth-inning bases-loaded single in the second game of the four-game Black World Series sweep. He also hurled for the 1947 Cleveland Buckeyes (NAL) champions and remained with them through 1948. Incomplete NAL statistics credit Bremer with a lifetime 46–26 record, but he probably earned over 75 NAL triumphs from 1937 through 1948 and over 200 career victories. Bremer's professional career ended in 1949 with his belated opportunity to pitch in minor league baseball, hurling 11 games for Cedar Rapids, IA (CA).

Bremer, who married Elizabeth Gertrude on December 4, 1937, had five sons and three daughters and worked for Gray's Drug Store and Harshaw Chemical in Cleveland before being forced into disability retirement.

BIBLIOGRAPHY: Eugene Bremer, Jr., letter to Merl F. Kleinknecht, July 11, 1995; Pedro Treto Cisneros, *Encyilopedia del Beisbol Mexicano* (Mexico, 1992); Dick Clark and Larry Lester, *The Negro Leagues Book* (Cleveland, OH, 1994); *Cleveland Call & Post*, 1942–1948; Robert Peterson, *Only the Ball Was White* (Englewood Cliffs, NJ, 1971); James A. Riley, *The Biographical Encyclopedia of the Negro Baseball Leagues* (New York, 1994).

Merl F. Kleinknecht

BRESNAHAN, Roger Philip "The Duke of Tralee" (b. June 11, 1879, Toledo, OH; d. December 4, 1944, Toledo, OH), player, coach, and manager, grew up in Toledo, where his family had settled after leaving Tralee, County Kerry, Ireland. As a stocky, powerful teenager playing on the city's sandlots, he quickly impressed local scouts. After a brief stint with Lima, OH (OSL), the right-handed pitcher signed with the Washington Senators (NL) late in 1897. He made his major league debut as a pitcher in August of that year and, in his first appearance, shut out the St. Louis, MO Browns, 3–0, on six hits. In the final month of the 1897 season, he made six more pitching appearances and compiled a perfect 4–0 record.

When Bresnahan held out for more money prior to the 1898 season, Washington released him. He drifted back to the minor leagues, playing briefly for Toledo, OH (ISL) in 1898 and Minneapolis, MN (WL) in 1899. After appearing in two games in 1900 for the Chicago Orphans (NL), he signed with John McGraw's* Baltimore Orioles (AL) in 1901. In July 1902, McGraw became manager of the New York Giants (NL) and persuaded Bresnahan and Oriole teammates Frank Bowerman, Joe McGinnity,* and John Cronin to jump to the Giants to help rebuild the struggling franchise.

Bresnahan spent the next six seasons with McGraw's New York Giants, who rose from the cellar in 1902 to finish second in 1903 and first in 1904 and 1905. Despite his bulky 5-foot 9-inch, 200-pound frame, he played center field in 1903 and 1904 and frequently hit in the leadoff position. In 1903 he enjoyed his best season offensively, getting 142 hits (including 42 for extra bases), stealing 34 bases, and batting .350. Bresnahan, who worked as a detective in the off-season, became the Giants' regular catcher in 1905 and quickly developed innovative catching techniques, game strategies, and natural leadership qualities. As the batterymate for Giants pitchers Christy Mathewson,* McGinnity, Red Ames,* Dummy Taylor, and Hooks Wiltse,* he won the nickname "The Duke of Tralee." In the 1905 World Series, he hit .313 and caught Mathewson's three shutouts over Connie Mack's* Philadelphia Athletics. Disregarding the taunts of players and fans, he began using shin guards in 1907 and paved the way for their rapid adoption throughout baseball. In 1908 he caught in 139 games and led NL batters with 83 walks.

In a three-way deal in December 1908, the New York Giants traded Bresnahan to the St. Louis Cardinals (NL). He served as player–manager there from 1909 through 1912, but the Cardinals hired Miller Huggins* as manager in 1913. After a long salary dispute with Bresnahan, the Cardinals sold him to the Chicago Cubs (NL) in June. From 1913 through 1915, Bresnahan shared the Cubs' catching duties with Jimmy Archer. As player–manager in 1915, he guided Chicago to a fourth place finish. From 1916 through 1923, he managed Toledo, OH (AA) and briefly held a controlling interest in the club.

Bresnahan coached for the New York Giants (NL) from 1925 to 1928 and helped develop young southpaw Carl Hubbell.* In 1931 he joined the Detroit Tigers (AL) coaching staff and stayed two seasons before retiring from the game. After returning to Toledo, he worked as turnkey of the city's municipal workhouse and later as a brewing company salesman. In the November 1944 general election, he ran unsuccessfully for county commissioner as a Democratic candidate. Bresnahan, who suffered from a chronic heart ailment, died one month later.

Bresnahan served pro baseball for one-third of a century as a player, coach, manager, and owner, appearing in 1,446 major league games and compiling a lifetime .279 batting average. Best known for his defensive skills and hard-nosed competitiveness, he played an instrumental role in the development of the modern-day catcher's position. Bresnahan, whom McGraw and

Branch Rickey* considered the best catcher they had ever seen, was inducted into the National Baseball Hall of Fame in 1945.

BIBLIOGRAPHY: Charles C. Alexander, *John McGraw* (New York, 1988); Roger Bresnahan file, National Baseball Library, Cooperstown, NY; Chicago *Daily Tribune*, December 5, 1944; Cappy Gagnon, "The Debut of Roger Bresnahan," *BRJ* 8 (1979), pp. 41–42; Frank Graham, *The New York Giants* (New York, 1952); Noel Hynd, *The Giants of the Polo Grounds* (New York, 1988); Eddie Gold and Art Ahrens, *The Golden Era Cubs, 1876–1940* (Chicago, IL, 1985); Irving A. Leitner, *Baseball: Diamond in the Rough* (New York, 1972); Craig Carter, ed., *TSN Daguerreotypes*, 8th ed. (St. Louis, MO, 1990); New York *Herald Tribune*, December 5, 1944; *The Baseball Encyclopedia*, 10th ed. (New York, 1996); Rob Rains, *The St. Louis Cardinals* (New York, 1992); Lowell Reidenbaugh, *Baseball's Hall of Fame-Cooperstown* (New York, 1993); G. H. Fleming, *The Unforgettable Season* (New York, 1981); David Quentin Voigt, *American Baseball*, vol. 2 (Norman, OK, 1970).

Raymond D. Kush

BRETT, George Howard (b. May 15, 1953, Glen Dale, WV), player, executive, and sportscaster, is the youngest son of accountant Jack Brett and bookkeeper Ethel Brett. His brother Kenneth pitched in the major leagues, while brothers John and Robert played minor league baseball. The Bretts moved in 1955 to Hermosa Beach, CA, where George starred in football and baseball at El Segundo High School. The easygoing, Brett attended El Camino, CA JC and Longview, MO CC.

The Kansas City Royals (AL) drafted him as a shortstop in 1971 and assigned him to Billings, MT, where he hit .291 and made the All-PrL team. In 1972, he led the CaL in sacrifice hits and assists for third basemen at San Jose, CA. At Omaha, NE in 1973, he batted .284, knocked in 117 runs, and made the AA All-Star team as third baseman. The 6-foot, 185-pound Brett, who batted left-handed and threw right-handed, joined the Kansas City Royals (AL) in late 1973 and started at third base in 1974. Batting instructor Charlie Lau* made Brett, who had never hit .300 in the minor leagues, a consistent spray line drive hitter, while Hal McRae* taught him to run the bases aggressively. In 1975 Brett batted .308, paced the AL with 195 hits and 13 triples, and led third basemen in nearly all offensive categories. In 1976 Brett again led the AL in triples, tying a major league mark for accomplishing the feat two consecutive seasons. He established a major league record for most consecutive games (6) with three or more hits from May 8 through 13, 1976.

As a major leaguer for 21 seasons, the sandy-haired Brett compiled a .305 batting average. He made 3,154 hits, including 665 doubles, 137 triples, and 317 HR, and knocked in 1,595 runs. Besides exceeding the .300 mark 11 seasons, Brett won AL batting titles with .333 in 1976, .390 in 1980, and .329 in 1990. He also paced the AL in hits, triples (1975, 1976, 1979), and slugging percentage three times (1980, 1983, 1985), and once each in doubles (1979) and total bases (1976). The only player besides Ty Cobb* to win three AL titles in hits and triples, he in 1979 became one of only five players to slug at least 20 doubles, 20 triples, and 20 HR the same season. Brett hit for the cycle on May 28, 1979 and slugged three HR in the same game on July 22, 1979 and April 20, 1983. Defensively, Brett possessed good hands and range at third base and often made errors because of inconsistent throws. Brett batted .292 in 10 All-Star games (1976–1979, 1981–1985, 1988) and .340 in six AL Championship Series (1976–1978, 1980, 1984–1985).

In 1980, Brett enjoyed among the finest batting performances of the modern era. From May to the All-Star break, he raised his batting average from .247 to .337. Brett then hit in 37 consecutive games from mid-July to mid-August to reach the .400 mark and finished the season with a sparkling .390. Besides recording the highest major league batting average since 1941, he tied John McGraw* for the highest hitting percentage by a third baseman. In 117 games, Brett compiled a .664 slugging percentage and a .461 on-base percentage and knocked in 118 runs to become the first player in 30 years to drive in over one run per game played. Brett slugged 24 HR and struck out only 22 times. He hit two HR in the AL playoffs, helping the Kansas City Royals defeat the New York Yankees. Although Brett batted .375 and made four extra-base hits in the World Series, the Royals lost to the Philadelphia Phillies. An AL MVP, he won the AL Silver Bat, Joe Cronin, and Fred Hutchinson awards and was named *TSN*, *Sport*, and AP Major League Player of the Year. The highly competitive, enthusiastic Brett negotiated a multiyear contract for $1 million per season.

In 1985, Brett paced the Royals to their second AL pennant and first World Series title and finished second in the MVP balloting. During the regular season, he finished first in slugging percentage (.585), second in batting average (.335) and on-base percentage (.436), and fifth in RBI (112), doubles (38), and runs scored (108), and belted a career-high 30 HR. Five Brett HR came in the final six victories that gave Kansas City its Western Division title. The AL playoff MVP, Brett batted .348 overall and hit two HR, one double, and one single and knocked in three runs in game three against the Toronto Blue Jays. In the World Series, he batted .370 against the St. Louis Cardinals.

After batting .306 in 1988, Brett in 1990 became the only major leaguer to win batting titles in three different decades. He also led the AL with 45 doubles in 1990. On September 30, 1992, he became the 18th player to join the exclusive 3,000 hit club with hits in all four at-bats against the California Angels. Brett retired after the 1993 season to become vice-president of baseball operations for the Royals. Since 1995, he also has served as a vice-president of the Major League Baseball Players Alumni Association. Brett was elected to the National Baseball Hall of Fame in 1999 and serves as a color analyst for Fox-Sports baseball telecasts.

At Yankee Stadium in July 1983, Brett hit a controversial ninth inning

HR, temporarily giving the Royals the lead. After the New York Yankees appealed, however, the umpire disallowed the HR because of pine tar on the hitting surface of Brett's bat. AL president Leland MacPhail, Jr.* later re-instated Brett's HR.

BIBLIOGRAPHY: George Brett file, National Baseball Library, Cooperstown, NY; Sid Bordman, *Expansion to Excellence* (Marceline, MS, 1981); John Garrity; *The George Brett Story* (New York, 1981); Robert Grayson, "The Class of '99," *SCD* 25 (December 25, 1998), pp. 80–81; *CB* (1981), pp. 33–36; John Benson et al., *Baseball's Top 100* (Wilton, CT, 1997); Steve Cameron and George Brett, *George Brett; Last of a Breed* (Dallas, TX, 1993); Ron Fimrite, "The Hits Keep Coming," *SI* 77 (October 5, 1992), pp. 24–26; A. W. Laird, *Ranking Baseball's Elite* (Jefferson, NC, 1990); Robert E. Kelley, *Baseball's Best* (Jefferson, NC, 1988); *TSN Baseball Register, 1985*; Gib Twyman, *Born to Hit: The George Brett Story* (New York, 1982); Dan Valenti, *Clout! The Top Ten Home Runs in Baseball History* (Lexington, MA, 1989).

David L. Porter

BREWER, Chester Arthur "Chet" (b. January 14, 1907, Leavenworth, KS; d. March 26, 1990, Whittier, CA), player, scout, and manager, was the son of William Brewer, a Methodist minister, and Minnie (Davis) Brewer. Brewer studied at the University of Mexico and became fluent in Spanish. The 6-foot 4-inch, 185-pound right-handed pitcher was known for his lively fastball and a devastating overhand sinker. His professional baseball career began with the Gilkerson Union Giants of Joliet, IL in 1924.

Brewer joined the Negro League in 1925 with the Kansas City, MO Monarchs (NNL). In his first full season with the Kansas City Monarchs in 1926, he compiled an 11–3 win–loss record and hurled eight complete games. Three years later, he led the NNL with 17 wins and 15 complete games and pitched 31 consecutive scoreless innings against the NNL's best. One of his greatest pitching performances came under the lights in 1930 against the Homestead, PA Grays. Brewer struck out 19 batters, including 10 in a row, but lost, 1–0, in 12 innings. He finished the 1930 season with 30 wins. Brewer won 34 games in 1933 and started the 1934 season with 16 straight victories, en route to 33 triumphs. Brewer spent 15 seasons with the Kansas City Monarchs (1925–1935, 1937, 1940–1941, and 1946) and five seasons with the Cleveland, OH Buckeyes (NAL, 1942–1943, 1946–1948) before retiring in 1948. Brewer also played briefly with the Washington, DC Pilots (EWL) in 1932, the New York Cubans (NNL) in 1936, the Philadelphia, PA Stars (NAL) in 1941, and the Chicago, IL American Giants (NAL) in 1946. Brewer claimed his greatest thrills were pitching a no-hitter against Satchel Paige* and the Santa Domingo team and two no-hitters in the 1939 MEWL.

After retiring as a player, Brewer scouted for the Pittsburgh Pirates (NL) from 1957 to 1974 and managed their rookie team. He worked for the Major League Scouting Bureau, where he discovered Enos Cabell,* Willie Crawford, Dock Ellis, Reggie Smith,* Bobby Tolan, Ellis Valentine, and Bob Watson.*

Brewer married Mary Margaret Davis in 1924. They had two children, Chester Eugene and Marian Louise. In 1973, he married Tina Blanchard. Five years later, the Ross Snyder Recreation Center in Los Angeles, CA was renamed the Chet Brewer Baseball Field to honor his commitment for teaching the mechanics of baseball and the importance of personal behavior to local youths. Brewer epitomized the "classic" man, being a sympathetic manager, a person of principle, a great storyteller, and a superbly conditioned athlete with immense competitive spirits.

BIBLIOGRAPHY: Janet Bruce, *The Kansas City Monarchs* (Lawrence, KS, 1985); Jack Etkin, *Innings Ago* (Kansas City, MO, 1987); John Holway, *Black Diamonds* (Westport, CT, 1989); Kansas City (MO) *Call*, October 19, 1934; August 25, 1939; Pittsburgh (PA) *Courier*, August 9, 1930; James A. Riley, *The Biographical Encyclopedia of the Negro Baseball Leagues* (New York, 1994).

Larry Lester

BRIDGES, Thomas Jefferson Davis "Tommy" (b. December 28, 1906, Gordonsville, TN; d. April 19, 1968, Nashville, TN), player, coach, and scout, was the elder of two children of Dr. Joe Gill Bridges and Florence (Davis) Bridges. He graduated from Gordonsville elementary and high schools and attended the University of Tennessee. He married Carolyn Jellicorse on March 21, 1930, had one daughter, and later wed Iona Veda Kidwell on May 17, 1950. The Bridges family included several generations of doctors and expected Tommy to carry on the tradition. In 1929, however, after four years at Tennessee, he left without a degree to play professional baseball. He was signed by Detroit Tigers (AL) scout Billy Doyle, who had seen him pitch for the University of Tennessee Volunteers, and joined Wheeling, WV (MAL) in midseason. At Evansville, IN (3IL) the following year, he struck out 189 batters in 20 games and was promoted to the Tigers. In his first major league appearance, in relief against the New York Yankees, he retired Babe Ruth* on a grounder and struck out Lou Gehrig.*

In 1932 Bridges shut out the Washington Senators, 12–0, coming within one out of a perfect game before yielding a pinch hit single to Dave Harris.* He hurled two other one-hitters and 33 career shutouts. He teamed with Eldon Auker* in 1936 to win the biggest double shutout of all time (14–0, 12–0) against the St. Louis Browns. The slender 5-foot 10½-inch, 155 pounder was quiet in demeanor; even his frequent laughter was silent. Besides demonstrating good speed, he gained fame for a sharp-breaking, down-and-out curve, the best thrown by any right-hander in the league. Less well recognized was his occasional spitter. Despite his personal control, Bridges was plagued by wildness on the mound. He issued more than 100 walks in each of six seasons and averaged .42 walks per inning.

During a 16-year career with the Tigers, Bridges won 194 games and lost

138 for a .584 winning percentage and a 3.57 ERA. He won 66 games from 1934 to 1936 and twice led the AL in strikeouts. He also pitched in the 1934, 1935, 1940, and 1945 World Series, winning four of five decisions. In his second triumph over the Chicago Cubs in 1935, he entered the ninth inning of the sixth game with the score tied. The Cubs' Stan Hack* led off with a triple, only to be stranded when Bridges retired the side on ten pitched balls.

Bridges served in the U.S. Army for two years and rejoined the Tigers for the 1946 season. He pitched for Portland, OR (PCL) from 1947 to 1949 and San Francisco, CA (PCL) and Seattle, WA (PCL) in 1950 and coached and scouted for the Cincinnati Reds (NL) in 1951. He scouted for the Tigers (AL) from 1958 through 1960 and New York Mets from 1963 to 1968 and worked for a Detroit tire company. Aside from baseball, he enjoyed hunting, fishing, and golf.

BIBLIOGRAPHY: William M. Anderson, *The Detroit Tigers* (South Bend, IN, 1996); Richard Bak, *A Place for Summer* (Detroit, MI, 1998); Fred Smith, *995 Tigers* (Detroit, MI, 1981); Clifford Bloodgood, "Tom Bridges of the Tigers," *BM* 50 (April 1933), pp. 507–508; Detroit *Free Press*, August 31, 1941, September 7, 1941, February 10, 1957; Joe Falls, *Detroit Tigers* (New York, 1975); Donald Honig, *Baseball When the Grass Was Real* (New York, 1975); Frederick G. Lieb, *The Detroit Tigers* (New York, 1946); Ronald G. Liebman, "The Most Lopsided Shutouts," *BRJ* 7 (1976), p. 53; Thomas Bridges file, National Baseball Library, Cooperstown, NY; *The Baseball Encyclopedia*, 10th ed. (New York, 1996).

A. D. Suehsdorf

BRIGGS, Walter Owen "Spike" (b. February 27, 1877, Ypsilanti, MI; d. January 17, 1952, Miami Beach, FL), club owner and president, was a son of locomotive engineer Rodney Davis Briggs and Ada (Warner) Briggs. He played first base and caught for the John S. Newberry Public School in Detroit, but left school at age 14 to become a car checker for the Michigan Central Railroad. He advanced to car department foreman before leaving the company eleven years later. Subsequently, he worked as a cement plant foreman, shipping clerk, and auto body trimmer before joining B. F. Everitt Company, Detroit car body makers, in 1904 as vice-president. In 1906, he became company president. Three years later, he organized the Briggs Manufacturing Company and merged B. F. Everitt with it. The new company rapidly became a major supplier of automotive bodies for the Ford and later Chrysler motor companies, making Briggs a multimillionaire.

A rabid lifetime baseball fan, Briggs acquired ownership of the Detroit Tigers (AL) in stages. At the invitation of club president Frank Navin,* he bought a 25 percent interest from the William Yawkey estate in 1920 and another 25 percent after part-owner John Kelsey died. He purchased the balance following Navin's death in late 1935. Briggs drew no salary, turned all profits into team operations, and spent his own money lavishly on the

Tigers. Reputedly, he put over $5 million into the remodeling of Briggs Stadium (formerly Navin Field). He provided liberal salaries for his players and advanced huge sums for the acquisition of Mickey Cochrane,* Al Simmons,* Fred Hutchinson,* and prize rookie Dick Wakefield. In 1941 *TSN* named Briggs baseball Executive of the Year for his acumen in operating the Tigers, salary generosity, faith in baseball, and sportsmanship. During his sole ownership, the Tigers won AL pennants in 1940 and 1945 and the World Series in 1945.

Briggs married Jane Cameron in 1904 and had five children: Grace Mary (Mrs. William D. Robinson), Elizabeth Jane (Mrs. Charles T. Fisher, Jr.), Walter Owen II "Spike," Susan Ann (Mrs. Everell Fisher), and Jane Cameron (Mrs. Philip A. Hart, Jr.). Briggs died of a kidney infection at his Miami Beach winter home. The energetic, willful Briggs became a major industrialist by expanding his automotive body company, promoting land developments in Florida and Arizona, and engaging in other diverse business enterprises. He remained undeterred by a paralysis of the legs, which confined him to a wheelchair during his final dozen years. He donated money frequently (often anonymously) for the civic betterment of Detroit and its people. His other sports interests included ownership of a racing stable and a 236-foot yacht. Son "Spike" succeeded him as president of the Tigers and served until 1956, when control of the Detroit club passed from the Briggs family to an eleven-man syndicate.

BIBLIOGRAPHY: William M. Anderson, *The Detroit Tigers* (South Bend, IN, 1996); Richard Bak, *A Place for Summer* (Detroit, MI, 1998); Walter Briggs file, National Baseball Library, Cooperstown, NY; Joe Falls, *Detroit Tigers* (New York, 1975); Frederick G. Lieb, *The Detroit Tigers* (New York, 1946); *NCAB* 51 (New York, 1969), p. 524; *The New England Historical and Genealogical Register*, vol. 110 (Boston, January 1956), p. 65; *NYT*, January 18, 1952, July 4, 1970; *TSN*, November 28, 1935, December 5, 1935, July 30, 1942, January 23, 1952, February 23, 1955, July 18, 1970; *WWWA* 3 (1951–1960), pp. 103–104.

                                                                          Frank V. Phelps

BRIGGS, Wilma "Briggsie," "Willie" (b. November 6, 1930, East Greenwich, RI), player, is the daughter of Fred Briggs, a dairy farmer and manager, and Edythe (Hathaway) Briggs, a housewife, and grew up with six brothers and four sisters. She was reared in a culture where baseball was considered very important, as her brothers welcomed her to their pick-up games. One of her brothers played in the Chicago Cubs (NL) system. Her baseball heroes included the legendary Jimmie Foxx* and her father. "My father was a great pitcher and catcher, but his greatest quality was that, as as a coach, he gave all of his players every opportunity to be successful," she commented.

The 5-foot 4-inch, 138-pound Briggs, who batted left-handed and threw right-handed, played outfield and first base for the Fort Wayne, IN Daisies (AAGPBL) from 1948 to 1953 and spent her final season in 1954 as a star for the South Bend, IN Blue Sox (AAGPBL). Baseball historians rank Briggs among the AAGPBL's stellar hitters. She helped Fort Wayne win pennants in both 1952 and 1953. Nicknamed "Briggsie" by sports writers, she steadily improved as a player. During her first two professional baseball seasons, she hit only two HR. Her HR output increased to an AAGPBL-leading nine in 1953. In 1954 she ranked second in the AAGPBL with 25 HR.

Before turning professional, Briggs played on her high school boys squad and on her father's Frenchtown Farmers team. She "credits Max Carey* with teaching her how to hit the opposite field, to bunt for a hit, and to protect the runners on base." In 1951, Briggs was voted the AAGPBL's best defensive outfielder with a .987 fielding percentage. In seven AAGPBL seasons, she batted .258 with 633 hits, 64 doubles, 43 HR, and 301 RBI and compiled a .963 fielding percentage. Her 43 HR ranked third best lifetime in the AAGPBL.

Subsequently, Briggs graduated from Barrington College, Rhode Island, with a Bachelor's degree in elementary education and taught for 23 years at Wickford Elementary School in North Kingstown, RI, until 1992. She played softball until age 62, often bowled, and golfs passionately.

Briggs, who is single, loved the intense professional competition and the widespread travel opportunities. Her career highlight involved hitting a grand-slam HR in front of her parents at South Bend, IN in 1954. Briggs, who liked the kindness of Daisies manager Bill Allington, remarked "when the players had nothing but cotton jerseys to wear under their ill-suited uniforms, Allington immediately procured wool jerseys for them."

Briggs enjoys reading poetry anthologies, especially Robert Burns, and *RD* non-fiction. She in 1990 was the first woman inducted into East Greenwich's Athletic Hall of Fame and was elected to the first AAGPBLPA Board of Directors. In 1991, she received the first annual "Game of Legends" Award for 38 years of contributing to women's softball in Rhode Island.

BIBLIOGRAPHY: Scott A.G.M. Crawford, telephone interview with Wilma Briggs, April 4, 1996; W. C. Madden, *The Women of the All-American Girls Professional Baseball League* (Jefferson, NC, 1997); AAGPBL files, Northern Indiana Historical Society, South Bend, IN; Tim Wiles, National Baseball Library, Cooperstown, NY, letter to Scott A.G.M. Crawford, December 14, 1995; Scott A.G.M. Crawford, telephone conversation with Dottie Collins, AAGPBLPA, February 1996; Barbara Gregorich, *Women at Play* (San Diego, CA, 1993).

Scott A.G.M. Crawford

BRILES, Nelson Kelley "Nellie" (b. August 5, 1943, Dorris, CA), player and sportscaster, of Scottish, English, Irish, Dutch, and German descent, is the third of five children of lumber mill workers. At Chico High School, Briles quarterbacked the T-formation in football, played basketball point guard, and pitched and played third base in baseball.

After graduating from high school in 1961, Briles majored in Spanish at

Santa Clara University. He finished 11–2 as a freshman pitcher, but team-mate Bob Garibaldi overshadowed him. Briles spent two and a half years at Santa Clara before his father died of a heart attack and his mother suffered a heart attack. He signed with the St. Louis Cardinals (NL) for a $50,000 bonus, using the money to put his brothers through junior college and to help pay his mother's medical bills.

In 1964, Briles finished 11–6 for Tulsa, OK (TL) with a 2.79 ERA, second best in the league. After being called up to the St. Louis Cardinals in 1965, he pitched only 82.1 innings. He started 17 games with a 3.21 ERA in 1966, but struggled to a 4–15 mark. The 5-foot 11-inch, 195-pound right-hander possessed an outstanding fastball, curve, and slider. Pitching coach Billy Muffett decided that Briles must have been tipping his pitches and convinced him to use a no-windup delivery in 1967. Thrust into a starting role after Bob Gibson* broke his leg, he compiled a 10–2 mark in the season's second half and 14–5 overall with a 2.43 ERA. His complete game victory in the third game of the World Series helped the Cardinals defeat the Boston Red Sox in seven games.

In 1968, Briles ended 19–11 with a 2.81 ERA, as the St. Louis Cardinals again won the NL pennant. In the World Series, he started two games and was charged with one loss. The Detroit Tigers defeated the Cardinals in seven games. Briles' performance suffered when the mound was lowered after the 1968 season. He compiled a 15–13 mark in 1969, but his ERA rose to 3.52. When a hamstring injury limited his effectiveness in 1970, he was traded to the Pittsburgh Pirates (NL) in January 1971.

At Pittsburgh, he returned to using a windup and developed such an emphatic follow-through that he frequently ended up flat on the ground after his delivery. He won eight of 12 decisions in 136 innings in 1971. His finest moment came when he pitched a two-hit, complete game shutout and drove in a run against the Baltimore Orioles in Game 5 of the World Series, which the Pirates took in seven games. In 1972 he won 14 and lost 11 with a 3.08 ERA in 195.2 innings, as the Pirates won the Eastern Division title. In 1973, he enjoyed his best year with Pittsburgh, leading the Pirates in starts (33), wins (14), innings (218.2), and complete games (7). Pittsburgh traded Briles to the Kansas City Royals (AL) in December 1973, but he suffered a knee injury and underwent surgery on May 1. Overall, he finished 11–13 in two years with Kansas City. The Kansas City Royals traded him to the Texas Rangers (AL) in November 1975. In 1976 he fared 11–9, with 12 no-decisions. He and Gaylord Perry* were the only Rangers pitchers with winning records. After appearing in 30 games for Texas in 1977, he was claimed on waivers by the Baltimore Orioles (AL) in September 1977. He pitched in only 16 games for the Orioles in 1978, ending 4–4 with a 4.64 ERA, and retired in January 1979.

In 14 major league seasons, Briles won 129 games and lost 112, with a 3.44 ERA. In 2,112.2 innings, he struck out 1,163 batters and walked only

547. "Thick-thighed, barrel-chested, and snub-nosed," as sportswriter Bob Broeg (SI) described him, the stocky, dark-haired Briles remained a fierce competitor who often pitched his best in the most important games.

The engaging, enterprising pitcher took additional college courses at Chico State College, performed in singing groups, and in 1969 started an electronics company specializing in video. He made a career as a solo singer and impressionist in Pittsburgh and in 1979 became the color commentator for KDKA-TV broadcasts of Pittsburgh Pirates baseball. Briles handled baseball broadcasts for USA Cable from 1981 through 1983 and broadcast for the Seattle Mariners (AL) in 1984 and 1985. He now works for the Pittsburgh Pirates as director of corporate relations.

He married Mary Virginia Moore, whom he had first met while he portrayed Joe Hardy in his high school's production of *Damn Yankees*, on January 30, 1965. They have four children, Kelley, David, Christina, and Sarah.

BIBLIOGRAPHY: Nelson Briles file, National Baseball Library, Cooperstown, NY; John T. Bird, *Twin Killing: The Bill Mazeroski Story* (Birmingham, AL, 1995); Bob Broeg, "Nelson Briles, The Almond-Knocker," *BD* 27 (June 1968), pp. 41–43; Bob Broeg and Jerry Vickery, *St. Louis Cardinals Encyclopedia* (Grand Rapids, MI, 1998); Bob Broeg, *Redbirds! A Century of Cardinals' Baseball* (St. Louis, MO, 1981); Richard L. Burtt, *The Pittsburgh Pirates, A Pictorial History* (Virginia Beach, VA, 1977); John Devaney, "Nellie Briles: No Fear of the Shadows," *Sport* 46 (December 1968), pp. 40–41; Christopher Fletcher, "Battling Bucs," *Pittsburgh* (October 1996), pp. 78–81; Ross Forman, "Former Baseball Players Reminisce at Fall Fest," *SCD* 21 (August 12, 1994), pp. 60–61; Chuck Greenwood, "Briles Was a Prime Time Player," *SCD* 23 (September 27, 1996), pp. 160–161; *The Baseball Encyclopedia*, 10th ed. (New York, 1996); Bob Smizik, *The Pittsburgh Pirates: An Illustrated History* (New York, 1990).

Luther W. Spoehr

BROCK, James Lee "Jim" (b. July 24, 1936, Phoenix, AZ; d. June 12, 1994, Mesa, AZ), coach, was the son of William Davis Brock, Sr., and Elsie Vanoy (Thomasson) Brock. His father, who was disabled by lung and respiratory problems and largely unemployed, spent considerable time toward making his son "a big league pitcher." Although failing in that mission, William probably spawned his son's single-minded passion for baseball.

Brock coached baseball at his hometown Mesa High School and Mesa JC, where his clubs won an unprecedented two consecutive national JC Championships. When Arizona State University coach Bobby Winkles* joined the California Angels (AL) organization in 1972, Brock replaced him as interim baseball coach. Arizona State still liked Winkles so much that it had left open his old job if the California position did not work out. Few imagined that Brock would surpass his legendary predecessor. Brock called the Arizona State position "the best baseball job in the country," the Sun Devils having won three NCAA College World Series titles under Winkles.

In his 1977 autobiography, entitled *The Devil's Coach*, Brock admitted that the Winkles aura concerned him. The fierce competitor and perfectionist, who disliked criticism, wrote, "If Arizona State won the National Championship, credit would be apportioned as follows: Players, 56 percent; Winkles, 43 percent; Brock, 1 percent. If A.S.U. didn't win, the blame would be placed on: Winkles, nothing; players, 6 percent; umpires, 3 percent; Brock, 91 percent."

Brock succeeded immediately, producing an NCAA record 64 victories against just 6 losses during his first season. The Sun Devils finished second behind the University of Southern California, losing 1–0 to the Trojans in the NCAA Championship final. Brock, named Coach of the Year for the first of four times, stated, "The fans hadn't eaten me alive for losing to U.S.C." He acknowledged that his intense drive magnified the pressure he experienced in the job and accounted for his sometimes severe coaching methods, conflicts with the NCAA, and occasional battles with university administrators. Brock credited his commitment to Christianity and his wife, Patsy Ann Futrell, with giving him a more tranquil attitude in later years. They had two children, Jim, Jr. and Cathi.

Brock led the Sun Devils to another second-place finish in 1973, third place in 1975 and 1976, and the NCAA Championship in 1977. His 1976 team set the Sun Devil record for victories with a 65–10 mark. Four of his teams won at least 60 games. Hubie Brooks and Bob Horner* starred on the 1977 Arizona State team. Brock's 1981 squad also won the NCAA title, featuring Alvin Davis and Donnie Hill. His 23-year 1,100–440 win–loss record at Arizona State included 13 College World Series appearances. Brock sent 64 players to the major leagues, including Brooks, Horner, Davis, Hill, Barry Bonds,* and Pat Listach. He ranks 14th among NCAA Division I coaches in career victories and 17th in winning percentage. Brock, who earned a Doctoral degree at Arizona State, died after a long bout with liver cancer.

BIBLIOGRAPHY: *Arizona State University Baseball Media Guide*, 1972–1994; Jim Brock and Joe Gilmartin, *The Devil's Coach* (Elgin, IL, 1977); *Official NCAA Baseball Records*, 1972–1994, *USAT*, June 13, 1994, *NYT*, June 14, 1994, p. D21.

Cappy Gagnon

BROCK, Louis Clark "Lou" (b. June 18, 1939, El Dorado, AR), player, is the son of Maud Brock and Paralee Brock and the seventh of nine children. When Maud deserted the family shortly after Louis' birth, Paralee moved to Colliston, LA just below the Arkansas border, and performed domestic and farm work to support the family. Brock attended all-black schools in Mer Rouge, LA and from 1954 to 1957 starred on the Union High School baseball and basketball teams. In 1957, he received a scholarship to Southern University at Baton Rouge. Although hitting a paltry .186 as a freshman, he impressed big league scouts with a .645 batting average his sophomore year. In 1959, he played in the Pan American games at Chicago. Brock married college sweetheart Katie Hay in December 1960 and has two children, Wanda and Louis, Jr.

After accepting a $30,000 bonus with the Chicago Cubs (NL) in 1961, Brock led the NoL the same year with 268 total bases, 181 hits, 117 runs, 33 doubles, and a .361 batting average at St. Cloud, MN (NoL). In September 1961, he was called up by the Cubs (NL). After two mediocre seasons in Chicago, Brock was sent on June 15, 1964 to the St. Louis Cardinals (NL) for Ernie Broglio and Bobby Shantz.* Although initially outraged, Cardinals fans quickly admired their new left fielder. The 5-foot 11½-inch, 170-pound Brock hit .348 and pilfered 33 bases the remainder of 1964, sparking the Cardinals to their first NL pennant since 1946. His major league career comprised 15 more seasons, all with St. Louis.

From 1965 through 1969, Brock averaged 100 runs, 190 hits, and 61 stolen bases per year. He dominated the 1967 and 1968 World Series, hitting .414 and .464 and setting World Series records with seven stolen bases in each. Although leading NL outfielders in errors seven times and striking out over 1,700 times, Brock compensated with his hitting and revolutionary daring on the basepaths. From 1970 through 1976, Brock collected 1,295 hits, swiped 478 bases and averaged .306 at the plate.

On September 10, 1974, Brock broke Maury Wills's* single-season major league theft record of 104 on his way to 118. Longtime teammate Tim McCarver* attributed Brock's success to his intimidation of infielders. In 1977, Brock surpassed Ty Cobb's* career stolen base record of 892. Brock hoped in 1978 to join boyhood hero Stan Musial* in the 3,000 hit club, but a dismal .221 season left him 100 hits short. At age 40 in 1979, Brock rebounded to hit .304 in his last campaign and made his 3,000th hit on August 13 against the Cubs' Dennis Lamp. Brock's 19-year major league career included 3,023 hits, 1,610 runs, a record 938 stolen bases, 486 doubles, 141 triples, and 149 HR. He stole 50 or more bases twelve consecutive seasons, another major league record.

Brock played healthy or injured, always with enthusiasm and determination. He demonstrated that speed could be a viable alternative to power, making the stolen bases as exciting as the HR. Former Cardinals skipper Red Schoendienst* commented in Brock's book, *Stealing Is My Game*: "He just loves to play ball. If you could play as well as him, wouldn't you?" Brock is very dedicated to the St. Louis community and has been involved with the Lou Brock Boys' Club since 1965. His civic awards include the B'nai B'rith Brotherhood Award, St. Louis Jaycees' Man of the Year, and the Roberto Clemente Award. Brock is engaged in the florist business in St. Louis and has several other commercial interests there. In 1985 he was elected to the National Baseball Hall of Fame. He works in retail and wholesale soft goods through Broc-World Products International.

BIBLIOGRAPHY: Louis Brock file, National Baseball Library, Cooperstown, NY; David Craft, *Redbirds Revisited* (Chicago, IL, 1990); John Benson et al., *Baseball's Top 100* (Wilton, CT, 1997); Louis Brock and Franz Schulze, *Stealing Is My Game* (Englewood Cliffs, NJ, 1976); Bob Broeg, *Redbirds: A Century of Cardinals Baseball* (St. Louis, MO, 1981); Bob Broeg and Jerry Vickery, *St. Louis Cardinals Encyclopedia* (Grand Rapids, MI, 1998); *CB* (1975), pp. 43–45; David L. Porter, ed., *African-American Sports Greats* (Westport, CT, 1995); Nila Gilcrest, "Katie Brock: In Every Way an All-Star," *TSN*, July 1, 1972, p. 15; Eddie Gold and Art Ahrens, *The New Era Cubs, 1941–1985* (Chicago, IL, 1985); Bill Guzman, *Munson, Garvey, Brock, and Carew* (New York, 1976); Rich Koster, "Tim McCarver: Twenty Years Behind the Mask," *BD* 38 (December 1979); Rob Rains, *The St. Louis Cardinals* (New York, 1992); Neal Russo, "At Age 32, Base Thief Brock Plots More, Bigger Heists," *TSN*, January 1, 1972, p. 33; Lowell Reidenbaugh, *Baseball's Hall of Fame-Cooperstown* (New York, 1993); Neal Russo, "Brock Still a Jet Fast Thief on 33rd Birthday," *TSN*, July 1, 1972, pp. 15, 20; Rich Westcott, *Diamond Greats* (Westport, CT, 1988).

Frank J. Olmsted

BRODIE, Walter Scott "Steve" (b. September 11, 1868, Warrenton, VA; d. October 30, 1935, Baltimore, MD), player, scout, and coach, was the son of Alexander M. Brodie, a tailor, Shakespearean actor, and Scottish immigrant, and Jeannette (LaMarque) Brodie, a Virginia native of French ancestry. Brodie, who married 15-year-old Caroline Amanda Henry in 1890 and had one son and one daughter, started playing semiprofessional baseball in Roanoke, VA in 1885 and 1886. He began his professional baseball career in 1887 as a catcher–outfielder first with Altoona, PA (PaStA) and Canton, OH (OSL). He played in 1888 for the Wheeling, WV Nailers (TSL), where his teammates included National Baseball Hall-of-Famer Ed Delehanty.* In 1889, he batted .302 for Hamilton, Canada (IL).

The 5-foot 9-inch, 175-pound Brodie joined the Boston Beaneaters (NL) in 1890. Brodie, among the swiftest, most durable center fielders of the 1890s, contributed to Boston's 1891 NL championship. His 727 consecutive game streak, a nineteenth-century record, began that year. An adequate batter in his first three major league seasons, he became an outstanding hitter with a .318 mark for the St. Louis Browns (NL) in 1893. Brodie moved to the Baltimore Orioles (NL) as center fielder for the championship 1894, 1895, and 1896 Orioles. The Orioles outfield of Joe Kelley* in left, Brodie in center, and Willie Keeler* in right ranked among the best in the game. Manager Ned Hanlon* traded Brodie to the Pittsburgh Pirates (NL) in 1897 for Jake Stenzel,* but reacquired him near the end of 1898.

Brodie jumped to the AL in 1901 with the Baltimore Orioles, managed by his former teammate John McGraw.* Brodie followed McGraw to the New York Giants (NL) in 1902 to close out his major league career. Brodie played on five championship teams, batted over .300 five times, and compiled a .303 career batting average, making 1,726 hits. During his playing days, his hijinks, durability, solid hitting, and fine fielding were publicized. *TSN* described him as "one of the notable clowns of the game," while McGraw's biographer labeled Brodie "a flake—a player who delighted in zany behavior."

Brodie continued playing in the minor leagues through 1910, making stops in Montreal, Canada (EL), Newark, NJ (EL), Providence, RI (EL), Binghamton, NY (NYSL), Birmingham, AL (SA), Norfolk VA (VSL), Portsmouth, VA (VSL), Roanoke, VA (VSL), and Wilmington, NC (ECaL). Baseball coaching assignments followed at Rutgers University from 1912 to 1914 and the U.S. Naval Academy from 1914 to 1922. In 1922 Brodie returned to Baltimore, MD, where he worked as a supervisor for the city Park Board until his death. In 1992, he was inducted into the Roanoke-Salem Hall of Fame.

BIBLIOGRAPHY: Charles C. Alexander, *John McGraw* (New York, 1988); James H. Bready, *The Home Team* (Baltimore, MD, 1959); Walter Brodie file, National Baseball Library, Cooperstown, NY; James H. Bready, *Baseball in Baltimore* (Baltimore MD, 1998); Craig Carter, ed., *TSN Daguerreotypes*, 8th ed. (St. Louis, MO, 1990); Frederick Ivor-Campbell et al., eds., *Baseball's First Stars* (Cleveland, OH, 1996); Harold Kaese, *The Boston Braves* (New York, 1948); Frederick G. Lieb, *The Baltimore Orioles* (New York, 1955); A. D. Suehsdorf, "Frank Selee, Dynasty Builder," *TNP* 4 (Winter 1985), pp. 35–41.

William E. Akin

BROUTHERS, Dennis Joseph "Dan," "Big Dan" (b. May 8, 1858, Sylvan Lake, NY; d. August 2, 1932, East Orange, NJ), player, coach, and scout, was reared in Wappingers Falls, NY and attended school there to age 16. He began semiprofessional ball in his late teens with the Wappingers Falls Actives, playing five years for various semipro and independent clubs and briefly stopping in 1879–1880 with the Troy, NY Haymakers (NL). From 1881 to 1885 Brouthers played for the Buffalo, NY Bisons and twice (1882, 1883) led the NL in batting. The hard-hitting first baseman proved the mightiest of the team's renowned "big four," which also included Hardy Richardson,* Jack Rowe,* and Deacon White.* In December 1884, he married Mary Ellen Croak of Wappingers Falls. They had four children, Leo, Allison, Margaret, and Lillian.

Sold as a group in late 1885 to the Detroit Wolverines (NL), the "big four" helped the Wolverines capture their first pennant in 1887. Brouthers spent three seasons in Detroit (1886–1888) and then played three years for Boston teams in three major leagues (NL, 1889; PL, 1890; AA, 1891). At Boston, he twice won his league's batting championship (1889, 1891) and twice helped his club win the pennants (1890, 1891).

Brouthers spent the remainder of his major league career in the NL. With the Brooklyn Bridegrooms in 1892, he won his fifth batting title. After joining the Baltimore Orioles in 1894, he helped win their first pennant and formed a lifelong friendship with teammate John McGraw.* Except for two games played in 1904 for McGraw's New York Giants, Brouthers finished his major league career with the Louisville Colonels in 1895 and Philadelphia Phillies in 1896.

Brouthers played minor league ball in the EL from 1896 to 1899 with

Springfield, MA, Toronto, Canada, and Rochester, NY, leading the EL in batting in 1897. He returned to the ball field intermittently after 1899, performing in 1904–1905 for Poughkeepsie, NY (HRL).

Brouthers remained active in baseball as a coach and scout (finding future New York Giants players Fred Merkle,* Larry Doyle,* and Buck Herzog*) and briefly owned a minor league club in Newburgh, NY. He worked many years until his death for McGraw's Giants as night watchman, press box chief, and stadium attendant. Mary Allen, his wife of over 47 years, died just two weeks after him and was survived by two daughters and two sons.

Christened Dennis but called "Dan" or "Big Dan," the 6-foot 2-inch, 207-pound Brouthers was physically large for his day. He batted and threw left-handed and reputedly possessed the sharpest batting eye in baseball. (He allegedly originated the familiar advice to hitters to "keep your eye on the ball.") As a major leaguer, he struck out less than once every seven games. From 1882 to 1892, he ranked among the top six batters in his league. His .342 lifetime batting average ranks fourth highest among his contemporaries and eighth highest of all time. In 1,673 games, he compiled 2,296 hits, 460 doubles, 106 HR, 1,523 runs, 1,296 RBI, and 256 stolen bases.

The premier power hitter of his era, Brouthers led his league seven times in slugging average (1881–1886, 1891), four times in total bases, three times in doubles, twice in HR, and once in triples. His .519 lifetime slugging average surpassed that of the next best 19th century slugger by a substantial margin. Brouthers was elected to the National Baseball Hall of Fame in 1945. In 1971, his home town of Wappingers Falls erected a monument to him at a Little League park by renaming it Brouthers Field.

BIBLIOGRAPHY: "Big Dan's Bat," *TSN*, February 5, 1898; Dan Brouthers file, National Baseball Library, Cooperstown, NY; Sam Crane, "Dan Brouthers," *NYJ*, December 11, 1911; Craig Carter, ed., *TSN Daguerreotypes*, 8th ed. (St. Louis, MO, 1990); Frederick Ivor-Campbell et al., eds., *Baseball's First Stars* (Cleveland, OH, 1996); Tom Meany, "McGraw Praises Brouthers," *NYWT*, August 4, 1932; Newark *Star Eagle*, August 3, 1932; *NYT*, August 3, 1932; Poughkeepsie (NY) *Evening Star*, August 3, 1932; *The Baseball Encyclopedia*, 10th ed. (New York, 1996); "Two Old Timers Talk Things Over," *NYWT*, June 2, 1931; Lowell Reidenbaugh, *Baseball's Hall of Fame-Cooperstown* (New York, 1993); *Wappingers Falls Past and Present 1871–1971* (Wappingers Falls, NY, 1971), pp. 47–49; Will Whitman, "Dan Brouthers Noted Batsman," Canton (NY) *Advertiser*, August 20, 1932.

Frederick Ivor-Campbell

BROWN, David "Dave," "Lefty" (b. 1896, San Marcos, TX; d. Denver, CO), player, enjoyed a brief, illustrious career as the era's top black left-handed pitcher. His baseball career began with the Dallas Black Giants in 1917 and 1918. After entering the top echelon of black baseball with Rube Foster's* Chicago American Giants in 1918, he soon became the ace pitcher of the powerful American Giants team. Brown remained with Chicago through

1922, helping the American Giants take the NNL's initial three championships from 1920 to 1922.

When the ECL was organized in 1923, Brown accompanied a bevy of
players leaving the NNL. He continued his pitching mastery with the New
York Lincoln Giants (ECL) during 1923 and 1924. He journeyed west for
the 1924–1925 CWL season to pitch with Santa Clara, CA, Brown's last
known professional team. The 1924–1925 season marked the last of three
seasons during which Brown hurled in the CWL. He posted a 17–12 career
mark in 31 CWL contests, but then vanished at the peak of his career.

When Foster signed Brown, the young pitcher possessed a criminal record. Since Brown had been convicted of robbery, Foster posted a $20,000
bond to have Brown placed in his custody. Brown's disappearance at the
beginning of the 1925 baseball season came under the cloud of a New York
homicide. Cocaine apparently was involved, with Brown allegedly murdering
another man in New York. He may have moved to the mid-west to avoid
the law and pitched under the alias "Lefty Wilson" for another five or six
years. He toured with Gilkerson's Union Giants in 1926, played with a Bertha, MN white team in 1927, and hurled for Sioux City, IA in 1929 and
Little Falls, MN in 1930. He died in Denver, CO, under mysterious circumstances. Whatever became of the talented, elusive Brown, he was considered
the best at pitching a baseball for a period of time.

BIBLIOGRAPHY: John B. Holway, *Blackball Stars* (Westport, CT, 1988); Robert W.
Peterson, *Only the Ball Was White* (Englewood Cliffs, NJ, 1970); James A. Riley, *The
All-Time All-Stars of Black Baseball* (Cocoa, FL, 1983); James A. Riley, *Biographical
Encyclopedia of the Negro Baseball Leagues* (New York, 1994); Charles E. Whitehead,
A Man and His Diamonds (New York, 1980).

                                                        Merl F. Kleinknecht

BROWN, James Kevin (b. March 14, 1965, Milledgeville, GA), player, graduated from Wilkinson County High School in Irwinton, GA and attended
Georgia Institute of Technology in Atlanta, where he earned *TSN* College
All-American honors as a pitcher in 1986. The Texas Rangers (AL) made
Brown the fourth overall pick in the June 1986 free agent draft. Brown
pitched only six minor league games in 1986 before winning his only start
for the Rangers. He won one of 12 decisions the next season at Tulsa, OK
(TL), Oklahoma City, OK (AA), and Charlotte, NC (FSL). In September
1988, Texas recalled Brown after he fashioned a 12–10 record at Tulsa.

The 6-foot 4-inch, 193-pound right-hander won 12, lost nine, and completed seven games for the Texas Rangers in 1989. With a four-seam fastball
in the mid 90s, a sinking fastball, an outstanding hard slider, a good change-
up, and an excellent move to first base, Brown quickly established himself
in the Texas rotation. He triumphed 12 times in 1990, but slipped to 9–12
in 1991. Brown led AL pitchers with 21 victories and 265.2 innings in 1992,
tossing 11 complete games while striking out 173 batters. He was the winning pitcher for the AL in the 1992 All-Star game. In 1993, Brown settled

for a $2.8 million one-year contract after losing an intense arbitration struggle with the Texas Rangers. He won 15, lost 12, and pitched 12 complete games despite missing the last half of spring training due to a rib cage stress fracture. Brown sought a four-year contract extension from Texas in 1994, but negotiations collapsed just before opening day. He struggled to a 7–9 record with a 4.82 ERA. Brown served as assistant player representative for the AL on the negotiating committee during the 1994 baseball strike.

Brown signed a free agent contract with the Baltimore Orioles (AL) in April 1995. He spent 3½ weeks on the disabled list in mid-season, finishing with 10 wins and nine defeats. Although having one of the best arms in baseball, he was perceived as aloof and a less than positive clubhouse influence. Brown moved on again, signing for $3.3 million per year with the Florida Marlins (NL) in December 1995. Using a sinker and slider to induce ground balls, he took advantage of Florida's slow infield. He won 17, lost 11, and led the NL with a 1.89 ERA. Brown, who allowed only 187 hits in 233 innings, pitched a scoreless inning for the NL in the 1996 All-Star game and finished second in the NL Cy Young voting. Brown again anchored the Marlins staff in 1997, when he won 16 games with a 2.69 ERA, struck out a career-high 205 batters, and made the NL All-Star Team. On September 24, he defeated the Montreal Expos to clinch the NL wild card playoff berth and give the Marlins their first post-season appearance. Brown pitched brilliantly with a 7–0 record and 1.84 ERA the final two months of the regular season and surrendered just one run in his only NL Division Series start against the San Francisco Giants. His two victories helped the Marlins defeat the Atlanta Braves in the NL Championship Series, but Brown lost both starts with an 8.18 ERA against the Cleveland Indians in the World Series. In December 1997, Florida traded him to the San Diego Padres (NL). His 18–7 record, 257 strikeouts, and 2.38 ERA helped San Diego capture the NL West division title, as he finished third in the NL Cy Young Award balloting. He hurled eight shutout innings to defeat the Houston Astros in the NL Division Series and blanked the Atlanta Braves in Game 2 of the NL Championship Series. He surrendered a three-run HR to Michael Tucker in a surprise relief appearance in Game 5 of the NL Championship Series and lost in the final Game 4 of the World Series to the New York Yankees. In December 1998, the Los Angeles Dodgers (NL) signed him to a record seven-year $105 million contract. No major leaguer had reached the $100 million barrier previously. In 1999, Brown compiled an 18–9 record and 3.00 ERA, ranking second in the NL in innings (252.1) and strikeouts (221). Through the 1999 season, Brown has won 157 games and lost 108, with 1,732 strikeouts, 66 complete games, 16 shutouts, and 2,430.2 innings in 349 games.

BIBLIOGRAPHY: James Kevin Brown file, National Baseball Library, Cooperstown, NY; *TSN Baseball Register, 1998*; John Dewan, ed., *The Scouting Report: 1994* (New York, 1994); Hank Hersch, "Texas Chainsaw Massacre," *SI* 77 (July 27, 1992), p. 58;

Zander Hollander, ed., *The 1997 Complete Handbook of Baseball*, 27th ed. (New York, 1997); Bob Kuenster, "Marlins Armed for a Pennant Run," *BD 56* (June 1997), pp. 22–25.

Frank J. Olmsted

BROWN, Larry "Iron Man" (b. September 5, 1905, Pratt City, AL; d. April 7, 1972, Memphis, TN), player and manager, excelled as a defensive catcher and subsequently became a playing manager during a 31-year Negro League baseball career. He played for at least 10 teams, often splitting seasons among two or three squads. Blessed with a rifle arm and quick release, Brown remained in great demand despite his average offensive skills. The 5-foot 8-inch, 180-pound Brown, noted for not removing his mask on pop flies, acquired the nickname of "Iron Man" because of his willingness to play every day. In 1930 he reportedly caught 234 games, sometimes making three appearances in one day.

Brown and his older sister were brought up by their mother until her death in 1918. After catching for Pratt City High School, Brown in 1919 worked as a mule driver for the Tennessee Coal and Iron Company. He played for the company nine with an occasional game for the Birmingham, AL Black Sox. He began a full-time professional baseball career on July 4, 1920, signing with Knoxville, TN, for $125 per month. After playing with the Pittsburgh, PA Keystones in 1921 and 1922, Brown split the 1923 season between the Indianapolis, IN ABCs (NAL) and the Memphis, TN Red Sox (NAL) and remained with the Red Sox in 1924 and 1925. After spending the 1926 campaign with the Detroit Stars (NNL), Brown batted .253 for Memphis in 1927. In late 1927, he moved to the Chicago American Giants (NNL) and started at catcher in the Negro World Series against the Atlantic City, NJ Bacharach Giants (ECL). Upon returning to Memphis, Brown hit .292 in 1928 and .289 in 1929 and led his club in games played, at bats, hits, and doubles in 1928.

Brown's defensive play in the CUWL attracted major league attention. After throwing out Ty Cobb* on five consecutive steal attempts in 1926, Brown allegedly was approached by the Detroit Tigers (AL) star Ty Cobb with the suggestion that the light-skinned catcher learn Spanish, pass as a Cuban, and accept his help into the major leagues. Rogers Hornsby* reportedly made a similar proposal, but Brown refused the offers.

In 1930 Brown batted .256 for the New York Lincoln Giants (NAL), managed by National Baseball Hall-of-Famer Pop Lloyd.* He moved to the Harlem Stars the next year and began the 1932 season with the New York Black Yankees (NAL), which folded at mid-year. Brown returned to the Chicago American Giants, which won the 1933 NNL championship. Chicago came within one game of repeating in 1934, losing a seven-game playoff series to the Philadelphia Stars. These two seasons marked the inaugural years for the East–West Negro League All-Star game. Fans voted Brown to start both years for the West squad. Brown spent 1935 and 1937 with the

Chicago American Giants, sandwiching around a season with the Philadelphia Stars (NAL). Brown's many moves may have resulted from an alcohol problem, but he spent 11 years from 1939 to 1948 as a Memphis Red Sox player–manager. Brown made four more All-Star teams from 1938 through 1941, batting .308 for his six All-Star appearances. Although statistics are spotty, Brown is credited with a .259 lifetime batting average for his 31-year career. After retiring in 1948 from baseball, Brown worked as a headwaiter in a Memphis, TN hotel for 23 years. He was married and had one son.

BIBLIOGRAPHY: Dick Clark and Larry Lester, eds., *The Negro Leagues Book* (Cleveland, OH, 1994); Phil Dixon and Patrick J. Hannigin, *The Negro Baseball Leagues* (Mattituck, NY, 1992); John Holway, *Voices From the Great Black Baseball Leagues* (New York, 1975); James A. Riley, *The Biographical Encyclopedia of the Negro Baseball Leagues* (New York, 1994).

David Bernstein

BROWN, Mordecai Peter Centennial "Three Finger," "Miner" (b. October 19, 1876, Nyesville, IN; d. February 14, 1948, Terre Haute, IN), player and manager, grew up in rural Indiana. Nicknamed "Three Finger" and "Miner," he played third base for the Coxville, IN semiprofessional team, composed mostly of miners. In 1901 he pitched for Terre Haute, IN (3IL), winning 23 games and losing eight. The following year saw him at Omaha, NE (WL), where his record was 27 wins, 15 losses.

During his major league career, he pitched for the St. Louis Cardinals (1903), Chicago Cubs (1904–1912, 1916), and Cincinnati Reds (1913) of the NL, and St. Louis Terriers, Brooklyn Tip-Tops, and Chicago Whales of the FL (1914–1915). Brown, whose career ERA was a near-record 2.06, threw 55 career shutouts and won 239 games and lost 130 for a .648 winning percentage. His outstanding pitching helped Chicago capture NL championships from 1906 to 1908 and in 1910. He won five World Series games, including two in relief, fielded superbly, and handled 108 chances without an error in 1908. He shared with Christy Mathewson* several World Series fielding records for pitchers. During a remarkable 1911 season, Brown won 16 of 27 starts, completed 21 games, and led the NL with 26 relief appearances and 13 saves.

After his major league career, Brown pitched for Columbus, OH (IL) in 1917–1918 and was player–manager for Terre Haute, IN (3IL) in 1919–1920. The Terre Haute resident managed a semiprofessional team and operated a filling station until he retired in 1945. In 1949, he was elected to the National Baseball Hall of Fame.

As a youth, "Three Finger" Brown caught his hand in a feed cutter and lost the top joint of his index finger and the use of his little finger. When his injured hand was still in a cast, he broke the other two fingers, which became permanently misshapen. With his crippled hand, Brown threw a natural sinker ball.

BIBLIOGRAPHY: John Benson et al., *Baseball's Top 100* (Wilton, CT, 1997); Mordecai Brown file, National Baseball Library, Cooperstown, NY; G. H. Fleming, *The Unforgettable Season* (New York, 1981); Warren Brown, *The Chicago Cubs* (New York, 1946); Paul C. Frisz, "Mordecai Peter Centennial Brown," *BRJ* 5 (1976), pp. 18–20; Ralph Hickok, *Who Was Who in American Sports* (New York, 1971); Noel Hynd, *The Giants of the Polo Grounds* (New York, 1988); Eddie Gold and Art Ahrens, *The Golden Era Cubs, 1876–1940* (Chicago, IL, 1985); Gene Karst and Martin J. Jones, Jr., *Who's Who in Professional Baseball* (New Rochelle, NY, 1973); *The Baseball Encyclopedia*, 10th ed. (New York, 1996); Bill Madden, *The Hoosiers of Summer* (Indianapolis, IN, 1994); Warren Wilbert and William Hageman, *Chicago Cubs—Seasons at the Summit* (Champaign, IL, 1997); *NYT*, February 15, 1948; Lowell Reidenbaugh, *Baseball's Hall of Fame-Cooperstown* (New York, 1993).

John E. Findling

BROWN, Raymond "Ray" (b. February 23, 1908, Ashland Grove, OH; d. 1968, Dayton, OH), player, was the ace pitcher for the Homestead, PA Grays (NNL) during their dynasty period, when they won nine consecutive pennants from 1937 to 1945. Before turning professional, Brown played high school baseball in Indian Lake, OH and attended Wilberforce University. He left before graduation to sign with the Homestead Grays and played there from 1932 through 1945 and in 1947 and 1948. The 6-foot 1-inch, 195 pounder, a versatile athlete, was an outstanding pitcher and a good hitter with power from both sides of the plate. Early in his career, he played center field when not starting on the mound. As the years passed, however, he concentrated more on his pitching. As the son-in-law of Homestead Grays' owner Cum Posey,* he was thought by some to have a preferred status on the team. Others considered the star hurler temperamental, but never questioned his ability and performance. He possessed a very effective knuckleball and curve, complemented with a sinker, slider, and fine fastball. Most of his 24-year career was spent in the Negro Leagues, but he also pitched in Mexico, Cuba, and Canada.

During Brown's tenure with the Grays, Homestead played in the first four Negro World Series (1942–1945) held between the NNL and the NAL and won the middle two. In World Series competition, Brown pitched seven games, posted a combined 3–2 win–loss ledger, and hurled a one-hit shutout of the Birmingham, AL Black Barons in the 1944 Classic. His best pitching gem came in 1945, when he pitched a perfect game in a seven-inning contest against the Chicago American Giants. He also appeared in two East-West All-Star Games (1935, 1940) without a decision.

With the great offensive support generated by the powerful bats in the Homestead Grays lineup, Brown enjoyed considerable success and ranks high in winning percentage among all-time Negro League pitchers. Throughout his Negro League career, he enjoyed long winning streaks. One stretch in 1936–1937 saw him credited with 28 straight victories. In 1938, the Homestead Grays fielded their strongest team during his tenure with the team. Brown finished the season with a 10–2 NNL record and ranked among five players designated by the Pittsburgh *Courier* as certain major league stars. He posted league marks of 18–3 (2.53 ERA) in 1940 and 10–4 (2.72 ERA) in 1941, the same year the big right-hander was credited with 27 straight wins against all levels of opposition. In 1942, he finished 13–6 with the Homestead Grays, who notched their sixth straight NNL pennant and lost to the Kansas City Monarchs in the World Series.

The Cuban favorite won more games in the CUWL than any other black American pitcher, posting a 46–20 record in his five seasons there. In 1936–1937, he led the CUWL in wins with a 21–3 record and hurled a no-hitter among his victories. He paced the PRWL in victories in 1941–1942 with a 12–4 ledger and a 1.82 ERA.

Brown left the Homestead Grays in 1946 and went to the MEL, where he finished 13–9 with a 3.52 ERA. Following a 15–11 mark and a 3.40 ERA in 1949, he left Mexico for the Sherbrooke, Canada (CaPL). He retired after the 1953 season, remarried, and settled in Canada for several years, before returning to the United States.

BIBLIOGRAPHY: Robert W. Peterson, *Only the Ball Was White* (Englewood Cliffs, NJ, 1970); Pittsburgh (PA) *Courier*, 1935–1946; James A. Riley, *The All-Time All-Stars of Black Baseball* (Cocoa, FL, 1983); James A. Riley, *The Biographical Encyclopedia of the Negro Baseball Leagues* (New York, 1994); James A. Riley, interviews with former Negro League players, James A. Riley collection, Cocoa, FL; Mike Shatzkin, ed., *The Ballplayers* (New York, 1990); *The Baseball Encyclopedia*, 10th ed. (New York, 1996).

James A. Riley

BROWN, Robert William "Bobby" (b. October 25, 1924, Seattle, WA), player and executive, is the son of William Christopher Brown, an executive with Schenley Distillery, and Myrtle Katherine (Berg) Brown. Brown, whose father started him playing baseball "before I can remember," attended Columbia High School in San Francisco CA from 1940 through 1942. After studying at Stanford University in 1942–1943 and the University of California at Los Angeles in 1943–1944, he enrolled in Tulane University's School of Medicine in 1944 and graduated in 1950. He since has been named to the Athletic Halls of Fame at both Stanford and Tulane.

Brown, whose sole competitive athletic interest was baseball, threw right-handed, batted left-handed, and found hitting his strong suit. He signed for a substantial bonus with the New York Yankees (AL) in 1946 and played that season with their Newark, NJ (IL) farm team, where he roomed with Yogi Berra.* (Berra once finished a comic book, turned to Brown, who was putting down a medical text, and asked, "How'd yours come out?") In 1946 Brown was named Outstanding New Jersey Athlete. Brown appeared briefly with the Yankees in 1946 and made the permanent team roster in 1947, leading the AL in pinch hits (9). Sharing duties at third base, he played against right-handed pitchers and never appeared in more than 113 games or accumulated over 363 at bats in a season. The 6-foot 1-inch, 180-pound Brown batted .279 lifetime and hit with some power, as 98 of his 452 major league hits went for extra bases. In 548 games, he slugged 62 doubles, 14 triples, and 22 HR, scored 233 runs, knocked in 237 runs, and walked 214 times. In four World Series (1947, 1949–1951), he batted .439 and made 8 extra-base hits among his 17 total hits. Brown was drafted into the U.S. Army during the 1952 season and missed the entire 1953 campaign. After appearing in 28 games in 1954, he retired to begin his medical internship.

From 1958 to 1984, Brown practiced cardiology in Fort Worth, TX. He lived there with his wife, Sara Kathryn (French) Brown, whom he had married on October 16, 1951. By 1984, Brown commented that he "wanted to either decrease my patient load or get into a different type of medicine." In 1984 he was offered the AL presidency, "an offer too tempting to turn down." By combining professional baseball and specialized medicine, Brown has already enjoyed an unorthodox career. The AL presidency gave him a third unconventional challenge. He served as AL president until August 1, 1994.

BIBLIOGRAPHY: Robert Brown file, National Baseball Library, Cooperstown, NY; Maury Allen, *Baseball; the Lives Behind the Seams* (New York, 1990); Dom Forker, *The Men of Autumn* (Dallas, TX, 1989); Mark Gallagher, *The Yankee Encyclopedia*, vol. 3 (Champaign, IL, 1997); *The Baseball Encyclopedia*, 10th ed. (New York, 1996); Tom Meany, *The Magnificent Yankees* (New York, 1952); Peter Golenbock, *Dynasty* (New York, 1975); Robert W. Creamer, *Stengel: His Life and Times* (New York, 1984); Luther W. Spoehr, correspondence with Robert W. Brown, 1985.

Luther W. Spoehr

BROWN, Thomas Tarlton "Tom," "Handsome" (b. September 21, 1860, Liverpool, England; d. October 25, 1927, Washington, DC), player, manager, and umpire, was one of the fleetest nineteenth-century baseball performers. He played for consecutive championship Boston Reds PL and AA teams in 1890 and 1891, respectively.

Although born in England, he moved with his parents, William H. Brown and Mary (Lucas) Brown, and two brothers to northern California as a child. He quit school in the eighth grade, apprenticing as a gold-beater and playing semipro baseball in the San Francisco Bay area. After starting his professional baseball career with Oakland, CA in 1882, Brown moved east and played for 10 different teams in the next 16 seasons. He batted .300 only once in the 1880s, but established himself among the major league's fastest base runners and best defensive outfielders. Albert Spalding* selected Brown as right fielder for the "All-American" team, which played the Chicago White Stockings on the 1888–1889 world tour.

Brown's best major league seasons followed the world tour. In 1890 he added speed to the Boston Reds (PL), scoring 146 runs and stealing 79 bases. The following year with the Boston Reds, he led the AA in hits (189), triples (21), runs (177), total bases, and stolen bases (106). With the Louisville Colonels (NL) in 1893, Brown paced the NL in stolen bases (66). After starting the 1895 season with the St. Louis Browns (NL), he was shipped to the Washington Senators (NL) and closed out his major league career there. A crowd favorite, Brown adopted the nation's capitol as his home. He piloted Washington to a first division finish in 1897, but his club fell to eleventh in 1898. Brown never managed again, compiling a 64–72–1 record for his two seasons at the helm. Subsequently, he umpired in the NYSL for six years from 1899 to 1905. In 17 major league seasons, he batted .265 with 1,951 hits, 64 HR, 736 RBI, and 657 stolen bases.

Brown resided in Washington until his death, operating a cigar store for 20 years and joining the Elks and the United Brethren Church. He suffered from emphysema and died in the Washington Tuberculosis Hospital. His wife, Christine, and their only child, Ethel May (Brown) Statton, preceded him in death.

BIBLIOGRAPHY: Thomas Brown file, National Baseball Library, Cooperstown, NY; Morris Bealle, *The Washington Senators* (Washington, DC, 1947); Peter Levine, "Business, Missionary Motives Behind 1888–89 World Tour," *BRJ* (1984), pp. 60–63; David Nemec, *The Beer and Whisky League* (New York, 1994); Frederick Ivor-Campbell et al., eds., *Baseball's First Stars* (Cleveland, OH, 1996); Shirley Povich, *The Washington Senators* (New York, 1954); Charles Westlake, *Columbus Baseball* (Columbus, OH, 1981).

William E. Akin

BROWN, Willard Jessie (b. June 26, 1911, Shreveport, LA; d. August 8, 1996, Houston, TX), player, starred from 1935 through 1956 in the NAL, MEL, PRWL, and TL. Brown and Hank Thompson* were the major leagues' first black teammates with the 1947 St. Louis Browns (AL), but rejection by team members and prevailing attitudes in this border city gave Brown little opportunity to display his talents. Before being released, he batted .179 in 21 games.

Brown played professionally with the Kansas City Monarchs (NAL) from 1935 through 1951, except for 1940 in Mexico, 1943–1945 in the U.S. Army, 1950 with Ottawa, Canada (BL), and his stint with the Browns. After playing in the Dominican Republic in 1952, Brown performed in the TL with Dallas, TX, Houston, TX, Austin, TX, San Antonio, TX, and Tulsa, OK from 1953 through 1956 and completed his career at Topeka, KS (WL).

Available statistics indicate a .351 batting average with 8 HR, 61 RBI, and 13 stolen bases on a 70-game MEL tour in 1940. From 1946 through 1948, he posted .348, .336, and .374 batting averages for the Monarchs and paced the NAL with 18 HR in 66 1948 contests. In two Negro World Series competitions, Brown hit .304 with three HR and 14 RBI in 11 games. His 10 RBI in the 1946 classic led all batters. He batted .309 in 588 games over five consecutive minor league seasons with 95 HR and 437 RBI. His best season in organized baseball came in 1954 with 35 HR, 120 RBI, and a .314 batting average for Dallas and Houston (TL).

Brown's winter league accolades included setting the Puerto Rican single season record with 27 HR (1947–1948) and 97 RBI (1949–1950). From 1946–1947 through 1949–1950 there, he claimed three HR crowns, four RBI titles, and three batting championships. The 5-foot 11-inch, 200-pound right-hander possessed great speed and proved an excellent outfielder with a strong arm. Brown played on five NAL championship teams with Kansas City (1937, 1939, 1941, 1942, 1946). The 1942 club swept the powerful Washington Grays in the Negro World Series, as Brown hit .412 in four games. He performed for two TL titlists, Dallas in 1953 and Houston the following year. Brown appeared in six Negro League All-Star games from 1936 through 1949.

BIBLIOGRAPHY: Baltimore *Afro-American*, September 20, 1947; Chicago *Defender*, September 28, October 5, 1946; Kansas City *Call*, September 20, 27, 1946; *Mexican League Individual Batting* (1940); Janet Bruce, *The Kansas City Monarchs* (Lawrence, KS, 1985); John B. Holway, *Black Diamonds* (Westport, CT, 1989); Larry Moffi and Jonathan Kronstadt, *Crossing the Line* (Jefferson, NC, 1994); National Baseball Hall of Fame, *Negro Players Reports*, No. 4 (April 1, 1972); *Negro American League Statistics* 1948; Newark (NJ) *News*, September 18, 24, 30, 1946; Newark (NJ) *Star Ledger*, September 30, 1946; New Jersey *Afro-American*, September 21, 28, October 5, 1946; Robert W. Peterson, *Only the Ball Was White* (Englewood Cliffs, NJ, 1970); Philadelphia *Afro-American*, September 19, 1942; Philadelphia *Tribune*, September 19, 1942; James A. Riley, *The All-Time All-Stars of Black Baseball* (Cocoa, FL, 1983); James A. Riley, *The Biographical Encyclopedia of the Negro Baseball Leagues* (New York, 1994); Pepe Seda, *Don Q Baseball Cues* (Ponce, PR, 1970); *TSN Official Baseball Guide, 1951, 1954–1957*; Jules Tygiel, *Baseball's Great Experiment* (New York, 1983).

Merl F. Kleinknecht

BROWNING, Louis Rogers "Pete," "Old Pete," "The Gladiator" (b. June 17, 1861, Louisville, KY; d. September 10, 1905, Louisville, KY), player, was the youngest of eight children and received minimal education at home. Nicknamed "Old Pete" or "The Gladiator," he played principally with the Louisville, KY Colonels (AA). One of baseball's most colorful players, the superstitious Browning invariably touched third base on his way to the dugout (believing it made him a better hitter), refused to cross puddles, and referred to his eyes as "lamps." The notoriously loquacious Browning fully enjoyed his stardom and often introduced himself as a "champion batter."

Partially deaf, Browning suffered from mastoiditis or an infection of the middle ear. This painful affliction may have caused his excessive drinking. Browning's club once left him behind when he was too intoxicated to find the train. "I can't hit the ball," Browning tragically commented, "until I hit the bottle." A writer observed, "Pete is a queer character. In spite of his faults he has the qualities of a popular favorite."

Baseball has seen few better natural hitters. During his major league career from 1882 to 1894, Browning compiled the eleventh highest batting average (.341) in major league baseball history. Browning loved to hit. A three-time batting champion (AA, 1882 and 1885; PL, 1890), Browning hit an incredible .402 in 1887 when walks counted as hits. Tip O'Neill* hit above .400 that year, with Browning placing second. After a .378 rookie season, he only twice hit below .300. "Browning," famed pitcher Charles Radbourne* declared, "is the most wicked hitter in the business," while another pitcher commented, "He can hit the ball anywhere." During his career, the powerful Browning slugged 295 doubles, 85 triples, and 46 HR among his 1,646 hits.

In May 1887, a reporter described his all-around baseball skills: "His work in center field has been capital, and some of his difficult catches have not been equalled on the local grounds [Louisville]. He is playing the best game of his life, and that is saying a great deal. The reason is clear—Pete is abstaining from drink." Although he disliked sliding, Browning ran the bases well and stole 103 bases in 1887. Primarily an outfielder, he also played the infield early in his career and even pitched. Since Browning insisted on bats made to his specifications, John Hillerich made him a special one known later as the Louisville Slugger. Browning's success generated demands from other players for made-to-order bats, enabling the Hillerich & Bradsby firm to launch a successful business.

Browning, contemporaries said, knew and thought only of baseball. After a game, his temper was "reckoned by the number of hits" he made. A longtime Louisville favorite, he jumped to the Cleveland Infants (PL) in 1890 because "they ain't treated me right here since 1886." The Louisville club retorted, "He was treated much better than he deserved." The feud failed to trouble Browning, whose .373 average won the PL batting title. After Browning's last major league appearance (three games in 1894), he played several seasons in the minors and retired. Returning to Louisville, he tried several careers unsuccessfully. An only slightly exaggerated tribute from 1890 noted, "Browning is the greatest hitter the world has ever produced."

BIBLIOGRAPHY: Louis R. Browning file, National Baseball Library, Cooperstown, NY; Louisville *Times*, September 11, 1905; Joseph Reichler, *The Great All-Time Baseball Record Book* (New York, 1981); *The Baseball Encyclopedia*, 10th ed. (New York, 1996); David Nemec, *The Beer and Whisky League* (New York, 1994); Harold Seymour, *Baseball: The Early Years* (New York, 1960); Robert Smith, *Pioneers of Baseball* (Boston, MA, 1978); *Spalding's Base Ball Guide, 1882–1893* (New York, 1882–1893); *SpL*, September 16, 1905; Robert L. Tiemann and Mark Rucker, eds., *Nineteenth Century Stars* (Kansas City, MO, 1989); Philip Von Borries, *Louisville Diamonds* (Paducah, KY, 1997); Philip Von Borries, *Legends of Louisville* (West Bloomfield, MI, 1993).

Duane A. Smith

BROWNING, Thomas Leo "Tom," "Pug" (b. April 28, 1960, Casper WY), player, pitched a perfect game against the Los Angeles Dodgers on September

16, 1988 to become only the third pitcher in NL history and the first in the Cincinnati Reds (NL) 119-year history to accomplish the feat. On June 9, 1994 he tragically collapsed on the mound after breaking his pitching arm.

He is the son of Billy D. Browning and C. Kay (Wagner) Browning. After attending Tennessee Wesleyan College in Athens, TN and Le Moyne College in Syracuse, NY, Browning was selected in the ninth round of the free agent draft by the Cincinnati Reds in June 1982. The tenacious 6-foot 1-inch, 190-pound left-hander led both the PrL and AA in strikeouts in 1982 and 1984, respectively. The Cincinnati Reds promoted him in September 1984, when he pitched a 5–1 victory over the Los Angeles Dodgers.

Browning finished the 1985 season with 11 consecutive triumphs, posting a 20–9 record and becoming the first Cincinnati Red to win 20 games as a rookie. He was chosen *TSN* Rookie Pitcher of the Year and finished second to Vince Coleman* in the NL Rookie of the Year voting. He posted another strong campaign in 1986 with 14 wins, but a torn muscle, suffered in early 1987, led to poor performances and demotion to Nashville, TN (AA). Pitching in Nashville restored Browning's mental toughness. After being recalled to the Reds, he compiled a 5–2 slate and 2.10 ERA over his last eight games. Browning's 10–13 season record marked his only losing campaign with the Reds.

Browning's September 16, 1988 perfect game, during which he never reached a three ball count on any hitter, highlighted his best overall season, when he posted an 18–5 record. The workhorse hurler led the NL in starts in 1986, 1988, and 1989 and paced the pitching staff of the 1990 World Champion Reds with a 15–9 record despite an injured ankle late in the season. He compiled a 1–1 mark in the 1990 NL Championship Series against the Pittsburgh Pirates and a 1–0 record in the World Series against the Oakland A's.

The Cincinnati Reds released Browning in October 1994. He signed a minor league contract with the Kansas City Royals (AL) in April 1995. After making two successful starts for Omaha, NE (AA), he joined the Kansas City Royals in May. The Royals soon placed him on the disabled list and released him in November. Browning reported to the Royals as a non-roster player in 1996, but retired from baseball after a few mediocre spring training starts. His career record of 123–90 and 3.94 ERA included 1,000 strikeouts in 1,921 innings.

Browning and his wife, Debbie, have four children, Tiffany, Tanner, Tucker, and Trevor.

BIBLIOGRAPHY: Thomas Browning file, National Baseball Library, Cooperstown, NY; Donald Honig, *The Cincinnati Reds* (New York, 1992); John Kuenster, "Tom Browning of the Reds, An Unheralded 20-Games Winner," *BD* 45 (March 1986), pp. 15–17; Ronald A. Mayer, *Perfect!* (Jefferson, NC, 1991); Mike Palercio, "The Bulldog," *RR* 1 (March 1988), p. 17; Bob Socci, "Virtuoso Performance," *RR* 8 (November 1988), pp. 15–17.

Richard D. Miller

BRUNANSKY, Thomas Andrew "Tom," "Bruno" (b. August 20, 1960, Covina, CA), player, is the son of Joseph L. Brunansky, Sr. and Margret Rae (McMullen) Brunansky of Hungarian descent. His father, a Class D professional baseball catcher and two-way lineman, would have played professional football for the Chicago Cardinals (NFL) if he had not been blacklisted for competing in an unsanctioned all-star game. His brother, Joseph, Jr., excelled at golf and as an All-America first baseman in college. Brunansky began his professional baseball career with Idaho Falls, ID (PL) in 1978 and reached the major leagues in 1981 with the California Angels (AL). After being traded to the Minnesota Twins (AL) in May 1982, he helped Kirby Puckett* adjust to the major leagues. He played for the St. Louis Cardinals (NL) from April 1988 to May 1990, the Boston Red Sox (AL) from May 1990 to October 1992, and the Milwaukee Brewers (AL) from January 1993 to June 1994. His major league career ended with the Red Sox in 1994.

The 6-foot 4-inch, 220-pound, right-handed streak hitter frequently batted well in only the first or second half of a season. Nevertheless, Brunansky hit 271 career HR and 306 doubles, with season highs of 32 HR for Minnesota in 1984 and 1987. An excellent outfielder, he led the NL with a .996 fielding average in 1988. His career highlights included hitting four straight HR with 9 RBI for the El Paso, TX Diablos (TL) in 1980 and belting an inside-the-park grand-slam HR in 1982, the first in the major leagues since 1979. Brunansky retired with a .245 lifetime batting average and made the AL All-Stars in 1985. He played in the AL Championship Series in 1987 for Minnesota and in 1990 for Boston, batting .412 with seven hits, four doubles, two HR, four walks, nine RBI, and a 1.000 slugging average in 1987. He hit only .200 with five hits, two RBI, and four walks in the 1987 World Series against St. Louis and only .083 in the 1990 AL Championship Series against the Oakland A's. He married Colleen Schumann and has two sons, Jason and Ryan.

BIBLIOGRAPHY: Jim Kaplan, "Bruno Is Breaking Out," *SI* 62 (May 27, 1985), pp. 56–58; Tom Brunansky file, National Baseball Library, Cooperstown, NY; Dave Monia and Dave Jarzyna, *Twenty-Five Seasons* (Minneapolis, MN, 1986); Bob Broeg and Jerry Vickery, *St. Louis Cardinals Encyclopedia* (Grand Rapids, MI, 1998); Robert Redmount, *The Red Sox Encyclopedia* (Champaign, IL, 1998); Mike Shatzkin, ed., *The Ballplayers* (New York, 1990); John Thorn et al., eds., *Total Baseball*, 5th ed. (New York, 1997); *WWIB*, 1995.

Victor Rosenberg

BRUSH, John Tomlinson, Jr. (b. June 15, 1845, Clintonville, NY; d. November 25, 1912, Louisiana, MO), owner and executive, owned the New York Giants (NL) baseball club and designed the existing baseball rules governing the World Series.

Brush, the son of John Tomlinson Brush, Sr., and Sarah Farar Brush, was orphaned at age four and brought up by his grandfather, Eliphalet Brush, in Hopkinton, MA. He entered the clothing business at age 17, enlisting in the Civil War in 1863. After the Civil War, he returned to the clothing business and eventually started his own company in Indianapolis, IN. Brush purchased the Indianapolis Hoosiers (NL) franchise in 1886 largely to publicize his clothing stores and became club president a year later.

The NL reduced its membership in 1889, dropping the Indianapolis Hoosiers. Brush consented only after retaining his owner's voting rights, being given stock in John B. Day's* troubled New York Giants (NL), and being promised the next open franchise. Brush in 1891 was granted rights to the Cincinnati Reds (NL), which he owned until 1902.

Brush purchased the New York Giants in 1902 and turned the franchise into a winning one, both on and off the field. He hired John McGraw* as field manager, giving him complete control over player dealings. Brush also penned a long-term lease and rebuilt the Polo Grounds, making it baseball's preeminent stadium for years.

Brush's lasting contribution to baseball, however, was creation of the rules organizing the World Series. The Pittsburgh Pirates (NL) met the Boston Pilgrims (AL) franchise in 1903 in a non-league-sanctioned championship, which Brush tried to halt in court. Brush's hatred of AL president Ban Johnson* made him oppose any series against the "minor league." His New York Giants won the 1904 NL pennant, but refused a challenge by the AL champion Boston Pilgrims.

Brush was criticized harshly by the newspapers and fans and changed his position in 1905. To oversee the World Series, he created several rules. These "Brush Rules," the majority of which are still used today, required the NL and AL champions to meet in the World Series. His other rules included the four-out-of-seven series format, a pool of 60 percent of the receipts to be divided between the players (with 70 percent going to the winners and 30 percent to the losers), and allowing only players on the respective clubs prior to September to play. Fittingly, Brush's New York Giants played in the first league-sanctioned World Series in 1905, defeating Connie Mack's* Philadelphia Athletics, four games to one. Brush's New York Giants lost two more World Series before his death, the 1911 World Series to the Philadelphia Athletics and the 1912 Classic to the Boston Red Sox.

Brush's business approach to team administration increased baseball's stature in the early 1900s. He suffered the debilitating effects of rheumatism and locomotor ataxia and died while traveling to California for his health. Brush married Agnes Ewart in 1869 and had a daughter, Eleanor. After his first wife died in 1888, Brush remarried in 1894 to Elsie Lombard and had another daughter, Natalie.

BIBLIOGRAPHY: John Brush file, National Baseball Library, Cooperstown, NY; Noel Hynd, *The Giants of the Polo Grounds* (New York, 1988); Frederick Ivor-Campbell et al., eds., *Baseball's First Stars* (Cleveland, OH, 1996); Charles C. Alexander, *John*

McGraw (New York, 1968); Lee Allen, *The Cincinnati Reds* (New York, 1948); Frank Graham, *The New York Giants* (New York, 1952); Gene Karst and Martin J. Jones, *Who's Who in Professional Baseball* (New Rochelle, NY, 1973); *NCAB*, vol. 15 (New York, 1914); *NYT*, November 27, 1912, p. 11; David Pietrusza, *Major Leagues* (Jefferson, NC, 1991); Joseph Reichler, *The World Series* (New York, 1979); Edward Mott Woolley, "Fortunes Made in Baseball," *LD* 45 (July 20, 1912), pp. 119–120.

Brian L. Laughlin

BRUTON, William Haron "Billy" (b. December 22, 1925, Panola, AL; d. December 5, 1995, Marshall, DE), player, was the son of Alvin Bruton, a tenant farmer. Upon graduation from Parker High School in 1943, Bruton spent two and a half years in the U.S. Army. Following his discharge in 1946, he moved north to Wilmington, DE and worked with Continental Can Company.

Bruton participated in baseball during his youth, but began playing softball in Wilmington city leagues. In 1949, former Negro League star Judy Johnson* noticed him. Johnson liked Bruton's catching style and recommended him to Philadelphia Athletics (AL) scout Bill Yancy. Since the Athletics did not need a catcher, Yancy referred Bruton to scout John Ogden of the Boston Braves (NL). Ogden lied about Bruton's age to persuade the Boston Braves to sign the 27-year-old prospect. Bruton began his professional baseball career with Eau Claire, WI (NoL) in 1950, hitting .302 and stealing 66 bases. In 1951, he performed for Denver, CO (WL) and the Milwaukee, WI Brewers (AA). Bruton credits Brewers manager Charley Grimm* and Boston Braves scout Jim Clarkson for getting him to the major leagues.

After a brief stint with the Boston Braves in September 1952, Bruton remained with the parent club in their new Milwaukee home in 1953. The rookie started in center field on opening day and immediately attracted attention around the NL. The 6-foot, 170-pound speedster won games almost single handedly with his timely hitting. After the first three weeks, Bruton led the NL in batting (.424), hits (14), triples (3), and stolen bases (5), ranked fourth in runs scored, and played outstanding defense. Such consistent performance made Bruton an instant hero with Milwaukee fans.

Bruton's asset remained speed, as he twice led the NL in triples and stole 207 career bases on a club laden with power hitters. Just after the 1957 All-Star break, he collided with shortstop Felix Mantilla while chasing a pop-up. Bruton suffered ligament damage and did not play again until late May 1958. Despite his absence, the Milwaukee Braves won the 1957 NL pennant and the World Series against the New York Yankees. In 1958, Bruton helped the Milwaukee Braves win a second consecutive NL pennant. Although stealing only four bases, he batted .280 in 100 games. The Braves lost the World Series to the New York Yankees, but Bruton led all players in hitting (.412) with two HR, five RBI, and three runs scored.

During 1959 against the St. Louis Cardinals, Bruton hit two of his three triples with bases loaded. Only one other player had achieved this single game feat. The 1960 campaign marked perhaps his best season, as he led the NL in triples (13) and runs scored (112) and batted .286, with 12 HR and 22 stolen bases. His production, however, was overshadowed by the Braves' need for a second baseman. In December 1960, Bruton was involved in a six-player trade with the Detroit Tigers (AL). He spent the last four seasons of his 12-year major league career with the Detroit Tigers. In 1961, he clouted a career-high 17 HR while batting .257 with 22 stolen bases.

Following the 1964 season, Bruton retired from baseball and returned to Wilmington, DE. He married Loretta Johnson in November 1950 and had four children. During his major league career, Bruton batted .273 with 94 HR and 207 stolen bases. After a 15-year hiatus, he resumed his employment with the Continental Can Company. He retired in 1988 to care for his ill father-in-law, "Judy" Johnson, and devote full time to his cabinet-making hobby. Bruton suffered a heart attack while driving near his Wilmington home.

BIBLIOGRAPHY: Martin Appel, *Yesterday's Heroes* (New York, 1988); William Bruton file, National Baseball Library, Cooperstown, NY; William Bruton file, Negro League Baseball Museum, Kansas City, MO; *Wilmington Defender*, December 7, 1995; Bob Buege, *The Milwaukee Braves: A Baseball Eulogy* (Milwaukee, WI, 1988); Bob Buege, "Milwaukee Madness," *OTBN* 6 (1994), pp. 12–14; Bob Buege, *Eddie Mathews and the National Pastime* (Milwaukee, WI, 1994); Gary Caruso, *The Braves Encyclopedia* (Philadelphia, PA, 1995); Leo Heiman et al., *When the Cheering Stops* (New York, 1990); Tom Meany, *Milwaukee's Miracle Braves* (New York, 1954); *Milwaukee Braves Yearbook*, 1957, 1959; Larry Moffi and Jonathan Kronstadt, *Crossing the Line* (Jefferson, NC, 1994); *NYT Biographical Service* 26 (December 1995), p. 1812; John Thorn et al., eds., *Total Baseball*, 5th ed. (New York, 1997).

Jerry J. Wright

BUCKNER, William Joseph "Bill" (b. December 14, 1949, Vallejo, CA), player and coach, starred in football and baseball at Napa, CA High School and was elected to the Northern California Football Hall of Fame. After graduating from Napa High School in 1968, he subsequently attended the University of Southern California and Arizona State University. His brothers, Robert and James, both played minor league baseball. The Los Angeles Dodgers (NL) selected Buckner in the second round of the June 1968 draft and assigned him to Ogden, UT (PrL), where he won the batting championship with a .344 average. In 1969, Buckner hit .307 for Albuquerque, NM (TL) and .315 for Spokane, WA (PCL). Buckner's .335 batting average in 1970 at Spokane ranked him third in the PCL.

After brief appearances with the Los Angeles Dodgers in 1969 and 1970, Buckner hit .277 his rookie 1971 season there. Although playing some games at first base, he was used primarily as an outfielder with the Dodgers. Buckner helped the Dodgers with the 1974 NL pennant by batting .314 and then hit .250 in the World Series against the Oakland Athletics. In April 1975, Buckner suffered a severely sprained left ankle while sliding into second base.

This led to an operation in September 1975 to remove a tendon. Bone chips were removed later from his left ankle during another operation, causing him to become a first baseman. Buckner was traded in January 1977 to the Chicago Cubs (NL) and remained there until being sent to the Boston Red Sox (AL) in May 1984.

An extremely competitive player, the left-hander proved an excellent contact hitter and rarely walked or struck out. The 6-foot, 185-pound Buckner hit to all fields and was an excellent student of pitchers, batting over .300 seven times. He led the NL with a .324 batting average in 1980 and 35 doubles in 1981 and tied for the NL lead with 38 doubles in 1983. In 1982, Buckner became the first Cub since Billy Williams* in 1970 to surpass 200 hits. Besides making 201 hits, he established career highs in runs (93) and walks (36) and knocked in 105 runs. Buckner also established a major league record for most assists by a first baseman (159), but broke the mark the next year with 161 assists and in 1985 with 184 assists. In 1985, Buckner batted .299 and ranked second in the AL in doubles (46) and third in hits (201) and tied for sixth in RBI (110). Buckner's games played (162), at bats (673), doubles, and RBI established career highs, while his hits tied a career peak. The next year, Buckner batted .269, tied for third in doubles (39), slugged 18 HR, and knocked in 102 runs in helping the Red Sox win the AL pennant. Buckner, who suffered from a strained achilles tendon and had two bad legs, batted .214 in the AL Championship Series against the California Angels. He hit only .188 in the World Series against the New York Mets and made an error that let in the winning run in game six. Buckner remained with Boston until being released in July 1987. He spent the rest of 1987 and through May 1988 with the California Angels (AL). Buckner joined the Kansas City Royals (AL) the rest of 1988 and in 1989 and finished his major league career with the Boston Red Sox in 1990. In 22 major league seasons, he batted .289 in 2,517 career games and recorded 1,077 runs scored, 2,715 hits, 498 doubles, 49 triples, 174 HR, 1,208 RBI, and 183 stolen bases. He coached for the Chicago White Sox (AL) in 1996 and 1997. He is married to Jody Schenck and has two children, Brittany and Kristen Ashley.

BIBLIOGRAPHY: *Boston Red Sox 1985 Media Guide*; William Buckner file, National Baseball Library, Cooperstown, NY; Jim Kaplan, "He's Off in a Zone of His Own," *SI* 57 (September 13, 1982), pp. 48–51; Eddie Gold and Arthur Ahrens, *The New Era Cubs, 1941–1985* (Chicago, IL, 1985); Peter Gammons, "The Hub Hails Its Hobbling Hero," *SI* 65 (November 10, 1986), pp. 26–28; Robert E. Kelley, *Baseball's Best* (Jefferson, NC, 1988); Louis Kraft, "Bill Buckner: The Odyssey of a Major League Survivor," *BD* 44 (May 1985), pp. 25–28; Dick Miller, "Bill Buckner: Profile of a Contact Hitter," *BD* 38 (August 1979), pp. 20–24; *The Baseball Encyclopedia*, 10th ed. (New York, 1996); Robert Redmount; *The Red Sox Encyclopedia* (Champaign, IL, 1998); Dan Shaughnessy, *The Curse of the Bambino* (New York, 1990); Steve Wulf, "Bouncing Back," *SI* 72 (March 19, 1990), p. 76; Dan Shaughnessy, *One Strike Away* (New York, 1987); Peter Golenbock, *Fenway* (New York, 1992).

Robert J. Brown

BUDIG, Gene Arthur (b. May 25, 1939, McCook, NE), executive, is the son of Arthur Budig and Angela (Schaal) Budig and earned a Bachelor of Science degree in 1962, a Master of Education degree in 1963, and a Doctor of Education degree in 1967 from the University of Nebraska-Lincoln. Budig married Gretchen Van Bloom on November 30, 1963 and has one son, Christopher, and two daughters, Mary Frances and Kathryn Angela. He joined the Air National Guard after graduation and was active for more than 29 years, retiring as a Major General in September 1992.

After serving as executive assistant to the governor of Nebraska from 1964 to 1967, Budig returned to his alma mater as administrative assistant to the chancellor. He subsequently became assistant professor of education administration, assistant vice-chancellor academic affairs, and assistant vice-president/director of public affairs there. A brief stint followed as vice-president and dean at Illinois State University in 1972. He then served as president at Illinois State from 1973 to 1977 and at West Virginia University from 1977 to 1981.

Budig moved to the University of Kansas as chancellor in 1981 and remained in that position until being named the seventh AL president on June 7, 1994. During 13 years at Kansas, he administered the construction of the largest academic building in the history of the Lawrence campus and other new centers and complexes. The school also raised a record $790 million from private sources for academic program enrichment during his tenure.

Budig took AL office on August 1, 1994, twelve days before the major league baseball strike began. During his first 18 months in office, he was involved in helping to settle the strike, form a new five-year national television contract with four networks, arrange a new five-year agreement with the Umpires Association, administer ownership changes in several cities, oversee the AL approval of new baseball-only parks in Milwaukee, Seattle, and Detroit, and suspend Roberto Alomar* following a spitting incident. Commissioner Bud Selig* eliminated the titles of league presidents in September 1999 and named Budig senior advisor to the commissioner.

BIBLIOGRAPHY: *WWA*, 49th ed. (1994), p. 471; Gene A. Budig file, AL Office, New York; Gene A. Budig file, National Baseball Library, Cooperstown, NY.

Jay Langhammer

BUFFINTON, Charles G. "Charlie" (b. June 14, 1861, Fall River, MA; d. September 23, 1907, Fall River, MA), player and manager, was the son of John Buffinton and Phoebe Buffinton. He married Alice Thornley and had three children. One of baseball's premier pitchers in the 1880s, Buffinton achieved early fame in only his second season. He helped pitch the Boston Beaneaters (NL) to the 1883 pennant with a 25–14 record and 34 complete games. From 1882 to 1892, the 6-foot 1-inch, 180-pound pitcher won 233 games, lost 153, notched at least 20 victories seven times, and compiled a 2.96 ERA. In his superlative 1884 season, he won 48 of 64 decisions for Boston, pitched eight shutouts, and walked only 76. He also struck out 417 batters, including eight consecutively against the Cleveland Blues, and won 13 games in a row. Besides pitching 587 innings, he registered 63 complete games. On August 9, he lost a no-hit game, 2–1, on errors.

A sore arm limited Buffinton's effectiveness in 1886, causing Boston to release him. Overcoming this physical problem, he enjoyed three successful seasons for the Philadelphia Quakers (NL). In 1890 he jumped to the PL, where he pitched for and managed the Philadelphia Quakers. In his last outstanding year (1891), he compiled a 29–9 record for the Boston Reds (AA). Occasionally he played outfield and first base, registering a .245 life-time batting average.

Contemporary sportswriters credited Buffinton with originating the drop ball and the hard overhand curve. In 1885 one commented, "There isn't a ball tosser in the country today who has more deceptive curves." Another remarked that his "perplexing curve . . . explodes in the dirt and gives catch-ers a workout." Every inch a gentleman, Buffinton exhibited outstanding character in an age when professional baseball still fielded rowdy elements. The Boston *Globe* eulogized him as a modest workman and a phenomenal ballplayer who helped to lay "the foundation of our great sport."

Among the highest paid players of the 1880s with a $2,800 salary, Buffin-ton benefited from the struggle between the rival PL and NL. Without warning, clubs slashed payrolls from 30 to 40 percent. Buffinton, who ob-jected strongly to this mid-year cut, refused to report in 1893. He never played major league baseball again and returned to Fall River to become a successful cotton and coal businessman.

BIBLIOGRAPHY: Charles Buffinton file, National Baseball Library, Cooperstown, NY; Gary Caruso, *The Braves Encyclopedia* (Philadelphia, PA, 1995); Harold Kaese, *The Boston Braves* (New York, 1948); *Herald News* (Fall River, MA), June 18, 1979; Joseph L. Reichler, *The Great All-Time Baseball Record Book* (New York, 1981); *The Baseball Encyclopedia*, 10th ed. (New York, 1996); Harold Seymour, *Baseball: The Early Years* (New York, 1960); *Spalding's Base Ball Guide, 1885–1893* (New York, 1885–1893); Robert L. Tiemann and Mark Rucker, eds., *Nineteenth Century Stars* (Kansas City, MO, 1989).

                                                                            Duane A. Smith

BUFORD, Donald Alvin "Don" (b. February 2, 1937, Linden, TX), player, instructor, coach, manager, and executive, moved at age five to California and graduated from Dorsey High School. After attending Los Angeles CC for a year and a half, he worked toward his B.S. degree in Physical Education at USC. The 5-foot 7-inch, 160 pounder returned punts and played left halfback in football, making the University of Notre Dame and UCLA All-

Opponent teams. He also played outfield for the Trojans baseball team, which won the NCAA College World Series in 1958.

The switch-hitting Buford, drafted in November 1959 by the Chicago White Sox (AL), was signed by Hollis Thurston and Doc Bennett and played 542 games in the minor leagues for six teams in six different leagues. He married Alescia R. Jackson, who owns a public relations company, on September 30, 1962 and has three sons, Don, Jr., a medical doctor, Daryl, and Damon.

His last minor league season with Indianapolis, IN (AA) came in 1963, when he led the AA in hits, runs scored, doubles, stolen bases, batting average, and assists by third basemen. The AA named him both Rookie of the Year and MVP, while *TSN* selected him Minor League Player of the Year.

The Chicago White Sox promoted Buford in 1963 and used him for a few games at a new position, second base. As a 27-year-old rookie in 1964, he tied the major league record for most double plays in a game by a second baseman. Two years later, he shared the AL mark for most games played and led the AL in sacrifice hits.

In November 1967, Chicago traded Buford to the Baltimore Orioles (AL) for Luis Aparicio.* Under manager Earl Weaver* in 1968, he received 11 MVP votes and fielded flawlessly. He also earned MVP votes in 1970 and 1971. He hit HR in three consecutive World Series against the New York Mets in 1969, the Cincinnati Reds in 1970, and the Pittsburgh Pirates in 1971. His major league career ended in 1972 with a .264 lifetime batting average, 1,203 hits, 93 HR, and 200 stolen bases.

Buford, called the "greatest lead-off man in the world" in Japan, had toured with the Baltimore Orioles there and signed in 1973 with the Taiheiyo, Japan Lions after a 16 percent pay cut by Baltimore. He played from 1973 through 1974 with the Nankai, Japan Hawks, retiring with a .270 batting average and 65 HR.

He then worked for Sears as personnel manager and for the Milwaukee Brewers (AL) as a scout and minor league instructor in 1980. From 1981 to 1984, he served as the first base coach for the San Francisco Giants (NL). The University of Southern California employed him as an assistant coach from 1985 through 1987. In 1992 and 1993, he managed the Hagerstown, MD Suns. His son, Damon, plays with the Chicago Cubs (NL). The Sherman Oaks, CA resident serves as the assistant director for player development for the Baltimore Orioles.

BIBLIOGRAPHY: Rich Marazzi, "Don Buford: A Good Man at the Top of the Order," *SCD* 21 (November 18, 1994), pp. 130–131; Don Buford file, National Baseball Library, Cooperstown, NY; James H. Bready, *Baseball in Baltimore* (Baltimore, MD, 1998); Ted Patterson, *The Baltimore Orioles* (Dallas, TX, 1995); *TSN*, August 21, 1965, September 30, 1967, March 3, 1968, July 25, 1970; *New York Daily News*, June 3, 1971; *BW*, May 26, 1992; *NYT*, May 20, 1973.

Thomas H. Barthel

BUHL, Robert Raymond "Bob" (b. August 12, 1928, Saginaw, MI), player, is the son of William Buhl, an automotive worker at General Motors' Saginaw Steering Gear. Buhl, encouraged by his father and exhibiting excellent athletic potential, excelled in city youth baseball programs and in baseball, basketball, and football at Saginaw Central High School, from which he graduated in 1946. Although a top high school pitcher, he was somewhat overlooked by pro scouts. Major league baseball looked toward stabilization with returning players from World War II.

After working eight months at a local General Motors plant, Buhl began his professional baseball career in 1947 with Madisonville, KY (KL). He moved up to Saginaw, MI (CL) in 1948, Hartford, CT (EL) in 1949, and Dallas, TX (TL) in 1950. A dispute occurred over Buhl's contract. Commissioner A. B. "Happy" Chandler* declared him a free agent following the 1950 campaign because he had signed while a high school senior. Boston Braves (NL) scout Earl Halshead immediately signed Buhl for the 1951 season, but the latter served two years as an Army paratrooper in Korea. He returned to the NL club in 1953 in their new Milwaukee home.

As a rookie, Buhl won his first two major league starts. He threw a two-hitter and a shutout en route to 13 wins, 8 losses, and a 2.97 ERA. The 1953 campaign marked the first of his six career double-figure win seasons, despite pitching in the shadows of Warren Spahn* and Lew Burdette.* A power pitcher with a herky-jerky motion and intense competitive nature, the 6-foot 2-inch, 190-pound right-hander used a large repertoire of pitches. The "Dodger Killer" defeated that team and their aces, Sandy Koufax* and Don Drysdale,* 23 times. Eight of those victories came in 1956, but the Braves lost the NL pennant to the Brooklyn Dodgers by one game on the last day of the season.

Late-season injuries prevented Buhl from reaching the 20-win seasonal milestone when he finished 18–8 in 1956, 18–7 in 1957, 15–9 in 1959, and 16–9 in 1960. But he finished among the NL's top ten in ERA seven times, hurling two one-hitters and four two-hitters. In 1958, Buhl shared the NL lead with four shutouts and ranked third with a 2.86 ERA. A sore shoulder and personality conflict with new Braves manager Birdie Tebbetts* forced Buhl's trade to the Chicago Cubs (NL) in April 1962. During a four-year stint with the Cubs, Buhl recorded 51 victories and 52 losses and won 12 games over his former Braves. In May 1966, Chicago traded him to the Philadelphia Phillies (NL) for Ferguson Jenkins.* With the Phillies, he won 6 and lost 8 games before his 1967 retirement. Buhl ranked among baseball's worst hitters even among pitchers. His lifetime .089 batting average included striking out 45 percent of the time. He made no hits in 70 at-bats in 1962 and did not get another hit until May 8, 1963.

During a 15-year major league career, Buhl compiled 166 wins against 132 losses, a 3.55 ERA, and a .557 winning percentage. He appeared in two 1957 World Series games against the New York Yankees and the 1960 All-

Star game and recorded 11 or more victories in 10 seasons. Buhl, who entered the insurance business in Saginaw, MI, married Joyce Miles in October 1951 and has four children. He worked as a maintenance manager for a trailer court in Florida and enjoys hunting and fishing near his Winter Haven, FL home.

BIBLIOGRAPHY: Robert Buhl file, National Baseball Library, Cooperstown, NY; Bob Buege, *The Milwaukee Braves: A Baseball Eulogy* (Milwaukee, WI, 1988); Bob Buege, "Milwaukee Madness," *OTBN* 6 (1994), pp. 12–14; Bob Buege, *Eddie Mathews and the National Pastime* (Milwaukee, WI, 1994); Gary Caruso, *The Braves Encyclopedia* (Philadelphia, PA, 1995); Eddie Gold and Art Ahrens, *The New Era Cubs, 1941–1985* (Chicago, IL, 1985); Tom Meany, *Milwaukee's Miracle Braves* (New York, 1954); *Milwaukee Braves Yearbook*, 1957–1959; John Thorn et al., eds., *Total Baseball*, 5th ed. (New York, 1997).

Jerry J. Wright

BUHNER, Jay Campbell "Bone" (b. August 13, 1964, Louisville, KY), player, is the son of David Buhner and Kay Buhner and grew up in League City, TX. He and his wife, Leah, have three children, Brielle, Chase, and Gunnar, and reside in Issaquah, WA.

Buhner played baseball at Clear Creek High School in League City, TX and matriculated at McLennan CC in Waco, TX in 1982. McLennan coach Rick Butler shaped him into a strong defensive outfielder. Buhner led McLennan in HR and helped them win the 1983 JC national title. The Atlanta Braves (NL) selected him in the ninth round of the 1983 free-agent draft. Buhner signed instead with the Pittsburgh Pirates (NL) in the second round of the January 1984 secondary free-agent draft. He played outfield at Watertown, NY (NYPL) in 1984, making the league's All-Star team.

After being traded in December 1984 to the New York Yankees (AL), Buhner spent the 1985 and 1986 seasons at Ft. Lauderdale, FL (FSL) and the 1987 and 1988 campaigns at Columbus, OH (IL). He also spent brief stints with the New York Yankees and led the IL in HR (31) in 1987. In July 1988, New York traded the right fielder to the Seattle Mariners (AL). Buhner began the 1989 season at Calgary, Canada (PCL) and has been the Mariners' regular right fielder since that June. His hard-playing approach to the game landed him on the disabled list four times with injuries ranging from a sprained right ankle to a broken right arm.

Buhner set a major league record for best RBI-to-hits ratio in a season with 121 RBI and 123 hits in 1995, breaking Jim Gentile's* 1961 record. *BA* named Buhner "Best Outfield Arm" in 1995, the year McLennan CC retired his jersey. The BBWAA selected him Houston Area Player of the Year in 1993 and 1995. In 1996, Buhner posted career bests in HR (44), RBI (138), doubles (29), and runs (107), making his first AL All-Star team and receiving the Gold Glove award. After clouting 40 HR in 1997, Buhner became just the 10th major league player to hit 40 or more HR three consecutive seasons.

Buhner and Ken Griffey, Jr.,* who slugged 56 HR in 1997, moved to third on the all-time list of top slugging teammates. Roger Maris* and Mickey Mantle* belted 115 for the 1961 New York Yankees, while Babe Ruth* and Lou Gehrig* clouted 107 for the 1927 New York Yankees. In the 1997 AL Division Series against the Baltimore Orioles, Buhner batted .231 with two HR.

Through the 1999 season, Buhner has batted .254 with 282 HR and 878 RBI. The 6-foot 3-inch, 210-pound right-handed power-hitter projects a fan-friendly manner. Seattle fans annually celebrate his shaved bald head at the "Buhner Buzz Night" fan promotion. Buhner remains very active with the Seattle chapter of the Cystic Fibrosis Foundation and the Juvenile Diabetes Association.

BIBLIOGRAPHY: Jay Buhner file, National Baseball Library, Cooperstown, NY; Gerry Callahan, "A Real Cutup," *SI* 84 (March 18, 1996), pp. 88–99; Mark Keast, "The Man Behind the Glare," *MM* 7 (1996), pp. 20–24; Ed Lucas and Paul Post, "Buhner Collecting for Future Generation," *SCD* 25 (January 23, 1998), p. 110; Seattle Mariners Information Guide, 1998.

Sarah L. Ulerick

BULKELEY, Morgan Gardner (b. December 26, 1837, East Haddam, CT; d. November 6, 1922, Hartford, CT), executive, was the son of Eliphalet Bulkeley and Lydia S. (Morgan) Bulkeley, descendants of *Mayflower* settlers. His father, an attorney and Connecticut State Senator and Representative, served as president of the Aetna Life Insurance Company. After attending East Haddam elementary school, Bulkeley moved with his family in 1846 to Hartford and continued his education through high school until age 15. He joined his uncle's dry goods business in Brooklyn, NY in 1852 as an errand boy and became a partner there within seven years. During the Civil War, he enlisted in the 13th New York Volunteers and fought in the Virginia peninsular campaign. Upon his father's death in 1872, Bulkeley returned to Hartford, founded the US Bank there, and was its president for seven years.

Bulkeley, who played amateur baseball, served in 1874 and 1875 as president of the professional Hartford Dark Blues (NA). When the NL was formed in February 1876, the distinguished banker was elected unanimously as its first president and agreed to serve one year. The initial NL season progressed reasonably well, as Bulkeley enhanced baseball's image by reducing gambling and drinking at games. A figurehead president, Bulkeley faced several awkward problems. NL attendance lagged, partly because Chicago captured the pennant easily. The New York Mutuals and Philadelphia Athletics, expecting to lose money, refused to make their last western trip. Bulkeley did not attend the December 1876 NL meeting, at which owners expelled those two clubs and elected William Hulbert* as president. For over 30 years, Bulkeley also was connected with the National Trotting Association.

Bulkeley presided over the Aetna Life Insurance Company from 1879 until his death, establishing two subsidiary companies. Under his management, Aetna became one of the soundest institutions in the industry, with $200 million in assets and 1,500 paid employees. He married Fannie Briggs (Houghton) on February 11, 1885, in San Francisco, CA and had two sons and one daughter. The Republican was elected as Hartford City Councilman (1875), Alderman (1876), and Mayor (1880–1888), Connecticut Governor (1889–1893), and U.S. Senator (1905–1911) and was a delegate to the Republican national convention in 1888 and 1896. He was awarded an honorary Master of Arts degree by Yale University in 1889 and Doctor of Laws degree by Trinity College in 1917. Upon his death, NL club owners praised him for "invaluable aid" as "a founder of the national game." In 1937 he was elected to the National Baseball Hall of Fame as a pioneer and executive.

BIBLIOGRAPHY: Morgan Bulkeley file, National Baseball Library, Cooperstown, NY; *ACAB* 1 (New York, 1887), p. 444; *BDAC* (Washington, D.C., 1961), p. 623; *DAB* 3 (New York, 1929), pp. 248–249; Eddie Gold, "Hall Would Be Home for Hulbert," *BHR* (1981), pp. 89–91; *NCAB* 10 (New York, 1900), p. 345; Frederick Ivor-Campbell et al., eds., *Baseball's First Stars* (Cleveland, OH, 1996); Lowell Reidenbaugh, *Baseball's Hall of Fame-Cooperstown* (New York, 1993); Harold Seymour, *Baseball: The Early Years* (New York, 1960); William J. Ryczek, *Blackguards and Red Stockings* (Jefferson, NC, 1992); Robert Smith, *Baseball's Hall of Fame* (New York, 1973); *WWWA* 1 (1897–1942), p. 163.

David L. Porter

BUNNING, James Paul David "Jim" (b. October 23, 1931, Southgate, KY), player and manager, played baseball at Xavier University in Cincinnati. The 6-foot 3-inch, 185-pound right-hander spent six years in the minor leagues at Richmond, IN (OIL) in 1950, Davenport, IA (3IL) in 1951, Williamsport, PA (EL) in 1952, Buffalo, NY (IL) in 1953, and Little Rock, AR (SA) in 1954 and 1955. He joined the Detroit Tigers (AL) in 1955 and 1956. After posting a 5–1 record in 1956, he enjoyed his best season of his 17-year major league career in 1957 with a 20–8 record and an AL-leading 267.1 innings pitched. Although having an uneven record from 1958 through 1963, he posted 17 and 19 wins in 1961 and 1962, respectively, and led the AL in strikeouts with 201 in both 1959 and 1960. After winning 118 games and losing 87 for the Detroit Tigers, he was traded in December 1963 to the Philadelphia Phillies (NL). He enjoyed three remarkable 19-win seasons and led the staff in innings pitched. After a 17–15 season in 1967, he spent the next campaign with the Pittsburgh Pirates (NL). He was traded to the Los Angeles Dodgers (NL) in August 1969 and finished his career with losing campaigns for the Philadelphia Phillies (NL) in 1970 and 1971. As an NL pitcher, he recorded well over 200 strikeouts in four consecutive seasons from 1964 through 1967. In 1967, he led the NL with 253 strikeouts and 302.1 innings pitched. Overall, he won 224 and lost 184 games for a .549 winning percentage and a 3.27 ERA and hurled over 100 victories in both leagues. He pitched no-hitters in each league, defeating the Boston Red Sox 3–0 in July 1958 and tossing a perfect game against the New York Mets in June 1964. In eight All-Star game appearances, he compiled an impressive 1.13 ERA. His 2,855 strikeout and only 1,000 walks rank him among the best control pitchers and strikeout artists in baseball history. He was the first pitcher since Cy Young* to win over 100 games and strike out over 1,000 batters in each league and retired second only to Walter Johnson* in career strikeouts. Bunning never played on a pennant-winning club, but his 17–11 record in 1961 helped the Detroit Tigers to a 101–61 season record and second place finish. Subsequently, he managed Philadelphia Phillies farm teams in 1972 and 1973 and then worked as a stockbroker, agent for major league players, and politician. A dominant figure in the MLBBPA, he helped establish the player's pension plan. He served as Ronald Reagan's local campaign manager in Campbell County, KY in 1980. In 1982 he was elected as a Republican to the Kentucky State Senate, defeating a 16-year incumbent. His campaign promised better representation of a badly depressed and underrepresented northern Kentucky region. In 1984 he won the Republican nomination for governor, but lost in the general election. In 1986, he was elected to the U.S. House of Representatives as a Republican from the Fourth Kentucky congressional district. He won re-election to five more House terms in a heavily Democratic district in 1988, 1990, 1992, 1994, and 1996 and edged Scott Baesler for the U.S. Senate in 1998. He and his wife, Mary Theis, whom he married in January 1952, have nine children. Since 1974 he has become a respected part of the business and political community in Cincinnati and northern Kentucky. Bunning's transition to a successful post-playing career is illustrated by his determination to gain his degree from Xavier, as he skipped spring training trips to finish a Bachelor of Science degree in economics in 1953. In 1996, he was elected to the National Baseball Hall of Fame.

BIBLIOGRAPHY: Jim Bunning file, National Baseball Library, Cooperstown, NY; Rich Westcott and Frank Bilovsky, *The New Phillies Encyclopedia* (Philadelphia, PA, 1993); Richard Bak, *A Place for Summer* (Detroit, MI, 1998); Stan Grosshandler, "These Players Excelled in Both Major Leagues!" *BD* 42 (November 1983), pp. 29–32; Robert Grayson, "Congressman Jim Bunning Finally Makes the Hall," *SCD* 23 (August 9, 1996), pp. 78–79; Herbert S. "Shan" Hoffman, "Jim Bunning," *TNP* 15 (1995), pp. 106–110; Ronald A. Mayer, *Perfect!* (Jefferson, NC, 1991); Gene Karst and Martin J. Jones, Jr., *Who's Who in Professional Baseball* (New Rochelle, NY, 1973); Edward Kiersh, *Where Have You Gone, Vince DiMaggio?* (New York, 1983); Joe Falls, *Detroit Tigers* (New York, 1975); Ralph Bernstein, *The Story of Jim Bunning* (Philadelphia, PA, 1965); Brent P. Kelley, *Baseball Stars of the 1950s* (Jefferson, NC, 1993); L. Van Dyne, "High and Inside," *Washingtonian* 27 (August 1992), pp. 72–73; Steve Wulf, "Jim Bunning," *SI* 66 (February 23, 1987), pp. 64–68.

Douglas A. Noverr

BURDETTE, Selva Lewis, Jr. "Lew" (b. November 22, 1926, Nitro, WV), player, coach, and scout, excelled as a right-handed pitcher for the Milwaukee Braves (NL). Nitro High School, from which he graduated, did not have a baseball team. Burdette pitched for the local America Vicose Plant and earned a baseball scholarship to the University of Richmond. After signing with the New York Yankees (AL), Burdette in 1947 pitched for Norfolk, VA (PiL) and Amsterdam, NY (CAL). At Quincy, IL in 1948, he led the 3IL in victories with 16. Burdette pitched for Kansas City, MO (AA) in 1949 and 1950 and made two appearances for the New York Yankees in late 1950. The following season, he compiled a 14–12 mark for San Francisco, CA (PCL) before being traded with $50,000 cash in August 1951 to the Boston Braves (NL) for veteran pitcher Johnny Sain.*

Over the next 13 years, Burdette combined with Warren Spahn* as one of the most successful righty–lefty pitching duos in baseball. Between 1953 and 1961, he won at least 13 games every season. His best campaigns included 19 wins in 1956 and 1960, 20 in 1958, and an NL-leading 21 in 1959. Burdette, who eight times recorded at least 15 triumphs, won 179 total games in Boston and Milwaukee Braves uniforms. In the 1957 World Series, Burdette started and won the second, fifth, and seventh games against the New York Yankees. He allowed only two earned runs in 27 innings for a 0.67 ERA. He established a World Series mark by pitching two shutouts and tied records with three wins and three complete games in a seven-game series. His fortunes were reversed in the 1958 World Series when he won one contest and lost two and allowed 17 runs in his three starts as the Yankees defeated the Braves. The five HR he allowed also tied a series mark.

Burdette paced the NL in ERA (2.70) in 1956 and shared the lead in shutouts (4) in 1959. He also led the NL once each in pitching percentage (1958), games started (1959), complete games (1960), and innings pitched (1961). He tossed a 1–0 no-hit victory against the Philadelphia Phillies on August 18, 1960, and on two separate occasions homered twice in the same game. The Braves in June 1963 traded Burdette to the St. Louis Cardinals (NL), where he pitched until June 1964. Burdette's other major league clubs included the Chicago Cubs (NL) in 1964 and 1965, Philadelphia Phillies (NL) in 1965, and California Angels (AL) in 1966 and 1967. His playing career ended in 1967 with Seattle, WA (PCL). In 626 major league games, Burdette recorded 203 wins, 144 losses (.585), 158 complete games, 33 shutouts, and a 3.66 ERA. He struck out 1,074 batters and employed numerous pitches, including, according to many NL hitters, an extremely effective spitball.

Burdette married Mary Ann Shelton on June 30, 1949 and has three children, Lewis, Madge, and Mary Lou. After retiring, Burdette scouted the southeastern area for the Central Scouting Bureau in 1968 and coached for the Atlanta Braves (NL) in 1972. He also worked as vice-president of a real estate firm in Sarasota, FL and as a public relations specialist for a cable television company in Athens, GA.

BIBLIOGRAPHY: Lew Burdette file, National Baseball Library, Cooperstown, NY; J. Buckley, Jr., "World Series: Kings of the Hill," *SI* 45 (October 7, 1991), pp. 45ff; Bob Buege, *The Milwaukee Braves: A Baseball Eulogy* (Milwaukee, WI, 1988); Gary Caruso, *The Braves Encyclopedia* (Philadelphia, PA, 1995); Gene Karst and Martin J. Jones, Jr., *Who's Who in Professional Baseball* (New Rochelle, NY, 1973); Craig Carter, ed., *TSN Daguerreotypes*, 8th ed. (St. Louis, 1990); *The Baseball Encyclopedia*, 10th ed. (New York, 1996); John Thorn et al., eds., *Total Braves* (New York, 1996); Eddie Gold and Art Ahrens, *The New Era Cubs, 1941–1985* (Chicago, IL, 1985).

Jack R. Stanton

BURGESS, Forrest Harrill "Smoky" (b. February 6, 1927, Caroleen, NC; d. September 15, 1991, Asheville, NC), player, coach, and scout, was the son of Loyd Luther "Smoky" Burgess, a textile worker who played semiprofessional baseball, and Ocie (Lewis) Burgess, both of English descent. After graduating from Tri High School in Caroleen in 1944, the left-handed batting catcher signed with the Chicago Cubs (NL) and played for Lockport, NY (PoL). In 1945 he moved up to Portsmouth, VA (PiL) and entered the U.S. Army, serving as a mail clerk in France. After appearing in one game for Los Angeles, CA (PCL) in 1946, he caught for Macon, GA (SAL) and Fayetteville, NC (TSL) and hit a TSL-leading .387 for 1947. In 1948 at Nashville, TN (SA), his .386 batting average topped the SA.

Burgess played for the Chicago Cubs and Los Angeles (PCL) in 1949, began the 1950 campaign with Springfield, MA (IL), and then rejoined the Chicago Cubs. After being traded to the Philadelphia Phillies (NL) in December 1951, he surpassed a .300 batting average twice in the next four years. In April 1955, he was traded to the Cincinnati Reds (NL). Burgess caught at least 90 games and hit at least .275 each season through 1958. The Pittsburgh Pirates (NL) acquired Burgess in January 1959. He hit .294 while sharing catching duties for the 1960 World Champions. He made the NL All-Star team in 1954, 1955, 1960, and 1961 and led NL catchers in fielding in 1960 and 1961. He was traded to the Chicago White Sox (AL) in September 1964 and stayed there until chronic ulcers forced his retirement following the 1967 season.

The 5-foot 8-inch, 185-pound Burgess lacked speed and possessed limited throwing ability, having suffered a shoulder injury in a jeep accident during World War II. Nonetheless, his .295 major league career batting average made "the little round man" a dangerous hitter. He achieved most fame as a pinch hitter in the early 1960s. His 145 career pinch hits rank second to Manny Mota,* and his 507 at-bats as a pinch hitter rank him first on the all-time list. In 18 major league seasons, Burgess made 1,318 hits, including 230 doubles and 126 HR, and drove in 673 runs.

Burgess, who married Margaret Head on July 21, 1945 and had two children, operated a service station and a car dealership in Forest City, NC. He later served as a scout and minor league hitting instructor for the Atlanta Braves (NL).

BIBLIOGRAPHY: Forrest Burgess file, National Baseball Library, Cooperstown, NY; Donald Honig, *The Cincinnati Reds* (New York, 1992); Eddie Gold and Art Ahrens, *The New Era Cubs, 1941–1985* (Chicago, IL, 1985); *The Baseball Encyclopedia*, 10th ed. (New York, 1996); Dick Groat and Bill Surface, *The World Champion Pittsburgh Pirates* (New York, 1961); *NYT*, September 17, 1991, p. D-21; Rich Westcott, *Diamond Greats* (Westport, CT, 1988); Bob Smizik, *The Pittsburgh Pirates: An Illustrated History* (New York, 1990).

Luther W. Spoehr

BURKETT, Jesse Cail "The Crab" (b. December 4, 1868, Wheeling, WV; d. May 27, 1953, Worcester, MA), player, manager, owner, coach, and scout, was the son of Granville Burkett and Eleanor Burkett and spent his youth fishing and swimming along the upper Ohio River. Burkett, whose early life is obscure, never knew his precise birthdate. He entered professional baseball as a pitcher in 1888, winning 27 games for Scranton, PA (CL). The following season, the 5-foot 8-inch, 155-pound left-hander posted an unbelievable 39–6 mark with Worcester, MA (AtA) and earned $125 per month. He purchased a house in Worcester and made it his permanent residence. In 1890, Burkett married Nellie McGrath of Worcester.

The Indianapolis, IN Hoosiers held Burkett's contract in 1890, but when the franchise folded that spring, the New York Giants (NL) signed him. He compiled a 3–10 log with a 5.56 ERA and fielded only .824, but batted .309 in 101 games. In 1891, he was sold to the Cleveland Spiders (NL) and assigned to Lincoln, NE (WA). A .349 batting average earned him a promotion in August to Cleveland. In his inauspicious first full big league season (1892), he hit .275 and committed 28 errors in left field. A speedy runner, he stole 36 bases, scored 119 runs, and often coupled fine bunting with speed to leg out infield hits.

At Cleveland, Burkett teamed with stars Cy Young,* Cupid Childs,* George Cuppy,* and Patsy Tebeau.* Nicknamed "The Crab" because of a cranky disposition, Burkett, who did not drink or smoke, often fought with umpires, managers, and fans. Off the field, the gentle Burkett took a special interest in children.

Burkett rarely showed power, but hit solid line drives. In 1893, he improved his batting average nearly 75 points to .348, scored 145 runs, and made a NL-leading 42 errors in the outfield. After hitting .358 in 1894, he complied consecutive .400 seasons. He paced Cleveland in 1895 with a NL-high .409 batting average on 225 hits and pilfered a career-high 41 stolen bases. Burkett led the NL the next season with a .410 average. In 1899 Burkett, Cy Young, and others were transferred to St. Louis by Frank Robison, who owned the Spiders and the St. Louis Cardinals. During three seasons in St. Louis, he hit .396, .363, and .376.

In 1902, Burkett jumped to the St. Louis Browns (AL) and saw his hitting slide. After batting .273 with the 1904 Browns, he was traded to the Boston Red Sox (AL) for rookie outfielder George Stone.* After Burkett led AL outfielders in errors and hit only .257 in 1905, the Red Sox released him. His brilliant major league career included 2,850 hits, 320 doubles, 182 triples, 1,720 runs, 952 RBI, 389 stolen bases, and a .338 batting average.

In 1906 Burkett bought the Worcester, MA (NEL) franchise and served as its owner, field manager, and outfielder through the 1913 season, hitting .325 in 483 games. From 1906 through 1909, Worcester finished first four times under Burkett's leadership. In 1916, he returned to the field as manager and utility player with Lawrence, MA, Hartford, CT, and Lowell, MA (EL). From 1917 to 1920, he coached baseball at Holy Cross College and scouted for the New York Giants (NL). After coaching for John McGraw's* New York Giants in 1921 and 1922, Burkett again managed the Worcester club for the next two seasons. He ended his managerial career with Lewiston, ME (NEL) in 1928 and 1929 and Lowell, MA (NEL) in 1933.

Burkett, who enjoyed reunions with old baseball friends and never lost his love of the game, retired to his Worcester home and later suffered from hardening of the arteries. In 1946, Burkett was elected to the National Baseball Hall of Fame.

BIBLIOGRAPHY: Bob Broeg and Jerry Vickery, *St. Louis Cardinals Encyclopedia* (Grand Rapids, MI, 1998); J. Thomas Hetrick, *Misfits* (Jefferson, NC, 1991); Jesse Burkett file, National Baseball Library, Cooperstown, NY; John Phillips, *The Spiders—Who Was Who* (Cabin John, MD, 1991); Martin Appel and Burt Goldblatt, *Baseball's Best: The Hall of Fame Gallery* (New York, 1977); Bob Broeg, *Redbirds: A Century of Cardinals' Baseball* (St. Louis, MO, 1981); Frederick Ivor-Campbell et al., eds., *Baseball's First Stars* (Cleveland, OH, 1996); John Lardner, "The Snake Pit and the Letter," *Newsweek* 43 (June 15, 1953), p. 91; *NYT*, May 28, 1953, p. 23; Lowell Reidenbaugh, *Baseball's Hall of Fame-Cooperstown* (New York, 1993).

Frank J. Olmsted

BURLESON, Richard Paul "Rick," "Rooster" (b. April 29, 1951, Lynnwood, CA), player and manager, is the son of Bill Gene Burleson and Jeanne (Rathbun) Burleson and attended Carriton JC in Norwalk, CA, California State University, Fullerton, and Whittier College. The 5-foot 10-inch, 160-pound shortstop, who batted and threw right-handed, signed with the Boston Red Sox (AL) in January 1970.

Burleson moved rapidly through the Boston Red Sox organization as shortstop for Winter Haven, FL (FSL) in 1970, Greenville, SC (WCL) and Winston-Salem, NC (CrL) in 1971, and Pawtucket, RI (EL) in 1972 and (IL) in 1973. He replaced Luis Aparicio* as starting Boston Red Sox shortstop in 1974, hitting .284. The confident, aggressive shortstop batted higher his rookie season than he had ever hit in the minor leagues. In 1975, Burleson knocked in a career-high 62 runs and hit .444 to help the Red Sox win the AL Championship Series against the Oakland Athletics and .292 in the World Series against the Cincinnati Reds.

Burleson remained with the Red Sox through 1980, making the 1977, 1978, and 1979 AL All-Star teams. His best major league season came in 1977, when he established career bests in batting average (.293), hits (194), doubles (36), and triples (7). Blessed with a tremendous throwing arm, Burleson in 1979 led the AL in fielding average (.980) and earned a Gold Glove. He paced the AL twice in putouts (1977, 1980) and once each in chances and assists (1980), setting a major league record for double plays by a short-stop with 147.

In December 1980, the Red Sox traded Burleson and Butch Hobson to the California Angels (AL) for Carney Lansford,* Mark Clear, and Rick Miller. He batted .293 in 1981, making the AL All-Star team for the final time and leading AL shortstops in chances, putouts, and assists. A rotator cuff injury on his throwing arm sharply curtailed his playing time from 1982 to 1984 and sidelined him the entire 1985 season. Burleson won AL Come-back Player of the Year honors in 1986, batting .284 in 93 games and .273 in the AL Championship Series against the Boston Red Sox. His major league career ended with the Baltimore Orioles (AL) in 1987.

During 13 major league seasons, Burleson batted .273 with 1,401 hits, 256 doubles, 50 HR, and 449 RBI in 1,346 games and compiled a .971 fielding average. He made the *TSN* AL All-Star Team in 1977 and 1981 and *TSN* Silver Slugger Team in 1981 and was named in 1983 to the All-Time Red Sox Dream Team. He managed San Bernardino, CA (CaL) in 1999 and San Antonio, TX (TL) in 2000. The La Habra, CA resident married Karen Crofoot in February 1974 and has three sons, James, Richard Chad, and Richard Kyle.

BIBLIOGRAPHY: Richard Burleson file, National Baseball Library, Cooperstown, NY; *TSN Baseball Register*, 1988; Peter Golenbock, *Fenway* (New York, 1992); John Thorn et al., eds., *Total Baseball*, 5th ed. (New York, 1997); Robert Redmount, *The Red Sox Encyclopedia* (Champaign, IL, 1998); Dan Shaughnessy, *The Curse of the Bambino* (New York, 1990); *WWA*, 44th ed., vol. I (1986–1987), p. 396.

David L. Porter

BURNS, George Henry "Tioga George," "The Tioga Kid," "General George" (b. January 31, 1893, Niles, OH; d. January 7, 1978, Kirkland, WA), player and manager, grew up in Tioga, PA. Nicknamed "Tioga George" and "The Tioga Kid" to help distinguish him from his contemporary, George Joseph Burns* (NL outfielder), the 6-foot 1½-inch, 185-pound right-hander spent his entire major league career in the AL. Burns quit Philadelphia Central High School at age 16 to pursue a professional baseball career. In 1913, the first baseman signed his first legitimate pro contract with Quincy, IL (CA) for $150 per month. Before playing a single game, however, he was sold to Burlington, IA (CA) with a $90 a month contract. In 1913, he also performed for Ottumwa, IA (CA) at $300 per month and Sioux City, IA (WL) before the Detroit Tigers (AL) bought his contract.

He began a 16-year major league career with Detroit in 1914 and played first base for the Tigers through the 1917 season. On March 8, 1918, he was sold to the New York Yankees (AL). The Yankees, however, immediately sent him to the Philadelphia A's (AL) for Ping Bodie. In 1918, he batted a spectacular .352 and led the AL with 178 hits. After marrying Marian R. Harris in April 1919, he had four daughters and became a devoted family man. On May 29, 1920, he was sold to the Cleveland Indians (AL). Cleveland survived a tight AL pennant race to capture its first championship, as Burns played a supporting role. Burns batted .300, splitting first base duties with Wheeler "Doc" Johnston in the 1920 World Series against the Brooklyn Robins and then hit .361 as part-time first baseman in 1921.

Burns, Joe Harris,* and Elmer Smith* were traded to the Boston Red Sox (AL) for Stuffy McInnis* on December 24, 1921. The highlight of his Red Sox career came on his unassisted triple play against Cleveland on September 14, 1923. On January 7, 1924, Boston traded Burns to the Cleveland Indians in a multi-player deal for William Wambsganss* of unassisted triple play fame. During this Cleveland stint, Burns enjoyed his best seasons with .310, .336, .358, and .319 batting averages. In 1926, he captured the AL MVP Award and led the AL in hits and doubles. Babe Ruth* did not receive a single vote for the trophy, although he joined Burns on the All-AL team. Burns' 216 hits included 64 doubles, a record not broken until 1931 and still among the best season totals ever.

In September 1928, Burns was released unconditionally by the Indians and signed by the New York Yankees (AL). New York once again sold him to the Philadelphia A's (AL) on June 19, 1929. He concluded his major league career after making unsuccessful pinch hit appearances in the 1929 World Series against the Chicago Cubs. In 1,866 major league games, Burns batted .307 and garnered 2,018 hits, 444 doubles, 72 triples, 72 HR, 901 runs, 951 RBI, and 154 stolen bases. He played in the PCL with Missions, CA (1930–1931), Los Angeles, CA (1931), Seattle, WA (1932–1934), and Portland, OR (1934). After managing Seattle (1932–1934) and Portland (1934–1935), he settled in the Seattle area to manage apartments. In 1947, he became a deputy sheriff of King County (Seattle), WA and held that position until retiring to Kirkland, WA.

BIBLIOGRAPHY: George H. Burns file, National Baseball Library, Cooperstown, NY; Craig Carter, ed., *TSN Daguerreotypes*, 8th ed. (St. Louis, MO, 1990); *The Baseball Encyclopedia*, 10th ed. (New York, 1996); Franklin Lewis, *The Cleveland Indians* (New York, 1949); John Thorn et al., eds., *Total Indians* (New York, 1996); Fred Smith, *995 Tigers* (Detroit, MI, 1981); Frederick G. Lieb, *Connie Mack* (New York, 1945); Jerome Romanowski, *The Mackmen* (Upper Darby, PA, 1979).

David B. Merrell

BURNS, George Joseph (b. November 24, 1889, Utica, NY; d. August 15, 1966, Gloversville, NY), player, manager, and coach, was the son of cigar-maker John Burns and participated in sandlot and amateur baseball. Burns began his professional career as a catcher for the Utica, NY Harps (NYSL) in 1909. Two years later, he became an outfielder and was sold for $4,000 to the New York Giants (NL). Burns played with the Giants for 10 years and developed into one of the era's best outfielders and hitters. During his first two years (1911–1912), he played little because manager John McGraw* wanted to groom him carefully. Burns became the regular left fielder in 1913 and married Mary Baker on October 7, 1914. The right-handed, 5-foot 7-inch, 160-pound outfielder exhibited excellent speed and possessed a strong arm. Defensively, he wore a special long-billed cap with blue sunglasses attached, which helped him master the Polo Grounds sunfield. Burns, who moved to center field in 1920 and combined with Irish Meusel* and Ross Youngs* to give McGraw the NL's best outfield, also became the Giants' leadoff hitter. Besides setting a then NL record of 459 consecutive games in the outfield, he led the NL in at bats and stolen bases twice and in walks and runs scored five times. He appeared in three World Series, batting .333 in the 1921 classic and leading the Giants with 11 hits. Burns made four hits in one game and delivered the game-winning safety in game four. In 1918, McGraw rated Burns next to Christy Mathewson* as the greatest player he had managed.

In December 1921, McGraw reluctantly traded Burns to the Cincinnati Reds (NL) to acquire third baseman Heinie Groh.* Burns enjoyed two solid seasons with the Reds, but declined at the plate in 1924 and was released. He joined the Philadelphia Phillies (NL) in 1925, hitting .292 in 88 games in his last major league season. Overall, Burns recorded 2,077 hits in 1,853 games and averaged 169 hits per season as a regular. Lifetime, he batted .287, scored 1,188 runs, knocked in 611 runs, collected 872 walks, and stole 383 bases. Between 1926 and 1930, Burns served as player–manager for various minor league teams, including Newark, NJ (IL) in 1926, Williamsport, PA (NYPL) in 1927 and 1928, Hanover, PA (BRL) in 1928, Springfield, MA (EL) in 1929, and San Antonio, TX (TL) in 1930. With the exception of his last minor league season, he hit at least .295 between 1926 and 1930. In 1931, he returned to the New York Giants (NL) as a coach. Burns lived in Gloversville, NY, where he operated his father's pool hall and became payroll clerk in a tannery. He retired in 1957 and resided in Gloversville until his death. Burns was survived by his second wife, Pauline Rezek, whom he married on October 18, 1952, and by two stepchildren.

BIBLIOGRAPHY: George Joseph Burns file, National Baseball Library, Cooperstown, NY; Frank Graham, *McGraw of the Giants* (New York, 1944); Noel Hynd, *The Giants of the Polo Grounds* (New York, 1988); Frank Graham, *The New York Giants* (New York, 1952); Paul MacFarlane, ed., *TSN Daguerreotypes of Great Stars of Baseball* (St.

Louis, MO, 1981); *NYT*, December 7, 31, 1921, August 16, 1966; Richard A. Puff, "Silent George Burns: A Star in the Sunfield," *BRJ* 12 (1983), pp. 119–125.

Douglas D. Martin

BURNS, Thomas Everett "Tommy" (b. March 30, 1857, Honesdale, PA; d. March 19, 1902, Jersey City, NJ), player and manager, entered professional baseball with Hornell, MI (NA) in 1878. Although Burns lacked outstanding minor league statistics, the Chicago White Stockings (NL) signed him to play shortstop in 1880.

The 5-foot 7-inch, 152-pound Burns hit .309 as a rookie and anchored the famous "stonewall infield," playing 474 games at shortstop and 704 games at third base. Hustling and determination made Burns a solid player. He did not smoke or drink, making him a favorite of manager Cap Anson.* On September 6, 1883, Burns set six major league records as the White Stockings scored 18 times in the seventh inning. These marks included most hits (3), total bases (8), and extra base hits (3) in an inning with two doubles and a HR. That season, he batted .294 and hit 37 doubles. On August 16, 1890, he helped set another major league record when he and teammate Malachi Kittredge both hit grand-slam HR in the same inning.

Burns proved a better third baseman, leading the NL several times in putouts, assists, and double plays. Only three White Stocking players, including Burns, did not jump to the short-lived PL in 1890. After Burns batted .277 in 1890, his production declined. He signed with the Pittsburgh Pirates (NL) in 1892 as player–manager, but was fired after 55 games. His .264 major league career batting average included 236 doubles, 69 triples, and 39 HR.

Burns then started a long managerial career with Springfield, MA (EL) from 1893 through 1897. When Anson was dismissed in 1898 as Chicago manager, Burns replaced him and led the White Stockings to a fourth place finish with an 85–65 mark. After Chicago slipped to eighth place the next year, Burns was fired. He managed Buffalo, NY (EL) in 1901. Jersey City, NJ (EL) signed Burns to manage for 1902, but he died of a heart attack.

BIBLIOGRAPHY: Thomas Everett Burns file, National Baseball Library, Cooperstown, NY; Art Ahrens and Eddie Gold, *Day by Day in Chicago Cubs History* (West Point, NY, 1982); Eddie Gold and Art Ahrens, *The Golden Era Cubs, 1876–1940* (Chicago, IL, 1985); Warren Brown, *The Chicago Cubs* (New York, 1946); Robert L. Tiemann and Mark Rucker, eds., *Nineteenth Century Stars* (Kansas City, MO, 1989); *The Baseball Encyclopedia*, 10th ed. (New York, 1996).

Duane A. Smith

BURNS, Thomas P. "Oyster," "Tommy" (b. September 6, 1864, Philadelphia, PA; d. November 11, 1928, Brooklyn, NY), player, was the son of Patrick Burns and Mary (Henderson) Burns, both Irish immigrants. The fiery competitor was nicknamed "Oyster" for liking to eat oysters and was called

"Tommy" during his playing days. Burns debuted professionally as a pitcher in 1883 with Harrisburg, PA (ISA), winning five of 13 decisions. He began 1884 with Wilmington, DE (EL), but bolted them shortly after the club entered the outlaw UA.

The 5-foot 8-inch, 183-pound right-hander signed with the major league Baltimore Orioles (AA) in 1884, ending his rookie season with a .298 batting average and 3.00 ERA. His batting average slipped to .231 in 78 games the next season with Baltimore, causing his demotion to the Newark, DE Domestics (EL). He spent the entire 1886 season there, helping Newark win the EL pennant.

Burns returned to the major leagues in 1887 and remained there through 1895. He spent 11 major league seasons as an outfielder, infielder, and pitcher with the Baltimore Orioles (AA) in 1887 and 1888, Brooklyn Trolley-Dodgers-Bridegrooms (AA) in 1888 and 1889, Brooklyn Bridegrooms (NL) from 1890 to 1895, and New York Giants (NL) in 1895. Burns led the AA in triples (19) in 1887 and the NL in HR (13) and RBI (128) in 1890, all career bests. He batted over .300 five times, including .341 in 1887 and .354 in 1894. Burns ended his major league career with a .300 batting average, 1,389 hits, at least 832 RBI, and a respectable 65 HR in a dead ball era. Besides leading the AA in saves in 1884 and 1885, he finished with eight wins and five losses for a .615 winning percentage.

As captain of the Baltimore Orioles, Burns developed a reputation as a fiery competitor. A *SL* editorial dated September 7, 1887 called him "obnoxious to many." In one particular game, he threw a ball at the Cleveland Blues pitcher "with the force caused by undue excitement." Burns later was relieved of his duties and fined $25 for the incident. After spending 1896 with Newark, NJ (AtL) and Grand Rapids, MI (WL) and 1897 with Hartford, CT (AtL), he retired to Brooklyn, NY.

BIBLIOGRAPHY: Thomas P. Burns file, National Baseball Library, Cooperstown, NY; Peter Filichia, *Professional Baseball Franchises* (New York, 1993); William F. McNeil, *The Dodgers Encyclopedia* (Champaign, IL, 1997); Frank Graham, *The Brooklyn Dodgers* (New York, 1945); James K. Skipper, Jr., *Baseball Nicknames* (Jefferson, NC, 1992); John Thorn et al., eds., *Total Baseball*, 5th ed. (New York, 1997); Robert L. Tiemann and Mark Rucker, eds., *Nineteenth Century Stars* (Kansas City, MO, 1989).

Scot E. Mondore

BURROUGHS, Jeffrey Alan "Jeff" (b. March 7, 1951, Long Beach, CA), player, attended Long Beach City College and married Deborah Gorman. They have two sons, Scott and Sean. The Washington Senators (AL) made Burroughs their first overall pick in the 1969 amateur draft. He began his professional baseball career with Wytheville, VA (ApL) in 1969 and spent nearly three seasons in the minor leagues.

Under the tutelage of manager Ted Williams,* the beefy Burroughs developed into a solid hitter. Burroughs became a starting outfielder with the

Texas Rangers (AL) in 1973, batting .279 with 30 HR and 85 RBI. The 1974 campaign marked a turning point for the 6-foot 2-inch, 200-pound right-hander, who batted .301, clouted 25 HR, and led the AL with 118 RBI to earn the AL MVP award. During the next two seasons with Texas, he also furnished impressive power numbers.

In December 1976, the Texas Rangers sent Burroughs to the Atlanta Braves (NL) for Ken Henderson, Dave May, Carl Morton, Roger Moret, Adrian Devine, and $250,000. Burroughs placed second in the NL with 41 HR and fourth with 114 RBI in 1977 and led the NL with 117 walks and a .436 on-base percentage in 1978. In December 1980, the Atlanta Braves shipped Burroughs to the Seattle Mariners (AL) for Carlos Diaz. Burroughs spent only the strike-shortened 1981 season with Seattle.

In April 1982, the Oakland Athletics (AL) acquired Burroughs as a DH. His power numbers steadily decreased. Burroughs finished his major league career in 1985 with the Toronto Blue Jays (AL). During 15 major league seasons, Burroughs batted .261 with 240 HR and 882 RBI. He was named to the 1974 AL All-Star team and appeared in the 1985 AL Championship Series against the Kansas City Royals.

Burroughs coached two Little League teams from Long Beach, CA to World Series championships. The 1992 team won by default, while the 1993 squad defeated a club from Panama. His son, Sean, played a key role in the 1993 title and plays in the San Diego Padres organization. Burroughs wrote *Jeff Burroughs' Instructional Guide for Little League Coaches and Parents* and co-authored *The Little League Team that Could* with Tom Hennessy.

BIBLIOGRAPHY: *Microsoft Complete Baseball*, CD-ROM (Redmond, WA, 1994); Jeff Burroughs file, National Baseball Library, Cooperstown, NY; Gary Caruso, *The Braves Encyclopedia* (Philadelphia, PA, 1995); *The Baseball Encyclopedia*, 10th ed. (New York, 1996); Phil Rogers, *The Impossible Takes a Little Longer* (Dallas, TX, 1991); Mike Shatzkin, ed., *The Ballplayers* (New York, 1990).

Chad Israelson

BUSCH, August Adolphus, Jr. "Gussie" (b. March 28, 1899, St. Louis, MO; d. September 29, 1989, St. Louis, MO), corporation executive and owner, was the son of Anheuser Busch and Alice (Zisemann) Busch and attended Fremont Public School and Smith Academy. Married four times and the father of eleven children, Busch wedded former secretary Margaret M. Snyder in 1981. Frequently compared to his dynamic grandfather Adolphus, Anheuser-Bush co-founder in 1865, he worked from vat scrubber to chief executive officer by 1946. His vigorous expansion program made the firm the national leader in 1953 and the world's largest brewery by his 1975 retirement.

Busch's lifestyle resembled "a Rhineland baron of old, devoted to hounds, horses, and magnificent entertainments" on his "Grant's Farm" estate in St. Louis County. Responsive to civic causes, Busch purchased the St. Louis

Cardinals (NL) baseball club in February 1953 for $3.75 million as a "sporting venture," to block the team's departure for Milwaukee. Although only marginally interested in baseball beforehand, Busch helped pioneer the now commonplace corporate executive's entry into big-time sports. With explosive energy, Busch spent $7 million on new players and farm system development and purchased and refurbished old Sportsman's Park. He piloted the drive to construct Busch Memorial Stadium in downtown St. Louis (1966), the last major sports complex to be built solely with private funds. Busch's efforts produced Cardinal NL pennants in 1964, 1967, 1968, 1982, and 1985 and three world championships.

Imbued with relentless drive, Busch frequently participated in spring training drills. His motto, "Work hard—love your work," fired his denunciation of inflationary player salaries when the Cardinal payroll in 1969 exceeded $1 million. Holdouts by top left-handed pitchers Steve Carlton* and Jerry Reuss* forced their departures because Busch regarded their attitude and outfielder Curt Flood's* court challenge to baseball's reserve clause as crass ingratitude. Busch stormed "I'm fed up. I can't understand what's happening here, or on our campuses in our great country." His gravelly voice and table-pounding vehemence demanded adamant owner resistance to the 1972 and 1981 strikes.

When inducted into Missouri's Sports Hall of Fame in his retirement year, Busch listed his lifelong dedications: (1) his wife and family, (2) the brewery, and (3) St. Louis. The city owed much to the "Big Eagle," especially for his retention of the Cardinals, only the best known of his many generosities to his community.

BIBLIOGRAPHY: Bob Broeg and Jerry Vickery, *St. Louis Cardinals Encyclopedia* (Grand Rapids, MI, 1998); Bob Broeg, *Redbirds: A Century of Cardinals' Baseball* (St. Louis, MO, 1981); *CB* (1973), pp. 69–71; "Gussie vs. the Cards," *Newsweek* 79 (June 19, 1972), p. 61; Leonard Koppett, "Busch, Beer, and Baseball," *NYT Magazine* (April 11, 1965), p. 32; William Leggett, "A Bird in Hand and a Burning Busch," *SI* 32 (March 23, 1970), pp. 18–23; Roy Malone et al., "Gussie Busch," St. Louis *Post-Dispatch*, August 25–29, 1975; Harold H. Martin, "The Cardinals Strike It Rich," *SEP* 225 (June 27, 1953), p. 22; *NYT*, September 30, 1989, p. 29; Rob Rains, *The St. Louis Cardinals* (New York, 1992); *WWA*, 42nd ed. (1982–1983), p. 466.

                                                            William J. Miller

BUSH, Guy Terrell "The Mississippi Mudcat" (b. August 23, 1901, Aberdeen, MS; d. July 2, 1985, Shannon, MS), player, was the son of a cotton farmer and attended the Tupelo, MS Military Academy for three years before beginning his professional baseball career in 1923 with Greenville, MS (CSL). After the 6-foot, 175-pound right-hander pitched a doubleheader shutout against Vicksburg, MS Chicago Cubs (NL) scout Jack Doyle* signed him to a $1,200 contract. The CSL disbanded in mid-season, after which Bush was promoted to the Chicago Cubs. The fear of big cities, however, kept him from the major league club and caused him to sign with the Milan-Trenton, IL (KL) team under an assumed name. After several weeks, he finally agreed to join the Chicago Cubs and made his major league debut in mid-September 1923. Bush split the 1924 season between Wichita Falls, TX (TL) and Chicago, compiling a 2–5 mark as a roster replacement for injured veteran pitcher Grover Cleveland Alexander.*

For the next decade, Bush both started and relieved as a mainstay of the Chicago Cubs' pitching corps. After compiling a lowly 6–13 mark in 1925, he rebounded with a 13–9 mark in 1926 and slipped to 10–10 in 1927. From 1928 through 1934, he averaged 17 victories per season as one of the NL's most impressive hurlers and compiled a composite .654 winning percentage. In 1929, Bush's 18–7 record, 3.66 ERA, and 18 complete games helped Chicago win the NL pennant. Three years later, his 19–11 mark and 3.21 ERA aided the Cubs in capturing another flag. The NL's highest-paid hurler for four years, Bush enjoyed his best season in 1933 with a 20–12 record, 2.75 ERA, and 20 complete games for the third-place Cubs.

After Bush posted an 18–10 mark in 1934, the Chicago Cubs traded him to the Pittsburgh Pirates (NL) that November. Bush finished with an 11–11 record the following season. After the Pirates released him midway through 1936, he signed with the Boston Braves (NL). After a disappointing 8–15 mark with the Braves in 1937, he was sold in February 1938 to the St. Louis Cardinals (NL) and appeared in just six games. Bush completed the 1938 season with Los Angeles, CA (PCL) and then quit baseball to manage his farm in Mississippi and gas stations in Chicago. After a five-year absence, he appeared in 10 games for Chattanooga, TN (SA) in 1944 and in four games with the Cincinnati Reds (NL) in 1945.

Bush finished with a 176–136 career mark and a 3.86 ERA. From 1925 to 1935, he averaged 41 games per year and led the NL in appearances (50) and saves (7) in 1929. Bush hurled a complete game in a 3–1 victory over the Philadelphia Athletics in the third contest of the 1929 World Series and lost the opening game of the 1932 World Series against the New York Yankees. On May 25, 1935, he pitched against the Boston Braves at Forbes Field and surrendered Babe Ruth's* final two career HR.

Bush worked with a Chicago sporting goods company and retired to his native Mississippi in the 1970s. He married Frances Richardson in 1927 and Delores Rosing in 1938.

BIBLIOGRAPHY: Warren Brown, *The Chicago Cubs* (New York, 1946); Guy T. Bush file, National Baseball Library, Cooperstown, NY; Chicago (IL) *Tribune*, July 4, 1985; Eddie Gold and Art Ahrens, *The Golden Era Cubs, 1876–1940* (Chicago, IL, 1985); Paul Green, *Forgotten Fields* (Waupaca, WI, 1984); Paul MacFarlane, ed., *TSN Daguerreotypes of Great Stars of Baseball* (St. Louis, MO, 1981); Mike Shatzkin, ed.,

The Ballplayers (New York, 1990); *TSN*, July 15, 1985; John Thorn et al., eds., *Total Baseball*, 5th ed. (New York, 1997); Warren Wilbert and William Hageman, *Chicago Cubs: Seasons at the Summit* (Champaign, IL, 1997).

Raymond D. Kush

BUSH, Leslie Ambrose "Bullet Joe" (b. November 27, 1892, Brainerd, MN; d. November 1, 1974, Fort Lauderdale, FL), player, was the son of a Northern Pacific Railroad conductor and attended two years of high school. He married Alice Marie Wray on November 6, 1937. He later wed and divorced S. E. McMahon.

The 5-foot 11-inch, 185-pound right-hander started his pitching career for Missoula, MT (UL) in 1912 and compiled a remarkable 29–12 win–loss record there. After Connie Mack* purchased him, he hurled for the Philadelphia Athletics (AL) from 1913 to 1917. He performed for the Boston Red Sox (AL) from 1918 to 1921 and New York Yankees (AL) from 1922 to 1924. The 1925 season found Bush a St. Louis Browns (AL) moundsman. As his skills diminished, Bush spent the 1926 campaign with the Washington Senators (AL) and the Pittsburgh Pirates (NL). In 1927, he variously was employed by Pittsburgh, the New York Giants (NL), and the Toledo, OH Mudhens (AA). Mack reacquired him for the 1928 season with the Philadelphia Athletics. He pitched for Portland, OR (PCL) and Newark, NJ (IL) in 1929 and Allentown, PA (EL) in 1930 and 1931, managing at his last stop.

Bush frequently finished among the first five AL hurlers in various pitching categories. In 1922 he won 26 of 33 decisions, recording the highest winning percentage (.788) and the second most victories. For the abysmal 36–117 1916 Philadelphia Athletics, he remarkably won 15 games. Although Philadelphia commited 314 errors in 1916, he accomplished eight shutouts and hurled a no-hit game against the Cleveland Indians on August 26. In 17 major league seasons, he won 195 games, lost 183 contests, and compiled a 3.51 ERA. Bush finished only 2–5 in World Series games, but his 2.67 ERA indicates that several losses comprised low-scoring affairs. Bush also helped himself at bat with a .253 lifetime average and is properly credited with having originated the forkball.

Despite such achievements, Bush experienced a nomadic career because his temperamental disposition infuriated managers. A 1919 spring training game saw him throw too hard at an obnoxious New York Giants batsman and weaken his arm for the season. In a 1922 World Series game against the New York Giants, he was ordered by Miller Huggins* to issue an intentional walk and screamed curses at the manager from the mound. Bush spent many years as a pari-mutuel clerk handling betting at New Jersey and Florida horserace tracks.

BIBLIOGRAPHY: *The Baseball Encyclopedia*, 10th ed. (New York, 1996); Leslie A. Bush file, National Baseball Library, Cooperstown, NY; Leslie A. Bush file, *TSN* Archives, St. Louis, MO; Frank Graham, *The New York Yankees* (New York, 1943); Mark Gallagher, *The Yankee Encyclopedia*, vol. 3 (Champaign, IL, 1997); Robert Redmount, *The Red Sox Encyclopedia* (Champaign, IL, 1998); Jerome Romanowski, *The Mackmen* (Upper Darby, PA, 1979); Frederick G. Lieb, *Connie Mack* (New York, 1945); Frederick G. Lieb, *The Boston Red Sox* (New York, 1947); Paul MacFarlane, ed., *TSN Daguerreotypes of Great Stars of Baseball* (St. Louis, MO, 1968).

Lowell L. Blaisdell

BUSH, Owen Joseph "Donie" (b. October 8, 1887, Indianapolis, IN; d. March 28, 1972, Indianapolis, IN), player, manager, and executive, was the son of Michael Bush and Ellen (Dolphin) Bush and had a sixth-grade education. After playing sandlot and semiprofessional baseball, he turned professional in 1905 as a shortstop with Sault Ste. Marie, MI (CCSL) and spent two seasons in the CL. He was drafted by the Detroit Tigers (AL) and assigned to Indianapolis, IN (AA), where he enjoyed a splendid 1908 season with the pennant-winning Indians.

In 1909, Bush supplanted the veteran shortstop Charley O'Leary and began a 13-year stretch as the linchpin of the Detroit Tigers infield. With the exception of Bobby Wallace,* he ranked as the best AL shortstop of his era. He epitomized what later became a well-recognized, affectionately regarded baseball type: the bold, feisty, bear-down, 5-foot 6-inch 140 pounder who always gave 100 percent. A switch-hitter skilled at working pitchers for walks and then for scoring, he usually batted in the leadoff or second spot ahead of Ty Cobb.* Afield, he possessed a strong arm and, according to baseball historian Fred Lieb (OS), "covered acres of ground."

His .250 career batting average spanned 16 major league years and 1,946 games. Primarily a singles hitter, he registered only 186 doubles, 74 triples, and nine HR. The 1,280 runs resulting from his 1,804 hits and 1,158 bases on balls gave him a scoring-effectiveness ratio of .43 percent, a mark achieved by few of the great sluggers. He scored more than 100 runs four times, with his 112 leading the AL in 1917. He stole 404 bases and, despite batting at the top of the order, compiled 436 RBI. Pitchers struck him out only 346 times.

His .936 career fielding average came in the era of pancake gloves. He tied Hugh Jennings* for most shortstop putouts in a single season (425, 1914) and ranks 11th for total career putouts with 4,038. His 10,846 total chances place him 10th all-time.

Bush played in only one World Series, batting .261 in the Detroit Tigers' seven-game loss to the Pittsburgh Pirates in 1909. He drove in three runs and stole three bases, but fanned five times and committed five errors.

In August 1921, the Washington Senators (AL) acquired Bush on waivers. His playing days ended and his managerial career began in 1923, when he piloted the Washington Senators to a 75–78 record and fourth-place finish.

Replaced by Stanley Harris,* Bush journeyed home to manage the Indianapolis Indians through 1926. Upon returning to the major leagues, he piloted the Pittsburgh Pirates to a NL pennant and a crushing four-game defeat by the New York Yankees in the World Series. Hard-nosed as ever, he disciplined great outfielder Kiki Cuyler* after an altercation by benching him for the World Series.

Dropped by the Pittsburgh Pirates, Bush moved to the doormat Chicago White Sox (AL) in 1930–1931 and, after winning the 1932 AA pennant with the Minneapolis Millers, ended his major league managing career with the Cincinnati Reds (NL) in 1933. His seven managerial seasons produced a 497–539 win–loss mark and .480 winning percentage. Back once more to the AA, he piloted Minneapolis to two pennants in four years (1934–1937) and served as manager and part-owner of the Louisville, KY Colonels (1939–1941). When the Colonels were sold, he rejoined the Indianapolis Indians as part-owner and manager (1942–1943) and served as club president (1952–1968). He scouted for the Boston Red Sox (AL) for three years and was scouting for the Chicago White Sox (AL) when the bachelor died in the house where he was born. Sixty-five years of his life were spent in organized baseball.

BIBLIOGRAPHY: William M. Anderson, *The Detroit Tigers* (South Bend, IN, 1996); Richard Bak, *A Place for Summer* (Detroit, MI, 1998); Joe Falls, *Detroit Tigers* (New York, 1975); *The Baseball Encyclopedia*, 10th ed. (New York, 1996); Donie Bush file, National Baseball Library, Cooperstown, NY; Peter J. Cava, Indianapolis, IN, to A. D. Suehsdorf, July 15, 1993; Richard M. Cohen et al., *The World Series* (New York, 1979); J. C. Kofoed, "The Greatest Shortstop in the American League," *BM* 15 (November 1915), pp. 65–67; Frederick G. Lieb, *The Detroit Tigers* (New York, 1946); Bill Madden, *The Hoosiers of Summer* (Indianapolis, IN, 1994); Dick Mittman, Indianapolis (IN) *News*, family data; Robert Obojski, *Bush League* (New York, 1975); John Thorn et al., eds., *Total Baseball*, 5th ed. (New York, 1997).

A. D. Suehsdorf

BUTLER, Brett Morgan (b. June 15, 1957, Los Angeles, CA), player, is the son of Jerry Butler and Betty (Weaver) Butler and grew up in Libertyville, IL. After graduating from Fremont, CA High School in 1975, Butler attended Arizona State University and twice made All-America in baseball at Southeastern Oklahoma State University. Scouts considered him too small, weak-armed, and not powerful. The Atlanta Braves (NL) selected the 5-foot 10-inch, 161-pound outfielder, who batted and threw left-handed, in the 23rd round of the June 1979 draft. He spent under four minor league seasons with Greenwood, SC (WCrL) and Gulf Coast, FL (GCL) in 1979, Anderson, SC (SAL) and Durham, NC (CrL) in 1980, and Richmond, VA (IL) in 1981 and 1982, earning IL MVP honors in 1981.

The Atlanta Braves gave the popular, flamboyant, confident Butler trials in 1981 and 1982 and made him starting center fielder and leadoff batter in

1983. In October 1983, the Braves traded him to the Cleveland Indians (AL). Butler played there from 1984 through 1987, stealing a career-high 52 bases in 1984 and batting .311 with a career-high 28 doubles and 14 triples in 1985.

The San Francisco Giants (NL) signed Butler in December 1987. He remained with San Francisco from 1988 through 1990, recording a career-high 192 hits in 1990. Butler helped the Giants win the NL West in 1989 and batted .286 against the Oakland A's in the World Series. In 1990, he batted .309 and tied a NL record on April 12 by walking five times.

In December 1990, the Los Angeles Dodgers (NL) signed Butler. Butler enjoyed his best seasons there from 1991 through 1994. In 1991, he made the NL All-Star team and established career highs in runs (112) and walks (108). Butler batted .309 in 1992 and a career-high .314 in 1994. The New York Mets (NL) signed him in April 1995, but returned him to the Los Angeles Dodgers that August. Butler batted .267 in the NL Championship Series against the Atlanta Braves. Throat cancer, discovered after a tonsillectomy, sidelined the born-again Christian for most of 1996. After 32 radiation treatments, he dramatically returned in September 1996. He retired following the 1997 season.

In 17 major league seasons, Butler batted .290 with 1,359 runs, 2,375 hits, 277 doubles, 131 triples, 578 RBI, 1,129 walks, and 558 stolen bases and ranks sixth in combined batting average and stolen bases. He led the NL four times in singles (1991–1994), three times in triples (1983, 1994–1995), twice in runs (1988, 1991) and fielding percentage (1991, 1993), and once in hits (1990) and walks (1991) and the AL once in triples (1986) and fielding percentage (1985). Defensively, the inveterate wall crasher and turf diver compiled a .992 fielding percentage. He and his wife, Eveline, have four children, Abbi, Stefanie, Katie, and Blake, and reside in Duluth, GA.

BIBLIOGRAPHY: Brett Butler file, National Baseball Library, Cooperstown, NY; Brett Butler and Jerry B. Jenkins, *Field of Hope* (Chicago, IL, 1997); William F. McNeil, *The Dodgers Encyclopedia* (Champaign, IL, 1997); *TSN Baseball Register*, 1998; Harry Stein, "Brett Butler: A Star Is Born," *Sport* 73 (June 1982), p. 46; Jeff Coplon, "The Butler Does It," *Sport* 77 (June 1986), pp. 32–33, 35–36, 40–41; Danny Knobler, "Baseball's Best Leadoff Hitters," *Sport* 81 (July 1990), pp. 40–42, 44–45; Tim Kurkjian, "Dodgers Blue," *SI* 84 (May 20, 1996), pp. 66, 69; Tom Verducci, "Back in Style," *SI* 85 (September 16, 1996), pp. 52–53.

David L. Porter

BUTTS, Thomas "Pee Wee," "Cool Breeze" (b. 1919, Sparta, GA; d. January 1973, Atlanta, GA), player, excelled as a Negro League shortstop and perhaps equaled white contemporaries Pee Wee Reese* and Phil Rizzuto.* From 1936 through 1952, Butts played with several Negro Leagues teams.

His baseball career ended in the minor leagues in 1955. He also played winter ball in Cuba, Mexico, and Puerto Rico.

His nickname "Pee Wee" derived from his slight 5-foot 9-inch, 145-pound physique. Nonetheless, the graceful, speedy Butts excelled in both baseball and football at Washington High School in Atlanta. After breaking his nose during a high school football game, he sported a crooked nose thereafter.

Butts quit high school to join the Atlanta Black Crackers (NAL). Opposing runners tried to intimidate the wispy Butts, but he sharpened his spikes, threw side-arm to first base, and forced on-coming runners to slide out of harm's way. The slick-fielding Butts, however, possessed an erratic arm.

The Atlanta Black Crackers struggled financially and became the Indianapolis, IN ABCs in 1939. Butts signed with the Baltimore Elite Giants (NNL) in 1939. When Butts made three throwing errors in his first game, manager Felton Snow nicknamed him "Cool Breeze" to calm the nervous youngster. His stint in the PRWL under E. Victor Harris,* considered the greatest Negro League manager, finally helped him defensively. Harris advised Butts to get more rest to improve his concentration and instructed him to stay down on the ball longer so that he would not have to rush throws.

Butts remained with Baltimore from 1939 to 1950, except for spending 1943 in the MEL. During his career, the right-handed Butts played with or against superstars James "Cool Papa" Bell,* Judy Johnson,* Josh Gibson,* Monte Irvin,* and Willie Mays.* With the Elite Giants, he roomed with future National Baseball Hall of Fame catcher Roy Campanella* and tutored second baseman and future Brooklyn Dodger star Jim "Junior" Gilliam.* When the Elite Giants dissolved after the 1950 season, Butts played with Winnipeg, Canada for manager Willie Wells.* Wells had been his main rival as the NNL's best shortstop. After the 1951 season, Judy Johnson convinced Butts to play minor league baseball. Butts spent a frustrating season with Lincoln, NE (WL) and returned to the Negro Leagues with the Birmingham, AL Black Barons (NAL) in 1953 and 1954 and the Memphis, TN Red Sox (NAL) in 1954. His last season in organized baseball came with Texas City, TX (BSL) in 1955.

Butts, a spray hitter, compiled an estimated .316 lifetime Negro League batting average and hit over .300 four times. His best season came in 1940, when he led the NNL in hitting with a .391 mark. The annual East-West All-Star game, the most important NNL event, included Butts six times.

Butts returned to Atlanta upon retirement from baseball and participated in an old-timers' game there in 1969. Family information remains sketchy, but he married.

BIBLIOGRAPHY: "Pee Wee" Butts file, National Baseball Library, Cooperstown, NY; John Holway, *Voices from the Great Black Baseball Leagues* (New York, 1975); John Holway, *Life in the Negro Leagues from the Men Who Lived It* (Westport, CT, 1989);

Robert Peterson, *Only the Ball Was White* (New York, 1970); "Pee Wee Butts," *Microsoft Complete Baseball* (Redmond, WA, 1994); James A. Riley, *The Biographical Encyclopedia of the Negro Baseball Leagues* (New York, 1994); Donn Rogosin, *Invisible Men: Life in Baseball's Negro Leagues* (New York, 1983).

Robert E. Weir

BYRD, William "Bill" "Daddy" (b. July 15, 1907, Canton, GA; d. January 4, 1991, Philadelphia, PA), player, grew up on a farm and was one of the last pitchers to throw a legal "spitter." He learned to throw the spitball as a youngster pitching with the Columbus, OH Blue Birds in 1933, but often only faked the spitter and used it as a psychological weapon. The 6-foot 1-inch, 215 pounder joined Tom Wilson's Columbus, OH Elite Giants (NNL) in 1935 and remained with the team for 16 years, as the franchise was relocated in Washington in 1937 and 1938 and finally in Baltimore, MD in 1938, 1939, and 1941 through 1950. During this time, he served as a stabilizing influence on the team and was like a father to the younger players.

The Baltimore Elite Giants' ace proved a gifted ballplayer, whose presence on the mound marked an unflinching dominance. Byrd, who once pitched and won a doubleheader, was always available for tough assignments. In addition to his spitball, he used a wide variety of other pitches and possessed excellent control of them all. His repertoire included a slow knuckler, fast knuckler, slider, round-house curve, fastball, and sinker. In Puerto Rico, he was called "El Maestro" and led the PRWL in victories with 15 during the winter season of 1940–1941.

Byrd, almost a perennial member of the East squad in the East-West game, made five pitching appearances between 1936 and 1946 and another as a pinch hitter in 1945. A good hitter from both sides of the plate, he honed his batting skills by hitting rocks with tree branches on the family farm in Canton, GA and posted season averages of .318 (1936), .286 (1941), .304 (1942), and .344 (1948).

Byrd maintained better than a .600 winning percentage in NNL games from 1932 to 1939 and suffered only one losing season over a 14-year period. In 1936, he was credited with a 20–7 record. After returning from a season in Caracas, Venezuela, he posted NNL marks of 7–3, 10–2, 9–4, 8–7, and 10–6 from 1941 through 1945. After posting his first losing season in 14 years in 1946, he added three winning seasons with records of 9–6, 11–6, and 12–3 from 1947 through 1949. His last full year in the NNL in 1949 saw the Baltimore Elite Giants win their only untainted pennant.

After beginning the 1950 season with the Baltimore Elite Giants, Byrd quickly retired with a lifetime record of 114–72. Byrd played semiprofessional ball while holding down a regular job at the General Electric Company in Philadelphia, PA, where he worked for 20 years until retiring in 1970. He and his wife, Hazel, had three daughters, Sylvia, Ruth, and Barbara.

BIBLIOGRAPHY: *Afro-American, 1935–1948; OBN* (1989), p. 14; John B. Holway, "The Original Baltimore Byrd," *BRJ* 19 (1990), pp. 23–27; Robert W. Peterson, *Only the Ball Was White* (Englewood Cliffs, NJ, 1970); James A. Riley, *The All-Time All-Stars of Black Baseball* (Cocoa, FL, 1983); James A. Riley, *The Biographical Encyclopedia of the Negro Baseball Leagues* (New York, 1994); James A. Riley, interviews with former Negro League players, James A. Riley collection, Canton, GA; Mike Shatzkin, ed., *The Ballplayers* (New York, 1990); *The Baseball Encyclopedia*, 10th ed. (New York, 1996).

James A. Riley

Hank Aaron
Unless otherwise credited, all photographs appearing in this volume are courtesy of
the National Baseball Hall of Fame Library, Cooperstown, NY.

Grover Cleveland Alexander

Adrian Constantine "Cap" Anson

Lucius Benjamin "Luke" Appling

Ernie Banks

James "Cool Papa" Bell

Johnny Bench

Yogi Berra

Wade Boggs

Barry Lamar Bonds
(Photo credit: National Baseball Hall of Fame Library,
Cooperstown, NY; courtesy of Mike Rucki)

GEORGE BRETT
FIRST BASE

George Brett

Lou Brock

Roy Campanella

Rod Carew

Steve Carlton

Alexander Cartwright

Oscar Charleston

Roger Clemens

Ty Cobb

Mickey Cochrane

Eddie Collins

Bill Dickey

Joe DiMaggio

Jean Faut Eastman

Buck Ewing

Bob Feller

Rollie Fingers

Whitey Ford

Jimmie Foxx

C

CABELL, Enos Milton, Jr. (b. October 8, 1949, Fort Riley, KS), player, is the son of Enos Cabell, Sr. and Naomi Cabell and graduated in 1967 from Los Angeles Gardena High School, where he starred in baseball and basketball. The 6-foot 5-inch, 185-pound right-handed Cabell enrolled at Harbor JC in Wilmington, CA, earning All-WSC honors in baseball.

The Baltimore Orioles (AL) signed Cabell as a free agent in September 1968. He won the ApL batting title at .374 with Bluefield, WV in 1969 and batted .284 for Stockton, CA (CaL) in 1970. Cabell earned a second minor league batting title at .311 with Dallas-Fort Worth, TX (TL) in 1971.

In 1972 Cabell batted .269 with Rochester, NY (IL) and debuted with the Baltimore Orioles September 17. Baltimore shuttled the infielder between the parent club and Rochester in 1973. He spent the entire 1974 season with the Orioles, batting .241 in 80 games.

The Baltimore Orioles traded Cabell to the Houston Astros (NL) in December 1974. He played six seasons with the Houston Astros and enjoyed his best season in 1978, batting .295 and leading Houston with 195 hits. The local BBWAA chapter named him the Astros MVP.

The Houston Astros dealt Cabell to the San Francisco Giants (NL) in December 1980. With the Giants, he batted .255 in 1981. The San Francisco Giants sent Cabell to the Detroit Tigers (AL) in March 1982. Cabell posted his best major league batting average there, hitting .311 in 1983.

The Houston Astros reacquired Cabell in February 1984 as a free agent and designated him team captain. Cabell hit .310. The development of Glenn Davis* as a first baseman led Houston to trade Cabell to the Los Angeles Dodgers (NL) in July 1985. Cabell finished the 1985 season at .272 and concluded his major league career in 1986 with a .256 batting average.

Cabell made 1,647 career hits in 15 major league seasons, batting .277 with 238 stolen bases, 60 HR, and 596 RBI. The versatile athlete played 888 games at third base, 655 at first base, and 112 in the outfield. The Houston Astros inducted him into their Hall of Fame in 1993.

He appeared in the AL Championship Series with Baltimore in 1974 and the NL Championship Series with Houston in 1980 and Los Angeles in 1985, batting only .184 in 13 games.

Cabell returned to Houston, where he owns an automobile dealership, Cabell Motors, and chairs the board of directors of Texas Southern University. He and his wife, Kathy, have three sons, Cordell, Marcus, and Stephen.

BIBLIOGRAPHY: Enos Cabell file, National Baseball Library, Cooperstown, NY; Enos Cabell biography (Houston, TX, 1995); *TSN Baseball Register*, 1986.

John Hillman

CALLAGHAN, Helen. *See* Helen Callaghan Candaele St. Aubin.

CALLAHAN, James Joseph "Nixey" (b. March 18, 1874, Fitchburg, MA; d. October 4, 1934, Boston, MA), player and manager, married Josephine Hardin in 1902 and had two sons and one daughter. His father died when he was young. At age 14, Callahan worked in a textile mill to support his mother. His pitching prowess led to offers from semiprofessional teams. At age 20, Callahan joined the Philadelphia Phillies (NL) and pitched nine games for them in 1894. The following year, he won 32 games for Springfield, MA (EL). After spending 1896 with Kansas City, MO (WL), he was sold to the Chicago Colts (NL). The 5-foot 10½-inch, 180-pound right-hander spent four years with Chicago, compiling records of 20–10 in 1898 and 21–12 in 1899. He pitched in the record 36–7 win over the Louisville Colonels on June 29, 1897. Callahan often played other positions when not pitching and performed a valuable utility role because he could play almost every position.

In 1901 Callahan jumped to the Chicago White Sox (AL) and compiled a 15–8 record. The next year, he finished 16–14 and hurled a no-hitter against the Detroit Tigers on September 20. During eight seasons, he boasted a 99–73 record and 3.39 ERA. In 1903 he became a full-time position player mainly in the outfield and also was named manager. His club wielded an 83–95 mark through mid-1904. After the 1905 season, he dropped out of organized baseball and founded the semipro Chicago Logan Squares. After the Chicago White Sox upset the Chicago Cubs in the 1906 World Series, the Logan Squares faced both teams in exhibitions. Callahan hurled a 2–1 victory over the White Sox, while the Logan Squares shut out the Cubs 1–0.

When the semipro business became unprofitable, Callahan returned to the Chicago White Sox in 1911. He played three more seasons and managed the White Sox again from 1912 through 1914. In 13 seasons, he batted .273 with 901 hits. He retired from baseball after managing the Pittsburgh Pirates

(NL) in 1916 and 1917. Callahan's career managerial record included 394 wins, 458 losses, and 14 ties. He lived in the Hyde Park area of Chicago and was found dead in bed at the Parker House in Boston, where he had visited actor George M. Cohan.

BIBLIOGRAPHY: Warren Brown, *The Chicago White Sox* (New York, 1952); James Callahan file, National Baseball Library, Cooperstown, NY; Eddie Gold and Art Ahrens, *The Golden Era Cubs, 1876–1940* (Chicago, IL, 1985); Frederick Ivor-Campbell et al., eds., *Baseball's First Stars* (Cleveland, OH, 1996); Chicago *Tribune*, October 5, 1934; *SL* 38 (November 9, 1901), p. 1; 57 (May 20, 1911), p. 1; *TSN*, October 18, 1902, p. 1.

William E. McMahon

CALLISON, John Wesley "Johnny" (b. March 12, 1939, Qualls, OK), player, spent 16 major league seasons as an outfielder. Callison, touted as the next Mickey Mantle,* began his professional baseball career in the Chicago White Sox (AL) organization at Bakersfield, CA (CaL) in 1957. He split the 1958 and 1959 campaigns between Indianapolis, IN (AA) and the Chicago White Sox. Chicago traded Callison in December 1959 to the Philadelphia Phillies (NL) for third baseman Gene Freese.

Callison enjoyed his most productive major league seasons with the Philadelphia Phillies from 1960 through 1969. From 1962 through 1965, Callison developed into a feared power hitter and one of the NL's premier defensive right fielders. He batted .300 in 1962, hit over 30 HR, and drove in over 100 runs in both 1964 and 1965 and scored over 100 runs in 1962 and 1964. He also led NL outfielders in assists from 1962 through 1965, years when Roberto Clemente* and Willie Mays* performed at their peaks.

Despite leading the NL in triples with 10 in 1962 and 16 in 1966 and in doubles with 40 in 1967, Callison experienced a power shortage for the rest of his major league career. He never again reached the 20 HR plateau. After averaging 91 RBI from 1962 through 1965, Callison slumped to 55 RBI per season the next four campaigns. In November 1969, Philadelphia traded Callison to the Chicago Cubs (NL) for Dick Selma and Oscar Gamble.* Callison's last productive season came in 1970, when he belted 19 HR and drove in 68 runs. Callison finished his major league career with the New York Yankees (AL) in 1972 and 1973 as a part-time outfielder.

During his major league career, Callison compiled a .264 batting average, 1,757 hits, 321 doubles, 226 HR, 926 runs, and 840 RBI. His biggest highlight came during the 1964 All-Star game. With two men out in the bottom of the ninth inning, he hit a dramatic three-run game-winning HR off Boston Red Sox reliever Dick Radatz.* In 1964, Callison finished second to Ken Boyer* of the St. Louis Cardinals in the NL MVP balloting. Basically a pull hitter, the three-time All-Star belted three HR in games against the Chicago Cubs in 1963 and during the infamous Phillies' ten-game losing streak in

1964. His 32 HR in 1965 remain the most hit by any left-hander in the history of Shibe Park/Connie Mack Stadium.

Callison sold cars and electronic equipment in Glenside, PA and worked as a bartender at Tomato's Bar in Doylestown, PA. In 1986, he underwent major surgery for a bleeding ulcer. While in intensive care, he suffered a serious heart attack and had bypass surgery. Callison, who married Dianne Lee Moore in March 1957, resides in Glenside, PA and has three daughters.

BIBLIOGRAPHY: John Callison file, National Baseball Library, Cooperstown, NY; Martin Appel, *Yesterday's Heroes* (New York, 1988); Johnny Callison and John Austin Sletten, *The Johnny Callison Story* (New York, 1991); Rich Westcott and Frank Bilovsky, *The New Phillies Encyclopedia* (Philadelphia, PA, 1993); *The Baseball Encyclopedia*, 10th ed. (New York, 1996); Mike Shatzkin, ed., *The Ballplayers* (New York, 1990); *TSN Baseball Register*, 1960, 1973; Allan Lewis, *The Philadelphia Phillies: A Pictorial History* (Virginia Beach, VA, 1981); Eddie Gold and Art Ahrens, *The New Era Cubs, 1941–1985* (Chicago, IL, 1985); Rich Westcott, *Diamond Greats* (Westport, CT, 1988).

John P. Rossi

CAMILLI, Adolph Louis "Dolph" (b. April 23, 1907, San Francisco, CA; d. October 21, 1997, San Mateo, CA), player, manager, coach, and scout, was the son of a farmer. Camilli played end in football for Sacred Heart Academy in 1924 and 1925, but rejected a football scholarship from St. Mary's College in California to play baseball. His brother, who fought as "Frankie Campbell," showed promise as a heavy-weight boxer. He died following a bout with Max Baer (IS) in 1931, the same year Camilli married Ruth Wallace of Sacramento, CA. Camilli had met Wallace while he was playing with the Sacramento Solons (PCL).

Camilli endured eight long years as a first baseman in the minor leagues from 1926 to 1933 before finally reaching the major leagues. He began his professional baseball career in 1926 at Logan, UT (UIL), hitting .311, and joined the San Francisco, CA Seals (PCL) later that year. The Seals returned him in mid-1927 to Logan (UIL). He spent the 1928 season with Salt Lake City, UT. With the Sacramento Solons (PCL) in 1929, a broken leg sidelined Camilli. In 1933, the Solons sold him to the Chicago Cubs (NL) for $25,000. The Cubs brought him up from Sacramento for 16 games at the end of the season. He belted his first major league HR against the Philadelphia Phillies, but compiled a disappointing .224 batting average.

In June 1934, the Chicago Cubs traded him to the Philadelphia Phillies (NL) for left-hander Don Hurst. Three years later, the skilled 5-foot 10½-inch, 185-pound left-hander batted a resounding .339 in 131 games, paced the NL with a .446 on-base percentage, and led NL first basemen in fielding. Brooklyn Dodger (NL) president Larry MacPhail* purchased Camilli in March 1938 for $45,000 and outfielder Pepper Morgan. The slugging first baseman usually drove in 100 runs each season with Brooklyn.

Camilli, a strong, silent, very sensitive individual, threatened to quit several times because of undue criticism. He refused to do beer commercials for fear the fans would criticize him and became a tough negotiator at contract time. In 1943, Branch Rickey* replaced MacPhail in Brooklyn. Rickey often had traded veterans, including first basemen Jim Bottomley,* Rip Collins,* and Johnny Mize* of the St. Louis Cardinals (NL) while they still possessed market value but had lost something in their swing. In July 1943, Rickey offered Camilli and veteran pitcher Johnny Allen* to the New York Giants (NL) for infielder Joe Orengo and pitchers Bill Lohrman and Bill Sayles. The proud, tired Camilli refused to report to the New York Giants, declining a $6,000 salary. He joined a class-action law suit by around 70 former players who retired before 1946 and were excluded from receiving a pension. Major League Baseball settled the suit, with the players receiving quarterly payments of $2,500 starting in September 1994.

The following season, Camilli served as player–manager of the Oakland, CA Oaks (PCL). He played in 113 games, hitting a respectable .289. Due to a wartime shortage of players, he resigned as manager of the Oaks in 1945. He signed with the Boston Red Sox (AL), hitting just .212 in 63 games. In 1948, he managed at Spokane, WA (PCL). Camilli piloted Dayton, OH (CL) in 1950 and Magic Valley, ID (PrL) in 1953 and spent the 1949, 1951, 1954, and 1955 seasons as a coach for Sacramento, CA (PCL). His last assignments involved scouting for the New York Yankees (AL) from 1960 to 1967 and for the Los Angeles Angels (AL) from 1969 to 1971.

During his 12-year major league career, Camilli hit .277 in 1,490 games with 239 HR, 936 runs scored, and 950 RBI. In 1941 Camilli captured the NL's MVP award, winning two-thirds of the Triple Crown with 34 HR and 120 RBI. He also led the NL with 115 strikeouts, a category he had taken previously in 1934. He also paced the NL in walks with 119 in 1938 and 110 in 1939. In 1941 Camilli played in his only World Series, hitting just .167 against the New York Yankees (AL). Doug, one of his five children, spent nine years with the Los Angeles Dodgers (NL) and Washington Senators (AL). Adolph and his wife, Ruth, retired to their Laytonville cattle ranch, 125 miles north of San Francisco, CA.

BIBLIOGRAPHY: Dolph Camilli file, National Baseball Library, Cooperstown, NY; *The Baseball Encyclopedia*, 10th ed. (New York, 1996); William F. McNeil, *The Dodgers Encyclopedia* (Champaign, IL, 1997); Al Figone, "Larry McPhail and Dolph Camilli," *TNP* 14 (1994), pp. 106–109; Gene Karst and Martin J. Jones, Jr., *Who's Who In Professional Baseball* (New Rochelle, NY, 1973); Peter Golenbock, *Bums* (New York, 1984); Richard Goldstein, *Superstars and Screwballs* (New York, 1991); Robert Obojski, "Dolph Camilli Reminisces About Baseball Career," *SCD* 21 (July 1, 1994), pp. 86–87; Rich Westcott and Frank Bilovsky, *The New Phillies Encyclopedia* (Philadelphia, PA, 1993); Ira Smith, *Baseball's Famous First Basemen* (New York, 1956).
William A. Borst

CAMINITI, Kenneth Gene "Ken" (b. April 21, 1963, Hanford, CA), player, is the son of Lee Caminiti, a Lockheed worker, and graduated from Leigh High School in San Jose, CA. Caminiti attended San Jose State University, where he played baseball two years and made the 1984 *TSN* College All-American team.

The Houston Astros (NL) selected the 6-foot, 220-pound third baseman in the third round of the June 1984 free agent draft. The switch-hitting Caminiti, who throws right-handed, began his professional baseball career with Osceola, FL (FSL) in 1985 and played for Columbia, SC (SL) in 1986 and 1987 and Tucson, AZ (PCL) in 1988.

Caminiti joined the Houston Astros in July 1987, clouting a triple and HR in his first game. He batted .255 and led Houston in doubles (31) in 1989, his first full major league season. Caminiti, who overcame a drinking problem, remained with the Houston Astros through 1994 and made the 1994 NL All-Star team. He ranks among the top ten career leaders in club doubles (180), HR (75), and RBI (445).

In December 1994, the Houston Astros sent Caminiti and five other players to the San Diego Padres (NL) for six players. Caminiti batted .302 with 26 HR in 1995, establishing a major league single-season record for most games (3) with switch-hit HR. In September 1995, he set another major league mark by clouting switch-hit HR in consecutive games against the Chicago Cubs.

Caminiti's best season came in 1996, when he became the first Padre to earn the NL MVP award. He accomplished career bests, batting .326 with 109 runs scored, 178 hits, 37 doubles, 40 HR, and 130 RBI. Caminiti broke Nate Colbert's club single-season HR mark and Dave Winfield's* team RBI record. Besides belting a HR in the All-Star game, he bettered his major league single season record by clouting switch-hit homers in four contests and his NL career standard for homering in most games (8) from both sides of the plate.

The intense, mentally tough Caminiti led San Diego to its first NL Division title since 1984. His 14 HR and 38 RBI in August established club records for a single month, while his dramatic tenth inning HR on September 27 sparked the Padres' crucial, three-game season-ending sweep of the Los Angeles Dodgers. He batted .300 with 3 HR in the NL Division Series loss to the St. Louis Cardinals. Postseason honors included making the *TSN* NL All-Star and Silver Slugger teams and earning his second consecutive *TSN* Gold Glove for his good hands, fine range, and powerful throwing arm. Caminiti earned another Gold Glove in 1997. His 29 HR and 82 RBI helped San Diego capture the NL West in 1998. After making just one hit in the NL Division Series against the Houston Astros, he batted .273 with two HR and four RBI to help San Diego defeat the Atlanta Braves in the NL Championship Series. Injuries slowed Caminiti in the World Series, where he made only one hit and two errors against the New York Yankees. In November 1998, the Houston Astros signed him to a $9.5 million, two-year contract. He batted .471 with three HR and eight RBI in the 1999 NL Division Series.

In 12 major league seasons, Caminiti has batted .274 with 1,452 hits, 289 doubles, 180 HR, 815 RBI, and a .951 fielding percentage. He ranked third in errors (194) in the 1990s. The Richmond, TX resident, who owns a motorcycle and 1955 Chevrolet, married Nancy Smith and has two daughters, Kendall and Lindsey.

BIBLIOGRAPHY: Ken Caminiti file, National Baseball Library, Cooperstown, NY; Michael Knisley, "Friends and Sluggers," *TSN*, September 16, 1996, pp. 7–9; Tom Verducci, "Scary Man," *SI 85* (September 9, 1996), pp. 48–50, 55; *TSN Baseball Register*, 1998; *San Diego Padres 1998 Media Guide.*

David L. Porter

CAMMEYER, William Henry (b. March 20, 1821, New York, NY; d. September 4, 1898, Brooklyn, NY), entrepreneur, executive, and manager, in 1862 built the first enclosed grounds designed specifically for baseball and pioneered the concept of baseball as a money-making venture. The son of John E. Cammeyer, proprietor of a New York tanning yard, and Catherine (Mead) Cammeyer, he married Margaret Anderson, a native of Scotland, in May 1849 and moved to the Williamsburg section of Brooklyn, NY that same year. He worked in his father's leather business, inheriting it upon the latter's death.

Upon seeing the growing interest in baseball and ice skating, Cammeyer in 1861 leased a large vacant plot of land in Williamsburg. He leveled the land and enclosed a field that could be flooded for skating in winter and used for baseball from spring through fall. From the first game on May 15, 1862, baseball was played at these Union grounds for 16 years. At one time or another most of Brooklyn's leading clubs, including the prominent Eckfords and Atlantics, made their home there. Cammeyer initially offered the grounds free to ball clubs and kept the proceeds from a ten cent admission charge, but soon the clubs demanded and received a share of the gate receipts.

In 1867 the Mutuals, a New York club which had been playing in Hoboken, NJ, moved to the Union grounds. The Mutuals were governed by New York politicians, including William M. "Boss" Tweed, and fielded players frequently accused of throwing games. In 1871 the Mutuals joined the new NA, baseball's first professional league. After Tweed's fall from political power, Cammeyer took control of the club and assumed its presidency in 1875. In 1876 the Mutuals joined the newly formed NL and, amid suspicions of game fixing and despite Cammeyer's efforts to thwart the gamblers, compiled a lacklustre 21–35 record through mid-September. Cammeyer, anticipating financial loss, cancelled his team's final trip to the NL's western cities. The Mutuals were expelled from the NL.

In 1877, Cammeyer's Union grounds hosted a final season of major league baseball. The Hartford, CT NL club played nearly all its home games there.

Cammeyer died of a "nervous disorder" following a lengthy illness. He was survived by his wife and seven of their 13 children.

BIBLIOGRAPHY: [Henry Chadwick], "The Gate-Money System," *TAC* 2 (February 20, 1868), p. 60; Donald Dewey and Nicholas Acocella, *Encyclopedia of Major League Baseball Teams* (New York, 1993); Daniel E. Ginsburg, *The Fix Is In* (Jefferson, NC, 1995); Richard Goldstein, *Superstars and Screwballs* (New York, 1991); Frederick Ivor-Campbell et al., eds., *Baseball's First Stars* (Cleveland, OH, 1996); Irving A. Leitner, *Baseball: Diamond in the Rough* (New York, 1972); Ed Maher, correspondence with Frederick Ivor-Campbell, 1992.

Frederick Ivor-Campbell

CAMNITZ, Samuel Howard "Howie" (b. August 22, 1881, Covington, KY; d. March 2, 1960, Louisville, KY), player, was the brother of major league baseball pitcher Harry Camnitz. The 5-foot 9-inch, 169-pound Camnitz, who batted and threw right-handed, began his professional baseball career with Greenwood, MS (CSL) in 1902. He moved in 1903 to Vicksburg, MS (CSL) and in 1904 to the Pittsburgh Pirates (NL). After having trouble concealing his pitches, Camnitz spent most of 1904 with Springfield, IL (3IL) and 1905 with Toledo, OH (AA). He returned to the Pittsburgh Pirates in 1906 and stayed there until traded in August 1913 to the Philadelphia Phillies (NL). In 1914, he jumped to the Pittsburgh Rebels (FL). During the 1915 season, Camnitz was released and retired from baseball.

Camnitz, who won 133 major league games and lost 106 decisions, enjoyed his best season in 1909, when his 25–6 record tied Christy Mathewson* for the best NL mark. His .806 winning percentage paced the NL. He also performed well in 1911 with a 20–15 mark and in 1912 with a 22–12 slate and compiled a career 2.75 ERA. He hurled 326 career games, starting 236 contests and completing 137 games. He started the second game of the 1909 World Series against the Detroit Tigers, but was replaced in the third inning and took the loss. Camnitz made his first major league start in 1906 with a 1–0 win over the Brooklyn Superbas, the first of seven victories by that score. He possessed outstanding control, averaging only 10.83 base runners per nine innings during his major league career. A careful student of the game, Camnitz studied box scores and related materials to determine which future opponents might give the most trouble. During his first FL season, he compiled a 14–19 record with a poor Pittsburgh Rebels club. In 1915, he was involved in a fight at a New York City hotel while on a road trip. The Pittsburgh Rebels suspended and then released him for violation of rules. Camnitz worked in the auto sales business for 40 years, retiring shortly before his death.

BIBLIOGRAPHY: *The Baseball Encyclopedia*, 10th ed. (New York, 1996); Samuel Howard Camnitz file, National Baseball Library, Cooperstown, NY; Robert Obojski, *Bush League* (New York, 1975); Marc Okkonen, *The Federal League of 1914–1915* (Garrett Park, MD, 1989); Frederick G. Lieb, *The Pittsburgh Pirates* (New York, 1948); Dennis De Valeria and Jeanne Burke De Valeria, *Honus Wagner: A Biography* (New York,

1996); William Hageman, *Honus: The Life and Times of a Baseball Hero* (Champaign, IL, 1996); Joseph L. Reichler, ed., *The Great All-Time Baseball Record Book* (New York, 1981).

Horace R. Givens

CAMPANELLA, Roy (b. November 19, 1921, Philadelphia, PA; d. June 26, 1993, Woodland Hills, CA), player, was one of five children of fruit and vegetable market owner John Campanella and Ida Campanella. He married Ruthe Willis in 1945 and had six children, including sons David, Tony, and Roy, Jr., and daughters Joyce, Beverly, and Depayton (Princess). He was legally separated from Ruthe in early 1960. Following her death, he married Mrs. Roxie Doles on May 5, 1964. From 1937 to 1945, he caught for the Baltimore Elite Giants (NNL) and appeared in the 1941, 1944, and 1945 All-Star games.

Campanella was the second black player approached to play professional baseball in the twentieth century. Brooklyn Dodger (NL) president Branch Rickey* met with Campanella in October 1945, after Chuck Dressen* made the arrangements. The 5-foot 9½ inch, 205-pound catcher began in the minor leagues in 1946 with Nashua, NH (NEL) and played for the Montreal, Canada Royals (IL) in 1947 and St. Paul, MN Saints (AA) in 1948 before joining the parent Brooklyn Dodgers (NL) in May 1948. At Nashua, manager Walter Alston* was indisposed one day and asked Campanella to serve as acting manager. Campanella thus became the first black to serve in that capacity in the white minor leagues.

Campanella caught for the Brooklyn Dodgers for 10 years (1948 to 1957) and, at his retirement, had slugged more career HR (242) and more single season HR (41 in 1953) than any other major league catcher. He also became the only catcher to play at least 100 games for nine consecutive seasons (1949–1957) and would have appeared in that many games his rookie season if he had not spent the first month in the minor leagues. His 142 RBI during 1953 established a then record for catchers.

In 1,215 major league games, he batted .276, made 1,161 hits, including 178 doubles, and knocked in 856 runs. Campanella holds the (NL) record for most consecutive years leading in chances accepted by a catcher (6) and tied the NL record for most years leading catchers in putouts (6). The NL MVP in 1951, 1953, and 1955, he was selected as catcher on *TSN* Major League All-Star teams in 1949, 1951, 1953, and 1955 and as the publication's Outstanding NL Player in 1953. Campanella, who appeared in the 1949, 1952–1953, 1955, and 1956 World Series, was named in 1969 to the National Baseball Hall of Fame.

A tragic automobile accident in January 1958 left him substantially paralyzed and terminated his playing career. Campanella's extraordinary courage in attempting to recover from this paralysis led to the book *It's Good to Be*

Alive, which subsequently became a made-for-television movie. Campanella worked with former teammate and roommate Don Newcombe* for the Los Angeles (NL) Baseball Club in the field of community services until his death.

BIBLIOGRAPHY: *Brooklyn Dodger Yearbooks*, 1949–1957; Roy Campanella, *It's Good to Be Alive* (New York, 1959); Ron Fimrite, "Triumph of the Spirit," *SI* 73 (September 24, 1990), pp. 94–100; David L. Porter, ed., *African-American Sports Greats* (Westport, CT, 1995); Richard Goldstein, *Superstars and Screwballs* (New York, 1991); Roy Campanella file, National Baseball Library, Cooperstown, NY; John Benson et al., *Baseball's Top 100* (Wilton, CT, 1997); Harvey Frommer, *Rickey and Robinson* (New York, 1972); Roger Kahn, *The Boys of Summer* (New York, 1972); Larry Moffi and Jonathan Kronstadt, *Crossing the Line* (Jefferson, NC, 1994); *NYT*, June 28, 1993, p. B-8; Murray Polner, *Branch Rickey: A Biography* (New York, 1982); Lowell Reidenbaugh, *Baseball's Hall of Fame-Cooperstown* (New York, 1993); Peter Golenbock, *Bums* (New York, 1984); Gene Schoor, *Roy Campanella: Man of Courage* (New York, 1959); Dick Young, *Roy Campanella* (New York, 1952).

Ronald L. Gabriel

CAMPANERIS, Dagoberto Blanco "Bert," "Campy" (b. March 9, 1942, Pueblo Nuevo, Matanzas, Cuba), player, is one of six children of a Cuban mechanic. Campaneris started to play organized baseball at age 11 and quickly became one of the best players in his region. Following graduation from Jose Tomas High School in Pueblo Nuevo, Campaneris in 1959 played for the Cuban national team in the Pan-American Games in San José, Costa Rica. Shortly thereafter, scout Bobby Delgado of the Kansas City Athletics (AL) signed the youngster to a contract. The young Cuban joined the Kansas City Athletics' Daytona Beach, FL (FSL) farm team in 1962. In an August game that year, Campaneris pitched two innings and threw left-handed to left-handed batters and right-handed to right-handed hitters. The Kansas City Athletics, however, convinced him to concentrate on his right-handed throwing ability.

After spending two years in the minors with various clubs, the 5-foot 10-inch, 160-pound Campaneris made his major league debut in July 1964 against the Minnesota Twins, hit a HR in his first at bat, and belted another HR later in the game. Only Bob Nieman of the St. Louis Browns had accomplished this feat previously. On September 9, 1965 against the California Angels, the talented Cuban became the first major league player in modern baseball history to play all nine positions in a single game. A solid infielder, Campaneris was selected to nine AL All-Star teams (1968–1975, 1977) as a shortstop. The shrewd Cuban, equally prolific on the base paths, led the AL in stolen bases six times (1965–1968, 1970, 1972). His most productive offensive campaign occurred in 1968, when he led the AL in hits (177) and stolen bases (62) and batted .276 for the Oakland Athletics (AL). One year later, Campaneris married Norma Fay of Kansas City, MO.

In November 1976, Campaneris was traded to the Texas Rangers (AL) and was named as the AL All-Star shortstop. Campaneris joined the California Angels (AL) in a May 1979 trade and ended his major league career with the New York Yankees (AL) in 1983. Nicknamed "Campy," he collected 2,249 career hits, batted .259, and swiped 649 bases. Campaneris ranks 14 on the all-time major league list in stolen bases. Campaneris also appeared in five AL Championship Series (1971–1975) and three World Series (1972–1974) with the Oakland Athletics. After two games of the 1972 AL Championship Series, Campaneris was suspended for the remainder of the series for flinging his bat at Detroit Tigers pitcher Lerrin La Grow. His most shining postseason performance came in the 1974 World Series, when he batted .353 in five games against the Los Angeles Dodgers.

BIBLIOGRAPHY: Bert Campaneris file, National Baseball Library, Cooperstown, NY; Gary Cartwright, "The Bert Campaneris Timetable," *Sport* 42 (May 1966), pp. 69–71; Bruce Markusen, *Baseball's Last Dynasty* (New York, 1998); Michael M. Oleksak and Mary Adams Oleksak, *Beisbol: Latin Americans and the Grand Old Game* (Grand Rapids, MI, 1991); John Thorn et al., eds., *Total Baseball*, 5th ed. (New York, 1997); *TSN*, August 8, 1964; *TSN*, April 25, 1970.

Samuel O. Regalado

CAMPBELL, Bruce Douglas (b. October 20, 1909, Chicago, IL; d. June 17, 1995, Fort Myers Beach, FL), player, was the son of Robert Russel Campbell, a housepainter, and Margaret Lucerne (Schaffer) Campbell. Campbell graduated from Lyons Township, IL High School in 1930. A neighbor spotted him playing semiprofessional baseball in Chicago and recommended him to Chicago White Sox (AL) vice-president Harry Grabiner. After receiving a tryout, Campbell signed a professional baseball contract in 1930 and played briefly with Indianapolis, IN (AA), Bloomington, IL (3IL), and the Chicago White Sox. In 1931, he hit .383 in 79 games with Little Rock, AR (SA) and .412 in five games with the White Sox. Campbell played in the AL through 1942, batting .290 in 1,360 games with Chicago, the St. Louis Browns, Cleveland Indians, Detroit Tigers, and Washington Senators. The solidly built 6-foot 1-inch, 180-pound outfielder with good power hit over .300 three times, belted 10 or more triples in six seasons, and produced 106 career HR and 766 RBI.

Campbell was hitting .325 with the Cleveland Indians in August 1935 when stricken by spinal meningitis. Although given only a 50–50 chance to live, he survived that attack and two others in October 1935 and May 1936. After recovering from his final attack, Campbell batted .372 in limited duty in 1936 and .301 in 134 games in 1937. Cleveland traded him in January 1940 to Detroit, where he batted .360 to pace the Tigers in the World Series against the Chicago Cubs.

After the 1942 season with the Washington Senators, Campbell joined the U.S. Army Air Corps and served as an engineer on B-24 bombers during World War II until his discharge in 1945. The Senators released him during spring training in 1946, after which he signed with Buffalo, NY (IL). In early July, he approached the AMVETS servicemen's organization for assistance in obtaining the balance of the $9,000 he contended was due him based on his 1942 baseball contract under the provisions of the Selective Service Act. Campbell claimed he was not given sufficient opportunity to get into playing condition to compete for a position before his release. On July 14, 1946, Buffalo released him.

Campbell's claim was adjudicated by the U.S. District Attorney in Washington, D.C. In August 1946, Washington Senators owner Clark Griffith* agreed to a financial settlement. Campbell hit .268 in 31 games for Minneapolis, MN (AA), ending his baseball career.

Campbell, who had resided in Fort Myers Beach, FL since 1935, built and sold homes in the area. He first married during World War II and married Adelaide Francis Freednour on July 13, 1961. In failing health from cancer, Campbell took his own life.

BIBLIOGRAPHY: *Who's Who in Major League Baseball* (Chicago, IL, 1933); Lee Allen, "Cooperstown Corner," *TSN*, May 4, 1968; Richard Bak, *A Place for Summer* (Detroit, MI, 1998); Richard Goldstein, *Spartan Seasons: How Baseball Survived the Second World War* (New York, 1980); Franklin Lewis, *The Cleveland Indians* (New York, 1949); Robert Milne, "The Browns Home-Run Slugger," *BM* (May 1934), pp. 561, 566; *The Baseball Encyclopedia*, 10th ed. (New York, 1996); Fort Myers (FL) *News-Press*, June 21, 1995; *NYT*, August 5–6, 13, 1935, May 3–4, 1936, July 10, 17, 20, August 2, 1946; *TSN*, August 8, 1935, May 7, June 25, July 25, 1936, July 24, 31, 1946.

Edward J. Tassinari

CANDAELE, Helen Callaghan. *See* Helen Callaghan Candaele St. Aubin.

CANDELARIA, John Robert "Candy" "Candyman" (b. November 6, 1953, Brooklyn, NY), player, spent most of his major league career with the Pittsburgh Pirates (NL). A left-handed pitcher, Candelaria attended Manhattan's LaSalle Academy and made the All-City basketball team in 1971 and 1972. The son of Puerto Rican parents, he was invited to try out for the 1972 Puerto Rican Olympic basketball team. He chose instead to sign with the Pittsburgh Pirates.

Candelaria enjoyed minor league success in 1973 at Charleston, SC (WCL), in 1974 at Salem, VA (CrL), and in 1975 at Charlestown, WV (IL) before joining Pittsburgh at midseason. In his rookie year, he won eight and lost six for Pittsburgh and struck out 14 Cincinnati Reds in the third game of the 1975 NL Championship Series. The 6-foot 6-inch, 250-pound Candelaria pitched the first and only no-run, no-hit game by a Pirate at Pittsburgh, defeating the Los Angeles Dodgers, 2–0, on August 9, 1976. In 1977, Candelaria experienced his best campaign. He won 20 and lost 5, becoming the first Pirate to win 20 games since Vernon Law* in 1960. His .800 winning percentage and 2.34 ERA both led the NL, as he was named to his only All-Star team. In the Pirates' 1979 championship season, Candelaria won 14 of 23 decisions and split two decisions with the Baltimore Orioles in the World Series.

The next several years saw Candelaria pitch well, but experience physical and emotional problems which diminished his effectiveness. In the wake of a major baseball drug scandal centered on Pittsburgh, Candelaria launched an abusive public campaign asking to be traded. His lackadaisical efforts on the field earned him the hostility of Pirates fans. He was shipped to the California Angels (AL) in August 1985.

With California, Candelaria's career rebounded. He was named AL Comeback Player of the Year in 1986 despite losing the deciding game of the AL Championship Series to the Boston Red Sox. After twice being on the disabled list for alcohol dependency treatment, Candelaria was sent to the New York Mets (NL) in September 1987. Subsequently, he pitched for the New York Yankees (AL) in 1988, the Montreal Expos (NL) in 1989, the Minnesota Twins (AL) and Toronto Blue Jays (AL) in 1990, and the Los Angeles Dodgers (NL) in 1991 and 1992, and ended his major league career with the Pittsburgh Pirates in 1993. In 19 major league seasons, he compiled 177 wins, 122 losses, a .592 winning percentage, and a 3.33 ERA. Candelaria resides in Laguna Hills, CA, with his second wife, Donna (Brown), and has one daughter.

BIBLIOGRAPHY: John Candelaria file, National Baseball Library, Cooperstown, NY; *The Baseball Encyclopedia*, 10th ed. (New York, 1996); Richard L. Burtt, *The Pittsburgh Pirates, A Pictorial History* (Virginia Beach, VA, 1977); Robert E. Kelly, *Baseball's Best* (Jefferson, NC, 1988); *NYT*, February 11, 1985, May 16, 1987, September 16, 1987; *New York Yankees 1989 Media Guide*; *Pittsburgh Pirates 1981 Media Guide*; *Pittsburgh Pirates 1985 Media Guide*; Bob Smizik, *The Pittsburgh Pirates: An Illustrated History* (New York, 1990).

Frank W. Thackeray

CANSECO, Jose, Jr. (b. July 2, 1964, Havana, Cuba), player, is the son of Jose Canseco, Sr., and the identical twin of Ozzie Canseco, former St. Louis Cardinals (NL) outfielder. He attended Coral Park High School in Miami, FL.

The Oakland Athletics (AL) selected Canseco in the 15th round of the free agent draft in June 1982. He played with Miami, FL (FSL) and Idaho Falls, ID (PrL) at third base and outfield. In 1983, Canseco's stops included Madison, WI (ML) and Medford, OR (NWL). He spent the entire 1984 season with Modesto, CA (CaL), batting .276 and hitting 15 HR. In 1985, Canseco played with Huntsville, AL (SL), Tacoma, WA (PCL), and 29 games with the Oakland Athletics (AL), batting .302. The next three seasons saw him with the Oakland Athletics from 1986 through 1988. After briefly appearing with Huntsville, AL (SL) in 1989, he spent full-time with the Oakland Athletics until traded to the Texas Rangers (AL) for three players and cash in August 1992.

The 6-foot 4-inch, 240-pound Canseco, who throws and hits right-handed, was named 1985 *TSN* Minor League Player of the Year. The 1986 season featured him being named AL Rookie Player of the Year by both *TSN* and the BBWAA. Canseco in 1988 batted .307 and led the AL with 42 HR, 124 RBI, and a .569 slugging percentage. *TSN* selected Canseco AL Player of the Year. He made the AL All-Star team in 1986, 1988, 1990, 1991, and 1992. The same years, he was named outfielder on the AL *TSN* Silver Slugger team. The BBWAA named him 1988 AL MVP. In 1984, Canseco led the CaL outfielders with eight double plays. He hit three HR in the same game on July 3, 1988 and June 13, 1994 and paced the AL with a career-high 44 HR in 1991.

From 1988 to 1990, Canseco appeared in three AL Championship Series and three World Series. In the 1989 World Series against the Los Angeles Dodgers, he batted .357 with one HR and three RBI. In 1989, Canseco received the then-largest major league raise, a $1.6 million one-year contract. On May 29, 1993, he made his pitching debut and worked the final inning of a 15–1 loss to the Boston Red Sox. He had been a high school pitcher and thrown a few times in the minor leagues. In July 1993, Canseco disclosed he had a torn elbow ligament. The injury probably was related to his pitching stint and sidelined him for the rest of the season. During the strike-shortened 1994 season, he batted .282 with 31 HR and 90 RBI and was named AL Comeback Player of the Year.

Canseco's off-season troubles, mainly speeding, caused continual problems for the Oakland Athletics management and led to his being traded. In December 1994, the Texas Rangers traded him to the Boston Red Sox (AL). Injuries continued to sideline him. In 1995, Canseco helped the Boston Red Sox win the AL wild card berth with a .306 batting average, 24 HR, and 81 RBI, but went hitless in the AL Division Series against the Cleveland Indians. After Canseco batted .289 with 28 HR and 82 RBI in 1996, the Oakland Athletics acquired him in a January 1997 trade. After struggling in 1997, he signed as a free agent with the Toronto Blue Jays (AL) and clouted 46 HR with 107 RBI in 1998. *TSN* named him to its AL Silver Slugger team in 1998. In December 1998, the Tampa Bay Devil Rays (AL) acquired him as a free agent. Although sidelined by back surgery in 1999, he still clouted 34 HR with 95 RBI in 113 games and made the AL All-Star team.

Through 1999, Canseco has batted .267 with 431 HR, 1,372 RBI, and 196 stolen bases.

BIBLIOGRAPHY: Jose Canseco file, National Baseball Library, Cooperstown, NY; John Benson et al., *Baseball's Top 100* (Wilton, CT, 1997); Barry Bloom, "Monster Basher," *Sport* 86 (June 1995), pp. 87–91; B. Buschel, "The Battle Is with Himself," *GQ* 59 (May 1989), pp. 224–229; Patrick Reusse, column, Minneapolis (MN) *Star Tribune*, September 28, 1988; *Texas Rangers Media Guide*, 1994; *TSN Official Baseball Register*, 1998; Ron Fimrite, "Kiss That One Goodbye," *SI* 65 (July 7, 1986), pp. 28–

30; Peter Gammons, "The Summer of His Discontent," *SI* 71 (October 2, 1989), pp. 72–74; *CB Yearbook* (1991), pp. 103–107; Richard Hoffer, "Try, Try Again," *SI* 80 (March 14, 1994), pp. 38–40; Scott Kelmhofer, "Canseco," *SCD* 22 (April 14, 1995), pp. 144–145; Ed Lucas and Paul Post, "Canseco Still Throws a Bash," *SCD* 25 (May 15, 1998), pp. 134–135; R. Kroichick, "Jose Canseco," *Sport* 83 (April 1992), pp. 20–24; R. Kroichick, "Double Damage," *Sport* 81 (October 1990), pp. 106–107; Rick Reilly, "Whaddaya Say, Jose?" *SI* 73 (August 20, 1990), pp. 42–46.

Stan W. Carlson

CARDENAL, Jose Rosario Domec (b. October, 7, 1943, Matanzas, Cuba), player and coach, attended Jose Marti School in Matanzas. A cousin of Bert Campaneris,* he entered professional baseball with El Paso, TX (TL) in 1961. Cardenal married Patricia Shannon in October 1964 and has one daughter. He played for Eugene, OR (PCL) and Tacoma, WA (PCL), reaching the major leagues briefly with the San Francisco Giants (NL) in 1963 and 1964. San Francisco traded the 5-foot 10-inch, 150-pound outfielder to the California Angels (AL) in November 1964. In his first AL game, he hit a HR off New York Yankee ace Whitey Ford.* He made the Topps Major League Rookie All-Star Team.

The colorful, exciting outfield speedster stole 329 career bases in a well-traveled career. He was traded to the Cleveland Indians (AL) in November 1967 and the St. Louis Cardinals (NL) in November 1969. He went to the Milwaukee Brewers (AL) in July 1971 and that December to the Chicago Cubs (NL). His six years with the Cubs marked his longest tenure with one club, as he became a fan favorite. In 1972, Cardenal was chosen Chicago Player of the Year. In October 1977, he was traded to the Philadelphia Phillies (NL) and batted .187 in the NL Championship Series. The New York Mets (NL) acquired him in August 1979. Cardenal ended his major league career in 1980 with the Mets and Kansas City Royals (AL), batting .200 against the Philadelphia Phillies in the World Series.

Cardenal enjoyed his best years with the Chicago Cubs, twice hitting over .300. His best season came in 1975, when he batted .317 with 68 RBI and 34 stolen bases. On May 2, 1976, he collected six hits, including a double and HR to help the Cubs defeat the San Francisco Giants, 6–5, in 14 innings. Cardenal spent 18 years in the major leagues with a .275 batting average, 138 HR, and 775 RBI.

He served as a minor league instructor for the Chicago White Sox (AL) and Chicago Cubs from 1981 through 1987 and worked for the Cincinnati Reds (NL) as a minor league outfield and base running instructor from 1987 through 1992. After coaching for the Cincinnati Reds in 1993 and St. Louis Cardinals (NL) in 1994 and 1995, he has coached with the New York Yankees (AL) since 1996.

BIBLIOGRAPHY: Jose Cardenal file, National Baseball Library, Cooperstown, NY; *Chicago Cubs 1977 Official Roster Book* (Chicago, IL, 1977); *Chicago Cubs Vineline* (May

1992); Eddie Gold and Art Ahrens, *The New Era Cubs, 1941–1985* (Chicago, IL, 1985); Rich Marazzi, "Former NL Flychaser Cardenal Had a Hand in Yankees' WS Victory," *SCD* 24 (September 12, 1997), pp. 80–81; *The Baseball Encyclopedia*, 10th ed. (New York, 1996).

Duane A. Smith

CARDENAS, Leonardo Lazaro "Leo," "Chico" (b. December 17, 1938, Pueblo Nuevo, Matanzas, Cuba), player, excelled as a premier major league short-stop during his 16-year major league career. His father, Rafael Cardenas, starred as an amateur shortstop and hit ground balls daily to his son. At age 16, Cardenas invited himself to a Cincinnati Reds (NL) tryout camp in Havana, Cuba. Scouts regarded Cardenas as "too skinny to play 154 games," but Paul Miller, manager of the Havana Sugar Kings, paid his way to the Reds 1956 spring training camp. After earning an assignment to Tucson, AZ (AMeL) in 1956, Cardenas spent two years with Savannah, GA (SAL) and moved to Havana, Cuba (IL) in 1959. He made the NA's All-Star Fielding team and played in the IL All-Star game, earning the title "Mr. Automatic." After Cardenas spent half of the 1960 season in Jersey City, NJ (IL), the Cincinnati Reds promoted him.

Always adept defensively, Cardenas also proved a strong hitter. As a Cincinnati regular from 1962 to 1968, he twice topped all NL shortstops in fielding and won a Gold Glove Award in 1965. The following year, he hit 20 HR to set a season record for Reds shortstops. In a June 6, 1966 double-header against the Chicago Cubs, he made six hits in eight at bats with four HR and eight RBI. The 5-foot 10-inch, 154-pound Cardenas substituted for a slumping Eddie Kasko in 1961 and hit .344 after the All-Star break to help the Reds win the NL pennant. Cincinnati traded Cardenas to the Minnesota Twins (AL) in November 1968. Cardenas contributed with both the glove and bat, helping the Twins garner a divisional championship in 1969. He batted .280 and led AL shortstops in assists, double plays, and putouts. His 570 putouts tied a 63-year-old AL league record. After spending three seasons with Minnesota, he played in 1972 with the California Angels (AL), 1973 with the Cleveland Indians (AL), and 1974–1975 with the Texas Rangers (AL).

Cardenas, selected for five All-Star teams (1964–1966, 1968), hit .333 as a pinch hitter in the 1961 World Series against the New York Yankees and appeared in the 1969–1970 AL Championship Series. Cardenas returned to Cincinnati upon retiring from baseball with a career .257 batting average, 118 HR, and 689 RBI. Cardenas, who worked for the Standard Oil Company in Cincinnati, married Gloria Jackson in September 1958 and had a son and three daughters. He later remarried and has two more children.

BIBLIOGRAPHY: Leo Cardenas file, National Baseball Library, Cooperstown, NY; Donald Honig, *The Cincinnati Reds* (New York, 1992); Roy McHugh, "Cincinnati's Spider," *Sport* 35 (September 1963), pp. 50–51, 91–94; Mike Lamey, "Will Cardenas

Make the Twins Forget Zoilo?" *BD* 28 (May 1969), pp. 40–43; Wade Swormstedt, "Former Reds Infielder Leo Cardenas Enjoys the Fans," *SCD* 18 (April 20, 1990), pp. 190–192.

Richard D. Miller

CAREW, Rodney Cline "Rod" (b. October 1, 1945, Gatun, Canal Zone), player and coach, is the son of construction worker Eric Carew and Olga Carew and has a brother, Eric, and three sisters, Sheridan, Diana, and Dorinne. Carew married Marilynn Levy, a native of North Minneapolis, in October 1970, and had three daughters, Charryse, Stephanie, and Michelle. Michelle died at age 18 after a seven-month battle with leukemia in April 1996. Carew was born on a train transporting his mother from Gatun to Gamboa and was delivered by Dr. Rodney Cline, for whom he was named. At age 11, he was hospitalized for six months with rheumatic fever. Carew then began playing Little League baseball and was taught by his uncle, Joe French. Within two years, Carew hit so well that he played with 17-year-olds. His family moved to Washington Heights near the Polo Grounds in New York City, but his father did not join them. Carew attended George Washington High School, worked in a grocery store, and played sandlot baseball with the Cavaliers on weekends.

In 1964 Carew signed with the Minnesota Twins (AL) for a $5,000 bonus. He played second base for Melbourne, FL and led the CRL in triples (3). After batting .325 at Melbourne, he hit .303 with Orlando, FL (FSL) in 1965 and was the first black player there. Although batting only .242 with Wilson, NC (CrL) in 1966, he was helped considerably by coach Vern Morgan.

In 1967 Carew joined the Minnesota Twins, batted .292, and won AL Rookie of the Year honors. The 6-foot, 182-pound Carew, who batted left and threw right-handed, played with Minnesota (1967–1978) as a second baseman and first baseman. He was traded to the California Angels (AL) for four players in February 1979 and played first base there. Carew won seven AL batting titles (1969, 1972–1975, 1977–1978) with averages of .332, .318, .350, .364, .359, .388, and .333. The AL MVP in 1977, he performed in the All-Star games in 1967–1969, 1971–1978, and 1983–1984. He was selected for the 1970, 1979, and 1982 squads, but withdrew because of injuries. In All-Star games, he made 10 hits and compiled a .244 batting average. Although never in a World Series, Carew played in four AL Championship Series (1967, 1970, 1979, 1982) and made 11 hits for a .220 batting average. *TSN* named him Major League Player of the Year (1977) and to its All-Star team (1967–1969, 1972, 1977–1978).

Carew's best season came in 1977, when he achieved career personal highs in at bats (616), batting average (.388), hits (239), triples (16), and runs (128) to lead the AL. That year he also hit 38 doubles, had 100 RBI, and tied his best HR output (14). His manager, Gene Mauch,* commented: "He's got everything—intelligence, strength, confidence, speed afoot, and hand-eye coordination. Many ballplayers are pleasant to manage, but managing Rodney is a privilege." Carew retired following the 1985 season.

In 2,469 career major league games, Carew compiled 9,315 at bats, 1,424 runs scored, 3,053 hits, 445 doubles, 112 triples, 92 HR, 1,015 RBI, 353 stolen bases, and a .328 batting average. On August 4, 1985 against the Minnesota Twins, Carew became the 16th major leaguer to make 3,000 career hits. He hit at least .300 for 15 consecutive seasons from 1969 to 1983 and led the AL in hits with 203 (1973), 218 (1974), and 239 (1977). He also made 200 hits in 1976 and led the AL in triples in 1973 (11) and 1977 (16) and in runs scored in 1977 (128). In 1969 Carew tied major league records by stealing home seven times and pilfering three bases in one inning. Defensively, Carew made 13,510 career putouts, 3,709 assists, 260 errors, and a .985 lifetime fielding percentage and led the AL in errors in 1968, 1974, and 1984. In 1991, he was elected to the National Baseball Hall of Fame. He coached for the California Angels from 1992 through 1999. The Milwaukee Brewers named him hitting coach in November 1999.

BIBLIOGRAPHY: Rod Carew file, National Baseball Library, Cooperstown, NY; Rod Carew with Frank Pace and Armin Keteylon, *Rod Carew's Art and Science of Hitting* (New York, 1986); *CB* (1978), pp. 63–66; Zander Hollander, ed., *Complete Handbook of Baseball, 1984* (New York, 1984); *NYT Biographical Service* 26 (December 1995), pp. 1914–1915; David L. Porter, ed., *African-American Sports Greats* (Westport, CT, 1995); George Rekela, "Carew Makes a Run at 400," *BRJ* 20 (1991), pp. 10–11; *TSN Baseball Register*, 1986; Tom Verducci, "Carew's Crew," *SI* 83 (July 17, 1995), pp. 28–30; *WWIB*, 71st ed. (New York, 1986), pp. 23–24; Jack Zanger, "It's Easier to Hustle in the Big Leagues," *Sport* 44 (November 1967), pp. 60–61, 72, 74.

Kevin R. Porter

CAREY, Max George "Scoops" (b. Maximillian Carnarius, January 11, 1890, Terre Haute, IN; d. May 30, 1976, Miami, FL), player, coach, and manager, was one of four sons of contractor Frank August Ernst Carnarius and Catherine Augusta (Astroth) Carnarius, both of German descent. In 1903, Carey's Lutheran parents enrolled him in a six-year, preministerial program at Concordia College in Fort Wayne, IN. After graduating in 1909, he spent the 1909–1910 academic year at Concordia Seminary in St. Louis, MO.

Carey played amateur baseball in college and in 1909 signed (as Max Carey) with South Bend, IN (CL) as a shortstop, third baseman, and outfielder and became a switch-hitter. He joined the Pittsburgh Pirates (NL) late in the 1910 season. Carey's lifetime .285 batting average featured a career-high .343 in the 1925 regular season and .458 for the victorious Pirates in the 1925 World Series against the Washington Senators. Best known as a base stealer, he led the NL 10 times between 1913 and 1925, establishing a career NL record of 738 thefts (since broken by Lou Brock*). He stole 51 bases in 53 attempts in 1922, 61 bases in 1913, and 63 in 1916. Against the New York Giants in an 18-inning game in 1922, he made six hits in six official at bats, added three walks and three stolen bases (including home), and made several spectacular catches. Carey, whose nickname, "Scoops," derived from his outstanding defensive ability, led NL outfielders in putouts nine times and established an NL career record of 6,363 putouts (eventually broken by Willie Mays*).

Carey was waived by the Pirates in 1926 after a dispute with management and played with the Brooklyn Dodgers (NL) until his 1929 retirement. In 2,476 games covering 20 years, he compiled 2,665 hits, 419 doubles, 159 triples, 70 HR, 1,545 runs, 800 RBI, and 1,040 walks. He coached with the Pittsburgh Pirates in 1930 and managed the Brooklyn Dodgers in 1932–1933 to a 146–161 win–loss record (.476) and one third-place finish.

Carey married Aurelia Behrens on June 22, 1913 and had two sons. He invested in the early 1920s in Florida real estate, but lost money in the 1929 stock market crash. After retiring as a player, he worked at business ventures and scouted for the Baltimore Orioles (AL) in 1955. He also managed Miami, FL (FECL) in 1940, Cordele, GA (GFL) in 1955, and Louisville, KY (AA) in 1956. Carey piloted the Milwaukee, WI Chicks (AAGPBL) in 1944 and Ft. Wayne, IN Daisies (AAGPBL) from 1950 to 1952. He left baseball in 1957 and worked as a racing official in Miami Beach, FL. He was elected to the National Baseball Hall of Fame in 1961 and died after a long illness. The long-legged, slender, 6-foot, 165-pound Carey, a swift, daring base runner and outfielder, easily made the transition to the lively ball era and demonstrated that speed could generate as much excitement as HR.

BIBLIOGRAPHY: Max Carey file, National Baseball Library, Cooperstown, NY; Richard Goldstein, *Superstars and Screwballs* (New York, 1991); Frederick G. Lieb, *The Pittsburgh Pirates* (New York, 1948); Lowell Reidenbaugh, *Baseball's Hall of Fame-Cooperstown* (New York, 1993); Dennis De Valeria and Jeanne Burke De Valeria, *Honus Wagner: A Biography* (New York, 1996); William Hageman, *Honus: The Life and Times of a Baseball Hero* (Champaign, IL, 1996); Bob Smizik, *The Pittsburgh Pirates: An Illustrated History* (New York, 1990).

Luther W. Spoehr

CARLTON, Steven Norman "Steve," "Lefty," "Ichabod" (b. December 22, 1944, Miami, FL), player, is the son of Joseph Carlton and Anne (Powers) Carlton. Joseph Carlton, a chicken farmer, later became a maintenance worker for Pan American Airways. Steve loved the Everglades and acquired the nickname "Ichabod" for his tall, lean physique. He played baseball throughout his youth, beginning in the North Miami Little League. Carlton attended North Miami High School from 1959 to 1963, winning eight of 10 decisions his senior year. He played American Legion ball in Miami and attended Miami-Dade CC. On the advice of Carlton's coach, St. Louis Cardinals (NL) scout Chase Riddle signed him on October 6, 1963 for a $5,000 bonus.

In 1964, Carlton compiled a 15–6 composite mark for Rock Hill, SC

(WCL), Winnipeg, Canada (NoL), and Tulsa, OK (TL). He married Beverly Ann Brooks in 1965 and has two sons, Steven and Scott. After pitching 15 games for St. Louis in 1965, he rejoined the Cardinals in late 1966. He won 27 composite games for the 1967–1968 Cardinals, appearing in both World Series. In 1969, Carlton sparkled with a 17–11 record and 2.17 ERA. On September 15, 1969, he broke the major league record by striking out 19 Mets in a 4–3 loss in New York. Carlton led the NL with 19 defeats in 1970, but rebounded with a 20–9 season the next year. His ratio of strikeouts and hits to innings pitched actually was better in 1970 than in 1971.

Carlton requested a $60,000 contract for 1972, but the Cardinals offered him only $55,000. Cardinals general manager Bing Devine traded the 6-foot 4-inch, 220-pound left-hander to the Philadelphia Phillies (NL) in February 1972 for right-hander Rick Wise.* Carlton pitched with the Phillies until 1986, making St. Louis regret the transaction. From 1972 through 1983, Carlton compiled a 37–12 edge over the Cardinals and registered his 100th and 300th victories against them.

The 1972 Phillies proved a terrible team with the exception of the spectacular Carlton. Philadelphia triumphed in only 59 games, with Carlton winning 27 or 46 percent. He led the NL in wins, ERA (1.97), innings pitched (346), and strikeouts (310), won 15 straight contests, and earned his first (NL) Cy Young Award. The press closely followed Carlton, predicting 30 wins for him in 1973. After Carlton struggled through a 13–20 year in 1973 and mediocre 1974 and 1975 seasons, the press began criticizing his interest in meditation and Eastern philosophies. Carlton began refusing interviews, a policy he continued until the middle of the 1986 season.

From 1976 to 1982, Carlton was the dominant NL pitcher with 137 wins. His slider, fastball, and curve, coupled with tremendous concentration and self-confidence, powered him to four 20-victory seasons with three more (NL) Cy Young awards. Carlton finished the 1983 campaign with a 15–16 record, but his 275 strikeouts paced the NL for the fifth time. On September 24, 1983, he became the sixteenth pitcher to win 300 games. Carlton remained with Philadelphia until July 1986, when the San Francisco Giants (NL) signed him. He completed 1986 with the Chicago White Sox (AL), split 1987 with the Cleveland Indians (AL) and Minnesota Twins (AL), and ended his major league career with Minnesota in 1988.

Carlton, a 10-time All-Star, appeared in the 1980 and 1983 World Series. Besides receiving the American Legion Graduate Award in 1971, he was named *TSN* Pitcher of the Year in 1972, 1977, 1980, and 1982 and won a Gold Glove in 1981. He finished his 24-year major league career with a 329–244 record and a 3.22 ERA, hurling 55 shutouts and striking out 4,136 batters in 5,217 innings. No NL pitcher or left-hander struck out more batters. Carlton compiled 20 or more victories six seasons and won in double figures 18 consecutive campaigns. A master of physical conditioning, Carlton regularly engages in Kung Fu workouts to stay in shape. In 1994, he was elected to the National Baseball Hall of Fame. He resides in Durango, CO on a 400-acre farm and does instructional work for the Phillies.

BIBLIOGRAPHY: Steve Carlton file, National Baseball Library, Cooperstown, NY; John Benson et al., *Baseball's Top 100* (Wilton, CT, 1997); Joe Curreri, "Carlton's (HOF) Slider Was Mean and Nasty," *SCD* 21 (August 12, 1994), p. 50; Ron Fimrite, "They're the Talks of Their Towns," *SI* 65 (July 14, 1986), pp. 22–24; Peter Gammons, "Lefty's Last Stand," *SI* 66 (March 30, 1987), pp. 48–49; Bob Broeg and Jerry Vickery, *St. Louis Cardinals Encyclopedia* (Grand Rapids, MI, 1998); Rich Westcott and Frank Bilovsky, *The New Phillies Encyclopedia* (Philadelphia, PA, 1993); Allen Lewis, *The Philadelphia Phillies: A Pictorial History* (Virginia Beach, VA, 1981); Kansas City *Star*, September 25, 1983; Robert E. Kelly, *Baseball's Best* (Jefferson, NC, 1988); John Kuenster, "Phils' Steve Carlton in Pursuit of His Third Cy Young Award," *BD* 39 (November 1980), pp. 17–19; John Kuenster, "Steve Carlton: He's Disciplined, Durable, and Still Competitive," *BD* 42 (November 1983), pp. 13–15; Allen Lewis, "Carlton Earns Legion Graduate Award," *TSN*, June 24, 1972, p. 23; Allen Lewis, "Super Steve Is Thinking Thirty," *TSN*, April 14, 1973, p. 3; Bus Saidt, "Steve Carlton: Silent, but Deadly," *BM* 144 (April 1980), pp. 42, 49, 52, 92–93; St. Louis *Globe-Democrat*, September 23, 1983; Martha Ward, *Steve Carlton: Star Southpaw* (New York, 1975); Steve Wulf, "Steve Carlton," *SI* 80 (January 24, 1994), pp. 48–49; Ken Young, *Cy Young Award Winners* (New York, 1994).

Frank J. Olmsted

CARNARIUS, Maximillian. *See* Max George Carey.

CARPENTER, Robert R. M., Jr. "Bob" (b. August 31, 1915, New Castle, DE), executive, is the son of Du Pont Chemical Company, vice president Robert R. M. Carpenter, Sr., and Margaretta (Du Pont) Carpenter, a member of the Du Pont family. His education included the Tower Hill School in Wilmington, DE and three years at Duke University. From 1944 to 1946, he served in the U.S. Army. He and his wife, Mary Kaye, who were married in June 1938, have two children, Robert R. M. III ("Ruly") and Mary Kaye. A sports enthusiast, Carpenter played end on the Duke University football team and dabbled in sports ownership as an employee in the public relations department of Du Pont. At the urging of Connie Mack* in the late 1930s, he bought the Wilmington, DE Blue Rocks (IL). He also briefly owned an ABL professional basketball franchise.

In 1943, Carpenter persuaded his father to buy him the ailing Philadelphia Phillies (NL) franchise for $400,000. The previous owner, William Cox, had been banned from baseball for gambling activities. The Carpenters controlled 80 percent of the Phillies stock. The Phillies, one of the weakest franchises in baseball, had suffered financially for many years and had sold numerous quality players, including Grover Cleveland Alexander,* Chuck Klein,* and Bucky Walters,* to pay their bills. Carpenter created a modern franchise by hiring excellent advisers, including seasoned general manager Herb Pennock.* To develop a minor league system, Carpenter spent over

$1 million on bonus players. By the late 1940s, the Phillies fielded a re-spectable team. Carpenter developed talent including Richie Ashburn,* Robin Roberts,* Curt Simmons,* and Willie Jones.* The Phillies, under the skillful direction of Eddie Sawyer, finished third in 1949, won the 1950 NL pennant, and lost the World Series in four games to the New York Yankees.

Carpenter, serving as his own general manager after Pennock's death in 1948, could not build on the success of the 1950 Whiz Kids. The team drifted toward mediocrity by the mid–1950s, despite the hiring of Roy Ha-mey as general manager in 1954. Hamey's administration failed largely be-cause the Phillies belatedly scouted black and Latin American talent and was the last NL team to have a black on its roster.

After Hamey resigned in 1959, Carpenter hired successful Milwaukee Braves executive John Quinn as general manager. Quinn and Carpenter re-built the Phillies as a contending ball club by dismantling the Whiz Kids. Through shrewd trades and a revamped farm system, the Phillies totally remodeled. After four straight cellar finishes (1958–1961), the Phillies again gained respectability and from 1962 to 1967 finished above .500 each year. In 1964, however, the Phillies suffered a terrible collapse, losing a 6½-game lead with only 12 games left. Nevertheless, the 92–70 record and the 1964 squad marked the club's best record since the 1950 pennant winners.

When the team declined in the late 1960s, Carpenter gradually turned over direction of the ball club to his son, Ruly. After being trained in every aspect of baseball administration, Ruly became Phillies president in 1973 and retained his father as chairman of the board. Under Ruly's direction, the Phillies ranked among the dominant NL powers, captured three con-secutive Eastern Division titles (1976–1978), and secured the club's first World Series victory in 1980 over the Kansas City Royals. In 1981, the Carpenters announced their intention to sell the team because of the impact that high player salaries were having on the financial structure of baseball. A financial group, led by club vice-president Bill Giles and including the Taft Broadcasting System and a consortium of local investors, purchased a controlling interest from the Carpenters for $30 million. The sale ended a 38-year era during which the Phillies became one of the healthiest major league franchises.

BIBLIOGRAPHY: Rich Westcott and Frank Bilovsky, *The New Phillies Encyclopedia* (Philadelphia, PA, 1993); *NYT*, July 11, 1990, p. D-20; Frederick G. Lieb and Stan Baumgartner, *The Philadelphia Phillies* (New York, 1953); Allen Lewis, *The Philadel-phia Phillies: A Pictorial History* (Virginia Beach, VA, 1981); Robin Roberts and C. Paul Rogers III, *The Whiz Kids and the 1950 Pennant* (Philadelphia, PA, 1996).

John P. Rossi

CARR, George Henry (b. 1895, Los Angeles, CA; d. unknown), player, starred at first base on several Negro League teams during the 1920s and 1930s. Carr began attracting national attention in the CWL, which typically consisted of one or two all-black clubs. From 1917 to 1920, he excelled with the Los Angeles White Sox. By 1920, Carr earned a regular spot at first base with the Kansas City, MO Monarchs (NNL). He remained with Kansas City through the 1922 season and switched to the Philadelphia, PA Hilldale Daisies (ECL) in 1923. Carr stayed with Hilldale until 1928, but played winter ball in 1925 and 1926 with the Philadelphia Royal Giants. He also played with the Atlantic City, NJ Bachrach Giants (ECL) in 1928 and 1929 and the New York Lincoln Giants (ECL) in 1928. Carr apparently left Negro League baseball until 1933, when he returned to the Atlantic City Bachrach Giants.

Carr, a 6-foot 2-inch, 230-pound switch hitter, combined power with a good batting average. With the Hilldale Daisies from 1923 to 1925, Carr batted .354 with 21 HR. The base-stealing threat pilfered 39 bases in 1923. He batted .367 in 1925 and .412 in 1927 and starred in the 1924 and 1925 Negro League World Series. Defensively, the versatile Carr also played third base, catcher, and outfielder.

Carr, who reportedly drank excessively and represented a disciplinary problem to his managers, lacked enough economic independence to live off of his baseball earnings. He drove a cab during his off-seasons in Kansas City and worked as a cook for a railroad company.

BIBLIOGRAPHY: Janet Bruce, *The Kansas City Monarchs* (Lawrence, KS, 1985); Dick Clark and Larry Lester, eds., *The Negro Leagues Book* (Cleveland, OH, 1994); John Holway, *Life in the Negro Leagues from the Men Who Lived It* (New York, 1991); James A. Riley, *The Biographical Encyclopedia of the Negro Baseball Leagues* (New York, 1994).

Joel S. Franks

CARRIGAN, William Francis "Bill" (b. October 22, 1883, Lewiston, ME; d. July 8, 1969, Lewiston, ME), player and manager, was signed by the Boston Pilgrims (AL) in 1906 after spending two years at Holy Cross College. The 5-foot 9-inch, 175-pound Carrigan, who batted and threw right-handed, was loaned to Louisville, KY (AA) for most of 1906 and 1907 and became a regular catcher for the Boston Red Sox (AL) in 1908. He batted .257 lifetime in 709 games, attaining a career high .296 in 1909. Carrigan achieved his greatest success after being appointed Boston Red Sox manager in mid-season 1913, succeeding Jake Stahl. Boston won AL pennants in 1915 and 1916 and both World Series, defeating the Philadelphia Phillies in 1915 and the Brooklyn Dodgers in 1916. During this period, he roomed with Babe Ruth* to keep the latter under control. Ruth later called Carrigan the greatest manager he had ever played for.

Upon retiring after the 1916 season, Carrigan returned to Lewiston, ME and managed his real estate and theater investments. He managed the Red Sox from 1927 to 1929, but Boston finished last each year. These poor teams dropped his career managerial record below the .500 mark. Carrigan's overall record as manager included 489 wins and 500 losses. After the 1929 season, he entered banking and became president of the Peoples Bank of Lewiston. Carrigan married Beulah Barret in 1915 and had two daughters, Constance and Buelah, and one son, William, Jr.

BIBLIOGRAPHY: William Carrigan file, National Baseball Library, Cooperstown, NY; Joseph L. Reichler, ed., *The Great All-Time Baseball Record Book* (New York, 1981); *The Baseball Encyclopedia*, 10th ed. (New York, 1996); Will Anderson, *Was Baseball Really Invented in Maine?* (Portland, ME, 1992); Jack Kavanagh, "Quit While You're Ahead," *TNP* 11 (1992), pp. 32–33; Peter Golenbock, *Fenway* (New York, 1992); Robert Redmount, *The Red Sox Encyclopedia* (Champaign, IL, 1998); Frederick G. Lieb, *The Boston Red Sox* (New York, 1947).

Horace R. Givens

CARROLL, Clay Palmer "Hawk" (b. May 2, 1941, Clanton, AL), player, ranked among the most effective relief hurlers in major league baseball from 1966 through 1976. He grew up in central Alabama, halfway between Birmingham and Montgomery, and worked in a cotton mill with his father when not in school. He left Clanton High School before graduation in 1961 to join spring training with the Milwaukee Braves (NL). Carroll spent three and one-half seasons in the minor leagues before being called up to the Milwaukee Braves in 1964. A 6-foot 1-inch, 188-pound right-hander, he started several games in the next few years. Most of his time, however, was spent working out of the Milwaukee bullpen. In 1966 the Braves franchise shifted to Atlanta, where he led the NL in games pitched (73) and compiled a 2.37 ERA.

On June 11, 1968, the Atlanta Braves traded Carroll to the Cincinnati Reds (NL), where he experienced his most productive seasons as a relief hurler. He also enjoyed a rare batting-pitching highlight on May 30, 1969 when he hit a HR in the 10th inning off Bob Gibson* of the St. Louis Cardinals to give the Reds a 4–3 win. In 1972, he again led the NL in games pitched with 65 and set a NL record with 37 saves. *TSN* named him the NL Fireman of the Year.

The Cincinnati Reds, managed by Sparky Anderson* and staffed by such batting stars as Johnny Bench,* Joe Morgan,* Tony Perez,* and Pete Rose,* dominated the NL in the 1970s. The Cincinnati Reds won five NL pennants and two World Series. Carroll proved very effective in postseason play. He worked in eight NL Championship Series games, winning two, saving one, and compiling a 1.50 ERA. In 14 World Series games, he triumphed twice, saved one, and had a 1.33 ERA. In the 1970 World Series against the Baltimore Orioles, he recorded the Cincinnati Reds' only victory. In 1975, he won the seventh and deciding World Series game over the Boston Red Sox. In his two-inning stint, he fanned Carlton Fisk.* Fisk the night before had hit his dramatic 12th-inning, game-winning HR off Pat Darcy.

Carroll sought a two-year contract from the Cincinnati Reds after their highly successful championship season in 1975. The Cincinnati Reds traded him to the Chicago White Sox (AL), who signed him to a one-year contract around $110,000. Carroll missed one-third of the 1976 season because of an injury and was traded to the St. Louis Cardinals (NL) in March 1977. He pitched well for the St. Louis Cardinals until traded back to the Chicago White Sox in August 1977. He appeared in only two games for the Pittsburgh Pirates (NL) in 1978 and closed out his baseball career with Vancouver, Canada (PCL) in 1979.

Carroll pitched in 731 major league games, winning 96 decisions, losing 73, and sporting an impressive 2.94 ERA. In 703 relief appearances, he compiled an even better 2.82 ERA and 143 saves. Among the firemen who hurled over 1,000 innings in relief, he recorded one of the lowest ERA.

During and after his pitching career, Carroll worked in a Bradenton, FL sporting goods business. He married Judy Haines in September 1964. He and his family were victims of a tragic shooting at their home on November 16, 1985. His second wife, Frances, and son, Brett, died of wounds, while Carroll, also shot, recovered after hospitalization. Carroll moved to Chattanooga, TN, where he currently resides.

BIBLIOGRAPHY: Bob Cairns, *Pen Men* (New York, 1993); Donald Honig, *The Cincinnati Reds* (New York, 1992); Greg Rhodes and John Erardi, *Big Red Dynasty* (Cincinnati, OH, 1997); Robert H. Walker, *Cincinnati and the Big Red Machine* (Bloomington, IN, 1988); Clay Carroll, "The Game I'll Never Forget," *BD* 40 (June 1981), pp. 69–73; Clay Carroll file, National Baseball Library, Cooperstown, NY; L. Robert Davids, *Baseball Briefs* (Washington, DC, 1987); John Thorn et al., eds., *Total Baseball*, 5th ed. (New York, 1993); *TSN Baseball Register*, 1979; *USAT*, November 18, 1985.

L. Robert Davids

CARTER, Gary Edmund (b. April 8, 1954, Culver City, CA), player and sportscaster, excelled as a scholar-athlete at Sunnyhills High School in Fullerton, CA, and captained the school's baseball, basketball, and football teams for two years. Selected in the third round of the 1972 free-agent draft, Carter rejected countless college scholarship offers to sign with the Montreal Expos (NL). Since his mother died of leukemia when he was 12 years old, he has remained close to his father, James, an aircraft parts inspector. Carter, completely devoted to his wife, high school sweetheart Sandy Lahm, and two daughters Christina and Kimberly, is a talkative, gung-ho athlete and applied the all-out approach to everything he did on the diamond.

After beginning his professional baseball career with Cocoa, FL (FECL) and West Palm Beach, FL (FSL), Carter moved to Quebec City, Canada (EL) and Peninsula, VA (IL) during the 1973 season. He played for Memphis, TN (IL) in 1974 and finished the season with Montreal. Used primarily as an outfielder for the Expos, Carter was named NL Rookie of the Year in

1975. He won the regular catching job in 1977, as special tutoring by Norm Sherry improved his performance greatly.

Carter hit three HR in games on April 20, 1977 and September 2, 1985 and tied a New York Mets record by slugging 13 HR in September 1985. His .294 batting average (1984), 106 RBI (1984), and 32 HR (1985) marked career highs. In 1978, Carter established a major league record for fewest passed balls (1). He led NL catchers in total chances (1977–1982), putouts (1977–1980, 1982), assists (1977, 1979–1980, 1982), and double plays (1978–1979, 1983). In 1980 and 1983, he paced NL catchers in fielding. Named to the NL All-Star team (1975, 1979–1988), Carter was voted the game's MVP in 1981 and 1984. His two HR in the 1981 classic tied a record for most HR in one game. The next year, he led All-Star balloting with nearly 3 million votes. He was named the catcher on *TSN* All-Star fielding team (1980–1982) and Silver Slugger team (1981–1982).

In 1981, Carter batted .421 in the Eastern Division playoffs and .438 in the NL Championship Series (the Expos' first), as Montreal lost to the Los Angeles Dodgers in five games.

Carter, named Montreal Player of the Year four times, was traded to the New York Mets (NL) in December 1984 for four players. During 1986, Carter batted .255, slugged 24 HR, and knocked in 105 runs to help lead the New York Mets to the NL pennant. Although hitting only .148 in the NL Championship Series against the Houston Astros, Carter excelled in the 1986 World Series. He batted .276, made 8 hits, slugged 2 HR, and knocked in 9 runs to help the Mets defeat the Boston Red Sox. He plated four runs in the 1988 NL Championship Series against the Los Angeles Dodgers. The Mets released Carter in December 1989. He played for the San Francisco Giants (NL) in 1990 and Los Angeles Dodgers (NL) in 1991 before ending his major league career with the Montreal Expos in 1992. In 19 major league seasons, he batted .262 with 2,092 hits, 371 doubles, 324 HR, and 1,225 RBI in 2,296 games. Carter announced for the expansion Florida Marlins (NL) from 1993 through 1996 and has broadcast for the Montreal Expos since 1997.

BIBLIOGRAPHY: George Kalinsky, *The New York Mets* (New York, 1995); Gary Carter file, National Baseball Library, Cooperstown, NY; Gary Carter and John T. Hough, *A Dream Season* (San Diego, CA, 1987); Ron Fimrite, "His Enthusiasm Is Catching," *SI* 58 (August 4, 1983), pp. 52–55, 58, 61; Ross Forman, "Gary Carter: Hall of Fame Bound?" *SCD* 25 (July 24, 1998), pp. 114–116; J. Friedman, "Strong, but a Stranger to Silences, Mets Catcher Gary Carter May Be Baseball's Happiest Warrior," *PW* 26 (September 15, 1986), pp. 117–118; Robert G. Kelly, *Baseball's Best* (Jefferson, NC, 1988); *NYT Biographical Service* 17 (October 1986), pp. 1208–1209; Mark Ribowsky, "The Selling of Gary Carter," *Sport* 72 (August 1981), pp. 49–54; *TSN Official Baseball Register, 1992.*

John L. Evers

CARTER, Joseph Cris, Jr. "Joe" (b. March 7, 1960, Oklahoma City, OK), player and sportscaster, is one of 11 children of Joseph Carter, Sr., a service station operator and truck driver, and Athelene Carter, a telephone worker. His brother, Fred, played outfield in the minor leagues. Carter majored in business administration at Wichita State University, earning *TSN* College All-American baseball team (1980, 1981) and *TSN* College Player of the Year (1981) honors.

The Chicago Cubs (NL) drafted the right-handed outfielder–first baseman as the second overall pick in June 1981 and assigned the 6-foot 3-inch, 225 pounder to Midland, TX (TL) and Des Moines–based Iowa Cubs (AA) from 1981 to 1984. Carter debuted briefly with the Chicago Cubs in 1983. In June 1984, Chicago traded the easygoing, generous Carter to the Cleveland Indians (AL). His best season came in 1986, when Cleveland secured its first winning season since 1968. Carter led the AL in RBI (121), reaching career highs in batting average (.302), runs scored (108), hits (200), and triples (9). In 1987, he became only the third major leaguer to attain 100 RBI, 30 HR, and 30 stolen bases the same season. Carter belted a career-best 35 HR with 105 RBI in 1989, tying major league records for most HR in two consecutive games (5) and most games in a single season with at least three HR (2).

In December 1989, the Cleveland Indians traded Carter to the San Diego Padres (NL) for three players. He knocked in 115 runs in 1990, but San Diego sent Carter and Roberto Alomar* that December to the Toronto Blue Jays (AL) for Fred McGriff* and Tony Fernandez.* The durable Carter in 1991 played every game for the third consecutive season. He batted .273 with 33 HR, 108 RBI, and a career-pinnacle 42 doubles, helping the Blue Jays capture the AL East Division crown. The Minnesota Twins defeated Toronto in the AL Championship Series. The Blue Jays repeated as AL East Division titlists in 1992, with Carter belting 34 HR and recording 119 RBI. Toronto vanquished the Oakland A's in the AL Championship Series and the Atlanta Braves in the World Series, as Carter batted .273 with two doubles, two HR, and three RBI and became the first player to start three consecutive World Series games at three different positions. In 1991 and 1992, he played in the All-Star Game and made the *TSN* AL All-Star and AL Silver Slugger teams. No major leaguer hit more HR between 1986 and 1993. Carter, an excellent fastball hitter, surpassed 30 HR in six seasons and 100 RBI in ten campaigns. He holds the AL career record for most games with at least 3 HR (5), but has averaged nearly 100 strikeouts since 1986.

In 1993, Carter made the AL All-Star team for the third consecutive season and tied a career high with 121 RBI, batting .254 and hitting 33 HR to help the Toronto Blue Jays capture a third consecutive AL East Division crown. Toronto prevailed over the Chicago White Sox in the 1993 AL Championship Series and the Philadelphia Phillies, four games to two, in the 1993 World Series. Carter belted a dramatic three-run HR in the ninth inning to give Toronto an 8–6 victory in Game 6, the first time a World Series had ended on a HR since 1960 and the only time a Fall Classic had concluded on a HR that rallied the losing team to victory. For the World Series, Carter batted .280 with two HR and eight RBI.

Carter set a major league record in 1994 by driving in 31 runs during April. During the strike-shortened 1994 season, he batted .271 with 27 HR and 133 RBI and again made the AL All-Star team. He remained with the Toronto Blue Jays through 1997, clouting 30 HR with 107 RBI in 1996 and knocking in 102 runs in 1997. The Baltimore Orioles (AL) signed him as a free agent in December 1997 and traded him to the San Francisco Giants (NL) in July 1998.

Through 1998, Carter batted .259 with 396 HR and 1,445 RBI. He holds the Toronto all-time record for most HR (203) and made five AL All-Star teams (1991–1994, 1996). The Leawood, KS resident and his wife, Diana, have three children, Kia, Ebony, and Jordan. He serves as a color analyst for the Toronto Blue Jays (AL).

BIBLIOGRAPHY: Joe Carter file, National Baseball Library, Cooperstown, NY; Ron Fimrite, "Pow! Wow!" *SI* 66 (April 6, 1987), pp. 74–76, 78, 80; Richard Hoffer, "Every Game Is a Home Game," *SI* 72 (April 16, 1990), pp. 78–80; *San Diego Padres 1990 Media Guide; TSN Official Baseball Register*, 1998; Jack Torry, *Endless Summers* (South Bend, IN, 1995); John Roehmis, ed., *A Series to Remember* (San Francisco, CA, 1993); Rick Weinberg, "Super Joe," *Sport* 83 (June 1992), pp. 22–23, 26, 28–29.

David L. Porter

CARTWRIGHT, Alexander Joy, Jr. (b. April 17, 1820, New York, NY; d. July 12, 1892, Honolulu, HI), the "Father of Modern Baseball," was the son of sea captain and marine surveyor Alexander Joy Cartwright and Ester Rebecca (Burlock) Cartwright. Cartwright attended school in New York City until 1836, when he left midway through the tenth grade to help support the family. From a lowly clerk, he advanced rapidly in the financial world. In 1842, he married Eliza Ann Gerrits Van Wie of Albany, NY. They had four children, Dewitt, Bruce, Kathleen Lee, and Alexander Joy Cartwright III.

A large, well-built man, Cartwright earned friends and continued success with his jovial, gregarious nature. In 1842 he joined a group of young bankers, lawyers, and merchants who regularly played baseball at Madison Square. At Cartwright's suggestion in September 1845, the Knickerbocker Base Ball Club became a permanent organization and established a constitution and by-laws. Cartwright and other officers divided club members into various teams for their biweekly games. In 1846, they began playing match games with other newly organized clubs. From 1846 through the 1870s, the Knickerbockers played at the Elysian Fields in Hoboken, NJ. According to

Albert Spalding,* "The organization of the Knickerbockers began the most important era in the history of the game."

Cartwright's rules, although overlooked for nearly a century, transformed baseball into a mature sport. His major innovations included rules establishing nine-member teams with unalterable batting order, nine-inning games, and 90 feet between bases and prohibiting throwing the ball at a runner to put him out. These rules, drawn up and published in 1846, were adopted by many baseball clubs.

Cartwright remained an active Knickerbockers player and officer until 1849, when he joined the gold rush. He taught baseball to fellow travelers, saloon keepers, soldiers, miners, and Indians across the Great Plains and along the Santa Fe and Oregon trails. In August 1849, he and former Knickerbocker Frank Turk introduced baseball in San Francisco. Cartwright then sailed for China, but illness forced him to make Honolulu his permanent home.

Success followed Cartwright to Hawaii, where his business became the prestigious Cartwright and Company. He became friend, adviser, and diplomatic envoy of the royal family. As one of Hawaii's leading citizens, he founded a bank, a hospital, the Honolulu fire and transportation departments, and the Masonic Lodge.

In 1852, Cartwright established Hawaii's first baseball field in Makiki Park. He organized teams and taught the game extensively, remaining an active player and an avid fan throughout his life. Consequently, baseball was played throughout the Hawaiian Islands before it was known in half of the United States. His family, which joined him in 1851, shared his enthusiasm for the sport. They read his diary and Knickerbocker Rules and played with the Knickerbocker baseball that he had brought from New York.

Despite Cartwright's popularity in Honolulu, Americans forgot him until plans were announced to celebrate in 1939 the centennial of Abner Doubleday's "invention of baseball." Bruce Cartwright then wrote the Centennial Committee about his grandfather's life and contribution to baseball. Consequently, Cartwright was inducted into the National Baseball Hall of Fame in 1938. In 1939 a replica of his Cooperstown plaque was placed in Honolulu City Hall, and Makiki Park was renamed Cartwright Park. A street and a baseball tournament also were named in his honor. Cartwright's innovative rules established him as the "Father of Modern Baseball," while his organization of the Knickerbocker Club and teaching of baseball across the United States and the Pacific sparked the growth and popularity of the game.

BIBLIOGRAPHY: Alexander Cartwright file, National Baseball Library, Cooperstown, NY; Martin Appel and Bert Goldblatt, *Baseball's Best* (New York, 1977); Brad Herzog, *The Sports 100* (New York, 1995); Seymour R. Church, *Base Ball* (Princeton, NJ, 1902); Robert W. Henderson, *Ball, Bat, and Bishop* (New York, 1947); Frederick Ivor-Campbell et al., eds., *Baseball's First Stars* (Cleveland, OH, 1996); Harold Peterson,

The Man Who Invented Baseball (New York, 1969); Albert G. Spalding, *America's National Game* (New York, 1911); Dean A. Sullivan, *Early Innings* (Lincoln, NE, 1995).

Mary Lou LeCompte

CARTY, Ricardo Adolfo Jacobo "Rico" (b. September 1, 1939, San Pedro de Macoris, DR), player and coach, grew up in the Dominican professional boxing world. His father worked as a foreman at the local sugar mill, while his mother toiled as a midwife. The elder Carty, however, also trained boxers and prepared his boy for a career in that sport. By age 16, young Carty had won 17 amateur bouts in his native country. Carty then joined various local baseball clubs in his hometown. In 1959, he was invited to join the Dominican Republic national baseball team bound for the Pan-American games in Chicago, IL. The following year, several major league scouts pursued the slugger. Carty mistakenly signed 10 professional baseball contracts. George Trautman,* NAML president, recognized the error as a matter of Carty's inexperience with contracts. Trautman did not suspend the Dominican, but gave the Milwaukee Braves (NL) exclusive rights for Carty's services.

Initially signed as a catcher, Carty spent four years in the Milwaukee Braves minor league system before debuting in the major leagues on September 15, 1963. In his first full major league season, Carty recorded a banner year with 22 HR and 88 RBI and finished second in NL batting with a .330 average. The right-handed slugger remained a steady force with the Milwaukee and Atlanta Braves, but was struck with tuberculosis in 1968. After the Braves had moved to Atlanta, he won the 1970 NL batting title with a .366 average, led the NL with a .456 on-base percentage, collected 175 hits, and belted 25 HR. During that season, Carty hit in 31 straight games for the longest hitting streak by a Latin player and, at that time, the third longest in NL history. He also appeared in his only All-Star contest as the first-ever write-in player. Off the field, Carty experienced problems in 1971, when he was involved in an altercation with Atlanta, GA policemen that led to the suspension of three officers.

Carty split the 1973 season with the Texas Rangers (AL), Chicago Cubs (NL), and Oakland Athletics (AL) and joined the Cleveland Indians (AL) for the 1974 campaign. After four years with the Cleveland Indians, the Dominican divided 1978 between the Toronto Blue Jays (AL) and Oakland Athletics and clouted a career-high 31 HR. He ended his major league career in 1979 with a second stint for the Toronto Blue Jays. During 15 major league seasons, Carty collected 1,677 hits and batted .299 with 204 HR and 890 RBI. Subsequently, Carty coached several years in the Dominican baseball leagues.

BIBLIOGRAPHY: Atlanta (GA) *Journal*, May 8, 1970, p. 4; Rico Carty file, National Baseball Library, Cooperstown, NY; Bob Buege, *The Milwaukee Braves: A Baseball Eulogy* (Milwaukee, WI, 1988); Gary Caruso, *The Braves Encyclopedia* (Philadelphia,

PA, 1995); "Carty a Born Hitter . . . Can He Reach .400?" *TSN*, July 4, 1970, p. 20; "Carty Kayoes His Hard-Luck Hoodoo," *TSN*, August 28, 1976, p. 3; Michael M. Oleksak and Mary Adams Oleksak, *Beisbol: Latin Americans and the Grand Old Game* (Grand Rapids, MI, 1991); John Thorn et al., eds., *Total Baseball*, 5th ed. (New York, 1997); John Thorn et al., eds., *Total Braves* (New York, 1996).

Samuel O. Regalado

CARUTHERS, Robert Lee "Bob," "Parisian Bob" (b. January 5, 1864, Memphis, TN; d. August 5, 1911, Peoria, IL), player and umpire, batted .282 in 10 major league seasons and compiled one of the highest winning percentages for pitchers (.688). The 5-foot 7-inch, 150-pound switch-hitter threw right-handed. He learned to play baseball in Chicago, IL where he moved in 1876 with his father, James P. Caruthers, a lawyer, Tennessee state's attorney, and Memphis judge, and his mother, the former Miss McNeil of Kentucky. After playing for two amateur clubs in Chicago (North End Club, 1882; Lake Views, 1883) and two professional WL clubs (Grand Rapids, MI, 1883; Minneapolis, MN, 1884), Caruthers joined the major league St. Louis Browns (AA) in September 1884.

Caruthers helped the Browns win three consecutive AA pennants (1885–1887), leading AA pitchers with 40 wins in 1885 and in winning percentage in 1885 (.755) and 1887 (.763). He also ranked fourth among the AA's batters in 1886 (.334) and fifth in 1887 (.357). In slugging he placed second in 1886 (.527), a fraction of a point below AA leading Dave Orr,* and third in 1887 (.547). From 1888 through 1891, Caruthers played for Brooklyn (AA, NL). In 1889, his AA-leading 40 wins, .784 winning percentage, and 7 shutouts helped bring Brooklyn its first AA pennant. When Brooklyn moved the next year to the NL and again won the championship, Caruthers won 23 games as a pitcher and played half his games in the outfield.

Used mainly as an outfielder, Caruthers concluded his major league career with St. Louis (1892), Chicago, (1893), and Cincinnati (1893) in the NL. After returning to the minors, he played outfield with Grand Rapids, MI (WL) in 1894, Jackson, MI (WA) in 1895, and Burlington, IA (WA) in 1896. Following his playing days, Caruthers umpired in the WL and 3IL. During the 1911 season, he suffered a nervous breakdown and died a few weeks later.

Caruthers, remembered primarily as a pitcher, won 218 major league games, lost only 99, registered six successive seasons of more than 20 victories, and compiled a 2.83 ERA. Among 19th century pitchers, his .688 major league winning percentage ranks him second behind Al Spalding* (.787). In 2,828.2 innings, he struck out 900 batters and hurled 24 shutouts. Caruthers pitched in early World Series with St. Louis (1885–1887) and Brooklyn (1889), winning 7 games, losing 8, and tying one. Twice defeating Chicago in 1886, he hurled a ten-inning 4–3 win in the final game to give St. Louis the AA's only World Series victory over an NL champion.

BIBLIOGRAPHY: Robert Caruthers file, National Baseball Library, Cooperstown, NY; Henry Chadwick Scrapbooks, Albert Spalding Collection, New York Public Library, vols. 6, 7; Craig Carter, ed., *TSN Daguerreotypes*, 8th ed. (St. Louis, MO, 1990); Robert L. Tiemann and Mark Rucker, eds., *Nineteenth Century Stars* (Kansas City, MO, 1989); David Nemec, *The Beer and Whisky League* (New York, 1994); Daniel Pearson, *Baseball in 1889* (Bowling Green, OH, 1993); William F. McNeil, *The Dodgers Encyclopedia* (Champaign, IL, 1997); *The Baseball Encyclopedia*, 10th ed. (New York, 1996); *SL*, August 12, 1911.

Frederick Ivor-Campbell

CASE, George Washington, Jr. (b. November 11, 1915, Trenton, NJ; d. January 23, 1989, Trenton, NJ), player, coach, and manager, was the son of George Washington Case, Sr., a farmer and self-employed businessman, and Clara (McIntyre) Case. His older half brother, William Clifford, encouraged him to participate in basketball and baseball at Trenton Central High School and Peddie School, where he graduated in 1936. A successful tryout with the Philadelphia Athletics (AL) prompted Joe Cambria, Albany, NY (IL) owner and part-time Washington Senators (AL) scout, to get permission from Philadelphia to let him play in 1936 for the Senators' York, PA (NYPL) farm team. York promptly relocated to Trenton, due largely to Clifford Case's influence. George Case stole 60 bases and batted .338, only .0002 behind the NYPL leader, for Trenton in 1937 and was named All-NYPL left fielder. The Washington Senators (AL) purchased him in August 1937. He finished the season with the Washington Senators, batting .289 in 22 games. During October 1937, he married Helen May Farrell of Trenton. They produced one son, George III, and one daughter, Robin.

An outfielder, Case played regularly nine seasons for the Washington Senators. The Senators traded him in December 1945 to the Cleveland Indians (AL) for one disappointing season. The Cleveland Indians returned him to the Washington Senators in March 1947 for a last part-time performance. A 6-foot, 180-pound, right-hand line drive hitter, he seldom homered or struck out as a leadoff batter and batted .282 in 1,226 games during 11 AL seasons. Case scored more than 100 runs in four seasons and led the major leagues in stolen bases five consecutive seasons from 1939 to 1943 and the AL in 1946. His highest stolen base production came with 61 in 1943. Unlike later eras, teams did not attempt steals when significantly ahead or behind. Back disabilities prevented him from sliding properly and disqualified him from military service. Clark Griffith* claimed Case, who stole bases on sheer speed, was the fastest runner in baseball history. Case never lost a match race to another baseball player and barely lost a 100-yard dash in 1946 to sprint-great Jesse Owens (OS) by less than a yard.

Case coached baseball at Rutgers University from 1950 through 1960, for the Washington Senators (AL) from 1961 into 1963, and for the Minnesota Twins (AL) in 1968. His managerial assignments included Hawaii (PCL) in

1965 and 1966, York, PA (EL) in 1967, and Oneonta, NY (NYPL) from 1969 through 1972. He also scouted for the Washington Senators and the Seattle Mariners (AL) and, being an excellent teacher, served as a minor league batting instructor. The modest, unassuming Case, liked and respected by his peers, enjoyed family life, duck hunting, and fishing. He started in 1939 making color movies of baseball scenes and associates, the best of which are preserved and currently marketed via videotape. Prior to his death from emphysema, he was elected to the Trenton, Washington, and New Jersey Sports Halls of Fame.

BIBLIOGRAPHY: George Case, Jr. file, National Baseball Library, Cooperstown, NY; Morris Bealle, *The Washington Senators* (Washington, DC, 1947); Harrington E. Crissey, Jr., *Teenagers, Graybeards and 4-F's, Vol. 2: The American League* (Trenton, NJ, 1982); Donald Honig, *Baseball Between the Lines* (New York, 1976); Richard Goldstein, *Spartan Seasons* (New York, 1980); Frederick G. Lieb, "Raised as Player by His Older Brother, George Case Inherits Speed from His Dad Who Was Noted Sprinter," *TSN*, August 18, 1938, p. 3; *NYT*, January 24, 1989, p. D-22; Robert Obojski, "George Case: The Stolen Base King of the Golden Era," *CSC* (July 1991), p. 24; Shirley Povich, *The Washington Senators* (New York, 1954); Shirley Povich, "1-Run Margin in Game—Case," *TSN*, December 27, 1945, p. 8; Bus Saidt, "Ballplayer George Case Dies at 73," Trenton (NJ) *Times*, January 24, 1989, pp. A1, A11, and "Case Will Be Missed By Many," Trenton (NJ) *Times*, January 24, 1989, pp. C1, C9; Rich Westcott, *Diamond Greats* (Westport, CT, 1988); John Phillips, *Winners* (Cabin John, MD, 1987).

Frank V. Phelps

CASEY, Hugh Thomas (b. October 14, 1913, Atlanta, GA; d. July 3, 1951, Atlanta, GA), player, was the son of James Casey, a police officer, and began his professional baseball career with Atlanta (SA) in 1932. The 6-foot 1-inch, 207-pound right-handed pitcher hurled for Charlotte, NC (PiL) in 1933, Atlanta in 1934, Los Angeles, CA (PCL) in 1936, Birmingham, AL (SL) in 1937, and Memphis, TN (SL) in 1938. In 1935, he compiled a 3.86 ERA without a decision for the Chicago Cubs (NL).

During 1938, Casey impressed Nashville manager Charley Dressen.* Dressen became a Brooklyn Dodgers (NL) coach and recommended the acquisition of Casey. With the Dodgers in 1939, Casey recorded a 15–10 mark and 2.93 ERA. He started 25 games, but developed into one of the first relief specialists. After 1941, Casey started only three of 201 games. Besides having great control, he did not hesitate to throw at hitters. His most famous pitch came during the fourth game of the 1941 World Series against the New York Yankees. With a 4–3 lead in the top of the ninth inning, Casey retired the first two hitters and threw a sharp breaking ball to Tommy Henrich* on a 3–2 count. Henrich missed the pitch, but reached first base because Dodger catcher Mickey Owen mishandled the ball. The Yankees scored four runs to win that contest, 7–4, and won the World Series, four games to one. In 1942, Casey led the NL with 13 saves.

Casey, who spent from 1943 to 1945 in military service, finished 11–5 with a 1.99 ERA and five saves in 1946 and 10–4 with a 3.99 ERA and NL-leading 18 saves in 1947. In the 1947 World Series against the New York Yankees, he set three records for relievers. He became the first pitcher to win a World Series game by throwing just one pitch, hurled the most contests (6), and finished the most games (6). The Dodgers released Casey after the 1948 season. The Pittsburgh Pirates (NL) signed him in the spring of 1949, but released him in August. He closed out the 1949 campaign with the New York Yankees (AL). In 1950, he returned to his hometown Atlanta Crackers and finished 10–4 before retiring. During his major league career, Casey compiled 75 wins, 42 losses, 55 saves, and a 3.45 ERA. In two World Series, he recorded two wins, two losses, and a 1.72 ERA.

Casey, a hard drinker and womanizer, married Kathleen Thomas in October 1937. They had no children. A Brooklyn court ruled against him in a paternity suit, declaring that he was the father of a child born to a Brooklyn woman. Still pleading his innocence, a despondent Casey committed suicide.

BIBLIOGRAPHY: Hugh Casey file, National Baseball Library, Cooperstown, NY; Donald Dewey and Nicholas Acocello, *The Biographical History of Baseball* (New York, 1995); Peter Golenbock, *Bums* (New York, 1984); Tom Knight, "Uncle Robbie and Hugh Casey," *BRJ* 22 (1993), pp. 105–106; William F. McNeil, *The Dodgers Encyclopedia* (Champaign, IL, 1997); Richard Goldstein, *Superstars and Screwballs* (New York, 1991); *TSN Official Baseball Register*, 1949; *TSN Complete Baseball Record Book*, 1997; John Thorn et al., eds., *Total Baseball*, 5th ed. (New York, 1997).

Robert J. Brown

CASH, David, Jr. "Dave" (b. June 11, 1948, Utica, NY), player and coach, is the son of David Cash, Sr., and enjoyed a solid 12-year major league career with four different NL teams. His major league clubs included the Pittsburgh Pirates (1969–1973), Philadelphia Phillies (1974–1976), Montreal Expos (1977–1979), and San Diego Padres (1980).

The 5-foot 11-inch, 170-pound right-handed hitter began his professional baseball career in the Pittsburgh Pirates organization at Salem, VA (ApL) in 1966. He won the batting title with a .335 average at Gastonia, NC (WCL) the next year. Upon joining the Pittsburgh Pirates in 1969, he was primarily a second baseman and played some games at both shortstop and third base. His impressive lifetime career offensive statistics featured a .283 batting average, 1,571 hits, and 732 runs scored, including a career-high 111 in 1975.

As a leadoff and number-two hitter, Cash averaged over 660 times at bat per season from 1974 through 1978, leading the NL three times. In 1975, he batted a then-record 699 times and struck out just 34 times. During his major league career, he proved a solid contact hitter and struck out just 309 times in over 5,500 at bats. Cash also led the NL in hits with 213 in 1975 and triples with 12 in 1976.

Cash came into his own in 1974, when the Pittsburgh Pirates traded him to the Philadelphia Phillies (NL) for pitcher Ken Brett. The team leader's slogan "Yes We Can" galvanized a maturing Phillies team, propelling them into NL pennant contention for the first time in a decade. With the Philadelphia Phillies, he also ranked among the NL's best second basemen and trailed only Joe Morgan* as an offensive and defensive star. Cash paired with Larry Bowa* to form a solid double play combination. They led the NL three consecutive years in double plays (1974–1976), with Cash leading all second sackers in fielding average in 1976 and 1978. Cash also was named to the NL All-Star team from 1974 through 1976.

Cash applied for free agency after the 1976 season and signed a three-year pact that November with the Montreal Expos (NL). He compiled one fine season with the Montreal Expos, hitting .289 with 188 hits and 42 doubles in 1977. He sagged badly thereafter and gradually lost his speed around second base, retiring after the 1980 season.

Cash and his wife, Pam, reside in Odessa, FL, and have two sons and one daughter. Cash worked as a stock broker and commodities broker from 1981 through 1987 and served as an instructor in the Philadelphia Phillies minor league system from 1988 through 1995. After coaching for the Philadelphia Phillies in 1996, he has coached with Rochester, NY (IL) in the Baltimore Orioles organization since 1997.

BIBLIOGRAPHY: Rich Westcott and Frank Bilovsky, *The New Phillies Encyclopedia* (Philadelphia, PA, 1993); David Cash file, National Baseball Library, Cooperstown, NY; Chuck Herron, "Dave Cash: Former NL All-Star Is Back in the Bigs," *SCD* 23 (June 21, 1996), pp. 154–156; Allen Lewis, *The Philadelphia Phillies: A Pictorial History* (Virginia Beach, VA, 1981); Richard L. Burtt, *The Pittsburgh Pirates: A Pictorial History* (Virginia Beach, VA, 1977); *Philadelphia Phillies Media Guide*, 1974–1976.

John P. Rossi

CASH, Norman Dalton "Norm," "Stormin' Norman" (b. November 10, 1934, Justiceburg, TX; d. October 12, 1986, Beaver Island, MI), player and sportscaster, attended San Angelo JC and starred in both baseball and football at Sul Ross State College. Upon graduation, he signed with the Chicago White Sox (AL) and spent the 1955 and 1956 seasons at Waterloo, IA (3IL), 1957 in military service, and part of 1958 at Indianapolis, IN (AA). After one season as a part-time White Sox player and appearing in the 1959 World Series, Cash was traded to the Cleveland Indians (AL) in December 1959. In April 1960, he was traded to the Detroit Tigers (AL).

A 6-foot, 190-pound first baseman, Cash played the next 15 years with the Detroit Tigers. In his second season with the Tigers (1961), Cash batted .361 to pace the AL. No major league ballplayer attained a higher seasonal average during the 1960s. In 1961, he led the AL in hits (193) and finished second in walks (124) and slugging average (.662). He hit 41 HR—the most ever recorded by a Tigers left-handed hitter—and batted in 132 runs. Cash played in both 1961 All-Star games and the 1966, 1971, and 1972 contests. Despite mediocre mobility, he led AL first baseman in fielding percentage in 1964 and 1967. In 1965 and 1971, he made the highest percentage of HR to at bats in the AL.

Cash never again approached his 1961 statistics, but became a Detroit Tigers mainstay until his retirement in 1974. Cash, who wed Myrta Harper in 1954, later married Dorothy Makoski in 1973. An integral part of the Tigers' 1968 world champions, he batted a team-high .385 against the St. Louis Cardinals in the seven-game World Series. At retirement, he ranked among the top ten Tigers players in games (2,018), at bats (6,593), runs (1,028), hits (1,793), doubles (241), RBI (1,087), and total bases (3,233). A lifetime .271 hitter, Cash ranked second to National Baseball Hall-of-Famer Al Kaline* in club HR and hit 377 career HR.

Well liked by his teammates, fans, and the press, the personable Cash remained in the Detroit area after his active career and served as a color commentator for Tigers games on cable television. Cash drowned while boating in Lake Michigan.

BIBLIOGRAPHY: *The Baseball Encyclopedia*, 10th ed. (New York, 1996); John Benson et al., *Baseball's Top 100* (Wilton, CT, 1997); Norm Cash file, National Baseball Library, Cooperstown, NY; William M. Anderson, *The Detroit Tigers* (South Bend, IN, 1996); Richard Bak, *A Place for Summer* (Detroit, MI, 1998); Joe Falls, *Detroit Tigers* (New York, 1975); Fred Smith, *995 Tigers* (Detroit, MI, 1981).

Sheldon L. Appleton

CAVARRETTA, Philip Joseph "Phil" (b. July 19, 1916, Chicago, IL), player, coach, and manager, is of Italian descent and attended Lane Tech High School for four years. The 5-foot 11½-inch, 175-pound Cavarretta married Lorayne Clares in 1936 and has three daughters. A brilliant high school player, Cavarretta turned professional in 1934 and played that year for Peoria, IL (CL) and Reading, PA (NYPL). At the season's end, he joined the Chicago Cubs (NL) and spent 20 years through 1953 there. He played 1954 and early 1955 with the Chicago White Sox (AL) and spent a season playing part-time with Buffalo, NY (IL). Cavarretta played first base primarily and sometimes as an outfielder.

Cavarretta starred with the Cubs. As a 19-year-old regular, he hit a HR on September 25, 1935 to clinch an NL pennant tie for the Chicagoans and kept alive their 21-game winning streak. Cavarretta led the NL in total hits (197) in 1944, batting (.355) in 1945, and pinch hits (12) in 1951. In 1945, he was named NL MVP. He batted .500 in three All-Star games and .317 in three World Series, appearing in 17 games. A batting star for the losing 1938 and 1945 Cubs, he hit .462 and .423, respectively. While managing the Cubs, he won a game with a bases-loaded pinch HR on July 29, 1951 to duplicate a feat accomplished by Rogers Hornsby* 20 years earlier. Lifetime, he batted .293 with 1,977 hits, 347 doubles, 99 triples, 95 HR, 990 runs scored, and 920 RBI and performed capably defensively.

Cavarretta managed the Chicago Cubs to a 169–213 record (1951–1953) and served as Detroit Tigers (AL) coach (1961–1963) and scout (1964). Cavarretta managed many years in the minor leagues, including stints with Buffalo NY (IL) from 1956 to 1958, Lancaster, PA (EL) in 1960, Salinas, CA (CaL) in 1965, Reno, NV (CaL) in 1966 and 1967, Waterbury CT (EL) in 1968, and Birmingham, AL (SL) from 1970 to 1972. He ended his association with baseball by serving as New York Mets (NL) minor league batting instructor (1973–1980). Cavarretta retired to Palm Harbor, FL and resides now in Villa Rica, GA.

BIBLIOGRAPHY: Thomas Aylesworth and Benton Minks, *The Encyclopedia of Baseball Managers* (New York, 1990); Warren Brown, *The Chicago Cubs* (New York, 1946); Eddie Gold and Art Ahrens, *The New Era Cubs, 1941–1985* (Chicago, IL, 1985); John Thom, *Champion Batsman of the 20th Century* (Los Angeles, CA, 1992); Jim Langford, *The Game Is Never Over* (South Bend, IN, 1980); *TSN*, August 22, 1935, May 31, 1945, January 4, 1948, July 25, 1970; Rich Westcott, *Diamond Greats* (Westport, CT, 1988); Warren Wilbert and William Hageman, *Chicago Cubs: Seasons at the Summit* (Champaign, IL, 1997).

Lowell L. Blaisdell

CAYLOR, Oliver Perry "O. P." (b. December 17, 1849, near Dayton, OH; d. October 19, 1897, Winona, MN), manager, official, journalist, was the son of farmers Henry Caylor and Mary Caylor. The small, fragile figure endured ill health throughout adulthood. Caylor, who graduated from Dayton High School as valedictorian, read law. Although securing admittance to the Cincinnati bar in 1872, he practiced law infrequently. As sporting editor of the *Cincinnati Enquirer*, Caylor soon gained popularity for his superb baseball coverage. In 1881, disagreements with publisher John McLean caused Caylor to switch to the *Cincinnati Commercial Gazette*. Caylor's fame as "the game's Boswell of the Mid-West" continuously enlarged. His columns appeared nationally in other newspapers and from 1886 to 1890 in *SL*. In his "peculiar, happy readable style," the honest, fearless reporter attacked anything and anybody he regarded as detrimental to baseball.

In November 1881, the dignified Caylor helped organize the AA and its local entry, the Cincinnati Red Stockings. The club, financed by Judge Justus Thorner, was formed from the "Reds," an amateur team Caylor had established earlier. Caylor became the Red Stockings secretary, business manager, and in 1885 and 1886 manager, although catcher Charlie "Pop" Snyder, the captain, actually directed the team on the field.

Events of 1887 severely frustrated Caylor. He founded the New York City-based *Daily Base Ball Gazette*, but it failed quickly when presidents John P. Day* of the New York Giants (NL) and Erastus Wiman of the New York Metropolitans (AA) refused to absorb further financial losses. Caylor joined the Metropolitans staff. In June, he succeeded Bob Ferguson* as manager. When the club finished seventh, however, he resigned in disgust. The AA expelled him on September 5 as the Metropolitans' representative from attending its councils for revealing confidences in print, an allegation he denied emphatically. His caustic wit and uncompromising attitudes had made him too many enemies. Thereafter, he implacably opposed the AA and firmly boosted the NL.

After a year's absence editing a newspaper in Carthage, MO, he returned to New York as editor of the *ST* in 1889 and 1890 and strongly opposed the PL. He served as baseball editor for the *New York Herald* from 1892 until his death from tuberculosis. Caylor was survived by a widow and a 14-year-old daughter.

BIBLIOGRAPHY: Oliver Perry Caylor file, National Baseball Library, Cooperstown, NY; J. Austin Fynes, ed., *Athletic Sports in America, England and Australia* (Philadelphia, PA, 1889); Frederick Ivor-Campbell et al., eds., *Baseball's First Stars* (Cleveland, OH, 1996); *The New York Clipper*, October 29, 30, 1897; Alfred H. Spink, *The National Game*, 2d ed. (St. Louis, MO, 1911); *SL*, September 14, 1887, October 23, 30, 1897.

Frank V. Phelps

CEDENO, Cesar Encarnacion (b. February 25, 1951, Santo Domingo, DR), player, grew up in Santo Domingo. His father, Diogene Cedeno, discouraged him from playing baseball in lieu of working at the family-owned store. Cedeno's mother, however, quietly supported his love for baseball and bought his first glove and pair of baseball shoes. As a high school player, Cedeno remained unheralded. In the fall of 1967, however, Houston Astros (NL) scouts Pat Gillick and Tony Pacheco saw the 16-year-old Dominican perform in an amateur game. Cedeno so impressed Gillick that the scout soon signed him to a contract.

Cedeno played his first professional game at age 17 and developed rapidly. With the Astros Oklahoma City, OK (AA) club, Cedeno batted .373, knocked in 61 runs, and hit 14 HR in 54 games in 1970. He joined the Astros in midseason of 1970 at age 19, becoming the youngest NL starting center fielder. In the remaining 90 games, Cedeno batted .310.

Manager Leo Durocher* saw great potential in Cedeno and called him the new Willie Mays.* Cedeno's 17 major league seasons indeed produced impressive numbers. No other major league player hit 20 or more HR and stole 50 or more bases in the same season for three consecutive years. Furthermore, he stole at least 50 bases six years in a row and led the NL in doubles in 1971 and 1972. He was named to the NL All-Star teams four times, won five consecutive Gold Glove awards (1972–1976), and was selected a *TSN* NL All-Star three times. In 1978 the Houston Astros rewarded him with a record-breaking $3.5 million contract for 10 years, the highest salary for a ballplayer at that time. Cedeno played his entire career in the

NL with the Houston Astros (1970–1981), Cincinnati Reds (1982–1985), St. Louis Cardinals (1985), and Los Angeles Dodgers (1986). Cedeno batted .285 lifetime with 2,087 hits, 436 doubles, 199 HR, 976 RBI, and 550 stolen bases.

Cedeno, however, experienced problems off the field. His most difficult moment came in December 1973, when he was arrested in the shooting death of a young woman. A Dominican court, amid much controversy, convicted him of involuntary manslaughter. In 1981, Cedeno climbed into the stands to confront a heckler and received a $5,000 fine and a brief suspension. These and other problems convinced him to enroll in the California Institute for Behavioral Medicine in Beverly Hills, CA in 1984 so he might control his anger. Cedeno retired as a major league player following the 1986 season. In 1989, he batted .331 with 23 RBI for the Gold Coast, FL Suns (SPBA). He married Cora Lefevre and has three sons, Cesar, Jr., Cesar Roberto, and Cesar Richard.

BIBLIOGRAPHY: Cesar Cedeno file, National Baseball Library, Cooperstown, NY; Arthur Daley, "Rendering unto Cesar," *NYT*, July 15, 1973; Tom Dowling, "Cesar Cedeno: The Shot Heard Round the Baseball World," *Sport 57* (August 1974), pp. 87–98; Abby Mendelson, "Whatever Happened to Cesar Cedeno?" *BQ* (Winter 1978–1979), pp. 45–46, 57; *Who's Who among Black Americans*, 5th ed. (Lake Forest, IL, 1988), p. 125.

Samuel O. Regalado

CEPEDA, Orlando Manuel Penne "The Baby Bull," "Cha-Cha" (b. September 17, 1937, Ponce, PR), player and scout, is the son of Peruchio Cepeda, Puerto Rico's most outstanding HR hitter. His father was nicknamed "The Bull," while Orlando became "The Baby Bull" and "Cha-Cha." After attending schools in Puerto Rico, he was signed in 1955 at age 17 by the New York Giants (NL). After a brief stint at Salem, VA (ApL), the 6-foot 2-inch, 205-pound first baseman–outfielder batted .393 for Kokomo, IN to lead the MOVL. In 1956 at St. Cloud, MN, the right-handed hitting and fielding Cepeda led the NoL with a .355 average. After hitting .309 with 25 HR for Minneapolis, MN (AA), he batted .312 with 25 HR in 1958 for the San Francisco Giants and was named NL Rookie of the Year. Cepeda hit the first major league HR on the West Coast against the Los Angeles Dodgers in the opening game on April 15, 1958.

During his 17-year major league career, Cepeda played for San Francisco, St. Louis Cardinals, and Atlanta Braves in the NL and Boston Red Sox and Kansas City Royals in the AL. He compiled a career .297 batting average with 2,351 hits, 417 doubles, 27 triples, and 379 HR, scored 1,131 runs, drove in 1,365 runs, and stole 142 bases. He led the NL in HR with 46 and RBI with 142 in 1961. Cepeda paced the NL with 111 RBI in 1967 at St. Louis and was selected as the NL's MVP. He played in two World Series with San Francisco and one with St. Louis, batting only .171 in 19 games.

Cepeda played for San Francisco from 1958 to 1966 and was traded to St. Louis in May 1966. One of baseball's most misunderstood players, he experienced a stormy stay in San Francisco and held out each spring for more money. He clashed continually with managers Alvin Dark* and Herman Franks,* who regarded him as lazy and indifferent. Fans irked him, once causing him to bean a San Francisco spectator. In 1965, he hurt his right knee and missed most of the season because of surgery. Although performing well with St. Louis, Cepeda was plagued by the knee injury the rest of his career.

After being traded to the Atlanta Braves (NL) in March 1969, Cepeda limped through half of the 1971 season and was forced to have surgery on his right knee. The Braves traded Cepeda in June 1972 to the Oakland A's (AL), where he was DH. In January 1973, the Boston Red Sox (AL) signed him as a free agent. In August 1974 he signed with Kansas City (AL) and the next year became one of baseball's first players arrested on drug charges. Federal agents found 160 pounds of marijuana in his car trunk at the San Juan, PR airport. Cepeda, who was convicted of drug smuggling, was sentenced to five years in prison and served ten months of that sentence. Subsequently, he operated a baseball school for children in San Juan, PR. Cepeda scouted for the Chicago White Sox (AL) in 1980 and served as community representative for the San Francisco Giants from 1989 through 1994. He was inducted into the PR Sports Hall of Fame in 1993 and the National Baseball Hall of Fame in 1999.

BIBLIOGRAPHY: Orlando Cepeda file, National Baseball Library, Cooperstown, NY; John Benson et al., *Baseball's Top 100* (Wilton, CT, 1997); Steve Bitker, *The Original San Francisco Giants* (Champaign, IL, 1998); Orlando Cepeda and Bob Markers, *High and Inside: The Orlando Cepeda Story* (New York, 1983); Ron Fimrite, "The Heart of a Giant," *SI* 75 (Fall 1991), pp. 58–64; Zander Hollander, ed., *The Complete Handbook of Baseball, 1972* (New York, 1972); Gene Karst and Martin J. Jones, Jr., *Who's Who in Professional Baseball* (New Rochelle, NY, 1973); Brent P. Kelley, *The Case For: Those Overlooked by the Baseball Hall of Fame* (Jefferson, NC, 1992); Edward Kiersch, *Where Have You Gone Vince DiMaggio?* (New York, 1983); Larry Moffi and Jonathan Kronstadt, *Crossing the Line* (Jefferson, NC, 1994); W. Ladson, "Didn't You Used to Be," *Sport* 80 (March 1989), p. 84; *The Baseball Encyclopedia*, 10th ed. (New York, 1996); Rich Westcott, *Diamond Greats* (Westport, CT, 1988).

James K. Skipper, Jr.

CEY, Ronald Charles "Ron" "Penguin" (b. February 15, 1948, Tacoma, WA), player, is the son of Frank Cey and Shirley (Robinson) Cey. The 5-foot 9-inch, 185-pound third baseman decided by age 8 to play baseball professionally. When selected by the New York Mets (NL) in 1966, however, he attended Washington State University instead. After the Los Angeles Dodgers (NL) chose him in the third round of the 1968 draft, he played in his home state for Tri-City, WA (NWL) and set NWL records for RBI, assists, and fielding percentage.

Cey, who threw and batted right-handed, took over in 1973 as the 43rd third baseman in the Los Angeles Dodgers' 16-year history. He led the NL in assists (328), accounted for 80 RBI, and earned Dodger Rookie of the Year honors. For a decade, he played on the longest continuous infield in major league history with Steve Garvey,* Davey Lopes,* and Bill Russell.* His short stride earned him the nickname "Penguin" from manager Tom Lasorda.*

Cey's 228 HR remains a Los Angeles–era Dodgers career record. He averaged over 80 RBI per season, including driving in over 100 runs in 1975 and 1977, and drew over 80 walks per campaign. He led NL third basemen in double plays (39) in 1973, recorded the most putouts (127) in the NL in 1980, and led the NL in fielding average in 1979 and 1984. Cey was selected to six All-Star Games and also appeared in four NL Championship Series, tying NL Championship Series records for most doubles in both four-game (3, 1974) and seven-game (7, 1977) series, most grand-slam HR in a game (1), and most RBI in an inning (4, seventh inning) on October 4, 1977. He played in the 1974, 1977, 1978, and 1981 World Series, tying the fall classic record for batting in all his team's runs in a game (4) against the New York Yankees on October 11, 1978. Cey recovered from a beaning incident against the New York Yankees in the 1981 World Series to win co-MVP honors.

Cey, who was traded to the Chicago Cubs (NL) in January 1983, paced the Cubs in RBI (90) and shared the club lead in HR (24). The following year, he led the Cubs with 97 RBI and 25 HR and played in the NL Championship Series against the San Diego Padres. He completed his career with the Oakland Athletics (AL), appearing in 45 games in 1987. During 17 major league seasons, Cey hit 328 career doubles and 316 HR, batted .261, attained a .445 slugging percentage, and ranked eighth among third basemen in career assists (4,018). He married Francis Fishbein of Chicago, IL on September 11, 1971. They have two children and live in Woodland Hills, CA.

BIBLIOGRAPHY: Ronald Cey file, National Baseball Library, Cooperstown, NY; *The Baseball Encyclopedia*, 10th ed. (New York, 1996); Peter Bonventre, "The Octopus," *Newsweek* 89 (October 24, 1977), p. 77; Eddie Gold and Art Ahrens, *The New Era Cubs, 1941–1985* (Chicago, IL, 1985); Bill James, *The Bill James Historical Baseball Abstract* (New York, 1986); Larry Keith, "In L.A. It's Up and Up and Away with Cey," *SI* 46 (May 16, 1977), pp. 24–28, 32; Robert E. Kelly, *Baseball's Best* (Jefferson, NC, 1988); Tommy Lasorda and David Fisher, *The Artful Dodger* (New York, 1985); William F. McNeil, *The Dodgers Encyclopedia* (Champaign, IL, 1997); Lawrence S. Ritter and Donald Honig, *The Image of Their Greatness* (New York, 1979); John Thorn et al., eds., *Total Baseball*, 5th ed. (New York, 1997); *WWA*, 44th ed. (1986–1987).

Gaymon L. Bennett

CHADWICK, Henry (b. October 5, 1824, Exeter, Devon, England; d. April 20, 1908, Brooklyn, NY), early promoter, shaper, chronicler, and conscience of baseball, was known as the "Father of Baseball" and later as "Father Chadwick." The son of English journalist James Chadwick, editor of the Exeter *Western Times*, he emigrated in 1837 with his parents to the United States. (His elder brother Edwin remained in England, where he gained international recognition as a pioneer in public health and sanitation.) The Chadwicks arrived a few days before Henry's 13th birthday and settled in Brooklyn, where Henry resided until his death. He began his journalistic career as a contributor to Brooklyn's *Long Island Star* in 1844. On August 19, 1848, he married Virginia native Jane Botts.

Although Chadwick had played baseball around 1847 or 1848, he did not see his first match between skilled players until nearly a decade later and quickly recognized baseball's potential for becoming America's national game. Over the next 50 years, Chadwick wrote voluminously about baseball in newspapers, magazines, pamphlets, and books. He reported its games, chronicled its development, taught its skills, recommended changes in its rules, and battled the drinking and gambling that threatened its integrity.

Chadwick covered baseball for more than 20 newspapers and magazines, most notably the Brooklyn *Eagle* (1856–1894 on the staff, freelance thereafter) and the New York *Clipper* (1857–1888). He originated the annual baseball guide in 1860 with *Beadle's Dime Base Ball Player* and edited *DeWitt's Guide* from 1869 to 1880 and *Spalding's Base Ball Guide* from 1881 to 1908. He wrote the first hardcover book devoted entirely to baseball (*The Game of Base Ball*, 1868) and numerous books and pamphlets on hitting, fielding, and base running, baseball jargon for British journalists, and other topics.

Chadwick influenced baseball's development unofficially through his writing and officially as a rules committee member of the NABBP (1858–1870) and the NL. To improve record keeping, he perfected the box score and devised the system for scoring games essentially still used today. Chadwick saw himself as a guardian of baseball's image and well-being, inveighing against drinking and rowdiness by players and fans and opposing disruptive influences like the outlaw PL of 1890. His opposition to gambling enabled baseball officials to stand firm against the persistent threats by gamblers to corrupt players and reduce baseball to a betting medium.

Though baseball dominated Chadwick's adult life, he pursued other interests. A songwriter and music teacher before becoming a baseball enthusiast, he continued to write music and play the piano. He also followed other sports and games, writing instructional guides on cricket, football, handball, and chess. He took particular delight in his family, which included his wife, two daughters, and numerous grandchildren and great-grandchildren.

The NL elected Chadwick an honorary member in 1894 and granted him a lifetime pension of $600 per year in 1896. In 1904, Chadwick was awarded the only medal given to a journalist by the St. Louis World's Fair. In 1938, he was elected to the National Baseball Hall of Fame.

BIBLIOGRAPHY: Brooklyn *Eagle*, April 20, 1908; Henry Chadwick, Scorebooks, Scrapbooks, Diaries, Albert Spalding Collection, New York Public Library; Henry Chadwick file, National Baseball Library, Cooperstown, NY; *DAB* 3 (1928), p. 587; *NYT*, April 21, 1908; Frederick Ivor-Campbell et al., *Baseball's First Stars* (Cleveland, OH, 1996); Thomas S. Rice, "Henry Chadwick," *TSN*, May 21, 1936; Allen E. Sanders, "Henry Chadwick, the 'Father of Baseball,'" source unidentified; Harold Seymour, *Baseball: The Early Years* (New York, 1960); Mac Souders, "Henry Chadwick," *BRJ* 15 (1986), pp. 84–85; Albert G. Spalding, *America's National Game* (New York, 1911); *SL*, April 25, May 2, 1908.

Frederick Ivor-Campbell

CHAMBERLAIN, Elton P. "Icebox" (b. November 5, 1867, Buffalo, NY; d. September 22, 1929, Baltimore, MD), player, grew up in Warsaw and Buffalo, NY. Before his 17th birthday, he played two professional baseball games at third base for Quincy, IL (NWL). The following year, he played for a Hamilton, Canada club. He spent much of the 1886 season with Macon, GA (SL) as a pitcher with a 13–20 record and an outfielder. He was signed later that year by the major league Louisville Colonels (AA) club, compiling a 0–3 mark. In 1887, his 18–16 win–loss record with Louisville established him as a major leaguer at age 19.

Chamberlain began the 1888 season with the Louisville Colonels, where he compiled a 14–9 win–loss record and 2.53 ERA. His season concluded with the St. Louis Browns (AA), where his brilliant 1.61 ERA and 11–2 record provided the impetus needed to catapult the club to their fourth straight AA pennant. In the World Series against the New York Giants, Chamberlain shut out the NL club in Game 2. He lost the fourth, sixth, and deciding eighth game, however, winning the meaningless tenth game.

The 1889 season proved the busiest and finest for the 5-foot 9-inch, 168-pound right-hander. Despite his chronic laziness (prompting his nickname "Icebox") and a brief suspension late in the 1889 campaign for allegedly careless play, Chamberlain hurled 421.2 innings and 44 complete games. He won 32 games, sharing third best in the AA, and lost 15 decisions. His 2.97 ERA places him fifth among career AA pitchers, while his 4.8 Total Pitcher Index (Pete Palmer's statistic for overall pitcher effectiveness) ranks third. Chamberlain combined with Charles "Silver" King,* who compiled a 35–16 record, to keep St. Louis in front of the AA through August. The St. Louis Browns, however, slipped to second place, two games behind the Brooklyn Bridegrooms.

In 1890, Chamberlain appeared in just five games with the St. Louis Browns, compiling a 3–1 record and high 5.91 ERA. He deserted the St. Louis Browns, returning home to Buffalo. The St. Louis Browns sold his contract to the Columbus, OH Buckeyes (AA), where he hurled an AA-high six shutouts and finished with a 12–6 record. His season ERA dropped to 2.83, fourth best in the AA.

Chamberlain won 22 games for the Philadelphia Athletics (AA) in 1891 and 19 for the Cincinnati Reds (NL) in 1892, but lost 23 games each season. Although pitching less the next two seasons, he compiled winning records of 16–12 and 10–9. He promised to pitch for the Cleveland Spiders (NL) in 1895, but signed instead with Warren, OH (IOL). He joined the Cleveland Spiders for the 1896 season, but was released in May after two ineffective appearances.

Altogether, Chamberlain won 157 major league games, lost 120 decisions, and compiled a 3.57 ERA in 2,521.2 innings. He is best remembered, though, for two games: On May 9, 1888, he pitched the final two innings of his 18–6 victory against the Kansas City Cowboys (AA) left-handed. In a Memorial Day 1894 game, he yielded four HR to Bobby Lowe* of the Boston Beaneaters.

BIBLIOGRAPHY: Al Kermisch, "Elton Chamberlain Another in Ambidextrous Class," *BRJ* 13 (1983), p. 48; J. Thomas Hetrick, *Chris Von der Ahe and the St. Louis Browns* (Lanham, MD, 1999); David Nemec, *The Beer and Whisky League* (New York, 1994); Daniel M. Pearson, *Baseball in 1889* (Bowling Green, OH, 1993); John Phillips, *The Spiders: Who Was Who* (Cabin John, MD, 1991); John Thorn et al., eds., *Total Baseball*, 5th ed. (New York, 1997); Robert L. Tiemann and Mark Rucker, eds., *Nineteenth Century Stars* (Kansas City, MO, 1989).

Frederick Ivor-Campbell

CHAMBLISS, Carroll Christopher "Chris" (b. December 26, 1948, Dayton, OH), player, coach and manager, participated in baseball at California schools while completing his education at Mira Costa JC and UCLA. The 6-foot 1-inch, 197-pound black first baseman was selected AA Rookie of the Year for Wichita, KS (AA) in 1970 and the AL Rookie of the Year the following season. After joining the Cleveland Indians (AL) in late May 1971, the left-handed–hitting, right-handed–throwing Chambliss batted .275 with 9 HR and 48 RBI. Much was expected from the 22-year-old, but he failed to exceed his rookie production over the next two seasons. The Indians traded Chambliss in April 1974 to the New York Yankees (AL), where he played for the next six seasons. Chambliss performed with the Atlanta Braves (NL) from 1980 through 1986 and briefly with the New York Yankees in 1988.

Chambliss's most productive period came from 1976 to 1983, when he averaged 16 HR per season and compiled 90 or more RBI for three consecutive years. An instrumental cog in the Yankees' pennant-winning successes between 1976 and 1978, he played a heroic role in the 1976 AL Championship Series against the Kansas City Royals with a sparkling .524 batting average. His ninth-inning HR won the decisive fifth game. Chambliss hit .313 in the losing 1976 World Series effort against the Cincinnati Reds. He also contributed to the Yankees' World Series title against the Los Angeles Dodgers in 1977, hitting .292 with 4 RBI. In the 1978 AL Championship Series, Chambliss belted .400 to help the Yankees again defeat the

Kansas City Royals. In 16 major league seasons, Chambliss finished with a .279 batting average, 2,109 hits, 972 RBI, and 185 HR. He managed Richmond, VA (IL) in 1992, coached for the St. Louis Cardinals (NL) from 1993 through 1995, and coached for the New York Yankees in 1988 and since 1996.

BIBLIOGRAPHY: Martin Appel, *Yesterday's Heroes* (New York, 1988); Chris Chambliss file, National Baseball Library, Cooperstown, NY; Mark Gallagher, *The Yankee Encyclopedia*, vol. 3 (Champaign, IL, 1997); Gary Caruso, *The Braves Encyclopedia* (Philadelphia, PA, 1995); Cleveland (OH) *Plain Dealer*, June 21, 1971, November 29, 1971, April 30, 1974; John Thorn et al., eds., *Total Baseball*, 5th ed. (New York, 1997).

James N. Giglio

CHANCE, Frank Leroy "Husk," "The Peerless Leader" (b. September 9, 1877, Fresno, CA; d. September 15, 1924, Los Angeles, CA), player and manager, played for the University of California in 1894–1895 and for an independent (probably semipro) team. Chance continued with baseball while studying dentistry at Washington College in Irvington, CA, where he was discovered in 1898 by Bill Lange,* former Chicago Colts outfielder. Upon Lange's recommendation, the Chicago Cubs (NL) signed Chance. Chance caught with Chicago until 1902, when manager Frank Selee* moved him permanently to first base. The good all-around player remained with Cubs from 1898 to 1912. Besides compiling a career .296 batting average, he led the NL in runs in 1906 (103) and in stolen bases in 1903 (67) and 1906 (57). In 20 World Series games, he hit .310 and stole 10 bases. He played very little after 1912 because of chronic headaches caused by several beanings. During his career, Chance made 1,273 hits, 200 doubles, 79 triples, 797 runs, 596 RBI, and 401 stolen bases.

During the 1905 season, new Cubs owner Charlie W. Murphy appointed Chance player–manager. In nearly eight years as mentor, Chance directed his team to four NL pennants and 100-game victory seasons and two world championships. In 1912, Chance quarreled bitterly with Murphy over the amount of money the owner was willing to pay to obtain quality players. When Murphy refused to spend more, Chance resigned in protest at the season's end. That winter Chance underwent surgery for his headaches, which were attributed to blood clots. After managing the New York Yankees (AL) in 1913 and 1914 to seventh-place finishes, Chance operated an orange grove in California. In 1916 and 1917, he was part-owner and manager of Los Angeles, CA (PCL). He managed the Boston Red Sox (AL) to last place in 1923 and would have piloted the Chicago White Sox (AL) the following year had he remained healthy. In 11 seasons as a major league manager, he compiled 946 wins and 648 losses for the sixth best percentage (.593).

A member of the Cubs' famed Joe Tinker* to John Evers* to Chance double play combination, he was elected with his teammates to the National

Baseball Hall of Fame in 1946. The origins of his nickname "Husk" are obscure, but Chicago baseball writer Charlie Dryden nicknamed him "Peerless Leader" for the championships the Cubs won under his direction.

BIBLIOGRAPHY: Frank Chance file, National Baseball Library, Cooperstown, NY; Thomas Aylesworth and Benton Minks, *The Encyclopedia of Baseball Managers* (New York, 1990); Eddie Gold and Art Ahrens, *The Golden Era Cubs, 1876–1940* (Chicago, IL, 1985); Warren Brown, *The Chicago Cubs* (New York, 1946); G. F. Fleming, *The Unforgettable Season* (New York, 1982); Ralph Hickok, *Who Was Who in American Sports* (New York, 1971); Gene Karst and Martin J. Jones, Jr., *Who's Who in Professional Baseball* (New Rochelle, NY, 1973); *The Baseball Encyclopedia*, 10th ed. (New York, 1996); *NYT*, September 16, 1924; Lowell Reidenbaugh, *Baseball's Hall of Fame-Cooperstown* (New York, 1993); Warren Wilbert and William Hageman, *Chicago Cubs: Seasons at the Summit* (Champaign, IL, 1997).

John E. Findling

CHANCE, Wilmer Dean (b. June 1, 1941, Wooster, OH), player, is the son of Wilmer Chance and Florence Chance and preferred his middle name. Of Swiss descent, he grew up on his parents' Ohio farm and rose early in the morning to help his father milk the cows. A star on championship basketball and baseball teams at Northwestern High School, the 6-foot 3-inch, 195-pound, right-handed pitcher signed with the Baltimore Orioles (AL) organization.

After spending the 1959–1960 seasons in the Baltimore Orioles farm system with Bluefield, WV (ApL) and Fox Cities, WI (3IL), Chance was selected by the Los Angeles Angels in the AL expansion draft in December 1960. In 1961, he pitched for Dallas–Fort Worth, TX (AA) and joined the Los Angeles Angels late in the season. Chance remained with the Los Angeles (and after 1965, California) Angels through the 1966 season. The California Angels traded him in December 1966 to the Minnesota Twins (AL), where he pitched from 1967 to 1969. Trades followed, as he spent most of the 1970 campaign with the Cleveland Indians (AL). The New York Mets (NL) acquired him in September 1970. In March 1971, Chance joined the Detroit Tigers (AL) for his final season.

His 11-year major league career was abbreviated by recurrent shoulder problems and squandered potential. Chance pitched 2,147.1 innings, winning 128 contests and losing 115 games for a .527 winning percentage. He struck out 1,534 batters, compiled a 2.92 ERA, and registered 33 shutouts. His best season came in 1964, when Chance used his blistering fastball to lead the AL in victories (20), ERA (1.65), complete games (15), innings pitched (278.1), and shutouts (11). Chance suffered only nine losses to register a .690 winning percentage and recorded 207 strikeouts. The 1964 season made the 23-year-old Chance the then-youngest recipient of the Cy Young Award and the highest salaried player ($41,000) in the brief history of the California Angels. Nonetheless, only in 1967, when his 20–14 win–

loss record, which included both a no-hitter and a five-inning (unofficial) perfect game, brought him the AL Comeback Player of the Year honors did Chance ever again approach his early brilliance. He led the AL in complete games (18) and innings pitched (283.2) that season.

Injuries and dissipation played a significant role in diminishing Chance's career. Early in his career, Chance came under the spell of hedonistic roommate "Bo" Belinsky. Chance's January 1961 marriage to Judith Carol Larson, which produced a son, ended in divorce. As an active player, Chance also pursued distracting, failed ventures as a billiards player–promoter and boxing manager–promoter. After the premature end of his baseball career, the Wooster, OH resident emerged as a midway barker and the peripatetic owner of a few carnival tent show games.

BIBLIOGRAPHY: Wilmer Chance file, National Baseball Library, Cooperstown, NY; Myron Cope, "Angel Who Doesn't Fear to Tread," *SEP* 238 (April 10, 1965), pp. 95–99; John Devaney, *Baseball's Youngest Big Leaguers* (New York, 1969); Bill Gallant, "Inside Dean Chance: Baseball's Winningest 'Loser,'" *All-Star Sports 2* (February 1968), pp. 14–17; Curry Kirkpatrick, "New Dean on List of Great No-Hitters: Dean Chance of Minnesota Twins," *SI* 27 (July 24, 1967), pp. 42–43; Bill Libby, "Chance of a Lifetime," *BD* 23 (December 1964), pp. 41–47.

William M. Simons

CHANDLER, Albert Benjamin "Happy" (b. April 18, 1898, Corydon, KY; d. June 15, 1991, Versailles, KY), commissioner, was the son of handyman–farmer Joseph Chandler and Callie Chandler. An impoverished, hard-working, ambitious youth, he completed high school and enrolled at Transylvania College in 1917 with "a red sweater on my back, a $5 bill in my pocket, and a song in my heart." Chandler, a sports enthusiast, played and coached football and participated in baseball in the RRVL and the BGL. After earning his law degree from the University of Kentucky, he began practicing law in Versailles, KY, and coached high school baseball there. Chandler married Mildred Watkins in 1925 and had four children.

The outgoing Chandler entered public life as a Democrat in 1928. He served as governor of Kentucky from 1935 to 1939 and 1955 to 1959 and as U.S. Senator from 1939 to 1945. An energetic campaigner, he proved a shrewd and colorful politician. In 1945 Leland McPhail, Sr.* promoted Chandler's selection as baseball commissioner, a position vacant since the death in 1944 of the stern Judge Kenesaw Mountain Landis.* Chandler became the goodwill ambassador baseball needed, but proved less pliant than sportswriters and baseball owners assumed he would be. He served as commissioner when Jackie Robinson* integrated organized baseball. Although scholars debate the commissioner's role in the controversies that surrounded Robinson's initial years with the Brooklyn Dodgers (NL), Chandler acted with fair-mindedness and spoke in favor of integration when anything less might have denied Robinson his opportunity.

Chandler acted decisively on the key issues of players' rights and the outlaw MEL, which in 1946 lured baseball stars with sizeable financial offers. He imposed a five-year ban from organized baseball on 18 jumpers, an edict which frightened magnates by nearly bringing a court ruling on the reserve clause. He also suspended Brooklyn Dodgers manager Leo Durocher* for the 1947 season for "an accumulation of unpleasant incidents . . . detrimental to baseball." In other instances, Chandler helped the players' association secure the radio and television revenue to bolster the new pension plan and supported a $5,000 minimum salary for major leaguers.

A clique of owners revolted against Chandler for arbitrarily jeopardizing the reserve clause and ordering investigations of the alleged gambling activities of one or two owners. Securing only nine of the 12 votes necessary for reelection, Chandler resigned in 1951 to resume an active role in Kentucky politics. An elder statesman in both sports and politics, Chandler in 1982 was elected to the National Baseball Hall of Fame. Upon this occasion, second baseman Joe Morgan* wired Chandler: "The Hall of Fame was made for people like you."

BIBLIOGRAPHY: Terry L. Birdwhistell, "A. B. 'Happy' Chandler," in Fred J. Hood, ed., *Kentucky: Its History and Heritage* (St. Louis, MO, 1978), pp. 208–220; Albert Chandler file, National Baseball Library, Cooperstown, NY; Albert B. Chandler file, Albert B. Chandler Collection and Albert B. Chandler Oral History Project, Margaret I. King Library, University of Kentucky, Lexington, KY; A. B. "Happy" Chandler with John Underwood, "How I Jumped from Clean Politics to Dirty Baseball," *SI* 34 (April 26, 1971), pp. 73–86, and (May 3, 1971), pp. 52–58; Albert B. Chandler with Vance Trimble, *Heroes, Plain Folks, and Skunks* (Chicago, IL, 1989); *CB* (1956), pp. 106–108; Daniel M. Daniel, "Senator Chandler Eminently Fitted for Vital Job as Baseball Commissioner," *BM* 75 (July 1945), pp. 255–257, 284–285; Frank Deford, "Happy Days," *SI* 67 (July 20, 1987), pp. 56–60; John Drebinger, "A Commissioner's Reign Ends," *BD* 10 (May 1951), pp. 399–400, 431–432; Milton Gross, "The Truth About Happy Chandler," *Sport* 6 (April 1959), pp. 53–62; Jerome Holtzman, *The Commissioners* (New York, 1998); Lexington (KY) *Herald*, June 24, 1983; *NYT*, June 16, 1991, p. 26; J. B. Shannon, " 'Happy' Chandler: A Kentucky Epic," in J. T. Salter, ed., *The American Politician* (Chapel Hill, NC, 1938), pp. 175–191; Jules Tygiel, *Baseball's Great Experiment: Jackie Robinson and His Legacy* (New York, 1983).

Lloyd J. Graybar

CHANDLER, Spurgeon Ferdinand "Spud" (b. September 12, 1907, Commerce, GA; d. January 9, 1990, South Pasadena, FL), player and scout, graduated from Carnesville, GA High School in 1928 and excelled in football, baseball, and track at the University of Georgia, where he received a Bachelor of Science degree in 1932. That same year Chandler began his professional baseball career with Springfield, MA (EL) and Binghamton, NY (NYPL). The 6-foot, 181-pound, right-handed pitcher hurled for Binghamton and Newark, NJ (IL) in 1933. Chandler divided the 1934 season among Newark and Syracuse, NY (IL) and Minneapolis, MN (AA). In 1935, he pitched with Oakland, CA (PCL) and Portland, OR (PCL) and returned to Newark for 1936 and part of 1937.

Chandler joined New York (AL) in 1937 and spent his entire 11-year major league career with the Yankees. He recorded a 7–4 won–lost record in 1937 and followed with 14–5, 3–0, 8–7, 10–4, and 16–5 marks. In 1943, he won 20, lost only 4, and led the AL with an .833 pitching percentage. His 1.64 ERA paced the majors, marking only the fourth time in AL history that a pitcher captured both laurels at once. Chandler topped the AL with 20 complete games, his 20 victories tying Dizzy Trout* of the Detroit Tigers for the AL lead. After serving in the military for much of the 1944 and 1945 seasons, Chandler won 20 and lost only 8 in 1946. His 2.46 ERA led the AL in 1947, when he posted a 9–5 record in his last major league season.

In 33.1 innings spanning four World Series (1941–1943, 1947), Chandler won two games, lost two decisions, and recorded a 1.62 ERA. The Yankees captured world championships in 1941, 1943, and 1947. His two victories in 1943 sparked the Yankees' World Series triumph over the St. Louis Cardinals in five games. Chandler in 1942 was credited with the win as the AL All-Stars defeated the NL 3–1. In 211 career major league games, Chandler won 109 decisions and lost 43 for a .717 percentage. He pitched 1,485 innings, allowed 1,327 hits, and struck out 614 batters, compiling a 2.84 ERA and 26 career shutouts. An exceptional batting pitcher, Chandler collected 110 hits in 548 plate appearances for a .201 average. On July 26, 1940 against the Chicago White Sox (AL), he slugged two HR in one game, including a grand slam off Pete Appleton. Chandler, who later scouted for the Yankees, married Frances Willard on October 19, 1939.

BIBLIOGRAPHY: Spud Chandler file, National Baseball Library, Cooperstown, NY; Donald Honig, *Baseball When the Grass Was Real* (New York, 1975); Mark Gallagher, *The Yankee Encyclopedia*, vol. 3 (Champaign, IL, 1997); Gene Karst and Martin J. Jones, Jr., *Who's Who in Professional Baseball* (New Rochelle, NY, 1973); *The Baseball Encyclopedia*, 10th ed. (New York, 1996); *NYT*, January 11, 1990, p. D-24; Frank Stevens, *Baseball's Forgotten Heroes* (Netcong, NJ, 1984); Rich Westcott, *Diamond Greats* (Westport, CT, 1988).

John L. Evers

CHAPMAN, John Curtis "Jack," "Death to Flying Things" (b. May 8, 1843, Brooklyn, NY; d. June 10, 1916, Brooklyn, NY), player and manager, began playing baseball as an outfielder with amateur clubs, including Putnam in 1860, Enterprise in 1861, the Atlantics of Brooklyn, NY from 1862 to 1866, and the Quaker Cities of Philadelphia, PA in 1867. He rejoined the Atlantics in 1868. The 5-foot 11-inch, 170-pound right-hander played right field on June 14, 1870 when the Atlantics defeated the Cincinnati Red Stockings 8–7 ending a 92-game winning streak. Chapman performed for the Eckford Club of Brooklyn in 1871 and played professionally for only three years with the Brooklyn Atlantics (NA) in 1874, St. Louis Brown Stockings (NA) in 1875, and Louisville, KY Grays (NL) in 1876. His managerial career included Louisville in 1876 and 1877, the Milwaukee Cream Citys (NL) in 1878, Worcester Ruby Legs (NL) in 1882, Detroit Wolverines (NL) in 1883–1884, and Buffalo, NY Bisons (NL) in 1885. He joined the Louisville Colonels (AA) as manager in 1889 and moved with them into the NL in 1892, being fired at mid-season. Chapman piloted minor league teams for many years with assignments in Buffalo, NY, Holyoke, MA, Springfield, MA, Syracuse, NY, Rochester, NY, and Toronto, Canada.

Manager Chapman's major league teams won only 351 contests and lost 502 games. His best season came in 1890, when Louisville won the AA pennant with an 88–44 record. In the 1890 World Series against the Brooklyn Bridegrooms, Louisville won three, lost three, and tied one game. He unfortunately piloted the 1877 Louisville Grays, which had four players banned for fixing games. Louisville appeared headed for the NL pennant before the scandal occurred. Chapman's playing record consisted of a .247 batting average. He acquired his nickname by making outstanding barehanded catches. Chapman, a highly respected man of dignity, provided black star Frank Grant* an opportunity to play for his Buffalo minor league teams from 1886 to 1889. Chapman, who married Mary Dee and had two daughters, Margaret and Elizabeth, became a salesman for a commercial house and lived in Brooklyn, NY.

BIBLIOGRAPHY: John Chapman file, National Baseball Library, Cooperstown, NY; Mike Shatzkin, ed., *The Ballplayers* (New York, 1990); Robert L. Tiemann and Mark Rucker, eds., *Nineteenth Century Stars* (Kansas City, MO, 1989); Geoffrey C. Ward and Ken Burns, *Baseball, an Illustrated History* (New York, 1994); *SL* 67 (June 24, 1916), p. 5.

William E. McMahon

CHAPMAN, Raymond Johnson "Ray" (b. January 15, 1891, Beaver Dam, KY; d. August 17, 1920, New York, NY), player, married Kathleen Daly in October 1919. The 5-foot 10-inch, 170-pound Chapman, the only major leaguer to suffer a fatal injury on the field of play, broke into professional baseball in 1910 with Davenport, IA (3IL). After a stop in Toledo, OH (AA) in 1911, he joined the Cleveland Naps (AL) briefly in 1912. The right-hander took over as the regular shortstop in 1913 and held that position with the Cleveland Naps and Indians until his death. A .278 lifetime batter, Chapman enjoyed perhaps the finest of his nine major league seasons in 1920. With 132 hits, 27 doubles, and an amazing 97 runs scored in only 110 games, he figured to place among the seasonal AL leaders in all three categories. His .303 batting average comprised his highest hitting mark since his rookie year.

A consummate team player, he set an AL record for sacrifice hits (67) in 1917 and led the junior circuit in sacrifices several other times. His defensive skills also abounded, as he always ranked among the league leaders in putouts, assists, and total fielding chances. Many contemporaries considered Chapman major league baseball's fastest runner. He often legged out infield grounders for hits, stretched singles into doubles, and stole 233 bases during his nine-year career. He totaled 1,053 hits and 671 runs scored in 1,050 major league games.

The circumstances of Chapman's death always have overshadowed his accomplishments. Batting against the submarine-ball pitcher Carl Mays* of the New York Yankees on a hot August 1920 afternoon in New York, he failed to avoid an inside pitch. The ball hit Chapman square in the temple, crushing his skull. Despite the heroic efforts of surgeons to save his life, he died the following morning. Understandably, some ill will was directed at Mays, who always maintained that the beaning was an accident. Mays had developed a reputation for throwing at opposing batsmen, leading the AL in that dubious category in 1917 and finishing second in 1918 and 1919. Threats of boycotts and a movement to bar Mays from organized ball permanently never materialized. Most people preferred to memorialize Chapman, who, according to Mays, was a "game and splendid fellow."

BIBLIOGRAPHY: *The Baseball Encyclopedia*, 10th ed. (New York, 1996); Raymond Chapman file, National Baseball Library, Cooperstown, NY; Richard Derby, "Beaning of Chapman Recounted," *BRJ* 13 (1984), pp. 12–13; Brent P. Kelley, *The Case For: Those Overlooked by the Baseball Hall of Fame* (Jefferson, NC, 1992); Franklin Lewis, *The Cleveland Indians* (New York, 1949); Mike Sowell, *The Pitch That Killed* (New York, 1989).

David S. Matz

CHAPMAN, William Benjamin "Ben" (b. December 25, 1908, Nashville, TN; d. July 7, 1993, Hoover, AL), player, manager, and coach, was the son of Harry C. "Tub" Chapman and Effie Chapman. His father, a minor league pitcher, left professional baseball after an arm injury and worked in the Birmingham, AL steel mills. Chapman became an outstanding athlete at Phillips High School, participating in baseball, football, basketball, and track. He attended Purdue University for one year on a football scholarship. The New York Yankees (AL) signed the 6-foot, 190-pound right-hander as a shortstop in 1928 and sent him to Asheville, NC (SAL). After hitting .336 and stealing 30 bases in 1928 there, he batted .336 and pilfered 26 bases the next year as a third baseman for St. Paul, MN (AA). The New York Yankees started Chapman, who batted .316 his rookie year, at third base and second base in 1930. In 1931, he moved to the outfield and combined his hitting ability with a strong arm and speed. New York used him at all three outfield positions before making him the regular center fielder in 1934.

The speedster led the AL in stolen bases in 1931 (61), 1932 (38), and 1933 (27) and tied for the AL lead in 1937 (35). Chapman's 13 triples in 1934 also topped the AL. In the 1932 World Series, he batted .294 to help the Yankees defeat the Chicago Cubs. Chapman, selected for the All-Star team in 1933, 1934, and 1935, was traded to the Washington Senators (AL) in 1936. Subsequently, he played with the Boston Red Sox (AL) in 1937 and 1938, Cleveland Indians (AL) in 1939 and 1940, and Washington Senators (AL) and Chicago White Sox (AL) in 1941. He briefly returned to the major leagues as a pitcher and outfielder with the Brooklyn Dodgers (NL) in 1944 and 1945 and the Philadelphia Phillies (NL) in 1945 and 1946. Chapman batted .302 lifetime and stole 287 career bases, including 14 thefts of home plate. In 1,717 major league games, he garnered 1,958 hits, 407 doubles, 107 triples, 90 HR, 1,144 runs scored, and 977 RBI. During 25 pitching appearances, he won 8 games and lost 6 in 141.1 innings for a 4.39 ERA.

Chapman also managed several clubs, beginning with Richmond, VA (PiL), in 1942 and 1944. He piloted the Philadelphia Phillies (NL) to four second-division finishes from 1945 to 1948 and a 197–277 (.416) overall mark. Chapman's other managerial assignments included Gadsden, AL (SEL) in 1949, Danville, VA (CrL) in 1950, Tampa, FL (FIL) in 1951 and 1953, and Toronto, Canada (IL) in late 1953. Subsequently, he sold insurance in Alabama. Chapman, who served as a coach with the Cincinnati Reds (NL) in 1952, married Ola Sanford on October 7, 1935 and had one son, William, Jr.

BIBLIOGRAPHY: Don Albaugh, "Ben Chapman: Jackie Robinson's Worst Nightmare," *SCD* 24 (September 26, 1997), pp. 146–147; Thomas Aylesworth and Benton Minks, *The Encyclopedia of Baseball Managers* (New York, 1990); Brooklyn *Eagle*, June 14, 1931; Ben Chapman file, National Baseball Library, Cooperstown, NY; Mark Gallagher, *Fifty Years of Yankee All Stars* (New York, 1984); Mark Gallagher, *The Yankee Encyclopedia*, vol. 3 (Champaign, IL, 1997); Frederick G. Lieb and Stan Baumgartner, *The Philadelphia Phillies* (New York, 1953); Rich Westcott and Frank Bilovsky, *The New Phillies Encyclopedia* (Philadelphia, PA, 1993); Craig Carter, ed., *TSN Daguerreotypes*, 8th ed. (St. Louis, MO, 1990); *NYT*, 1930–1948; New York *World Telegram*, 1928–1948; *NYT*, July 8, 1993, p. D-19; Murray Palmer, *Branch Rickey* (New York, 1982); *The Baseball Encyclopedia*, 10th ed. (New York, 1996); Jackie Robinson, *I Never Had It Made* (Greenwich, CT, 1972); St. Louis *Star*, July 29, 1931; Jules Tygiel, *Baseball's Great Experiment* (New York, 1983).

Robert J. Brown

CHARLESTON, Oscar McKinley "The Black Ruth" (b. October 12, 1896, Indianapolis, IN; d. October 6, 1954, Philadelphia, PA), player and manager, ranked among the greatest Negro baseball players and was the son of jockey and construction worker Tom Charleston and Mary (Jeannette) Charleston. After attending school in Indianapolis until his sophomore year, he enlisted in the U.S. Army at age 15 and was shipped to the Philippines. He played his first baseball there with the Negro 24th Infantry and by 1914 became the only black player in the MnL. In 1915 the 6-foot 1-inch, 180-pound Charleston returned to Indianapolis and starred immediately as a center fielder for the ABCs, leading them to a championship the following year.

His incredible speed, including clocking 23 seconds in the 220 yard dash with the Army track team, enabled him to play shallow, just behind second base. He caught short liners and bloop flies there, chased down long flies, and demonstrated a powerful throwing arm. According to Elwood "Bingo" De Moss,* "Oscar was the only player I've ever seen who could turn twice while chasing a fly and then take it over his shoulder. He had an uncanny knowledge of judging fly balls." His unparalleled speed and ability to detect flaws in a pitcher's motion became obvious assets on the basepaths. Above all, the "Black Babe Ruth" demonstrated natural fastball hitting ability by hitting to every part of the ballpark with enormous power. Hitting and speed, coupled with a swinging bunt, made Charleston a consistent offensive threat.

He joined Rube Foster's* Chicago American Giants as an outfielder in 1919, but returned to the ABCs (NNL) two years later. In 1921, the left-handed slugger batted .434, stole 34 bases, and led the NNL in doubles, triples, and HR. The next season, he hit .370 and again paced the NNL in HR. During the 1920s, he also played with the St. Louis Giants, Harrisburg, PA Hilldales (ECL), and Philadelphia Hilldales (ANL). With Harrisburg, he led the ECL in batting in 1924 and 1925 and in doubles and HR the latter year. After the ECL broke up, he led the ANL in 1928 by batting .363 for Philadelphia. In 1930, he joined Cum Posey's* great Homestead, PA Grays, featuring "Double Duty" Radcliffe,* Ted Page,* Smoky Joe Williams,* and Josh Gibson.* With other Grays stars, he jumped to the Pittsburgh Crawfords (NNL) in 1932. Owner Gus Greenlee* outbid Posey for Charleston's services and enabled him to play at Greenlee Field, the nation's only black-owned stadium. By this time, Charleston had moved from outfield to first base. His great speed diminished, but he became player–manager of his teams from the late 1920s onward. Charleston starred with the Crawfords until 1936, batting .280 and .372 his first two seasons although well past his prime as a player. Through 1954 he managed various teams, including the Toledo, OH Crawfords, Indianapolis Crawfords, and Philadelphia Stars. In 1954 Charleston led the Indianapolis Clowns to a Negro World Championship, his first as a manager.

Charleston's legendary feats included a lifetime .376 league batting average, a .326 mark against white major leaguers, and a .361 average for nine CUWL seasons. As a CUWL rookie, he averaged .405. He reputedly hit four HR in a single exhibition game against the St. Louis Cardinals in 1921 and occasionally played all nine positions in a game to display his versatility. From 1933 to 1935, he started the first three Negro All-Star games. When Branch Rickey* searched for an appropriate black player to sign with the Brooklyn Dodgers (NL), Charleston scouted the Negro leagues for him. Charleston, who died of a heart attack, was survived by his wife Jane; he had no children. In 1976, Charleston was elected to the National Baseball Hall of Fame as perhaps the greatest all-around player in Negro League history.

BIBLIOGRAPHY: James Bankes, *The Pittsburgh Crawfords* (Dubuque, IA, 1991); Chicago *Defender*, October 23, 1954; Oscar Charleston file, National Baseball Library, Cooperstown, NY; David L. Porter, ed., *African-American Sports Greats* (Westport, CT, 1995); John Holway, *Voices from the Great Black Baseball Leagues* (New York, 1975); John B. Holway, *Blackball Stars* (Westport, CT, 1988); Robert W. Peterson, *Only the Ball Was White* (Englewood Cliffs, NJ, 1970); Pittsburgh *Courier*, October 16, 1954; James A. Riley, *The All-Time All-Stars of Black Baseball* (Cocoa, FL, 1983); James A. Riley, *The Biographical Encyclopedia of the Negro Baseball Leagues* (New York, 1994).

Gerald E. Brennan

CHASE, Harold Homer "Hal," "Prince Hal" (b. February 13, 1883, Los Gatos, CA; d. May 18, 1947, Colusa, CA), player and manager, generally was rated the greatest fielding first baseman in major league history. Chase starred for Santa Clara University in 1903 and for Los Angeles, CA (PCL) in 1904 before the New York Highlanders (AL) purchased his contract for a reported $2,700.

Chase's career with the Highlanders (predecessor of the Yankees) from 1905 to 1913 was marked by his brilliant fielding and controversial behavior. Nicknamed "Prince Hal" by fans, he ranged far from first base to cut off grounders and scoop up bunt hits and developed into a respectable batter excelling at the hit-and-run play. His reputation for discontentment and dishonesty, however, also grew. He defied organized baseball by playing winter ball in the outlawed CaL under a false name for awhile. Amid rumors questioning his honesty, he left New York in midseason 1908 to play in California. Despite new accusations by Chase's manager, George Stallings,* that he tried to throw a game, New York Highlanders owner Frank Farrell exonerated him and appointed him playing manager late in the 1910 season. He managed the New York Highlanders to a sixth-place finish in 1911 with 76 wins and 76 losses.

Chase's stardom and fan appeal may have shielded him from punishment by baseball authorities. When manager Frank Chance* reported Chase for throwing baseball games in 1913, New York traded the first baseman in June to the Chicago White Sox (AL). Unhappy there after 58 games in 1914, he jumped to the Buffalo Buffeds (FL) for the 1914 and 1915 campaigns and led the FL with 17 HR in 1915. After the FL collapsed, Chase played with the Cincinnati Reds from 1916 to 1918 and led the NL with a .339 batting average and 184 hits in 1916. Manager Christy Mathewson* suspended him in 1918 for crookedness, when an investigation produced 14 allegations of misconduct. Chase escaped punishment and was traded to the New York Giants (NL) in February 1919, his last major league season. In 1,919 games, he made 2,158 hits, 322 doubles, 124 triples, 57 HR, 980 runs, 941 RBI, 363 stolen bases, and .291 batting and .391 slugging averages.

The most damaging evidence against Chase surfaced in 1920. A teammate from the 1918 Cincinnati Reds testified that he and Chase bribed a Cincinnati pitcher and gambled $500 on the outcome. The fix failed, but Chase's check survived to record his involvement. Chase was also indicted in the Chicago Black Sox scandal, but avoided testifying and later privately admitted to having prior knowledge of the fixed World Series of 1919. Chase was accused of attempted bribery of a PCL player in 1920 and was barred from that and three other California leagues. Chase, whose private life was marred by two divorces, apparently spent his remaining years as player and manager for teams in Arizona and Mexico. Although portrayed by one historian as the "archetype of all crooked ball players" and by an earlier sportswriter as the player with a "corkscrew brain," Chase died without ever admitting any wrongdoing.

BIBLIOGRAPHY: Hal Chase file, National Baseball Hall of Fame, Cooperstown, NY; Dan Gutman, *Baseball Babylon* (New York, 1992); Daniel E. Ginsburg, *The Fix Is In* (Jefferson, NC, 1995); Eliot Asinof, *Eight Men Out* (New York, 1963); Mark Gallagher, *The Yankee Encyclopedia*, vol. 3 (Champaign, IL, 1997); Robert C. Hoie, "The Hal Chase Case," *BHR* (1981), pp. 34–41; Martin D. Kohout, "The Prince of Darkness," *TNP* 11 (1992), pp. 21–22; Frederick G. Lieb, *Baseball as I Have Known It* (New York, 1977); *NYT*, 1905–1920, May 19, 1947; Richard Scheinin, *Field of Screams* (New York, 1994); Harold Seymour, *Baseball: The Golden Age* (New York, 1971).

Joseph E. King

CHENEY, Laurance Russell "Larry" (b. May 2, 1886, Belleville, KS; d. January 6, 1969, Daytona Beach, FL), player, was a lanky, 6-foot 1½-inch, 185-pound right-handed spitball pitcher who broke into the major leagues with the Chicago Cubs (NL) in 1911 with a 1–0 record. His first full major league season in 1912 proved spectacular with 28 complete games and a 26–10 record. He led the NL in victories and complete games and hit a career high .226, including his only major league HR.

Cheney, who married Paula Behrmann, continued to pitch brilliantly the next two seasons with 21–14 and 20–18 for third- and fourth-place teams and led the NL in appearances with 54 and 50 respectively. His most famous game during this span occurred on September 14, 1913, when he allowed 14 hits and still shut out the New York Giants 7–0. No other major league pitcher ever allowed that many hits in a shutout. The Chicago Cubs used him as a starter and reliever in 1913, with his 11 saves leading the NL. Wildness plagued him in 1914, as shown by his NL-leading 140 walks. In two other seasons, he also walked more than 100 batters.

When Cheney dropped to an 8–9 record in 1915, the Chicago Cubs traded him to the Brooklyn Robins (NL). The spitballer enjoyed another good season in 1916, when he helped the Robins win the NL pennant with his 18–12 record, 15 complete games, and 1.92 ERA. He appeared in one game in the 1916 World Series against the Boston Red Sox. He never recaptured his earlier success, dropping to 11–13 in 1918 and 3–10 with the Robins, Boston Braves (NL), and Philadelphia Phillies (NL) in 1919. His lifetime record included 116 wins, 100 losses, and a 2.70 ERA. Besides completing 132 of 313 games, he walked 733 batters and struck out 926.

BIBLIOGRAPHY: Art Ahrens and Eddie Gold, *Day by Day in Chicago Cubs History* (West Point, NY, 1982); Warren Brown, *The Chicago Cubs* (New York, 1946); Frank Graham, *The Brooklyn Dodgers* (New York, 1945); Eddie Gold and Art Ahrens, *The Golden Era Cubs, 1876–1940* (Chicago, IL, 1985); *The Baseball Encyclopedia*, 10th ed. (New York, 1996); Warren Wilbert and William Hageman, *Chicago Cubs: Seasons at the Summit* (Champaign, IL, 1997).

Duane A. Smith

CHESBRO, John Dwight "Jack," "Happy Jack" (b. June 5, 1874, North Adams, MA; d. November 6 1931, Conway, MA), player and coach, became one of the few pitchers to lead both major leagues in won–lost percentage with .677 and .824 for the Pittsburgh Pirates (NL) in 1901 and 1902 and .774 for the New York Highlanders (AL) in 1904. The 5-foot 9-inch, 180-pound right-hander exhibited great endurance in his most outstanding season (1904). Chesbro's 41 victories remain the modern era and AL record, while his 51 starts and 48 complete games rank second, and his 454.2 innings stands third. As a youth, Chesbro played with the Houghtonville, MA Nine and several other western Massachusetts sandlot teams. In 1894, he began working for the state mental hospital in Middletown, NY and was nicknamed "Happy Jack" because of his pleasant disposition. Although working with patients, he maintained principal interest in the hospital baseball team and learned about pitching from coach Pat McGreehy.

Chesbro began his minor league career in 1895 with Albany, NY (NYSL). After the Albany club disbanded, he joined Johnstown, NY (NYSL) and compiled a 7–10 combined season record. After the NYSL folded on July 6, 1895, he then logged a 3–0 mark for Springfield, MA (EL). In 1896, he married Mabel Shuttleworth and played for Roanoke, VA (VL) until it failed on August 20. Chesbro spent the rest of 1896 as a semipro in Cooperstown, NY, becoming perhaps the only National Baseball Hall-of-Famer to pitch there regularly. He performed for Richmond, VA (AtL) in 1897 and 1898 and boasted a 17–4 mark through July 1899, when he was sold to the Pittsburgh Pirates (NL) for $1,500. After appearing in 19 games for Pittsburgh in 1899, he was involved in one of the most complex deals ever made. The Louisville Colonels (NL) were about to be abolished and conducted a dispersal sale, in which 14 players, including Honus Wagner,* Deacon Phillippe,* Rube Waddell,* and Fred Clarke,* moved to Pittsburgh for Chesbro and five others. The players traded to Louisville then rejoined Pittsburgh when the two clubs merged and participated on the second-place Pirates team in 1900.

Chesbro enjoyed his first 20-win season and led the NL with a .677 won–

lost percentage as the Pirates captured their initial NL pennant in 1901. The next season, Chesbro led the Pirates to another pennant with an NL-leading 28 victories and 8 shutouts (including three consecutive shutouts twice). Besides losing only 6 decisions, Chesbro compiled a 12-game winning streak from May 16 to July 24. During the 1902 season, he began throwing his famous spitball for Pirates manager–outfielder Clarke. Chesbro seized an opportunity to earn more money by jumping with pitcher Jesse Tannehill* to manager Clark Griffith's* New York Highlanders for their first AL season in 1903. Chesbro logged a 21–15 mark for the fourth-place Highlanders, while the Pirates won their third straight NL pennant and lost their first World Series.

Chesbro's 1904 season was the finest any pitcher has enjoyed in the twentieth century, as he completed each of his first 30 starts and 48 of 51 overall. On August 10, he was relieved for the first time in a 5–1 loss to the Chicago White Sox. Chicago also knocked him out again on September 30 in three innings. Counting four relief appearances, Chesbro's innings totaled a remarkable 454.2. Besides striking out 239 batters and allowing only 338 hits, Chesbro recorded a 14-game winning streak from May 14 through July 4. Unfortunately, this great season ended on an unhappy note for Chesbro and the New York team. Chesbro won his 41st game on Friday, October 7, putting New York one-half game ahead of Jimmy Collins'* Boston Red Sox. Since Saturday's doubleheader was moved to Boston to avoid a conflict with a Columbia University football game, manager Griffith wanted Chesbro to stay in New York and rest for the season's final games on Monday, October 10. Owner Frank Farrell, however, persuaded Chesbro to journey to Boston, where he was knocked out for only the third time in a 13–2 loss. The Boston Red Sox also won the second game, 1–0, putting New York 1½ games behind. Chesbro started the first game in New York on October 10 against Boston's Bill Dinneen.* Both pitchers were deadlocked 2–2 when Boston's Lou Criger reached base. With two men out and Criger on third base, Chesbro worked the count to no balls and two strikes on Fred Parent. Chesbro's next pitch, a powerful spitball, was a wild pitch and allowed Criger to score the winning run. Many writers claimed that catcher Jack Kleinow should have been charged with the passed ball, but the damage was done. Although New York won the second game 1–0, Boston captured the AL pennant.

Chesbro pitched 1,407 innings from 1903 through 1906, but an ankle injury in 1907 slowed him considerably. He lost four games in nine appearances in 1909, was sold to Boston for the waiver price, and lost his only decision there, falling short of 200 career victories. After leaving major league baseball, he built a chicken farm in Conway, MA, coached baseball at Amherst College, and played semipro baseball. In 1912, he launched an unsuccessful comeback with the New York Highlanders and then could not even make his town team. At Conway, he operated a sawmill and lumber yard and raised chickens. Griffith persuaded him to join the Washington Senators (AL) as a coach in 1924, but financial problems caused his release on Memorial Day. Chesbro was named to the National Baseball Hall of Fame in 1946 with 198 career victories. In 392 major league games, he lost only 132 games, completed 260 of 332 starts, struck out 1,265 and walked only 690 batters in 2,896.2 innings, hurled 35 shutouts, and compiled a 2.68 ERA. Chesbro led his league three times in winning percentage; twice in wins, appearances, and games started; and once each in complete games, innings, and shutouts.

BIBLIOGRAPHY: Martin Appel and Bert Goldblatt, *Baseball's Best* (New York, 1977); John Chesbro file, National Baseball Library, Cooperstown, NY; Harry Grayson, *They Played the Game* (New York, 1945); Lowell Reidenbaugh, *Baseball's Hall of Fame-Cooperstown* (New York, 1993); Mark Gallagher, *The Yankee Encyclopedia*, vol. 3 (Champaign, IL, 1997); Frank Graham, *The New York Yankees* (New York, 1943).

David B. Merrell

CHILDS, Clarence Algernon "Cupid," "Paca" (b. August 14, 1867, Calvert County, MD; d. November 8, 1912, Baltimore, MD), player, came from a large family in the rural Chesapeake backwaters. He entered professional baseball as a teenager in the NCL and played with Petersburg, VA (VL) in 1886 and Shamokin, PA (CPL) in 1887. In 1888 Childs, who threw right-handed but batted from the left side, made his major league debut as a second baseman in two games for the Philadelphia Quakers (NL). He finished the 1888 season with Kalamazoo, MI (TSL) and the following year played for the Syracuse, NY Stars (IL).

In 1890 Childs remained in Syracuse, which became a major league franchise in the wobbly AA. After hitting .345 and leading the AA with 33 doubles, he joined the Cleveland Spiders (NL) the next year. In eight seasons with Cleveland (1891–1898), he built a reputation as a durable second baseman and a consistent hitter and averaged nearly .320 at the plate in that span. In 1892, he led all second sackers with a .938 fielding percentage and scored an NL-leading 136 runs. At Cleveland, he averaged over 750 chances at second base each season and in 1896 led the NL with 369 putouts and 496 assists.

Before the 1899 season, Cleveland owners Frank Robison and Stanley Robison transferred the Spiders' best players to the St. Louis Browns (NL), which they had recently acquired in auction. Consequently, Childs, player–manager Patsy Tebeau,* Cy Young,* Bobby Wallace,* and five other Cleveland players were sent to St. Louis. After playing there one season, Childs joined the Chicago Orphans (NL) and in 1900 again led the NL with 759 total chances at second base. He was released by Chicago in early July 1901 and finished the season with Toledo, OH (WA). He divided the following season between Jersey City, NJ (EL) and Syracuse, NY (NYSL), spent 1903 with Montgomery, AL (SA), and closed his career with Scranton, PA (NYSL) in 1904.

Upon leaving pro baseball, Childs returned to Baltimore and became moderately well-to-do in the real estate business. A series of unsuccessful deals, however, brought him a sizeable financial loss, after which he became a local coalyard operator. Following a lengthy illness, he was hospitalized in October 1912 and died early the next month. Former teammates contributed liberally to a fund established to defray his medical expenses and provided his wife and 8-year-old daughter a modest sum on which to live.

At the peak of his career in the mid–1890s, the stocky 5-foot 8-inch, 185-pound infielder—nicknamed "Paca" and "Cupid"—was considered the NL's quickest second baseman and one of its heaviest hitters. At Cleveland, Childs and longtime shortstop Eddie McKean* formed one of the game's most respected keystone combinations. He appeared in 1,456 major league games, playing all but one at second base. In his major league career, Childs collected 1,720, hits, scored 1,214 runs, and posted a .306 batting average.

BIBLIOGRAPHY: Clarence Childs file, National Baseball Library, Cooperstown, NY; Baltimore *Sun*, November 9, 1912; Chicago *Daily Tribune*, November 9, 1912; Craig Carter, ed., *TSN Daguerreotypes*, 8th ed. (St. Louis, MO, 1990); J. Thomas Hetrick, *Misfits!* (Jefferson, NC, 1991); Frederick Ivor-Campbell et al., eds., *Baseball's First Stars* (Cleveland, OH, 1996); John Phillips, *The Spiders—Who Was Who* (Cabin John, MD, 1991); *The Baseball Encyclopedia*, 10th ed. (New York, 1996); David Quentin Voigt, *American Baseball*, vol. 1 (Norman, OK, 1966).

Raymond D. Kush

CHYLAK, Nestor, Jr. "Nunny" (b. May 11, 1922, Peckville, PA; d. February 17, 1982, Dunmore, PA), umpire and executive, was one of four children born to Nestor Chylak, the owner of a bar-restaurant, and Melanie "Nellie" (Shipskie) Chylak, a department store clerk. The Greek Catholic of Ukran-ian descent grew up in Olyphant, PA, graduated from high school in 1940, and studied engineering at Rutgers University in 1941–1942 and St. Thomas University (now the University of Scranton) in 1946–1947. He served in the infantry with the Rangers during World War II from 1942 to 1946. He was wounded seriously and nearly blinded during the Battle of the Bulge, re-ceiving the Silver Star and the Purple Heart. As a civil engineer with the Pennsylvania State Highway Department, Chylak officiated local college baseball and basketball games. He never attended an umpire school, but moved rapidly through the minor leagues as an umpire in the PoL (Class D), 1947, CAL (Class C), 1948, NEL (Class B), 1949, EL (Class A), 1950–1951, and IL (Class AAA), 1952–1953.

Chylak umpired in the AL from 1954 to 1978, working six All-Star games (1957, 1960—both games, 1964, 1973, 1978), 15 games in three AL Cham-pionship Series (1969, 1972, 1973), and 31 games in five World Series (1957, 1960, 1966, 1971, 1977). As umpire-in-chief, he forfeited a game to the

Texas Rangers when disorderly Cleveland Indians fans stormed the field during the ninth inning of "Beer Night" in Cleveland, OH on June 14, 1974. The 6-foot, 200-pound Chylak, a model umpire, combined firm discipline with tact and a sense of humor. Peers and sportswriters generally regarded Chylak as the best AL umpire of his generation. Chylak received in 1972 the coveted Umpire of the Year Award from the AL Somers Umpire School. On retiring in 1978 after suffering a mild stroke, he served as assistant supervisor of AL umpires from 1979 through 1981. Chylak died of an apparent heart attack. AL president Lee MacPhail* accurately stated: "He was considered an outstanding teacher and certainly one of the finest umpires in major league baseball in modern times. We are sure he will be a candidate for eventual Hall of Fame recognition."

Chylak, who married Sue Maria Shemet in 1956 and had two sons, Robert and William, was an avid photographer and popular banquet speaker. In 1985, the Pennsylvania Sports Hall of Fame inducted him posthumously. The Veterans Committee elected him to the National Baseball Hall of Fame in 1999.

BIBLIOGRAPHY: Nestor Chylak file, National Baseball Library, Cooperstown, NY; Nestor Chylak file, *TSN* Archives, St. Louis, MO; Sue Chylak, letters to Larry R. Gerlach, January 4, 9, 1989; Gene Karst and Martin J. Jones, Jr., *Who's Who in Professional Baseball* (New Rochelle, NY, 1973); *Scrantonian* (PA), February 21, 1982; *TSN Baseball Register*, 1954–1958, 1968–1978.

Larry R. Gerlach

CICOTTE, Edward Victor "Eddie" (b. June 19, 1884, Springwells, MI; d. May 5, 1969, Detroit, MI), player, figured prominently in baseball's greatest scandal by helping throw the 1919 World Series to the Cincinnati Reds. Cicotte began a three-year minor league pitching apprenticeship in 1905. From the Detroit area, he spent a brief stint in 1905 with the Detroit Tigers (AL). Finding his size unimpressive, Detroit let Atlanta, GA (SAL) have him. After pitching well there, Cicotte spent 1906 with Des Moines, IA (WL) and 1907 with Lincoln, NE (WL) and enjoyed very successful seasons.

Cicotte reached the major leagues in 1908 and performed reasonably well for four and one-half years with the Boston Red Sox (AL). Sold in July 1912 to the Chicago White Sox (AL), he gradually advanced to great success over the next eight and one-half seasons. Had he not been expelled from baseball by Commissioner Kenesaw Mountain Landis* after the 1920 season, Cicotte surely would have been selected to the National Baseball Hall of Fame. A contemporary of outstanding pitchers Grover Cleveland Alexander* and Walter Johnson,* Cicotte led AL hurlers twice in winning percentage, innings pitched and total wins, and once in ERA. He won 28 games in 1917 and 29 games in a 140-game schedule in 1919, helping the White Sox garner two AL pennants and one world championship. During his major league career, he won 208 games, lost only 149 times, struck out 1,374 batters in 3,223 innings, and compiled an impressive 2.37 ERA.

A pitching artist, the 5-foot 9-inch, 175-pound Cicotte finessed hitters via the first complete mastery of the knuckleball and through his superb control. Reputedly a trick-pitch magician, he utilized the spitball and its spinoffs, the shine, and emery balls. Babe Ruth,* the game's premier slugger, never slammed a HR off him, and commented, "That froggie can pitch!"

Cicotte ruined an otherwise admirable career by joining seven other "Black" Sox to lose the 1919 World Series deliberately. In return for pitching ineptly in two games, he received $10,000 from gamblers. His motives included worry over a large, unpaid farm mortgage and resentment toward the team's owner, Charles A. Comiskey.* In 1918 Comiskey paid Cicotte only $7,000, a much lower salary than was paid to some pitchers with less skill. After public disclosure of the scandal in 1920, Cicotte expressed remorse for his deed. Thereafter, Cicotte lived inconspicuously in the Detroit area, worked many years for the Ford Motor Company, and also enjoyed modest success as a strawberry grower. His use of a pseudonym protected his wife and three children from adverse publicity.

BIBLIOGRAPHY: Edward Cicotte file, National Baseball Library, Cooperstown, NY; Warren Brown, *The Chicago White Sox* (New York, 1952); Eliot Asinof, *Eight Men Out* (New York, 1963); Lowell L. Blaisdell, "Cicotte the Ruth Slayer," *BRJ* 20 (1991), p. 66; Dan Gutman, *Baseball Babylon* (New York, 1992); Daniel E. Ginsburg, *The Fix Is In* (Jefferson, NC, 1995); Frederick G. Lieb, *Baseball as I Have Known It* (New York, 1977); Victor Luhrs, *The Great Baseball Mystery* (New York, 1966); *NYT*, May 9, 1969; *TSN*, May 24, 1969; Bill Veeck, *The Hustler's Handbook* (New York, 1965).
                                                                    Lowell L. Blaisdell

CLARK, Jack Anthony (b. November 10, 1955, New Brighton, PA), player, is the son of Ralph C. Clark and Jennie B. (Tooch) Clark. In 1958 the Clarks moved to Covina, CA, a Los Angeles suburb. Clark grew up rooting for the San Francisco Giants (NL) and idolizing Juan Marichal,* Gaylord Perry,* Willie Mays,* and Roberto Clemente.* He did not attend many Los Angeles Dodger (NL) games, but watched the San Francisco Giants on television. In June 1973, the San Francisco Giants drafted Clark out of Gladstone High School, Azusa, CA, as a pitcher. After Clark pitched five games at Great Falls, MT (PrL), the Giants converted the right-hander to an outfielder and third baseman. Clark responded with a .321 batting average. He batted over .300 in 1974 and 1975 at Fresno, CA (CaL) and Lafayette, LA (TL), but led both leagues in errors at third base. Clark shifted to the outfield in 1976 and batted .323 to earn a second straight September recall to the San Francisco Giants.

In 1977, Clark won the right field job for the San Francisco Giants and hit .252 in 136 games. The following season, the 6-foot 3-inch, 200-pound Clark blossomed offensively with a .306 batting average, 25 HR, and 98 RBI and was heralded by many sportswriters as "baseball's next superstar." Clark predicted that eventually he would bat .400, but his outspokenness caused some people to regard him as arrogant. Although never reaching superstar status with the Giants, he averaged 23 HR per season from 1978 to 1983, drove in 103 runs in 1982, and set the Giants club record with a 26-game hitting streak in 1978. In 1984, he batted .320 in 57 games before surgery for a knee injury sidelined him the rest of the season. Clark, who lost favor in San Francisco by complaining about a losing team attitude, was traded to the St. Louis Cardinals (NL) in February 1985 for four players.

Clark enjoyed his greatest impact as a St. Louis Cardinal from 1985 to 1987 after being moved to first base. In 1985, Clark represented the Cardinals' only power threat with 22 HR. Manager Whitey Herzog* considered Clark "one of the those guys you build your lineup around." Clark blasted one of the most memorable HR in NL Championship Series history, as his two-out, ninth-inning, three-run HR against the Los Angeles Dodgers in the sixth game gave the Cardinals the 1985 NL pennant. Clark experienced his finest season in 1987, achieving career highs of 35 HR, 106 RBI, and 93 runs while leading the NL with a .461 on-base percentage, .597 slugging percentage, and 136 walks. On September 9, 1987, he tore ligaments in his right ankle. Clark pinch-hit once in the 1987 NL Championship Series against the San Francisco Giants and missed the entire World Series against the Minnesota Twins.

Clark left the St. Louis Cardinals in January 1988 to sign a $3 million, two-year contract with the New York Yankees (AL). He slugged 27 HR and drove in 93 runs as the Yankees' DH in 1988, but was sent to the San Diego Padres (NL) in a five-player deal that October. With San Diego, Clark continued to pound HR and collect walks. From 1987 to 1990, he averaged 121 walks per season. He recorded his 1,000th career RBI during the first week of the 1990 campaign. In December 1990, Clark joined the Boston Red Sox (AL) as a free agent. Clark in 1991 joined Bobby Bonds* as the only players to hit 25 HR in a season with five different clubs. His major league career ended with the Boston Red Sox in 1992. In 18 major league seasons, Clark batted .267 with 1,826 hits, 332 doubles, 340 HR, and 1,180 RBI in 1,994 games. Clark and his wife, Tammy, have two daughters, Danika and Rebekah, and one son, Anthony.

BIBLIOGRAPHY: John Benson et al., *Baseball's Top 100* (Wilton, CT, 1997); Jack Clark, "The Game I'll Never Forget," *BD* 47 (July 1989), pp. 57–58; Whitey Herzog and Kevin Horrigan, *White Rat* (New York, 1987); Robert E. Kelly, *Baseball's Best* (Jefferson, NC, 1988); Kevin Kernan, "A New Start—Again for Jack Clark," *BD* 47 (March 1989), pp. 62–64; B. Nightengale, "Jack Clark," *Sport* 82 (April 1991), pp. 82–84; Bob Oates, "Jack Clark: A Giant with a Big Future," *BD* 38 (May 1979), pp. 32–34; Rob Rains, *The St. Louis Cardinals* (New York, 1992); Rick Reilly, "This Is the House That Jack Built," *SI* 75 (July 22, 1991), pp. 60–65; Ralph Wiley, "Jack the Ripper," *SI* 67 (July 20, 1987), pp. 38–41; Jack Clark file, National Baseball

Library, Cooperstown, NY; Bob Broeg and Jerry Vickery, *St. Louis Cardinals Encyclopedia* (Grand Rapids, MI, 1998); *San Diego Padres 1990 Media Guide*; Mike Shatzkin, ed., *The Ballplayers* (New York, 1990); Ozzie Smith and Rob Rains, *Wizard* (Chicago, IL, 1988); W. Ladson, "Riches to Rags," *Sport* 85 (January 1994), pp. 34–37; Jill Lieber, "Jack Clark," *SI* 81 (August 1, 1994), pp. 46–47.

Frank J. Olmsted

CLARK, William Nuschler, Jr. "Will," "The Thrill" (b. March 13, 1964, New Orleans, LA), player, is the son of William Clark, Sr., sales representative for a pest control company, and Letty Clark and made High School Baseball All-America at Jesuit High School in New Orleans, where he broke Rusty Staub's* records. After graduation from high school, he spent three years at Mississippi State University (SEC) and was named a baseball All-America during his sophomore year in 1984. He was chosen for the 1984 U.S. Olympic team, which won a silver medal at the Los Angeles, CA Summer Games. Clark won the Golden Spikes Award as the nation's best collegiate player in 1985. The San Francisco Giants (NL) selected Clark as a first-round draft choice in 1985. Clark played at Fresno, CA (CaL), where he batted .309 with 10 HR and 48 RBI.

In 1986, Clark emerged as the San Francisco Giants first baseman. On opening day, the 6-foot, 190-pound left-handed hitter became the 53rd player to homer in his first major league at bat when he connected on a pitch thrown by Nolan Ryan* of the Houston Astros at the Houston Astrodome. In his rookie season, he hit .287, produced 41 RBI, and slugged 11 HR in only 111 games. Any notions of a sophomore jinx in 1987 were dispelled when his statistics improved to a .308 batting average, 91 RBI, 35 HR, and a .580 slugging average. Since then, he has become one of the game's best players. Known for his consistency and competitiveness, he studies videotapes of his hitting to find ways of improving. Clark has led the NL in RBI (109) in 1988, bases on balls (100) in 1988, runs scored (104) in 1989, and slugging percentage (.536) in 1991. In 1991, his 303 total bases tied for the NL lead. Starting in 1988, he appeared on five consecutive NL All-Star teams. Although not possessing great range, he furnishes fine defensive play and led NL first basemen in double plays in 1987 (130), 1988 (126), 1990 (118), 1991 (115), and 1992 (130). The sure-handed Clark also topped all others at his position in total chances in 1988 (1,608), 1989 (1,566), and 1990 (1,587). In 1991, he paced all NL first basemen with a .997 fielding percentage and won his first Gold Glove Award.

Clark performed in the 1987 and 1989 NL Championship Series, batting a combined .489 average and earning the 1989 NL Championship Series MVP Award. In the first game, he belted two HR, including a grand slam, and drove in a record six RBI. He also established records for a five-game series with 13 hits, six long hits, eight runs scored, 24 total bases, .650 batting average, and a 1.200 slugging average. Clark played four games in his only

World Series appearance in 1989, hitting .250 against the Oakland A's. In December 1993, the Texas Rangers (AL) signed Clark as a free agent. During the strike shortened 1994 season, he batted .329 with 80 RBI and made the AL All-Star team. He batted .302 with 16 HR and 92 RBI in 1995 and .326 with 51 RBI in 1997. New York Yankees pitchers held him to only two hits in the 1996 AL Division Series. His .305 batting average, 23 HR, and 102 RBI helped Texas win the AL West in 1998, but New York Yankees pitchers held him to one hit in the AL Division Series. In December 1998, the Baltimore Orioles (AL) signed him to an $11 million, two-year contract. Through 1999, Clark amassed a career .302 batting average with 410 doubles, 263 HR, 1,135 RBI, and a .493 slugging average. In 1999, he was named to the USA Baseball All-Time Team. He remains single and resides in South Lake, TX. Clark and Troy Aikman own the Fog City Diner in Dallas, TX.

BIBLIOGRAPHY: William Clark file, National Baseball Library, Cooperstown, NY; T. De Marco, "Will to Win," *Sport* 85 (May 1994), pp. 38–41; Rom Fimrite, "The Bay Area Bombers," *SI* 68 (April 4, 1988), pp. 44–49; *1993 San Francisco Giants Media Guide*; Paul Post, "Clark's Career Led off with a Bang," *SCD* 24 (February 28, 1997), pp. 146–147; Ray Ratto, "The Thrill of It All," *Sport* 81 (July 1990), pp. 24–28; E. M. Swift, "Will Power," *SI* 72 (May 28, 1990), pp. 74–86; Casey Tefertiller, "Clark Figures to Be a Giant Force in the 90's," *Baseball America's Baseball 90*, pp. 126–127; John Thorn et al., eds., *Total Baseball*, 5th ed. (New York, 1997); *TSN Official Baseball Register*, 1998.

Robert J. Brown

CLARK, William Watson "Watty," "Lefty," "Needle" (b. May 16, 1902, St. Joseph, LA; d. March 4, 1972, Clearwater, FL), player, manager, and executive, was the son of James R. Clark and Laura Clark and was of Scotch-Irish ancestry. The 6-foot ½-inch, 175-pound left-handed Clark grew up in Louisiana and attended Mississippi College in Clinton, MS, where he earned a B.A. degree in 1924. He played college football and started his baseball career as a freshman, although he had not played baseball before. Clark won 36 games, lost four, and tied two during his four college seasons. He pitched batting practice for the Cleveland Indians (AL) as a senior and then finished 1–3 for the Indians in 12 games.

Clark also pitched for Peoria, IL (3IL) for the rest of the 1924 season and for New Orleans, LA (SA) in 1925 and Terre Haute, IN (3IL) in 1925 and 1926. After posting a 19–9 record at Terre Haute in 1926, he was sold for $3,000 to the Brooklyn Robins (NL) and compiled a 7–2 mark in 27 appearances in 1927. Clark married Rebekah Nelson of Clearwater, FL on May 18, 1928 during his second full major league season. He pitched 12 major league seasons and remained with the Brooklyn Robins/Dodgers until June 1933, when he and Lefty O'Doul* were traded to the New York Giants (NL) for Sam Leslie.* He returned to the Brooklyn Dodgers in 1935 and concluded his major league career there in 1937.

Clark's most active season came in 1929, when he led the NL in games started (36), innings pitched (279), hits allowed (295), and losses while compiling a 16–19 record. His best season (1932) saw him finish 20–12 and again lead the NL in games started at 36. Overall, Clark compiled a 111–97 win–loss mark with a respectable 3.66 ERA. Although completing the 1933 season with the pennant-winning New York Giants, he did not appear in the World Series against the Washington Senators.

Clark's nickname of "Needle" derived from his days as a relief pitcher in Brooklyn, where his teammates likened him to Sherlock Holmes' famous remark, "Quick Watson, the Needle." Clark, a hard-luck pitcher, maintained his serenity and pitched well even in defeat, averaging over 38 games per season during the height of his career with the Robins and Dodgers. He attributed much of his success to Wilbert Robinson,* his initial manager at Brooklyn.

Subsequently, Clark appeared in three games with Minneapolis, MN (AA) in 1938 and in eight games with Reidsville, NC (BL) in 1939, producing a 29–23 record as manager before being named club president on June 23. He eventually worked as a building contractor.

BIBLIOGRAPHY: William Watson Clark file, National Baseball Library, Cooperstown, NY; *TSN Baseball Register*, 1953; Harold "Speed" Johnson, ed., *Who's Who in Major League Baseball*, 1933 (Chicago, IL, 1933); W. F. McNeil, *The Dodgers Encyclopedia* (Champaign, IL, 1997); Richard Goldstein, *Superstars and Screwballs* (New York, 1991); Frank Graham, *The Brooklyn Dodgers* (New York, 1945).

Michael J. McBride

CLARKE, Fred Clifford "Cap" (b. October 3, 1872, Winterset, IA; d. August 14, 1960, Winfield, KS), player, manager, and executive, was the son of farmer William D. Clarke and Lucy (Cutler) Clarke and brother of major league outfielder Joshua Clarke. The Clarkes moved to Winfield, KS when Fred was age two, but returned to Iowa near Des Moines five years later. Clarke attended Dickenson, IA public shools, delivered newspapers under Des Moines circulation manager Edward Barrow,* and played baseball for the Des Moines Stars and Mascots. A left fielder, Clarke joined the Carroll, IA semipro club in 1891 and began his professional career the next year with Hastings, NE (NeSL). After splitting 1893 between St. Joseph, MO (WA) and Montgomery, AL (SL), he hit .311 in 1894 for Savannah, GA (SL). He married Annette Gray in October 1898 and had two daughters, Helen Donahoe and Muriel Sullivan.

In 1894, Clarke joined the Louisville, KY Colonels (NL) for a $100 guarantee and $175 a month if he remained with the team. Using a light bat, Clarke auspiciously debuted with a record four singles and one triple in five times at the plate. The 5-foot 10-inch, right-handed Clarke batted .312 lifetime, made 2,672 hits, and scored 1,619 runs in 2,242 games for the Louisville Colonels (1894–1899) and Pittsburgh Pirates (1900–1915). Although only 165 pounds, he slugged 361 doubles, 220 triples, and 67 HR and knocked in 1,015 runs. Clarke batted over .300 eleven seasons, including five consecutively, and surpassed the .350 mark in 1897 and 1903. He hit safely in 31 consecutive games in 1895 and batted a career-high .390 in 1897 for Louisville, finishing second to Willie Keeler.* Besides stealing over 30 bases seven seasons and pilfering 506 career bases, Clarke led the NL in doubles (32) and slugging percentage (.532) in 1903 and in walks (80) in 1909. Defensively, he handled nearly 5,000 chances and led NL left fielders in percentage nine times. Twice tying major league records, Clarke made four assists in an August 1910 game and 10 putouts in an April 1911 contest. He often made spectacular catches with somersault dives.

Clarke piloted Louisville (1897–1899) and Pittsburgh (1900–1915), ranking high among major league managers with 1,602 victories and recording an impressive .576 win–loss percentage. An energetic, aggressive, inspirational leader, he stressed physical conditioning, practice, dedication, and desire. In 1897, Louisville appointed 24-year-old Clarke as baseball's first "boy manager." Although not faring well initially, Clarke's club improved dramatically when it merged with Pittsburgh in 1900. Outstanding batters Clarke, Honus Wagner,* and Ginger Beaumont,* along with excellent pitchers Deacon Phillippe,* Jesse Tannehill,* Sam Leever,* Jack Chesbro,* Vic Willis,* and Albert Leifield,* transformed Pittsburgh from a perennial second division team to a premier club. Under Clarke's adept guidance, the Pirates captured pennants from 1901 to 1903 and in 1909, placed second five times, and finished in the second division only twice. From 1901 through 1913, the New York Giants and the Chicago Cubs were the only other teams to win NL pennants. Clarke helped the Pirates take the 1903 pennant by hitting .351, but his club lost to the Boston Red Sox in the first modern World Series. In 1909, he sparked the Pirates to their first World Series title by slugging two HR against the Detroit Tigers. His World Series records included five sacrifice hits and four walks in one game. As Pittsburgh manager, Clarke earned only $3,600 annually. After retiring as manager, he raised wheat and livestock on a profitable 1,320 acre ranch near Winfield, KS. Clarke, who served briefly in the mid–1920s as Pirates coach and vice-president and later presided over non-professional baseball leagues, was elected to the National Baseball Hall of Fame (1951), Iowa Sports Hall of Fame (1951), and Kansas Sports Hall of Fame.

BIBLIOGRAPHY: Martin Appel and Burt Goldblatt, *Baseball's Best: The Hall of Fame Gallery* (New York, 1977); Fred Clarke file, National Baseball Library, Cooperstown, NY; Jerry E. Clark, *Anson to Zuber: Iowa Boys in the Major Leagues* (Omaha, NE, 1992); Des Moines (IA) *Register*, April 15, 1951, August 15, 1960; Frederick Ivor-Campbell et al., eds., *Baseball's First Stars* (Cleveland, OH, 1996); Lowell Reindenbaugh, *Baseball's Hall of Fame-Cooperstown* (New York, 1993); Frederick G. Lieb, *The Pittsburgh Pirates* (New York, 1948); George S. May, "Major League Baseball Players from Iowa," *The Palimpsest* 36 (April 1955), pp. 133–165; Tom Meany,

Baseball's Greatest Teams (New York, 1949); *NYT*, August 15, 1960; David L. Porter, correspondence with Mrs. Neal (Clarke) Sullivan, June 27, 1984; *The Baseball Encyclopedia*, 10th ed. (New York, 1996); Robert Smith, *Baseball's Hall of Fame* (New York, 1973); Winfield (KS) *Daily Courier*, August 15, 1960; Arthur D. Hittner, *Honus Wagner: The Life of Baseball's "Flying Dutchman"* (Jefferson, NC, 1996); William Hageman, *Honus: The Life and Times of a Baseball Hero* (Champaign, IL, 1996); Dennis De Valeria and Jeanne Burke De Valeria, *Honus Wagner: A Biography* (New York, 1996); Philip Von Borries, *Legends of Louisville* (West Bloomfield, MI, 1993).

David L. Porter

CLARKSON, John Gibson (b. July 1, 1861, Cambridge, MA; d. February 4, 1909, Belmont, MA), player, was one of five sons of wealthy manufacturer Thomas G. Clarkson and the brother of ballplayers Arthur "Dad" and Walter Clarkson. Clarkson, who married Ella Bar in March 1886 and was inducted in 1963 into the National Baseball Hall of Fame, attended Webster Grammar School and Comer's Business School in Cambridge. In a whirlwind 12-year major league career, Clarkson won 328 games (tenth on the all-time list), lost 176 decisions, compiled a .648 winning percentage, completed 485 starts, and recorded a lifetime 2.81 ERA. He led the NL in wins, appearances, complete games, innings, and strikeouts in 1885, 1887, and 1889; in shutouts in 1885 and 1889; and in ERA in 1889.

A pitcher for Adrian "Cap" Anson's* Chicago White Sox (NL) from 1884 to 1887, Clarkson led the team to pennants in 1885 and 1886. After winning 53 of the club's 87 victories in 1885, he performed similarly in 1886. Clarkson was traded to the Boston Beaneaters (NL) in 1888 and maintained his incredible form there. He won 49 of Boston's 83 victories in 1889 and combined with Charles "Kid" Nichols* to win or save 69 of Boston's 87 victories in 1891. A superlative fielder, Clarkson led the NL in assists and total fielding chances in 1885 and 1889 and recorded an amazing eight putouts in one game on his 24th birthday. On July 27, 1885, he pitched a no-run, no-hit game to beat the Providence, RI Grays, 6–0.

Anson praised Clarkson as "one of the greatest of pitchers," but observed that the handsome, high-strung young hurler needed continual ego boosting. Anson claimed that Clarkson "pitched on praise" and stated, "He won't pitch if scolded." Although quiet, Clarkson was not inhibited. He once threw a lemon instead of a regular baseball to prove that it was too dark to continue play. Peers regarded him as a calculating, scientific player who studied and pitched to each batter's individual weaknesses. With his long, cradling fingers and deep-set, dark eyes, he dominated NL batters partly by sheer intimidation. In 1884, he relied on his will power and superbly controlled curveball to strike out seven consecutive batters.

Clarkson began his career with Worcester, MA (NEL) in 1882, played with Saginaw, MI (NWL) in 1883, and was sold in early 1884 to Chicago. In 1888, Chicago owners made national headlines by selling Clarkson and battery mate Mike "King" Kelly* to Boston for a record $10,000 each. Four years later, Boston traded Clarkson to the second-place Cleveland Spiders (NL). Although performing well that season, Clarkson exhibited declining skills thereafter. He retired after the 1894 season and purchased a Cambridge cigar store, which he operated until his death from complications of pneumonia.

BIBLIOGRAPHY: John Clarkson file, National Baseball Library, Cooperstown, NY; Warren Brown, *The Chicago Cubs* (New York, 1946); Glenn Dickey, *The History of National League Baseball* (New York, 1979); Harold Kaese, *The Boston Braves* (New York, 1948); *NYT*, August 6, 1963; Craig Carter, ed., *TSN Daguerreotypes*, 8th ed. (St. Louis, MO, 1990); Frederick Ivor-Campbell et al., eds., *Baseball's First Stars* (Cleveland, OH, 1996); John Phillips, *The Spiders—Who Was Who* (Cabin John, MD, 1991); Eddie Gold and Art Ahrens, *The Golden Era Cubs, 1876–1940* (Chicago, IL, 1985); Warren Wilbert and William Hageman, *Chicago Cubs: Seasons at the Summit* (Champaign, IL, 1997); John Thorn et al., eds., *Total Braves* (New York, 1996); Gary Caruso, *The Braves Encyclopedia* (Philadelphia, PA, 1995); Daniel Pearson, *Baseball in 1889* (Bowling Green, OH, 1993); *The Baseball Encyclopedia*, 10th ed. (New York, 1996).

Alan R. Asnen

CLEMENS, William Roger "Rocket" (b. August 4, 1962, Dayton, OH), player, ranked among the leading AL pitchers from 1986 through 1998. The youngest of five children of Bill Clemens, a truck driver, and Bess (Wright) Clemens, he moved from Dayton to Vandalia, OH with his mother after his parents divorced. His mother married Woody Booher, a tool-and-die-maker who died in 1971. After his family moved to Texas in 1977, he attended Dulles High School in Sugar Land as a sophomore and graduated from Spring Woods High School in Houston in 1980. He earned letters in football, basketball, and baseball, compiling a 31–6 pitching record in three seasons. He attended Houston's San Jacinto JC in 1980–1981 and transferred to the University of Texas at Austin. He won 28 games against seven defeats the next two years and twice pitched the deciding game of the NCAA College World Series, losing in 1982 and winning the next year.

Clemens was drafted by the Boston Red Sox (AL) and completed the 1983 season with Winter Haven, FL (FSL) and New Britain, CT (EL), where he clinched the EL playoff title with a three-hit shutout. He began 1984 at Pawtucket, RI (IL) and was promoted on May 11 to the Boston Red Sox. An arm injury ended his season on August 31 with a 9–4 record. The next year, a shoulder injury ended his season in mid-August with his record at 7–5. Clemens's shoulder was repaired surgically two weeks later.

Clemens burst into stardom at the start of the 1986 season with 14 straight wins, including a record-setting 20–strikeout game against the Seattle Mariners on April 29. He started and won the All-Star Game with three perfect innings and pitched the Boston Red Sox to the AL East title with an AL-high 24 wins against only 4 losses. Clemens's .857 winning percentage, 2.48 ERA, and 5.0 TPI (Total Pitcher Index, Pete Palmer's measure for pitchers' overall effectiveness) also topped the AL, helping earn him both the AL Cy Young and MVP awards. In the AL Championship Series against the California Angels, Clemens lost the opener and won the deciding seventh game. He pitched in two World Series games against the New York Mets without a decision.

Clemens remained at or near the top among AL pitchers. In 1987, he held out through March for more pay and began slowly with a 4–6 record. His 16–3 finish, however, gave him a share of the AL lead with 20 wins and earned him his second AL Cy Young Award. His .690 winning percentage, 18 complete games, and seven shutouts also paced the AL. Clemens's record slipped a bit to 18–12 in 1988, but his 14 complete games, eight shutouts, and 291 strikeouts led the AL and helped the Boston Red Sox win another AL East title. He pitched in one AL Championship Series game with no decision. After finishing 17–11 in 1989, Clemens in 1990 enjoyed perhaps his finest season. His 21–6 record helped the Boston Red Sox earn their third AL East crown in five years, while his career-best 1.93 ERA and 6.2 TPI led the AL and four shutouts shared the AL lead. Clemens's two AL Championship Series appearances, though, produced a 0–1 record. Umpire Terry Cooney expelled him from Game 4 for swearing.

Clemens continued to top the AL in 1991 and 1992 with 2.62 and 2.41 ERAs, four and five shutouts, and a 5.3 TPI each year. In 1991 he also led the AL with 241 strikeouts and 271.1 innings pitched and compiled an 18–10 record, earning his third AL Cy Young Award. In 1992, he posted an 18–11 win–loss record.

A 1993 groin injury that sidelined Clemens for nearly a month in mid-season, late-season elbow pain, and concern over his mother's illness contributed to Clemens's first losing record, an 11–14 mark, and a career-worst 4.46 ERA. During the strike-shortened 1994 season, he compiled a 9–7 mark with a 2.85 ERA. Injuries limited Clemens to a 10–5 record in 1995 and one appearance in the AL Division Series against the Cleveland Indians. Although winning only 10 of 23 decisions in 1996, he tied his major league record by striking out 20 Detroit Tigers on September 18.

In November 1996, the Toronto Blue Jays (AL) acquired Clemens as a free agent. He earned *TSN* AL Pitcher of the Year honors, made *TSN* All-Star team, and won his fourth AL Cy Young award in 1997, leading the AL in victories (21), ERA (2.05), complete games (9), shutouts (3), innings pitched (264), and strikeouts (292). He lost only seven decisions and made his first All-Star game appearance since 1992. Clemens finished 20–6 with a 2.65 ERA and 271 strikeouts in 1998, winning his last 15 decisions. He led AL hurlers in ERA and strikeouts and shared the AL lead in victories. Clemens earned an unprecedented fifth AL Cy Young Award.

The Toronto Blue Jays traded him to the New York Yankees (AL) in

February 1999. In 1999, he hurled seven shutout innings in the AL Division Series and compiled a 1–0 record and 1.17 ERA in the World Series. Through 1999, Clemens hurled 3,462.1 innings in 480 games with 247 wins, 134 losses, a .648 winning percentage, 45 shutouts, 3,316 strikeouts, and 3.04 ERA. He made Major League Baseball's All-Century Team and ranked third in wins (152) in the 1990s.

Clemens married Debbie Lynn Godfrey in November 1984 and has four sons, including Koby Aaron and Kory.

BIBLIOGRAPHY: Roger Clemens file, National Baseball Library, Cooperstown, NY; John Benson et al., *Baseball's Top 100* (Wilton, CT, 1997); Richard J. Brenner, *Roger Clemens, Darryl Strawberry* (New York, 1989); S. Buckley, "Rocket Science," *Sport* 84 (May 1993), pp. 56–59; G. Callahan, "Commanding Presence," *SI* 86 (March 31, 1997), pp. 120–124; B. Buschel, "Fastballs from the Edge," *NYT Magazine*, June 2, 1991, pp. 42–45; N. Carfardo, "Roger Clemens," *Sport* 82 (May 1991), pp. 65–68; Peter Gammons, "Striking Out Toward Cooperstown," *SI* 64 (May 12, 1986), pp. 26–28; P. Carlson, "What's 23 Years Old and Goes K-K-K . . . ? Red Sox Strike-out Ace Roger Clemens," *PW* 25 (May 19, 1986), pp. 128ff; Jack Lautier, *Fenway Voices* (Camden, ME, 1990); Peter Golenbock, *Fenway* (New York, 1992); Robert Redmount, *The Red Sox Encyclopedia* (Champaign, IL, 1998); *CB Yearbook*, 1987, pp. 115–119; Roger Clemens with Peter Gammons, *Rocket Man: The Roger Clemens Story* (Lexington, MA, 1987); John P. McCarthy, *Baseball's All-time Dream Team* (Cincinnati, OH, 1994); Leigh Montville, "A Moment of Madness," *SI* 73 (November 26, 1990), pp. 110–120; Steve Rushin, "Roger, Over and Out," *SI* 74 (May 13, 1991), pp. 36–38; Mike Shalin, "Clemens Goes Home to Texas," Boston (MA) *Herald*, September 23, 1993, pp. 112, 114; Bruce Newman, "The Fireball Express," *SI* 68 (June 6, 1988), pp. 74–76; *NYT Biographical Service* 17 (May 1986), pp. 561–562; John Thorn et al., eds., *Total Baseball*, 5th ed. (New York, 1997); Ken Young, *Cy Young Award Winners* (New York, 1994).

Frederick Ivor-Campbell

CLEMENTE, Roberto "Bob" (b. Clemente y Walker, August 18, 1934, Carolina, PR; d. December 31, 1972, San Juan, PR), player, was the son of sugar mill worker and sugar cane cutter Melchor Clemente and Luisa (Walker) Clemente. The youngest of seven children, he adopted his island's passion for year-round baseball. By age 14, he competed against Negro League and major league professionals in exhibition matches. He first played profession-ally for the Santurce Crabbers in winter ball during 1952–1953, impressing major league talent hounds Branch Rickey* and Al Campanis. After another season with the Crabbers, he signed a $10,000 bonus with the Brooklyn Dodgers (NL) and spent the 1954 season with the Dodgers' Montreal, Canada (IL) farm team. Despite the organization's best efforts to hide him from rival scouts, he was drafted by the Pittsburgh Pirates (NL) in November 1954. He joined the Pirates in 1955 and spent his entire major league career with Pittsburgh.

During the 1960s, the 5-foot 11-inch, 185-pound Clemente became base-ball's best all-around right fielder, winning NL batting titles in 1961, 1964,

1965, and 1967. He paced the NL in hits (1967) and triples (1969), tied for the lead in hits (1964), and topped NL outfielders in assists four times (1959–1960 and 1966–1967). In his major league career, he batted above .300 13 times en route to becoming the 11th major leaguer to reach the 3,000 hit mark. Although lacking the HR power of Willie Mays* or Hank Aaron,* he proved a fearsome hitter, especially in clutch situations. In 2,433 games, he batted .317 with 440 doubles, 166 triples, 240 HR, 1,416 runs scored, 1,305 RBI, and 1,230 strikeouts. In the field, he mastered the Forbes Field and Three Rivers Stadium caroms and possessed an awe-inspiring throwing arm. He led the Pirates to world championships in 1960 and 1971. His all-around talents earned him the NL MVP Award in 1966. Clemente hit safely in every game of his two World Series appearances, capturing the Babe Ruth* Award for his efforts in the 1971 fall classic.

Clemente's accomplishments dramatized the arrival of more Latin American ballplayers, including Tony Oliva* from Cuba, Juan Marichal* from the Dominican Republic, and Orlando Cepeda* from his own Puerto Rico. Although Mexicans and Cubans had preceded him, Clemente became the first Latin superstar. He was sensitive to and outspoken about the discrimination encountered by Latin players on account of race and language, telling one reporter in 1965: "The Latin player doesn't get the recognition he deserves. Neither does the Negro unless he does something really spectacular." Clemente's belief that writers ignored Latin and black accomplishments was underscored by his low ranking in the 1960 MVP voting and low finish in the selection of the 1960s Player of the Decade. Spending his career in Pittsburgh no doubt contributed to a lack of publicity, only partially rectified by attention given Clemente's outstanding performance in 1971 World Series. Throughout his career, Clemente was plagued by headaches, muscle pulls, stomach pains, and especially back problems, which had been aggravated by a 1956 auto accident. However, critics labeled him a hypochondriac and suggested that he missed too many games.

Clemente became a folk hero in Puerto Rico. He married Vera Cristina Zabala on November 14, 1964 and insisted that all his children, Roberto, Luis Roberto, and Enrique Roberto, be born on his native island. In 1970, some 300,000 Puerto Ricans signed a salutory telegram as part of a "Roberto Clemente Night" in Pittsburgh. He participated in various Puerto Rican community projects, especially the creation of the "Sports City" complex to help underprivileged children improve their athletic skills. In December 1972, he helped organize relief efforts for victims of a Nicaraguan earthquake. He died when a plane carrying relief supplies to that country crashed shortly after takeoff. The widespread grief in Puerto Rico caused the governor's inaugural ceremonies to be canceled out of respect. Clemente's premature death prompted the National Baseball Hall of Fame Committee to waive its five-year rule. Clemente was voted into the shrine (the first Latin American to be so honored) eleven weeks after his funeral.

BIBLIOGRAPHY: Roberto Clemente file, National Baseball Library, Cooperstown, NY; Roy Blount, Jr., *The Baseball Hall of Fame 50th Anniversary Book* (New York, 1988); Peter C. Bjarkman, *Baseball with a Latin Beat* (Jefferson, NC, 1994); Myron Cohen, "Aches and Pains and Three Batting Titles," *SI* 24 (March 7, 1966), pp. 30–34; J. Feldman, "Clemente Went to Bat for All Latino Ballplayers," *Smithsonian* 24 (September 1993), pp. 128–136; Edward Grossman, "Pride of the Pirates," *Commentary* 57 (January 1974), pp. 72–76; Arnold Hano, *Roberto Clemente: Batting King* (New York, 1974); Brad Herzog, *The Sports 100* (New York, 1995); Roger Kahn, "Golden Triumphs, Tarnished Dreams," *SI* 45 (August 30, 1976), pp. 32–36, 62; Craig Carter, ed., *TSN Daguerreotypes* (St. Louis, MO, 1990); Bruce Markusen, *Roberto Clemente: The Great One* (Champaign, IL, 1998); Jim O'Brien, *Remembering Roberto* (Pittsburgh, PA, 1994); David L. Porter, ed., *African-American Sports Greats* (Westport, CT, 1995); Larry Moffi and Jonathan Kronstadt, *Crossing the Line* (Jefferson, NC, 1994); Steve Wulf, "Amoa Roberto!" *SI* 77 (December 28, 1992–January 4, 1993), pp. 114–118; John T. Bird, *Twin Killing: The Bill Mazeroski Story* (Birmingham, AL, 1995); Richard L. Burtt, *The Pittsburgh Pirates: A Pictorial History* (Virginia Beach, VA, 1977); Bob Smizik, *The Pittsburgh Pirates: An Illustrated History* (New York, 1990); "Old Aches and Pains," *Time* 89 (May 26, 1967), p. 56; "Viva Roberto," *Ebony* 22 (September 1967), pp. 38–41; Kal Wagenheim, *Clemente* (New York, 1973).

James W. Harper

CLEMENTS, John J. "Jack" (b. July 24, 1864, Philadelphia, PA; d. May 23, 1941, Norristown, PA), player, manager, and umpire, broke into the major leagues in 1884 at age 19 with the Keystone Baseball Club of Philadelphia (UA). After Keystone dropped out of the UA in August, Clements moved across town to the Philadelphia Phillies (NL) and played there the next 13 years. A rarity as a left-handed throwing catcher, he lacked outstanding defensive skills. As a left-hander hitter, however, the 5-foot 8½-inch, 204-pound Clements developed into one of the best-hitting catchers and one of the better sluggers of the dead ball pre–1920 era. He pioneered in the use of a chest protector in 1884, surviving early laughter to become the first major leaguer to catch 1,000 games.

In 1890 Clements emerged as one of the NL offensive leaders, ranking third in batting average at .315 and second in slugging average with .472. From 1890 through 1896, Clements averaged .317 in batting and .484 in slugging percentage. His 57 HR in that span placed him among the top 10 major leaguers.

Clements' .310 batting average in 1891 ranked fourth in the NL, while his career-high 17 HR in 1893 placed second only to teammate Ed Delahanty's* 19. A broken ankle sidelined him much of the following season, but he recovered to hit .394 and compile a .612 slugging average in 1895. Both figures marked personal bests and ranked him third in the NL, as did his 13 HR.

In 1898 Clements moved on to the St. Louis Cardinals (NL), where he led NL catchers in fielding average (.971) for the only time in his career.

His major league career wound down with the Cleveland Spiders (NL) in 1899 and the Boston Beaneaters (NL) in 1900. He finished the 1900 season with Providence, RI (EL) and caught for Worcester, MA (EL) in 1901 and for Springfield, MA (CtSL) in 1902. After his playing days, he worked several years for sporting goods manufacturer A. J. Reach* in Philadelphia, PA. He toiled for the Dunbar Furnace Company in Connellsville, PA and for a baseball manufacturer in Perkasie, PA. A son, John, became a minor league catcher.

Over his 17-year major league career, Clements batted .286, to rank tenth-best all-time among catchers with over 1,000 games. His average of 1.8 HR per 100 at bats places third among 19th-century players and sixth among all dead ball era players. He played in 1,157 major league games, numbering 226 doubles, 60 triples, and 77 HR among his 1,226 hits. He managed the Philadelphia Phillies for 19 games in Harry Wright's* absence in 1890 to a 13–6 record and served temporarily as an NL umpire during 1892.

BIBLIOGRAPHY: Jack Clements file, National Baseball Library, Cooperstown, NY; John Phillips, *The Spiders: Who Was Who* (Cabin John, MD, 1991); John Thorn et al., eds., *Total Baseball*, 5th ed. (New York, 1997); Robert L. Tiemann and Mark Rucker, eds., *Nineteenth Century Stars* (Kansas City, MO, 1989); Allan Lewis, *The Philadelphia Phillies: A Pictorial History* (Virginia Beach, VA, 1981); Rich Westcott and Frank Bilovsky, *The New Phillies Encyclopedia* (Philadelphia, PA, 1993); Frederick G. Lieb and Stan Baumgartner, *The Philadelphia Phillies* (New York, 1953).

Frederick Ivor-Campbell

CLIFT, Harlond Benton "Blackie," "Darkie" (b. August 12, 1912, El Reno, OK; d. April 27, 1992, Yakima, WA), player and coach, was the son of Alvin Benton Clift and Amy Jane (Hulse) Clift. He married Cora Douglass in July 1936 and had two sons. Clift, whose first name was frequently misspelled "Harland," was nicknamed "Blackie" or "Darkie" at his first spring training with the St. Louis Browns (AL) when the veterans thought his first name was "Harlem."

After having spent the 1932 season with Wichita Falls–Longview, TX (TL) and the 1933 campaign with San Antonio, TX (TL), Clift joined the St. Louis Browns in 1934 and became one of the best third basemen in the major leagues. He remained with the Browns until August 1943, when he was traded to the Washington Senators (AL). Clift played only eight games for the Senators in 1943 because of complications from the mumps. The off-season saw him injure his left shoulder when thrown from a horse. Clift never really recovered from that injury and spent most of the 1944 season on the voluntarily retired list. After the 1945 campaign, Clift retired as an active player. He served as a coach for the San Francisco, CA Seals (PCL) through 1953 and then operated his father's cattle ranch in Yakima, WA.

Clift compiled an excellent record both offensively and defensively. He led the major leagues in walks with 111 in 1939 and set the Browns' record and third baseman record for runs scored in 1936 with 145. The most productive hitter among his era's third basemen exhibited more power than any previous player at that position. In 1937, he established a major league record for third basemen with 29 HR. Clift increased it the next year to 34, a mark unbroken until the 1950s. During his major league career, Clift made 1,558 hits, belted 309 doubles, 62 triples, and 178 HR, and batted .272. No-hit games were spoiled three times by Clift.

An exceptional fielder with range and reliability, Clift in 1937 set records for a third baseman with 603 chances accepted and 405 assists. These marks remained unbroken until the baseball season was extended from 154 contests to 162 games. Clift's role in 50 double plays at third base that year ranks him second lifetime. Clift, a member of the Browns' Hall of Fame and third baseman on the Browns' all-time team, lived in retirement in Yakima, WA.

BIBLIOGRAPHY: Harlond Clift file, National Baseball Library, Cooperstown, NY; Bill Borst, ed., *Ables to Zoldak*, vol. 1 (St. Louis, MO, 1988); Bill Borst, *Still Last in the American League* (West Bloomfield, MI, 1992); Bill Borst, ed., *The Brown Stocking*, vol. 1 (St. Louis, MO, 1985); Bill Borst, *The St. Louis Browns, An Informal History* (St. Louis, MO, 1978); Brent P. Kelley, "A Chat with a Premier Third Baseman of the 30's," *SCD* 16 (January 13, 1989), pp. 120–122; Brent P. Kelley, *The Early Stars* (Jefferson, NC, 1997), Brent P. Kelley, *The Case For: Those Overlooked by the Baseball Hall of Fame* (Jefferson, NC, 1992); William B. Mead, *Even the Browns* (Chicago, IL, 1978); *NYT Biographical Service* 23 (April 1992), p. 532; Shirley Povich, *The Washington Senators* (New York, 1954); John Thorn et al., eds., *Total Baseball*, 5th ed. (New York, 1997).

Ralph S. Graber

COBB, Tyrus Raymond "Ty," "The Georgia Peach" (b. December 18, 1886, Narrows, GA; d. July 17, 1961, Atlanta, GA), player and manager, was the eldest of three children born to William Herschel Cobb and Amanda (Chitwood) Cobb. Cobb grew up in Royston, GA under the dominant influence of his father, variously a school teacher and principal, mayor, publisher of the Royston *Record*, state senator, and county school commissioner. William stressed academics and urged Ty to become a doctor or lawyer, but Cobb preferred balls and bats to books.

Cobb, who batted left-handed but threw right-handed, made his professional debut in 1904 at age 17 with Augusta, GA (SAL). Released after two games, he played with a semipro team in Anniston, AL before rejoining Augusta at the end of the season. He started the 1905 season with Augusta, but in August joined the Detroit Tigers (AL). He retired 24 years later holding 43 major league regular season career records. As a measure of Cobb's greatness, many of those career marks remained as of 1999 among the best in history: first in runs (2,246) and batting average (.366); second in hits (4,189) and triples (295); fourth in games (3,035), at bats (11,434), doubles (724), and stolen bases (892); and fifth in RBI (1,937).

Cobb epitomized "scientific" baseball, which featured aggressive base running and precision batting to counter the overpowering pitching of the dead ball era. He was above average as an outfielder and was peerless on offense. No one ever ran the bases with more daring and guile than Cobb, who perfected the hook slide or "fade away." With a split grip (hands apart) on the bat, the 6-foot 1-inch, 175-pound Cobb won nine consecutive AL batting titles from 1907 to 1915 and added three more from 1917 to 1919. After his second year with Detroit, he hit at least .320 for 22 consecutive years, capped by brilliant .401, .410, and .420 marks. His best season was 1911, when he led the AL in every offensive category except HR and set personal career highs in hits (248), runs (147), RBI (127), batting average (.420), and slugging percentage (.621). As a measure of his overall dominance, Cobb led the AL 12 times in batting average, eight times in slugging percentage and hits, six times in stolen bases, five times in runs scored, four times in triples and RBI, and three times in doubles. He had at least 200 hits for nine seasons and stole a career-high 96 bases in 1915.

Cobb, whose prime came during the dead ball era, hit only 117 career HR. But he once led the AL in HR and HR percentage (1909), became at age 38 the first modern player to hit five HR in two games (1925), and had a .512 career slugging percentage. As player–manager of the Tigers from 1921 to 1926, he proved superb as a strategist but poor at handling players. Under his leadership the team finished no higher than second place (1923) and posted an overall .519 winning percentage with 479 wins and 444 losses. Unable to give up the game, Cobb played for Connie Mack's* Philadelphia Athletics in 1927 and 1928 and hit .357 and .323 there before retiring at age 41.

Cobb's brilliance was due more to a careful mastery of skills combined with a maniacal will to succeed than to native talent. His unrelenting quest to be the best featured an aggressive style of play simultaneously admired and abhorred by teammates, opponents, and fans alike. Cobb exhibited in extreme form all the aggressive, extroverted human characteristics—bravery, egotism, unyieldingness, hypersensitivity. He also proved to have a dyspeptic personality, being obstinate, obsessive, paranoid, vituperative, and racist. As a result, he engaged in numerous verbal and physical assaults on and off the field. Some of the ugliest encounters involved blacks, as Cobb, by lineage and upbringing an ardent defender of the Old South, could not abide the lack of "proper" deference shown by northern blacks. No misanthrope, however, he made countless private acts of generosity and charitable contributions, including $100,000 each for a hospital in Royston and a Georgia college scholarship fund.

Retirement for Cobb proved traumatic and tragic. A millionaire thanks to wise investments, he never found anything more meaningful to fill 33 years than playing golf and balancing bank accounts. Without baseball, his life lacked meaning. He experienced two divorces (from Charlie Marion Lombard, whom he married in 1908, and from Frances Fairburn Cass, whom he married in 1949) and the alienation of his five children, Tyrus, Jr., Shirley, Roswell Herschel, Beverly, and James Howell. Increasingly critical of modern baseball and its players, he spent the last years of his life fighting the ravages of cancer and loneliness with drugs and alcohol.

The irascible personality that made Cobb's personal life so miserable also drove him to levels of unparalleled athletic achievement. The affliction was congenital, for Cobb admitted that he had been "a bad boy with a vying disposition." Two traumatic experiences in his late teens set his temperament for life. The first was a burning desire to win approval from a stern and distant father, who sent him off to professional baseball with the admonition, "Don't come home a failure." The effort to please became an obsession the next year, when his mother, ostensibly by accident, killed his father with a shotgun. The second incident was the unmercifully cruel hazing given by the Tigers to the cocky, young southern rookie in 1906. From then on, Cobb battled the world en route to baseball glory.

When the initial balloting was held in 1936 for election to the National Baseball Hall of Fame, Cobb received the most votes (222) and came within four ballots of unanimity. One of baseball's greatest performers, he was surely the game's greatest competitor. As contemporary great George Sisler* explained, "The greatness of Ty Cobb was something that had to be seen and to see him was to remember him forever." Cobb made Major League Baseball's All-Century Team and ranked 20th among ESPN's top century athletes.

BIBLIOGRAPHY: Charles C. Alexander, *Ty Cobb* (New York, 1984); William M. Anderson, *The Detroit Tigers* (South Bend, IN, 1996); Joe Falls, *Detroit Tigers* (New York, 1975); Mark Alvarez, "Say It Ain't So, Ty: The Cobb-Speaker Scandal," *TNP* 14 (1994), pp. 21–29; Richard Bak, *Ty Cobb: His Tumultuous Life and Times* (Dallas, TX, 1994); Richard Bak, *A Place for Summer* (Detroit, MI, 1998); Ty Cobb, *Busting 'Em and Other Stories* (New York, 1914); Ty Cobb file, National Baseball Library, Cooperstown, NY; Larry Ammen, "Cobb on a Rampage" *BRJ* 20 (1991), pp. 39–42; Ty Cobb, "They Don't Play Baseball Any More," *Life* 32 (March 17, 1952), pp. 136ff, and (March 24, 1952), pp. 63ff; Ty Cobb with Al Stumpf, *My Life in Baseball* (Garden City, NY, 1961); *CB* (1951), pp. 111–113; John D. McCallum, *Ty Cobb* (New York, 1975); John P. McCarthy, *Baseball's All-Time Dream Team* (Cincinnati, OH, 1994); Richard Seheinin, *Field of Screams* (New York, 1994); Leigh Montville, "The Last Remains of a Legend," *SI* 77 (Fall 1992), pp. 60–64; Fred Smith, *995 Tigers* (Detroit, MI, 1981); *NYT*, July 18, 1961; Brent P. Kelley, *In the Shadow of the Babe* (Jefferson, NC, 1995); J. Lapointe, "Three Who Made History; Cobb, Louis, and Howe," *Sport* 80 (May 1989), p. 60; John Thom, *Champion Batsman of the 20th Century* (Los Angeles, CA, 1992); *The Baseball Encyclopedia*, 10th ed. (New York, 1996); Al Stumpf, "Ty Cobb's Wild Ten-Month Fight to Live," *True* 14 (December 1961), pp. 38ff; Al Stumpf, *Cobb: A Biography* (Chapel Hill, NC, 1994).

Larry R. Gerlach

COCHRANE, Gordon Stanley "Mickey," "Black Mike" (b. April 6, 1903, Bridgewater, MA; d. June 28, 1962, Lake Forest, IL), player, coach, manager, executive, and scout, was the son of Scotch-Irish immigrants John Cochrane and Sarah (Campbell) Cochrane. His father worked as a coachman and caretaker for a wealthy Boston family and partly owned a local movie theater. Cochrane graduated from Bridgewater High School in 1921 and participated in all sports there. He became one of the finest all-around athletes at Boston University (1921–1924), excelling in baseball, football, track and field, basketball, and boxing. Cochrane especially starred as a halfback in football and captained the 1923 squad. In 1921 against Tufts University, Cochrane dropkicked a 53-yard field goal for a Terrier record.

Cochrane began playing professional baseball with Dover, DE (ESL) in 1923 and used the name "Frank King" to protect his amateur status. In 1924, his contract was sold to Portland, OR (PCL). After batting .333 in 1924, Cochrane was purchased by Connie Mack's* Philadelphia Athletics (AL) for a reported $50,000 and five players. Cochrane became the Athletics' regular catcher in 1925, compiling a .331 batting average in 134 games. With intensive coaching from veteran Ralph "Cy" Perkins, he improved his catching and caught 100 or more games 11 successive seasons from 1925 to 1935.

Cochrane excelled as a hitter (slugging three HR in one game), catcher, base runner, and team leader. Mack considered him the greatest single factor in winning AL pennants for the 1929–1931 Athletics, a team that included stars Al Simmons,* Jimmie Foxx,* and Lefty Grove.* In 1928, Cochrane was named AL MVP. He helped the Athletics win the 1929 and 1930 World Series, but performed poorly in the 1931 classic lost to the St. Louis Cardinals.

In December 1933, the Detroit Tigers (AL) bought Cochrane from Philadelphia for $100,000 and catcher John Pasek and appointed him manager. Cochrane's Tigers in 1934 won the first AL pennant for Detroit since 1909, but lost the World Series to the Cardinals. The Tigers captured their second consecutive AL pennant in 1935 and the world championship in seven games over the Chicago Cubs. Detroit finished second to the New York Yankees in 1936 and 1937. On May 25, 1937, Cochrane suffered a severe head injury when hit with a ball pitched by Irving "Bump" Hadley of the Yankees. His skull was fractured in three places, abruptly ending his exciting, productive, colorful playing career. Confined to the bench, Cochrane did not give the Tigers the leadership they desired and was released as field manager in August 1938.

In 13 major league seasons, Cochrane led two teams to five AL pennants and compiled a lifetime .320 batting average (.357 in 1930). In 1932, he slugged 23 HR and knocked in 112 runs. In 1,482 career games, Cochrane made 1,652 hits, 1,041 runs, 333 doubles, 64 triples, 119 HR, 832 RBI, and 64 stolen bases. In 31 World Series games, he batted .245, collected 27 hits, 17 runs, 4 doubles, and 2 HR, and batted in 6 runs. As a manager for five seasons, Cochrane won 348 of 600 games for a .582 percentage.

During World War II, Cochrane served as an officer in the U.S. Navy's fitness program, operated the athletic program at Great Lakes Naval Training Station, and coached their baseball team. Cochrane and his wife, the former Mary Hohr, had two daughters and a son, Gordon, Jr., who died in World War II. Following the war, Cochrane represented a trucking line and operated a dude ranch in Wyoming. He returned to baseball in 1950 as a coach and general manager of the Philadelphia Athletics (AL) and scouted for the New York Yankees (AL) in 1955 and for Detroit (AL) in 1960. In 1961, he was named vice-president of the Tigers and remained in that position until his death. He battled depression, alcohol dependence, and cancer. He was elected to the National Baseball Hall of Fame in 1947.

BIBLIOGRAPHY: Mickey Cochrane file, National Baseball Library, Cooperstown, NY; William M. Anderson, *The Detroit Tigers* (South Bend, IN, 1996); E. Baker, "The Road Not Taken," *GQ* 61 (September 1991), pp. 300–303; Charles Bevis, *Mickey Cochrane; The Life of a Baseball Hall of Fame Catcher* (Jefferson, NC, 1998); John Benson et al., *Baseball's Top 100* (Wilton, CT, 1997); Richard Bak, *A Place for Summer* (Detroit, MI, 1998); Bob Broeg, *Super Stars of Baseball* (St. Louis, MO, 1971); Gene Karst and Martin J. Jones, Jr., *Who's Who in Professional Baseball* (New Rochelle, NY, 1973); Craig Carter, ed., *TSN Daguerreotypes*, 8th ed. (St. Louis, MO, 1990); A. W. Laird, *Ranking Baseball's Elite* (Jefferson, NC, 1990); Fred Smith, *995 Tigers* (Detroit, MI, 1981); Joe Falls, *Detroit Tigers* (New York, 1975).

John L. Evers

COCKRELL, Phillip Williams "Fish" (b. Phillip Williams, October 6, 1898, Augusta, GA; d. March 31, 1951, Philadelphia, PA), player, manager, umpire, was the son of James Williams, a sharecropper farmer, and was the fourth of seven children. He possessed an athletic flair and keen interest in baseball. In the summer of 1913, the 15-year-old began a five-year baseball career with the Havana Red Sox of Watertown, NY and the New York Lincoln Giants to help support his family. Cockrell completed high school in 1917 and graduated from Paine College in Augusta, GA in 1921.

The 5-foot 8-inch, 160-pound, right-handed spitballer joined the Hilldale Daisies of Philadelphia in May 1918, compiling a 6–3 record. Following a 2–2 season performance in 1920, Cockrell registered a 5–5 record with the independent Atlantic City, NJ Bacharach Giants in 1921. He finished 15–1 with the Hilldale Daisies (ECL), recording two victories over Rube Foster's* Chicago American Giants in the World Series. Foster attempted to lure Cockrell to his club in 1923, but Hilldale owner Ed Bolden gave him a modest raise and promises of bigger paydays.

Cockrell remained with the Hilldale Daisies through 1931, compiling 128 wins and 66 losses with 259 strikeouts, eight shutouts, and six no-hitters. From 1923 to 1925, the Hilldale Daisies won the ECL pennant and played the NNL champion Kansas City Monarchs in the Negro League World Series. Hilldale lost all three World Series, but Cockrell fared 24–8, 10–1, and 14-2 during those seasons. Although winning 10 games and losing three in 1926, Cockrell missed eight games from injuries received when white park security bodily hauled him from the field after he attacked an umpire for reversing a decision. Club owner Bolden suspended him for five days and fined him $100.

Following a disappointing 1927 season, Cockrell won only 8 games against 12 losses in 1928. The Hilldale Daisies continued to lack cohesion and harmony in 1929 under temperamental manager Oscar Charleston.* In mid-May, Cockrell replaced Charleston and guided the club to a second place finish. The defections of Judy Johnson,* Jake Stephens, and Charleston weakened Hilldale in 1930, but Cockrell hurled a 5–0 shutout for his sixth no-hitter against Cape May, NJ. Still under Cockrell's management in 1931, Hilldale regained much of its early success with a 120–34–4 record behind his own 23–3 pitching performance. In his final season with Hilldale, Cockrell won only two games against seven losses in 1932.

Cockrell, who experienced mediocre seasons with the Bacharach Giants and Philadelphia Stars, retired following the 1934 season. Cockrell umpired in the NNL from 1936 to 1946. In 1951 Cockrell was a homicide victim, mistakenly shot by a jealous husband as he left a Philadelphia bar.

BIBLIOGRAPHY: Dick Clark and Larry Lester, eds., *The Negro Leagues Book* (Cleveland, OH, 1994); Phil Dixon, *The Negro Baseball Leagues* (Mattituck, NY, 1992); John B. Holway, *Black Diamonds* (Westport, CT, 1989); Neil Lanctot, *Fair Dealing and Clean Playing* (Jefferson, NC, 1994); Phillip Cockrell file, National Baseball Library, Cooperstown, NY; Negro Leagues Baseball Museum, Kansas City, MO; T. S. O'Connell, "Age Never Slowed This Speedster Down," *SCD* 18 (June 21, 1991), pp. 184–186; Robert Peterson, *Only the Ball Was White* (New York, 1970); Mark Ribowsky, *A Complete History of the Negro Leagues, 1884 to 1955* (New York, 1995); James A. Riley, *The Encyclopedia of the Negro Baseball Leagues* (New York, 1994); Mike Shatzkin, ed., *The Ballplayers* (New York, 1990).

Jerry J. Wright

COLAVITO, Rocco Domenico "Rocky" (b. August 10, 1933, New York, NY), player, coach and scout, is the son of Rocco Colavito and Angelina (Spofadino) Colavito, both of Italian descent. The youngest of five children, Colavito attended Public School No. 4 and Theodore Roosevelt High School in New York City. At age 16, he began playing semipro baseball and signed in 1951 for a $3,000 bonus as a pitcher–outfielder with the Cleveland Indians (AL). In 1951 Colavito slugged 23 HR and knocked in 111 runs for Daytona Beach, FL (FSL). The next year, he played for Cedar Rapids, IA (3IL) and Spartanburg, SC (TSL). At Reading, PA in 1953, he led the Class A EL with 28 HR and 121 RBI. He played in 1954 and 1955 with Indianapolis, IN, pacing the AA in 1954 with 38 HR and 116 RBI. After starting the 1956 season with San Diego, CA (PCL), he was summoned by Cleveland.

The 6-foot 3-inch, 190-pound, rifle-armed outfielder became one of the most popular, productive Indians players. In 1956, he slugged 21 HR and then slumped in batting average the next year. He hit 41 HR, drove in 113 runs, batted .303, and topped the AL in slugging percentage (.620) in 1958. The next year his 42 circuit clouts, including four HR on June 10 against the Baltimore Orioles, tied for the AL lead. A controversial April 1960 trade sent Colavito to the Detroit Tigers (AL) for AL batting champ Harvey Kuenn.* Between 1960 and 1963, Colavito provided considerable power for the Detroit Tigers. In 1964 he slugged 34 HR and drove in 102 runs for the Kansas City Athletics (AL). After Cleveland purchased Colavito in January 1965, he responded with 26 HR and led the AL with 108 RBI and 93 walks. He also set an AL record for outfielders by recording 234 consecutive errorless games from September 6, 1964 to June 15, 1966. In 1966 he belted 30 HR, but his overall offensive production slipped significantly. He joined the Chicago White Sox (AL) in June 1967 and finished his playing career in 1968 with the Los Angeles Dodgers (NL) and New York Yankees (AL).

In 14 major league seasons, Colavito hit 374 HR and surpassed 100 RBI six times. For his career, he compiled 1,159 RBI, 1,730 hits, 283 doubles, and 951 walks and batted .266 as a major leaguer. He also pitched in two games, compiling a 1–0 record and a 0.00 ERA in 5.2 innings. He made *TSN* All-Star team in 1961 and played in eight All-Star games from 1959 through 1966. After scouting for the New York Yankees in 1969 and 1973, he coached for the Cleveland Indians (1976–1978) and Kansas City Royals (1982–1983). Married in October 1954 to Carmen Perroti, Colavito has three children and owns a mushroom farm in Temple, PA.

BIBLIOGRAPHY: William M. Anderson, *The Detroit Tigers* (South Bend, IN, 1996); Martin Appel, *Yesterday's Heroes* (New York, 1988); John Benson et al., *Baseball's Top 100* (Wilton, CT, 1997); Richard Bak, *A Place for Summer* (Detroit, MI, 1998); Jack Torry, *Endless Summers* (South Bend, IN, 1995); Rocky Colavito file, National Baseball Library, Cooperstown, NY; Rocky Colavito, "Secrets of a Home Run Hitter," *Official Baseball Annual* (New York, 1963); Joe Falls, *Detroit Tigers* (New York, 1975); John Phillips, *Winners* (Cabin John, MD, 1987); Ross Forman, "Rocky Colavito," *SCD* 25 (August 7, 1998), pp. 100–102; Brent P. Kelley, *The Case For: Those Overlooked by the Baseball Hall of Fame* (Jefferson, NC, 1992); Fred Smith, *995 Tigers* (Detroit, MI, 1981); John Thorn et al., eds., *Total Indians* (New York, 1996); Hy Goldberg, "Colavito: Can He Save the Indians?" *Dell Sports* (July 1965), pp. 36–37, 76–77; Craig Carter, ed., *TSN Daguerreotypes*, 8th ed. (St. Louis, MO, 1990); Terry Pluto, *The Curse of Rocky Colavito* (New York, 1994); *Time* 74 (August 24, 1959), pp. 50–55, 92 (September 6, 1968), p. 77.

Douglas D. Martin

COLEMAN, Vincent Maurice "Vince," "Vincent Van Go" (b. September 22, 1961, Jacksonville, FL), player, graduated from Raines High School in Jacksonville, where he lettered in baseball and football. Coleman, a 1982 graduate of Florida A&M University with a Bachelor of Arts degree in physical education, placekicked for the football team and stole 65 bases on the baseball squad his junior year. The St. Louis Cardinals (NL) signed Coleman, who employed his blazing speed to share the ApL lead with 43 stolen bases for Johnson City, TN in 1982. The following year, he set a professional baseball record by pilfering 145 bases with Macon, GA (SAL) to earn the SAL MVP award. His 101 stolen bases with the Louisville, KY Redbirds (AA) in 1984 topped the AA. The Cardinals made the 6-foot 1-inch, 182-pound Coleman a switch hitter.

Coleman set a major league rookie record with 110 stolen bases for St. Louis in 1985, enabling the Cardinals to become the first NL team since the 1912 New York Giants to swipe 300 bases. He stole 107 bases and 109 bases the next two seasons and tied a NL record by leading in stolen bases six consecutive seasons. Coleman established a major league record with his 50th consecutive successful theft attempt on July 26, 1989. He reached the 500 stolen base plateau in 804 games, the fastest pace in major league history. A better than 80 percent base stealing success rate kept him in the leadoff spot. Coleman, however, averaged 105 strikeouts per season in six years with the Cardinals. He played in the 1988 and 1989 All-Star games. A tarpaulin machine rolled over Coleman's leg, causing a chip fracture, before the fourth game of the 1985 NL Championship Series against the Los Angeles Dodgers. He missed the entire 1985 World Series, won by the Kansas City Royals. Coleman made only four hits and fanned 10 times, as the St. Louis Cardinals succumbed to the Minnesota Twins in the seven game 1987 World Series.

After joining the New York Mets (NL) in December 1990, Coleman missed much of 1991 and 1992 with hamstring and rib cage injuries. He was convicted of a misdemeanor for throwing an M-80 firecracker into a crowd outside Dodgers Stadium in Los Angeles, injuring three people and prompting his trade to the Kansas City Royals (AL) in January 1994. In 1995, Coleman batted .288 and stole 42 bases for the Kansas City Royals and Seattle Mariners (AL). Coleman split 1996 between the Cincinnati Reds (NL), Indianapolis, IN (AA), and Vancouver, Canada (PCL) and appeared briefly with the Detroit Tigers (AL) in 1997. In 13 major league seasons, he played in 1,371 games, made 1,425 hits, scored 849 runs, drove in 346 runners, hit 28 HR, stole 752 bases, and batted .264. He signed a minor league contract with the St. Louis Cardinals in January 1998, but retired that season.

BIBLIOGRAPHY: Vincent Coleman file, National Baseball Library, Cooperstown, NY; Bob Broeg and Jerry Vickery, *St. Louis Cardinals Encyclopedia* (Grand Rapids, MI, 1998); John Dewan, ed., *The Scouting Report: 1994* (New York, 1994); Jack Herman, "In-Vince-ible," *Redbird Review* (August 1988), pp. 5, 19; Zander Hollander, ed., *1994 Complete Handbook of Baseball*, 24th ed. (New York, 1994); Kip Ingle, *St. Louis Cardinals 1988 Media Guide* (St. Louis, MO, 1988); Franz Lidz, "Invincible," *SI* 74 (April 15, 1991), pp. 104–106; Ozzie Smith with Rob Rains, *Wizard* (Chicago, IL, 1988); Rob Rains, *The St. Louis Cardinals* (New York, 1992).

Frank J. Olmsted

COLLINS, Dorothy Wiltse "Dottie" (b. September 23, 1923, Inglewood, CA), player, is the only child of Daniel Wiltse, a Standard Oil Company welder/ lead burner, and Eleanor Wiltse of English–German–Italian background. "My dad started training me when I was just knee-high," she recalled, "he wanted a pitcher." After starting as a nine-year-old bat-girl in the Los Angeles Parks Department Softball League, Collins pitched in the California State Championships at age 11—before 25,000 people at Wrigley Field in Los Angeles, CA. She graduated from high school in 1941 and played softball from 1936 to 1944.

The 5-foot 7-inch, 125-pound Collins pitched in the AAGPBL for six seasons from 1944 to 1948 and in 1950, mostly under her maiden name. She compiled a 20–16 record with a league-high 205 strikeouts for the Minneapolis, MN Millerettes in 1944, when the team won only 44 games, but also set an AAGPBL record by hitting 44 batters that season. She spent most of her AAGPBL career as the lead pitcher for the Fort Wayne, IN Daisies. Her best season came in 1945, when she finished 29–10 with an AAGPBL single-season record 293 strikeouts, 17 shutouts, and a 0.83 ERA. Her .744 winning percentage tied for league best. Collins also won 22 games in 1946 and 20 games in 1947, when she led AAGPBL pitchers with a .965 fielding percentage. In each of her first four seasons, she struck out over 200 batters. She finished 117–76 for her career with a 60.6 winning percentage, 1,004 strikeouts, and a 1.81 ERA. On August 28, 1945, Collins pitched and won both games of a doubleheader against the Rockford Peaches. She met Harvey Collins after the second game and married him in March 1946. They have two children, Patricia and Daniel. Collins cut her 1948 season short when she was four months pregnant and did not play the following season. She returned in 1950, compiling a 13–8 record.

Collins pitched right-handed, both underhand and overhand, successfully. The AAGPBL changed from underhand delivery to sidearm and then to overhand over the course of her career. One of her coaches, who marveled that she could throw a curveball underhanded, never saw another pitcher do that with a softball.

Collins worked for General Electric Company in Fort Wayne after her baseball career and played golf, winning the Ft. Wayne City Championship in 1971. In 1987 she helped form the AAGPBL's Player's Association, serving as treasurer, board member, newsletter editor, and general spokesperson.

BIBLIOGRAPHY: AAGPBL files, Northern Indiana Historical Society, South Bend, IN; Barbara Gregorich, *Women at Play* (San Diego, CA, 1993); Susan E. Johnson, *When Women Played Hardball* (Seattle, WA, 1994); W. C. Madden, *The Women of the All-American Girls Professional Baseball League* (Jefferson, NC, 1997); Jim Sargent, "Dottie Wiltse: Pitching in the AAGPBL in the 1940s," *SCD* 24 (October 3, 1997), pp. 156–157.

Dennis S. Clark

COLLINS, Edward Trowbridge, Sr. "Eddie," "Cocky" (b. May 2, 1887, Millerton, NY; d. March 25, 1951, Boston, MA), baseball and football player, manager, and executive, was the son of railroad freight agent John Rossman Collins and Mary Meade (Trowbridge) Collins. He graduated from Irving School in Tarrytown, NY in 1903. Collins began playing baseball at an early age, but considered football his favorite game. A varsity quarterback at Columbia University, he graduated from there in 1907. After playing semipro baseball, Collins was signed by the Philadelphia Athletics (AL). He played 20 games with the Athletics during the 1906 and 1907 seasons and four games with Newark, NJ (EL) in 1907, using the name "Sullivan" to retain his collegiate eligibility. In 1908, Collins became a regular second baseman for Philadelphia and helped lead Connie Mack's* Athletics to four AL pennants (1910–1911, 1913–1914) and three world championships (1910–1911, 1913).

The 5-foot 9-inch, 170-pound second baseman threw right-handed, batted left-handed, and starred in the famous $100,000 infield, which included Stuffy McInnis,* Jack Barry,* and Frank "Home Run" Baker.* In 1914 Collins was named the AL MVP, but was sold to the Chicago White Sox (AL) following the Athletics loss to the Boston Braves in the World Series. Collins remained with Chicago for 12 years, managing the White Sox two seasons. He played on the world championship 1917 club and in 1919 was one of the Chicago players making an honest effort to defeat the Cincinnati Reds in the World Series. Eight teammates were accused of trying to fix the classic, known as the "Black Sox" scandal. In 1920, Collins achieved a career-high .372 batting average. With Collins as player–manager (1925–1926), the White Sox finished fifth both seasons and won 160 of 307 games. Chicago released him after the 1926 season. Collins returned to Philadelphia as player–coach and made his last appearance during the 1930 season.

Collins, who holds the record for longest service as an active AL player (25 years), led the AL in runs scored three times (1912–1914) and stolen bases four times (1910, 1919, 1923–1924). He twice stole six bases in one game, a major league record. His 81 thefts in 1910 and 224 hits in 1920 remain club records. Collins made at least five hits in one game five times and set the all-time World Series record for most stolen bases (14), since equalled by Lou Brock.* He retains major league records by second basemen for most years (21), most games (2,650), most assists (7,630), most chances accepted (14,591), and most years leading the AL in fielding average (9) and ranks second with 6,526 putouts.

Collins ranks high on the all-time major league lists in several categories. He compiled a .333 lifetime batting average (23rd) and batted over .300 17 times (3rd), including nine consecutive times. In 2,826 games (13th), he batted 9,949 times (19th), scored 1,821 runs (12th), and collected 3,315 hits (8th). His hits included 2,641 singles (3rd), 438 doubles, and 187 triples

(12th). He amassed 4,268 total bases (38th), received 1,499 bases on balls (15th), knocked in 1,300 runs, and compiled a .429 slugging average. Collins stole 743 bases (7th), including 17 steals of home (9th). In six World Series, he played in 34 games, batted 128 times, scored 20 runs, collected 42 hits, including 7 doubles and 2 triples, recorded 11 RBI, and compiled a .328 batting average.

After coaching with Philadelphia (AL) in 1931 and 1932, Collins the following season became vice-president, treasurer, and business manager for the Boston Red Sox (AL). He served in this capacity until his death, helping build the Red Sox into consistent AL pennant contenders. Collins, who in 1939 was elected to the National Baseball Hall of Fame, married Mabel Doane on November 3, 1910 and had two sons, Edward, Jr. and Paul. Edward, Jr., played baseball for the Philadelphia Athletics (AL) between 1939 and 1942.

BIBLIOGRAPHY: Eliot Asinof, *Eight Men Out* (New York, 1963); Connie Mack, *My 66 Years in the Big Leagues* (Philadelphia, PA, 1950); Frederick G. Lieb, *Connie Mack* (New York, 1945); Edward Collins file, National Baseball Library, Cooperstown, NY; Peter Golenbock, *Fenway* (New York, 1992); Robert Redmount, *The Red Sox Encyclopedia* (Champaign, IL, 1998); John Benson et al., *Baseball's Top 100* (Wilton, CT, 1997); Bob Broeg, *Super Stars of Baseball* (St. Louis, MO, 1971); Craig Carter, ed., *TSN Daguerreotypes*, 8th ed. (St. Louis, MO, 1981); A. W. Laird, *Ranking Baseball's Elite* (Jefferson, NC, 1990); Lowell Reidenbaugh, *Baseball's Hall of Fame-Cooperstown* (New York, 1993); *TSN Official Baseball Record Book, 1998.*

John L. Evers

COLLINS, Harry Warren "Rip," "Two Gun" (b. February 26, 1896, Weatherford, TX; d. May 27, 1968, Bryan, TX), player, was the son of Henry Warren Collins and Marie (Davidson) Collins. After graduating from high school in Austin, he starred in four sports at Texas A&M University. The 6-foot 1-inch, 205-pound Collins served in the U.S. Army in World War I prior to his major league career, which began as a pitcher in 1920 with the New York Yankees (AL).

Although Collins won 14 games with two shutouts as a rookie, his ERA ballooned to 5.44 in 1921. His only World Series action came in October 1921, when he pitched two-thirds of an inning against the New York Giants in Game 3. In December 1921, the New York Yankees sent Collins and three other players to the Boston Red Sox (AL) for Sad Sam Jones,* Joe Bush,* and Everett Scott.* After a solid 14–11 season with Boston, he was traded with Del Pratt* to the Detroit Tigers (AL) in October 1922 for four players and $25,000.

Collins compiled a 44–40 record for Detroit the next five seasons, primarily as a starter. He finished his major league career in St. Louis with the Browns (AL) from 1929 to 1931. The right-handed Collins was described as a pitcher with a million dollars worth of talent and 25 cents worth of enthusiasm for baseball. His true interests included hunting, fishing, and partying. He claimed to have started drinking at age six and appropriately was nicknamed after a pre-Prohibition brand of whiskey.

Collins married Letty Parmele on September 10, 1917 and later married his second wife, Ruth Duff, on November 26, 1948. They subsequently moved to Bryan, TX, where he worked as a security officer and sheriff. Although never a baseball star, he finished with a respectable 108–82 career record, a .568 winning percentage, and 3.99 ERA.

BIBLIOGRAPHY: "Rip Collins Dead at 72," *Bryan Daily Eagle*, May 28, 1968, p. 1; "Rip Collins," *Microsoft Complete Baseball* CD-ROM (Redmond, WA, 1994); Rip Collins file, National Baseball Library, Cooperstown, NY; Mike Shatzkin, ed., *The Ballplayers* (New York, 1990); Fred Smith, *995 Tigers* (Detroit, MI, 1981); Richard Bak, *A Place for Summer* (Detroit, MI, 1998); Frederick G. Lieb, *The Detroit Tigers* (New York, 1946); Bill Borst, ed., *Ables to Zoldak*, vol. 1 (St. Louis, MO, 1988); Bill Borst, *The St. Louis Browns, An Informal History* (St. Louis, MO, 1978).

Kent M. Krause

COLLINS, James Anthony "Ripper" (b. March 30, 1904, Altoona, PA; d. April 15, 1970, New Haven, CT), player, coach, manager, scout, and broadcaster, was of Scotch and German descent and received his nickname as a boy. He hit the team's only baseball so hard that when it struck a fence nail, the cover ripped off. He attended Nanty Glo Elementary School in Nanty Glo, PA through the fifth grade and was employed in the coal mines around Altoona when a minor league scout offered him a contract. The scout, however, refused him a five-dollar bonus, prompting Collins's return to the coal mines.

Collins entered professional baseball in 1923, splitting games between Wilson, VA (VL) and York, PA (NYPL). He briefly quit baseball in 1924, but returned to hit .327 and .313 with Johnstown, PA (MAL) in 1925 and 1926. The switch-hitting Collins batted .388 with 101 RBI at Danville, IL (3IL) in 1928 and crushed 38 HR while driving in 134 for Rochester, NY (IL) the next season. The parent St. Louis Cardinals (NL) did not promote him, however, because future National Baseball Hall-of-Famer Jim Bottomley* played first base. In 1930, the 5-foot 9-inch, 163-pound Collins forced the St. Louis Cardinals' hand. At Rochester, he annihilated pitching with 234 hits, 40 HR, 165 runs scored, 180 RBI, and a .376 batting average.

In 1931, Collins batted .301 while sharing duties with Bottomley at first base for the St. Louis Cardinals. St. Louis traded Bottomley to the Cincinnati Reds (NL) and installed Collins as full-time first baseman. Collins responded with 21 HR and 91 RBI in 1932, blending in with "Gashouse Gang" members Dizzy Dean,* Paul Dean, Pepper Martin,* and Leo Durocher.* A noted prankster, he also loved to sing. With Dazzy Vance,* Martin, and Dizzy Dean, he formed a quarter who sang on KMOX radio in St.

Louis, MO in 1933. He and other St. Louis Cardinals made newspaper advertisements for Camel cigarettes.

In 1934, Collins enjoyed his finest major league season. Manager Frankie Frisch* converted him into a disciplined hitter. Collins powered an NL-high 35 HR, still a Cardinal record for a switch-hitter, led the NL with a .615 slugging percentage, and had 200 hits, 128 RBI, and a .333 batting average. His .367 batting average sparked the St. Louis Cardinals' seven-game World Series victory over the Detroit Tigers. Collins followed with 23 HR and 122 RBI the next season. In 1936, a young, power-hitting first baseman, Johnny Mize,* joined the St. Louis Cardinals. The St. Louis Cardinals traded Collins to the Chicago Cubs (NL) in October 1936.

The Chicago Cubs released Collins after the 1938 season. He returned to the minor leagues and collected 402 hits and 239 RBI in two seasons with the Los Angeles, CA Angels (PCL). The 36-year-old Collins married Jeanne Houser on October 17, 1940. They had three sons and one daughter.

In 1941, Collins played 49 games for the Pittsburgh Pirates (NL). Collins served as player–manager for Albany, NY (EL) from 1942 to 1946. In 1944 the 40-year-old Collins batted .396, the highest average in professional baseball that year. After managing the San Diego, CA Padres (PCL) in 1947 and 1948, he spent several years in radio broadcasting and worked in promotions for Wilson Sporting Goods. In 1962, he served as one of 10 coaches with the Chicago Cubs in the rotating manager scheme. He then scouted for the St. Louis Cardinals until his death. His major league career totals included 1,084 games, 1,121 hits, 135 HR, 659 RBI, and a .296 batting average. Collins's minor league career covered 1,611 games with 1,837 hits, 1,061 runs, 193 HR, 928 RBI, and a .331 batting average.

BIBLIOGRAPHY: James Collins file, National Baseball Library, Cooperstown, NY; Bob Broeg, *Redbirds: A Century of Cardinals' Baseball* (St. Louis, MO, 1981); Bob Broeg and Jerry Vickery, *St. Louis Cardinals Encyclopedia* (Grand Rapids, MI, 1998); Eddie Gold and Art Ahrens, *The Golden Era Cubs, 1876–1940* (Chicago, IL, 1985); L. Robert Davids, ed., *Minor League Baseball Stars* (Cooperstown, NY, 1978); G. H. Fleming, *The Dizziest Season* (New York, 1984); Gene Karst and Martin Jones, Jr., *Who's Who in Professional Baseball* (New Rochelle, NY, 1973); Rob Rains, *The St. Louis Cardinals* (New York, 1992); Lowell Reidenbaugh, *Baseball's Hall of Fame-Cooperstown* (New York, 1993).

                                                                          Frank J. Olmsted

COLLINS, James Joseph "Jimmy" (b. January 16, 1870, Buffalo, NY; d. March 6, 1943, Buffalo, NY), player and manager, was the son of policeman Anthony Collins and Alice (O'Hara) Collins. Collins moved to Buffalo at age two, graduated from St. Joseph's Collegiate Institute there, and worked for the Lackawanna Railroad. He married Sarah Edwina Murphy on July 4, 1907 and had two daughters. Collins began his professional career as a third baseman and then as an outfielder with Buffalo, NY (EL), batting .286 in

1893 and .352 in 1894. The Boston Beaneaters (NL) purchased Collins and loaned him for one year to the Louisville Colonels (NL), where he was shifted back to third base. After returning to the Boston Beaneaters (NL) in 1896, he soon became recognized as the premier third baseman of his era. An innovative third baseman, Collins played far off the bag and rushed in on batters when bunts were anticipated. Managers Connie Mack* and John McGraw* both picked Collins as best third baseman on their all-time nines. Although only 5-feet 7½-inches and 160 pounds, Collins led the NL in HR in 1898 with 15. From 1896 to 1900 with Boston, he batted .296, .346, .328, .277, and .304. In 1899, he handled 629 chances at third base.

Collins jumped to the Boston Pilgrims (AL) in 1901 as player–manager at a $5,500 salary and 10 percent of the profits over $25,000. His Boston team finished second in 1901 and third in 1902, but won the AL pennant in 1903 and defeated the Pittsburgh Pirates five games to three in the first modern World Series. Collins was dismissed as manager in 1906, when his team plunged to a 44–92 record. His overall record as Boston manager comprised 464 wins and 389 losses for a .544 percentage. In July 1907, he was traded to the Philadelphia Athletics (AL) and closed out his major league career there the following season. During 14 major league seasons, he batted .294, made 1,999 hits, 352 doubles, 1,055 runs, and 983 RBI and fielded .928.

Collins managed Minneapolis, MN (AA) in 1910 and Providence, RI (EL) in 1911. He was employed by the city of Buffalo for many years and was working as a street inspector when he died. For 22 years he directed the Buffalo Municipal League, one of the nation's most extensive amateur baseball programs. Collins earned as much as $18,000 as a player–manager and held much real estate in the Buffalo area, but lost most of his wealth in the Depression. In 1945, he was elected to the National Baseball Hall of Fame.

BIBLIOGRAPHY: James Collins file, National Baseball Library, Cooperstown, NY; Thomas Aylesworth and Benton Minks, *The Encyclopedia of Baseball Managers* (New York, 1990); Lee Allen, *The American League Story* (New York, 1961); Buffalo *Courier-Express*, March 6, 7, 1943; Buffalo *Evening News*, March 7, 1943; Craig Carter, ed., *TSN Daguerreotypes*, 8th ed. (St. Louis, MO, 1990); Frederick Ivor-Campbell et al., eds., *Baseball's First Stars* (Cleveland, OH, 1996); Lowell Reidenbaugh, *Baseball's Hall of Fame-Cooperstown* (New York, 1993); John Thorn et al., eds., *Total Braves* (New York, 1996); Gary Caruso, *The Braves Encyclopedia* (Philadelphia, PA, 1995); Harold Kaese, *The Boston Braves* (New York, 1948); Robert Redmount, *The Red Sox Encyclopedia* (Champaign, IL, 1998); Harold Seymour, *Baseball: The Early Years* (New York, 1960).

Joseph M. Overfield

COLLINS, John Francis "Shano" (b. December 4, 1885, Charlestown, MA; d. September 10, 1955, Newton, MA), player and manager, performed as an outfielder with the Chicago White Sox (AL) and the Boston Red Sox (AL) from 1910 to 1925 and epitomized the early days of professional baseball when New England Irishmen dominated the game.

Collins, the son of Irish immigrants John T. Collins and Hannah (Corcoran) Collins, began his professional baseball career as a shortstop with Haverhill, MA (NEL) in 1907 and progressed to Springfield, MA (CtL) in 1909. The "tall, lean and leathery" sure fielder, fast runner, and hard hitter was sold to the Chicago White Sox before the 1910 season. After spending two years as a reserve, he started in 1912, principally in the outfield. In the 1917 and 1919 AL pennant years, the 6-foot, 185-pound right-hander played mainly in right field and spelled the left-handed Nemo Leibold against left-handed pitchers. As one of the players most conspicuously loyal to the management, he was not approached to participate in the Black Sox scandal. When the scandal ringleader, Chick Gandil,* did not return for the 1920 season, Collins replaced him at first base and enjoyed his best season with a .303 batting average. In March 1921, however, he and Leibold were traded to the Boston Red Sox for Harry Hooper.* Collins played in the outfield and at first base for the Red Sox until June 1925, when he became manager of the team's affiliate at Pittsfield, MA (EL). After piloting at Des Moines, IA (WL) and Nashua, NH (NEL), he was selected manager of the Boston Red Sox in 1931. He brought a weak team home sixth, but resigned abruptly after a losing streak in June 1932 and ended his active life in baseball. Collins batted .264 with 1,687 hits and 709 RBI in 1,799 games and produced a 73-134 win–loss managerial record at Boston.

Collins painted for the Kenmore Hotel in Boston until retiring in 1951. He was survived by his wife, Elizabeth (Doyle) Collins, and their three daughters and one son.

BIBLIOGRAPHY: Eliot Asinof, *Eight Men Out* (New York, 1963); Boston *Globe*, December 11, 1955, p. 62; Warren Brown, *The Chicago White Sox* (New York, 1952); John Francis Collins file, National Baseball Library, Cooperstown, NY; Daniel E. Ginsburg, *The Fix Is In* (Jefferson, NC, 1995); Robert Redmount, *The Red Sox Encyclopedia* (Champaign, IL, 1998); Thomas Aylesworth and Benton Minks, *The Encyclopedia of Baseball Managers* (New York, 1990).

George W. Hilton

COMBS, Earle Bryan "The Kentucky Colonel," "The Gentleman from Kentucky" (b. May 14, 1899, Pebworth, KY; d. July 21, 1976, Richmond, KY), player and coach, was of Scotch-German ancestry and one of six children of hill farmer James J. Combs and Nannie (Brandenburg) Combs of Owsley County, KY. To become a school teacher, Combs attended Eastern Kentucky State Normal School in Richmond. A talented athlete, he competed on the college basketball and track squads and played shortstop and outfield for the baseball nine. In his last season before graduation in 1921, he batted .591.

To pay for his education, Combs taught between college terms at one-room schools. He soon discovered that he could earn more than twice as much playing semipro baseball. In 1921, his second of two summers in the semipros, he hit .444 for Harlan, KY and was signed by the Louisville Colonels (AA). Combs immediately starred for the Colonels, batting .344 in 1922. His .380 batting average the following year ranked second highest in a league in which Al Simmons* and Bill Terry* also played. The New York Yankees (AL), outbidding several teams, acquired Combs for $50,000 plus two players. The previous year, Combs had married Ruth McCollum of Levi, KY; they had three sons.

Combs held out in spring training in 1924, vowing to return to teaching if he were not paid the share of the purchase price promised him by the Louisville front office. The highly principled Combs insisted: "I am not a dumb animal to be brow beaten, cowed, lashed, coerced, or goaded into anything I do not think is right. I am a human being and I intend to stay one whether I play with the New York Yankees or not."

The dispute was settled to Combs' satisfaction. He soon replaced veteran center fielder Whitey Witt, but a leg injury cut short his season. Although not a polished minor league fielder, Combs developed into an accomplished ballhawk for the Yankees. Limited only by a somewhat weak throwing arm, he possessed ideal range to play between Bob Meusel* and Babe Ruth* and became "the keystone in baseball's greatest outfield."

When Combs joined the Yankees, manager Miller Huggins* already had begun rebuilding the club into what would become by 1927 perhaps the greatest team ever. In that memorable year, Combs peaked with a .356 batting average and led the AL in times at bat (648), hits (231), and triples (23). As leadoff batter, Combs often reached base to set the stage for Ruth, Lou Gehrig,* and other sluggers in the middle of the lineup. The speedy 6-foot, 185 pounder, Combs often drove balls into the outfield gaps and stretched singles into doubles. For eight consecutive years, he scored over 100 runs and hit over 30 doubles. Three times he led the AL in triples. From 1924 to 1934, Combs' average dipped slightly under .300 only once.

Combs had slowed down by 1934 and moved to left field, but still hit over .300. A fractured skull, suffered when he crashed into the left field wall in St. Louis in August 1934, ended his major league career as a regular and prompted his decision to retire following the 1935 campaign. Although his feats were often overshadowed by those of his more colorful teammates, Combs gained recognition as the era's best leadoff man. Nicknamed "The Kentucky Colonel" and "The Gentleman from Kentucky," he hit .350 in four World Series and compiled a lifetime .325 batting average. In 1,455 games, he made 1,866 hits, 309 doubles, 154 triples, 1,186 runs, and 632 RBI.

Combs remained with the Yankees as a coach until 1944, helping polish the skills of Joe DiMaggio.* Subsequently, Combs coached with the St. Louis Browns (AL) in 1947, Boston Red Sox (AL) from 1948 to 1952, and

Philadelphia Phillies (NL) in 1954. Combs, who settled on his 400 acre farm near Richmond, KY, participated in various business and civic projects. He served with pride as a member and then chairman of the Board of Regents of Eastern Kentucky University, his alma mater. Remembering his own youth, he anonymously paid the fees of several EKU students.

Elected to the National Baseball Hall of Fame in 1970, Combs said it was "the last thing I ever expected. I thought the Hall of Fame was for superstars, not just average players like I was." Those who saw him perform knew otherwise. "His value to a club was appreciated by the fans," wrote John Kieran* in the *NYT* near the end of Combs' playing career. "But not to the extent it was appreciated by the managers. Miller Huggins had two personal favorites: Lou Gehrig* and Earle Combs."

BIBLIOGRAPHY: Dave Anderson et al., *The Yankees* (New York, 1979); Earle Combs file, National Baseball Library, Cooperstown, NY; Earle Combs Scrapbook and Correspondence, Eastern Kentucky University Archives, Richmond, KY; Knoxville (TN) *News-Sentinel*, April 26, 1964; Mark Gallagher, *The Yankee Encyclopedia*, vol. 3 (Champaign, IL, 1997); Frank Graham, *The New York Yankees* (New York, 1943); Louisville *Courier-Journal*, March 24, 1922, February 9, 1924, April 27, 1944, April 7, 1953; John Mosedale, *The Greatest of All: The 1927 New York Yankees* (New York, 1974); *NYT*, July 26, 1976; "One of Baseball's Best," *TBA* (September-October 1983), pp. 5, 6, 14; "Recognition Dinner: Earle B. Combs," Souvenir Program, Eastern Kentucky University, March 10, 1970; Richmond (KY) *Daily Register*, July 22, 1976; Ira L. Smith, *Baseball's Famous Outfielders* (New York, 1954); Leo Trachtenberg, *The Wonder Team* (Bowling Green, OH, 1995); John J. Ward, "The Greatest Leadoff Man in the American League," *BM* 40 (December 1927), pp. 317, 324.

Lloyd J. Graybar

COMISKEY, Charles Albert "Charlie," "Old Roman," "Commy" (b. August 15, 1859, Chicago, IL; d. October 26, 1931, Eagle River, WI), player, manager, and owner, was the son of Irish immigrants, Chicago politician John Comiskey and Annie (Kearns) Comiskey. Comiskey grew up in Chicago and briefly attended St. Mary's College in Dodge City, KS. In 1876, he began playing semiprofessional baseball. Three years later, Ted Sullivan hired the center fielder to play for the Dubuque, IA Rabbits (NWL). In 1882, Comiskey joined the St. Louis Browns (AA) and was converted to a first baseman. He served as player–manager in 1883 and from 1885 to 1894, winning AA titles from 1885 through 1888 with the Browns. One of the highest-paid players, Comiskey earned $6,000 in 1889. In 1890 he jumped to the Chicago Pirates (PL), a cooperative organization not recognizing the reserve clause. After the PL venture failed, Comiskey in 1891 rejoined the Browns. He moved in 1892 to the Cincinnati Reds when the AA merged with the NL. In 1,390 career games, he made 1,530 hits and batted .264. His 11-year managerial career included 839 wins and 540 losses for a .608 mark (3rd best).

Comiskey, who retired after the 1894 season, purchased the Sioux City, IA franchise (WL) and quickly moved it to St. Paul, MN. In 1900, WL president Ban Johnson* renamed the loop the AL and shifted its clubs into larger cities. Comiskey's team moved to the South Side of Chicago, one-half mile from the old PL grounds, and was renamed the White Stockings. The AL proclaimed itself a major league in 1901 and quickly gained public acceptance by recruiting outstanding players.

Renamed the White Sox in 1902, Comiskey's club scored a great box office success and fared pretty well on the diamond. The 1906 White Sox, nicknamed the "Hitless Wonders" for their lack of batting prowess, won the AL pennant and defeated the powerful Chicago Cubs in the city's only crosstown World Series. In 1910 Comiskey opened a modern fire-resistant park at Thirty-fourth and Shields, site of the old Brotherhood Park. The ballpark, only the third built of cement and steel, seated about 30,000 spectators. In 1917, the White Sox won their second AL pennant and defeated the New York Giants in the World Series. After a disappointing 1918 campaign shortened by World War I, the White Sox in 1919 returned to first place on the feats of Eddie Collins,* Eddie Cicotte,* Ray Schalk,* Lefty Williams,* and Shoeless Joe Jackson.* Although heavily favored in the World Series, the White Sox lost to the Cincinnati Reds, five games to three. In September 1920, newspapers revealed that eight players had fixed the outcome of the Series. Jackson, Cicotte, and Williams confessed their involvement to the grand jury. The miserly Comiskey had paid the corrupted players poorly for several years. A court acquitted the players in 1921 after the confessions were lost, but Commissioner Kenesaw Mountain Landis* barred them permanently from organized baseball. When Jackson sued for back pay in 1924, Comiskey's attorney conveniently produced the missing documents. Comiskey never rebuilt a formidable club after the Black Sox scandal, as the White Sox finished in the first division only once during the rest of his life. Son J. Louis, the sole child of his marriage to Nan Kelley in 1882, inherited the team when Comiskey died in 1931.

Comiskey founded and owned the White Sox for over 30 years. Experts blamed him in large part for the 1919 scandal because his tight-fisted management took advantage of the less sophisticated players. In 1939, he was voted into the National Baseball Hall of Fame.

BIBLIOGRAPHY: Charles Comiskey file, National Baseball Library, Cooperstown, NY; Adrian Anson, *A Ball Player's Career* (Chicago, IL, 1900); Eliot Asinof, *Eight Men Out* (New York, 1963); Gustav Axelson, *"Commy": The Life Story of Charles A. Comiskey* (Chicago, IL, 1919); Chicago *Tribune*, 1900–1920, October 26, 1931; Dave Condon, *The Go-Go Chicago White Sox* (New York, 1960); Frederick Ivor-Campbell et al., eds., *Baseball's First Stars* (Cleveland, OH, 1996); Richard Lindberg, *Sox* (New York, 1984); Richard Lindberg, *Who's on Third? The Chicago White Sox Story* (South Bend, IN, 1983); Warren Brown, *The Chicago White Sox* (New York, 1952); J. Thomas Hetrick, *Chris Von der Ahe and the St. Louis Browns* (Lanham, MD, 1999);

Dan Gutman, *Baseball Babylon* (New York, 1992); Daniel E. Ginsburg, *The Fix Is In* (Jefferson, NC, 1995); Richard C. Lindberg, *Stealing First in a Two-Team Town* (Champaign, IL, 1994); Eugene C. Murdock, *Ban Johnson, Czar of Baseball* (Westport, CT, 1982); *NCAB* 24 (New York, 1935), p. 173; *NYT*, 1883–1921, October 26, 1931; *The Baseball Encyclopedia*, 10th ed. (New York, 1996); Steven A. Riess, *Touching Base* (Westport, CT, 1980); Harold Seymour, *Baseball: The Golden Age* (New York, 1971); *TSN*, 1900–1931; David Q. Voigt, *American Baseball*, vol. 2 (Norman, OK, 1970).

Steven A. Riess

CONCEPCION, David Ismael (Benitez) (b. June 17, 1948, Aragua, Venezuela), player, is the son of a truckdriver and attended Agustin Codazzi High School in Aragua. Concepcion considered basketball his favorite sport and did not contemplate a professional baseball career. After his high school graduation, Concepcion's part-time play for the local Aragua team impressed his coach, Wilfredo Calvino, a Cincinnati Reds (NL) scout. Calvino signed Concepcion to a professional baseball contract in 1967. The frail Venezuelan spent two years in the minor leagues, where the Cincinnati Reds focused on his play as a shortstop.

The Cincinnati Reds promoted Concepcion to the parent club in 1970 and made him a full-time starter in 1972. During the decade, he served as a vital member on one of major league baseball's most powerful teams. The media dubbed the Cincinnati club "the Big Red Machine." The Cincinnati Reds named him team captain in 1973. Concepcion contributed 167 hits and 82 RBI in 1974 and won the Roberto Clemente Award as the top Latin American major league player in 1977. His most productive offensive season came in 1978, when he collected 170 hits and compiled a .301 batting average. No Cincinnati Reds shortstop had batted .300 since Joe Tinker* in 1913.

The Venezuelan's main prowess, however, remained as a fielder. In 1977, he led NL shortstops in fielding percentage. A steady force at shortstop, Concepcion collected five Gold Glove awards during the 1970s and helped the Reds win three NL Championship Series and two World Series. Concepcion, hampered by an injured elbow in 1980, even introduced and perfected the method of bouncing a fielded ball on the artificial turf on throws to first base. His bat at times also made an impact during championship play. In the 1976 World Series triumph against the New York Yankees, the thin shortstop batted an impressive .357. Concepcion also participated in three NL Championship Series and led Cincinnati with a .455 batting average against the Pittsburgh Pirates in 1975. He hit better than .300 three times and was named the Reds' MVP in 1981.

After the 1988 season, the Cincinnati Reds released the nine-time NL All-Star (1973, 1975–1982). In 1989, his attempt to make the California Angels (AL) roster failed. Concepcion returned to his native Venezuela, where he managed his hometown Aragua Tigres. Concepcion concluded his major league career with 2,326 hits, 950 RBI, and a .267 batting average. He appeared in 2,178 games at shortstop, surpassed in the NL by only Ozzie Smith* and Larry Bowa.* Concepcion ranks among Reds leaders in doubles (389), games, hits, stolen bases (321), runs, and RBI. Concepcion and his wife, Delia (Montenegro), have three children, David Alejandro, David Eduardo, and Daneska.

BIBLIOGRAPHY: David Concepcion file, National Baseball Library, Cooperstown, NY; Stephen Goode, "A New Generation of Latino Athletes," *Nuestro* 9 (September 1985), pp. 26–32; Donald Honig, *The Cincinnati Reds* (New York, 1992); Michael M. Oleksak and Mary Adams Oleksak, *Beisbol: Latin Americans and the Grand Old Game* (Grand Rapids, MI, 1991); Greg Rhodes and John Erardi, *Big Red Dynasty* (Cincinnati, OH, 1997); "Shortstop: Dave Concepcion: All Decade Team," *BM* 15 (April 1980), p. 19; John Thorn et al., eds., *Total Baseball*, 5th ed. (New York, 1997); Robert H. Walker, *Cincinnati and the Big Red Machine* (Bloomington, IN, 1988).

Samuel O. Regalado

CONE, David Brian (b. January 2, 1963, Kansas City, MO), player, is the son of Edward Cone, who worked for Swifts Meatpacking, and Joan Cone and graduated from Rockhurst High School in Kansas City, MO, where he played football and basketball and participated on the track and field team. Major league scouts spotted him playing in the Ban Johnson League in Kansas City. The Kansas City Royals (AL) selected Cone in the third round of the June 8, 1981 free agent draft. He won 6 of 10 decisions for the Royals Blue team (GCL) in 1981. Cone captured 16 victories and lost just 3 while recording a 2.09 ERA for Charlotte, SC (SAL) and Fort Myers, FL (FSL) in 1982. His entire 1983 season was spent on the disabled list. Averaging about 5.5 walks per nine innings, the 6-foot 1-inch, 190-pound right-hander recorded losing records at Memphis, TN (SL) in 1984 and Omaha, NE (AA) in 1985. In 1986, Cone moved to the Omaha bullpen and improved his control. After Cone won 8 games and saved 14 others, Kansas City promoted him in late season.

In need of a catcher, the Kansas City Royals traded Cone to the New York Mets (NL) for Ed Hearn in March, 1987. The Mets returned him to a starting role. Cone won five of 11 decisions despite missing two and a half months with injuries. Almost invincible in 1988, he triumphed 20 times and lost only three decisions while leading the NL with a .870 winning percentage and posting a 2.22 ERA. Cone favored a cross-seam fastball, but also effectively employed a split-fingered pitch, hard slider, change, and curve. His fastballs regularly were clocked in the mid-90s. For the next four seasons, Cone anchored the Mets' starting rotations. He led NL hurlers with 233 strikeouts in 1990 and with 241 strikeouts in 1991. In the 1988 NL Championship Series, he split two decisions. The Mets, however, fell to the Los Angeles Dodgers in seven games.

The Toronto Blue Jays (AL), looking for help down the stretch, traded third baseman Jeff Kent and outfielder Ryan Thompson to the Mets for Cone in August 1992. Cone won four games for Toronto, giving him 17 victories. His combined 261 strikeouts paced the major leagues. He again won one of two decisions in the AL Championship Series against the Oakland Athletics. He started two games without a decision in the World Series, as the Blue Jays defeated the Atlanta Braves in six games.

In December 1992, Cone rejoined Kansas City with a three-year, $18 million contract. In 1993 he won only 11 of 25 decisions, but received less run support than any other regular AL starter. During the strike-shortened 1994 campaign, Cone climbed to spectacular heights. He won 16 games, lost only five, recorded a 2.94 ERA, and took home the AL Cy Young Award. In a cost-cutting move, however, the Royals traded Cone back to the Toronto Blue Jays for three prospects in April 1995. Cone produced a 9–6 record through July 1995, when the last place Blue Jays traded him to the New York Yankees (AL) for three minor league pitchers. Cone won nine of 11 decisions for the Yankees, helping New York into post-season play. He finished 1–0 in two starts in the AL Division Series, but the Seattle Mariners ended the Yankees' pennant hopes. Cone jumped out to a 4–1 start in 1996 after signing a three-year, $19.5 million contract with the Yankees. He returned in September from surgery for an aneurysm in his shoulder to win three more games that helped the Yankees win the AL Eastern Division title. Cone defeated the Atlanta Braves in the third game of the World Series, which the Yankees won in six games. His 12–6 record and 222 strikeouts helped the Yankees make the AL Division playoffs in 1997. He compiled a 20–7 record with 209 strikeouts and a 3.55 ERA, helping New York dominate the AL East with the second most victories in major league history. He shared the AL lead in victories and ranked fifth in strikeouts. Cone blanked the Texas Rangers in the clinching rain-delayed Game 3 of the AL Division Series and compiled a brilliant 1.13 ERA in the AL Championship Series against the Cleveland Indians. He also triumphed in Game 3 of the World Series against the San Diego Padres. Cone finished second in the AL with a 3.44 ERA in 1999 and pitched a perfect game for a 6–0 win over the Montreal Expos on July 18. He compiled a 1–0 record and 2.57 ERA in the AL Championship Series and a 1–0 record and 1.29 ERA in the World Series.

Cone, a passionate, aggressive pitcher who takes his emotions to the mound, pitched in the 1988 and 1992 All-Star games for the NL and the 1994, 1997, and 1999 All-Star games for the AL. He has tossed three one-hitters and on October 6, 1991 struck out 19 Philadelphia Phillies in a three-hit shutout. Through 1999, Cone had pitched 390 games and 2,590 innings with 180 wins, 102 losses, 2,420 strikeouts and a 3.19 ERA. He and wife, Lynn, reside in Leawood, KS.

BIBLIOGRAPHY: David Cone file, National Baseball Library, Cooperstown, NY; Roger Angell, "Conic Projection," *NY* 72 (May 20, 1996), pp. 49–53; J. E. Bradley, "The Headliner," *SI* 78 (April 5, 1993), pp. 92–102; John Dewan, ed., *The Scouting Report: 1994* (New York, 1994); John Harper, "David Cone Hopes to Extend His Winning Ways in '91," *BD* 50 (June 1991), pp. 48–50; Hank Hersch, "Reeling and Dealing," *SI* 77 (September 7, 1992), pp. 10–12; Zander Hollander, *The Complete*

Handbook of Baseball 1996, 26th ed. (New York, 1996); Bob Klapisch, "Met Pitchers Thrived on 'Heat' in '88," *BD* 49 (February 1989), pp. 62–64; Bob Klapisch, "David Cone," *Sport* 84 (July 1993), pp. 52–57; *NYT Biographical Service* 19 (October 1988), pp. 1094–1095; *NYT Biographical Service* 22 (April 1991), pp. 337–338; Frank J. Olmsted, telephone interview with Rev. Chris Pinne', S. J., July 29, 1995; J. Poses, "Beers with . . . David Cone," *Sport* 80 (May 1989), pp. 16ff.

Frank J. Olmsted

CONIGLIARO, Anthony Richard "Tony," "Tony C." (b. January 7, 1945, Revere, MA; d. February 24, 1990, Salem, MA), player and sportscaster, was the son of Sal Conigliaro, a businessman, and Teresa Conigliaro of Swampscott, MA. Conigliaro catapulted from St. Mary's High School in Lynn, MA to the Boston Red Sox (AL) in two years. His only minor league baseball experience came in 1963 with Wellsville, NY (NYPL), where he hit .363 and collected 42 doubles, 24 HR, and 74 RBI in 83 games.

Despite breaking an arm in spring training and suffering other injuries, the 19 year old enjoyed a sensational rookie season with the Boston Red Sox in 1964. The handsome 6-foot 3-inch, 185-pound Italian-American batted .290 and hit 24 HR, quickly becoming a popular local hero. Conigliaro, whom critics labeled brash and headstrong, exuded confidence, collecting 32 HR and 82 RBI in 1965. He became the youngest ballplayer to lead the major leagues in HR and, by July 1967, the youngest ever to reach 100 HR.

No major leaguer, however, ever experienced more tragedy. On August 18, 1967, the hard-throwing Jack Hamilton of the California Angels beaned Conigliaro on the head. Conigliaro missed the remainder of the 1967 AL pennant-winning season and the 1968 campaign. The right-hander, plagued by double vision which physicians thought permanent, tried out as a pitcher in the instructional league. His eyesight improved there. Consequently, Conigliaro won the AL's Comeback Player of the Year award in 1969, hitting 20 HR, driving in 82 runs, and batting .255. He enjoyed his best major league season in 1970, producing 36 HR, 116 RBI, and batting .266.

Yet the Boston Red Sox traded the right fielder to the California Angels (AL) in October 1970 after realizing his vision was worsening. His poor performance there in 1971 contributed to his decision to retire. Conigliaro operated a nightclub near Boston for the next three years before trying a comeback in 1975 with the Boston Red Sox as a DH. But the hitting success of rookie Jim Rice* soon led a slumping Conigliaro to retire. He then began a career as a sportscaster for the next seven years, mostly in San Francisco, CA. On January 9, 1982, the 37-year-old bachelor, in apparent top physical condition, suffered a heart attack while his brother, Billy, a former major leaguer, was driving him to the airport. Conigliaro suffered severe brain damage, preventing him from speaking and using his limbs. After a slight recovery, he died of pneumonia and kidney failure. Conigliaro's abbreviated eight-year major league career included 166 HR, 516 RBI, and .264 batting average in 876 major league games. He played in the 1967 All-Star game.

BIBLIOGRAPHY: Tony Conigliaro file, National Baseball Library, Cooperstown, NY; Tony Conigliaro questionnaire furnished by Richard Topp, Chicago, IL; David Cataneo, *Tony C* (Nashville, TN, 1997); Tony Conigliaro with Jack Zanger, *Seeing It Through* (New York, 1970); Peter Golenbock, *Fenway* (New York, 1992); Wil A. Linkugel and Edward J. Pappas, *They Tasted Glory* (Jefferson, NC, 1998); Jack McCallum, "Faith, Hope, and Tony C.," *SI* 57 (July 5, 1982), pp. 58–62, 64, 66–67, 69–70, 72; Howard Liss, *The Boston Red Sox* (New York, 1982); Mike Lupica, "A Brother's Keeper," *Esquire* 111 (March 1989), pp. 77–80; Peter Gammons, Obituary, *SI* 72 (March 5, 1990), p. 72; *NYT Biographical Service* 21 (February 1990), p. 187; Robert Redmount, *The Red Sox Encyclopedia* (Champaign, IL, 1998); John Thorn et al., eds., *Total Baseball*, 5th ed. (New York, 1997).

James N. Giglio

CONLAN, John Bertrand "Jocko" (b. December 6, 1899, Chicago, IL; d. April 16, 1989, Scottsdale, AZ), baseball player and umpire and boxing referee, was the son of Chicago policeman Audley Conlan and Mary Ann Conlan. He attended All Saints Parochial School and enrolled two years at De La Salle High School in Chicago. In 1912 and 1913, he served as batboy at Comiskey Park for the Chicago White Sox (AL). After playing with Chicago semipro teams, he entered professional baseball with Tulsa, OK (WL). He was traded to Wichita, KS (WL) and played outfield there in 1920, 1922, and 1923, but was suspended in 1921. The fast, 5-foot 7½-inch, 165-pound center fielder enjoyed six good IL seasons, three at Rochester, NY and three at Newark, NJ. A knee injury cost him an opportunity in 1926 with the Cincinnati Reds (NL). After spending 1930 with Toledo, OH (AA) and the next two years with Montreal, Canada (IL), he quit baseball. The injury-ridden Chicago White Sox, however, lured him out of retirement in 1934. A left-handed batter, he hit .249 in 63 games in 1934 and .286 in 65 games in 1935 for the White Sox.

Between games of a July 1935 doubleheader between Chicago and the St. Louis Browns (AL), umpire Red Ormsby suffered heat prostration and could not continue. Conlan, sidelined by a sprained thumb, volunteered to substitute for Ormsby in the second game and the next day and performed impressively and efficiently. Consequently, Conlan officiated in the NYPL during 1936 and 1937 and in the AA in 1938, 1939, and 1940. He advanced to the NL in 1941 and quickly established his authority, ejecting 26 players and managers during the season. Conlan remained an active NL umpire through the 1967 season, umpiring in six World Series, six All-Star games, and four pennant-deciding NL playoffs. Besides being the only big league arbiter of his time who made all his signals with his left hand, he was the only NL umpire to wear an outside chest protector.

In 1925, before umpiring baseball, he had become a licensed New York State boxing referee. He married Ruth Anderson in January 1926 and had two children, John (an Arizona state senator), and Ruth (Mrs. Page Watson).

Conlan, whose brother Joe had a pitching trial with the Brooklyn Robins (NL) in 1920, was elected to the National Baseball Hall of Fame in 1974.

BIBLIOGRAPHY: Martin Appel and Burt Goldblatt, *Baseball's Best: The Hall of Fame Gallery* (New York, 1977); John B. Conlan file, National Baseball Library, Cooperstown, NY; Larry R. Gerlach, ed., *The Men in Blue* (New York, 1980); Paul Green, "Jocko Conlan," *SCD* 10 (October 28, 1983), pp. 52–60; Sam Levy, "Jocko Conlan, New National League Umpire . . . ," *TSN*, February 20, 1941; *NYT*, April 18, 1989, p. B–7; Lowell Reidenbaugh, *Baseball's Hall of Fame-Cooperstown* (New York, 1993); *TSN Baseball Register, 1958; TSN*, January 12, 1949, July 4, 1951.

Frank V. Phelps

CONNOLLY, Thomas Henry, Sr. "Tom," "Tommy" (b. December 31, 1870, Manchester, England; d. April 28 1961, Natick, MA), umpire, was the dean of AL arbiters. Connolly had at least one younger sister and one younger brother, both of whom were born in England. His brother, Francis, umpired professionally in the AA. Connolly played cricket in England as a youth, but never saw a baseball game there. The Connollys migrated in 1885 to Natick, MA, where Tom became batboy for a local baseball team. Although he never played baseball, he assiduously studied the rule book and eventually became the nation's leading authority on baseball rules. NL arbiter Tim Hurst discovered Connolly officiating for a YMCA club in Natick and secured him a professional umpiring job in the NEL. Connolly officiated in the NEL from 1894 to 1897 and joined the NL in 1898. In 1900, he quit because NL president Nicholas Young* failed to back his rulings.

AL president Ban Johnson* hired Connolly in 1901 for the league's inaugural season. In April 1901, Connolly umpired the Cleveland-Chicago contest behind home plate at Comiskey Park in the first AL game ever played. He also officiated at the first AL contests at Shibe Park in Philadelphia, Fenway Park in Boston, and Yankee Stadium in New York City. Besides calling the first World Series in 1903 between the Boston Pilgrims and Pittsburgh Pirates, he officiated in seven subsequent fall classics. Connolly ranked with Bill Klem,* Billy Evans,* Tim Hurst, and Silk O'Loughlin* among the finest all-time major league umpires. The slim, quiet, subdued Connolly, who once described an umpire as "one with poise and without rabbit ears," did not try to please the crowd or engage in theatrical gestures. He lacked the color of Klem, but commanded great respect from players for his fairness.

Although ejecting 10 players his first season, Connolly once went 10 full seasons without ousting a protester. Teams usually did not become too demonstrative in objecting to Connolly's calls. Detroit Tigers star Ty Cobb* once remarked, "You can go just so far with Tommy. Once you see his neck get red it's time to lay off." During an AL pennant race, Connolly once aroused the ire of Detroit Tigers fans by calling Cobb out for crossing home plate while at bat. Cobb had hit the third pitch of an intentional walk for a triple, which would have scored a runner from second base. Connolly an-

other time retorted to irate Cleveland Indians manager Tris Speaker,*
"You're out of the game, of course. And if you don't change your thinking,
you'll be out of baseball."

In June 1931, new AL president William H. Harridge* appointed Connolly as the first AL umpire-in-chief. Nearly every AL club owner and manager had complained about the poor quality of umpiring that season.
Headquartered in Chicago, Connolly supervised AL umpires, scouted the
minor leagues for umpiring talent, and advised Harridge on playing rules.
Connolly retired as AL umpire-in-chief in January 1954 at age 83 and was
replaced by Cal Hubbard* (FB). Connolly, who the previous year had become the first umpire elected to the National Baseball Hall of Fame, had
married Margaret L. Davin in 1902, with whom he had eight children. Four
sons, Thomas, Jr., Edward, Francis, and Arthur, and three daughters, Margaret, Helen, and Mrs. Richard Kilroy, survived him. His wife had died in
1943 after five years of illness.

BIBLIOGRAPHY: Lee Allen, *The Hot Stove League* (New York, 1955); Martin Appel
and Burt Goldblatt, *Baseball's Best: The Hall of Fame Gallery* (New York, 1977); Thomas Connolly file, National Baseball Library, Cooperstown, NY; *NYT*, June 3, 1931;
January 14, February 11, 1954; April 29, 1961; David L. Porter, correspondence with
Frank V. Phelps, March 30, 1986, David L. Porter Collection, Oskaloosa, IA; David
L. Porter, telephone conversation with Frank V. Phelps, April 3, 1986; Lowell Reidenbaugh, *Baseball's Hall of Fame-Cooperstown* (New York, 1993); Robert Smith, *Baseball's Hall of Fame* (New York, 1973); *TSN*, August 5, 1943; May 10, 1961.

David L. Porter

CONNOR, Roger (b. July 1, 1857, Waterbury, CT; d. January 4, 1931, Waterbury, CT), player, manager, and owner, was the son of immigrants from
County Kerry, Ireland and the brother of major league player Joseph Connor. Connor graduated from Waterbury schools, married a local woman,
and had one adopted daughter. He entered organized baseball in 1876 as a
left-handed-throwing third baseman with the Waterbury, CT Monitors (EL)
and played there for two years. From 1878 to 1879, he became a power
hitter for the Holyoke, MA (EL) squad. Rival Springfield, MA (EL) manager
Bob Ferguson* became mentor in 1880 of the Troy, NY Haymakers (NL)
and signed Connor.

Connor played with Troy through the 1882 season, shifting to first base
when a shoulder injury restricted his mobility. He transferred to the New
York Gothams (renamed "Giants" in 1885) in 1883, when the Troy franchise was moved to New York City. Connor remained with the New York
Giants through 1889, joined the New York Giants of the rival PL in 1890,
and returned to the Giants in 1891. After being traded to the Philadelphia
Phillies (NL) in 1892, he again returned to the Giants in 1893. Still a solid
performer, Connor was traded to the St. Louis Browns (NL) in the mid-
season of 1894 and played through the 1897 season.

The 6-foot 3-inch, 220-pound Connor compiled a .317 batting average over 18 major league seasons, hit over .300 12 times, and paced the NL in 1885 with a .371 batting average. Connor, affectionately called "Dear Old Roger" by the Giants fans, led the NL in triples twice and ranked fifth in career triples with 233. The most productive HR hitter of the dead ball era, Connor slugged more round trippers (138) than any pre–twentieth century player. His career achievements included 441 doubles, 1,620 runs scored, and 1,322 RBI.

An effective base runner for a big man, Connor stole 244 bases. He mastered a crowd-pleasing "come-up slide," sliding into a base feet first and bouncing to his feet instantly. Although not a superior fielding first baseman, he dug low throws out of the dirt, presented a large target, and led the NL in fielding twice.

Connor cut a dashing figure with his broad handlebar mustache and his confident bearing and personality. He organized the Giants' chapter of the BPBBP in 1885. Connor managed unsuccessfully with the St. Louis Browns in 46 games in 1896 and two years later purchased the Waterbury club. Connor served as pilot and first baseman there through 1902, retiring as an active player at age 45. For many years he served as school maintenance inspector in Waterbury. In 1976 Connor belatedly was elected to the National Baseball Hall of Fame.

BIBLIOGRAPHY: Roger Connor file, National Baseball Library, Cooperstown, NY; Martin Appel and Burt Goldblatt, *Baseball's Best: The Hall of Fame Gallery* (New York, 1977); Noel Hynd, *The Giants of the Polo Grounds* (New York, 1988); Frederick Ivor-Campbell et al., eds., *Baseball's First Stars* (Cleveland, OH, 1996); James D. Hardy, Jr., *The New York Giants Baseball Club* (Jefferson, NC, 1996); J. Thomas Hetrick, *Chris Von der Ahe and the St. Louis Browns* (Lanham, MD, 1999); Lowell Reidenbaugh, *Baseball's Hall of Fame-Cooperstown* (New York, 1993).

                                                                                    Fred Stein

COOLEY, Duff Gordon "Sir Richard," "Dick" (b. March 29, 1873, Leavenworth, KS; d. August 9, 1937, Dallas, TX), player, manager, and owner, began his baseball career in Topeka, KS (WL) in 1893. He joined the St. Louis Browns (NL) club that season, debuting on July 27. On September 30, he garnered six hits, including a double and triple, against the Boston Beaneaters.

The 5-feet 11-inch, 158-pound outfielder, nicknamed "Sir Richard" for his aristocratic manner, remained with the St. Louis Browns until the Philadelphia Phillies (NL) acquired him in 1896. He spent four years in Philadelphia before being traded to the Pittsburgh Pirates (NL) for Tully Sparks and Heinie Reitz in February 1900. In May 1901, Pittsburgh sold him to the Boston Beaneaters (NL). Cooley moved to the AL in October 1904, when the Detroit Tigers purchased his contract. When the outfielder broke his leg in 1905, rookie Ty Cobb* took his place in the lineup in late August.

Detroit sold Cooley to the Boston Beaneaters in October 1905, but he re-tired instead.

The left-handed hitting Cooley batted over .300 for five of his 13 major league seasons. His highest batting average occurred in his rookie 1893 sea-son, when he hit .346. He led the NL in at-bats in 1897 with 566. Cooley retired with a .294 batting average, 1,576 hits, 847 runs scored, and 557 RBI.

Cooley returned to Topeka in 1906 to own the local WA baseball fran-chise and managed the Topeka, KS White Sox to championships in 1906 and 1908. He sold the club in 1911 and owned the Salt Lake City, UT (UtA) team from 1911 to 1913. The former major leaguer affiliated briefly with the San Diego, CA club (PCL).

The Kansas native left baseball and moved to Dallas, TX, where he worked as a salesman. He died of heat stroke with chronic alcoholism a contributing cause. Cooley was divorced from his ex-wife, Louise, and had no children.

BIBLIOGRAPHY: *The Baseball Encyclopedia*, 10th ed. (New York, 1996); Duff Cooley file, National Baseball Library, Cooperstown, NY; John Thorn et al., eds., *Total Baseball*, 5th ed. (New York, 1997); Rich Westcott and Frank Bilovsky, *The New Phillies Encyclopedia* (Philadelphia, PA, 1993); Frederick G. Lieb and Stan Baumgart-ner, *The Philadelphia Phillies* (New York, 1953); J. Thomas Hetrick, *Chris Von der Ahe and the St. Louis Browns* (Lanham, MD, 1999).

John Hillman

COOMBS, John Wesley "Jack," "Colby Jack," "Iron Man" (b. November 18, 1882, LeGrand, IA; d. April 15, 1957, Palestine, TX), player, coach, and manager, was the son of an Iowa farmer. He moved to Maine with his parents at the age of four. Coombs grew up on a farm and attended Colburn Classic High School in Waterville, ME, where he learned to pitch. He stud-ied chemistry at Colby College and starred on the baseball team there. In 1906, he signed with Connie Mack's* Philadelphia Athletics (AL) for the then fabulous sum of $2,400. He planned to use his baseball earnings to become a chemist, but instead made baseball a career. Coombs never played minor league baseball. After blanking the Washington Senators in his major league debut, Coombs a month later pitched an entire 24-inning game to defeat the Boston Red Sox. By pitching 42 innings in a ten-day period, he hurt his arm and finished the season with a 10–10 record. From 1907 to 1900, he compiled a mediocre 25–25 record.

Relying heavily on an improved curve ball developed with Mack's assis-tance, in 1910 he won 31 of 40 decisions and pitched 13 shutouts to head the star-studded staff that included Eddie Plank* and Chief Bender.* Mack discovered that Coombs' breaking pitches became more effective when his arm was tired. In the 1910 World Series against the Chicago Cubs, Coombs won three games in five days and improved as the World Series progressed. He and Christy Mathewson* were considered among the games' greatest pitchers. In 1911 Coombs, nicknamed "Iron Man," led the Athletics with 28 victories and just 9 losses and greatly helped his club overcome a seemingly insurmountable Detroit Tigers lead. During a crucial game with Detroit, a Coombs fastball broke the wrist of rookie first baseman Del Gainor. Gainor, a potential superstar, never regained full use of his wrist and never fulfilled his promise. In the third game of the 1911 World Series, Coombs bested Mathewson on a HR by Frank Baker.*

In 1912 Coombs won 21 and lost 10, but his club finished 15 games behind Boston. Although Coombs was a teetotaler, his teammates drank excessively to cause the Athletics' poor performance. During spring training in San Antonio, TX in 1913, he was stricken with typhoid fever that settled in his spine and nearly caused his death. The next two seasons, he pitched only a few innings. Having lost both velocity and control, he no longer compared with Mathewson. After being released by the Athletics, he won 43 and lost 43 for the Brooklyn Dodgers (NL). Coombs, a popular figure in Philadelphia, managed the Phillies (NL) for part of the 1919 season to only 18 victories in 62 decisions. Manager Hugh Jennings,* a close friend, hired Coombs in 1920 to coach Detroit Tigers (AL) pitchers. During 14 seasons, he won 158 games, lost 110 decisions for a .590 percentage, compiled a 2.78 ERA, and struck out 1,052 batters in 2,320 innings.

Coombs retired from professional baseball after the 1920 season. He coached at Princeton and Duke universities, where he developed several major league players. Coombs and his wife, Mary, who had no children, enjoyed campus life. He encouraged his players to visit him at his home in the evenings to talk baseball. The highly knowledgeable Coombs wrote a baseball textbook still used by coaches. Coombs maintained that the players of his era performed better than those he coached.

BIBLIOGRAPHY: Jack Coombs file, National Baseball Library, Cooperstown, NY; Jerry E. Clark, *Anson to Zuber: Iowa Boys in the Major Leagues* (Omaha, NE, 1992); Jack Coombs, "My Greatest Diamond Thrill," *TSN*, November 2, 1944; "Mack's Great Expectations," *LD* 36 (March 8, 1913), pp. 543–546; Frederick G. Lieb, *Connie Mack* (New York, 1945); Connie Mack, *My Sixty-Six Years in the Big Leagues* (Philadelphia, PA, 1950); Anthony J. Papalas, interview with Bo Farley, November 12, 1983, Greenville, NC.

Anthony J. Papalas

COOPER, Arley Wilbur (b. February 24, 1892, Bearsville, WV; d. August 7, 1973, Encino, CA), player and manager, began his professional baseball career in 1911 as a pitcher with Marion, OH (OSL) and posted a 17–11 mark there. In 1912 the lanky 5-foot 11-inch, 165-pound southpaw compiled a 16–9 record with Columbus, OH (AA) before joining the Pittsburgh Pirates (NL) late in the season. Cooper made an impressive debut with the Pirates, hurling an 8–0 shutout against the St. Louis Cardinals in his first major league game and compiling a 3–0 record with a 1.66 ERA in six mound appearances. The following season, he was used primarily in relief and posted a modest 5–3 record in 30 games. When Pirates manager Fred Clarke* put him into the starting rotation in 1914, he responded with 19 complete games, a 2.13 ERA, and a 16–15 record.

After posting a dismal 5–16 mark in 1915, Cooper rebounded in 1916 with 16 complete games, a 1.87 ERA, and a 12–11 record that included seven shutout losses. In the middle of the season, he married Edith Warden. For the next eight campaigns (1917–1924), Cooper ranked among the NL's most durable, successful left-handed pitchers, averaging over 35 starts, 295 innings, 26 complete games, and 20 wins per season. In October 1924, he figured in one of the period's biggest trades. Pirates owner Barney Dreyfuss* traded Cooper, infielder Rabbit Maranville,* and first baseman Charlie Grimm* to the Chicago Cubs (NL) for pitcher Vic Aldridge, infielder George Grantham,* and rookie first baseman Al Niehaus.

In 1925, Cooper started 26 games, completed 13 contests, and posted a 12–14 record for the last place Cubs. After a 2–1 start in 1926, Chicago sold him for the waiver price to the Detroit Tigers (AL) in early June. He went winless for the Tigers in four decisions and finished the season with Toledo, OH (AA). Cooper pitched in the minor leagues at Oakland, CA (PCL) in 1927–1928, Shreveport, LA (TL) in 1929, and Shreveport and San Antonio, TX (TL) in 1930. He retired from professional baseball after managing McKeesport, PA (PSA) in 1935, Jeannette, PA (EL) in 1936, and Greensburg, PA (PSA) in 1937.

Cooper compiled a lifetime 216–178 major league win–loss mark (.548 winning percentage) and hurled 35 career shutouts, including eight 1–0 complete game wins. He struck out 1,252 batters in 3,480 innings and recorded a 2.89 ERA. Twice he led the NL in complete games (1919 and 1922). Cooper also paced the NL with 327 innings pitched (1921) and 22 victories (1921). A better than average right-handed batter, Cooper made 293 career hits and led all major league pitchers with a .346 batting average (36 hits in 104 at bats) in 1924. With 202 victories during his 13 years with Pittsburgh, he remains the Pirates' all-time winningest pitcher.

BIBLIOGRAPHY: Arley Wilbur Cooper file, National Baseball Library, Cooperstown, NY; Richard L. Burtt, *The Pittsburgh Pirates: A Pictorial History* (Virginia Beach, VA, 1977); Morris Eckhouse and Carl Mastrocola, *This Date in Pittsburgh Pirate History* (New York, 1980); Eddie Gold and Art Ahrens, *The Golden Era Cubs, 1876–1940* (Chicago, IL, 1985); Frederick G. Lieb, *The Pittsburgh Pirates* (New York, 1948); Charlie Grimm with Ed Prell, *Baseball, I Love You!* (Chicago, IL, 1968); Craig Carter, ed., *TSN Daguerreotypes*, 8th ed. (St. Louis, MO, 1990); *The Baseball Encyclopedia*, 10th ed. (New York, 1996); *TSN*, August 25, 1973.

                                                                Raymond D. Kush

COOPER, Cecil Celester (b. December 20, 1949, Brenham, TX), player and executive, is the youngest of 13 children. Cooper's mother died when he was 10, while his father worked as an itinerant laborer. Two of Cooper's older brothers, John and Sylvester, played baseball with the barnstorming Indianapolis, IN Clowns. Cooper grew up with his eldest sister, Helen, in Independence, TX (population 300), about 70 miles northwest of Houston. Cooper attended all-black Packard High School until his senior year, when he transferred to the integrated Brenham High School. He played for two state high school championship baseball teams and later attended Blinn JC and Prairie View AM College. The 6-foot 2-inch, 190-pound Cooper was selected by the Boston Red Sox (AL) in the sixth round of the June 1968 free agent draft.

Cooper spent nearly six seasons in the Red Sox minor league system with Jamestown, NY (NYPL), Greenville, SC (WCL), Danville, IL (ML), Winston-Salem, NC (CrL), and Pawtucket, RI (IL). He joined Boston during the 1971 season, but started both the 1972 (Louisville, KY, AA) and 1973 (Pawtucket) seasons in the minors before being recalled. In 1974 Cooper became a regular first baseman with the Red Sox.

Cooper became a star after being traded to the Milwaukee Brewers (AL) on December 6, 1976 for first baseman George Scott* and outfielder Bernie Carbo. Cooper already had shown flashes of brilliance, compiling a .327 batting average in the minor leagues and a .283 mark with the Red Sox. But he blossomed as a fielder and hitter with the Brewers. After the trade, Cooper batted at least .300 seven straight seasons. Cooper also won the Gold Glove Award twice and led AL first basemen in chances with 1,068 in 1981 and 1,550 in 1983, and in double plays from 1980 through 1983. He was named the first baseman on *TSN* AL All-Star team from 1979 to 1982. In Cooper's finest season (1980), he led the majors with 122 RBI and the AL with 355 total bases. He placed second in the majors with 219 hits and a .352 batting average. From 1979 to 1983, Cooper compiled more hits (942) and RBI (535) than any other baseball player. His .320 batting average over that span trailed only George Brett* and Rod Carew.* The four-time All-Star played in World Series with the 1975 Red Sox and 1982 Brewers, setting a record in the 1982 series with ten assists by a first baseman. He retired following the 1987 season. In 17 major league seasons, he batted .298 with 2,192 hits, 415 doubles, 241 HR, 1,012 runs, scored, and 1,125 RBI. He won the 1983 Roberto Clemente* Award for humanitarianism and participated in Athletes for Youth, an organization that offers recreation and counseling to Milwaukee youth. Cooper and his wife, Octavia, who married in February 1983, have one daughter, Kelly, and reside in Katy, TX. In 1998, Milwaukee appointed him director of player development.

BIBLIOGRAPHY: Cecil Cooper file, National Baseball Library, Cooperstown, NY; Anthony Cotton, "No Condolences, Please," *SI 53* (September 22, 1980), p. 60; Ron Fimrite, " 'I'm the Lou Gehrig of My Time,' " *SI 59* (September 22, 1983), pp. 52–54; Howard Liss, *The Boston Red Sox* (New York, 1982); Robert E. Kelly, *Baseball's Best* (Jefferson, NC, 1988); Robert Redmount, *The Red Sox Encyclopedia* (Champaign,

IL, 1998); Peter Golenbock, *Fenway* (New York, 1992); *Milwaukee Brewers Press Guide*, 1984; *NYT*, June 27, 1982; *TSN Baseball Register*, 1988.

Eric C. Schneider

COOPER, Morton Cecil "Mort" (b. March 2, 1914, Atherton, MO; d. November 17, 1958, Little Rock, AR), player, ranked among the dominant right-handed NL pitchers during the World War II era. With his catcher-brother Walker Cooper,* he formed one of the more renowned sibling batteries in baseball history. The product of the St. Louis Cardinals (NL) farm system joined the parent club in 1939 after six years of apprenticeship with Des Moines, IA (WL) in 1933, Elmira, NY (PoL) in 1934, Columbus, OH (AA) from 1934 to 1937, and Houston, TX (TL) in 1938, winning 13 games his last two seasons.

In his first major league season, Cooper won 12 of 18 decisions in 1939 and shared NL Rookie of the Year honors with teammate Bob Bowman. The 1940 and 1941 campaigns saw him produce 11–12 and 13–9 records. The Cardinals narrowly lost out to the Brooklyn Dodgers in the NL 1941 pennant race. Cooper engaged in the first of several legendary matchups with Whitlow Wyatt,* with the contests often finishing 1–0. The 1942 campaign, the first of three consecutive NL pennants for the Cardinals, resulted in Cooper's greatest single-season performance. His feats included NL-leading 22 wins, 10 shutouts, a 1.78 ERA, only 7 losses, and the MVP award. After Cooper lost the 1942 World Series opener, St. Louis swept the New York Yankees in the next four games. Cooper enjoyed comparable success in 1943. His NL-tying 21 wins (against 8 losses), NL-leading .724 winning percentage, and 2.30 ERA featured consecutive one-hitters against the Brooklyn Dodgers and Philadelphia Phillies. He split two decisions with the New York Yankees in the 1943 World Series, opening his second effort with five consecutive strikeouts. In 1944, Cooper compiled a 22–7 record, led the NL with seven shutouts, boasted a 2.46 ERA, and divided two decisions with the St. Louis Browns in the World Series.

In May 1945, St. Louis traded Cooper in a sensational deal to the Boston Braves (NL) for Charlie "Red" Barrett. Barrett won 21 games for his new team, but Cooper experienced arm trouble and struggled to a 7–4 mark. Cooper never pitched effectively again in his brief post–World War II career, compiling a 13–11 record for the Braves in 1947, a 3–10 mark for Boston and the New York Giants (NL) in 1947, and concluding his career briefly with the Chicago Cubs (NL) in 1949. The 6-foot 2-inch, 210-pound Cooper married Bernadine Owen in October 1936 and enjoyed hunting and fishing. In a relatively brief seven-year stint with the Cardinals, he won 105 and lost 50 to rank as the all-time team leader in winning percentage (.677) and posted 28 shutouts. His complete major league career included 128 wins, 75 losses, and a 2.97 ERA.

BIBLIOGRAPHY: Morton Cooper file, National Baseball Library, Cooperstown, NY; Bob Broeg and Jerry Vickery, *St. Louis Cardinals Encyclopedia* (Grand Rapids, MI,

1998); *The Baseball Encyclopedia*, 10th ed. (New York, 1996); Bob Broeg, *Redbirds: A Century of Cardinals' Baseball* (St. Louis, MO, 1981); Rob Rains, *The St. Louis Cardinals* (New York, 1992); Frederick G. Lieb, *The St. Louis Cardinals* (New York, 1945); *TSN* Baseball Register, 1940–1948.

Leonard H. Frey

COOPER, William Walker (b. January 8, 1915, Atherton, MO; d. April 11, 1991, Scottsdale, AZ), player and coach, ranked among the strongest, most effective NL catchers during 18 seasons with six different major league franchises. The brother of pitcher Mort Cooper,* he starred with the St. Louis Cardinals (NL) and New York Giants (NL) in the 1940s and possessed a formidable throwing arm and long-ball power. Cooper clinched the 1942 St. Louis World Series victory over the New York Yankees by picking off Joe Gordon* at second base in the decisive fifth game.

Before joining the St. Louis Cardinals in 1941, Cooper spent six seasons in the Cardinals farm system. He posted outstanding batting figures of .336 at Asheville, NC (PiL) in 1939 and .302 at Columbus, OH (AA) in 1940. Cooper started as catcher for the Cardinals' 1942 World Championship squad, batting .281 in 125 games. During the 1943 and 1944 seasons, he registered All-Star batting credentials with .318 and .317 batting marks and over 150 combined RBI. Most of the 1945 campaign was lost to U.S. Naval service. In January 1946, he was dealt to the New York Giants (NL) for the then-huge sum of $175,000. He enjoyed his greatest single offensive season the next year with a .305 batting average, 35 HR, and 122 RBI.

Cooper moved to the Cincinnati Reds (NL) in June 1949, Boston Braves (NL) in May 1950, Milwaukee Braves (NL) in 1953 when the franchise transferred, and Pittsburgh Pirates (NL) and Chicago Cubs (NL) in 1954. Cooper posted .313 batting averages in 1950 and 1951. He rejoined the St. Louis Cardinals in 1956 and concluded his major league career there in 1957. Cooper finished his major league career with a .285 batting average, made 1,341 hits, slugged 173 HR, and knocked in 812 runs in 1,473 games. He batted .300 in the 1942–1944 World Series with the St. Louis Cardinals and hit safely in all five games in the 1943 classic. Following his major league playing career, he coached for the St. Louis Cardinals in 1957 and Kansas City Royals (AL) in 1960 and entered law enforcement work in Missouri. The 6-foot 3-inch, 205-pound Cooper married Doris Triplett in October 1937 and had two daughters, Sarah and Jane. Sarah won the Miss Missouri Beauty Pageant and married Don Blasingame, an NL infielder of the 1960s.

BIBLIOGRAPHY: William Walker Cooper file, National Baseball Library, Cooperstown, NY; Bob Broeg and Jerry Vickery, *St. Louis Cardinals Encyclopedia* (Grand Rapids, MI, 1998); *The Baseball Encyclopedia*, 10th ed. (New York, 1996); Bob Broeg, *Redbirds: A Century of Cardinals' Baseball* (St. Louis, MO, 1981); *SCD* 18 (May 24, 1991), p. 10; Rob Rains, *The St. Louis Cardinals* (New York, 1992); Frederick G. Lieb,

The St. Louis Cardinals (New York, 1945); Noel Hynd, *The Giants of the Polo Grounds* (New York, 1988); Fred Stein, *Under Coogan's Bluff* (Glenshaw, PA, 1978); Gary Caruso, *The Braves Encyclopedia* (Philadelphia, PA, 1995); *TSN Baseball Register*, 1942–1957.

Leonard H. Frey

CORCORAN, Lawrence J. "Larry" (b. August 10, 1859, Brooklyn, NY; d. October 14, 1891, Newark, NJ), player and umpire, ranked among the sport's great early pitchers. Besides winning 170 games for Cap Anson's* Chicago White Stockings (NL) between 1880 and 1884, he became the first major leaguer to pitch three no hitters. The diminutive right-hander began his career in 1877 with the Mutuals of Brooklyn and moved upstate to pitch for the Livingstons of Geneseo, NY. He turned professional with Buffalo, NY's first organized team, an independent with no league affiliation. After two years with Springfield, MA (IA, 1878; NA, 1879) he was acquired by the Chicago White Stockings. In his first season (1880), he won 43 games, hurled 536 innings, compiled a 1.95 ERA, scored his first no-hitter, and led the NL with 268 strikeouts. He paced the league with 31 victories in 1881 and .692 winning percentage and another 1.95 ERA in 1882.

Known for his speed, Corcoran alternated with slower Fred Goldsmith* through three championship seasons. He also exhibited an effective, troublesome curve and good control and proved a plucky fielder who was adept at holding runners on base. When not pitching, Corcoran played shortstop or the outfield. Lifetime, he batted a meager .223, but his 287 hits included 47 doubles, 15 triples, and 2 HR. He also tallied 192 runs in 1,289 times at bat. During an 1884 game with the Buffalo Bisons, Corcoran tried to relieve the pain of an inflamed right index finger by pitching alternately with his right and left hands. After being hit hard for four innings, he was removed from the box. He was sent to shortstop, where he played the remainder of the game, and made three hits, including two triples. Eleven days later, the sufficiently recovered Corcoran blanked the Providence, RI Grays for his third no-hitter.

His effectiveness was destroyed by a sore arm. From 1885 until the close of his career in 1887, he won 7 and lost 6 for Chicago White Stockings, New York Giants (NL), and Indianapolis Hoosiers (NL), and batted .185 in 21 games as an outfielder and shortstop with Washington Statesmen (NL). In eight seasons, Corcoran completed 256 of 268 starts, struck out 1,103 batters in 2,392.1 innings, hurled 22 shutouts, registered 177 wins and 89 losses, and recorded a 2.36 ERA. His .665 winning percentage ranks as the sixth highest of all time.

He struggled through several minor league seasons, trying to regain his touch, and umpired in the AtL in 1890. He died from kidney disease, leaving his wife Gertrude and four children. His brother lost one complete game as a pitcher for the Chicago White Stockings in 1884.

BIBLIOGRAPHY: Lawrence Corcoran file, National Baseball Library, Cooperstown, NY; Eddie Gold and Art Ahrens, *The Golden Era Cubs, 1876–1940* (Chicago, IL, 1985); Al Kermisch, "From a Researcher's Notebook," *BRJ* 11 (1984), p. 66; Newark (NJ) *Evening News*, October 15, 1891; Joseph Overfield, "Christo Von Buffalo: Was He the First Baseball Cartoonist?" *BRJ* 10 (1981), pp. 147–150; *The Baseball Encyclopedia*, 10th ed. (New York, 1996); Harold Seymour, *Baseball: The Early Years* (New York, 1960); *SL*, July 22, 1885, p. 5; Robert L. Tiemann and Mark Rucker, eds., *Nineteenth Century Baseball Stars* (Kansas City, MO, 1989); Warren Wilbert and William Hageman, *Chicago Cubs: Seasons at the Summit* (Champaign, IL, 1997); David Quentin Voigt, *American Baseball*, vol. 1 (University Park, PA, 1983).

A. D. Suehsdorf

CORCORAN, Thomas William "Tommy," "Corky" (b. January 4, 1869, New Haven, CT; d. June 25, 1960, Plainfield, CT), player and umpire, was the second of five children of laborer Peter J. Corcoran and Mary (McNally) Corcoran. He married Dasie M. Sykes in 1898 and Gladys May Dawley on December 5, 1925 and had four children by the first marriage and three by the second. An active amateur and semipro player around New Haven, Corcoran was recruited in 1886 as a pitcher and infielder for a Little Rock, AR semipro team and turned professional the following year with Lynn, MA (NEL). He first played shortstop full-time at Wilkes Barre, PA (CL) in 1888 and returned to New Haven for a successful 1889 season with the city's AA team. His excellent fielding earned him a position with Ned Hanlon's* Pittsburgh Burghers franchise of the ill-fated PL in 1890. After the BPBP collapse, Corcoran joined the Philadelphia Athletics (AA) and led the AA in putouts (300) and fielding average (.911). When Philadelphia did not survive the merger of the AA with the NL, Corcoran signed with the Brooklyn Bridegrooms (NL). He played five seasons there and achieved his top career batting mark of .300 in 1894. His best seasons came from 1893 through 1897, when Corcoran averaged .286 and slugged 15 HR.

In 1897, the Cincinnati Reds (NL) acquired him for two players and cash. For the next 10 years, he excelled as the Reds' shortstop and team captain. He led the NL in fielding average in 1904 (.936) and 1905 (.952), in assists in 1898 (561) and 1905 (531), and in double plays in 1902 (49) and 1905 (67). In 1903 against the St. Louis Cardinals, he set the major league record for assists by a shortstop in a nine-inning game (14). The New York Giants (NL) signed the 38-year-old veteran in 1907 as bench strength behind rookie second baseman Larry Doyle.* Released later in the year, he became playing manager at Uniontown, PA (POML) and managed New Bedford, MA (NEL) in 1908.

Over an 18-year major league career, Corcoran compiled modest averages at bat (.256) and afield (.924). "My work didn't show in the statistics," he told interviewers. Nevertheless, his overall record is impressive: 2,200 games (2,073 at shortstop), 2,252 hits, 1,184 runs, 155 triples (47th all-time), 387 stolen bases, and 1,135 RBI. Initially a barehanded fielder, he ranks fourth in total chances (12,612), fifth in putouts (4,550), sixth in assists (7,106), and seventh in average chances per game (6.1).

A wide-ranging shortstop with a strong and accurate arm who never earned more than $4,600 a year, Corcoran also proved an excellent sign stealer. At Philadelphia, he once uncovered an electric signaling device buried in the third base coaching box. His keystone partners included Yank Robinson at Pittsburgh, Monte Ward* and Tido Daly* at Brooklyn, and Bid McPhee* and Miller Huggins* at Cincinnati. After retirement as a player, he umpired in the CtL (1912), NYSL (1913–1914), FL (1915), and IL (1919). He lived on his 160-acre farm at Voluntown, CT, where he was an occasional fox hunter and amateur field-dog trainer.

BIBLIOGRAPHY: Lee Allen, *The Cincinnati Reds* (New York, 1948); Cincinnati (OH) *Enquirer*, January 30, 1960; Thomas W. Corcoran file, National Baseball Library, Cooperstown, NY; Hartford (CT) *Courant*, June 27, 1960; Frank Graham, *The Brooklyn Dodgers* (New York, 1945); Frederick Ivor-Campbell et al., eds., *Baseball's First Stars* (Cleveland, OH, 1996); William F. McNeil, *The Dodgers Encyclopedia* (Champaign, IL, 1997); Paul MacFarlane, ed., *TSN Daguerreotypes of Great Stars of Baseball* (St. Louis, MO, 1981); Norwich (CT) *Bulletin*, April 15, 1956; January 5, 1957; January 4, 1958; January 3, 26, 1960; *NYT*, January 3, 1960; *The Baseball Encyclopedia*, 10th ed. (New York, 1996); *Spalding's Baseball Guide*, 1890–1900 (New York, 1890–1900); *SL*, July 14, 1906.

A. D. Suehsdorf and Duane A. Smith

COVELESKI, Harry Frank "Cove," "The Giant Killer" (b. Harry Frank Kowalewski, April 23, 1886, Shamokin, PA; d. August 4, 1950, Shamokin, PA), player, was the son of Anthony Kowalewski, a coal miner, and Ann Kowalewski, Polish immigrants. His brothers, Frank and John, played minor league baseball, while Harry, a pitcher, is enshrined in the National Baseball Hall of Fame. The four brothers left school at early ages to work in the mines.

In 1907, Coveleski jumped from the Shamokin sandlots to pitch for the Kane, PA (ISL) club until it disbanded in mid-season. After joining the independent Wildwood, NJ Ottens, he in late September made the Philadelphia Phillies (NL) and allowed no earned runs in 20 innings. The Phillies in 1908 optioned him to the Lancaster, PA Red Roses (TSL), where the 6-foot, 180-pound lefthander converted his side arm delivery to over arm and won 22 games. After being recalled near the season's end, Coveleski gained instant fame as "The Giant Killer" by vanquishing the torrid New York Giants three times in five days. Coveleski's feat forced a playoff game for the NL pennant, which the Giants lost to the Chicago Cubs.

The ex-miner failed to fulfill his early promise, posting a disappointing 6–10 win–loss record in 1909. Philadelphia traded him in January 1910 to the Cincinnati Reds (NL) for pitcher Ad Brennan. Coveleski performed poorly during April 1910 and was assigned to the Birmingham, AL Barons

(SL), where he won 21 games. The Reds recalled him, but released him after absorbing a humiliating 16–4 defeat by the Giants.

Coveleski hurled the next three seasons for the Chattanooga, TN Lookouts (SL), finishing 12–23 in 1911, 13–12 in 1912, and 28–9 in 1913. The husky southpaw married Cecilia Glassie in September 1913 and had one son, William. The Detroit Tigers (AL) gave him another major league chance. Coveleski succeeded brilliantly with records of 22–12 in 1914, 22–13 in 1915, and 21–11 in 1916. Only Walter Johnson* hurled better in the AL over that span. Arm trouble limited Coveleski to marks of 4–6 in 1917 and 0–1 in 1918. His 1919 comeback effort with the Little Rock, AR Travelers (SL) failed.

After leaving baseball, Coveleski owned and operated a tavern in Shamokin. Despite "The Giant Killer" achievement, he did not use his blazing fast ball and assorted curves effectively until midway through his career. His impressive 9-year major league record produced 81 wins, 55 losses, and a 2.39 ERA.

BIBLIOGRAPHY: Harry Coveleski file, National Baseball Library, Cooperstown, NY; William M. Anderson, *The Detroit Tigers* (South Bend, IN, 1996); Richard Bak, *A Place for Summer* (Detroit, MI, 1998); Fred Smith, *995 Tigers* (Detroit, MI, 1991); Don Basenfelder, "Harry Coveleski, 'Giant Killer' of '08," *TSN*, November 6, 1941; G. H. Fleming, *The Unforgettable Season* (New York, 1982); "Harry Coveleski, Southpaw Pitcher of the Philadelphia National League Club," *SL* (December 19, 1908), p. 1; "Harry Coveleski Dies; Famed as 'Giant Killer,' " *TSN*, August 16, 1950, p. 20; Frederick G. Lieb, *The Detroit Tigers* (New York, 1946); John Thorn et al., eds., *Total Baseball*, 5th ed. (New York, 1997); Franklin W. Yeutter, " 'Giant Killer' Calls Lip Smartie Like McGraw," *TSN*, January 15, 1947, p. 11.

Frank V. Phelps

COVELESKI, Stanley Anthony "Stan" (b. Stanislaus Kowalewski, July 13, 1889, Shamokin, PA; d. March 20, 1984, South Bend, IN), player, was born of Polish immigrant parents. Coveleski, the youngest of five boys of Anthony Kowalewski, a coal miner, and Ann Kowalewski, left St. Stanislaus Elementary School after the fourth grade and began working in the coal mines. For an 11-hour, six-day week, the 12-year-old Coveleski earned $3.75. Coveleski's introduction to baseball proved quite unusual, considering his eventual success. He suspended a can from a tree limb with a piece of string, gave it a swing, and tried to hit it with a rock. His uncanny accuracy attracted the attention of some local baseball people. After pitching only five amateur baseball games, he signed his first professional contract in 1908 with Shamokin, PA (AtL).

In 1912, Coveleski received his first major league experience when the Philadelphia Athletics (AL) promoted him late in the season. He passed this test with a 2–1 record in three starts and remains one of the few players to pitch a shutout in his first major league appearance. His next major league opportunity came with the Cleveland Indians (AL) in 1916. During a nine-year stay there, he compiled a 172–123 record for a .583 winning percentage. The 5-foot 11-inch, 166-pound Coveleski enjoyed four consecutive 20-win seasons, including the 1920 World Series championship campaign. In the 1920 World Series against the Brooklyn Dodgers, he won 3 games, allowed only 15 hits, walked 2 batters, allowed 2 runs, pitched 3 complete games and compiled a brilliant 0.67 ERA.

Cleveland traded Coveleski to the Washington Senators (AL) in December 1924, believing that he already had seen his best years. In 1925, his record included a 20–5 mark, an AL-leading .800 winning percentage and a 2.84 ERA. He also made a second, less successful, World Series appearance, losing two games to the Pittsburgh Pirates. After helping the New York Yankees (AL) late in the 1928 season with a 5–1 record in 12 appearances, Coveleski retired his aged, sore right arm to a service station business in South Bend. He was elected to the Cleveland Indians Hall of Fame in 1966, the National Baseball Hall of Fame in 1969, and the Polish-American Hall of Fame in 1976.

Six decades after his retirement from baseball, his record still remains impressive. He compiled a 215–142 career mark for a .602 winning percentage and a 2.89 lifetime ERA, won 20 or more games five times, triumphed in 13 consecutive games in 1925, hurled 38 career shutouts, and pitched a 19-inning complete-game victory against the New York Yankees. In 3,082 innings pitched, he struck out 981 batters and walked 802. He led the AL in shutouts (9) in 1917 and (5) in 1923, strikeouts (133) in 1920, ERA in 1923 (2.76) and 1925 (2.84), and winning percentage (.800) in 1925. He and his brother, Harry,* combined for a 296–197 record, placing them among the best in that category. Coveleski, an introverted figure known for his loyalty to team and family, gained plaudits for his control and ranked among the best spitball pitchers. He and 16 other hurlers were allowed to continue using the spitball after the pitch was banned in 1920.

BIBLIOGRAPHY: *SEAL*, vol. 1 (1981–1985), pp. 188–190; Cleveland *Plain Dealer*, 1916–1925, March 21, 23, 1984; Stanley Coveleski file, National Baseball Library, Cooperstown, NY; Gene Karst and Martin J. Jones, Jr., *Who's Who in Professional Baseball* (New Rochelle, NY, 1973); Eugene Murdock, *Baseball Players and Their Times* (Westport, CT, 1991); Lawrence S. Ritter, *The Glory of Their Times* (New York, 1966); *NYT*, July 27, 29, 1969; Morris Bealle, *The Washington Senators* (Washington, DC, 1947); Shirley Povich, *The Washington Senators* (New York, 1954); Franklin Lewis, *The Cleveland Indians* (New York, 1949); John Thorn et al., eds., *Total Indians* (New York, 1996); *The Baseball Encyclopedia*, 10th ed. (New York, 1996); Joseph L. Reichler, *The Great All-Time Record Book* (New York, 1981); Lowell Reidenbaugh, *Baseball's Hall of Fame-Cooperstown* (New York, 1993).

John E. Neville

COWENS, Alfred Edward, Jr. "Al," "A. C." (b. October 25, 1951, Los Angeles, CA), player, is the son of Alfred Cowens and Peggy Cowens and excelled as a football player at Centennial High School in Compton, CA. The Kansas City Royals (AL) selected him in the 84th round of the June 1969 free agent draft. The 6-foot 2-inch, 205-pound right-handed Cowens played third base, shortstop, and the outfield at Kingsport, TN (ApL) in 1969. He batted .283 at Billings, MT (PrL) the next season. Cowens progressed through the Royals' system primarily as an outfielder at Waterloo, IA (ML) and San Jose, CA (CaL) in both 1971 and 1972, and Jacksonville, FL (SL) in 1972 and 1973. He captured SL Player of the Year honors in 1973.

Cowens made the 1974 Kansas City Royals as a fourth outfielder and batted .242, often as a late inning defensive replacement. In 1975, he shared right field duties with Vada Pinson* and improved his batting average to .277. As the regular right fielder the next season, Cowens batted .265 and stole a career-high 23 bases. He adopted an aggressive batting style from hitting coach Charlie Lau.* His best season came in 1977, when he established career highs with 162 games, 189 hits, 98 runs, 14 triples, 23 HR, 112 RBI, and a .312 batting average, to pace the Royals to 102 victories and an AL West title. Cowens finished second to Rod Carew* in the 1977 AL MVP voting and was selected Royals' Player of the Year. His power surge amazed others because he clouted only three HR in 1976 and just five HR in 1978. He batted .274 in 1978 and .295 in 1979 despite suffering a broken jaw when hit by Texas Ranger reliever Ed Farmer. Cowens batted .200 in the 1976, 1977, and 1978 AL Championship Series with the New York Yankees triumphing in all three series.

The Kansas City Royals traded Cowens to the California Angels (AL) in December 1979. California dealt him to the Detroit Tigers in May 1980. Cowens batted .268 in 1980 and .261 with only 18 RBI in 1981. Detroit sold him to the Seattle Mariners (AL) during spring training in 1982. His five seasons in Seattle resulted in peaks and valleys. In 1982, he belted 20 HR, batted .270, and produced a career-best 39 doubles. Cowens hit only seven HR and batted just .205 the next season, but rebounded to produce 15 HR, 34 doubles, 78 RBI, and a .277 batting average in 1984. In 1985, he hit .265 with 14 HR and 32 doubles. The emergence of outfielders Danny Tartabull* and Phil Bradley relegated Cowens to the bench in 1986. In June 1986, Seattle released him. Cowens finished his major league career with 1,494 hits, 276 doubles, 68 triples, 108 HR, 704 runs, 717 RBI, 120 stolen bases, and a .270 batting average in 1,584 games. He released the ball quickly in the outfield, possessed an accurate arm, and won a *TSN* Gold Glove in 1977, but never played in an All-Star game.

Cowens, who married Velma McClendon, has two sons, Purvis and Dante, and lives in Los Angeles, CA.

BIBLIOGRAPHY: Al Cowens file, National Baseball Library, Cooperstown, NY; Zander Hollander, ed., *The Complete Handbook of Baseball*, 13th ed. (New York, 1983); Kansas City Royals, *Grandslam* (Kansas City, MO, 1976); Marybeth Sullivan, ed., *The Scouting Report: 1986* (New York, 1986).

Frank J. Olmsted

COX, Robert Joe "Bobby" (b. May 21, 1941, Tulsa, OK), player and manager, attended high school in Selma, CA and Reedley JC in California. The Los Angeles Dodgers (NL) signed Cox to a professional baseball contract in 1959. The Chicago Cubs (NL) selected Cox from the Los Angeles Dodgers in the minor league draft in November 1964. In 1966, Cox was acquired by the Atlanta Braves (NL). The 6-foot, 185-pound second and third baseman, who threw and batted right-handed, completed his minor league career with stops including Reno, NV (CaL) in 1960, Salem, OR (NWL) and Panama City, FL (AlFL) in 1961, Salem in 1962, Albuquerque, NM (TL) and Great Falls, MT (PrL) in 1963, Albuquerque in 1964, Salt Lake City, UT (PCL) in 1965, Tacoma, WA (PCL) and Austin, TX (TL) in 1966, and Richmond, VA (IL) in 1967.

In December 1967, the Atlanta Braves traded Cox to the New York Yankees (AL) for two players. Cox spent 1970 with Syracuse, NY (IL) and was released by the New York Yankees in September 1970. Fort Lauderdale, FL (FSL), a Yankee affiliate, signed Cox in July 1971 and released him as a player the following month. Cox's only major league experience as a player came with the New York Yankees in 1968 and 1969. He appeared in 135 games in 1968 and 85 contests in 1969, compiling a .225 career major league batting average. He pitched in three games for Fort Lauderdale in 1971, losing one decision and boasting a 5.40 ERA.

Cox, a minor league instructor for the New York Yankees organization from October 1970 to March 1971, served as player–manager for Fort Lauderdale in 1971. The following season, he managed West Haven, CT (EL). West Haven won the EL pennant and defeated Three Rivers, Canada in three straight games in a postseason playoff. From 1972 to 1976, Cox managed Syracuse, NY (IL) to two second-place and two third-place finishes. He became a major league manager in 1978, piloting the Atlanta Braves (NL) for four seasons. Atlanta finished sixth his first two years and fourth the next two in the NL West.

The Toronto Blue Jays (AL) hired Cox as manager in 1982. In Cox's first season there, the Toronto Blue Jays finished sixth in the AL East. Toronto rose to fourth place in 1983 and second in 1984. In 1985, the Toronto Blue Jays came in first in the AL East and lost to the Kansas City Royals in the AL Championship Series. Out of baseball after the 1985 season, Cox returned as manager of the Atlanta Braves (NL) in June 1990 and replaced Russ Nixon with the Braves in sixth place. In 1991, the Atlanta Braves finished first in the NL West and defeated the Pittsburgh Pirates in the NL Championship Series. Atlanta was defeated by the Minnesota Twins, four games to three, in the World Series.

In 1992, the Atlanta Braves repeated as NL West titlist and again defeated Pittsburgh in the NL Championship Series. The Braves, however, lost to the Toronto Blue Jays in the six game World Series. In 1993, Atlanta took the NL West, but fell to the Philadelphia Phillies in the six-game NL Championship Series. During the strike-shortened 1994 season, Cox guided the Braves to a 68–46 mark and a second-place NL East Division finish. He managed the Braves to first place in the NL East with records of 90–54 in 1995, 96–66 in 1996, 101–61 in 1997, a franchise record 106–56 in 1998, and 103–59 in 1999. The Braves in 1999 became the fourth major league franchise to record three consecutive 100-victory seasons. In 1995, the Braves defeated the Colorado Rockies in the NL Division Series, Cincinnati Reds in the NL Championship Series, and Cleveland Indians, 4–2, in the World Series. Atlanta vanquished the Los Angeles Dodgers in the 1996 NL Division Series and came from behind to defeat the St. Louis Cardinals in the 1996 NL Championship Series, but lost, 4–2, to the New York Yankees in the World Series. The Florida Marlins eliminated the Braves in the 1997 NL Championship Series after Atlanta bested the Houston Astros in the NL Division Series. The Atlanta Braves swept the Chicago Cubs in the 1998 NL Division Series, but were upset, 4–2, by the San Diego Padres in the NL Championship Series. The Braves won the 1999 NL Division Series and the NL Championship Series but lost the World Series.

In four AL seasons, Cox's teams achieved 355 wins and 292 losses. In 14 seasons, his NL teams have won 1,166 games while losing 912. Altogether, Cox's major league managerial totals include 1,521 wins and 1,204 losses for a .558 winning percentage. He ranked first in managerial wins (900) in the 1990s. Cox coached the AL All-Star team in 1985. The BBWAA named him AL Manager of the Year in 1985, while *TSN* designated him Major League Manager of the Year. In 1991, he was chosen NL Manager of the Year by both *TSN* and the BBWAA. The BBWAA designated him NL Manager of the Year again in 1995. In 1999, he was chosen *TSN* Manager of the Year for a third time. Cox is a racing car enthusiast. He and his wife, Pamela, have three children, Kami, Keisha, and Skyla.

BIBLIOGRAPHY: Bobby Cox file, National Baseball Library, Cooperstown, NY; *Atlanta Braves Media Guide*, 1998; Leonard Koppett, *The Man in the Dugout* (New York, 1993); Alexander Wolff, "Out of Control," *SI* 82 (May 15, 1995), pp. 34–36; John Thorn et al., eds., *Total Braves* (New York, 1996); Gary Caruso, *The Braves Encyclopedia* (Philadelphia, PA, 1995); *TSN Official Baseball Register*, 1998.

Stan W. Carlson

CRAIG, Roger Lee (b. February 17, 1930, Durham, NC), player, scout, coach, and manager, is the son of John Craig, a salesman, and graduated in 1949 from Durham High School, where he played baseball and basketball. After Craig attended North Carolina State University, the Brooklyn Dodgers (NL) signed him in 1950. The 6-foot 4-inch, 191-pound right-handed pitcher divided the his first professional baseball season between Newport News, VA (PiL) and Valdosta, GA (GFL) and spent 1951 with Newport News. After military service in 1952 and 1953, he hurled for Newport News, Elmira, NY (EL) and Pueblo, CO (WL) in 1954, and Montreal, Canada (IL) in 1955.

Craig pitched for the Brooklyn Dodgers (NL) from 1955 through 1957 and the Los Angeles Dodgers (NL) from 1958 through 1961. The New York Mets (NL) selected him in the 1961 expansion draft and started him in 1962 and 1963. He toiled in 1964 with the St. Louis Cardinals (NL),

1965 with the Cincinnati Reds (NL), and 1966 with the Philadelphia Phillies (NL). His best season came in 1959, when he finished 11–5 with a 2.06 ERA and shared the NL lead with four shutouts. With the New York Mets in 1963, he tied the NL record for most consecutive games lost in a season with 18. In 12 major league seasons, he compiled 74 wins, 98 losses, and a 3.83 ERA. His World Series appearances in 1955, 1956, 1959, and 1964 produced 2 wins, 2 losses, and a 6.49 ERA.

Craig scouted for the Los Angeles Dodgers in 1967 and managed Albuquerque, NM (TL) in 1968. He served as pitching coach for the San Diego Padres (NL) from 1969 to 1972 and in 1976 and 1977, minor league pitching instructor for the Los Angeles Dodgers in 1973, and pitching coach for the Houston Astros (NL) in 1974 and 1975. He piloted the San Diego Padres in 1978 and 1979, achieving the club's first winning record. The Detroit Tigers (AL) hired him as a pitching coach from 1980 to 1984, when they won the AL pennant and World Series. After scouting for the Tigers in 1985, he managed the San Francisco Giants (NL) to a 586–566 record from September 1985 to 1992.

Craig championed the split-fingered fast ball and pioneered in calling pitches from the dugout. The Giants won the NL Western Division in 1987, where AP named him Major League Manager of the Year. Craig piloted the Giants to a NL pennant in 1989 before being swept by the Oakland Athletics in the World Series. He compiled a 738–737 record in 10 seasons as a major league manager. He married Carolyn Anderson in December 1951 and has four children, Sherri, Roger, Jr., Teresa, and Vicki.

BIBLIOGRAPHY: Donald Dewey and Nicholas Acocella, *The Biographical History of Baseball* (New York, 1995); Roger Craig file, National Baseball Library, Cooperstown, NY; Rich Marazzi, "1955: The 'Boys of Summer' Have Their October," *SCD* 21 (May 12, 1995), pp. 140–142; Thomas Aylesworth and Benton Minks, *The Encyclopedia of Baseball Managers* (New York, 1990); William F. McNeil, *The Dodgers Encyclopedia* (Champaign, IL, 1997); Richard Goldstein, *Superstars and Screwballs* (New York, 1992); *The Baseball Encyclopedia*, 10th ed. (New York, 1996); *San Diego Padres 1976 Media Guide*; *San Francisco Giants 1992 Media Guide*; *TSN Complete Baseball Record Book*, 1997; Leonard Koppett, *The Man in the Dugout* (New York, 1993).

Robert J. Brown

CRAMER, Roger Maxwell "Doc," "Flit" (b. July 22, 1905, Beach Haven, NJ; d. September 9, 1990, Manahawkin, NJ), player and coach, was the son of butcher John Roger Cramer and Eva Jean (Spraigue) Cramer and attended Manahawkin, NJ Grade School and Barnegat High School. He married Helen Letts of Manahawkin on December 25, 1927 and had two children, Elaine and Joan. A left-handed hitter and right-handed throwing outfielder, the 6-foot 2-inch, 185-pound Cramer played in the AL from 1929 through 1948. Nicknamed "Doc," he led the AL in at bats seven times, a major league record, and in singles five times. Frequently ranking among AL leaders in hits, in 1940 he tied Barney McCosky* and Rip Radcliff* for most hits with 200. He was named to the AL All-Star team on five occasions.

In July 1928, former Philadelphia Athletics catcher Cy Perkins discovered Cramer pitching for a semi-pro team in Beach Haven, NJ and persuaded Athletics manager Connie Mack* to sign him. The blue-eyed youngster debuted as an infield-pitcher in 1929 at Martinsburg, WV (BRL), hitting .404 to win the batting championship. Cramer joined the Athletics in late 1929 and remained there through 1935, learning the game's finer points from National Baseball Hall-of-Famer Eddie Collins.* Subsequently, Cramer played with the AL's Boston Red Sox (1936–1940), Washington Senators (1941), and Detroit Tigers (1942–1948). The outfielder starred in the 1945 World Series and helped the Tigers defeat the Chicago Cubs, four games to three. Cramer made 11 hits (all singles) for a .379 batting average, scored 7 runs, and drove in 4 tallies.

During his 20-year major league career, Cramer batted .296, made 2,705 hits, 396 doubles, and 109 triples, scored 1,357 runs, and knocked in 842 tallies. Cramer twice recorded six hits in six consecutive times at bat (on June 20, 1932, at Comiskey Park in Chicago and on July 13, 1935, at Shibe Park in Philadelphia) to tie a major league record, and made a single, double, triple, and HR in a June 10, 1934 contest. An outstanding, agile fielder, Cramer was considered one of the fastest "big men" during his career. He led AL outfielders in putouts in 1936 and 1938 and in fielding in 1945, made 5,412 career putouts to rank eighth on the all-time list, and ranks among the top 50 in all-time at bats. Cramer coached for the Tigers (1948), Seattle, WA (PCL, 1950), and Chicago White Sox (AL, 1951–1953). An avid hunter, Cramer worked as a carpenter in Manahawkin.

BIBLIOGRAPHY: Roger Cramer file, National Baseball Library, Cooperstown, NY; Richard Bak, *Cobb Would Have Caught It* (Detroit, MI, 1991); Connie Mack, *My 66 Years in the Big Leagues* (Philadelphia, PA, 1950); Frederick G. Lieb, *Connie Mack* (New York, 1945); Joe Falls, *Detroit Tigers* (New York, 1975); Donald Honig, *Baseball: When the Grass Was Real* (New York, 1975); Harold (Speed) Johnson, *Who's Who in Major League Baseball* (Chicago, IL, 1933); Stanley Kuminski, "Singles Are Important Too," *BRJ* 3 (1974), pp. 60–63; Craig Carter, ed., *TSN Daguerreotypes*, 8th ed. (St. Louis, MO, 1990); Ted Taylor, "Does Doc Cramer Belong in the Hall of Fame?" *SCD* 25 (June 12, 1998), pp. 90–91; Rich Westcott, *Diamond Greats* (Westport, CT, 1988); Robert Redmount, *The Red Sox Encyclopedia* (Champaign, IL, 1998); Peter Golenbock, *Fenway* (New York, 1992); Fred Smith, *995 Tigers* (Detroit, MI, 1981); William M. Anderson, *The Detroit Tigers* (South Bend, IN, 1996).

B. Randolph Linthurst

CRANDALL, Delmar Wesley "Del" (b. March 5, 1930, Ontario, CA), player, manager, and sportscaster, graduated from Fullerton Union High School and broke into professional baseball in 1948 as a catcher with Leavenworth, KS (WA). His .304 batting mark with Leavenworth in 1948 and .351 average in 38 games the next year with Evansville, IN (3IL) earned him a promotion to the Boston Braves (NL) for the remainder of the 1949 season. The 19-year-old rookie catcher never returned to the minor leagues. In his 16-year major league career, he hit 179 HR, drove in 657 runs, and compiled a .254 batting average.

The 6-foot 1-inch, 180-pound Crandall excelled behind the plate for the Milwaukee Braves (NL), leading NL catchers in assists six times (1953–1954, 1957, 1958–1960), in fielding percentage four times (1956, 1958–1959, 1962), and in putouts three times (1954, 1958, 1960). *TSN* gave him four Gold Glove awards (1958–1960, 1962). Crandall caught three no-hit games, including one each by Jim Wilson, Warren Spahn,* and Lew Burdette.* Authorities generally regarded him as one of the best catchers of his era, as evidenced by his selection as an NL All-Star in 1953–1956, 1958–1960, and 1962.

Crandall spent most of his career as a member of the Milwaukee Braves organization, but also performed brief stints with the San Francisco Giants (NL) in 1964, Pittsburgh Pirates (NL) in 1965, and Cleveland Indians (AL) in 1966. He played on Milwaukee's NL pennant teams of 1957 and 1958. The Milwaukee Braves' 1957 World Series triumph over the New York Yankees ranked as his greatest thrill as a player.

After his playing career ended, Crandall managed at the minor league level beginning with Albuquerque, NM (TL) in 1969. His 1970 Albuquerque club captured the TL championship with a win–loss record of 83–52, an achievement that brought Crandall TL Co-Manager of the Year honors.

After piloting Evansville, IN (AA) in 1971 and briefly the next year, Crandall returned to Milwaukee on May 29, 1972 to take over as the manager of the AL Brewers. In nearly four years as the Brewer skipper, he compiled a record of 271 wins and 338 losses. Crandall won 93 games and lost 131 as the manager of the Seattle Mariners (AL) in 1983 and 1984. He also worked as a radio broadcaster for the Chicago White Sox (1985–1988) and with the Milwaukee Brewers (1989–1994). He managed San Bernardino, CA (CaL) in 1996 and 1997 and has served as special adviser to player development for the Los Angeles Dodgers (NL) since November 1998.

Crandall married Frances Sorralls on March 18, 1951 and has six children, including Del, Jr. and Billy. Crandall, a nondrinker and nonsmoker, developed a reputation as the consummate family man and is widely respected for his integrity and character.

BIBLIOGRAPHY: *The Baseball Encyclopedia*, 10th ed. (New York, 1996); Del Crandall file, National Baseball Library, Cooperstown, NY; *Lead Off:* 1992 Milwaukee Brewers official game program, p. 57; John Thorn et al., eds., *Total Braves* (New York, 1996); Bob Buege, *The Milwaukee Braves: A Baseball Eulogy* (Milwaukee, WI, 1988); Gary Caruso, *The Braves Encyclopedia* (Philadelphia, PA, 1995).

David S. Matz

CRANDALL, James Otis "Doc" (b. October 8, 1877, Wadena, IN; d. August 17, 1951, Bell, CA), player, manager, and coach, performed 24 years as a major league and especially a top minor league pitcher. He attended his hometown grammar school. The 5-foot 10½-inch, 180-pound right-hander married Bertha Caldwell in 1905 and had a son and a daughter.

Crandall began pitching professionally in 1906 and 1907 with Cedar Rapids, IA (3IL). From 1908 through 1913—except for a midseason momentary stop with the St. Louis Cardinals (NL) in the latter year—he mostly relieved for manager John McGraw's* New York Giants (NL). The versatile Crandall also pinch-hit and occasionally played in the infield. When the FL appeared in 1914 and 1915, he pitched and played second base for the St. Louis Terriers. After briefly appearing with the St. Louis Cardinals in 1916, he pitched that year for Oakland, CA (PCL) and Los Angeles, CA (PCL). With the exception of a brief appearance with the Boston Braves (NL) in the 1918 war year, he pitched for Los Angeles from 1917 through 1926. In 1927–1928, he played and managed at Wichita, KS (WL). Crandall returned to the PCL and performed for Sacramento, CA (PCL) and Los Angeles again in 1928–1929, closing his playing career. He coached for the Pittsburgh Pirates (NL) from 1931 to 1934, Des Moines, IA (WA) in 1935, Seattle, WA (PCL) in 1937, and Sacramento in 1938. In later life, he worked as a security guard.

Crandall, probably the very first clearly demarcated relief pitcher, enjoyed considerable success with the New York Giants. He twice finished second in pitchers' winning percentage, led four times in relief wins, and appeared four times among the (retroactive) relief save leaders. He relieved well in the 1911, 1912, and 1913 World Series, winning one decision and also serving as pinch hitter. With the St. Louis Terriers in 1915, he won 21 games as a starting pitcher. His nearly 10-year major league career featured 102 wins, 62 losses, a .622 winning percentage, a 2.92 ERA, and a .285 batting average. During his West Coast tenure, Crandall reached stardom as a spitball pitcher while winning 20 or more games five seasons. In the minor leagues, Crandall won 249, lost 163, compiled a .606 winning percentage, enjoyed a 2.96 ERA, and batted .263.

BIBLIOGRAPHY: *The Baseball Encyclopedia*, 10th ed. (New York, 1996); James Crandall file, National Baseball Library, Cooperstown, NY; *Minor League Baseball Stars*, vol. 2 (Manhattan, KS, 1985); *NYT*, August 18, 1951; Noel Hynd, *The Giants of the Polo Grounds* (New York, 1988); Charles C. Alexander, *John McGraw* (New York, 1988); Ray Robinson, *Matty: An American Hero* (New York, 1993).

Lowell L. Blaisdell

CRAVATH, Clifford Carlton "Gavvy," "Cactus" (b. March 23, 1881, Escondido, CA; d. May 23, 1963, Laguna Beach, CA), player and manager, was nicknamed "Gavvy" and "Cactus." In 1903 he married Californian Myrtle

Wilson, with whom he had two daughters. They also brought up a nephew, Jeff Cravath, who coached the University of Southern California football team in the post–World War II years. An outfielder, Cravath played for Los Angeles, CA (PCL) from 1903 through 1907. After being sold to the Boston Red Sox (AL) in 1908, he hit only .256 with one HR in 94 games. The Red Sox sold him in August 1908 to the Chicago White Sox (AL), who dealt him in May 1909 to the Washington Senators (AL). After being released in 1911 to Minneapolis, MN (AA) he hit 29 HR. The Philadelphia Phillies (NL) purchased his contract in 1912 for $9,000.

At Baker Bowl, Cravath quickly led the HR hitters of the dead ball era. His 24 HR in 1915 set the major league mark for this century until Babe Ruth* hit 29 in 1919 for the Boston Red Sox. Cravath's slugging helped the Phillies win their first NL pennant in 1915. The same year, he led the NL in RBI and runs scored. In the fifth game of the 1915 World Series, Cravath made an unforgettable play. During the first inning with the bases loaded, none out, and the count on Cravath three balls and two strikes, manager Pat Moran* gave the slugger the bunt sign. The Red Sox converted the bunt into a double play, denying the Phillies a big inning.

In 1919, the Phillies fell into the cellar at midseason. Cravath reluctantly replaced Jack Coombs* as manager and continued through the 1920 season as player–manager. His two cellar-dwelling teams won only 40 percent of their games. He served as player–manager of Salt Lake City, UT (PCL) in 1921 and as a pinch hitter for Minneapolis (AA) in 1922. Subsequently, he prospered in real estate in Laguna Beach, CA and became justice of the peace and court judge.

A practical joker known for his modesty and geniality, the muscular right-handed hitter led the NL in HR five times (1913–1915, 1917–1919) and tied for the lead once, hit to all fields with power, and excelled as the outstanding slugger of the pre-Ruthian era. During an 11-year major league career, he made 1,134 hits, smashed 232 doubles, 83 triples, and 119 HR, batted in 719 runs, and hit .287. His 128 RBI in 1913 proved remarkable for his era.

BIBLIOGRAPHY: Gavvy Cravath file, National Baseball Library, Cooperstown, NY; Rich Westcott and Frank Bilovsky, *The New Phillies Encyclopedia* (Philadelphia, PA, 1993); Brent P. Kelley, *The Case For: Those Overlooked by the Baseball Hall of Fame* (Jefferson, NC, 1992); Allen Lewis, *The Philadelphia Phillies: A Pictorial History* (Virginia Beach, VA, 1981); Allen Lewis and Larry Shenk, *This Date in Philadelphia Phillies History* (Briarcliff Manor, NY, 1979); Frederick G. Lieb and Stan Baumgartner, *The Philadelphia Phillies* (New York, 1953); Tom Meany, *Baseball's Greatest Teams* (New York, 1949); *NYT*, May 24, 1963; Ira Smith, *Baseball's Famous Outfielders* (New York, 1954); *TSN*, June 8, 1963.

                                                                    Ralph S. Graber

CRAWFORD, Henry Charles "Shag" (b. August 30, 1916, Philadelphia, PA), player and umpire, is one of six children born to Harry Crawford, a barber, and Mary (McKeown) Crawford. He obtained his unusual nickname not from shagging balls, as is usually assumed, but from teasing reference by playmates to his "shaggy" clothes. Crawford quit Philadelphia's West Catholic High School to help support the family by working for Baldwin's Locomotive Works in Eddystone, PA and playing semipro baseball. He signed with the Philadelphia Phillies (NL) and caught briefly with Centreville, MD (ESL) in 1937 and Hutchinson, KS (WA) in 1938. He served in the U.S. Navy from 1943 to 1946 and was on board the destroyer *Walke* when it was hit by a Kamikaze plane during the invasion of Luzon. After World War II, he resumed delivering milk and umpiring sandlot games. His professional umpiring career began when AL umpire Johnny Stevens recommended him to the Class C CAL in June 1950. Crawford umpired in the Class A EL (1951–1953) and the Class AAA AA (1954–1955) before being promoted to the NL at the unusually advanced age of 39.

In 20 major league seasons, the 6-foot 1-inch, 185-pound Crawford umpired three All-Star games (1959, 1963, 1968), three World Series (1961, 1963, 1969), and two NL Championship Series (1971, 1974). Known for his slow, deliberate, and strong ball–strike calls, he pioneered the now common style of crouching low and placing a hand on the catcher's back. Crawford umpired home plate on August 11, 1965 when Juan Marichal* of the San Francisco Giants hit Los Angeles Dodgers catcher John Roseboro* in the head with a bat. He courageously tackled Marichal to prevent further violence. Crawford worked tirelessly to advance his profession by joining the staff of the Al Somers Umpire School 1969 and helping organize the NL's umpire association in 1964. A member of the MLUA's board of directors, he declined an assignment to work the 1975 World Series because it would violate the agreement with the league to rotate umpires in postseason assignments. The NL retired him after the season.

Crawford married Vivian L. Gallagher in 1940 and has four children. His eldest son, Joey, referees in the NBA, while his second child, Jerry, umpires in the NL.

BIBLIOGRAPHY: Shag Crawford file, National Baseball Library, Cooperstown, NY; Jack Mann, "The Battle of San Francisco," *SI* 23 (August 30, 1965), pp. 12–15; *TSN*, September 14, 1965; Larry R. Gerlach, ed., *The Men in Blue: Conversations with Umpires* (New York, 1980); Shag Crawford, telephone conversation with Larry R. Gerlach, June 23, 1996.

Larry R. Gerlach

CRAWFORD, Samuel Earl "Sam," "Wahoo Sam" (b. April 18, 1880, Wahoo, NE; d. June 15, 1968, Hollywood, CA), player and umpire, ended his schooling after five grades and learned the barbering trade. After playing much semipro baseball around Nebraska, Crawford in 1899 joined Chatham, Canada (CnL). A muscular 6-foot, 190 pounder who batted and threw left-handed, Crawford quickly advanced to Columbus OH-Grand Rapids MI

(WL) and to the Cincinnati Reds (NL). Two years later (1901), he batted .330 and led the major leagues with 16 HR. In 1903, the established NL star jumped his Cincinnati contract and signed with the Detroit Tigers in the new AL for a salary of $3,500.

After batting .335 his first season at Detroit, Crawford slumped for three years. Under the fiery rookie manager Hughey Jennings* and alongside the brilliant young Ty Cobb* in the Detroit outfield, Crawford in 1907 hit .323 to help the Tigers win the AL championship. Detroit repeated in 1908 and 1909, as Crawford continued to hit well above .300. In 1908 he led the AL with 7 home runs, making him the only player to top both major leagues in HR. In the Tigers' three straight World Series losses, however, he averaged only .243.

Although Detroit won no more pennants during Crawford's years there, Crawford remained a strong, durable performer. In 1911, he batted a career-high .378 (to Cobb's league-leading .420). Although not fast, Crawford proved a clever base runner, stealing 41 bases in 1912. Crawford disliked the suspicious, easily riled Cobb, who was convinced that Crawford resented his spectacular achievements and bigger salaries. When Crawford left the Tigers in 1917, he still felt considerable bitterness toward Cobb. During 19 major league seasons, Crawford compiled a lifetime .309 batting average, made 2,961 base hits, drove home 1,525 runs, and smashed 458 doubles, 97 HR, and an unsurpassable 309 triples.

Crawford returned to California, where for several years he had made his off-season home, and played four seasons for Los Angeles, CA in the strong PCL. Although considerably slower, he still hit .360, .332, and .318 before retiring as a player in 1921. During the late 1930s, he umpired for a few years in the PCL. Crawford held various jobs outside baseball, handled his money wisely, and provided comfortably for his wife, Mary, whom he married when he was age 62, and son Samuel, Jr.

Despite their earlier enmity, Cobb always admired Crawford's ballplaying talents and for years campaigned to get him into the National Baseball Hall of Fame. In 1957, the Veterans Committee voted Crawford into membership.

BIBLIOGRAPHY: Samuel Crawford file, National Baseball Library, Cooper: .own, NY; Charles C. Alexander, *Ty Cobb* (New York, 1984); Joe Falls, *Detroit Tigers* (New York, 1975); Richard Bak, *Ty Cobb: His Tumultuous Life and Times* (Dallas, TX, 1994); Richard Bak, *A Place for Summer* (Detroit, MI, 1998); William M. Anderson, *The Detroit Tigers* (South Bend, IN, 1996); Fred Smith, *995 Tigers* (Detroit, MI, 1981); Frederick G. Lieb, *The Detroit Tigers* (New York 1946); Craig Carter, ed., *TSN Daguerreotypes*, 8th ed. (St. Louis, MO, 1990); Lawrence Ritter, *The Glory of Their Times* (New York, 1966); *TSN*, June 29, 1968; Lowell Reidenbaugh, *Baseball's Hall of Fame-Cooperstown* (New York, 1993).

Charles C. Alexander

CREIGHTON, James "Jim" (b. April 15, 1841, Brooklyn, NY; d. October 18, 1862, Brooklyn, NY), player, was the son of James Creighton and Jane Creighton. Creighton grew up in King's County, NY, where he earned nationwide fame pitching for hometown teams. As baseball's popularity soared, he became America's earliest diamond hero and the first martyr. After his death, some clubs adopted his name. He revolutionized the game by pitching aggressively and throwing with speed and spin. Before Creighton developed his underhand snap with the Niagaras of Brooklyn, pitchers tossed the ball easily to the batter.

After joining the Niagaras in 1858 as a second baseman, Creighton began pitching the following year. The Star Club of Brooklyn, a high-ranked junior team, then lured him into their organization. On September 3, 1859, he defeated the big-time Brooklyn Excelsiors, 17–12, but lost 15–12 to the formidable Brooklyn Atlantics because of team fielding lapses. Creighton joined the Excelsiors the next year, making that well-traveled club nearly invincible with his innovative pitching strategy. After the Excelsiors visited Boston, Boston Lowell moundsman and captain James D'Wolff Lovett commented: "Creighton had a great influence upon my success as a pitcher. I noted him very carefully and found that his speed was not due to mere physical strength, but that this later was supplemented by a very long arm and a peculiar wrist movement, very quick and snappy." Henry Chadwick* praised Creighton's "head work" or intelligent style, while conservatives deemed his controversial form illegal.

A marvelous hitter, Creighton established an undefeated record by completing one entire season without being put out. A hitting feat against the Unions of Morisania, NY ended Creighton's career and life at age 21. Creighton ruptured an internal organ while hitting a HR. John Chapman, who attended the game, reported: "He did it hitting a home run. When he crossed the rubber he turned to George Flanley and said 'I must have snapped my belt,' and George said 'I guess not.' It turned out that he suffered a fatal injury. Nothing could be done for him, and baseball met with a severe loss." After a few days of internal hemorrhaging, he died.

BIBLIOGRAPHY: Henry Chadwick, *The American Game of Baseball* (New York, 1868); James Creighton file, National Baseball Library, Cooperstown, NY; Brad Herzog, *The Sports 100* (New York, 1995); James D'Wolf Lovett, *Old Boston Boys and the Games They Played* (Boston, MA, 1906); Preston D. Orem, *Baseball 1845–1881* (Altadena, CA, 1961); Albert Spalding, *America's National Game* (New York, 1911); Robert L. Tiemann and Mark Rucker, eds., *Nineteenth Century Stars* (Kansas City, MO, 1989); William F. McNeil, *The Dodgers Encyclopedia* (Champaign, IL, 1997); Richard Goldstein, *Superstars and Screwballs* (New York, 1991).

Mark D. Rucker

CRONIN, Joseph Edward "Joe" (b. October 12, 1906, San Francisco, CA: d. September 7, 1984, Osterville, MA), player, manager, and executive, was the son of teamster Jerry Cronin and homemaker Mary (Caroline) Cronin and graduated in 1924 from Sacred Heart High School in San Francisco. He married Mildred Robertson on September 27, 1934 and had four children, Thomas, Michael, Maureen, and Kevin. Cronin, who exhibited high morality, strong Christian faith, honesty, fairness, and an excellent memory, fully appreciated the psychology and history of baseball. The extremely modest Cronin believed that baseball did more for him than he contributed to it and was the first ballplayer to rise through the ranks to become AL president. A jovial, friendly person, Cronin admired and exhibited loyalty, dedication, determination, and ability.

After being signed by the Pittsburgh Pirates (NL) in 1924, he played second base and shortstop the next year for Johnstown, PA (MAL). In 1926, he performed for New Haven, CT (EL) and appeared briefly for Pittsburgh. Cronin spent 1927 as a bench reserve for Pittsburgh and early 1928 with Kansas City, MO (AA). On July 28, 1928, the Washington Senators (AL) bought his contract and used him that season as backup for Bobby Reeves. From 1929 to 1934, he started there at shortstop and managed the club the final two years. His 1933 team won the AL pennant, but lost the World Series to the New York Giants, four games to one. In October 1934, the Boston Red Sox (AL) paid a record $250,000 and traded one player for his services. At Boston, he played shortstop from 1935 to 1945 and managed from 1935 to 1947. His 1946 club won the AL pennant, but lost the World Series to the St. Louis Cardinals, four games to three. Named the All-Time Washington Senators shortstop, he received the AL MVP Award in 1930 and was selected as *TSN* shortstop from 1930 to 1934 and in 1938 and 1939. Cronin led AL shortstops three times each in putouts and assists, twice in fielding percentage and doubles, and once in triples. With Boston in 1943, Cronin set an AL record by slugging five pinch hit HR. Besides batting a career .300 mark for Boston, he hit for the cycle on August 2, 1940, becoming the sixth Red Sox player to do so.

During his 20-year major league career, he appeared in 2,124 games for three teams. In 7,579 times at bat, he made 1,482 singles, 515 doubles, 118 triples, and 170 HR, received 1,059 walks, batted in 1,424 runs, scored 1,233 times, and compiled a .301 batting average. Afield, he averaged .951, made 4,290 putouts, and handled 6,048 assists. The successful manager guided Washington to a 165–139 record and Boston to a 1,071–916 mark. During his fifteen managerial seasons, he finished with 1,236 wins and 1,055 losses for a .540 mark. Cronin, who holds the Red Sox record for managerial longevity and most victories, was elected in 1956 to the National Baseball Hall of Fame. In 1982 Boston fans selected him as second-team manager of their all-time "dream team."

Cronin served as Red Sox vice-president, treasurer, and general manager from 1948 to 1959, as AL president from 1959 to 1973, and as chairman of the AL board from 1973 to 1984. In addition, he became a director of the

National Baseball Hall of Fame in 1959, chairman of its Veterans Committee in 1970, and president of the BPAA in 1977. His impact upon baseball included helping to incorporate the Reorganization Agreement into the AL constitution and adding new teams to the AL. Red Sox owner Thomas Yawkey* took a paternal, benevolent attitude toward his team personnel and staff, while manager Cronin ideally complemented his owner's admired personal philosophy and deservedly was acclaimed as Yawkey's devoted, loyal standard-bearer.

BIBLIOGRAPHY: Joseph Cronin file, National Baseball Library, Cooperstown, NY; *SEAL*, vol. 1 (1981–1985), pp. 195–197; *Boston Red Sox Media Guide*, 1984; Ellery H. Clark, Jr., *Boston Red Sox: 75th Anniversary History* (Hicksville, NY, 1975); Ellery H. Clark, Jr., Red Sox Analytical Letter Collection, correspondence with Joe Cronin, Dom DiMaggio, and Bob Doerr; Ellery H. Clark, Jr., *Red Sox Fever* (Hicksville, NY, 1979); Ellery H. Clark, Jr., *Red Sox Forever* (Hicksville, NY, 1977); Ellery H. Clark, Jr., Red Sox Interviews, Joe Cronin, June–August 1983; Mrs. Cronin, August 1983; Peter Golenbock, *Fenway* (New York, 1992); *The Baseball Encyclopedia*, 10th ed. (New York, 1996); Morris Bealle, *The Washington Senators* (Washington, DC, 1947); Robert Redmount, *The Red Sox Encyclopedia* (Champaign, IL, 1998); Frederick G. Lieb, *The Boston Red Sox* (New York, 1947); Shirley Povich, *The Washington Senators* (New York, 1954); Ed Linn, *The Great Rivalry* (New York, 1991); Boston *Globe*, September 8, 1984; *NYT*, September 8, 1984; *TSN*, September 17, 1984.

Ellery H. Clark, Jr.

CROSETTI, Frank Peter Joseph "Frankie" "The Crow" (b. October 4, 1910, San Francisco, CA), player and coach, is the son of Domenic Crosetti, a stevedore, rancher, and garbage collector, and Rachel (Monteverde) Crosetti and played sandlot baseball. His professional career began as a shortstop with the San Francisco Seals (PCL). The New York Yankees (AL) purchased his contract in 1929. He made a key contribution as a Yankees rookie in 1932, helping the team win its first world championship in four seasons. In his 17 seasons with the New York Yankees, he performed on nine AL pennant winners and eight World Series champions. He epitomized the typical New York Yankees star of the 1930s and 1940s, being tough, talented, and dedicated to winning.

From 1932 to 1940 and again in 1943 and 1945, Crosetti was the regular New York Yankees shortstop. Crosetti, who played 62 games at third base in 1941, originally retired during the 1944 season, but returned in 1945. In 1941 and from 1946 to 1948, he was a utility infielder.

In 1938, Crosetti led AL shortstops with 352 putouts, 506 assists, and 120 double plays. The following year, he paced AL shortstops in fielding (.968), putouts (323), and double plays (118). The fleet-footed Crosetti led the New York Yankees in stolen bases for three consecutive seasons (1936–1938) and paced the AL with 27 stolen bases in 1938. He set a major league record for times at bat in a 154-game season with 757. His skills included being

adept at the hidden ball and play and being one of baseball's best sign stealers.

In 1936 and 1939, Crosetti was selected for the AL All-Star team. As a
player and coach, he wore the New York Yankees pinstripes for a record 23
World Series. The World Series appearances involved eight as a player and
15 as a coach. His only World Series HR was hit off the legendary Dizzy
Dean* of the Chicago Cubs in 1938.

From 1949 to 1968, the New York Yankees employed Crosetti as a third-
base coach. He also coached for the Seattle Pilots (AL) in 1969 and Minnesota Twins (AL) in 1970 and 1971. Always in great shape, he worked and
played as hard and long as the regulars. In his prime, he remained an underrated player.

In his 17 major league seasons as a New York Yankee, Crosetti batted
.245 in 1,683 games with 1,541 hits and 1,006 runs scored. His extra base
hits included 260 doubles, 65 triples, and 98 HR. In his seven World Series
appearances, he played in 29 games.

At rookie and spring training camps, Crosetti served as infield instructor.
Crosetti was one of the first New York Yankees that young Mickey Mantle*
met in 1951. Mantle possessed an old, beaten-up glove, causing Crosetti to
buy him a new one. Crosetti married Norma Devincenzi on October 22,
1938 and has two children, John and Ellen.

BIBLIOGRAPHY: Frank Crosetti file, National Baseball Library, Cooperstown, NY;
Dave Anderson et al., *The Yankees* (New York, 1979); *The Baseball Encyclopedia*, 10th
ed. (New York, 1996); Frank Crosetti, letter to Stan W. Carlson, January 1993; Frank
Graham, *The New York Yankees* (New York, 1943); David Halberstam, *Summer of '49*
(New York, 1989); Mark Gallagher, *The Yankee Encyclopedia*, vol. 3 (Champaign, IL,
1997); Dom Forker, *The Men of Autumn* (Dallas, TX, 1989); Dom Forker, *Sweet
Seasons* (Dallas, TX, 1991); *New York Yankee Media Guide*, 1992; John Thorn et al.,
eds., *Total Baseball*, 5th ed. (New York, 1997).

                                                                  Stan W. Carlson

CROSLEY, Powel, Jr. (b. September 18, 1886, Cincinnati, OH; d. March 28,
1961, Cincinnati, OH), executive, was the son of attorney and real estate
developer Powel Crosley, Sr. and Charlotte (Utz) Crosley. The tall, restless
Crosley was more interested in gadgetry than scholarship and graduated
from the Ohio Military Institute in 1905. He attended the University of
Cincinnati and pitched for its baseball team, but dropped out to engage in
advertising, sales, and peddling novelties. Earlier he even had chauffeured
to learn more about cars, his first and most enduring enthusiasm. He married
Gwendolyn Aiken of Cincinnati in 1910 and had two children. Following
her death in 1939, he was married three more times: to Marrianne Richards
in 1943 (divorced 1944), to Eva Brokaw in 1952 (died 1955), and to Charlotte K. Wilson in 1956 (divorced 1960).

After early failures in automobile manufacturing, the innovative Crosley
bought into a growing auto accessories company during World War I. He

acquired control and expanded his business interests to include production of radio and broadcasting equipment and other mass market appliances, the most successful being the Shelvador refrigerator.

In 1934 Leland MacPhail, Sr.,* who was operating the bankrupt Cincinnati Reds (NL) for a local bank, interested Crosley in purchasing a share of the team and becoming the club's president. Crosley claimed that civic pride motivated him to acquire an interest in and then control of the Reds in 1936, but his ownership of the popular, profitable radio station WLW probably figured in his decision. Utilizing his business expertise, he promised Reds fans a "new deal." In 1935, he received permission to introduce major league night games. The first night game was played on May 24, matching the Philadelphia Phillies and the Reds. It was witnessed by over 20,000 fans, perhaps 10 times more than would have turned out for an afternoon game. Drawing barely 200,000 fans in 1934 and finishing in last place since 1931, the Reds progressed during Crosley's regime. Under general managers MacPhail and Warren Giles,* the Reds made the first division by 1938 and won consecutive NL pennants in 1939–1940. In the 1940 World Series, Crosley's club triumphed over the Detroit Tigers.

During Crosley's lifetime, the Reds never again achieved the same success. The Reds' modest farm system did not have the top caliber players to replace such aging stars from the 1939–1940 champions as catcher Ernie Lombardi* and pitcher Bucky Walters.* The Reds returned to the second division by 1945 and remained there until 1956.

After World War II, Crosley contracted his business interests. In 1945, he sold his appliance company and radio stations to the Aviation Corporation (AVCO). He hoped to manufacture a four-cylinder compact car for the postwar market, but sales lagged. In 1952, Crosley sold his auto business to the General Tire and Rubber Company. He spent more time at his island retreats off the Georgia coast and Lake Ontario than with the Reds. Nevertheless, he placed astute baseball men in control of the club. Under new general manager Gabe Paul,* the Cincinnati farm system in the mid–1950s became more productive. With young sluggers Wally Post* and Frank Robinson* joining established star Ted Kluszewski,* the Reds in 1956 tied the then NL HR record.

Crosley died before the Reds won their next NL pennant in 1961, but remained a good owner throughout his control of the club. He let experienced baseball men handle club operations, made the team profitable, and kept the Reds in Cincinnati. Rejecting opportunities to move his franchise to Los Angeles, CA or New York, Crosley insisted that the Reds remain in Cincinnati and be controlled after his death by a family-directed foundation. Profits from the Reds went to charities. Crosley's baseball philosophy essentially remained unchanged: "I do . . . not want to see Cincinnati, the birthplace of major league baseball, become a minor league town. While Cincinnati is the smallest city in the big leagues, the love of baseball is deep rooted."

BIBLIOGRAPHY: Lee Allen, *The Cincinnati Reds* (New York, 1948); William H. Beezley, "Crosley, Powel, Jr.," *DAB*, Supp. 7 (1961–1965), pp. 154–155; Powel Crosley, Jr., interview, October 4, 1938, Cincinnati Baseball Club Press Releases, February 5, 1934 and November 6, 1936, all in Powel Crosley, Jr. file, National Baseball Library, Cooperstown, NY; Forrest Davis, "The Crosley Touch—And Go!" *SEP* 222 (September 30, 1939), pp. 18, 51–57; Lloyd J. Graybar, interview with Pat Harmon, November 28, 1983; Donald Honig, *The Cincinnati Reds* (New York, 1992); "Love's Labor Lost," *Time* 60 (July 28, 1952), p. 70; *NYT*, February 5, 1934, July 1, September 19, 1936, July 19, October 26, November 3, 1960, March 29, 30, 1961; Gabe Paul to Lloyd J. Graybar, November 29, 1983; Gerard Piel, "Powel Crosley, Jr.," *Life* 22 (February 17, 1947), pp. 47–48, 50–54; Joe Rice, *Cincinnati's Powel Crosley Jr.: Industrialist, Pioneer Radio Builder* (Covington, KY, 1976); *TSN*, April 5, 1961.

Lloyd J. Graybar

CROSS, Lafayette Napoleon "Lave" (b. May 12, 1866, Milwaukee, WI; d. September 6, 1927, Toledo, OH), player and manager, was the son of Czechoslavakian immigrants and brother of less successful big league players Amos Cross and Frank Cross. He played amateur ball in the Cleveland area before becoming a professional with Sandusky, OH in 1884. His major league career began with the Louisville, KY Colonels (AA) in 1887. He moved to the Philadelphia Athletics (AA) in 1889, jumped to the Philadelphia Quakers (PL) in 1890, then returned to the AA squad in 1891, the AA's last year. He remained in Philadelphia with the Phillies NL team through the 1897 season. In the next three years, he saw action with the Cleveland Spiders, Brooklyn Bridegrooms and St. Louis Cardinals, all of the NL. In 1901 Connie Mack* lured him to join the Philadelphia Athletics in the newly formed AL, where he remained through 1905. Cross moved to the Washington Senators (AL) in 1906 and ended his 21 year major league career in 1907 following an ankle injury. In 1907 he joined New Orleans as player manager. He later played at Charlotte, NC and Haverhill, MA, retiring in 1912.

One of the game's most versatile, durable, and popular stars, Cross played 2,275 major league games, appearing in every position except pitcher: 1,721 at third base, 324 as catcher, 119 as outfielder, 65 at shortstop, 60 at second base, and 7 at first base. With a lifetime .292 batting average, .382 slugging average, 2,645 hits, 411 doubles, 135 triples, and 47 HR, Cross held an honored place in the history of the game. He once hit for the cycle and holds the record for most assists in a game by a second baseman (15 in 12 innings). He remains tied for third in most assists by a third baseman, with 10 in 10 innings. He played third base with a catcher's mitt, a then legal ploy that enabled him to knock down many a hard drive and throw out the runner. He managed the Cleveland Spiders (NL) briefly (1899), winning 8 and losing 30 for a .211 percentage. Cross played without distinction in one

World Series (1905) as a third baseman. He worked as a machinist at Willys Overland Automobile Manufacturing in Toledo and was survived by his wife and a daughter.

BIBLIOGRAPHY: Lave Cross file, National Baseball Library, Cooperstown, NY; Frederick Ivor-Campbell et al., eds., *Baseball's First Stars* (Cleveland, OH, 1996); J. Thomas Hetrick, *The Misfits!* (Jefferson, NC, 1991); John Phillips, *The Spiders—Who Was Who* (Cabin John, MD, 1991); David Nemec, *The Beer and Whisky League* (New York, 1994); Rich Westcott and Frank Bilovsky, *The New Phillies Encyclopedia* (Philadelphia, PA, 1993); Frederick G. Lieb and Stan Baumgartner, *The Philadelphia Phillies* (New York, 1953); Frederick G. Lieb, *Connie Mack* (New York, 1945); Connie Mack, *My 66 Years in the Big Leagues* (Philadelphia, PA, 1950); Joseph L. Reichler, *The Great All-Time Baseball Record Book* (New York, 1981); *The Baseball Encyclopedia*, 10th ed. (New York, 1996).

Robert G. Weaver

CROWDER, Alvin Floyd "General" (b. January 11, 1899, Winston-Salem, NC; d. April 3, 1972, Winston-Salem, NC), player, manager, and executive, was the son of George Crowder and Emma (Munke) Crowder. He grew up in Winston-Salem and became seriously interested in baseball while serving in the United States Army. He pitched in the minor leagues in San Francisco, CA (PCL), Waterbury, CT (EL), Rochester, NY (IL), Winston-Salem, NC (PiL), and Birmingham, AL (SL) before reaching the major leagues in 1926. He was nicknamed "General" after World War I General Enoch Crowder, supervisor of the draft, but the two were not related.

The 5-foot 10-inch, 170-pound Crowder joined the Washington Senators (AL) in 1926, but was traded to the St. Louis Browns (AL) in July 1927. The right-hander compiled a superb 21–5 mark for the Browns in 1928 and led the AL with an .808 winning percentage. In 1929 he paced the AL in shutouts with four. Crowder was traded back to the Washington Senators in June 1930, winning 18 games in both 1930 and 1931. In 1932 he recorded 15 straight triumphs en route to a 26–13 mark, as his 26 victories and 327 innings pitched paced the AL. He led the AL again the next season in appearances (52) and wins with a 24–15 mark. Washington traded Crowder to the Detroit Tigers (AL) in August 1934. He retired following the 1936 season with a 167–115 record and 4.12 ERA.

Crowder pitched in the 1933 World Series for the Washington Senators and the 1934 and 1935 fall classics for the Detroit Tigers. He lost one game each in the 1933 World Series against the New York Yankees and the 1934 World Series against the St. Louis Cardinals, but won one contest in the 1935 fall classic against the Chicago Cubs. Crowder maintained that his biggest baseball thrill came in pitching the inaugural 1933 All-Star game. He also gained a measure of fame for his success against the feared New York Yankees. Walter Johnson* wrote of Crowder at his peak that "He's got everything—speed, curve, control and sense. He's the best worker I've ever seen."

Crowder subsequently owned, managed, and occasionally played for Winston-Salem, NC in the late 1930s and early 1940s. He also worked as a Winston-Salem businessman until ill health forced his retirement in the 1950s. He and his wife, Joanna (Brockwell) Crowder, had two children, Kathryn and Alvin, Jr. Crowder belongs to the North Carolina Sports Hall of Fame.

BIBLIOGRAPHY: Frank Lane, "Baseball's Greatest Pitcher in 1932," *BM* 50 (May 1933), pp. 537–539; Mal Mallete, "Old Yank-Stopper Crowder Predicts They Will Stay Up Another Decade," *TSN*, July 2, 1958, p. 11; Winston-Salem *Journal*, April 4, 1972; Alvin Crowder file, National Baseball Library, Cooperstown, NY; Shirley Povich, *The Washington Senators* (New York, 1954); Bill Borst, ed., *Ables to Zoldak*, vol. 1 (St. Louis, MO, 1988); Bill Borst, *The St. Louis Browns, An Informal History* (St. Louis, MO, 1978); Fred Smith, *995 Tigers* (Detroit, MI, 1981); Charles Bevis, *Mickey Cochrane: The Life of a Baseball Hall of Fame Catcher* (Jefferson, NC, 1998).

Jim L. Sumner

CRUTCHFIELD, John William "Jimmie" (b. March 25, 1910, Ardmore, MO; d. March 31, 1993, Chicago, IL), player, was the son of John H. Crutchfield and Carrie (Cooper) Crutchfield and attended elementary school in Ardmore and two years of high school in Moberly, MO. Crutchfield began his Negro League professional career in 1930 as an outfielder with the Birmingham, AL Black Barons (NNL) and started the 1931 season with the Indianapolis ABC's (NNL). During that season, he was acquired by the Pittsburgh Crawfords (NNL) and played there throughout the 1936 season. Crutchfield later performed for the Newark, NJ Eagles (NNL) and Cleveland Buckeyes (NAL), with a brief stint in 1943 in the U.S. Army.

Known as "The Black Lloyd Waner*" because of his ability to play hit and run, Crutchfield compiled a lifetime .270 batting average while displaying enthusiasm, hustle, and sportsmanship. Crutchfield was playing for the Indianapolis ABC's against the Pittsburgh Crawfords in 1931, when Pittsburgh offered him $50 to stay. Crutchfield strengthened the Crawfords team, playing with legendary black stars Josh Gibson,* Satchel Paige,* Judy Johnson,* and "Cool Papa" Bell.* Crutchfield's most noteworthy honors included selection to four East-West All-Star games. As a member of the Pittsburgh Crawfords in 1934, 1935, and 1936, Crutchfield was selected as the starting right fielder. In 1941, while playing for the Chicago American Giants, he was named to the squad as an outfielder and played left field. His best season came in 1935, when he batted .308.

Crutchfield later served as a resource person for Robert W. Peterson's *Only the Ball Was White* and for Craig Davidson's Negro Leagues film, *The Sun Was Always Shining Someplace*. Upon retiring from baseball, Crutchfield worked 26 years for the U.S. Postal Service. He married Julia Robertson Marshall in 1947 and resided in Chicago.

BIBLIOGRAPHY: James Bankes, *The Pittsburgh Crawfords* (Dubuque, IA, 1991); *NYT Biographical Service* 24 (April 1993), p. 483; Robert W. Peterson, *Only the Ball Was White* (Englewood Cliffs, NJ, 1970); James A. Riley, *The Biographical Encyclopedia of the Negro Baseball Leagues* (New York, 1994); Robert L. Ruck, *Sandlot Seasons: Sport in Black Pittsburgh* (Urbana, IL, 1986); William A. Sutton, correspondence with Jeff Kernan, William A. Sutton Collection, Columbus, OH.

William A. Sutton

CRUZ, Jose "Cheo" (Dilan) (b. August 8, 1947, Arroyo, PR), player and coach, is the brother of former major leaguers Hector Cruz and Tommy Cruz. After graduating from Carmen Bozello de Heyke School in Arroyo, PR, he was signed by veteran St. Louis Cardinals (NL) scout Chase Riddle in October 1966. He displayed consistency at the plate and in the outfield from 1967 to 1969 in the Cardinals farm system at St. Petersburg, FL (FSL), Modesto, CA (CaL), and Little Rock–based Arkansas (TL). After starting well at Tulsa, OK (AA) in 1971, Cruz batted .274 in 83 games for St. Louis and played center field between Lou Brock* and Matty Alou.* Cruz married Hilda Vazquez on November 18, 1972. He batted only .235 and .227 as a regular in 1972 and 1973, thus losing his starting job to rookie sensation Bake McBride.* In 1973, his younger brothers, Hector and Tommy, joined the Cardinals. In October 1974, St. Louis sold him to the Houston Astros (NL) for a mere $20,000.

At Houston, hitting instructor Deacon Jones made Cruz a more disciplined hitter. By laying off bad pitches, Cruz improved his batting average and drew more walks. The 6-foot, 185-pound left-handed Cruz still maintained an unorthodox batting style, raising his right foot high in the air as he strode into a pitch. Cruz became one of the most consistent longtime ballplayers in Astros history. He patrolled the spacious reaches of the Astrodome outfield from 1975 to 1987, batted at least .300 six times, and pilfered a career-high 44 bases in 1977. Cruz may have attempted the longball more often in another home ballpark, but became more productive as a line-drive hitter in the dead air and far reaches of the Astrodome. He was named NL Player of the Month in July 1984, when he batted .443. In 13 seasons with the Astros, Cruz batted .292 and established Houston records for games (1,870), at bats (6,629), hits (1,937), triples (80), and RBI (942).

Despite his longevity and productivity, Cruz attracted little national attention. He never played in a World Series and batted only once for the NL in the 1985 All Star game. He signed with the New York Yankees (AL) as a free agent in February 1988, but hit only .200 in 38 games that year in his final major league season. Cruz played outfield for the Orlando, FL Juice in the SPBA's 1989–1990 maiden season and batted .306 with 49 RBI. His career major league totals included 2,251 hits, 1,036 runs, 165 HR, 1,077

RBI, and 317 stolen bases in 2,353 games. Cruz, who was named to *TSN*'s Silver Slugger team in 1983 and 1984, has coached for the Houston Astros since 1996.

BIBLIOGRAPHY: Jose Cruz file, National Baseball Library, Cooperstown, NY; Phil Elderkin, "Jose Cruz: A Steady Hitter with an Unorthodox Style," *BD* 43 (August 1984), pp. 67–68; Marty Hendin, ed., *St. Louis Souvenir Yearbook* (St. Louis, MO, 1974); Harry Shattuck, "Jose Cruz of the Astros: Underrated No Longer!" *BD* 40 (February 1981), pp. 55–58; Jayson Stark, "Jose Cruz: The Big League's Most Unheralded Star," *BD* 44 (August 1985), pp. 39–42.

Frank J. Olmsted

CUCCINELLO, Anthony Francis "Tony," "Chick" (b. November 8, 1907, Long Island City, NY; d. September 21, 1995, Tampa, FL), player, coach, scout, and manager, was the son of Samuel Cuccinello, an engineer with Consolidated Edison, and Amelia (Barberesi) Cuccinello and began his long professional baseball career in 1926 with Syracuse, NY (IL). After only four games, he was sent to Lawrence, MA (NEL) for the remainder of the 1926 season and 1927 campaign. After 127 games at Danville, IL (3IL) in 1928, he was sold to the Cincinnati Reds (NL). The Cincinnati Reds optioned him to Columbus, OH (AA) for the rest of the 1928 season and 1929 campaign and recalled him in 1930. Cuccinello enjoyed two outstanding major league seasons while playing several infield positions, batting .312 in 1930 and .315 in 1931.

Cuccinello was traded to the Brooklyn Dodgers (NL) in March 1932 and played there through 1935. In December 1935, the Brooklyn Dodgers sent him to the Boston Bees (NL) in a multiplayer deal. In June 1940, the Boston Bees traded him to the New York Giants (NL). In 1941, hobbled by a knee injury, he was assigned to the New York Giants farm team in Jersey City, NJ (IL) as player–manager. He agreed to pilot Jersey City again in 1942, but secured his release so that he could join the Boston Braves (NL) as a player–coach. After being let go on July 19, 1943, he was signed the same day by the Chicago White Sox (AL) and played there until unconditionally released on January 5, 1946. After spending a year out of baseball, he returned in 1947 to manage Tampa, FL (FIL).

Known as an intelligent player, Cuccinello coached for Indianapolis, IN (AA) in 1948, the Cincinnati Reds (NL) from 1949 to 1951, Cleveland Indians (AL) from 1952 to 1956, Chicago White Sox (AL) from 1957 to 1966, Detroit Tigers (AL) in 1967 and 1968, and Chicago White Sox (AL) again in 1969. He scouted for the New York Yankees (AL) until 1985. He coached on three AL pennant winners, the 1954 Cleveland Indians, 1960 Chicago White Sox, and 1968 Detroit Tigers. Detroit won the 1968 World Series.

His 1,704 major league games included 1,205 at second base, 468 at third base, and five at shortstop. Cuccinello batted .280 with 1,729 hits, recording 334 doubles, 46 triples, and 94 HR. He drove in 884 runs, scored 730 runs, drew 579 walks, and stole 42 bases. In 1939, he established a major league record for the longest errorless game (23 innings) by a second baseman. He was selected to NL All-Star teams in 1933 and 1938.

Cuccinello's brother, Al, played infield for the New York Giants (NL) in 1935, while his nephew, Sam Mele,* was an AL outfielder and managed the Minnesota Twins (AL). Cuccinello married Clara Caroselli in October 1932 and resided in Tampa, FL. He had two sons, Anthony, Jr., and Joseph, and one daughter, Darlene Ann.

BIBLIOGRAPHY: Tony Cuccinello file, National Baseball Library, Cooperstown, NY; Lee Allen, *The Cincinnati Reds* (New York, 1948); Frank Graham, *The Brooklyn Dodgers* (New York, 1945); Harold Kaese, *The Boston Braves* (New York, 1948); William F. McNeil, *The Dodgers Encyclopedia* (Champaign, IL, 1997); Gary Caruso, *The Braves Encyclopedia* (Philadelphia, PA, 1995); Robert L. Tiemann, *Dodger Classics* (St. Louis, MO, 1983); *TSN Official Baseball Register*, 1969; Rich Westcott, *Diamond Greats* (Westport, CT, 1988).

Ralph S. Graber

CUELLAR, Miguel Angel Santana "Mike" (b. May 8, 1937, Santa Clara, Las Villas, Cuba), player and coach, received only three years of formal education and worked extensively with his family in Cuba's sugar mills. He played amateur baseball on the Cuban plantation teams, but hoped to escape rural life. In 1956, he enlisted in the Cuban army to pursue a baseball career. His manager, an army captain, routinely threatened professional baseball scouts with prison if they pursued Cuellar's services because the latter excelled as a pitcher. Cuellar, however, signed his first professional baseball contract in 1956 with the Havana, Cuba Sugar Kings (IL), a Class AAA club affiliated with the Cincinnati Reds (NL). In his 1957 debut, the 6-foot, 165-pound southpaw struck out seven consecutive batters in 2.2 innings of no-hit relief work. The 1957 campaign saw Cuellar lead the IL with a 2.44 ERA.

Cuellar's forgettable 1959 major league debut with the Cincinnati Reds featured a soaring 15.75 ERA in only four innings of work. Five years later, the Cuban returned to the major leagues armed with a potent screwball. After spending the 1964 season with the St. Louis Cardinals (NL), Cuellar performed with the Houston Astros (NL) from 1965 to 1968, Baltimore Orioles (AL) from 1969 to 1976, and California Angels (AL) in 1977. He was elected to four All-Star squads, the 1967 NL aggregate and 1970, 1971, and 1974 AL teams. Cuellar's greatest seasons came with the Baltimore Orioles, where he won at least 20 games four times. In 1969, Cuellar finished with a 23–11 win–loss mark as one of four Baltimore pitchers to garner at least 20 victories and shared the AL Cy Young Award. Strangely, he led the AL in wins (24–8), winning percentage (.750), and complete games (21) the following year, but earned no accolades. Overall, Cuellar compiled a lifetime 185–130 major league win–loss record, 1,632 strikeouts, 36 shutouts, and a 3.14 ERA. He threw four one-hitters, seeing two no-hitters broken up with two outs in the ninth inning. He also posted a 2–0 World Series record in 1969 and 1971 against the New York Mets and Pittsburgh Pirates, respectively. Retirement followed Cuellar's brief appearance with the California Angels in 1977. During 1984, he was inducted into the Cuban Baseball Hall of Fame in Miami, FL. Cuellar, who lives in Levittown, PR, with his wife, Emma (Jimenez) Cuellar, coaches for Duluth, MN (NoL).

BIBLIOGRAPHY: Mike Cuellar file, National Baseball Library, Cooperstown, NY; Art Berke, *Unsung Heroes of the Major Leagues* (New York, 1976); Doug Brown, "Si, Si Senor—Cuellar Is Some Pitcher," *TSN*, June 28, 1969; Rich Marazzi, "Cuban-Born Mike Cuellar Was Orioles' Mound Magician," *SCD* 24 (July 11, 1997), pp. 90–91; Ted Patterson, *The Baltimore Orioles* (Dallas, TX, 1995); James H. Bready, *Baseball in Baltimore* (Baltimore, MD, 1998); Daniel Okrent and Harris Lewine, *The Ultimate Baseball Book* (Boston, MA, 1981); John Thorn et al., eds., *Total Baseball*, 5th ed. (New York, 1997).

                                                                      Samuel O. Regalado

CULLENBINE, Roy Joseph (b. October 18, 1913, Nashville, TN; d. May 28, 1991, Mt. Clemens, MI), player, was the son of an itinerant tap dancer and a former member of a girl's softball team. The family settled in Detroit, MI, where Cullenbine played football at Eastern High School. He skipped scholastic baseball because a local rule prohibited him from taking part in MuL baseball games if he performed on the high school team. When Cullenbine played in the MuL, he also served as a batboy for the Detroit Tigers (AL) under manager Bucky Harris* in 1930. In 1932, scout "Wish" Eagan saw Cullenbine working out at Navin Field and landed him a job on Harry Heilmann's* All-Stars. Cullenbine signed as an outfielder with Shreveport, LA (EDL) and transferred later that year to Greenwood, MS (EDL). Fort Worth, TX (TL) marked his next stop that season. In 1935 Cullenbine joined Springfield, IL (3IL), where his .338 mark won the 6-foot 1-inch, 185-pound switch-hitter a promotion to Beaumont, TX (TL) before the end of the season. He hit .285 in 1936 and joined the Toledo, OH Mud Hens (AA) in 1937, where he played third base for manager Fred Haney. Cullenbine played in 25 games for the Detroit Tigers before the end of the 1938 season and appeared in 75 games with them in 1939. In a historic decision in 1940, Judge Kenesaw Mountain Landis* decreed that his contract had not been properly handled when he was ascending in the Detroit Tigers chain, making Cullenbine a free agent.

The Brooklyn Dodgers (NL) signed Cullenbine for $25,000, but he did not produce and inspired taunts of "Larry the $25,000 Lemon" in the local press. He was hitting just .180 in late May, when the St. Louis Browns (AL) acquired him for Joe Gallagher. The St. Louis Browns advised him to cut down on his weight. In 1941, he blossomed into an AL All-Star, hitting .317. He tied an AL record by scoring five runs in the first game on July 31, 1941 and a major league record by tripling and doubling in the fifth inning on June 3, 1941. General manager Bill DeWitt of the St. Louis Browns quickly tired of Cullenbine and derided his lack of aggressiveness at the plate. During his 10 major league seasons, Cullenbine drew 853 walks to go with his 1,072 hits, an inordinately high percentage. Browns manager Luke Sewell* called him one of the "laziest human beings you ever saw." In June 1942, the St. Louis Browns shipped Cullenbine and Bill Trotter to the Washington Senators (AL) for Mike Chartak and Steve Sundra. Two months later, Washington waived Cullenbine to the New York Yankees (AL). Cullenbine hit .364 in September and played in his first World Series against the St. Louis Cardinals.

Cullenbine was shipped with Buddy Rosar to the Cleveland Indians (AL) for Roy Weatherly and Oscar Grimes in December 1942 and was named to the 1943 AL All-Star team. After Cullenbine played in eight games in 1945, the Cleveland Indians returned him to the Tigers for Don Ross and Dutch Meyer. This trade enabled Cullenbine to be on his second pennant winner. He led the AL that season with 113 free passes, batted .335 in 1946, and hit 24 HR in 1947 for the Detroit Tigers. Cullenbine compiled a .276 lifetime batting average in 1,181 games with 110 HR and 599 RBI. In 12 World Series games, he batted .244 with six RBI. He married Margaret Bader in February 1938 and later became the divorced father of three children.

BIBLIOGRAPHY: Roy Cullenbine file, National Baseball Library, Cooperstown, NY; Bill Borst, ed., *Ables to Zoldak*, vol. 1 (St. Louis, MO, 1988); *NYT*, May 30, 1991, p. D–20; Mike Shatzkin, ed., *The Ballplayers* (New York, 1990); Fred Smith, *995 Tigers* (Detroit, MI, 1981); William M. Anderson, *The Detroit Tigers* (South Bend, IN, 1996); Bill Borst, *The St. Louis Browns, An Informal History* (St. Louis, MO, 1978); Bill Borst, *Still Last in the American League* (West Bloomfield, MI, 1992).

William A. Borst

CUMMINGS, William Arthur "Candy" (b. October 18, 1848, Ware, MA; d. May 16, 1924, Toledo, OH), player and executive, excelled as an effective right-handed pitcher in amateur club baseball, the NA, and the NL. At age 17, he started playing baseball in New York City. His slight 5-foot 9-inch, 120-pound frame accounted for his nickname. Between 1866 and 1871, Cummings played for several independent teams in the New York City area. He pitched primarily for the Excelsior Club of Brooklyn in 1866 and 1867 and the Star of Brooklyn the next four seasons. During that period, Cummings allegedly invented the curveball. Henry Chadwick* occasionally supported the Cummings claim, but reported seeing curveball pitchers in the 1850s.

In 1871, Chadwick named Cummings the leading U.S. amateur pitcher. Cummings turned professional in 1872, joining the New York Mutuals (NA). In the NA, he pitched for the Baltimore Lord Baltimores in 1873, Philadelphia Athletics in 1874, and Hartford Dark Blues in 1875. Cummings starred in the NA, winning 33, 28, 28, and 35 games from 1872 to 1875. In

1875, he hurled six shutouts and compiled an impressive 1.73 ERA. His NL career was limited to the 1876 and 1877 seasons, reflecting the heavy pitching loads of previous years. He won 16 and lost 8 for the Hartford Dark Blues in 1876 and compiled a 5–14 record in his final season with the Cincinnati Red Stockings.

Unable to accept that his skills were declining, Cummings became president of the rival IA. This loose confederation of independent teams failed quickly and ended Cummings' connection with organized baseball. Cummings played semi-pro ball in Albany, NY and Ware, MA through 1884. He settled in Athol, MA, where he owned a paint and wallpaper store for 32 years. He moved to Toledo, OH to live with his son, Arthur. In 1939 he was elected to the National Baseball Hall of Fame.

BIBLIOGRAPHY: William Cummings file, National Baseball Library, Cooperstown, NY; Frederick Ivor-Campbell et al., eds., *Baseball's First Stars* (Cleveland, OH, 1996); William J. Ryczek, *Blackguards and Red Stockings* (Jefferson, NC, 1992); Paul MacFarlane, ed., *TSN Hall of Fame Fact Book* (St. Louis, MO, 1982); *The Baseball Encyclopedia*, 10th ed. (New York, 1996); Lowell Reidenbaugh, *Baseball's Hall of Fame-Cooperstown* (New York, 1993).

Gordon B. McKinney

CUPPY, George Joseph "Nig" (b. George Maceo Koppe, July 3, 1869, Logansport, IN; d. July 27, 1922, Elkhart, IN), player, made his major league debut in 1892 with the Cleveland Spiders (NL) under fiery manager Oliver "Pat" Tebeau.* Cuppy, a right-handed pitcher who stood 5-feet 7-inches and weighed 160 pounds, quickly attracted attention for his "contortions in the box," "fair share of speed," and "curve of greater or lesser intensity." Cuppy's first major league season saw him win 28 games and combine with Spider ace Cy Young* for 64 wins, forming one of the NL's most potent mound duos.

During his seven seasons with Cleveland from 1892 through 1898, Cuppy joined Young, second baseman "Cupid" Childs,* shortstop Ed McKean,* and catcher "Chief" Zimmer* in sparking the Spiders to first-division finishes each season, a feat equaled only by Frank Selee's* Boston Beaneaters (NL). From 1892 through 1896, Cuppy averaged 24 wins and 32 complete games per season and recorded an impressive .645 winning percentage. He finished fourth in league ERA (2.51) in 1892 and compiled the third best ERA (3.12) in 1896. In 1894 he pitched three shutouts, tying for the NL lead with Kid Nichols* of the Boston Beaneaters and Amos Rusie* of the New York Giants.

Cuppy posted a 10–6 mark in 19 games in 1897 and finished with a modest 9–8 record in 18 games in 1898. The following season, Cuppy and other star Cleveland players were transferred to the St. Louis Perfectos (NL) roster by owner Christopher Von der Ahe,* who hoped to build a team strong enough to break the championship monopoly by the Boston Beaneaters and the Baltimore Orioles. Cuppy compiled an 11–8 record for the Perfectos in 1899, but the team, despite the presence of Tebeau, Young, Childs, Bobby Wallace,* and Jesse Burkett,* finished a distant fifth. In January 1900 St. Louis sold Cuppy to the Boston Beaneaters (NL), where he won eight of 12 decisions in 17 games. His major league career ended the following season with a 4–6 mark in 13 games for the Boston Pilgrims (AL).

Altogether, Cuppy won 162 games and lost 98 for a .623 winning percentage and completed 224 of his 262 major league starts. After his retirement from baseball, he returned to Elkhart, IN and married Olive Depew on November 15, 1910. He died of Bright's disease at his farm home.

BIBLIOGRAPHY: *The Baseball Encyclopedia*, 10th ed. (New York, 1996); Chicago (IL) *Tribune*, April 28, 1892; July 28, 1922; George Cuppy file, National Baseball Library, Cooperstown, NY; Bill Madden, *The Hoosiers of Summer* (Indianapolis, IN, 1994); John Phillips, *Who Was Who* (Cabin John, MD, 1991); J. Thomas Hetrick, *The Misfits!* (Jefferson, NC, 1991); J. Thomas Hetrick, *Chris Von der Ahe and the St. Louis Browns* (Lanham, MD, 1999); Frederick G. Lieb, *The St. Louis Cardinals* (New York, 1945); J. G. Taylor Spink, comp., *TSN Daguerreotypes of Great Stars of Baseball* (St. Louis, MO, 1961); John Thorn et al., eds., *Total Baseball*, 5th ed. (New York, 1997); Robert L. Tiemann and Mark Rucker, eds., *Nineteenth Century Stars* (Kansas City, MO, 1989); David Quentin Voigt, *American Baseball*, vol. 1 (Norman, OK, 1966).

Raymond D. Kush

CURRIE, Reuben (b. 1899, Kansas City, MO; d. 1969, Chicago, IL), player, was a star right-handed pitcher for some of the finest Negro League teams of the 1920s and 1930s. He first attracted attention on Kansas City sandlots, hurling for the Kansas City, MO Tigers in 1917. In 1920, Currie joined the hometown professional Kansas City Monarchs (NNL). Aside from pitching for the Los Angeles White Sox winter team in 1921, Currie remained with the Monarchs through the 1923 season. He pitched for the Philadelphia, PA Hilldale Daisies (ECL) in 1924 and 1925, compiling a career best 13–2 mark in 1925. After hurling for the Philadelphia Royal Giants winter team, he played for the Chicago American Giants (NNL) in 1926 and 1927 and the Detroit Stars (NNL) in 1928. During his first nine seasons, he compiled an 80–57 mark. Currie spent 1930 with the Baltimore Black Sox (ANL) and finished up his Negro League career in 1932 with the Kansas City Monarchs. Currie appeared in four consecutive World Series from 1924 to 1927, performing brilliantly in the first two.

The 6-foot 4-inch, 195-pound Currie generally outsmarted batters. Kansas City Monarch teammate Chet Brewer* called Currie a masterful, curve ball pitcher with "good control." Brewer described him as "just a class pitcher," who "looked like a professor out there on the mound, like a big time teacher." Currie proved a ruthless competitior when facing hitters. Ernest "Willie" Powell claimed that "Rube always knew what their weakness was. You want to know what their weakness is: A fast ball between the eyes."

BIBLIOGRAPHY: Janet Bruce, *The Kansas City Monarchs* (Lawrence, KS, 1985); Dick Clark and Larry Lester, eds., *The Negro Leagues Book* (Cleveland, OH, 1994); John B. Holway, *Life in the Negro Leagues from the Men Who Lived It* (New York, 1991); James A. Riley, *The Biographical Encyclopedia of the Negro Baseball Leagues* (New York, 1994).

Joel S. Franks

CUTSHAW, George William "Clancy" (b. July 29, 1887, Wilmington, IL; d. August 22, 1973, San Diego, CA), player, married Evelyn Myrtle Barber on June 16, 1908. SABR voted Cutshaw the top defensive second baseman of the 1910–1919 decade over Johnny Evers* and Larry Doyle.* His .980 fielding percentage in 1919 ranks among the top marks of the first half century. He led NL second basemen in one of the five defensive categories on 18 occasions, 12 better than Evers. Cutshaw enjoyed in 1915 the seventh best NL defensive performance by any fielder, regardless of position.

Cutshaw played baseball at the University of Notre Dame, until turning professional in 1908. From 1909 through 1911, he played for Oakland, CA (PCL). In 1911, he made the PCL All-Star team as second baseman and led the PCL with 89 stolen bases. Cutshaw began his major league career in 1912 with the Brooklyn Superbas (NL), starting at second base for the next six seasons. He initially batted second ahead of future National Baseball Hall of Famers Casey Stengel* and Zack Wheat* but later batted cleanup behind Wheat and in front of Stengel. From 1913 to 1917, Cutshaw produced nine more RBI than Wheat. He lost out to teammate Jake Daubert* for the Chalmers Award in 1913 as the NL's MVP. Daubert led the NL in batting at .350, but Cutshaw produced six more doubles, six more triples, five more HR, 28 more RBI, and 14 more stolen bases. Cutshaw won the clinching game of the 1916 NL pennant race with a pivotal HR over the right field fence at Ebbets Field.

On January 8, 1918, Brooklyn traded Cutshaw and Stengel to the Pittsburgh Pirates (NL) for future National Baseball Hall of Famer Burleigh Grimes.* During his 12 major league seasons, the intelligent "underrated" Cutshaw excelled at the hit and run play and base stealing. He stole home six times and led the NL in sacrifice hits with 37 in 1920. Cutshaw paced the NL in fewest strikeouts in 1914, 1916, and 1918 and played in all of his team's games in 1915, 1918, and 1919. On August 9, 1915, he became the first twentieth-century National Leaguer to make six hits in six at bats in a game. On August 4, 1913, he belted two inside the park HR in a contest against the Chicago Cubs.

Cutshaw finished his major league career with the Detroit Tigers (AL) in 1922 and 1923. Manager Ty Cobb* called him "a master of the position" and declared he "was simply great, in ways that didn't show to the fans and sportswriters." On April 22, 1922, Cutshaw made five putouts and eight assists in a game against the Cleveland Indians. In 1,516 major league games, he batted .265 with 1,487 hits, 653 RBI, and 271 stolen bases. Cutshaw returned to the PCL in 1924 for three seasons with Seattle, WA and retired to San Diego, CA as a citrus grower.

BIBLIOGRAPHY: George Cutshaw file, National Baseball Library, Cooperstown, NY; Brent P. Kelley, *The Case For: Those Overlooked by the Baseball Hall of Fame* (Jefferson, NC, 1992); *NYT*, September 29, 1916; Arthur Daley, *Times at Bat* (New York, 1950); Ty Cobb and Al Stump, *My Life in Baseball* (Garden City, NY, 1961); Richard Goldstein, *Superstars and Screwballs* (New York, 1991); Frank Graham, *The Brooklyn Dodgers* (New York, 1945); Fred Smith, *995 Tigers* (Detroit, MI, 1981).

Cappy Gagnon

CUYLER, Hazen Shirley "Kiki" (b. August 30, 1898, Harrisville, MI; d. February 11, 1950, Ann Arbor, MI), player, coach, and manager, was the son of George Cuyler and Anna Cuyler. His father, a Coast Guardsman and probate judge, played semipro baseball in Canada in the late 1800s. Hazen, who first played baseball at age nine, starred in high school baseball, track and field, basketball, and football. He also pitched and played outfield for several semipro organizations in northeastern Michigan and served a two-year U.S. Army stint. He married Bertha Kelly on January 8, 1919 and had two children, Harold and Kelly. While Cuyler was employed for Buick Motors in Flint, MI, the Bay City, MI (MOL) club signed him in 1921 and sold his contract to the Pittsburgh Pirates (NL). He played outfield for Charleston, SC (SAL) in 1922 and Nashville, TN (SA) in 1923. The latter year, he earned MVP honors by averaging .340 at the plate and leading the SA in six categories.

Cuyler appeared briefly with Pittsburgh from 1921 through 1923. For the Pittsburgh Pirates in 1924, he posted one of baseball's greatest rookie seasons with a .354 batting average. In 1925, he enjoyed an even better season with a .357 batting average, led the NL in triples (26) and runs scored (144), and drove in the run that won the World Series against the Washington Senators. Besides batting over .300 eight other seasons, he paced the NL in runs scored (113) in 1926 and doubles (42) in 1934. In August 1927, Pirate manager Donie Bush* benched Cuyler following a disagreement. Cuyler stayed there through the World Series, but then was traded in November to the Chicago Cubs (NL). During seven years there, he averaged .325, helped the club capture NL pennants in 1929 and 1932, and batted .360 in 1929 and .355 in 1930. Cuyler joined the Cincinnati Reds (NL) in July 1935 and ended his playing career with the Brooklyn Dodgers (NL) in 1938. In 18 major league seasons, he batted .321 with 2,299 hits, 394 doubles, 157 triples, 128 HR, 1,305 runs scored, and 1,065 RBI.

Cuyler managed Chattanooga, TN (SA) to first, fourth, and third place finishes from 1939 through 1941. After coaching for the Chicago Cubs (NL) from 1941 through 1943, he managed the Atlanta, GA Crackers (SA) in 1944. The Crackers made the SA playoffs in 1945 and won the SA championship the next year under Cuyler's tutelage. After two disappointing seasons, however, Cuyler joined Joe McCarthy's* Boston Red Sox (AL) as a coach in 1949. The quiet Cuyler, who neither drank nor smoked, excelled as a powerful line drive hitter, fleet runner, and talented outfielder with an outstanding arm. He led the NL four times in stolen bases between 1926 and 1930 and finished second two other times. His base-stealing career ended, however, after two leg injuries in the early 1930s. For many years, Cuyler toured the off-season with his All-Star basketball team. Cuyler died of a heart attack while fishing near Glennie, MI, and was elected in 1968 to the National Baseball Hall of Fame.

BIBLIOGRAPHY: Hazen Cuyler file, National Baseball Library, Cooperstown, NY; *Alcona* (MI) *County Herald*, February 17, 1950; Hazen Cuyler Scrapbook Collection, Alcona County Library, Harrisville, MI; *The Baseball Encyclopedia*, 10th ed. (New York, 1996); *TSN*, February 1950; Lowell Reidenbaugh, *Baseball's Hall of Fame-Cooperstown* (New York, 1993); Frederick G. Lieb, *The Pittsburgh Pirates* (New York, 1948); Richard L. Burtt, *The Pittsburgh Pirates: A Pictorial History* (Virginia Beach, VA, 1977); Eddie Gold and Art Ahrens, *The Golden Era Cubs, 1876–1940* (Chicago, IL, 1985); Warren Wilbert and William Hageman, *Chicago Cubs: Seasons at the Summit* (Champaign, IL, 1997).

Gerald E. Brennan

D

DAHLEN, William Frederick "Bill," "Bad Bill" (b. January 5, 1870, Nelliston, NY; d. December 5, 1950, Brooklyn, NY), player and manager, came from upstate New York and was the son of a masonry contractor. He attended the local elementary school and graduated from Fort Plain (NY) High School. For the next two years, he attended Clinton Liberal Institute and played on its baseball team.

In 1890 the 5-foot 9-inch, 170-pound infielder entered professional baseball with Cobleskill, NY (NYSL). The right-handed hitting Dahlen joined Cap Anson's* Chicago Colts (NL) club the following year and played there for eight seasons. He later played for the Brooklyn Superbas (1899–1903), New York Giants (1904–1907), and Boston Doves (1908–1909) in the NL. From 1910 through 1913, Dahlen managed the Brooklyn Superbas (Dodgers). He guided the team to two sixth- and two seventh-place finishes, compiling 251 wins against 355 losses.

As a regular shortstop, Dahlen played for championship teams with the Brooklyn Superbas in 1899 and 1900 and the New York Giants in 1904 and 1905. His clever base running and aggressive fielding earned the respect of opposing NL players and managers. Dahlen led NL shortstops in fielding average once and in assists four times and compiled 8,133 assists. His 1,080 errors remain a major league record.

A .272 lifetime hitter, he made 2,457 hits, 413 doubles, 163 triples, and 84 HR, drove in 1,233 runs, and stole 547 bases. In 1894, he belted a career-high 15 HR and set a major league record by hitting safely in 42 consecutive games from June 20 to August 7. After being held hitless on August 7, he began another streak by hitting in 28 straight games. This mark was surpassed three years later by Willie Keeler,* who hit in 44 consecutive games.

Married to Jeanette Hoglund in December 1903, Dahlen had a daughter and later worked on the docks for the Brooklyn Post Office and as an attendant at Yankee Stadium. He also owned a filling station. The steady, durable Dahlen spanned baseball's developing years from the 19th century into its modern era and shares the major league record with his 20 years at shortstop.

BIBLIOGRAPHY: Arthur R. Ahrens, "The Daily Dahlen of 1894," *BRJ* 4 (1975), pp. 57–60; Warren Brown, *The Chicago Cubs* (New York, 1946); Gene Karst and Martin J. Jones, Jr., *Who's Who in Professional Baseball* (New Rochelle, NY, 1973); *NYT*, December 6, 1950; *TSN*, December 11, 1950; Robert L. Tiemann and Mark Rucker, eds., *Nineteenth Century Stars* (Kansas City, MO, 1989); Eddie Gold and Art Ahrens, *The Golden Era Cubs, 1876–1940* (Chicago, IL, 1985); Thomas Aylesworth and Benton Minks, *The Encyclopedia of Baseball Managers* (New York, 1990); Richard Goldstein, *Superstars and Screwballs* (New York, 1991); Ray Robinson, *Matty: An American Hero* (New York, 1993); Noel Hynd, *The Giants of the Polo Grounds* (New York, 1988).

                                                                    Joseph Lawler

DALRYMPLE, Abner Frank (b. September 9, 1857, Warren, IL; d. January 25, 1939, Warren, IL), player, attended Warren grade schools and began working odd jobs at age 12. Dalrymple earned $45 per month as a brakeman at the Illinois Central Railroad Company and showed promise by age 14 as a baseball fielder and hitter. He played for several semiprofessional teams before starting his 19-year professional baseball career with the Milwaukee, WI West Ends (KA) in 1878.

The 5-foot 10½-inch, 175-pound Dalrymple, who batted left-handed and threw right-handed, joined the major leagues with the Milwaukee Brewers (NL) in 1878. He set a high standard by winning the NL batting title with a career-best .354 mark. Dalrymple in 1879 joined the Chicago White Stockings (NL), owned by Albert Spalding* and managed by Cap Anson.* He signed with Chicago for $2,500 and collected $300 per month to roam left field.

Dalrymple remained with Chicago through 1886, enjoying several great seasons as a leadoff hitter. He led the NL with 91 runs and 126 hits in 1880 and 11 triples in 1885, helping the White Stockings win NL pennants from 1880 to 1882 and in 1885 and 1886. Following his major league career, he fondly relayed stories about hiding balls in his uniform and pulling them out at the opportune time. In 1880 Ezra Sutton* of the Boston Red Stockings hit a HR which was called an out when Dalrymple pulled the hidden ball from his blouse and acted as if he had caught it on the fly. This incident helped Chicago win the game. On July 3, 1883, he and Anson both collected four doubles in the 31–7 annihilation of the Buffalo, NY Bisons.

After struggling with the Pittsburgh Alleghenys (NL) in 1887 and 1888, Dalrymple drifted to the minor leagues with Denver, CO (WA) in 1889 and 1890 and Milwaukee, WI (WA) in 1891. His major league career ended with a .311 batting average for the Milwaukee Brewers (AA) in 1891. He spent the next four minor league seasons with Spokane, WA (PNL) in 1892, Macon, GA (SL) in 1893, Indianapolis, IN (WL) in 1894, and Evansville, IN (SL) in 1895.

In 12 major league seasons, Dalrymple batted .288 with 813 runs, 1,202 hits, 217 doubles, 43 HR, and 407 RBI. He retired to Warren, IL and was employed as a conductor with the Northern Pacific Railroad. He worked 36 years and eight months with the railroad before retiring at age 70 and died after a lengthy illness.

BIBLIOGRAPHY: Abner Dalrymple file, National Baseball Library, Cooperstown, NY; Peter Filichia, *Professional Baseball Franchises* (New York, 1993); Warren Brown, *The Chicago Cubs* (New York, 1946); Eddie Gold and Art Ahrens, *The Golden Era Cubs, 1876–1940* (Chicago, IL, 1985); John Thorn et al., eds., *Total Baseball*, 5th ed. (New York, 1997); Robert L. Tiemann and Mark Rucker, eds., *Nineteenth Century Stars* (Kansas City, MO, 1989); Warren Wilbert and William Hageman, *Chicago Cubs: Seasons at the Summit* (Champaign, IL, 1997).

Scot E. Mondore

DALY, Thomas Peter "Tom" "Tido" (b. February 7, 1866, Philadelphia, PA; d. October 29, 1939, Brooklyn, NY), player, manager, and scout, was the brother of Joe Daly, who played briefly in the major leagues from 1890 to 1892. Daly began his baseball career as a catcher with Millville, PA and Trenton, NJ (IL) in 1884. In 1886 he helped Newark, NJ win the IL pennant.

The 5-foot 7-inch, 170-pound catcher made his major league debut with the Chicago White Stockings (NL) in 1887, compiling the best fielding average (.935) among NL catchers. Daly played for the Chicago White Stockings two years and accompanied them on an international barnstorming tour in the winter of 1888–1889, but was released on their return. After spending 1889 with the Washington Senators (NL), he joined the Brooklyn Bridegrooms (NL) in 1890.

The switch-hitting right-hander batted .243 to help the Brooklyn Bridegrooms capture the NL pennant and participated in his first post-season series. The Brooklyn Bridegrooms played to a 3–3 draw with the Louisville, KY Cyclones (AA) in the World Series, as Daly made only four hits in 22 at bats. After moving to the infield in 1892, he performed for Brooklyn at second base from 1893 to 1901 except for 1897.

Daly left the Brooklyn Bridegrooms in 1897 to play for his former catching mate, Connie Mack,* who was managing Milwaukee, WI (WL). He returned to Brooklyn in 1898 and helped the renamed Superbas to the NL pennant again in 1900, hitting .312. His pinnacle season came in 1901, when he batted .315 and led the NL with 38 doubles.

Daly returned to Chicago in 1902, with the new White Sox (AL). The following year, he moved in June to the Cincinnati Reds (NL) and finished strong with a .293 batting average in 80 games as their regular second baseman. In 16 major league seasons, Daly compiled a .278 batting average with 262 doubles, 103 triples, and 49 HR. He collected 687 bases on balls, walking an average of once every nine plate appearances. A speedy base runner, he chalked up 385 steals.

Daly managed Providence, RI (EL) in 1904, Altoona, PA (TSL) in 1905 and 1906, and Johnstown, PA (TSL) in 1907 and scouted for the Cleveland Naps (AL) in 1911 and 1912 and the New York Yankees (AL) from 1913 to 1915. Daly resided in Brooklyn until his death from a yearlong illness.

BIBLIOGRAPHY: *The Baseball Encyclopedia*, 10th ed. (New York, 1996); Thomas P. Daly file, National Baseball Library, Cooperstown, NY; Frank Graham, *The Brooklyn Dodgers* (New York, 1945); Frederick Ivor-Campbell et al., eds., *Baseball's First Stars* (Cleveland, OH, 1996); William F. McNeil, *The Dodgers Encyclopedia* (Champaign, IL, 1997); Mike Shatzkin, ed., *The Ballplayers* (New York, 1990); John Thorn et al., eds., *Total Baseball*, 5th ed. (New York, 1997).

Gaymon L. Bennett

DANCER, Faye "Tiger," "Fanny" (b. April 24, 1925, Santa Monica, CA), player, is the daughter of James Dancer, an appliance store owner, and the third of four children. Her family loved sports, with her father sponsoring a men's local softball team for many years. Dancer played independent softball while attending Santa Monica City High School. Following graduation in 1941, she played professional softball in a southern California league. The 5-foot 6-inch 145-pound, blonde, freckled-faced Dancer joined five other California girls Bill Allington brought to the Midwest to play on AAGPBL teams and was paid $75 a week.

In 1944, Dancer joined the Minneapolis, MN Millerettes (AAGPBL) and helped them win the pennant. The team lacked fan support and victories, but rookie Dancer batted .274 with 75 RBI. Her 155 hits included 44 for extra bases and two grand-slam HR. The Millerettes moved to Fort Wayne, IN in 1945 and were renamed the Daisies. From 1945 to 1947, Dancer became one of the AAGPBL's most talented, colorful, and fun-loving players as an outfielder, first baseman, and pitcher. She always entertained the crowd, thriving on their attention. Since fans paid her way, she involved herself in the community, had fun, and gave the fans their money's worth on the field. Dancer frequently turned cartwheels and backflips en route to her outfield position. Superstitiously, she had fans rub a glass eye during a game to bring the team good luck and sought their support when an umpire's call went against her.

Dancer's off the field antics included coating light bulbs with limburger cheese in the room of new chaperones and sneaking out of hotels after curfew to sample a city's nightlife and drink beer. She consorted with dubious characters, including a midget in Fort Wayne who brought beer to the players and a gangster in Peoria, IL. Dancer never allowed her antics to interfere with playing baseball. She frequently played with injuries, sustained from diving for fly balls or running into teammates or stands. For the Fort Wayne Daisies, Dancer batted .195 with a league-best 3 HR, 29 RBI, and 29 stolen bases in 1945 and .279 with 16 HR, 73 RBI, and 26 stolen bases in 1946. After 29 games with the Daisies in 1947, Dancer was traded to the Peoria, IL Redwings and completed the season with a .286 batting average, 10 HR, 84 RBI, and 20 stolen bases. For the Redwings in 1948, she batted .272 with 6 HR and 58 RBI and ranked second behind Sophie Kurys* with 30 stolen bases. Numerous injuries forced Dancer's retirement following that season.

Dancer returned to the Peoria Redwings in 1950, but a herniated disk from a sliding injury and a chipped vertebra forced her permanent retirement after only 49 games. She batted .309, with 10 HR and 69 RBI. Although very talented and popular, Dancer never played in an All-Star game or World Series. Over a six-year career, she batted .269 with 893 hits, 388 RBI, 54 HR, and 147 stolen bases. She also compiled an 11–11 win–loss record with a 2.28 ERA.

Dancer's most memorable experience involved playing baseball for Jim Thorpe's (FB) barnstorming team in 1947. Some of Thorpe's disgruntled players walked out, constituting a breach of contract. Dancer and teammates played two games to keep the Olympian out of jail. Dancer returned to Santa Monica, CA and became an electronics technician for Howard Hughes' aircraft plant. In 1955, she and AAGPBL star Lavonne "Pepper" Paire-Davis* opened an electronics business.

BIBLIOGRAPHY: AAGPBL Collection, Joyce Sports Research Collection, Hesburgh Library, University of Notre Dame, South Bend IN; Gai Berlage, *Women in Baseball* (Westport, CT, 1994); Lois Browne, *Girls of Summer* (Toronto, Canada, 1992); Susan M. Cahn, "No Freaks, No Amazons, No Boyish Bobs," *CH* 18 (Spring 1989), pp. 26–41; Harold T. Dailey, AAGPBL Records, Pattee Library, Pennsylvania State University, University Park, PA; Jay Feldman, "Glamour Ball," *SH* 1 (May/June 1987), pp. 59–69; Jack Fincher, "The Belles of the Ball Game Were a Hit with Their Fans," *Smithsonian* 20 (July 1989), pp. 88–97; Barbara Gregorich, *Women at Play* (San Diego, CA, 1993); Susan E. Johnson, *When Women Played Hardball* (Seattle, WA, 1994); Sue Macy, *A Whole New Ball Game* (New York, 1993); Faye Dancer file, National Baseball Library, Cooperstown, NY; Faye Dancer file, Northern Indiana Historical Society, South Bend, IN; W. C. Madden, *The Women of the All-American Girls Professional Baseball League* (Jefferson, NC, 1997); Jack Stenbuck, "Glamour Girls of Big League Ball," *MD* 27 (July 1946), pp. 70–73.

Jerry J. Wright

DANDRIDGE, Raymond Emmitt "Hooks," "Ray" (b. August 31, 1913, Richmond, VA; d. February 12, 1994, Palm Bay, FL), player, manager, and scout, was the son of Archie Dandridge, a textile worker, and Alberta (Thompson) Dandridge. He attended school in Richmond, VA and Buffalo, NY and was a Golden Gloves boxer and football quarterback. The Detroit Stars (NNL) signed him as they barnstormed north during spring training in 1933. Dandridge, a sandlot ballplayer, impressed Detroit manager "Candy Jim" Taylor,* who played him at shortstop. Dandridge performed the next season for the Newark, NJ Dodgers, who moved him to third base, and the Newark Eagles (NNL).

During his 16-year Negro League career, Dandridge was its premier third baseman. He played in the late 1930s in the Newark Eagles' "million dollar infield," which supposedly would have been worth $1 million if they were white. The 5-foot 7-inch, bowlegged Dandridge also played for the New York Cubans (NNL) and winter ball in Venezuela, Cuba, Puerto Rico, and Mexico. In 1944, manager Cum Posey* ranked Dandridge among the greatest players in the Negro Leagues. "There never was a smoother-functioning master at third base than Dandridge," Posey remarked, "and he can hit that apple, too."

Dandridge played for Vera Cruz in Mexico during the 1940s, but returned to the United States to manage and play for the New York Cubans in 1949. He was sold that year to the Minneapolis, MN Millers (AA), the New York Giants' farm club. Dandridge told the Giants he was 29 years old, although he was actually 36 at the time. In 1949, he was selected the AA Rookie of the Year. The next season, he hit .311 and was named the AA MVP for the champion Millers. Although Sal Maglie* and Monte Irvin* urged the Giants (NL) to promote Dandridge, New York did not comply perhaps because of his age, informal quotas, and Dandridge's popularity in Minneapolis. In 1953, Dandridge played for Oakland, CA (PCL), but hurt his arm and was released. When his arm recovered, he played in 1955 with Bismarck, ND and then retired. He returned to Newark, where he tended bar, scouted for the Giants, and worked as a recreational director.

Considered by many the best third baseman never to make the major leagues, Dandridge regretted that he was not given the opportunity. "The only thing I ever wanted to do was hit in the major leagues . . . I just wanted to put my left foot in there. I just would have liked to have been up there for one day, even if it was only to get a cup of coffee."

In 1987, Dandridge was inducted into the National Baseball Hall of Fame. He was survived by his second wife, Henrietta, and three children.

BIBLIOGRAPHY: Martin Appel, *Yesterday's Heroes* (New York, 1988); Joseph Durso, "Hall of Fame Doors Open for Dandridge," *NYT Biographical Service* 18 (March 1987), pp. 174–175; John B. Holway, *Blackball Stars* (Westport, CT, 1988); *NYT*, February 14, 1994, p. 88; John B. Holway, "Dandy at Third: Ray Dandridge," *TNP* 1 (Fall 1982), pp. 7–9; Raymond Dandridge file, National Baseball Library, Cooperstown, NY; Robert W. Peterson, *Only the Ball Was White* (New York, 1970); David L. Porter, ed., *African-American Sports Greats* (Westport, CT, 1995); Lowell Reidenbaugh, *Baseball's Hall of Fame-Cooperstown* (New York, 1993); James A. Riley, *The Biographical Encyclopedia of the Negro Baseball Leagues* (New York, 1994); Donn Rogosin, *Invisible Men: Life in Baseball's Negro Leagues* (New York, 1983); Jules Tygiel, *Baseball's Great Experiment* (New York, 1983).

Robert L. Ruck

DANNING, Harry "Harry the Horse" (b. September 6, 1911, Los Angeles, CA), player and coach, is the son of Robert Danning, proprietor of a used furniture store, and Jenny (Goldberg) Danning, of East European-Jewish descent. Danning, a graduate of Los Angeles High School, played sandlot, scholastic, and semipro baseball. His brother Ike, who appeared in two games for the 1928 St. Louis Browns (AL), encouraged Danning to sign a contract with the New York Giants (NL) organization in 1931. The 6-foot 1-inch, 190-pound catcher spent the 1931–1933 seasons in the Giants farm system with Bridgeport, CT (EL), Winston-Salem, NC (PiL), and Buffalo, NY (IL) and went hitless in two at bats with the New York Giants in September 1933.

Danning spent his entire major league career from 1933 to 1942 with the New York Giants. A reserve catcher until Gus Mancuso was injured during the 1937 season, he emerged as one of the top major league catchers of the 1938–1942 period. Hard work enabled him to develop strong defensive skills. A fine handler of pitchers, Danning adeptly caught "low-ball" hurlers. He led NL catchers twice in putouts (1939–1941), assists (1939–1940), and double plays (1939–1940). A good contact hitter, Danning possessed solid power and recorded personal highs of 16 HR in 1939 and 91 RBI in 1940. Between 1937 and 1942, he batted .288, .306, .313, .300, .244, and .279. He compiled a career .285 batting average with 847 hits, including 57 HR, 26 triples, and 162 doubles, 363 runs scored and 397 RBI in 890 games.

During World War II, Danning served in the U.S. Army from 1942 to 1945. A knee injury prevented Danning from resuming his playing career after the war. In 1947, he coached for the Hollywood, CA Stars (PCL). On January 11, 1940, Danning married Diane Nygord. They had one daughter, Vicki. Following his retirement from baseball, he resided in Millbrae, CA and served as an agency manager for Metropolitan Life Insurance.

Danning, who appeared in the World Series twice (1936, 1937) and was selected for four NL All-Star teams (1938, 1939, 1940, 1941), remains the best Jewish catcher in major league baseball history. He lives in Valparaiso, IN.

BIBLIOGRAPHY: Harry Danning file, National Baseball Library, Cooperstown, NY; Frank Graham, *The New York Giants* (New York, 1952); Peter Levine, *Ellis Island to Ebbets Field: Sport and the American Jewish Experience* (New York, 1992); Erwin Lynn, *The Jewish Baseball Hall of Fame* (New York, 1987); Harold Ribalow, *The Jew in American Sports*, rev. ed. (New York, 1959); Barry Schweid, "Harry the Horse," *BRJ* 27 (1998), pp. 79–80; Robert Slater, *Great Jews in Sports* (Middle Village, NY, 1983); Rick Van Blair, "Flashback—Harry Danning: Catching Star of Another Era," *BD*

53 (October 1994), pp. 63–66; Peter Williams, *When the Giants Were Giants* (Chapel Hill, NC, 1994); Fred Stein, *Under Coogan's Bluff* (Golenshaw, PA, 1978).

William M. Simons

DARK, Alvin Ralph "Blackie," "Cap," "The Swamp Fox" (b. January 7, 1922, Comanche, OK), player and manager, was the third of four children of an itinerant oil rigger. He entered Louisiana State University in 1941 and made both the 1942 and 1943 All-American football teams, the latter as a U.S. Marines ROTC student at Southwestern Louisiana Institute. Dark married Adrienne Vyra Managan in October 1946 and had four children. In 1970, he married Jacolyn Rockwood and adopted her two children.

After World War II military service, Dark entered professional baseball in 1946 with the Boston Braves (NL) organization. In 1947, he played shortstop and batted .303 for Milwaukee, WI (AA). The 1948 BBWAA NL Rookie of the Year, Dark tied an NL record with a 23-game hitting streak for the Braves. Traded with roommate and keystone partner Eddie Stanky* to the New York Giants (NL) in December 1949, Dark in 1951 was named team captain by manager Leo Durocher* and led the NL with 41 doubles. Dark made three All-Star teams, was voted *TSN* All-Star shortstop in 1954, and played in three World Series. Besides batting a solid combined .415 in the 1951 and 1954 World Series, he tied a record for the most singles (7) in a four-game series (1954). His popularity as a player peaked with the Giants' victory over the Cleveland Indians in 1954. Dark rode in the lead car of the tickertape parade through Manhattan with Willie Mays,* who credited him as one of the greatest influences in his career. Dark's most memorable day came on October 3, 1951, when he led off the ninth inning and scored the first run in the playoff game rally against the Brooklyn Dodgers. The classic game ended with Bobby Thomson's* famed "shot heard 'round the world." As a manager Dark utilized innovative strategy, including having a new relief pitcher intentionally walk the first batter faced and having pitchers take batting practice instead of shagging flies in the outfield. Dark played with the St. Louis Cardinals (1956–1958), Chicago Cubs (1958–1959), Philadelphia Phillies (1960) and Milwaukee Braves (1960) of the NL, compiling a .289 career batting average. In 1,828 games, he made 2,089 hits, 358 doubles, 126 HR, 1,064 runs scored, and 757 RBI.

Nicknamed "Blackie" and "Cap" as a player, Dark was called "The Swamp Fox" as San Francisco Giants manager because of his southern Louisiana childhood and his tactic of watering down the dirt area around first base to slow down Maury Wills* and other NL base stealers. Dark piloted the Giants from 1961 to 1964, capturing the 1962 NL pennant. He managed the Kansas City Athletics (AL) in 1966 and 1967 after a year's absence from baseball because of alleged racial remarks. From 1968 to 1971, Dark piloted the Cleveland Indians (AL) and assumed many of general manager Gabe Paul's* functions. An arrogant, stormy player and manager, Dark joined

Charley Finley's* Oakland Athletics (AL) as pilot in 1974 as a softspoken "reborn Christian." Players, whom he characterized as an "incredibly talented bunch of backbiters," constantly chastised him for his apparent lack of aggressiveness. Nonetheless, he guided the A's to the 1974 and 1975 World Series, becoming only the third mentor to manage AL and NL teams to the fall classic. His managerial career ended in 1977 after one season leading the San Diego Padres (NL) because of "irreconcilable differences" with team owner Ray Kroc. He later served as director of development for the Chicago White Sox (AL). As a manager 13 seasons, Dark compiled a 994–954 mark (.510). His autobiography, *When in Doubt, Fire the Manager* (written with John Underwood), was published in 1980. He belongs to the Oklahoma Sports Hall of Fame, Louisiana Sports Hall of Fame, and LSU Sports Hall of Fame.

BIBLIOGRAPHY: Alvin Dark file, National Baseball Library, Cooperstown, NY; Anthony J. Connor, *Baseball for the Love of It* (New York, 1982); Noel Hynd, *The Giants of the Polo Grounds* (New York, 1988); Thomas Aylesworth and Benton Minks, *The Encyclopedia of Baseball Managers* (New York, 1990); Gary Caruso, *The Braves Encyclopedia* (Philadelphia, PA, 1995); Alvin Dark and John Underwood, *When in Doubt, Fire the Manager* (New York, 1980); Glenn Dickey, *The History of American League Baseball* (New York, 1980); Glenn Dickey, *The History of National League Baseball* (New York, 1979); Charles Einstein, *Willie Mays* (New York, 1963); Charles Einstein, *Willie's Time* (New York, 1979); Brent P. Kelley, *Baseball Stars of the 1950s* (Jefferson, NC, 1993); Leonard Koppett, *The Man in the Dugout* (New York, 1993); Robert Obojski, "Alvin Dark Interviewed," *SCD* 23 (November 15, 1996), pp. 130–131; Bruce Markusen, *Baseball's Last Dynasty* (New York, 1998); *The Baseball Encyclopedia*, 10th ed. (New York, 1996); John Thorn, *The Relief Pitcher* (New York, 1979); John Thorn et al., eds., *Total Braves* (New York 1996).

Alan R. Asnen

DARLING, Ronald Maurice, Jr. "Ron" (b. August 19, 1960, Honolulu, HI), player, became one of the few players of Asian Pacific ancestry to star in the major leagues. Darling, the son of Ronald M. Darling, Sr. and brother of Eddie Darling, a minor league first baseman, first attracted national attention as a Yale University pitching ace. He entered professional ball with Tulsa, OK (TL) in 1981 and pitched for the New York Mets (NL) from 1983 until 1991. He moved in July 1991 to the Montreal Expos (NL) and finished the 1991 season with the Oakland Athletics (AL). His career ended with the Oakland A's in 1995.

The 6-foot 3-inch, 195-pound right-hander enjoyed some fine seasons— particularly for the New York Mets. His best seasons included 1985, when he won 16, lost six, and achieved a 2.90 ERA, and 1986, when he won 15, lost six and dropped his ERA to 2.81. In 1988, Darling recorded a career-high 17 victories and lost just nine with a fine 3.25 ERA.

Darling's other career highlights included being selected as an NL All-

Star in 1985 and pitching in three 1986 World Series games against the Boston Red Sox, splitting two decisions. He started the final seventh game, but was not the pitcher of record when the Mets came from behind to win the world championship. Darling also appeared in the NL Championship Series for the Mets in 1986 and 1988 and the AL Championship Series for the Oakland Athletics in 1992. In 1989, Darling's all-around athleticism earned him the Gold Glove Award. With the Mets, Darling won the Thurman Munson Award in 1988 for his community work. During his major league career, Darling compiled a 136–116 record and 3.87 ERA. He married Tony O'Reilly and has two children, Tyler and Jordan.

BIBLIOGRAPHY: Ronald Darling file, National Baseball Library, Cooperstown, NY; Mike Lupica, "Simply Darling," *Esquire* 111 (April 1989), pp. 67ff; "Team Spirit," *HB* 122 (May 1989), pp. 150–153; "Darling Returns to the Classroom," *NYT Biographical Service* 18 (October 1987), pp. 1123–1124; Peter Gammons, "More Than a Media Darling," *SI* 66 (April 6, 1987), pp. 56–58; Kristin McMurran, "That Lady in the Locker Room Is Mets Pitcher Ron Darling's Model Wife," *PW* 26 (October 13, 1986), pp. 51–52; *TSN Baseball Register*, 1966; Amy Unterburger, ed., *Who's Who Among Asian Americans*, 1994/95 (Detroit, MI, 1994).

Joel S. Franks

DAUBERT, Jacob Ellsworth "Jake" (b. April 7, 1884, Shamokin, PA; d. October 9, 1924, Cincinnati, OH), player, came from the Pennsylvania anthracite region, where his father, Jacob, and two brothers worked as coal miners. Daubert attended an elementary school in Shamokin before moving with his family to nearby Llewellyn, PA around 1896. At age 11 he began working as a breaker boy, separating slate and other impurities from coal. As a teenager, Daubert followed his brothers into baseball by pitching for local teams. With the Lykens, PA semipro club, the 5-foot 10-inch, 160-pound left-hander occasionally filled in at first base. He showed great ability there and eventually abandoned pitching altogether.

In 1907, Daubert entered professional baseball with Kane, PA (ISL) and Marion, OH (OPL). The Cleveland Indians (AL) drafted Daubert the following year, but he failed to make the team. He was sent to Nashville, TN (SA) and spent the next two seasons polishing his batting skills. After hitting .314 for Memphis, TN (SA) in 1909, he was sold to the Brooklyn Dodgers (NL). As a rookie in 1910, Daubert won the first base job and remained there for Brooklyn until 1918. In his first major league season, Daubert batted .264, hit 15 triples, and displayed outstanding defense.

Beginning in 1911, Daubert became the NL's finest all-around first baseman, hit over .300 in each of the next six seasons, and played brilliantly on defense. In 1913 and 1914, he won consecutive batting championships with .350 and .329 averages, respectively. During this stretch, he led all first basemen in assists once (1915) and in fielding average twice (1912, 1916). In

1913 Daubert received the Chalmers Award as the NL's MVP. Five years later, he paced the NL in triples (15).

Daubert played a key role in Brooklyn's first pennant-winning season in 1916, directing play defensively as team captain and performing with his accustomed reliability at first base. In the World Series, however, he hit only .176 as the Dodgers lost to the Boston Red Sox, four games to one.

A salary dispute with Dodgers' owner Charles Ebbets* led to Daubert's trade to the Cincinnati Reds (NL) in March 1919. Appointed captain of his new team, he helped the Reds capture their first pennant and defeat the Chicago White Sox in the World Series that fall. In 1922, the 37-year-old veteran enjoyed an outstanding season and attained personal highs in nearly every offensive and defensive category. In 156 games for Cincinnati, Daubert made 205 hits, scored 114 runs, hit 12 HR, and batted .336. Besides hitting a NL-leading 22 triples, he also paced the NL in putouts and double plays and tied for the lead in fielding average. Late in the 1924 season, Daubert became ill and was ordered back to his Schuylkill Haven, PA home to rest. Within the next month, he died from complications following an appendectomy.

Daubert, a regular his entire 15-year major league career, batted .303 with 2,326 hits in 2,014 games. Daubert compiled 250 doubles, 165 triples, 56 HR, 1,117 runs scored, 722 RBI, and 251 stolen bases. He surpassed the .300 mark ten times and set the NL career record for sacrifice hits with 392. His four sacrifice hits in one 1914 game remain a major league record.

Daubert, who married Gertrude Viola Acaley in September 1903 and had a son and a daughter, owned and operated a coal and ice business in Schuylkill Haven in the off-season. A talent for business and leadership led to his election as a vice-president of the Baseball Players' Fraternity, an early successful players' union. Daubert displayed consistency at bat and in the field, earning the respect of teammates and opponents alike. Considered by many the equal of the more colorful Hal Chase* at first base, the well-spoken, modest Daubert ranked among the most popular players of his time.

BIBLIOGRAPHY: Jake Daubert file, National Baseball Library, Cooperstown, NY; Frank Graham, *The Brooklyn Dodgers* (New York, 1945); Gene Karst and Martin J. Jones, Jr., *Who's Who in Professional Baseball* (New Rochelle, NY, 1973); F. C. Lane, "Jake Daubert—A Self-Made Success," *BM* 12 (February 1914), pp. 33–48; *New York World*, October 10, 1924; *NYT*, October 11, 1924; Donald Honig, *The Cincinnati Reds* (New York, 1992); Richard Goldstein, *Superstars and Screwballs* (New York, 1991); William F. McNeil, *The Dodgers Encyclopedia* (Champaign, IL, 1997); John Thom, *Champion Batsman of the 20th Century* (Los Angeles, CA, 1992).

Joseph Lawler

DAULTON, Darren Arthur (b. January 3, 1962, Arkansas City, KS), player, is the son of David Daulton, Sr., a construction builder, and Carol C. Daulton and graduated in 1980 from Arkansas City High School, where he participated in football, baseball, and wrestling. Daulton, who also attended Cowley County, KS CC, was married to Lynne Austin and has one son, Zachary Ryan.

The Philadelphia Phillies (NL) selected the 6-foot 2-inch, 200-pound catcher, who bats left and throws right-handed, in June 1980. Daulton began his professional baseball career with Helena, MT (PrL) in 1980 and caught for Spartanburg, SC (SAL) in 1981 and Peninsula, VA (CrL) in 1982. He joined the Philadelphia Phillies for two games following the 1983 season at Reading, PA (EL), where he made the EL All-Star team. Daulton caught for Portland, OR (PCL) in 1984 and part of 1985 before returning to the Philadelphia Phillies. With the exception of spending 29 games with Clearwater, FL (FSL) and Portland-based Maine (IL) in 1987 and three games with Scranton, PA (IL) and Reading in 1991, Daulton played from 1985 to July 1987 with the Philadelphia Phillies. Injuries sidelined him for parts of eight seasons, as he completed only the 1989–1990 and 1992–1993 campaigns. Daulton has undergone surgery seven times on his left knee and once on his right knee.

In 1990, Daulton led all NL catchers in games, walks, runs, doubles, on-base percentage, and assists and shared the NL lead in HR and double plays. He paced the NL with 109 RBI in 1992, becoming only the fourth catcher in major league history to win the RBI title and the first NL player to capture an RBI crown with fewer than 500 times at bat. His career highs in hits (131), triples (5), HR (27), and RBI (109) enabled him to make the 1992 *TSN* Silver Slugger team. Besides pacing the Phillies in RBI (105) for the second straight season in 1993, Daulton also topped all NL catchers with 1,057 total chances and 19 double plays and was selected starting catcher for the first time while making his second All-Star appearance. The same season, he established career highs in games (147), runs (90), hits (131), and doubles (35) and became the first Philadelphia catcher to walk 100 times in a season. Daulton led the Phillies in a six-game triumph over the Atlanta Braves in the 1993 NL Championship Series before losing to the Toronto Blue Jays in the six-game World Series. Despite an injury, Daulton paced Philadelphia in HR and RBI in 1994 and compiled a career-high .300 batting average. After missing nearly all of the 1996 season, he was traded to the Florida Marlins in July 1997 and batted .250 with one RBI in the NL Championship Series against the Atlanta Braves. His .389 batting average, two doubles, one HR, and two RBI helped the Marlins win the 1997 World Series against the Cleveland Indians.

Daulton retired as a player in January 1998. In 14 major league seasons, Daulton appeared in 1,161 games, scored 511 runs, made 891 hits, belted 137 HR, produced 588 RBI, and compiled a .245 batting average. Daulton performed in 22 post-season games with 18 base hits, 14 runs scored, three HR, nine RBI, and a .281 batting average.

BIBLIOGRAPHY: Darren Daulton file, National Baseball Library, Cooperstown, NY; Paul Hagen, "The Blue Collar Catcher," *Sport* 84 (May 1993), pp. 51–53; Leigh Montville, "Leading Man," *SI* 79 (October 11, 1993), pp. 46–48; Rich Westcott and Frank Bilovsky, *The New Phillies Encyclopedia* (Philadelphia, PA, 1993); *Philadelphia Phillies Media Guide*, 1997; Dave Rosenbaum, *If They Don't Win It's a Shame* (Tampa, FL, 1998); *TSN Official Baseball Register*, 1998; *USAT Baseball Weekly*, August 30–September 5, 1995, p. 64.

John L. Evers

DAUS, George August. *See* George August Dauss.

DAUSS, George August "Hooks," "Hookie" (b. George August Daus, September 22, 1889, Indianapolis, IN; d. July 27, 1963, St. Louis, MO), player, was one of three sons of machinist John Dauss and Annie Dauss. He attended a local elementary school and spent one year at Manual Training High School in Indianapolis. On May 29, 1915, he married Olie M. Speake. He joined South Bend, IN (CL) in 1909, but his manager thought him undersized and never pitched him in an official game. After shutting out Duluth, MN (MWL) in an exhibition game, however, he was promptly signed by that club. He advanced to St. Paul, MN (AA) in 1911 and was acquired by the Detroit Tigers (AL) late in 1912.

Dauss became one of few Tigers to spend their entire major league career with Detroit, the largest contingent of one-team players in either circuit. In 15 seasons, he won 222 games and lost 182 to pace all pitchers in Tigers history. The club's mediocre record, however, obscured his impressive performance. Detroit won no pennants and finished better than fourth in only five of his years. Nonetheless, he achieved 10 winning seasons and scored more than 15 victories seven times. His best pitching years were 1915 (24 wins) and 1919 and 1923 (21 each). His career ERA was 3.30, while his .550 winning percentage exceeded the Tigers' team record of .514.

A stocky right-hander, Dauss threw a serviceable fastball. He was nicknamed "Hooks" or "Hookie" because of a tantalizing curve ranking among the AL's best. He combined good control with a placid, friendly nature, leading some to believe he lacked aggressiveness on the mound. He led the AL in hit batsmen in 1914 (19), 1916 (16), and 1921 (15), however, and ranks tenth highest on the lifetime list with 121. A capable fielder, he made 1,128 assists to place high among pitchers. After a heart condition forced his retirement in 1927, he operated a farm in Missouri and worked for Pinkerton's National Detective Agency in St. Louis.

BIBLIOGRAPHY: George Dauss file, National Baseball Library, Cooperstown, NY; Detroit *Free Press*, March 29, 1924; Terry Bohn, "Hooks Dauss's 1911 Season," *BRJ* 25 (1996), pp. 112–113; Ted DiTullio, "The One-Team Players," *BRJ* 7 (1978), pp. 33–35; Raymond Gonzalez, "Pitchers Giving Up Home Runs," *BRJ* 10 (1981), pp. 24–25; Alex J. Haas, "Batters Hit by Pitchers," *BHR* (1981), pp. 84–86; Indianapolis (IN) *News*, July 28, 1963; Indianapolis *Star*, July 27, 1963; Gene Karst and Martin L. Jones, *Who's Who in Professional Baseball* (New Rochelle, NY, 1973); Frederick G. Lieb, *The Detroit Tigers* (New York, 1946); Bill Madden, *The Hoosiers of Summer* (Indianapolis, IN, 1994); Charles C. Alexander, *Ty Cobb* (New York, 1984); Fred Smith, *995 Tigers* (Detroit, MI, 1981); Richard Bak, *Ty Cobb: His Tumultuous Life and Times* (Dallas, TX, 1994); William M. Anderson, *The Detroit Tigers* (South Bend, IN, 1996); Richard Bak, *A Place for Summer* (Detroit, MI, 1998); Joe Falls, *Detroit Tigers* (New York, 1975); *Baseball Encyclopedia*, 10th ed. (New York, 1996).

                                                                                                    A. D. Suehsdorf

DAVIS, Charles Theodore "Chili" (b. January 17, 1960, Kingston, Jamaica), player, is the son of William Davis and Jenny (Baux) Davis and a 6-foot 3-inch, 217-pound right-handed outfielder and switch-hitting DH. Davis did not play baseball until age 10 when his parents moved from Jamaica to Los Angeles, CA, where in 1977 he graduated from Dorsey High School.

The San Francisco Giants (NL) selected Davis in the 11th round of the June 1977 free-agent draft and assigned him to Cedar Rapids, IA (ML) in 1978. He spent 1979 at Fresno, CA (CaL) and 1980 at Shreveport, LA (TL). Davis appeared in eight games for the San Francisco Giants in 1981 before being sent to Phoenix, AZ (PCL), where he compiled a .350 batting average, 19 HR, 75 RBI, and 40 stolen bases in just 88 games. From 1982 through 1987, he played full time with the San Francisco Giants except for 10 games at Phoenix in 1983. Davis' best seasons with the San Francisco Giants included 24 HR, 81 RBI, and a .315 batting average and career bests in hits (167), runs scored (87), and triples (6). He played in the 1987 NL, Championship Series loss to the St. Louis Cardinals, collecting only three hits and a .150 batting average.

The San Francisco Giants granted Davis free agency in November 1987. He signed with the California Angels (AL) in December 1987 and played three seasons there, establishing career bests in games played (158) during the 1988 season and being selected team MVP in 1989. After being granted free agency in December 1990, Davis joined the Minnesota Twins (AL) in January 1991. He enjoyed a big season in the Minnesota Twins 1991 World Championship run, batting .277, driving in 93 runs, and posting career highs with 34 doubles and 29 HR. In the AL Championship Series, Davis batted .294 with five hits in Minnesota's triumph over the Toronto Blue Jays and batted .222 with 2 HR in the Twins' World Series victory over the Atlanta Braves.

Minnesota granted Davis, who remains single, free agency in November 1992. He again signed with the California Angels in December 1992. In 1993, he led the California Angels with a career-high 112 RBI, fourth on the club's all-time list, and established a major league record for the most RBI without a sacrifice fly. On July 23, 1994, Davis became the 178th major league player to attain 1,000 career RBI. Besides batting a career-best .318

in 1995, Davis posted a club record .561 slugging average in 1994. He ranked third on the Angels all-time list in career slugging average. He has belted seven career grand-slam HR and switch hit HR in one game 10 times, but went hitless in the 1984, 1986, and 1994 All-Star games. After Davis batted .292 with 95 RBI in 1996, California traded him to the Kansas City Royals (AL) in October 1996. In 1997, he led the Kansas City Royals with a career-high 30 HR. The New York Yankees (AL) acquired Davis as a free agent in December 1997. Injuries limited him to 35 games in 1998. He batted .364 with one double, one HR, and four RBI to help the New York Yankees defeat the Cleveland Indians in the AL Championship Series and hit .286 with two RBI in New York's sweep of the San Diego Padres in the World Series. He retired in December 1999 after his 19 HR and 78 RBI helped New York win the AL East Division.

In 19 major league seasons, Davis scored 1,240 runs and made 2,380 hits in 2,436 games. He has compiled a .274 batting average with 424 doubles, 30 triples, 350 HR, and 1,372 RBI, recording 1,194 walks, 1,698 strikeouts, and 142 stolen bases.

BIBLIOGRAPHY: Charles Davis file, National Baseball Library, Cooperstown, NY; Zander Hollander, ed., *The Complete Handbook of Baseball 1994*, 24th ed. (New York, 1994); *TSN Official Baseball Register*, 1998; *USAT Baseball Weekly Almanac*, 1995.

John L. Evers

DAVIS, Curtis Benton "Curt," "Coonskin" (b. September 7, 1903, Greenfield, MO; d. October 13, 1965, Covina, CA), player, was one of five children of William R. Davis, a real estate broker, and Ida (Brown) Davis. He began his professional baseball career in 1928 as a pitcher with Salt Lake City, UT in the short-lived Class C UIL after working as a lumberjack and playing for two seasons with semiprofessional baseball teams in Vernonia, OR and Ashland, OR. After enjoying a 16–8 season at Salt Lake as a teammate of pitcher Thornton Lee,* he joined the San Francisco Seals (PCL) in 1929. Not until 1934, however, at age 30, did Davis reach the major leagues with the Philadelphia Phillies (NL).

A 6-foot 2-inch, 185-pound right-hander with a sidearm delivery, Davis appeared in an NL-leading 51 games in 1934. He won 19 while losing 17 for the seventh-place Phillies and achieved a 2.95 ERA, the lowest for any Philadelphia starter since 1920. The Philadelphia Phillies recorded another seventh-place finish in 1935, as Davis took 16 of 30 decisions. During these two years, no other Philadelphia Phillies pitcher garnered more wins than losses.

In May 1936, the Philadelphia Phillies traded Davis with outfielder Ethan Allen* to the Chicago Cubs (NL) for a washed-up Chuck Klein.* A sore arm sidelined Davis for half the 1937 season, but he returned to compile a 10–5 record. The next spring, the Chicago Cubs sent Davis, two other players, and $185,000 to the St. Louis Cardinals (NL) for Dizzy Dean.* As the deal turned out, Davis was the prize. Following a 12–8 season in 1938, he reached his peak with 22 victories to lead the 1939 St. Louis Cardinals into second place. In June 1940, the St. Louis Cardinals traded a fading Davis and Joe Medwick* to the Brooklyn Dodgers (NL) for $15,000 and three players. Although then age 37, Davis enjoyed several good, first-division campaigns under the flamboyant manager Leo Durocher.* In 1941, his 13–7 record helped the Brooklyn Dodgers take the NL pennant. Davis was bested, 3–2, by Red Ruffing* in the opening game of the World Series, in which the New York Yankees prevailed.

Davis' major league career ended in 1946 with 158 wins (including 26 in relief), 131 losses, and a 3.42 ERA. His Total Pitcher Index (TPI) rating in *Total Baseball* lists him 78th all-time and 21st in his era. He was selected a NL All-Star twice, being hit hard in relief of Carl Hubbell* in the 1936 game and not playing in 1939.

In retirement, Davis became a real estate salesman. He was married three times: to Lillian Preston in October 1936, to Della F. Haggberg in 1954, and to Lennis Hutchison in 1959. He had no children.

BIBLIOGRAPHY: *The Baseball Encyclopedia*, 10th ed. (New York, 1996); Curt Davis file, National Baseball Library, Cooperstown, NY; *TSN*, October 27, 1965; William F. McNeil, *The Dodgers Encyclopedia* (Champaign, IL, 1997); Leo Durocher and Ed Linn, *Nice Guys Finish Last* (New York, 1975); Richard Goldstein, *Superstars and Screwballs* (New York, 1991); Rich Westcott and Frank Bilovsky, *The New Phillies Encyclopedia* (Philadelphia, PA, 1993); Frederick G. Lieb and Stan Baumgartner, *The Philadelphia Phillies* (New York, 1953); John Thorn et al., eds., *Total Baseball*, 5th ed. (New York, 1996).

A. D. Suehsdorf

DAVIS, Eric Keith (b. May 29, 1962, Los Angeles, CA), player, is the son of Jimmy Davis and Shirley Davis and grew up in Los Angeles, where he won All-City honors as a shortstop in baseball and as a basketball player at Fremont High School. His close friend Darryl Strawberry* played with him on a CML baseball team. After Davis graduated from high school in 1980, the Cincinnati Reds (NL) signed him as an eighth-round draft choice. Davis declined basketball scholarships from several colleges.

Davis played professional baseball at Eugene, OR (NWL) in 1980 and 1981, being converted to the outfield. His subsequent minor league stops included Cedar Rapids, IA (ML) in 1982 and Waterbury, CT (EL) and Indianapolis, IN (AA) in 1983. With Wichita, KS (AA) in 1984, the 6-foot 3-inch, 185-pound hitter displayed midseason statistics of a .314 batting average, 14 HR, 34 RBI, and 27 stolen bases. The Cincinnati Reds promoted him and made him the regular center fielder until an injury sidelined him. In 1985, his playing time was split between the Cincinnati Reds and Denver, CO (AA).

In his first full season with the Cincinnati Reds in 1986, Davis batted a .277 with 27 HR, 71 RBI, and a career-high 80 stolen bases. Only Rickey Henderson* previously had hit over 20 HR while stealing 80 or more bases in a season. The following year appeared to mark the blossoming of a great career. He was named the NL Player of the Month for April and May and set NL records by having 19 HR through May and hitting three grand-slam HR in May. On August 2, the earliest date of any season, he joined the 30/30 Club with at least 30 or more HR and stolen bases. The center fielder finished 1987 with a .293 batting average, 37 HR, 100 RBI, and 50 stolen bases. Davis, who won Gold Glove awards in 1987, 1988, and 1989, was named to the *TSN* Silver Slugger team in 1987 and 1989 and made the NL All-Star team in 1987 and 1989.

Injuries limited his production, as Davis never played in more than 135 games in a season. He spent considerable time on the disabled list, being sidelined some in 1984, 1989, 1990, 1991, 1992, 1995, and 1997. In Game 4 of the 1990 World Series against the Oakland Athletics, he suffered a lacerated right kidney while trying to make a diving catch. The Cincinnati Reds traded Davis to the Los Angeles Dodgers (NL) in November 1991. The Los Angeles Dodgers hoped that he would form part of a great offensive combination with his longtime friend and teammate Darryl Strawberry. Injuries to both, however, prevented that from happening. In August 1993, the Los Angeles Dodgers traded Davis to the Detroit Tigers (AL). The Detroit Tigers released Davis in October 1994. He temporarily retired in 1995 and signed with the Cincinnati Reds in January 1996. Davis earned *TSN* NL Comeback Player of the Year honors in 1996, batting .287 with 26 HR and 83 RBI. In December 1996, the Baltimore Orioles (AL) acquired him as a free agent. Despite battling colon cancer, he batted .304 in 1997 and .327 with 28 HR and 89 RBI in 1998. In November 1998, the St. Louis Cardinals (NL) signed him as a free agent.

Through 1999, Davis has amassed a .269 batting average with 883 runs scored, 272 HR, 872 RBI, and 347 stolen bases. Through 1994, his 335 thefts made him the all-time stolen base percentage leader with 85.9 percent (among those with 300 career attempts). He and his wife, Sherrie, have two daughters, Erica and Sacha, and reside in Woodland Hills, CA.

BIBLIOGRAPHY: Eric Davis file, National Baseball Library, Cooperstown, NY; Jim Brosnan, "The Cincinnati Kid," *Life* 10 (August 1987), pp. 78–81; Chuck Johnson, "Reds' Davis Gets Results by 'Going on Gut Instincts,'" *USAT*, April 14, 1989, p. C7; *Los Angeles Dodgers 1993 Media Guide*; Hal McCoy, "Aches, Pains and Superstardom," *TSN*, March 2, 1987, p. 22; Donald Honig, *The Cincinnati Reds* (New York, 1992); Sam McManis, "The Reds' Menace," *Sport* 78 (March 1987), pp. 22–24; Jay Mariotti, "The Ultimate Player—Do Reds Have Him?" *TSN*, June 19, 1987, pp. 10–11; Leigh Montville, "Unbroken Spirit," *SI* 88 (March 16, 1998), pp. 46–48; Ron Rappoport, "Eric Davis Soaks It Up," *Sport* 81 (June 1990), pp. 52–54, 56, 60; Charles Siebert, "Say Hey! Is Eric Davis the Next . . . ," *NYT Magazine* (May 3,

1987), pp. 42ff; John Thorn et al., eds., *Total Baseball*, 5th ed. (New York, 1997); *TSN Official Baseball Register*, 1998; Ralph Wiley, "These Are Red Letter Days," *SI* 66 (May 25, 1987), pp. 36–38.

                                                                                              Robert J. Brown

DAVIS, George Stacey (b. August 23, 1870, Cohoes, NY; d. October 17, 1940, Philadelphia, PA), player, manager, and scout, was the son of Wales native Abram Davis and English-born Sarah (Healy) Davis. He began his baseball career in 1889 with an Albany, NY independent minor league team. He joined the Cleveland Spiders (NL) in 1890 as an infielder and outfielder. In 1893, he was traded to the New York Giants (NL) and played shortstop for the Giants through the 1901 season. Davis managed the Giants in 1895 and 1900–1901, producing 107 wins and 139 losses (.435). Davis jumped to the Chicago White Stockings (AL) in 1902 and then returned to the Giants in 1903, violating the recent "peace treaty" between the two leagues. AL president Ban Johnson* and Chicago owner Charles Comiskey* obtained a court injunction (defeating Davis' attorney, John Montgomery Ward*) that kept Davis out of all but four games in 1903 and forced him to return to Chicago in 1904. With Chicago through 1909, he helped the White Stockings' "hitless wonders" win the 1906 World Series by batting .308 with six RBI in three games. He served as player-manager of Des Moines, IA (WL) in 1910 and then retired.

The 5-foot 9-inch, 180-pound right-hander proved a stylish-fielding shortstop and a dangerous, intelligent switch-hitter, batting .295 in 2,377 games. His 2,660 hits included 451 doubles, 163 triples, and 73 HR. He also stole 616 bases, scored 1,539 runs, drove in 1,437 tallies, and led the NL with the 136 RBI in 1897. He made six hits in six times at bat on August 15, 1895, slugged three triples in an April 23, 1894 contest, and hit two doubles, one triple, and one HR on May 18, 1906. He batted .300 or better nine consecutive seasons in a dead ball era and set a record in 1893 with a 33-game hitting streak. Defensively, he led the league in double plays five times and total chances and fielding average four times. Davis scouted for the New York Yankees (AL) in 1915 and the St. Louis Browns (AL) in 1917, but little is known of his post-baseball career. He evidently sold automobiles for a time and married Jane (Holden) Davis. A steady, solid performer on the field and briefly an object of controversy off it, Davis both enjoyed the benefits of his sport's popularity and was frustrated by its economic consolidation. In 1998, the Veterans Committee elected him to the National Baseball Hall of Fame.

BIBLIOGRAPHY: Warren Brown, *The Chicago White Sox* (New York, 1952); Frank Graham, *The New York Giants* (New York, 1952); William F. Lamb, "George Davis: Forgotten Great," *TNP* 17 (1997), pp. 3–8; John Phillips, *The Spiders—Who Was Who* (Cabin John, MD, 1991); George Davis file, National Baseball Library, Cooperstown, NY; Lee Lowenfish, "The Later Years of John M. Ward," *TNP* 2 (Fall

1982), pp. 66–69; *The Baseball Encyclopedia*, 10th ed. (New York, 1996); *1998 National Baseball Hall of Fame and Museum Yearbook*.

Luther W. Spoehr

DAVIS, Glenn Earle (b. March 28, 1961, Jacksonville, FL), player, was a 6-foot 3-inch, 212-pound first baseman who threw and batted right-handed. The son of Gene Davis and Margaret Davis, he married Teresa Beesley in 1984. His father played professional baseball for 10 years, but alcoholism caused his parents' divorce. His mother blamed baseball and often forcibly took Davis off the neighborhood diamond to keep him from bad company. He rebelled by drinking, playing with guns, and driving fast cars amid periods of utter despair. He termed his early life "a crossword puzzle." His unrelated classmate "Storm" Davis, later a major league pitcher, brought Glenn to his own home. His new family consoled him with religion, as "the Lord entered my life." Davis found a new focus, signing with the Houston Astros (NL) in 1981 as a first baseman.

A real power hitter, Davis reached the major leagues with the Houston Astros in 1984. He batted .271 with 20 HR in 1985 and .265 with 31 HR and 101 RBI in 1986. Houston manager Hal Lanier regretted that Davis lost power potential in his home field, the "cavernous" Astrodome. But Davis wisely concentrated on just "hitting the ball hard." Opposing teams tried shifting their second basemen to the left side of the infield against him. Davis, who played in the 1986 and 1989 All-Star games, worked hard on defense to become a more all-around player.

Not wanting his large contract, however, Houston dismayed Astros fans by trading Davis in January 1991 to the Baltimore Orioles (AL) for three young players. But a neck injury, which damaged his spinal accessory nerve, cut deeply into his playing time mostly as a DH. His best season with Baltimore came in 1992, when he batted .276 with 13 HR in just 106 games. His major league career rapidly faded, causing his release in September 1993. To that point, he batted .259 with 190 HR and 603 RBI in 10 major league seasons. He spent 1995 in Japan with the Hanshin Tigers. He played in the NL in 1996, hoping for another turn in the major leagues. By then, Davis found an infinitely greater goal for his life through helping disadvantaged children. Upon recalling his own unfortunate childhood, he in 1990 personally contributed $250,000 to establish the Glenn Davis Home for Boys in Columbus, GA. His wife, Teresa, founded a similar school for girls. Their sincere compassion for troubled youth impressed many, especially those in the schools and hospitals they visited regularly.

BIBLIOGRAPHY: John Thorn et al., eds., *Total Baseball*, 5th ed. (New York, 1997); *The Baseball Encyclopedia*, 10th ed. (New York, 1996); Mike Shatzkin, ed., *The Ballplayers* (New York, 1990); Bruce Newman, "Sorry Past, Bright Future," *SI* 65 (August 25, 1986), pp. 27–34; *TSN*, October 22, 1984; *TSN*, August 26, 1985; *TSN*, August 4, 1986, p. 14; *TSN*, August 7, 1986; *TSN*, March 2, 1987; *TSN*, August 1, 1988;

TSN, February 20, 1989; *TSN*, April 10, 1989; *TSN*, January 21, 1991; Neil Hohlfeld, "Davis a Champion for Troubled Kids," *USAT*, April 30, 1990; "Northern Exposure: Davis Hopes to be Seen, as Was Strawberry, in Minor League," *St. Louis Post-Dispatch*, August 14, 1996, p. 8D; *WWIB, 1994*, 79th ed.; *TSN Official Baseball Register, 1994*; Glenn Davis file, National Baseball Library, Cooperstown, NY; J. Friedman, "A Painful Childhood Behind Him, Houston Astro Glenn Davis Only Slugs Baseballs Now," *PW* 26 (August 25, 1986), pp. 53ff; M. Moran, "Fulfillment for Astros' Davis," *NYT Biographical Service* 17 (July 1986), pp. 848–849.

William J. Miller

DAVIS, Harry H. "Jasper" (b. July 19, 1873, Philadelphia, PA; d. August 11, 1947, Philadelphia, PA), player, manager, coach, and scout, graduated from Girard College in 1891 and worked in business. In 1894, Providence, RI (EL) signed the 5-foot 10-inch, 180-pound batter and infielder. Davis played first base for Pawtucket, RI (NEL) in 1895 and joined the New York Giants (NL) in 1896. After performing for the Pittsburgh Pirates (NL) from 1896 to 1898 and Louisville, KY Colonels (NL) and Washington Senators (NL) in 1898, he returned to Providence in 1899. In 1897, he led the NL in triples with 28. The New York Giants had traded him to the Pittsburgh Pirates between two games of a doubleheader involving the two teams. Davis participated at first base for the Giants in the first game and at the same position for the Pirates in the second game.

Davis's early career saw him suffer from rheumatism in his legs, causing his 1900 announcement to retire from baseball. Manager Connie Mack* of the Philadelphia Athletics (AL) induced Davis to return. With the Athletics, Davis led the AL in HR from 1904 through 1907, in doubles in 1902, 1905, and 1907, in RBI in 1905 and 1906, and in runs scored in 1905. He belted 43 doubles in 1902, 10 HR in 1904, 47 doubles and 8 HR with 83 RBI in 1905, 12 HR with 96 RBI in 1906, and 35 doubles with 8 HR in 1907. His major league career statistics included 1,841 hits, 361 doubles, 145 triples, 75 HR, 951 RBI, and 1,001 runs scored. Davis, the first Philadelphia Athletics captain, served as acting manager on numerous occasions. He piloted the Cleveland Naps (AL) as a player–manager to a 54–71 record and sixth-place finish in 1911 and resigned before the completion of the season. He coached for the Athletics from 1913 to 1917 and in 1919, when he joined the City of Philadelphia Common Council.

Davis was reelected several times to the council and worked in the Philadelphia Tax Office, the scrap iron and steel business, and as a private detective. From 1918 through 1927, the Philadelphia Athletics employed him as a scout. Davis married Eleanor Hicks on March 1, 1898 and had two sons and one daughter.

BIBLIOGRAPHY: Thomas Aylesworth and Benton Minks, *The Encyclopedia of Baseball Managers* (New York, 1990); Frederick G. Lieb, *Connie Mack* (New York, 1945); Connie Mack, *My 66 Years in the Big Leagues* (Philadelphia, PA, 1950); *The Baseball*

Encyclopedia, 10th ed. (New York, 1996); Harry H. Davis file, National Baseball Library, Cooperstown, NY; Ira L. Smith, *Baseball's Famous First Basemen* (New York, 1956).

Horace R. Givens

DAVIS, Herman Thomas "Tommy" (b. March 21, 1939, Brooklyn, NY), player and coach, grew up in Brooklyn, graduated in 1956 from Boys High, and lettered in baseball, basketball, and track and field there. During his senior year, he captained the basketball team, was selected for the All-City basketball team, and was chosen as the school's best athlete. After signing his first professional baseball contract with the Brooklyn Dodgers (NL), Davis hit .325 in 43 games as an outfielder for Hornell, NY (PoL), in 1956. During the next three minor league seasons, he hit above .300 and played first, second, and third base and the outfield. His minor league assignments included Kokomo, IN (ML) in 1957 and Victoria, TX (TL) and Montreal, Canada (IL) in 1958. In 1957 with Kokomo, he led the ML in batting average (.357), at bats (518), runs scored (115), and hits (185). At Spokane, WA in 1959, he led the PCL in batting average (.345), hits (211), at bats (612), and games played (153).

Davis hit .276 in his first full season with the Los Angeles Dodgers (NL) in 1960. With the Dodgers, the 6-foot 2-inch, 200-pound right-hander played mainly as an outfielder and occasionally at third and first base. He led the NL in 1962 with a .346 batting average, 153 RBI, and 230 hits and also belted 27 HR and scored 120 runs. In 1963, he again paced the NL with a .326 batting average to help the Dodgers win the NL pennant and batted .400 in the World Series sweep of the New York Yankees. Davis tied World Series records for most triples in a game and four-game series (2), most putouts by an outfielder in an inning (3), and most putouts by a left fielder in a game (6). He broke an ankle sliding into second base on May 1, 1965 and never regained his former speed. In 1966, he batted .313 to help the Dodgers capture another NL pennant and hit .250 in the World Series sweep by the Baltimore Orioles.

Davis tied a major league record for most clubs belonged to (10). From 1967 to 1976, his clubs included the New York Mets (NL) in 1967, Chicago White Sox (AL) in 1968, Seattle Pilots (AL) from October 15, 1968 to August 31, 1969, Houston Astros (NL) from August 31, 1969 to June 22, 1970, Oakland Athletics (AL) from June 22 to September 16, 1970 and March 29, 1971, to July 6, 1972, Chicago Cubs (NL) from September 16 to December 22, 1970 and July 6 to August 18, 1972, Baltimore Orioles (AL) from August 18, 1972 to June 2, 1976, California Angels (AL) from June 2 to September 20, 1976, and Kansas City Royals (AL) for the remainder of the 1976 season. At Baltimore, Davis became the prototype of the DH and set the standard for offensive output with his .289 batting average. His 18-year major league career produced a .294 batting average, 2,121 hits, 1,052 RBI, 811 runs scored, 272 doubles, 153 HR, and 136 stolen bases. Davis married Shirley Johnson on February 6, 1957 and has four children, Lauren, Leslie, Carlyn, and Herman Thomas III. He coached for the Seattle Mariners (AL) in 1981 and served as a hitting instructor for the California Angels (AL) in 1980 and Los Angeles Dodgers from 1984 through 1988.

BIBLIOGRAPHY: William F. McNeil, *The Dodgers Encyclopedia* (Champaign, IL, 1997); Bob Cottrol, "T. Davis, dh, Alive and Loved in Baltimore," *BS* 4 (August 1974), pp. 26–27, 54–55, 98; Tommy Davis file, National Baseball Library, Cooperstown, NY; Paul MacFarlane, ed., *TSN Daguerreotypes of Great Stars of Baseball* (St. Louis, MO, 1981); Larry Moffi and Jonathan Kronstadt, *Crossing the Line* (Jefferson, NC, 1994); Walter Alston, *A Year at a Time* (Waco, TX, 1974); Walter Alston with Si Burick, *Alston and the Dodgers* (New York, 1966); *The Baseball Encyclopedia*, 10th ed. (New York, 1996); *TSN Official Baseball Record Book, 1998* (St. Louis, MO, 1998); Barry Sparks, "Tommy Davis," *SCD* 25 (April 3, 1998), pp. 160–161.

Robert J. Brown

DAVIS, John Howard "Johnny," "Cherokee," "Chief" (b. February 16, 1918, Ashland, VA; d. November 17, 1982, Ft. Lauderdale, FL), player, was a slugging outfielder for the Newark, NJ Eagles (NNL) during the 1940s. He finished runner-up twice for the NNL HR title and played in the 1944, 1945, and 1949 All-Star games. The 6-foot 3-inch, 215-pound right-handed pull-hitter joined Monte Irvin,* Larry Doby,* and Lennie Pearson as the "Big Four," powering the Eagles to the 1946 NNL Championship. In Newark's World Series victory over the Kansas City Monarchs, he slammed the game-winning double in the decisive seventh game. Following the World Series, he performed on Satchel Paige's* All-Star team against Bob Feller's* All-Stars on a cross-country barnstorming tour.

Davis' road to baseball stardom involved trouble, as he grew up in several orphanages and foster homes. After completing the ninth grade, he enlisted in the U.S. Merchant Marine at age 17. He was discharged four years later and played with the Mohawk Giants of Schenectady, NY in 1940. During this time, he encountered trouble with the law and was incarcerated in a New York State penitentiary. After Newark Eagles owner Abe Manley secured his release, he played outfield with the Eagles from 1941 through 1950. Davis spent 1951 with Drummondville, Canada (CPrL), 1952 with San Diego, CA (PCL), 1953 with Ft. Lauderdale, FL (FIL), where he established the all-time FIL HR record, and 1954 with Montgomery, AL (SAL).

Davis, also a hard-throwing pitcher, fanned 15 batters in a 1948 game for the Newark Eagles. Besides starring in the VWL, he in 1944 hurled a no-hitter in the PRWL and led the PRWL in strikeouts. He won the PRWL MVP award in the winter of 1947–1948 and led the PRWL in HR in 1951–1952.

After retiring from baseball, Davis was employed in an auction gallery in

Fort Lauderdale. He and his wife, Ada, married August 29, 1952 and had two daughters.

BIBLIOGRAPHY: *Afro-American*, 1941–1948; *Chicago Defender*, 1943–1946; John B. Holway, *Black Diamonds* (Westport, CT, 1989); *Newark Herald*, 1946; James Overmyer, *Effa Manley and the Newark Eagles* (Metuchen, NJ, 1993); Robert W. Peterson, *Only the Ball Was White* (Englewood Cliffs, NJ, 1970); *The Pittsburgh Courier*, 1941–1948; James A. Riley, "Johnny Davis," *BRJ* 11 (1982), pp. 36–38; James A. Riley, *The All-Time All-Stars of Black Baseball* (Cocoa, FL, 1983); James A. Riley, *The Biographical Encyclopedia of the Negro Baseball Leagues* (New York, 1994); James A. Riley, interviews with former Negro League players, James A. Riley collection, Cocoa, FL; *The Baseball Encyclopedia*, 10th ed. (New York, 1996).

James A. Riley

DAVIS, LaVonne Paire "Pepper" (b. May 29, 1924, Los Angeles, CA), player, grew up playing baseball with her older brother, Joe, and started playing baseball at age nine for Sattinger's grocery store of Santa Monica, CA in 1933. Victories earned the players free groceries during the Depression. The 5-foot 4-inch, 138-pound Paire entered the AAGPBL during its inaugural season in 1944 with five other California high school girls. She batted .241 for the Minneapolis Millerettes in 1944 and stayed in the AAGPBL through 1953, playing for the Fort Wayne, IN Daisies in 1945, Racine, WI Belles in 1946 and 1947, Grand Rapids, MI Chicks from 1948 through 1952, and Fort Wayne in 1952 and 1953. The versatile Paire caught, played shortstop and third base, and even pitched.

Paire exhibited an aggressive catching style, leading to a broken collarbone her rookie year against the Racine Belles. She suffered numerous injuries thereafter, but kept on playing. Paire played in 458 games as a catcher, 298 games at shortstop, and 143 games at second base. A lifetime .225 hitter with 400 RBI, she made good contact and led the AAGPBL in 1945 with the fewest strikeouts (6). The same season, she paced the Fort Wayne Daisies with 39 RBI. She knocked in 70 runs in 1946 and led the AAGPBL with 71 RBI in 1950. Defensively, Paire demonstrated good range and a strong arm and led all catchers in fielding in 1950 with a .979 percentage. She also played on five championship clubs while with Minneapolis (1944), Racine Belles (1946), Grand Rapids (1948), and the Fort Wayne Daisies (1952–1953).

Paire also toured in Latin America following the 1948 season, playing baseball and promoting women's participation in the game. Her final contribution to the AAGPBL came in writing their "Victory Song" in 1945.

Subsequently, Paire played amateur softball and bowled. She worked for Hughes Aircraft Company, married, and had three children, William, Robert, and Susan. She retired in 1963 to Van Nuys, CA and serves as the spokesperson for the WNABA, including women between the ages of 18 and 65. She is included in a Women in Baseball display, opened at the

National Baseball Hall of Fame in 1988, and served as technical advisor for the movie *A League of Their Own*.

BIBLIOGRAPHY: Barbara Gregorich, *Women at Play* (New York, 1993); Gai Berlage, *Women in Baseball* (Westport, CT, 1994); W. C. Madden, *The Women of the All-American Girls Professional Baseball League* (Jefferson, NC, 1998); Lois Browne, *The Girls of Summer* (New York, 1992); Sharon Roepke, *Diamond Gals* (Flint, MI, 1988); Vince Lupo, "Pepper Adds a Spice to Women's Ball," *SCD* 21 (November 25, 1994), p. 210; Rich Marazzi, "A Chat with the Legendary Ladies of Baseball," *SCD* 22 (July 14, 1995), pp. 150–152.

Leslie Heaphy

DAVIS, Lorenzo "Piper" (b. July 3, 1917, Piper, AL; d. May 21, 1997, Birmingham, AL), player and manager, performed in the Negro Leagues from 1942 through 1950 and played in the minor leagues from 1951 through 1958. His father, John Davis, worked in the coal mines, while his mother, Georgia (Cox) Davis, was a homemaker. Lorenzo followed in his father's footsteps until a mining accident there convinced him that baseball provided a safer career. He honed his athletic skills playing baseball, basketball, and football for Westfield High School. Davis briefly attended Alabama State College and Miles College, but found the cost too high even with a partial scholarship.

Davis left the mines to work for Alabama's Cast Iron and Pipe Company and also played on their company baseball team in the Steel and Industrial League. Davis began playing professional baseball with the Omaha, NE Tigers in 1936 and worked his way up to the Birmingham, AL Black Barons (NAL) in 1942. He became the Barons' player–manager in 1948 and 1949, helping to develop Willie Mays,* and performed four times for the West All-Stars during the 1940s, getting at least one hit in each game and knocking in four runs. He played for the Harlem Globetrotters basketball team during the off-season because owner Abe Saperstein (IS) also was connected with the Birmingham Black Barons.

In 1950, the Boston Red Sox (AL) signed Davis. Although never having the opportunity to play major league baseball, Davis performed for Scranton, PA (EL), Ottawa, Canada (BL), Fort Worth, TX (TL), Oakland, CA (PCL), Los Angeles, CA (PCL), and San Francisco, CA (PCL) in the minor leagues. He led Scranton in batting, HR, RBI, and stolen bases in May 1950, when the Boston Red Sox released him for "economical reasons." He also spent at least eight winters playing throughout Latin America.

Other players described Davis as a "smooth infielder" with "outstanding hands." Many contemporaries believed Davis actually played first base better than second base, where he spent most of his career. Davis helped Birmingham win NAL championships in 1943, 1944, and 1948, batting .353 and leading the NAL in RBI.

Davis scouted for the Detroit Tigers (AL), St. Louis Cardinals (NL), and

Montreal Expos (NL) in the 1970s and 1980s and was elected to the Alabama Sports Hall of Fame in 1993.

BIBLIOGRAPHY: James A. Riley, *The Biographical Encyclopedia of the Negro Leagues* (New York, 1994); Brent P. Kelley, "Piper Davis: Willie's Father," *RS* (July 1995), pp. 22, 24, 26, 28; "Negro Leaguer Piper Davis," *SCD* 24 (June 20, 1997), p. 10; *NYT Biographical Service* 28 (May 1997), p. 809; James A. Riley, "The Man Who Made Mays," *TDL* (July 1993), pp. 35–38, 46, 50; Kevin Scarbinsky, "Born Too Soon," Birmingham (AL) *News*, July 19, 1987, pp. 1C, 8C; Shelley Smith, "Remembering Their Game," *SI* 77 (July 6, 1992), p. 92.

Leslie Heaphy

DAVIS, Virgil Lawrence "Spud" (b. December 20, 1904, Birmingham, AL; d. August 14, 1984, Birmingham, AL), player, manager, coach, and scout, was of German and English heritage. He batted .300 lifetime in the major leagues and caught for the St. Louis Cardinals' (NL) championship Gas House Gang of 1934.

After his father died, he was brought up by his mother in the Lakeview section of Birmingham. His childhood love of potatoes led his family to nickname him "Spud." He started playing baseball at Birmingham Central High School and then transferred to Gulf Coast, MS Military Academy, where he captained the football team and played basketball and baseball. He briefly attended the University of Alabama and played semiprofessional football before beginning his professional baseball career.

Davis played semiprofessional baseball in Louisiana while in high school and batted .356 for Gulfport, LA (CSL) in 1926. The New York Yankees (AL) acquired Davis and farmed him to Reading, PA (IL), where he hit .308 in 1927. Despite his impressive offensive statistics, the Yankees were concerned about his growing weight problem and sold him to Buffalo, NY (IL). Branch Rickey,* however, soon drafted him for the St. Louis Cardinals.

The right-handed Davis began his major league career in 1928 with the St. Louis Cardinals. After Davis appeared in only two games, St. Louis traded the rookie to the Philadelphia Phillies (NL) for experienced catcher Jimmie Wilson.* Davis logged five outstanding seasons from 1929 through 1933 for the Phillies, batting .342, .313, .326, .336, and .349.

St. Louis sent Wilson in November 1933 to Philadelphia for the hard-hitting Davis. Davis batted .300 and drove in 65 runs as the regular catcher in 1934, helping the Cardinals regain the NL pennant. Davis, described as "a perfect gentleman," never fit in with the raucous Gas House Gang of "Dizzy" Dean* and "Pepper" Martin.* In the 1934 World Series against the Detroit Tigers, manager Frankie Frisch* started popular Bill DeLancey as his catcher and limited Davis to two pinch hit appearances. Although Davis hit .317 and .273, the Cardinals finished second and third in 1935 and 1936. Friction increased between Davis and star pitcher Dean, who demanded that the catcher be traded. The usually quiet Davis threatened to punch Dean.

St. Louis obliged Dean by selling Davis to the Cincinnati Reds (NL) in December 1936. After Davis experienced a mediocre year in 1937, the Reds traded him to the Philadelphia Phillies in June 1938 for pitcher Bucky Walters.* Davis shared catching duties with Wally Millies and rebounded in 1939 to bat .307 with the Philadelphia Phillies. He batted .326 in 1940 after being sold to the Pittsburgh Pirates (NL), where he completed his playing career. Frankie Frisch, who now managed Pittsburgh, retained Davis as a coach from 1941 through 1946. When Frisch quit in September 1946, Davis managed the Pirates to a 1–2 record. He scouted for the Pirates from 1947 to 1949 and returned to the coaching box with the Chicago Cubs (NL) from 1950 to 1953.

In 16 major league seasons, Davis batted .308 with 1,312 hits and 647 RBI in 1,458 games, but the 6-foot 1-inch catcher, whose playing weight varied from 197 to 240 pounds, belted only 77 career HR. Davis retired to Birmingham, AL with his wife, Helen (Ball) Davis, whom he had married in April 1928. He was inducted into the Alabama Sports Hall of Fame in 1977.

BIBLIOGRAPHY: Virgil Davis file, National Baseball Library, Cooperstown, NY; William E. Akin, "Alabama's All-Time All-Stars," *ID* (July 11, 1971), pp. 9–12; Lee Allen, *The Cincinnati Reds* (New York, 1948); Donald Honig, *The Cincinnati Reds* (New York, 1992); Robert E. Hood, *The Gashouse Gang* (New York, 1976); Frederick G. Lieb, *The Pittsburgh Pirates* (New York, 1948); Frederick G. Lieb and Stan Baumgartner, *The Philadelphia Phillies* (New York, 1953); G. H. Fleming, *The Dizziest Season* (New York, 1984); Robert Gregory *Diz* (New York, 1992); Rich Westcott and Frank Bilovsky, *The New Phillies Encyclopedia* (Philadelphia, PA, 1993).

William E. Akin

DAVIS, William Henry "Willie" (b. April 15, 1940, Mineral Springs, AR), player and manager, the son of Lorenzo "Piper" Davis, a Negro League player, moved to Los Angeles, CA as a youth. An outstanding athlete at Theodore Roosevelt High School, he was selected All-City in baseball, basketball, and track and field. Davis, whose 25-foot 5-inch broad jump established an All-City track record, batted right-handed and pitched for the school baseball team. After graduating in 1958, he signed with the Los Angeles Dodgers (NL). To make the greatest use of Davis' speed, Dodgers scout Kenny Myers converted him to an outfielder and left-handed batter. He began the 1959 season by playing seven games with Green Bay, WI (3IL) and then was assigned to Reno, NV (CaL), where he won the batting title with a .365 average and led the league in runs scored (135), hits (187), doubles (40), triples (16), and outfield putouts (302). These accomplishments earned Davis selection to the All-Star team and Rookie of the Year and MVP honors. At Spokane, WA in 1960, Davis won the PCL batting championship with a .346 average and paced the PCL in runs scored (126), hits (216), triples (26), and stolen bases (30). In 1960, Davis was named to the PCL and Class AAA All-Star teams and selected as *TSN* Minor League Player of the Year.

Davis joined the Los Angeles Dodgers in late 1960, batting a career-high .318. He played his first full season with the Dodgers in 1961 and remained there until traded to the Montreal Expos (NL) in December 1973. The Texas Rangers (AL) acquired him in a December 1974 trade. He was sent in June 1975 to the St. Louis Cardinals (NL) and swapped to the San Diego Padres (NL) that October. After spending the 1976 season with the Padres, Davis played Japanese baseball for two years. He returned to the United States and played his final major league season with the California Angels (AL) in 1979. He served as player-manager for Aguila, Mexico (MEL) in 1980.

Considered among baseball's fastest players, the 5-foot 11-inch, 180-pound center fielder covered a wide area with his speed while making great defensive plays. Nevertheless, he led NL outfielders in errors (15) in 1962 and tied for most miscues (12) in 1974. During the 1966 World Series against the Baltimore Orioles, he made three errors in the fifth inning of Game two. This established records for most errors by an outfielder in an inning and a game. Davis led NL outfielders in putouts with 400 in 1964 and 404 in 1971 and won Gold Glove awards in 1972 and 1973. His daring base running made him a constant threat to steal or take extra bases. Davis hit inside-the-park HR four times and stole a career-high 42 bases in 1964. During the 1965 World Series against the Minnesota Twins, he tied Honus Wagner's* fall classic record by stealing three bases in one game. Davis also appeared in the 1963 World Series against the New York Yankees, but only compiled a .167 composite batting average in three fall classics.

As a batter, Davis established a Los Angeles Dodgers record by hitting in 31 consecutive games in 1969 and surpassed .300 averages from 1969 through 1971. Davis, who led the NL in triples in 1962 (10) and 1970 (16), was elected to the NL All-Star team in 1971 and 1973 and chosen as an outfielder on *TSN* 1971 All-Star team. Dodgers manager Walter Alston* selected Davis as club captain in 1973. His major league career produced a .279 batting average, 2,561 hits, 1,053 RBI, 1,217 runs scored, 395 doubles, 138 triples, 182 HR, and 398 stolen bases.

BIBLIOGRAPHY: Willie Davis file, National Baseball Library, Cooperstown, NY; Walter Alston, *A Year at a Time* (Waco, TX, 1976); Walter Alston with Si Burick, *Alston and the Dodgers* (New York, 1966); *Los Angeles Dodgers 1985 Media Guide; Los Angeles Dodgers Yearbook, 1962*; William F. McNeil, *The Dodgers Encyclopedia* (Champaign, IL, 1997); Rich Marazzi and Len Fiorito, *Aaron to Zipfel* (New York, 1985); *The Baseball Encyclopedia*, 10th ed. (New York, 1996); Joseph L. Reichler, ed., *The Baseball Trade Register* (New York, 1984); Gene Schoor, *The Complete Dodgers Record Book* (New York, 1984); *TSN Official World Series Records*, 1985; Richard Wittingham, *The Los Angeles Dodgers: An Illustrated History* (New York, 1982).

Robert J. Brown

DAWSON, Andre Nolan "Hawk" (b. July 10, 1954, Miami, FL), player, grew up and resides in Miami. The 6-foot 3-inch, 190-pound Dawson played baseball at Southwest Miami High School and three years at Florida A&M University. The nephew of Theodore Taylor, an outfielder in the Pittsburgh Pirates organization from 1967 to 1969, he married Vanessa Turner on December 16, 1978. They have three children.

The Montreal Expos (NL) selected Dawson, a center fielder, as the 251st player chosen in the 1975 free agent draft. Dawson played only 186 minor league games before joining the Expos. In 1975, he played 72 games at Lethbridge, Canada (PrL), hitting .330 with 13 HR and 50 RBI. Dawson started the 1976 season with Quebec City, Canada (EL), batting .357 in 40 games, and was promoted to Denver, CO (AA). In his first month at Denver, Dawson hit 14 HR with 28 RBI and finished the season with a .350 batting average. After the playoffs, the Expos purchased his contract.

Dawson started slowly in the majors. During the remainder of the 1976 season, he hit only .235 in 24 games. Dawson began the 1977 season as part-time outfielder and struggled at the plate until June, when manager Dick Williams* made him the permanent center fielder. Dawson then batted .282, knocked in 65 runs, stole 21 bases, and won the NL Rookie of the Year Award.

Dawson developed into an All-Star center fielder and won Gold Glove awards from 1980 through 1983. He twice (1981 and 1983) finished runner-up in the voting for NL MVP and was named *TSN* NL Player of the Year in 1981. Major league players voted Dawson the best all-around player in a *NYT* 1983 poll. On July 30, 1978, he hit two HR in the third inning to tie a major league record. From 1980 to 1983, he hit .302 and averaged 24 HR, 87 RBI, and 31 stolen bases. During the same period, he averaged 398 put-outs and under 8 errors per season. He led the NL in both putouts and chances from 1981 through 1983. Dawson belted 3 HR, including two in a 12-run fifth inning, and tied a club record with 8 RBI to help the Montreal Expos defeat the Chicago Cubs, 17–15, on September 24, 1985. Only two other major leaguers have slugged 2 HR in the same inning twice. His 23 HR in 1985 included seven in a five-game stretch in late September.

The Chicago Cubs (NL) signed Dawson as a free agent in March 1987. In 1987, Dawson earned the NL MVP award, leading the NL with 49 HR and 137 RBI while batting .287. He won his seventh Gold Glove and fourth *TSN* Silver Slugger award. Dawson spent 1993 and 1994 with the Boston Red Sox (AL) and ended his major league career with the Florida Marlins (NL) in 1995 and 1996. He underwent eight knee operations and made the NL All-Star team eight times (1981–1983, 1987–1991). In 21 major league seasons, he batted .279 with 2,774 hits, 503 doubles, 438 HR, and 1,591 RBI.

BIBLIOGRAPHY: Bruce Anderson, "A Bargain at Any Price," *SI* 66 (June 1987), pp. 36–37; Mike Bryan, *Baseball Lives* (New York, 1989); "Andre Dawson: Baseball's First 40–40 Man," *Sport* 73 (April 1982), p. 49; Andre Dawson with Tom Bird, *Hawk*

(Grand Rapids, MI, 1994); Walter Leary, "The $2 Million Gamble That Paid Off," *Ebony* 43 (May 1988), pp. 42ff; Jack Friedman, "No Series for the Cubbies, but At Least They Have Andre the Awesome," *PW* 28 (October 5, 1987), pp. 121–122; David Whitford, "The Last Laugh," *Sport* 78 (December 1987), pp. 16–18; *Montreal Expos Press Guide 1984*; *NYT*, July 4, 1983; David L. Porter, ed., *African-American Sports Greats* (Westport, CT, 1995); *TSN Baseball Register, 1996.*

Eric C. Schneider

DAY, John B. (b. September 23, 1847, Colchester, MA; d. January 25, 1926, Cliffside, NJ), owner, executive, and manager, founded the New York Giants (NL) baseball club and turned it into one of baseball's premier franchises. Day, a lifelong bachelor and successful Connecticut tobacco manufacturer, supported several independent baseball teams. In 1883, Day and Boston sportsman Jim Mutrie* formed the Metropolitan Exposition Company and were awarded the New York Giants NL franchise. They also received the New York Mets (AA) in 1884. Day signed many players from the failed Troy, NY Trojans (NL) franchise and pitcher John Montgomery Ward* from the Providence, RI Grays (NL). The New York Giants and the New York Mets both played in the original Polo Grounds until Day sold the New York Mets in 1885. A canvas fence was raised to separate the two diamonds. After the New York Mets won the 1884 AA championship, Day funneled off the club's talent to the New York Giants because the NL charged twice as much for tickets.

The New York Giants enjoyed success both on and off the field, winning NL pennants in 1888 and 1889 and becoming one of the NL's most valuable franchises. Day, a popular owner with the players, paid some of the best salaries and spared no expense on travel for the team. The onset of the Brotherhood war, however, radically changed Day's fortunes. The BPBP, the players association formed in 1885, began to seek funding for their own teams and started the PL in 1890. Most of the Giants squad defected to the BPBP PL. The battle for fans proved especially fierce in New York with five teams, including two NL and three PL, competing during the season. Day still fielded a New York Giants team, but the club failed to remain competitive.

The BPBP war crippled Day financially. To keep the New York Giants from ruin, Day appealed to the NL for assistance. The NL provided nearly $80,000 in 1891, with several NL owners receiving stock in the troubled club. The NL owners recognized the importance of a New York franchise and loaned Day players to help the Giants. Day sold a share of his New York Giants club to Edward B. Talcott, owner of a BPBP team, and resigned his club presidency after a disastrous 1892 season. He sold his remaining share of the New York Giants to Andrew Freedman* in 1895 for $48,000. In 1899, Day returned to the New York Giants as manager and guided the club to ninth place and a 29–35 record through July 5. Day, who never regained his lost fortune, served as inspector of NL umpires until his health forced him to resign in the early 1920s. In 1916, the NL voted to give Day a pension for life. Day died of a paralytic stroke.

BIBLIOGRAPHY: Charles C. Alexander, *Our Game* (New York, 1991); Lee Allen, *The Giants and the Dodgers* (New York, 1964); James M. DiClerico and Barry J. Bavelee, *The Jersey Game* (New Brunswick, NJ, 1991); Frank Graham, *New York Giants* (New York, 1952); Noel Hynd, *The Giants of the Polo Grounds* (New York, 1988); Frederick Ivor-Campbell et al., eds., *Baseball's First Stars* (Cleveland, OH, 1996); James D. Hardy, Jr., *The New York Giants Baseball Club* (Jefferson, NC, 1996); *NYT*, December 14, 1916, p. 12; January 26, 1925, p. 12; David Pietrusza, *Major Leagues* (Jefferson, NC, 1991); Steven A. Riess, *Touching Base* (Westport, CT, 1980).

Brian L. Laughlin

DAY, Leon (b. October 30, 1916, Alexandria, VA; d. March 13, 1995, Baltimore, MD), player, performed as an infielder, outfielder, and right-handed pitcher in the Negro and minor leagues. The son of glass factory gas producer Ellis Day and Hattie (Lee) Day, he grew up in Baltimore's Mount Winan's district. He quit school in the tenth grade and participated in sandlot baseball with the local athletic club. In 1934, Day played second base for the semipro Baltimore, MD Silver Moons and switched to the Baltimore Black Sox (NNL) in midseason. The diminutive 5-foot 7-inch, 145-pound Day jumped in 1935 to the Brooklyn Eagles (NNL), where manager "Candy Jim" Taylor* converted him to a pitcher. He pitched in his first Negro East-West All-Star Game in Chicago, striking out three batters. In 1937, he moved with the Eagles to Newark, NJ. The soft-spoken Day played with Newark, NJ (NNL) from 1937 through 1946, but missed the 1938 season due to a monetary dispute and the 1944 and 1945 seasons because of U.S. Army service. Day married Helene Johnson on July 17, 1939; they had no children. Using a no-windup delivery, Day possessed a sharp curve and a good fastball and frequently struck out batters. He whiffed five of seven batters he faced and was credited with the win in the 1942 East-West All-Star Game. In seven All-Star games, he struck out a record 14 hitters. His 18 strikeouts in a 1942 game set a Negro League record. On opening day in 1946, Day hurled a no-hitter against the Philadelphia Stars. In 1946, he led the NNL in strikeouts, compiled a 13–4 record, and pitched in two Negro World Series games against the Kansas City Monarchs.

Day performed well in the winter leagues. An excellent hitter, he played in Puerto Rico in 1935–1936, 1940–1941, and 1941–1942 and hit .307, .330, and an NNL-leading .351 those three years. In Cuba in 1937–1938, he won seven and lost three. After the 1943 season, Day entered the U.S. Army and participated in the Normandy landings. He played baseball in the service, twice defeating Ewell Blackwell* of the Cincinnati Reds (NL) in 1945.

Day played with the Mexico City Reds (MEL) in 1947 and 1948 and briefly in the CUL in 1947–1948. He returned to the NNL in 1949, helping the Baltimore Elite Giants win the pennant. In 1950 and 1951, he played semipro ball with the Winnipeg, Canada Buffalos. Entering organized baseball, he played 14 games with Toronto, Canada (IL) in 1951. With Scranton, PA (EL) the following season, he compiled a 13–9 record, batted .314, and led pitchers in fielding. He completed his career by playing semipro ball in Canada with Edmonton, Winnipeg, and Brandon from 1953 to 1955.

Day later worked for the Tragfer Bakery Company, Revere Brass and Copper, and Liberty Security Company as a security guard. In Newark, he was employed with Conmar Zipper Company as a substitute mail carrier and as a bartender at former Negro Leaguer Len Pearson's lounge. After his first wife died, Day married his second wife, Geraldine, in November 1980. A great pitcher and second baseman, the quiet gentleman helped pioneer the integration of minor league baseball. Considered the equal of Leroy "Satchel" Paige* by National Baseball Hall of Famer Monford Irvin,* Day exhibited skills establishing the excellence of Negro League play. In 1995, he was elected to the National Baseball Hall of Fame. His quick wit and delightful sense of humor belied his fiercely competitive nature.

BIBLIOGRAPHY: Leon Day file, National Baseball Library, Cooperstown, NY; Terry A. Baxter, correspondence with L. Robert Davids, 1984, Terry A. Baxter Collection, Cedar Rapids, IA; Terry A. Baxter, correspondence with Leon Day, 1984, Terry A. Baxter Collection, Lee's Summit, MO; Terry A. Baxter, correspondence with Jorge Figueroda, 1984, Cuban League Statistics, Terry A. Baxter Collection, Lee's Summit, MO; Terry A. Baxter, correspondence with Cliff Kachline, 1984, Terry A. Baxter Collection, Lee's Summit, MO; Terry A. Baxter, telephone interview with Monte Irvin, 1984; Ross Forman, "Negro League Great Leon Day Profiled," *SCD* 21 (April 22, 1994), pp. 150–151; John B. Holway, "One Day at a Time," *BRJ* 12 (1983), pp. 137–143; John B. Holway, *Blackball Stars* (Westport, CT, 1988); *NYT*, March 15, 1995, p. B12; James Overmyer, *Effa Manley and the Newark Eagles* (Metuchen, NJ, 1993); Robert W. Peterson, *Only the Ball Was White* (Englewood Cliffs, NJ, 1970); James A. Riley, *The All-Time Stars of Black Baseball* (Cocoa, FL, 1983); James A. Riley, *The Biographical Encyclopedia of the Negro Baseball Leagues* (New York, 1994); Donn Rogosin, *Invisible Men: Life in Baseball's Negro Leagues* (New York, 1983); Jules Tygiel, *Baseball's Great Experiment* (New York, 1983).

Terry A. Baxter

DEAN, Jay Hanna "Dizzy" (b. January 16, 1910, Lucas, AR; d. July 17, 1974, Reno, NV), player and sportscaster, was the son of itinerant farm workers Albert Dean and Alma (Nelson) Dean and the younger brother of major league pitcher Paul. Dean, who attended public school only through the second grade, married Patricia Nash on June 6, 1931. They had no children. One of sport's most colorful personalities, Dean was nicknamed "Dizzy" because of his eccentric behavior. Dean began his professional career in 1930 with St. Joseph, MO (WL), where he won 17 and lost eight. The same year, he won eight of 10 decisions with Houston (TL) and pitched a three-hit, full game victory for the St. Louis Cardinals (NL). His strengths included a high, hard pitch, a fast curve (which he called his "crooky"), and control. After posting a 26–10 record and striking out 303 in 304 innings at Houston in 1931, he joined the Cardinals in 1932. Dean became the staff mainstay until injured in the 1937 All-Star game. After being hit on the toe by an Earl Averill* line drive, Dean aggravated his arm by returning to activity too soon and lost his pitching effectiveness.

From 1932 through 1936, Dean won 120 games and lost 65 and struck out 962 in 1,530 innings. He enjoyed spectacular 30–7 and 28–12 seasons in 1934 and 1935 and led the NL in strikeouts four times and in innings pitched three times. In 1937, the year of his critical injury, he won 13 of 23 decisions and compiled excellent statistics. In April 1938, the Cardinals traded him to the Chicago Cubs (NL). From 1938 until his release in mid-May 1941, however, Dean won only 16 games, lost 8, and struck out merely 68 in 226 innings. In 1947, he pitched four innings for the St. Louis Browns (AL) as a promotional stunt, surrendering only three hits and one walk and allowing no runs.

With a lifetime record of 150 wins and 83 losses, Dean compiled a 3.02 ERA, struck out 1,163, and walked only 453 batters in 1,967.1 innings. Dean won two games over the Detroit Tigers in the 1934 World Series and also appeared in the 1938 fall classic. In the Gashouse Gang's 1934 World Series, Dean bragged considerably, played a tuba, and squeezed the tail of an over-sized toy tiger. In the final game, Dean pitched the Cardinals to an 11–0 rout. Dean struck out 17 Chicago Cubs in 1933, at the time an NL record. With Pepper Martin,* Dean played numerous practical jokes in dugouts and hotels around the circuit. He was elected to the National Baseball Hall of Fame in 1953.

As a radio and television announcer, Dean provoked controversy with his peculiar wording ("purply passed" and "slud"), repeated use of "ain't," and constant mispronunciation of players' names ("Scarn" for Skowron, "Slooter" for Slaughter,* "Stingle" for Stengel*). Despite all criticisms, Dean remained very popular with his audiences. From the 1940s to 1965, Dean's version of the "Wabash Cannonball" was heard on the airwaves of St. Louis Cardinals and New York Yankees broadcasts and CBS and NBC Game of the Week telecasts.

BIBLIOGRAPHY: Dizzy Dean file, National Baseball Library, Cooperstown, NY; Bob Broeg and Jerry Vickery, *St. Louis Cardinals Encyclopedia* (Grand Rapids, MI, 1998); Allen Churchill, "Close-up of the Undizzy Mr. Dean," *NYT*, April 22, 1951, pp. 15ff; Robert Gregory, *Diz* (New York, 1992); Rob Rains, The St. Louis Cardinals (New York, 1992); Jack Kavanagh, "Dizzy Dean vs. Carl Hubbell," *BRJ* 21 (1992), pp. 33–35; G. H. Fleming, *The Dizziest Season* (New York, 1984); Ted Shane, "His Dizziness—Jerome Herman Dean," *RD* 59 (August 1951), pp. 98–103; Curt Smith, *America's Dizzy Dean* (St. Louis, MO, 1978); Vince Staten, *Ol' Diz: A Biography of Dizzy Dean* (New York, 1992).

                                                                                                    John E. DiMeglio

DE CINCES, Douglas Vernon "Doug" (b. August 29, 1950, Burbank, CA), player, attended Pierce JC in Woodland Hills, CA and UCLA and signed with the Baltimore Orioles (AL) in 1970. He started at third base with Rochester, NY (IL) in 1973. Manager Earl Weaver* liked his play in spring training and promoted him to the Orioles in 1974. Although progressing steadily, the 6-foot 2-inch, 190-pound De Cinces played in the shadow of Brooks Robinson,* whose brilliant third base play won universal admiration. "Nobody is going to move out Brooks Robinson," De Cinces observed, but "I'm going to go out and play." He remained a utility infielder until Robinson retired following the 1977 campaign.

As starting third baseman, De Cinces provided the Baltimore Orioles with a steady glove and shotgun arm for the next three seasons. He batted .286 with 28 HR and 80 RBI in 1978, his very best campaign with Baltimore. His only World Series appearance came in 1979 against the Pittsburgh Pirates. In seven games, he batted .200 with five hits. He suffered from a spinal disorder in his lower back and consequently batted just .230 in 1979. Surgery clearly was an option, but De Cinces performed exercises prescribed by Orioles trainer Ralph Salvon. He batted .263 in only 100 games in 1981. His affliction endured to varying degrees. The arrival of heralded rookie Cal Ripken, Jr.,* however, ended De Cinces' career with the Orioles. Baltimore traded him in January 1982 to the California Angels (AL). There, his back improved for a time. He posted his best major league season in 1982, hitting .301 with 30 HR and 97 RBI. Most notably, De Cinces clouted three HR in separate games on August 3 and August 8 and also played in his only All-Star game. His final major league season came in 1987 with the California Angels and the St. Louis Cardinals (NL). "Playing hurt might benefit the team, but at the time it doesn't benefit you," De Cinces admitted. Nevertheless, Orioles and Angels fans much admired his determination and perseverance. In 1,649 major league games, he batted .259 with 237 HR and 879 RBI.

BIBLIOGRAPHY: Doug De Cinces file, National Baseball Library, Cooperstown, NY; Ray Buck, "Wings' De Cinces Wants Show Time with Orioles," *TSN*, June 2, 1973; Ken Nigro, "Knife for De Cinces," *TSN*, August 16, 1980; Ken Nigro, "De Cinces Ducks Knife At Least for Awhile," *TSN*, November 1, 1980; Ken Nigro, "Big Test for De Cinces's Ailing Back," *TSN*, March 7, 1981; "Angel Policy Irks De Cinces's Agent," *TSN*, July 18, 1983; Tom Singer, "De Cinces Doesn't Plan on Being Next Carew," *TSN*, June 23, 1986; John Thorn et al., eds., *Total Baseball*, 5th ed. (New York, 1997); Mike Shatzkin, ed., *The Ballplayers* (New York, 1990); *TSN Official Baseball Register*, 1988; James H. Bready, *Baseball in Baltimore* (Baltimore, MD, 1998); Ted Patterson, *The Baltimore Orioles* (Dallas, TX, 1995).

William J. Miller

DEDEAUX, Raoul Martial "Rod" (b. February 17, 1915, New Orleans, LA), player and coach, grew up in Los Angeles, CA, where he worked as a trucking executive and became the nation's most successful college baseball coach.

Glendale, CA served as the residence of both Dedeaux and Casey Stengel,* arguably the two most distinguished American baseball mentors. Stengel led the most major league teams (7) to World Series Championships, while Dedeaux guided the most college teams (11) to World Series titles. Both mentors spiced their interviews with distinctive speaking styles and a creative use of language. Dedeaux claimed that Stengel influenced his coaching philosophy, stating, "A little clowning always helps." According to Dedeaux, Stengel possessed the best brain in baseball "even long before his success with the [New York] Yankees."

Dedeaux, an All-City shortstop for Hollywood, CA High School, attended the University of Southern California. By his graduation in 1935, he had started three seasons in baseball, made the All-PCC squad his final two campaigns, and captained the USC Trojans. Manager Stengel signed Dedeaux to a Brooklyn Dodgers (NL) contract. Dedeaux briefly appeared with the 1935 Brooklyn Dodgers, making one hit in four at-bats, and became only the third Trojan to make the major leagues. Few realized that the University of Southern California campus would become a gold mine for major league scouts.

After becoming the Trojan mentor in 1942, Dedeaux developed that dynasty. In 44 seasons from 1942 through 1986, Dedeaux guided the Trojans to 11 NCAA championships in baseball. No other college baseball team has captured more than four NCAA championships. Dedeaux, named CBCA College Baseball Coach of the Year six times, won 28 PCC, PEC, and PTC baseball titles in a very competitive league and became the second winningest Division I college baseball coach with 1,332 victories. His 45-year record also included 571 losses and 11 ties for a .699 winning percentage. Fifty of Dedeaux's players, including Tom Seaver,* Fred Lynn,* Dave Kingman,* Steve Kemp, Roy Smalley,* and Mark McGwire,* made the major leagues. Dedeaux commanded strong loyalty from his former players, who praised his attention to fundamentals, development of a winning attitude, and charisma.

For many years, Dedeaux lobbied intensively for the inclusion of baseball as an Olympic sport. At the Tokyo, Japan 1964 Summer Olympic Games, he coached the U.S. baseball team. Baseball was featured there as a demonstration sport. In 1984, Dedeaux's dream was fulfilled when baseball formally was introduced as a full medal sport. Dedeaux coached the U.S. baseball team, which won the silver medal. He also served as president of Dart Transportation, a successful worldwide trucking firm.

BIBLIOGRAPHY: *The Baseball Encyclopedia*, 10th ed. (New York, 1996); Los Angeles (CA) *Times*, 1942–1986; *Official NCAA Baseball Records*, 1942–1986; *University of Southern California Baseball Media Guide, 1986*.

Cappy Gagnon

DELAHANTY, Edward James "Ed," "Big Ed" (b. October 30, 1867, Cleveland, OH; d. July 2, 1903, Niagara Falls, Canada), player, was the son of James

Delahanty, a teamster, and Bridget (Croke) Delahanty and joined Frank, James,* Joseph, and Thomas to form the largest brother combination in major league baseball. In 1888, he started his major league career with the Philadelphia Quakers (NL) and later starred there in one of the greatest outfields in baseball history. Between 1891 and 1895, Delahanty teamed with Billy Hamilton* and Sam Thompson* to form one of the few all National Baseball Hall of Fame outfields.

Although renowned as a hitter, Delahanty exhibited considerable speed and proved a fine fielder. The 6-foot 1-inch, 170-pound Delahanty stole 455 bases under the liberal scoring rules that prevailed before 1900. His ability to steal 29 bases at age 33 under modern rules confirmed his speed and base running skills. The swift Delahanty hit 185 triples for 13th place on the all-time list. Despite playing with the fleet Hamilton in the same outfield, Delahanty performed at center field in 1891 and 1892. Although not playing center field in 1896, Delahanty led NL outfielders in chances per game.

In his 16-year major league career, he compiled a .346 batting average to rank fourth best in major league history. Delahanty knocked in 1,464 runs and made 2,596 hits, including 522 doubles, 185 triples, and 101 HR. He three times hit at least .400 for a season and led the NL with a .410 mark in 1899. He paced the AL in hitting in 1902 with a .376 average. Besides his two batting titles, Delahanty led his league in doubles and slugging percentage five times, RBI three times, HR twice, and hits and triples once. Conscious of his value as a star, Delahanty jumped to the Cleveland Infants (PL) in 1890 and Washington Nationals (AL) in 1902 to gain pay increases. He died while still an active player by falling off a bridge at Niagara Falls and being swept over the falls. Delahanty was elected to the National Baseball Hall of Fame in 1945.

BIBLIOGRAPHY: John Benson et al., *Baseball's Top 100* (Wilton, CT, 1997); Frederick Ivor-Campbell et al., eds., *Baseball's First Stars* (Cleveland, OH, 1996); P. Keats, "Hall of Famer Ed Delahanty: A Source for Malamud's *The Natural*," *AmLit* 62 (March 1990), pp. 102–104; John Thom, *Champion Batsman of the 20th Century* (Los Angeles, CA, 1992); Rich Westcott and Frank Bilovsky, *The New Phillies Encyclopedia* (Philadelphia, PA, 1993); Frederick G. Lieb and Stan Baumgartner, *The Philadelphia Phillies* (New York, 1953); Shirley Povich, *The Washington Senators* (New York, 1954); Edward Delahanty file, National Baseball Library, Cooperstown, NY; Lowell Reidenbaugh, *Baseball's Hall of Fame-Cooperstown* (New York, 1993); Jerrold Casway, "The Best Outfield Ever?" *BRJ* 27 (1998), pp. 3–7; Paul MacFarlane, ed., *TSN Hall of Fame Fact Book* (St. Louis, MO, 1983); *The Baseball Encyclopedia*, 10th ed. (New York, 1996); Mike Sowell, *July 2, 1903* (New York, 1992); Lewis Schied, "The Tragedy of Ed Delahanty," *BRJ* 20 (1991), p. 80.

Gordon B. McKinney

DELAHANTY, James Christopher "Jim" (b. June 20, 1879, Cleveland, OH; d. October 17, 1953, Cleveland, OH), player, was one of the six baseball-playing sons of James Delahanty, a teamster, and Bridget (Croke) Delahanty, Irish immigrants. Ed,* who is enshrined in the National Baseball Hall of Fame, Tom, Joe, Jim, and Frank performed in the major leagues between 1889 and 1915. Will, the youngest, lost his opportunity to reach the major leagues because of injuries. Jim, the next most accomplished to Ed, played 13 NL and AL seasons from 1901 through 1915. The 5-foot 10½-inch, 170-pound infielder, who batted and threw right-handed, compiled a major league career .283 batting average in the dead ball era and registered 1,159 hits despite frequent injuries. A versatile fielder, Delahanty played every position except catcher. Although a mediocre outfielder, he excelled in the infield and especially at second base.

Like his brothers, Delahanty honed his baseball skills on Cleveland sandlots. He began his professional baseball career in 1896 as a third baseman for Lima, OH (OSL) before the league disbanded. After a year's absence, Delahanty played with the Montgomery, AL Senators (SL), the Allentown, PA Peanuts (AtL), and the Worcester, MA Farmers (EL) from 1898 through 1900. The Chicago Cubs (NL) purchased him for 1901, but a broken kneecap ended his season after 17 games. Chicago traded him to the New York Giants (NL) in February 1902. Delahanty appeared in seven games before being shipped to the Little Rock, AR Travelers (SL), where he hit .329 in 1902 and a SL-leading .382 in 1903. He then played regularly at various positions for the Boston Beaneaters (NL) in 1904 and 1905, the Cincinnati Reds (NL) in 1906, the St. Louis Browns (AL) in 1907, and the Washington Senators (AL) from 1907 through 1909.

After the Washington Senators traded him to the Detroit Tigers (AL) in August 1909, the quiet Clevelander attained his peak performances. During the 1909 World Series against the Pittsburgh Pirates, Delahanty led all hitters with a .346 batting average. He batted .294 in 1910 and a career-best .339 in 1911, recording 184 hits. Illness and injuries caused his mid-season 1912 release to the Minneapolis, MN Millers (AA). After remaining with the Millers through 1913, he split 1914 between the Brooklyn Tip-Tops (FL) and the Hartford, CT (CtL) club.

Delahanty, who worked for the Cleveland Street Repair Department for many years, was survived by his widow, Hester, and a daughter, Mrs. Eunice Smith.

BIBLIOGRAPHY: James Delahanty file, National Baseball Library, Cooperstown, NY; Ed Bang, "Famous Families of the Game—The Delahantys," *TSN*, November 6, 1946; Shirley Povich, *The Washington Senators* (New York, 1954); W. D. Soden, "The Greatest Family in the History of the Game," *BM* 9 (September 1912), pp. 17–22; "Jim Delahanty" (obituary), *TSN*, October 28, 1953; John Thorn et al., eds., *Total Baseball*, 5th ed. (New York, 1997); Bill Borst, ed., *Ables to Zoldak*, vol. 1 (St. Louis, MO, 1988).

Frank V. Phelps

DeMAGGIO, Dominic Paul. *See* Dominic Paul DiMaggio.

DeMAGGIO, Joseph Paul. *See* Joseph Paul DiMaggio.

DEMAREE, Joseph Franklin "Frank" (b. Joseph Franklin Dimaria, June 10, 1910, Winters, CA; d. August 30, 1958, Los Angeles, CA), player and manager, was the son of Franklin Demaree and Louisa (Seiferman) Demaree, Sacramento Valley fruit ranchers, both of whom were deaf. As a teenager, Demaree participated in baseball, basketball, track and field, and tennis. After graduating from high school in Woodland, CA in 1927, he played shortstop and the outfield on semiprofessional baseball teams in Woodland, Willows, CA, and Maryville, CA. Demaree, who batted and threw right-handed, joined Sacramento, CA (PCL) as an outfielder near the close of the 1930 season, batting .228. With Sacramento, he hit a solid .312 with 210 hits in 180 games in 1931 and a robust .364 in 1932. In July 1932, Sacramento sold Demaree to the Chicago Cubs (NL). He hit .250 in 23 games for Chicago that season, belting his first major league HR in the 1932 World Series against the New York Yankees.

In 1933, the 5-foot 11½-inch, 185-pound Demaree batted a respectable .272 as a replacement for Chicago Cub outfielder Kiki Cuyler,* who had broken his leg during spring training. But Cub manager Charlie Grimm* assigned Demaree in 1934 to Los Angeles, CA (PCL) for more seasoning. Demaree batted .383 with 190 runs, 269 hits, 45 HR, 173 RBI, and 41 stolen bases, earning PCL MVP honors. He rejoined the Chicago Cubs in 1935, batting .325 to help Chicago capture the NL pennant and hitting .250 with two HR against the Detroit Tigers in the World Series. Demaree enjoyed his finest major league season in 1936, hitting .350 with 212 hits, 96 RBI, and 300 total bases. In 1937, he collected 199 hits and attained personal career highs in HR (17) and RBI (115).

The Chicago Cubs traded Demaree in December 1938 to the New York Giants (NL), where he batted .304 with 170 hits in 1939 and .302 with 139 hits in 1940. The Giants sold him in July 1941 to the Boston Braves (NL). Used sparingly, he stayed with the Braves through the 1942 season, joined the St. Louis Cardinals (NL) in 1943, and ended his major league career with the St. Louis Browns (AL) in 1944. Demaree finished the 1944 season with Portland, OR (PCL) and returned there the following year to hit .304 in 136 games. He managed the Wisconsin Rapids, WI (WSL) in 1948 and San Bernadino, CA (SuL) in 1950.

During 12 major league seasons, Demaree batted .299 with 72 HR and 591 RBI. He started as an outfielder for the NL in the 1936 and 1937 All-Star games and appeared in the 1932, 1935, 1938, and 1943 World Series. Subsequently, Demaree scouted for the Chicago White Sox (AL) and was employed by United Artists Studio in Hollywood, CA at the time of his death. He married Nadine Mitchell in December 1931.

BIBLIOGRAPHY: Chicago (IL) *Tribune*, September 1, 1958; Joseph F. Demaree file, National Baseball Library, Cooperstown, NY; Eddie Gold and Art Ahrens, *The Golden Era Cubs, 1876–1940* (Chicago, IL, 1985); Mike Shatzkin, *The Ballplayers* (New York, 1990); J. G. Taylor Spink, *Daguerreotypes: Hall of Fame Members and Other Immortals* (St. Louis, MO, 1961); John Thorn et al., eds., *Total Baseball*, 5th ed. (New York, 1997).

Raymond D. Kush

DeMONTREVILLE, Eugene Napoleon "Gene" (b. March 26, 1874, St. Paul, MN; d. February 18, 1935, Memphis, TN), player and manager, was a diminutive shortstop and second baseman known for heavy hitting and weak fielding. DeMontreville's poor fielding skills caused him to play for seven different clubs in his 11-year major league career, despite being a lifetime .303 batter with 1,096 hits.

DeMontreville grew up in a French-Canadian section of St. Paul, MN. His parents disapproved of his obsession with baseball, but he still played sandlot baseball. His brother Lee appeared in 26 games for the St. Louis Browns (AL) in 1903. DeMontreville compensated for his small 5-foot 8-inch, 165-pound stature by developing a keen batting eye. He completed St. Paul High School and made his professional baseball debut with Buffalo, NY–Binghamton, NY–Scranton, PA (EL) in 1894. DeMontreville made a brief major league appearance with the Pittsburgh Pirates (NL) in 1894, but spent the following season with Toronto, Canada (EL) and the Washington Senators (NL). He started for the Washington Senators in the 1896 season, hitting .343 and knocking in 77 runs. The next season, DeMontreville batted .341 and drove in 93 runs. He, however, also led the NL in errors in both campaigns, committing 97 in 1896 and 91 the next in a mere 133 games.

The NL expanded to a 154-game schedule in 1898, when the Washington Senators sold their inept fielding shortstop to the Baltimore Orioles (NL). One team owner later admitted that 40 hits were added to DeMontreville's "official" record to enhance his sale value. Orioles manager John McGraw* moved him to second base. DeMontreville hit .328, but McGraw disliked his 60 errors and sold him to the Chicago Orphans (NL).

His batting average slipped to .280 in 1899, prompting the Orphans to sell him to the Brooklyn Superbas (NL) the following January. After hitting only .244 in 1900, DeMontreville was sold to the Boston Beaneaters (NL) in February 1901. He batted .300 that season, hitting safely in 23 straight games, knocking in 72 runs, and leading NL second baseman with a .954 fielding percentage. In 1902, his batting average dropped to .260 with Boston. DeMontreville played for the Washington Senators in the newly formed AL in 1903, but his .273 batting average did not compensate for his weak fielding. He broke his foot that year and spent much of it managing Worcester, MA-Montreal, Canada (EL). His major league career ended with the St. Louis Browns (AL) in 1904. He later played with Indianapolis, IN (AA) in 1904, Toledo, OH (AA) in 1905 and 1906, Birmingham, AL (SL) in 1907 and 1908, and New Orleans, LA (SL) in 1909 and 1910, managing the team the latter year.

DeMontreville married Dorothy Kelley in 1905 and settled in Memphis, TN, where he became the superintendent of the Mid-South Fair Association. He compiled nearly as many errors (439) as career RBI (497).

BIBLIOGRAPHY: "Gene DeMontreville," *Microsoft Complete Baseball* (Redmond, WA, 1994); Eugene DeMontreville file, National Baseball Library, Cooperstown, NY; *The Baseball Encyclopedia*, 10th ed. (New York, 1996); Shirley Povich, *The Washington Senators* (New York, 1954); Harold Seymour, *Baseball: The Early Years* (New York, 1960); David Quentin Voigt, *American Baseball*, vol. I (University Park, PA, 1983).
Robert E. Weir

DE MOSS, Elwood "Bingo" (b. September 5, 1889, Topeka, KS; d. January 26, 1965, Chicago, IL), player and manager, began his baseball career with the Topeka, KS Giants in 1905. Although originally a shortstop, he switched to second base after pitching a game and injuring his throwing arm. By 1915, he was considered the best second baseman in black baseball—perhaps the best ever. Being an adept gloveman, he retained his preeminent position until the mid–1920s. His speed gave him unusually wide range afield. De Moss, whose impeccable defensive skills served as a model for later second basemen, excelled in all phases of baseball. He proved a fine spray hitter who hit line drives to right field and could pull the ball if the situation warranted. An excellent bunter and a skilled hit-and-run artist, he almost always made contact at the plate as second-place hitter in the lineup and rarely struck out. His speed made him a threat on the basepaths, while his enthusiasm on the bench contributed as much to his team as his ability on the field. De Moss played for various teams but enjoyed his most productive years with C. I. Taylor's* Indianapolis, IN ABCs (1915, 1916, 1926) and Rube Foster's* Chicago American Giants (1913, 1917–1925). His 1911 Indianapolis club captured the championship. As team captain, he helped the American Giants win four titles (1917, 1920–1922) and batted .303 in 1921. His hustle and team play were suited to Foster's aggressive managerial style. After his playing days ended in 1930, he managed in the Negro Leagues through 1945, utilizing the skills he had learned from Taylor and Foster with the Detroit Stars (1927–1930), Cleveland Giants (1933), Chicago Brown Bombers (1942–1943), and Brooklyn Brown Dodgers (1945).

BIBLIOGRAPHY: John B. Holway, *Voices from the Great Black Baseball Leagues* (New York, 1975); Robert W. Peterson, *Only the Ball Was White* (Englewood Cliffs, NJ, 1970); James A. Riley, *All-Time All-Stars of Black Baseball* (Cocoa, FL, 1983); James

A. Riley, *The Biographical Encyclopedia of the Negro Baseball Leagues* (New York, 1994); Paul Debono, *The Indianapolis ABCs* (Jefferson, NC, 1997).

Gerald E. Brennan

DENNY, John Allen (b. November 8, 1952, Prescott, AZ), player, is the son of Clarence Denny and Dixie (Rader) Denny. His parents divorced when he was five years old, forcing his mother to work three jobs. After growing up in Prescott, he attended Yavapai JC and Southern Illinois University in Edwardsville. The St. Louis Cardinals (NL) selected the moody, 6-foot 3-inch, 190-pound pitcher, who batted and threw right-handed, in the 29th round of the June 1970 draft. He spent over five minor league seasons with Sarasota, FL (GCL) in 1970, St. Petersburg, FL (FSL) in 1971, Modesto, CA (CaL) in 1972, Little Rock–based Arkansas (TL) in 1973, and Tulsa, OK (AA) in 1974 and 1975, having a brief trial with the St. Louis Cardinals in 1974.

Denny, who pitched for the St. Louis Cardinals from 1975 to 1981, enjoyed a 10–7 rookie season. After posting an 11–9 record and leading the NL with a 2.52 ERA in 1976, he finished with a 14–11 mark and 2.96 ERA in 1978. Inconsistency troubled him, as his record slipped to 8–11 with a 4.85 ERA in 1979. St. Louis traded Denny to the Cleveland Indians (AL) in December 1979. After faring 8–6 in 1980 and 10–6 in 1981, he struggled with a 6–11 mark in 1982.

In September 1982, the Philadelphia Phillies (NL) acquired the determined, introspective Denny. Denny's career peaked in 1983, when he won the NL Cy Young Award with a 19–6 record and career-best 2.37 ERA. Besides pacing the NL in victories, he won 76 percent of his decisions to capture best winning percentage honors. *TSN* named Denny NL Pitcher of the Year, Comeback Player of the Year, and to its NL All-Star team. Although losing his only decision in the NL Championship Series against the Los Angeles Dodgers, he compiled a 1–1 mark and 3.46 ERA in the World Series against the Baltimore Orioles. Denny split 14 decisions with a 2.45 ERA in an injury-riddled 1984 campaign and struggled with an 11–14 mark and 3.82 ERA in 1985. His major league career ended with the Cincinnati Reds (NL) in 1986.

During 13 major league seasons, Denny compiled a 123–108 mark with a 3.59 ERA, 18 shutouts, and 1,146 strikeouts in 2,148.2 innings. He combined an excellent curveball and change up with effective control, walking only three batters per game. Although suffering from weak ankles, Denny fielded well. The Tucson, AZ resident married Patricia Torkelson in September 1973 and has three sons, John, Mark, and Christopher. A born-again Christian, he serves on the FCA board of directors.

BIBLIOGRAPHY: John Denny file, National Baseball Library, Cooperstown, NY; Bob Broeg and Jerry Vickery, *St. Louis Cardinals Encyclopedia* (Grand Rapids, MI, 1998); *TSN Baseball Register*, 1986; *WWA*, 44th ed. (1986–1987), p. 692; Bruce Newman,

"This Card Is Certainly No Joker," *SI* 46 (June 20, 1977), pp. 44ff; Richard K. Rein, "Prayers of Born Again Pitcher John Denny Were Answered with an Award-Winning Season," *PW* 21 (April 9, 1984), pp. 83–84; Rich Westcott and Frank Bilovsky, *The New Phillies Encyclopedia* (Philadelphia, PA, 1993).

David L. Porter

DERRINGER, Samuel Paul "Duke" (b. October 17, 1906, Springfield, KY; d. November 17, 1987, Sarasota, FL), player, was the son of tobacco farmer and businessman Samuel P. Derringer and caught for the Springfield High School baseball team. He volunteered to pitch in a game that his team was losing, struck out eight batters the final few innings, and was converted to a pitcher. Derringer's performance for the Coalwood, WV mining baseball team in 1926 impressed St. Louis Cardinals (NL) scout Jack Ryan, who signed him. The 6-foot 4-inch, 210-pound, right-handed Derringer pitched two seasons each at Danville, IL (3IL) and Rochester, NY (IL). Derringer won 25 games at Danville and 40 decisions at Rochester, leading the Rochester, NY Red Wings to two pennants (1929–1930).

Derringer became a starting pitcher for the defending NL champion St. Louis Cardinals in 1931, compiling an 18–8 mark and becoming the first rookie to lead the NL in winning percentage (.692). After helping the Cardinals win the pennant, Derringer suffered two losses to the Philadelphia Athletics in the World Series. He was traded to the Cincinnati Reds (NL) for Leo Durocher* in May 1933 and hurled for the Reds from 1933 through 1942. Derringer captured 22 victories, the NL's third best, for a sixth-place club in 1935. Although suspended briefly by manager Chuck Dressen* in 1936 for failing to slide into home plate in a game with the New York Giants, Derringer still paced the NL in games (51). From 1938 through 1940, Derringer won 21, 25, and 20 contests to enjoy the peak years of his career. In 1939, he lost only seven decisions and led the NL with a .781 winning percentage. Derringer paced the NL in complete games (26) in 1938, pitched one-hit games against the Cardinals and Chicago Cubs in 1940, and appeared on the NL All-Star team in 1935 and 1939 through 1941. In 1939 and 1940, he helped Cincinnati take consecutive NL pennants. Derringer lost a 2–1 heartbreaker to the New York Yankees in the first game of the 1939 World Series, but returned to win two games and lead the Reds to the world championship against the Detroit Tigers in 1940. In the seventh game, Derringer hurled a 2–1 complete-game victory. After being traded to the Chicago Cubs in January 1943, Derringer won 16 games in 1945 to help Chicago capture the NL pennant in his last major league season. In 1946, he recorded nine victories for Indianapolis, IN (AA).

Derringer, whose three different major league clubs made World Series appearances, ranks second on the all-time Cincinnati club list with 171 victories and first with 150 losses. In his 15 major league seasons, Derringer pitched in 579 games, struck out 1,507 batters, and walked 761 hitters. He ranks high on the all-time major league lists for pitchers in numerous statistical categories. Derringer compiled 223 victories, 212 losses, and 251 complete games, pitched 3,645 innings, allowed 1,652 runs, captured 10 1–0 complete game victories, and had a 3.46 lifetime ERA. These impressive accomplishments were made by a pitcher who had been told in 1927 by Boston Braves manager Lee Fohl, "Kid, you'll never be a big league pitcher. Your curveball isn't good enough."

Derringer married three times, including to Eloise Brownback on October 17, 1937 and Mary Jane Stein on September 3, 1944. Following his retirement from baseball, Derringer was employed as a salesman for a plastics company.

BIBLIOGRAPHY: Paul Derringer file, National Baseball Library, Cooperstown, NY; Craig Carter, ed., *TSN Daguerreotypes* (St. Louis, MO, 1990); Gene Karst and Martin J. Jones, Jr., *Who's Who in Professional Baseball* (New Rochelle, NY, 1973); *NYT*, November 18, 1987, p. A-28; Donald Honig, *The Cincinnati Reds* (New York, 1992); Lee Allen, *The Cincinnati Reds* (New York, 1948); Eddie Gold and Art Ahrens, *The Golden Era Cubs, 1876–1940* (Chicago, IL, 1985); Walter Brown, *The Chicago Cubs* (New York, 1946); Frederick G. Lieb, *The St. Louis Cardinals* (New York, 1945); Ritter Collett, *The Cincinnati Reds* (Virginia Beach, VA, 1976); *TSN*, May 7, 1936, September 26, 1940; *TSN Official Baseball Record Book, 1998*.

David S. Matz and John L. Evers

DEVLIN, Arthur McArthur "Art" (b. October 16, 1879, Washington, DC; d. September 18, 1948, Jersey City, NJ), player and manager, batted and threw right-handed with a 6-foot, 175-pound frame. Devlin played football and baseball at Georgetown University in 1900 and 1901 and signed with New Bern, NC (NCSL). He played in 1903 for Newark, NJ (EL) and in 1904 joined the New York Giants (NL), where he remained until 1911. In December 1911, the New York Giants sold him to the Boston Braves (NL). Devlin played with Boston through 1913. After the Boston Braves released him, he signed as playing manager for Oakland, CA (PCL) in 1914, moved to Montreal, Canada (IL) in 1915, and managed Lebanon, PA (PSL) in 1916. Since the PSL closed shortly after opening day, Devlin joined Rochester, NY (IL) for the balance of the 1916 season. His last baseball assignment came in 1917–1918 as manager of Norfolk, VA (VL).

Devlin played most infield positions, but was considered the era's finest third baseman. Sportswriter Grantland Rice (OS) named Devlin to his All-Time All-Star team. Devlin batted .269 lifetime with 1,185 base hits and proved a good base runner early in his career, stealing 285 bases. In 1905, he stole 59 bases to share the NL lead. The following year, he stole 54 bases to finish three behind NL leader Frank Chance.* Leg injuries the latter part of Devlin's career reduced his stolen bases total. He played for the New York Giants in the 1905 World Series against the Philadelphia Athletics, batting .250 with three stolen bases. Although not a power hitter, Devlin hit a grand-slam HR in his first major league at bat with the New York Giants. The NL briefly suspended Devlin in 1910 for fighting with an abusive fan in Brooklyn, NY. In 1906, Devlin married Ilma Wilk, the daughter of Frederick Wilk, a vice-president of the Union Trust Company in Chicago, IL.

BIBLIOGRAPHY: *The Baseball Encyclopedia*, 10th ed. (New York, 1996); Arthur Devlin file, National Baseball Library, Cooperstown, NY; Noel Hynd, *The Giants of the Polo Grounds* (New York, 1988); Charles C. Alexander, *John McGraw* (New York, 1988); Joseph L. Reichler, ed., *The Great All-Time Baseball Record Book* (New York, 1981).

Horace R. Givens

DEVLIN, James Alexander "Jim" (b. 1849, Philadelphia, PA; d. October 10, 1883, Philadelphia, PA), player, ranked during his final two major league baseball seasons among the finest all-time pitchers. Little is known of the first two-thirds of his brief life, but he reportedly played third base at age 22 or 23 for an Easton, PA club in 1872. The following year, he batted .242 as a reserve infielder for the Philadelphia White Stockings (NA). With the Chicago White Stockings (NA), though, he played more regularly and boosted his batting average to .286 in 1874 and .289 in 1875. The latter season also marked his pitching debut, as he won seven games and lost 16 decisions with a 1.93 ERA.

The newly organized Louisville, KY Grays in 1876 recruited Devlin to play in the NL's inaugural season. Devlin single-handedly carried the Louisville Grays to a fifth-place finish, pitching for the NL's weakest offensive team. The 5-foot 11-inch, 175-pound right-hander finished fourth in the NL with 30 wins, while compiling the NL's second-best ERA (1.56). His 35 losses led the NL, but his team scored no runs in 40 percent of those setbacks. Devlin led the NL in the workhorse categories of games (68), complete games (66), and innings pitched (622), topped the NL in strikeouts with 122, and batted .315, outperforming his nearest teammate by 42 points. His NL-leading 7.3 Total Baseball Ranking (an overall performance rating devised by Pete Palmer) for 1876 places him among the top 100 major league single-season performers at all positions and number 31 among pitchers.

The Louisville Grays fielded a stronger team in 1877. Devlin's effectiveness declined somewhat, partly because he joined some of his teammates in a gambling conspiracy to lose several games. Nevertheless, his win–loss record improved to 35–25. The Louisville Grays led the NL in mid-August, but a suspicious seven-game losing streak dropped the Grays to a second-place finish. Devlin pitched every inning of every game, with his workhorse statistics and 5.9 TBR again leading the NL. He planned to leave Louisville for the St. Louis Browns (NL) in 1878. After the crookedness of the "Louisville Four" was uncovered in October 1877, Devlin admitted his involvement and was expelled from baseball.

Devlin's frequent pleas for reinstatement met with sympathy, but firm rejection. Although Devlin found work and respect as a Philadelphia police officer, his wife, Kate, and son, James, Jr., were left "in straitened circumstances" when he died from tuberculosis six years after his expulsion.

In five major league seasons, Devlin batted .287 with 340 hits in 266 games. In three seasons as a pitcher, he hurled 1,405 innings, completed 151 of his 153 starts, and compiled a 72–76 win–loss record.

BIBLIOGRAPHY: James Devlin file, National Baseball Library, Cooperstown, NY; John E. Findling, "The Louisville Grays' Scandal of 1877," *JSH* 3 (Summer 1976), pp. 176–187; Dan Gutman, *Baseball Babylon* (New York, 1992); Daniel E. Ginsburg, *The Fix Is In* (Jefferson, NC, 1995); Albert G. Spalding, *America's National Game* (New York, 1911); John Thorn et al., eds., *Total Baseball*, 5th ed. (New York, 1997); Robert L. Tiemann and Mark Rucker, eds., *Nineteenth Century Stars* (Kansas City, MO, 1989); William J. Ryczek, *Blackguards and Red Stockings* (Jefferson, NC, 1992); Philip Von Borries, *Legends of Louisville* (West Bloomfield, MI, 1993).

Frederick Ivor-Campbell

DICKEY, William Malcolm "Bill" (b. June 6, 1907, Bastrop, LA; d. November 12, 1993, Little Rock, AR), player, coach, and manager, was one of the seven children of railroader John Dickey and Laura Dickey. The family moved to Little Rock, AR, which he made his primary home. After attending grammar school in Kensett, AR, the Scotch-Irish youngster starred for Searcy High School and spent one year at Little Rock JC. After playing one year of semipro ball, Dickey signed his first professional contract in 1925 at age 17 and caught the next few seasons with minor league teams at Little Rock, AR (SA), Muskogee, OK (WA), Jackson, MS (CSL), Minneapolis, MN (AA), and Buffalo, NY (IL). In October 1932, he married Violet Ann Arnold; he had one daughter, Vicki.

Dickey was promoted to the New York Yankees (AL) at the end of 1928, became regular catcher the next year, and caught over 100 games for a record 13 consecutive years. With powerful Yankees teams, the tall, slender (6-foot 1½-inch, 185-pound) backstop compiled a .313 lifetime batting average over 17 major league seasons. One of the better clutch hitters, he batted over .300 eleven times, drove in at least 100 runs on four occasions, and slugged 202 career HR. Dickey, who tied a major league record by slugging grand-slam HR in two consecutive games in August 1937, made *TSN* Major League All-Star team in 1932–1933, 1936, 1938–1939, and 1941. The great left-handed hitting catcher's top batting mark (.362) came in 1936. The following season, he drove in 133 runs and belted 29 HR. In 1,789 career games, he compiled 1,969 hits, 343 doubles, and 1,209 RBI. A fine defensive catcher and thrower, he proved a masterful handler of pitchers. During his tenure, the Yankees played in eight World Series and lost only to the St. Louis Cardinals in 1942. He also appeared in seven All-Star contests. Although not a fast runner, Dickey demonstrated extreme agility.

Along with Mickey Cochrane,* Gabby Hartnett,* Yogi Berra,* Roy Campanella,* Johnny Bench,* Mike Piazza,* and Ivan Rodriguez,* Dickey ranks among the best catchers in major league history. Many experts place him first. The quiet-spoken gentleman took control of the game on the field. In a rare display of anger, he fractured the jaw of Washington Senators outfielder Carl Reynolds* following a play at the plate in 1932. A fine and 30-day suspension followed.

After spending 1944 and 1945 in the U.S. Navy, Dickey finished his playing career in 1946. During that year, he succeeded Joe McCarthy* as New York Yankees manager, compiled a 57–48 record (.543), and left the position in September. After managing at Little Rock, AR (SA) in 1947, he returned to New York as a coach under Casey Stengel.* He coached for the Yankees through 1957 and scouted for them in 1959. During this period, he imparted his baseball knowledge to great Yankees backstop Berra.

Dickey, a close friend of Lou Gehrig* on and off the field, was the first Yankee to learn of his fatal illness. He remained an avid hunter, fisherman, and golfer and until 1972 was a successful investment salesman in Little Rock. Dickey was elected to the National Baseball Hall of Fame in 1954. His younger brother, George Willard "Skeets" Dickey, caught six seasons for Boston Red Sox (AL) and Chicago White Sox (AL).

BIBLIOGRAPHY:William Dickey file, National Baseball Library, Cooperstown, NY; Mark Gallagher, *The Yankee Encyclopedia*, vol. 3 (Champaign, IL, 1997); Dave Anderson et al., *The Yankees* (New York, 1979); Martin Appel and Burt Goldblatt, *Baseball's Hall of Fame Gallery* (New York, 1977); Violet Arnold (Mrs. Bill Dickey), "I Married a Ballplayer," *SEP* 240 (May 28, 1949), pp. 34ff; Harry T. Paxton, "World Series Fever: I've Had It," *SEP* 222 (October 6, 1951), p. 31; Stanley Frank, "Iron Man in a Mask," *SEP* 211 (June 17, 1939), pp. 17ff; Frank Graham, *The New York Yankees* (New York, 1943); Frank Graham, *Baseball Extra* (New York, 1954); Gene Karst and Martin J. Jones, Jr., *Who's Who in Professional Baseball* (New Rochelle, NY, 1973); *NYT*, 1928–1943, 1946, 1949–1957, November 14, 1993, p. B7; *The Baseball Encyclopedia*, 10th ed. (New York, 1996); Christy Walsh, ed., *Baseball's Greatest Lineup* (New York, 1952), pp. 133–145; Rich Westcott, *Diamond Greats* (Westport, CT, 1988).

Frank P. Bowles

DICKSON, Murry Monroe (b. August 21, 1916, Tracy, MO; d. September 21, 1989, Kansas City, KS), player, compiled a 172–181 win–loss record while often pitching for noncompetitive teams. Dickson, a product of rural western Missouri, was signed by the St. Louis Cardinals (NL) in 1939 as a $65-a-month shortstop. After converting to a pitcher, the right-handed Dickson first appeared with the St. Louis Cardinals in 1939 following 22 wins at Houston, TX (TL). His first major league victory did not come until 1942. After spending 1944 and 1945 in the military service, Dickson returned to the St. Louis Cardinals in 1946 in time to play a major role in their world championship season. Dickson compiled a 15–6 record in 1946, as his .714 winning percentage led the NL. He started two games in the 1946 World

Series against the Boston Red Sox (AL), losing one contest and pitching one run ball through seven innings in the seventh game. In 1947 and 1948, the slender 5-foot 10½-inch, 157 pounder led the Cardinals in innings pitched.

In January 1949, the Pittsburgh Pirates (NL) bought Dickson for the then huge sum of $125,000. The strikingly inept Pirates teams used Dickson as the workhorse of their staff. He mastered at least eight pitches and threw them from various angles. In 1951 Dickson recorded his only 20-victory season, finishing 20–16 with a poor Pirates club. He won 14 games for a 1952 Pirates team that fared 42–112, the worst record in Pittsburgh history. From 1952 through 1954, he led the NL in losses.

Dickson moved to the Philadelphia Phillies (NL) in January 1954 and returned to the St. Louis Cardinals in May 1956. After the 1957 season, the alleged spitballer joined the Kansas City Athletics (AL). In August 1958, the New York Yankees (AL) acquired Dickson for their annual pennant drive. He relieved twice in the 1958 World Series against the Milwaukee Braves, pitching four innings without a decision. Dickson concluded his major league career with the Kansas City Athletics in 1959.

During his 18 major league seasons, Dickson relieved almost as often as he started. The late bloomer, who won 158 games after his 29th birthday, pitched 149 complete games, hurled 27 shutouts, and compiled a 3.66 ERA. After leaving baseball, the reclusive Dickson, who loved to fish and trap-shoot, worked as a carpenter in the Kansas City area and lived on a private lake near Leavenworth, KS. Dickson married Julia Wood in February 1939 and had a son, Steven, and a daughter, Donna. After Julia died of cancer, a second marriage was short-lived.

BIBLIOGRAPHY: Murry Dickson file, National Baseball Library, Cooperstown, NY; Bob Broeg and Jerry Vickery, *St. Louis Cardinals Encyclopedia* (Grand Rapids, MI, 1998); *The Baseball Encyclopedia*, 10th ed. (New York, 1996); Richard L. Burtt, *The Pittsburgh Pirates, A Pictorial History* (Virginia Beach, VA, 1977); Brent P. Kelley, *100 Greatest Pitchers* (Greenwich, CT, 1988); NYT, September 22, 1989, p. A-28; Bob Smizik, *The Pittsburgh Pirates: An Illustrated History* (New York, 1990); TSN, October 2, 1989, p. 58; John Thorn and John B. Holway, *The Pitcher* (New York, 1987).

Frank W. Thackeray

DIERKER, Lawrence Edward "Larry" (b. September 22, 1946, Hollywood, CA), player, sportscaster, and manager, is the son of Charles Dierker and Marilynn (Keller) Dierker and made All-League in baseball and basketball at Taft High School. He attended the University of California, Santa Barbara and the University of Houston. His brother, Richard, pitched in the Baltimore Orioles (AL) organization. Eighteen major league teams scouted Dierker, who signed as a free agent with the Houston Colt 45s (NL) in 1964. After hurling just 39 innings for Cocoa, FL (CRL), the 6-foot 4-inch, 205-pound right-handed pitcher joined the Colt 45s.

Dierker compiled a 137–117 mark with Houston from 1964 to 1976. He still holds franchise records for most starts (320), complete games (106), innings pitched (2,295), and shutouts (25) and ranks second in victories, combining a live fastball, curveball, screwball, slider, and change up with excellent control. His major league debut, a 7–1 loss to the San Francisco Giants, came on his 18th birthday at Colt Stadium. In October 1966, he fell three outs short of pitching a perfect game in a 1–0 setback to the New York Mets. Military service shortened his 1967 campaign.

In 1969, Dierker became the first Houston Astro to win 20 games and hurl 20 complete games. He finished with a 20–13 record, attaining career bests in ERA (2.33), strikeouts (232), and innings (305.1) and making the NL All-Star team. After winning 16 of 28 decisions in 1970, Dierker logged a 12–6 mark with a 2.72 ERA in 1971 and made the NL All-Star team again. He fared 15–8 with a 3.40 ERA in 1972 and hurled a 6–0 no hitter against the Montreal Expos on July 9, 1976.

In November 1976, the Houston Astros traded Dierker and Jerry De-Vanon to the St. Louis Cardinals (NL) for Joe Ferguson and Bobby Detherage. He struggled in 1977 and was released by the Cardinals in March 1978. During 14 major league seasons, the Houston resident compiled a 139–123 record and 3.31 ERA with 1,493 strikeouts and just 711 walks in 2,333.2 innings.

Dierker served as television and radio color analyst for the Houston Astros from 1979 to 1996 and replaced Terry Collins as manager in October 1996. In 1997, he guided Houston to a Central Division title with an 84–78 record. The Atlanta Braves swept the Astros in the NL Division Series. In 1998, Houston established a franchise record 102–60 mark under Dierker to take the NL Central Division, but lost the NL Division Series in four games to the San Diego Padres. The BBWAA designated him 1998 NL Manager of the Year. On June 13, 1999, he collapsed in the dugout and suffered a grand mal seizure in the eighth inning of the team's game against the San Diego Padres at the Astrodome. After brain surgery, he return July 15 and guided the Astros to a third consecutive NL Central Crown with a 97–65 record. The Astros lost the NL Division Series. Dierker married Julia Lane Campbell on July 15, 1975 and has three children, Ashley, Julia, and Charles.

BIBLIOGRAPHY: Larry Dierker file, National Baseball Library, Cooperstown, NY; *TSN Baseball Register*, 1998; *Houston Astros Media Guide*, 1998.

David L. Porter

DIHIGO, Martin (b. May 25, 1905, Mantanzas, Cuba; d. May 20, 1971, Cienfuegos, Cuba), player and manager, was considered the most versatile Negro League performer. The 6-foot 1-inch, 190-pound right-hander, who excelled as a batter and pitcher and at all defensive positions except catcher, played summers in the U.S. Negro Leagues through 1936. In 1923, the youthful Dihigo made his initial American appearance as a second baseman, first baseman, and pitcher for the touring Cuban Stars. After performing with the Cuban Stars (ECL) through 1927, he played with the Homestead, PA Grays in 1928, Philadelphia, PA Hilldale Daisies (ANL) in 1929 and the early 1930s, and New York Cubans (NNL) in 1935 and 1936.

The casual, popular, humorous Dihigo starred offensively in the U.S. Negro Leagues, hitting .302 in 1925 and .370 in 1927 for the Cuban Stars. He paced the ECL with 18 HR in 1926 and shared the ECL lead in HR the next year (10). At Hilldale in 1929, he captured the ANL batting crown with a superlative .408 mark. Dihigo enjoyed his best American season in 1935, batting .308 and managing the New York Cubans to the second half NNL title. For the East squad in the 1935 All-Star Game, Dihigo started in center field, batted third in the lineup, and finished as the losing relief pitcher. The Cubans lost a seven-game playoff for the 1935 NNL title to the formidable Pittsburgh Crawfords. Defensively, Dihigo possessed an extremely powerful throwing arm, wide range, and considerable speed. According to manager Cum Posey,* Dihigo's "gifts afield have not been approached by any man— black or white."

Right-handed Dihigo excelled mainly as a pitcher in Latin America. Throughout his career, Dihigo performed winters in the Cuban Leagues. Besides enjoying outstanding 11–2, 14–10, 11–5, and 14–2 seasons, he compiled an impressive 115–60 lifetime CUL mark. Dihigo twice hit over .400 there, once making five hits in the final season game to edge teammate Willie Wells* for the batting title. Dihigo starred summers in the MEL from 1937 to the 1950s, recording an impressive 119–57 overall pitching slate. In 1938, he finished at 18–2 with a 0.90 ERA and led the MEL with a .387 batting average. His MEL statistics four years later included a 22–7 pitching mark, league leadership in strikeouts and ERA, and a .319 batting average. Dihigo hurled the first MEL no-hitter and also tossed no-hitters in Venezuela and Puerto Rico.

In 1945, Dihigo played one full season with the Homestead Grays (NNL) and helped them to first and second half NNL titles. The Cuban and Mexican Baseball Hall of Fame member served as Cuban Minister of Sports at the time of his death and in 1977 became the first Cuban elected to the National Baseball Hall of Fame. New York Giants (NL) manager John McGraw* lauded Dihigo as the greatest natural baseball player he had ever seen, while Negro Leaguer Walter Leonard* called him "the greatest all-around player" and "the best ball player of all time, black or white."

BIBLIOGRAPHY: Martin Dihigo file, National Baseball Library, Cooperstown, NY; Peter C. Bjarkman, *Baseball With a Latin Beat* (Jefferson, NC, 1994); John B. Holway, *Blackball Stars* (Westport, CT, 1988); Paul MacFarlane, ed., *TSN Hall of Fame Fact Book* (St. Louis, MO, 1983); Robert W. Peterson, *Only the Ball Was White* (Englewood Cliffs, NJ, 1970); Lowell Reidenbaugh, *Baseball's Hall of Fame-Cooperstown* (New York, 1993); James A. Riley, *The All-Time All-Stars of Black Baseball* (Cocoa, FL, 1983); James A. Riley, *The Biographical Encyclopedia of the Negro Baseball Leagues* (New York, 1994).

David L. Porter

DiMAGGIO, Dominic Paul "Dom," "The Little Professor" (b. Domenic DeMaggio, February 12, 1917, San Francisco, CA), player, is the son of

Joseph DiMaggio and Rosalie (Mercurio) DiMaggio and the younger brother of National Baseball Hall-of-Famer Joe DiMaggio* and of NL outfielder Vince DiMaggio. Educated in the San Francisco public schools, he became one of the most outstanding defensive outfielders of the immediate post–World War II era. He was probably the most underrated ballplayer of his day because of his size, his professorial appearance (he wore glasses), his lack of power, and especially because he lived in the constant shadows of his legendary brother, Joe, and his Boston Red Sox (AL) teammate Ted Williams.* DiMaggio, one of the premier center fielders of the 1940s, still was chosen for eight All-Star Games, led the AL twice in at-bats (1948, 1951) and runs scored (1950, 1951), compiled 1,680 hits, and batted .298 lifetime in his 11-year career with Boston from 1940 through 1942 and 1947 through 1953. The most talented defensive outfielder in Red Sox history revolutionized centerfield play. He fielded his outfield post like an infield position, fearlessly charging all ground balls, gunning down misadventurous base runners, and displaying a speed, range, and anticipation on fly balls matched only by his brother, Joe.

His career offensive statistics did not reach the standards of Williams or his brother, Joe, but DiMaggio hit over .300 in four of his ten full-time campaigns and never batted below .283 for a single season. He topped AL center fielders in putouts in 1942 and 1948 and in assists in 1940 and 1947. World War II service caused him to miss three full seasons (1943–1945) in the prime of his career. DiMaggio's best seasons came in 1946, 1949, and 1950. In 1946, he led Boston to an AL flag with sparkling defensive play and a .316 batting average. He challenged his brother's legendary 56-game hitting streak in 1949, reaching safely 34 consecutive games. The string ended in Game 35 on a brilliant catch by brother, Joe. His best overall season came in 1950, when he hit a career-high .328 and paced the junior circuit in stolen bases (15), triples (11), and runs scored (131). DiMaggio, who also enjoyed another 27-game hitting streak in 1951, left major league baseball at the outset of the 1953 season. A dispute had developed with new Boston manager Lou Boudreau* because the aging outfielder faced limited playing time.

The extremely intelligent, serious DiMaggio became a remarkably successful businessman as owner of a plastics manufacturing firm in New England and scored large financial successes by capitalizing on his business acumen rather than by merely exploiting his famous baseball name. DiMaggio's later life has not been without trauma, however. His abortive attempt to return to baseball as part of a syndicate that bid to purchase the Boston Red Sox from the Yawkey family proved disappointing. He began suffering in the late 1970s with a painful case of Paget's disease, a serious bone affliction that brought about considerable back and hip deterioration. By language, demeanor, and behavior, DiMaggio always seemed more serious, more scholarly, and ultimately more successful than most in his workmanlike approach to both life and the game of baseball.

BIBLIOGRAPHY: Dominic DiMaggio file, National Baseball Library, Cooperstown, NY; David Halberstam, *Summer of '49* (New York, 1989); Brent P. Kelley, *The Case For: Those Overlooked by the Baseball Hall of Fame* (Jefferson, NC, 1992); Jerry Nason, ed., *Famous American Athletes of Today*, 10th series (Boston, MA, 1947); Rich Marazzi and Len Fiorito, *Aaron to Zuverink* (New York, 1982); Thomas Meany, "Hey, DiMag!: The Great Story of Two Brothers," *Sport* 3 (September 1947), pp. 59–69; Robert Redmount, *The Red Sox Encyclopedia* (Champaign, IL, 1998); Peter Golenbock, *Fenway* (New York, 1992); Frederick G. Lieb, *The Boston Red Sox* (New York, 1947); Mike Shatzkin, ed., *The Ballplayers* (New York, 1990).

Peter C. Bjarkman

DiMAGGIO, Joseph Paul "Joe," "Joltin' Joe," "The Yankee Clipper" (b. Joseph DeMaggio, November 25, 1914, Martinez, CA; d. March 8, 1999, Hollywood, FL), player, was the second youngest of nine children of fisherman Joseph DiMaggio and Rosalie (Mercurio) DiMaggio and the brother of major league center fielders Dominic* and Vincent. A San Francisco sportswriter misspelled the original family name, DeMaggio, but the outstanding success of the trio of sons led the family to accept the new spelling. DiMaggio attended San Francisco public schools through the eleventh grade. He was married and divorced twice (Dorothy Arnold, 1939–1947; Marilyn Monroe, 1954) and had one son.

At age 17, DiMaggio played three games at shortstop for the San Francisco, CA Seals (PCL). During the next three seasons, he played outfield for the same team and hit .340, .341, and .398. In 1933, he hit safely in 61 consecutive games for San Francisco. DiMaggio spent his entire major league career (1936 to 1951) with the New York Yankees (AL). As a rookie in 1936, he hit .323, slugged 29 HR, tied for the AL lead in triples with 15, and paced the AL's outfielders with 22 assists. From 1943 through 1945, DiMaggio served in the military.

Noted as a class ballplayer with a powerful arm, DiMaggio gracefully covered center field in vast Yankee Stadium. Many baseball authorities regard DiMaggio as the all-time greatest center fielder. The large Yankee Stadium dimensions notably affected the pull hitter's lifetime statistics, but DiMaggio still ranked among the sport's best. At Yankee Stadium, DiMaggio hit .315 and slugged one HR in every 22.7 at bats. By contrast, he hit .333 and slugged one HR in every 16.2 at bats on the road. Before enlisting in the military, "the Yankee Clipper" averaged .339 at the plate and hit a HR every 18.2 at bats. In his post-military career, DiMaggio compiled a .304 career batting average and slugged a HR every 20 at bats. If World War II had not occurred, DiMaggio probably would have enjoyed a significantly better career. Numerous injuries and ailments, including a very painful heel bone spur, also shortened his career.

DiMaggio compiled a .325 career batting average, winning AL batting titles with .381 in 1939 and .352 in 1940. During his career, he also hit 361 HR (including AL titles with 46 in 1937 and 39 in 1948) and won two RBI crowns. His 2,214 lifetime hits included 881 for extra bases. In 1941, he set an all-time major league record by hitting safely in 56 consecutive games. Averaging .408 during this span, DiMaggio made 91 hits in 223 at bats.

The team's quiet leader and "Big Guy" for 13 seasons, DiMaggio led the Yankees to ten AL pennants and eight world championships. Although unable to play the first two months of the 1949 season because of a disabling heel injury, DiMaggio in late June hit four HR and made a game-saving catch to help the Yankees sweep the Boston Red Sox in a three-game series at Fenway Park. DiMaggio's effort helped the Yankees win the 1949 AL pennant by a single game over the Red Sox.

Besides being the AL's MVP in 1939, 1941, and 1947, DiMaggio was selected as *TSN* All-Star center fielder eight times, received the most votes at all positions from 1937 through 1941, and was named their 1939 Major League Player of the Year. Despite these achievements, DiMaggio was not elected to the National Baseball Hall of Fame until his second year of eligibility (1955).

DiMaggio hosted a post-game telecast his first year of retirement, served as spring training coach and executive vice-president for the AL Oakland Athletics (1968–1969), represented a major New York bank, partly owned DiMaggio's Restaurant at San Francisco's Fisherman's Wharf, and served on the board of directors of the AL Baltimore Orioles (1980). He served as vice-president of the Association of Baseball Players of America. To a younger generation, DiMaggio's television appearances in commercials made him familiar as "Mr. Coffee." An American icon, he was a very private, complex man with a mystique and aura surrounding him. DiMaggio made Major League Baseball's All-Century Team and ranked 21st among ESPN's top century athletes.

BIBLIOGRAPHY: Joe DiMaggio file, National Baseball Library, Cooperstown, NY; Maury Allen, *Where Have You Gone, Joe DiMaggio?* (New York, 1975); Dave Anderson et al., *The Yankees* (New York, 1979); Marty Appel, "Remembering the Great Joe DiMaggio," *SCD* 26 (January 7, 1999), pp. 131–132; Dave Anderson, "The Longest Hitting Streak in History," *SI* 15 (July 17, 1961), pp. 36–38ff; John Benson et al., *Baseball's Top 100* (Wilton, CT, 1997); George DeGregorio, *Joe DiMaggio: An Informal Biography* (New York, 1990); Joe DiMaggio, *The DiMaggio Albums* (New York, 1989); "DiMaggio's 57 Varieties," *NYT Biographical Service* 18 (August 1987), pp. 840–841; Joseph Durso, *DiMaggio: The Last American Knight* (Boston, MA, 1995); Phil Elderkin, "Was DiMaggio the Last Hero?" *WM* 4 (July 1991), pp. 22–23; David Halberstam, *Summer of '49* (New York, 1989); Roger Kahn, *Joe & Marilyn: A Memory of Love* (New York, 1986); Christopher Lehmann-Haupt, *Me and DiMaggio* (New York, 1986); Carl Lundquist, "The Magnificent Yankee," *TNP* 11 (1992), pp. 34–37; Jack B. Moore, *Joe DiMaggio: A Bio-Bibliography* (Westport, CT, 1986); Tom Mortensen, "Joltin' Joe Portrayed as a Great Player, Complex Personality," *SCD* 24 (November 14, 1997), p. 12; Michael Seidel, *Streak; Joe DiMaggio and the Summer of '41* (New York, 1988); Al Silverman, *Joe DiMaggio: The Golden Year 1941* (Englewood Cliffs, NJ, 1969); Wilfred Sheed, "Where Have You Gone, Joe DiMaggio?" *Life* 12

(October 1989), pp. 94–98; James Stewart-Gordon, "Unforgettable Joe DiMaggio," *RD* 109 (August 1976), pp. 173–176ff; Glenn Stout, *DiMaggio: An Illustrated Life* (New York, 1995); Gay Talese, "Silent Season of a Hero," *Esquire* 66 (July 1966), pp. 40–43.

John E. DiMeglio

DIMARIA, Joseph Franklin. *See* Joseph Franklin Demaree.

DINNEEN, William Henry "Bill," "Big Bill," "Wild Bill" (b. April 5, 1876, Syracuse, NY; d. January 13, 1955, Syracuse, NY), player and umpire, was the son of Thomas Dinneen and Catherine (Murray) Dinneen. One of the greatest right-handed pitchers of the early modern era, he enjoyed an outstanding 40-year career in major league baseball. The 6-foot 1-inch, 190-pound Dinneen began his professional baseball career at age 19 with Toronto, Canada (EL) in 1895. After reaching the major leagues with the Washington Senators (NL) in 1898, he pitched for the Boston Beaneaters (NL) from 1900 to 1901, moved cross-town to the Boston Pilgrims–Red Sox (AL) from 1902 to June 1907, and finished his playing career with the St. Louis Browns (AL) from 1907 to 1909. He won 20 or more games four times (1900, 1902–1904), but suffered arm problems for the rest of his career. His best year came in 1903, when he triumphed in 21 of 34 decisions and became the first pitcher to win three games in a twentieth-century World Series. Dinneen lost only one contest to the Pittsburgh Pirates, completing all four games with two shutouts and a 2.01 ERA. The 1904 campaign featured him setting an AL record by pitching 37 consecutive complete games (337.2 successive innings) from April 16 to October 10. During his 12-year major league career, he completed 306 of 352 starts and pitched 3,074.2 innings. He boasted a lifetime 3.01 ERA and a .490 winning percentage with 170 wins and 179 losses. On September 27, 1905, he hurled a no-hitter against the Chicago White Sox in his first outing of the month.

Dinneen joined the AL umpire staff on September 12, 1909, less than two weeks after the St. Louis Browns released him. No other person ever broke into the major leagues with no previous umpiring experience. During 29 campaigns as an umpire, Dinneen worked 45 games in eight World Series (1911, 1914, 1916, 1920, 1924, 1926, 1929, 1932). Known as an "umpire baiter" as a player, Dinneen possessed a quick temper as an arbiter and privately was nicknamed "Redneck" by players. His 1922 ejection of Babe Ruth* for "shameful and abusive language" led to a five-day suspension for the New York Yankees (AL) slugger. Dinneen, renowned for his work behind the plate, received praise from AL president Will Harridge*: "If there ever was a finer umpire, especially on balls and strikes than Dinneen, I don't know who he was." The only man who both pitched and called no-hit major league games, Dinneen umpired six no-hitters and ranks second only to Silk O'Loughlin's* record seven no-hit games. Illness forced his retirement in 1937.

Dinneen, an avid fisherman and skilled chef, possessed a voracious appetite. His culinary specialities included trout, pancakes, and pies, especially his "Million Dollar Lemon Pie." Dinneen married Margaret Quinn in 1906 and had one daughter and three sons. His surname, which he took great pains to see was spelled correctly with three "n"s, came from Dinane, which was derived from the ancient Irish name O'Dinehan and meant "grandson of the defiant."

BIBLIOGRAPHY: *The Baseball Encyclopedia*, 10th ed. (New York, 1996); Bill Borst, ed., *Ables to Zoldak*, vol. 1 (St. Louis, MO, 1988); Butler Funeral Home, Syracuse, NY, letter to Larry R. Gerlach, May 3, 1991; Bill Dinneen file, National Baseball Library, Cooperstown, NY; Bill Dinneen file, *TSN* Archives, St. Louis, MO; Gene Karst and Martin J. Jones, Jr., *Who's Who in Professional Baseball* (New Rochelle, NY, 1973), pp. 249–250; Frederick G. Lieb, *The Boston Red Sox* (New York, 1947); John Thorn et al., eds., *Total Baseball*, 5th ed. (New York, 1997).

Larry R. Gerlach

DISMUKES, William "Dizzy" (b. March 15, 1890, Birmingham, AL; d. June 30, 1961, Campbell, OH), player, manager, coach, and executive, was associated with many fine Negro League teams. Dismukes, a product of Stillman College in Alabama, began his professional baseball career as a submarine pitcher with the East St. Louis, IL Imperials in 1908. The next year, he played with the Kentucky Unions from nearby Lovejoy, IL. The Minneapolis, MN Keystones signed him in 1910, but he finished the season under legendary manager C. I. Taylor* with the West Baden, IL Sprudels.

In 1911, the 6-foot, 180-pound, right-handed submarine pitcher defeated Howie Camnitz* of the Pittsburgh Pirates (NL) 2–1. The Pittsburgh Pirates, playing without shortstop Honus Wagner,* were held to four hits and one unearned run. Later that season, a rubber-armed Dismukes won three games in two days against the tough Indianapolis, IN ABCs. One game lasted 12 innings. In 1912, he pitched his first no-hitter, a 1–0 win, against the Chicago, IL American Giants. Dismukes remained with the West Baden Sprudels through the 1913 season. After a brief stay with the Brooklyn, NY Royal Giants, he joined the Indianapolis, IN ABCs in 1915. During a 20-game winning streak that season, he pitched his second no-hitter, a 5–0 triumph over the Chicago, IL American Giants.

Upon entering the military in 1918, Dismukes joined the 803rd Pioneer Infantry baseball team in Nantes, France. His squad won the championship of southern France. After fulfilling his military obligation, he returned in 1920 to the Indianapolis ABCs (NNL) and served as player–manager there through part of the 1924 campaign. He pitched briefly with the Birmingham, AL Black Barons (NNL) in 1924, Memphis, TN Red Sox (NNL) in 1925, St. Louis, MO Stars (NNL) from 1926 through 1929, and Columbus, OH Blue Birds (NNL) in 1933 and 1934 and managed the powerhouse 1932 Detroit, MI Wolves in the short-lived EWL.

From 1942 to 1952, Dismukes served as business manager of the Kansas City, MO Monarchs (NAL). As black players were integrating the major leagues, the New York Yankees (AL) hired him as a scout in 1953. After two years in the Yankee organization, he served with the Chicago Cubs (NL) in a similar capacity in 1955 and 1956. His peers often described him as an outstanding manager with a mathematician's mind and great administrative skills. Personally, Dismukes was known for his arbitration abilities with ball players and upper management.

BIBLIOGRAPHY: Indianapolis (IN) *Freeman*, September 16, 1911, May 15, 1915, May 22, 1915, July 31, 1915; Kansas City (MO) *Call*, March 17, 1950, January 23, 1953; Larry Lester, interview with John "Buck" O'Neil, December 6, 1992; James A. Riley, *The Biographical Encyclopedia of the Negro Baseball Leagues* (New York, 1994); Michael Shatzkin, ed., *The Ballplayers* (New York, 1990); James Overmyer, *Effa Manley and the Newark Eagles* (Metuchen, NJ, 1993); Janet Bruce, *The Kansas City Monarchs* (Lawrence, KS, 1985).

                                                                                    Larry Lester

DIXON, Herbert Albert "Rap" (b. September 2, 1902, Kingston, GA; d. July 20, 1944, Detroit, MI), player, performed as an outfielder for numerous Negro League teams and was the eldest of five children of steelworker John Dixon and Rose (Goodwin) Dixon. Young "Rap," whose nickname was derived from Virginia's Rappahannock River and denoted his southern origin, began his baseball career with the semipro Steelton, PA Keystone Giants. After completing two years at Steelton High School, he turned professional in 1922 with the Harrisburg, PA Giants (ECL). When the ECL dissolved and the Harrisburg team disbanded in 1928, Dixon joined the Baltimore Black Sox (ANL). The next season, he made 14 straight hits in games against the powerful Homestead, PA Grays and helped Baltimore become the ANL champions. In 1930, in the first game ever played by black teams at Yankee Stadium, Dixon hit three HR into the right field stands.

After a stint with the Chicago American Giants (NNL) in 1931, he batted .343 and hit 15 HR for the Pittsburgh Crawfords (1934) and played with the Philadelphia Stars (1933–1934). In the first Negro All-Star Game at Comiskey Park, Chicago, in 1933, Dixon played right field for the East team. Batting second, he made one hit, stole a base, scored twice, and made no errors afield. Dixon helped the Stars win the NNL championship in 1934 and then joined an elite group of black stars invited to play winter ball in the strong PuL. Dixon played the next season with the Brooklyn Eagles and ended his playing career in 1936 with the Homestead Grays. He also managed the Baltimore Black Sox. After retiring from baseball, he was employed at the Steelton plant of the Bethlehem Steel Company. He was married to Rose Yarbrough in 1932 and had no children.

Negro Leaguers surviving from Dixon's time assess his skills consistently. A lean 6 footer who threw right-handed and batted left-handed, Dixon proved an intelligent hitter with good power and excelled with men on base in close games. He is credited with a .304 career batting average and hit .362 in 13 exhibitions against major league pitching between 1926 and 1931. A swift runner afield and on the bases, he possessed a strong, accurate throwing arm. One contemporary described him as having "a Clemente arm." Although fellow players considered him "temperamental," he ranks among the Negro Leagues' legitimate candidates for the National Baseball Hall of Fame.

BIBLIOGRAPHY: Herbert Dixon file, National Baseball Library, Cooperstown, NY; John B. Holway, *Voices from the Great Black Baseball Leagues* (New York, 1975); Robert W. Peterson, *Only the Ball Was White* (Englewood Cliffs, NJ, 1970); James A. Riley, *The All-Time All-Stars of Black Baseball* (Cocoa, FL, 1983); James A. Riley, *Biographical Encyclopedia of the Negro Baseball Leagues* (New York, 1994); Donn Rogosin, *Invisible Men: Life in Baseball's Negro Leagues* (New York, 1983); Art Rust, Jr., *Get That Nigger Off the Field!* (New York, 1976); A. D. Suehsdorf, telephone interviews with: Leon Day, May 10, 1984; Paul Dixon, October 4, 5, December 30, 1983; Monte Irvin, August 29, 1983; William "Judy" Johnson, September 21, 1983; Walter "Buck" Leonard, September 21, 1983; Ted Page, October 3, 1983; Norman C. "Tweed" Webb, December 18, 1983.

A. D. Suehsdorf

DOAK, William Leopold "Spittin' Bill" (b. January 28, 1891, Pittsburgh, PA; d. November 26, 1954, Bradenton, FL), player, enjoyed three superlative seasons and endured many losing ones in the St. Louis Cardinals' (NL) wilderness years between 1913 and 1923. He was the son of W. A. Doak, a civil engineer, and Bertha R. Doak. Doak began his professional baseball career as a pitcher with Wheeling, WV (IOL) in 1910 after completing four years at Union High School in Pittsburgh, PA. Following stops at Columbus, OH (AA) and Akron, OH (OPL), he was given a two-inning tryout by the Cincinnati Reds (NL) in 1912. He returned to Akron and then was sold to the St. Louis Cardinals for $500.

The St. Louis Cardinals plunged into the cellar during Doak's and manager Miller Huggins's* first year in 1913, but then rose to third place in 1914. Doak compiled a 19–6 record and led the NL with a sparkling 1.72 ERA in 1914. He pitched 256 innings and earned seven shutouts, including a 1–0 triumph over Grover Cleveland Alexander* of the Philadelphia Phillies. The slow, careful right-hander based his repertoire on the spitter and a "slow drop." Doak's written request on behalf of spitballers in 1920 persuaded the joint rules committee of the major leagues to lighten its ban on the pitch by allowing each club two active players who would be permitted to throw spitters to the end of their careers. The final list comprised 17 hurlers, including Doak. His only 20-win season also came that year, when the Cardinals finished fifth. For third-place St. Louis in 1921, he won 15 while losing only 6 and led the NL in pitching percentage (.714) and ERA (2.58).

The St. Louis Cardinals traded Doak to the Brooklyn Robins (NL) in June 1924 for Leo Dickerman, a far inferior right-hander. Doak, now 33 years old, helped the Robins to a second-place finish with an 11–5 record. Three of his wins, including two two-hit shutouts, came in the space of eight days. He left baseball in 1925–1926 to participate in the Florida land boom as partner in a real estate firm in his new home town of Bradenton, FL. He rejoined the Robins in 1927 and ended his career with the St. Louis Cardinals in 1929. Lifetime, his statistics totaled 169 wins and 157 losses, 2,782.2 innings pitched, 34 shutouts, and 1,014 strikeouts.

For many years, Doak operated a Bradenton, FL candy store. He also coached boys' baseball at all levels, once leading Bradenton High School to a state championship, and taught golf professionally at the local country club. He designed the successful "Bill Doak baseball glove" in 1918. An evolutionary model, it provided a deep pocket and thongs laced between thumb and fingers. Produced by the Rawlings Sporting Goods Company, the glove earned him royalties up to $25,000 a year and remained popular at his death. He married Jessie Marie Porter on his birthday in 1914 and had three children.

BIBLIOGRAPHY: Bradenton (FL) *Herald*, November 28, 1954; William Doak file, National Baseball Library, Cooperstown, NY; Frederick G. Lieb, *The St. Louis Cardinals* (New York, 1945); Bob Broeg and Jerry Vickery, *St. Louis Cardinals Encyclopedia* (Grand Rapids, MI, 1998); Harold Seymour, *Baseball: The Golden Age* (New York, 1971); John Thorn et al., eds., *Total Baseball*, 5th ed. (New York, 1997).

A. D. Suehsdorf

DOBSON, Joseph Gordon "Joe," "Curly," "Burrhead" (b. January 20, 1917, Durant, OK; d. June 23, 1994, Jacksonville, FL), player, was the youngest of 14 children. Of Scotch-Irish descent, he was educated in Coolidge, AZ public schools. Although losing his left thumb and part of his forefinger in an accident at age nine, the right-handed Dobson starred as an amateur pitcher and made his professional debut with 19 wins for Troy, AL (AlFL) in 1937. He was promoted to New Orleans, LA (SL) in 1938 and joined the Cleveland Indians (AL) in 1939. In two seasons with the Indians, Dobson pitched mainly in relief and battled his control.

The Cleveland Indians sent Dobson to the Boston Red Sox (AL) in a six-player December 1940 deal. Dobson hit his stride in Boston, winning over 10 games primarily as a starter in two of his first three seasons and setting an AL record in 1943 for consecutive errorless games by a pitcher with 156. Dobson then spent two years in the U.S. Army. In 1946, he won 13 games to help the Boston Red Sox win their first AL pennant since 1918. In the 1946 World Series against the St. Louis Cardinals, Dobson made three mound appearances and allowed only four hits and no earned runs in 12.2

innings. He threw a sparkling four-hitter to win his Game 5 start and performed well in relief of starter Dave "Boo" Ferris in Game 7. The Cardinals, however, tallied once against Dobson's successor in the eighth inning to win the World Series.

Dobson's next two seasons marked his best statistically, as he won 18 games with a 2.95 ERA in 1947 and 16 games with five shutouts in 1948. He made the 1948 AL All-Star team. The Red Sox closed the 1948 season with a disappointing loss to the Cleveland Indians in a one-game title playoff. Dobson's ERA rose significantly in 1949 and 1950, but he won 29 games altogether and enjoyed good offensive support from his power-hitting teammates. In December 1950, Boston traded Dobson to the Chicago White Sox (AL) in a five-player deal for pitchers Bill Wight and Ray Scarborough. The winner of 106 games in Boston, Dobson turned in two workmanlike seasons in Chicago before slumping badly in 1953. He closed his major league career with two brief mound appearances for the Boston Red Sox in 1954.

The 6-foot 2-inch, 205 pounder never overpowered batters and did not compile impressive strikeout numbers. He recorded 137 lifetime victories and only 103 losses for a .571 winning percentage and 3.62 ERA. Dobson, who married Marguerite Weiss in January 1939 and after her death married Maxine Evelyn Lee in 1945, operated a store and tourist cottages in Munsonville, NH. He later returned to baseball as a business manager in the FSL.

BIBLIOGRAPHY: Joe Dobson file, National Baseball Library, Cooperstown, NY; *WWIB*, 1951; *TSN Baseball Register, 1944*; Jack Lautier, *Fenway Voices* (Camden, ME, 1990); Peter Golenbock, *Fenway* (New York, 1992); David Halberstam, *Summer of '49* (New York, 1989); Robert Redmount, *The Red Sox Encyclopedia* (Champaign, IL, 1998); Rich Marazzi and Len Fiorito, *Aaron to Zuverink* (New York, 1981).

Lloyd J. Graybar

DOBY, Lawrence Eugene "Larry" (b. December 13, 1924, Camden, SC), player, coach, manager, and executive, is the son of David Doby and Etta Doby. His father, a semipro baseball player, died when Larry was eight years old. He and his mother then moved to Paterson, NJ, where she worked as a domestic. Doby, a four-sport letterman at Paterson East Side High School, entered Long Island University in 1940 on a basketball scholarship. He soon transferred to Virginia Union University in Richmond and left school in 1943, when drafted to join the U.S. Navy. Stationed at the Great Lakes Naval Training School, Doby became aware of racial discrimination because the base had segregated white and black baseball teams. Doby starred on the latter and was signed to a professional contract by the Newark, NJ Eagles (NNL). In 1947–1948, he played basketball with the Paterson, NJ Crescents (ABL). He married Helen F. Curvey on August 10, 1946 and has one daughter, Christine Lynn.

In 1946, Doby helped lead the Newark Eagles to a Negro World Series championship and started in the East–West (Negro Leagues) All-Star Game. The following year, he led the NNL in batting average and HR when Bill Veeck* of the Cleveland Indians (AL) paid Newark $15,000 for him. Doby joined the Indians and on July 4, 1947 became the first black to play in the AL. An AL player through 1959, Doby hit well and possessed excellent power and speed. Under the tutelage of National Baseball Hall of Famer Tris Speaker,* he became a premier center fielder and often climbed fences to catch balls.

Doby's 1950 performance earned him Cleveland Baseball Man of the Year honors and a position on the BWAA All-Star team. He led the AL with a .442 on-base percentage in 1950. In 1952, he became the first black to win a major league HR crown, pacing the AL with 32 HR, 104 runs scored, and a .542 slugging percentage. He topped the AL with 32 HR and 126 RBI in 1954. Doby played in six major league All-Star games from 1949 through 1954 and was selected as starting center fielder in 1950. He posted a .300 batting average and slugged a pinch-hit HR in the 1954 contest.

Doby, a member of the Cleveland Indians 1948 world championship and 1954 AL pennant teams, played there through 1955 and rejoined them for the 1958 season. He spent 1956 and 1957 with the Chicago White Sox (AL) and split the 1959 season between the Detroit Tigers (AL) and Chicago. A lifetime .283 batter, he slugged 243 doubles and 253 HR and drove in 970 runs. Doby played in 1960 with San Diego, CA (PCL) and spent his final professional season in 1962 with the Chunichi Dragons in Japan. During the next two decades he served in various capacities with the Montreal Expos (NL), Cleveland Indians (AL), and Chicago White Sox (AL). Doby managed Chicago the last half of the 1978 season to 37 wins and 50 losses. He worked as director of community affairs for the New York Nets (NBA) from 1983 through 1990 and for the Office of the Commissioner of Major League Baseball in the 1990s. He currently is employed as assistant to AL President Gene Budig* and for Major League Baseball Properties. In 1998, the Veterans Committee elected him to the National Baseball Hall of Fame.

BIBLIOGRAPHY: Larry Doby file, National Baseball Library, Cooperstown, NY; "As Baseball Honors Robinson, Has It Forgotten Doby?" *NYT Biographical Service* 18 (March 1987), pp. 286–287; Brent P. Kelley, *The Case For: Those Overlooked by the Baseball Hall of Fame* (Jefferson, NC, 1992); Larry Doby, "Playing Hardball," *PW* 29 (May 9, 1988), pp. 97ff; Leon Hardwick and Effa Manley, *Negro Baseball* (Chicago, IL, 1976); Craig Carter, ed., *TSN Daguerreotypes* (St. Louis, MO, 1990); John Phillips, *Winners* (Cabin John, MD, 1987); Joseph Thomas Moore, *Pride Against Prejudice* (New York, 1988); Larry Moffi and Jonathan Kronstadt, *Crossing the Line* (Jefferson, NC, 1994); *NYT Biographical Service* 28 (February 1997), pp. 308–310; James A. Riley, *The Biographical Encyclopedia of the Negro Baseball Leagues* (New York, 1994); A. C. Toepel, "Doby in Shadows of the Spotlight," *SCD* 24 (July 18, 1997), pp. 64–66; Art Rust, Jr., *Get That Nigger Off the Field!* (New York, 1976); *TSN Official Baseball*

Guide, 1979; Jules Tygiel, *Baseball's Great Experiment* (New York, 1983); Rich West-cott, *Diamond Greats* (Westport, CT, 1988); A. S. "Doc" Young, *Great Negro Baseball Stars* (New York, 1953).

Merl F. Kleinknecht

DOERR, Robert Pershing "Bobby" (b. April 7, 1918, Los Angeles, CA), player, coach, and scout, is the son of telephone company supervisor Harold Doerr and Frances (Herrnberger) Doerr. A 1935 graduate of Fremont High School in Los Angeles, he married Monica Terpin on October 24, 1938 and had one son. Doerr began his professional baseball career with Hollywood, CA (PCL) in 1934 and 1935 and San Diego, CA (PCL) in 1936. Doerr played second base for the Boston Red Sox (AL) from 1937 through 1951 except for military service in 1945 and served as team captain during the post–World War II period. A .980 career fielder, Doerr once held the AL record for consecutive chances without an error by a second baseman (414), led AL second basemen in double plays five times, fielding percentage and putouts four times, and assists three times, and set a World Series record for assists by a second baseman (31). Recent sophisticated performance measures show Doerr as the best fielding second baseman of the 1940s.

A straightaway hitter upon joining the Red Sox, he was converted to a pull hitter by the Boston brass to take advantage of the Fenway Park wall. The new stroke paid dividends at Fenway, where Doerr compiled a .315 career batting average with 145 HR. On the road, however, Doerr frequently hit many long flyouts and batted only .261 with 78 HR. Notable performance contrasts included 1942 (.342 home, .243 away), 1944 (.351 home, .286 away), and 1950 (.344 home, .238 away). In 13 full major league seasons, Doerr hit below .300 only three times in Boston, with one of those being .299, and above .300 only twice on the road. Doerr batted .288 during his career, with 2,042 hits, 381 doubles, 89 triples, 223 HR, 1,094 runs scored, and 1,247 RBI. In his lone World Series (1946), he batted .409 with 9 hits against the St. Louis Cardinals.

A competitive, honest, quiet leader, Doerr twice made the only hits off Bob Feller* in one-hit games. He scouted for the Red Sox from 1957 to 1966 and coached with Boston from 1967 to 1969. The expansionist Toronto Blue Jays (AL) lured him out of retirement to coach hitting from 1977 through 1981. *TSN* named him the AL's MVP in 1944, while Boston fans voted him the all-time Red Sox second baseman in 1969. Doerr, who resides in Agness, OR, worked with the cattle business and spent a decade as a fishing guide on the Rogue River in Southwestern Oregon. In 1986 the Veterans Committee elected him to the National Baseball Hall of Fame.

BIBLIOGRAPHY: Robert Doerr file, National Baseball Library, Cooperstown, NY; Ellery H. Clark, Jr., *Boston Red Sox: 75th Anniversary Edition* (Hicksville, NY, 1975); John DiMeglio, interviews and correspondence with Bobby Doerr, 1984, John

DiMeglio Collection, Mankato, MN; Peter Golenbock, *Fenway* (New York, 1992); David Halberstam, *Summer of '49* (New York, 1989); Frederick G. Lieb, *The Boston Red Sox* (New York, 1947); Jack Lautier, *Fenway Voices* (Camden, ME, 1990); Rich Marazzi, "HOF Second Baseman Bobby Doerr Interviewed," *SCD* 21 (May 27, 1994), pp. 150–152; Rich Westcott, *Diamond Greats* (Westport, CT, 1988); Lowell Reidenbaugh, *Baseball's Hall of Fame-Cooperstown* (New York, 1993).

John E. DiMeglio

DONALDSON, John Wesley (b. February 20, 1892, Glasgow, MO; d. April 14, 1970, Chicago, IL), player and scout, was a poised left-handed pitcher with pin-point control. After completing Avon Grammar School in Glasgow, he attended George Smith College in Sedalia, MO for one year. Donaldson's hard, sharp-breaking curve proved to be his money pitch. He starred from 1913 to 1917 for J. L. Wilkinson's* multiracial Des Moines, IA All-Nations ballclub, averaging around 20 strikeouts per game and pitching three consecutive no-hitters in 1913. In 1916, Donaldson pitched All-Nations to series victories over the two top black teams, Rube Foster's* Chicago American Giants and C. I. Taylor's* Indianapolis ABCs.

Donaldson's wide assortment of curves, combined with a good fastball and change-up, made him one of the best left-handers in the history of black baseball. Wilkinson called Donaldson the most amazing pitcher he had ever seen, while National Baseball Hall-of-Famer John Henry Lloyd* regarded him as the toughest pitcher he had ever faced. New York Giants (NL) manager John McGraw* assessed Donaldson's value at $50,000 had the latter been white. In 1917, a NYSL manager reportedly offered Donaldson $10,000 to pass as a Cuban and pitch for his team.

Donaldson's baseball career spanned parts of three decades. After starting in 1912 with a barnstorming combination of baseball and showbiz talent called the Tennessee Rats, he pitched for Chicago Union Giants and the the Chicago Giants in 1917, Indianapolis ABCs and Brooklyn Royal Giants in 1918, Detroit Stars in 1919, and Kansas City Monarchs from 1920 through 1924, 1931, and 1934. His prime seasons often were spent barnstorming across the Midwest playing against white semiprofessional teams, resulting in fragmentary records on him. Donaldson's extra-inning strikeout totals included 27 batters in a 12-inning game and 35 in an 18-inning contest.

Besides being an outstanding pitcher, the tall, lean, graceful athlete possessed good all-around playing skills. He could hit with some authority and fielded smoothly, often playing at shortstop or in the outfield. Following arm trouble, he continued as an everyday player with the Kansas City Monarchs. After leaving the Monarchs in 1923, Donaldson formed his own touring baseball team, the John Donaldson All-Stars, and performed into the next decade. He also pitched for the Bertha, MN Fishermen in 1924 and 1927, Moose Jaw, Canada in 1925, Lismore, MN in 1926, and St. Cloud,

MN in 1930. Donaldson worked as a shipping clerk in the Chicago post office and scouted for the Chicago White Sox (AL).

BIBLIOGRAPHY: Janet Bruce, *The Kansas City Monarchs* (Lawrence, KS, 1985); Robert W. Peterson, *Only the Ball Was White* (Englewood Cliffs, NJ, 1970); James A. Riley, *The All-Time All-Stars of Black Baseball* (Cocoa, FL, 1983); James A. Riley, *The Biographical Encyclopedia of the Negro Baseball Leagues* (New York, 1994); James A. Riley, interviews with former Negro League players, James A. Riley Collection, Canton, GA.

James A. Riley

DONATELLI, August Joseph "Augie" (b. August 22, 1914, Heilwood, PA; d. May 24, 1990, St. Petersburg, FL), player and umpire, was one of eight children born to Italian immigrants Antonio Donatelli, a coal miner, and Vencenza (DiSantis) Donatelli. Upon graduation from high school, he became a coal miner like his father and also played portions of three seasons as an infielder in the lower minor leagues. A B-17 tailgunner during World War II, Donatelli was shot down during the first daylight raid on Berlin, Germany and spent 15 months as a German prisoner of war. He began his umpiring career by officiating softball games in prisoner of war camps. After the war, he used the GI bill to attend Bill McGowan's* Umpiring School and graduated first in his class. A "born" umpire, Donatelli advanced to the major leagues in only four years. He spent 1946 in the Class C PrL, started 1947 in the Class A SAL, advanced at midseason to the Class AAA IL, and joined the NL in 1950.

Donatelli, one of the most respected and influential major league umpires during his 24-year career, was known for his hustle, unerring judgment, and refusal to tolerate verbal abuse from players or managers. Baseball writers voted him in 1955 as the NL's best base umpire after he had spent only five years in the major leagues. Donatelli's most memorable moment occurred while umpiring home plate. In the fourth game of the 1957 World Series, he resolved a dispute over whether New York Yankees pitcher Tommy Byrne had hit Nippy Jones of the Milwaukee Braves on the foot by a pitch by awarding Jones first base after finding a smudge of black shoe polish on the ball. In 1961, he inadvertently started a style of umpiring balls and strikes that became a standard technique for NL umpires. After finding it necessary to rest on one knee to provide relief from hemorrhoidal pain, he retained the position for the rest of his career because it afforded a better view of low, outside pitches. His most important contribution to the umpiring profession and baseball history was being the principal organizer of the NL umpires' union in 1964. The union, reorganized as the MLUA with the addition of AL arbiters in 1968, brought about greatly improved salaries, benefits, and working conditions for umpires. A crew chief for 14 years, he umpired four All-Star games (1953, 1957, 1961, and 1969), two NL Championship Series (1969, 1972), and five World Series (1955, 1957, 1961, 1967,

1973). In 1973, his fellow arbiters voted him the Al Somers Award as the Outstanding Major League Umpire of the previous year.

Donatelli, who had been on the staff of the Al Somers Umpire School for 30 years, retired after the 1973 season. He became the chief instructor of the ESUTS and then scouted umpiring prospects for the NL. Donatelli, who married Mary Lou Lamont in 1946 and had four children, died in his sleep of a heart attack.

BIBLIOGRAPHY: Harold C. Burr, "Donatelli Drops into Ump Role," *BD* 9 (June 1950), pp. 23–24; Augie Donatelli file, National Baseball Library, Cooperstown, NY; Peter Levine, ed., *Baseball History: An Annual of Original Baseball Research* (Westport, CT, 1989); *NYT*, May 26, 1990, p. 15; *TSN*, March 3, 1973, June 4, 1990.

Larry R. Gerlach

DONLIN, Michael Joseph "Mike," "Turkey Mike" (b. May 30, 1878, Peoria, IL; d. September 24, 1933, Hollywood, CA), player, manager, and scout, was the sixth child of railroad conductor John Donlin and Maggie (Cayton) Donlin. He attended elementary school in Erie, PA and worked as a machinist before entering professional baseball with Los Angeles, CA (CaL) in 1897. He married actress and vaudeville star Mabel Hite on April 10, 1906. After her death, he wed vaudevillian Rita Ross on October 20, 1914. Donlin had no children through either marriage.

Originally a wild-throwing minor league pitcher, the versatile Donlin became a star major league outfielder and occasionally played first base and shortstop. In his 12 checkered seasons with six teams, he played more than 100 games only five times. A broken ankle shelved him for most of the 1906 season. He sat out 1907 because New York Giants manager John McGraw* would not meet his salary demands and spent 1909, 1910, and 1913 performing on the vaudeville circuit.

Yet for his 1,049 games, including 431 with the Giants, Donlin ranked among the best. He led the NL in only one statistic (124 runs in 1905), but proved a strong, consistent left-handed batter. Donlin topped .300 in all but two seasons and compiled a .333 lifetime average. During his major league career, the 5-foot 9-inch, 170-pound Donlin made 1,282 hits, 669 runs, 176 doubles, 97 triples, and 51 HR, batted in 543 runs, and stole 213 bases.

Donlin was a flamboyant personality on and off the field. A strutting walk earned him his nickname, while his pugnacity made him a particular favorite of McGraw during his five seasons in New York. "Oh, you Mabel's Mike!" Giants fans used to yell after a rollicking play. But aggression combined with hard drinking often got him into serious trouble. He was arrested several times and missed most of the 1902 season with the Cincinnati Reds (NL) after a six-month jail sentence for assault.

Donlin's close association with McGraw began in 1900. He had started his sophomore season with the St. Louis Cardinals (NL), who had acquired him from the Santa Cruz, CA Sandcrabs (CaL), when McGraw quit the Baltimore Orioles (NL) to be the Cardinals' third baseman. When McGraw agreed to manage the new Baltimore Orioles (AL) in 1901, Donlin joined him. He hit .348 and batted six for six one day against the Detroit Tigers before moving to Cincinnati Reds (NL) in 1902. In July 1904, McGraw, now piloting the New York Giants, bought him from the Reds for cash.

With immortal Christy Mathewson,* Donlin became the most popular of the 1905 Giants by hitting .356 in 150 games and performing well in the famous five-shutout World Series. He played only one complete season (1908) thereafter. In August 1911, the Giants sold the 33-year-old Donlin to the Boston Braves (NL). The Braves traded him to the Pittsburgh Pirates (NL), for whom he played 77 games in 1912. He then ignored a waiver claim by the Philadelphia Phillies (NL). He returned to vaudeville and played 36 games for Jersey City, NJ (IL) before finishing his career with the New York Giants as a utility player in 1914.

He briefly managed Memphis, TN (SA) in 1917 and the following year scouted the Pacific Coast for the Boston Braves. Thereafter, he concentrated on the stage and movies. Although never the actor he fancied himself, he received respectable reviews and numerous small parts in both silent films and talkies.

BIBLIOGRAPHY: Baltimore *Evening Sun*, April 12, 1962; Detroit *Free Press*, November 30, 1947; Noel Hynd, *The Giants of the Polo Grounds* (New York, 1988); Christy Mathewson, *Pitching in a Pinch* (Briarcliff Manor, NY, 1977); Michael Donlin file, National Baseball Library, Cooperstown, NY; Brent P. Kelley, *The Case For: Those Overlooked by the Baseball Hall of Fame* (Jefferson, NC, 1992); Charles C. Alexander, *John McGraw* (New York, 1988); New York *Sun*, September 25, 1933; *NYT*, September 25, 1933; "Post-Playing Careers," *BRJ* 9 (1980), pp. 1–5; *The Baseball Encyclopedia*, 10th ed. (New York, 1996); Richard Scheinin, *Field of Screams* (New York, 1994); Harold Seymour, *Baseball: The Early Years* (New York, 1960); Harold Seymour, *Baseball: The Golden Years* (New York, 1971); *SL*, February 16, 1907; *TSN*, January 25, 1945; Ray Robinson, *Matty: An American Hero* (New York, 1993).

A. D. Suehsdorf

DONOHUE, Peter Joseph "Pete" (b. November 5, 1900, Athens, TX; d. February 23, 1988, Fort Worth, TX), player, graduated from North Side High School in Fort Worth. He moved directly from TCU to the Cincinnati Reds (NL), debuting on July 1, 1921. Astyanax Douglass, his former TCU teammate, influenced his decision to join the Cincinnati Reds. Donohue received a $5,000 signing bonus and posted a 7–6 record his rookie season in 1921.

The 6-foot 3-inch, 174-pound right-hander won 18 and lost nine in 1921. Donohue blossomed into one the NL's best hurlers over the next four seasons, recording 21 wins in 1923 and 1925 and 20 victories in 1926. From July 1921 to July 1925, he defeated the Philadelphia Phillies 20 consecutive times.

Donohue led the NL in innings pitched (285.2) and starts (38) in 1926 and almost boosted Cincinnati to the NL pennant. In September 1926, Donohue shut out the New York Giants. He relieved the next day and started the third game of the World Series, but the New York Giants hitters tagged him early and forced him to leave the game. The overwork took a large toll on the hurler, who never achieved another winning season.

The Cincinnati Reds traded Donohue and outfielder Ethan Allen* to the New York Giants (NL) for infielder Pat Crawford in May 1930. After Donohue posted an 8–9 1930 season, the Giants released him. The slender righthander never won another major league game, although pitching briefly for the Cleveland Indians (AL) in 1931 and Boston Red Sox (AL) in 1932. Before retiring from baseball, Donohue pitched for Jersey City, NJ (IL) and Minneapolis, MN (AA). He compiled a lifetime major league record of 134 wins, 118 losses, 571 strikeouts, and 2,112.1 innings pitched in 12 seasons. The slightly built Donohue always battled hitters fiercely. Many baseball historians credit him with the development of the change-up as an integral part of a pitcher's repertoire.

Donahue opened Berry Brothers and Donohue Dry Cleaners in Fort Worth and golfed almost daily at Colonial CC. Although given a lifetime pass to NL games, Donohue never used it until presenting it at a Texas Rangers (AL) game in the 1970s. After being informed that the pass could only be used for NL games, he refused even to listen to Rangers radio broadcasts. Donohue married Frances Meyer of Louisville, KY in 1930 and had one daughter, Judy.

BIBLIOGRAPHY: *The Baseball Encyclopedia*, 10th ed. (New York, 1996); Peter Donohue file, National Baseball Library, Cooperstown, NY; Lee Allen, *The Cincinnati Reds* (New York, 1948); Donald Honig, *The Cincinnati Reds* (New York, 1992).

John Hillman

DONOVAN, Patrick Joseph "Patsy" (b. March 16, 1865, County Cork, Ireland; d. December 25, 1953, Lawrence, MA), player and manager, was the son of an immigrant and American Civil War veteran. His father, Gerald, had returned to Ireland to take a wife. At age three, Donovan was brought by his parents from Ireland to Massachussetts. Donovan played outfield for Lawrence-Salem, MA (NEL) in 1886 and 1887 and London, Canada (IL) in 1888 and 1889. He began his major league career with the Boston Nationals (NL) in 1890 as an outfielder for manager Frank Selee,* but an injury cut his rookie year short. He enjoyed his best years with the Pittsburgh Pirates (NL, 1893–1899), hitting over .300 six times and learning the finer points of the game from manager Connie Mack* (1894–1896). Due to a disputed play at second base involving Donovan, Mack was ejected from a game for the only time in his career. A good outfielder, a speedy base runner, and a scrappy, intelligent player, Donovan in 1900 led the NL with 45 stolen bases as a St. Louis Cardinal. His career 518 stolen bases, 2,253 hits, 736 RBI, and .301 batting average revealed his impressive combination of speed and power.

He managed the Pittsburgh Pirates (1897, 1899) and St. Louis Cardinals (1901–1903). After a contractual dispute with St. Louis, the National Commission permitted Donovan in 1904 to become player–manager of the Washington Senators (AL). Legal questions forced him to miss spring training. Besides batting only .229, he managed a last-place club. Although his playing career was virtually over, he continued to manage. Donovan managed the Brooklyn Superbas (NL) to second division finishes from 1906 through 1908, but achieved a good record against the New York Giants. He became one of John McGraw's* most hated rivals and always saved his premier pitcher, Nap Rucker,* for the Giants. Donovan ended his major league managing career with the Boston Red Sox (AL) in 1910 and 1911. He never managed a team above fourth place, but lacked good personnel and left Boston the year before it acquired the players making it the dominant AL team. As a minor league manager, he greatly influenced National Baseball Hall of Famer Joe McCarthy.* McCarthy considered Donovan one of the nation's finest baseball minds. Despite his solid achievements as player and manager, Donovan was best remembered as the "discoverer" of Babe Ruth.* He scouted Ruth in Baltimore, MD and recommended that the Red Sox purchase his contract. His minor league managerial assignments included Buffalo, NY (IL) from 1915 through 1917, Syracuse, NY (IL) in 1918, Newark, NJ (IL) in 1919, Jersey City, NJ (IL) in 1921 and from 1924 through 1926, Springfield, MA (EL) in 1923, Providence, RI (EL) in 1927, and Attleboro, MA (NEL) in 1928. He scouted New England for the New York Yankees (AL) from 1931 to 1946 and coached baseball at Phillips Exeter Academy.

BIBLIOGRAPHY: Patsy Donovan file, National Baseball Library, Cooperstown, NY; Malcolm Bingay, *Of Me I Sing* (New York, 1949); Detroit Baseball Club Letterbooks, vols. 3–4, Ernie Harwell Collection, Detroit Public Library, Detroit, MI; Detroit *News*, December 10, 1923; G. H. Fleming, *The Unforgettable Season* (New York, 1981); Thomas Aylesworth and Benton Minks, *The Encyclopedia of Baseball Managers* (New York, 1990); Frederick G. Lieb, *The Pittsburgh Pirates* (New York, 1948); Frederick Ivor-Campbell et al., eds., *Baseball's First Stars* (Cleveland, OH, 1996); Bob Broeg and Jerry Vickery, *St. Louis Cardinals Encyclopedia* (Grand Rapids, MI, 1998); Frederick G. Lieb, *The Detroit Tigers* (New York, 1946); *TSN*, January 6, 1954.

Anthony J. Papalas

DONOVAN, Richard Edward "Dick" (b. December 7, 1927, Boston, MA; d. January 6, 1997, South Weymouth, MA), player, performed as a solid right-handed pitcher with five major league teams from 1950 through 1965 and compiled a 122–99 career win-loss record with a 3.67 ERA.

The 6-foot 3-inch, 210-pound Donovan grew up near Boston and signed with the Boston Braves (NL) upon graduating from North Quincy High

School, although briefly attending Boston University. After pitching for Hartford, CT (EL) in 1945, Donovan served in the U.S. Navy in 1946 and hurled for Fort Lauderdale, FL (FIL) in 1947, Evansville, IN (3IL) in 1948, and Hartford and Milwaukee, WI (AA) in 1949 and 1950. He debuted with the Boston Braves in 1950, but did not earn a major league victory until 1955.

Donovan pitched for Milwaukee in 1951 and 1952 and the Atlanta Crackers (SA) in 1953 and 1954, appearing in just 17 major league games with the Boston Braves and the Detroit Tigers (AL). The Chicago White Sox (AL) purchased his contract in September 1954, finally giving the 27-year-old his chance. He responded in 1955 with a 15–9 record and 3.32 ERA and made the AL All-Star team. Success came when Donovan perfected a sinker and slider, the latter being his best pitch. He also developed superb control, walking only 495 batters in over 2,017.1 innings.

In 1957, Donovan finished 16–6 and topped the AL with a .727 winning percentage and 16 complete games. He pulled a tendon in his right arm in 1959 and slipped to a 9–10 mark. Donovan, however, pitched very well in the 1959 World Series, losing heart-breaking Game 3, 2–1, to Don Drysdale* of the Los Angeles Dodgers. Two days later, Bob Shaw, Billy Pierce,* and Donovan combined to blank the Dodgers 1–0, the first three-man shutout in World Series history.

Donovan improved his record in 1960 to 6–1, appearing mostly in relief. The Washington Senators (AL) selected him in the 1961 expansion draft. Besides finishing 10–10, he led the AL with a 2.40 ERA and made the AL All-Star team. The Senators traded Donovan and two other players to the Cleveland Indians (AL) for outfielder Jimmy Piersall* in October 1961.

In 1962, Donovan enjoyed his only 20-win season with a 20–10 mark for the Indians, repeating as an AL All-Star, leading the AL with 5 shutouts and slugging four HR. He won one-quarter of Cleveland's 80 victories, earning the Indians Man of the Year award. His record fell to 11–13 in 1963, 7–9 in 1964, and 1–3 in 1965 before retiring in June.

Subsequently, Donovan worked as a stock broker for Bache Halsey Stuart and as a realtor for his own firm in Quincy, MA. Donovan, who married Patricia Casey in February 1959 and had two children, resided in Cohasset, MA.

BIBLIOGRAPHY: *Boston Herald,* July 17, 1977; Dick Donovan, *Microsoft Complete Baseball* (Redmond, WA, 1994); Dick Donovan file, National Baseball Library, Cooperstown, NY; Richard Lindberg, *Who's on Third?* (South Bend, IN, 1983); Danny Peary, ed., *We Played the Game: 65 Players Remember Baseball's Greatest Era, 1942–1964* (New York, 1994); *The Baseball Encyclopedia,* 10th ed., (New York, 1996); Bob Vanderberg, *Sox: From Lane and Fain to Zisk and Fisk* (Chicago, IL, 1982).

                                                                                    Robert E. Weir

DONOVAN, William Edward "Wild Bill" (b. October 13, 1876, Lawrence, MA; d. December 9, 1923, Forsyth, NY), player and manager, was the son of Gerald Donovan and younger brother of Patrick "Patsy" Donovan.* He grew up in Philadelphia and played his first baseball at Fairmount Park. Donovan began his major league career as a pitcher with the Washington Senators (NL) in 1898 and the following year joined the Brooklyn Superbas (NL), winning 25 games in 1901. He jumped to the Detroit Tigers (AL) in 1903 and played there until 1912, becoming one of the city's most popular athletes. The large, handsome, good-natured Donovan packed Bennett Park to capacity every time he faced Rube Waddell.* When Detroit trained in Augusta, GA in the spring of 1905, he admired a teenage outfielder playing for the Augusta Tourists and brought Tyrus Cobb* to the attention of Detroit manager William Armour.

Although easygoing, Donovan became one of the game's best scrappers. During spring training in 1907, he broke up a fight between Charlie Schmidt and Cobb and saved the "Georgia Peach" from serious injury. Donovan's most memorable achievement came in a 17-inning, 9–9 game against the Philadelphia Athletics at the end of the 1907 season. Donovan surrendered most of the runs in the first few innings, but then became nearly unhittable. In a late inning fracas, he knocked out Monte Cross with one punch. Donovan stayed in the game because the police mistakenly arrested Detroit first baseman Claude Rossman. At Windsor, Canada across the Detroit River, Donovan met and married the beautiful daughter of a saloon keeper. The fashionable, graceful Mrs. Donovan was often photographed in the Detroit newspapers. Donovan, who lived beyond his means, constantly asked part-owner and general manager Frank Navin* for salary advances. A teetotaler, he mainly needed the money to keep his wife in the latest fashions. Donovan beat up and nearly killed a Detroit mobster, Bill Constantine, who pursued his wife. The Donovans' highly publicized, stormy marriage ended in divorce without any children.

Donovan pitched well in the 1907, 1908, and 1909 World Series, but bad fortune and a weak infield prevented him from winning more than one game. In two 1907 World Series games against the Chicago Cubs, he struck out 16 batters. A passed ball by Charlie Schmidt in the ninth inning led to an unearned run and a 12-inning tie game. In the second game of the 1908 World Series against the Cubs, he pitched a shutout for seven innings. A questionable eighth-inning call by one umpire, however, led to a six-run outburst. Donovan allowed only two runs in Game 5, but the Cubs shut out Detroit. He won the second game of the 1909 World Series against the Pittsburgh Pirates, but the primarily warm-weather pitcher lost the crucial seventh game on a cold day. Donovan, who experienced arm trouble the last five years of his career, achieved a 186–139 mark (.572 winning percentage) and a 2.69 ERA.

From 1915 to 1917, he managed the New York Yankees (AL) to losing records. Navin, an admirer who kept Donovan's picture on his office wall, sent promising first baseman Wally Pipp* to help rescue Donovan's New

York club. Donovan suffered the managerial fate of his brother, Patsy, leaving a mediocre team on the verge of becoming a superpower. Donovan managed the Philadelphia Phillies (NL) to an eighth-place finish in 1921 and also piloted Providence, RI (IL) in 1913 and 1914, Jersey City, NJ (IL) in 1919 and 1920, and New Haven, CT (EL) in 1922–1923. He died in an automobile-train crash near Forsyth, NY.

BIBLIOGRAPHY: William Donovan file, National Baseball Library, Cooperstown, NY; Thomas Aylesworth and Benton Minks, *The Encyclopedia of Baseball Managers* (New York, 1990); Charles Alexander, *Ty Cobb* (New York, 1984); Richard Bak, *Ty Cobb: His Tumultuous Life and Times* (Dallas, TX, 1994); Mark Gallagher, *The Yankee Encyclopedia*, vol. 3 (Champaign, IL, 1997); Rich Westcott and Frank Bilovsky, *The New Phillies Encyclopedia* (Philadelphia, PA, 1993); Malcolm Bingay, *Of Me I Sing* (New York, 1949); Detroit Baseball Club Letterbooks, vols. 3–4, Ernie Harwell Collection, Detroit Public Library, Detroit, MI; Detroit *News*, December 10, 1923; G. H. Fleming, *The Unforgettable Season* (New York, 1981); Frederick G. Lieb, *The Detroit Tigers* (New York, 1946); *TSN*, January 6, 1954.

                                                                    Anthony J. Papalas

DOUGHERTY, Patrick Henry "Patsy" (b. October 27, 1876, Andover, NY; d. April 30, 1940, Bolivar, NY), player, performed as an outfielder for three teams and was noted mainly as a fast base runner and excellent bunter. A lifelong resident of the New York–Pennsylvania oilfield, he pitched for the town team at Bolivar, NY. Fielder Jones,* who played for nearby Shinglehouse, PA, recognized his talent and remembered it. Dougherty completed Bolivar High School and spent a year at Westbrooks Academy, an Olean, NY business school. He turned professional with Bristol, CT (CtL) in 1896 and progressed through the minor leagues to Olean, NY, Canandaigua, NY, Homestead, PA, and Bridgeport, CT. Dougherty led the CtL in batting as a pitcher in 1901 and the CaL in batting in winter ball, but never pitched in the major leagues.

Manager Jimmy Collins* of the Boston Red Sox (AL) brought Dougherty to the major leagues as an outfielder. Dougherty hit .342 in 1902 and .331 in 1903, marks he never again approached. He clouted two HR in a game against the Pittsburgh Pirates in the 1903 World Series. No other player followed suit until Harry Hooper* in 1915. The 6-foot-2-inch, 190-pound left-handed batter hit poorly against left-handers and spitballers, but was reportedly the fastest AL runner to first base.

In June 1904, Red Sox owner John I. Taylor traded Dougherty to the New York Highlanders (AL) for Bob Unglab and cash. After Dougherty hit .263 in 1905, manager Clark Griffith* threatened him with a $600 salary cut. The dispute caused Dougherty to leave the Highlanders after 12 games to return to the oilfield. In June 1905, manager Fielder Jones brought his Chicago White Sox (AL) to Olean for an exhibition game and signed Dougherty. Dougherty played in 75 games for the 1906 World Champions and performed regularly with the White Sox until 1911 as one of the strongest hitters on extremely weak-hitting teams. In 1,233 major league games, he batted .284 with 1,294 hits, 17 HR, and 261 stolen bases. He led the AL in hits with 195 in 1905, stolen bases with 47 in 1908, and in runs scored both in 1905 and 1906 with 107 and 113, respectively.

Before the 1912 season, Dougherty abruptly announced he had made enough money from baseball and began his business career. After serving as ISL president in 1916, he joined the State Bank of Bolivar in 1918. At the time of his death, he served as assistant cashier. He married Florence K. Mott on February 15, 1904; they had five children.

BIBLIOGRAPHY: *The Baseball Encyclopedia*, 10th ed. (New York, 1996); Lee Allen, "Cooperstown Corner," *TSN*, October 5, 1968; Patrick Henry Dougherty file, National Baseball Library, Cooperstown, NY; Warren Brown, *The Chicago White Sox* (New York, 1952); Frederick G. Lieb, *The Boston Red Sox* (New York, 1947); Robert Redmount, *The Red Sox Encyclopedia* (Champaign, IL, 1998).

George W. Hilton

DOUTHIT, Taylor Lee "The Ballhawk" (b. April 22, 1901, Little Rock, AR; d. May 28, 1986, Fremont, CA), player, graduated from the University of California, where he starred in basketball and baseball. The 5-foot 11½-inch, 175-pound Douthit, who batted and threw right-handed, signed originally with the St. Louis Cardinals (NL). After playing outfield for Fort Smith, AR in 1923, he split 1924 between the Cardinals and St. Joseph, MO and 1925 between the Cardinals and Milwaukee, WI.

Douthit joined the St. Louis Cardinals to stay in 1926 and scored five runs in one game, one short of the major league record. He batted .291 lifetime with 1,201 hits, batting .308 in 1926, .336 in 1929, and .303 in 1930. Douthit appeared in the 1926, 1928, and 1930 World Series with St. Louis, batting just .140. An excellent leadoff hitter and wide-ranging fielder, he was nicknamed "The Ballhawk." Douthit, who led the NL three times in putouts and twice in errors, scored 665 career runs, including 111 in 1928 and 128 in 1929. He batted safely in 22 straight games in 1930 and made nine consecutive hits in 1931 just before being traded in June to the Cincinnati Reds (NL). The Reds sold him to the Chicago Cubs (NL) for the waiver price in April 1933. Arthritis of the hip caused him to retire after that season and to enter the family insurance business in northern California.

BIBLIOGRAPHY: Taylor Douthit file, National Baseball Library, Cooperstown, NY; Joseph L. Reichler, ed., *The Great All-Time Baseball Record Book* (New York, 1981); *The Baseball Encyclopedia*, 10th ed. (New York, 1996); Frederick G. Lieb, *The St. Louis Cardinals* (New York, 1945); Bob Broeg and Jerry Vickery, *St. Louis Cardinals Encyclopedia* (Grand Rapids, MI, 1998).

Horace R. Givens

DOWNING, Brian Jay (b. October 9, 1950, Los Angeles, CA), player, graduated from Magnolia High School near Anaheim Stadium in Anaheim, CA and attended Cypress, CA JC. He married Cheryl Neumann on October 24, 1974 and has three sons, Bradley, Brandon, and Brent.

The 5-foot 10-inch, 194-pound right-hander made his major league debut with the Chicago White Sox (AL) at third base in May 1973 after only three years of minor league experience. His first major league hit, an inside-the-park HR, came off Mickey Lolich* of the Detroit Tigers. After converting to catcher in 1974, he ranked second among AL receivers in putouts (730) and total chances (822) in 1975. In his final season with Chicago, he batted .284 in 1977.

In December 1977, the California Angels (AL) acquired Downing in a trade. He batted .326 in 1979, third best in the AL, but fractured his left ankle on a play at home plate in April 1980. In 1982, he played 158 games in the outfield without committing an error. His 330 chances established an AL record, breaking the 314 mark held by Roy White.* The same year, he belted 6 HR as a lead-off batter. He established another AL record in 1983 for most consecutive errorless games (244), shattering Al Kaline's* standard.

Downing shared the 1984 Owner's Trophy as the Angels' Co-MVP and led his club in games played (156), hits (148), doubles (28), total bases (249), and RBI (91). On April 24, 1984, Downing, Bobby Grich,* and Reggie Jackson* hit consecutive HR against Dennis Boyd of the Boston Red Sox at Fenway Park. In 1986, Downing's first three hits were HR.

Downing was selected AL Player of the Month for April 1987, batting .352 with 9 HR and 22 RBI. He finished the 1987 season with career highs in runs scored (110), HR (29), and AL-leading walks (106) and broke the Angels record for leadoff HR (7). In 1988 he became a DH and the first Angel ever to have five consecutive seasons with at least 20 HR. His 25 HR that year fell one shy of breaking Frank Robinson's* club record for most HR by a DH. He recorded his 200th career HR on May 22, 1988 against the Boston Red Sox.

During 1989, Downing surpassed Jim Fregosi* for career games played with the Angels and led all DH in game appearances. He became the Angels' all-time leader in hits (1,409), singling off Nolan Ryan* of the Texas Rangers in the ninth inning on June 14. His 1989 batting average dramatically improved 41 points to .283, but his HR production dropped markedly. Downing, who played in a club-record 13th season with the Angels in 1990, joined the Texas Rangers (AL) as a free agent in 1991 and performed as a DH. His major league career ended with Texas in 1992. In 20 major league seasons, he batted .267 with 2,099 hits, 360 doubles, 275 HR, 1,188 runs scored, and 1,073 RBI and compiled a .995 fielding percentage.

BIBLIOGRAPHY: Brian Downing file, National Baseball Library, Cooperstown, NY; *California Angels Media Guides*, 1979–1990; *TSN Official Baseball Register*, 1974–1992; John Thorn et al., eds., *Total Baseball*, 5th ed. (New York, 1997).

Darryl R. Zengler

DOYLE, Dorothy Harrell "Snookie" (b. February 4, 1924, Los Angeles, CA), player, is the daughter of William D. Harrell and Catherine Harrell. Her mother's ancestry was Welsh and German, while her father's heritage was Scotch, Irish, and Cherokee. Doyle graduated from Fremont High School in 1942 and played softball in the Los Angeles City Leagues. She married during World War II, but divorced her first husband.

In 1944, Doyle was recruited by AAGPBL scout Bill Allington. The 5-foot 4-inch, 127-pound right-hander arrived in Chicago, IL on June 6, 1944 and was assigned to the Rockford, IL Peaches. For nine seasons, Doyle starred as shortstop and ranked among the AAGPBL leading hitters. An early AAGPBL member, she made the All-Star team four consecutive years from 1947 to 1950 and again in 1952. Nicknamed "Snookie" by her grandmother, Doyle led the Rockford Peaches in RBI from 1947 to 1950. She possessed a keen eye for pitches, garnering 203 career walks and striking out only 95 times. Doyle made 667 career hits, scored 326 runs, drove in 306 runs, and completed her career with a .228 batting average. She helped bring championship honors to the Rockford team in 1945, 1948, 1949, and 1950. In 1948 she batted .251 and led the Peaches with 58 RBI. She also led Rockford in RBI in 1949 and 1950. Defensively, she ranked among the league's leading shortstops with 1,533 putouts and 2,085 assists. The Rockford Peaches and the South Bend, IN Blue Sox were the only teams to remain in the AAGPBL during its 12-year history from 1943 to 1954.

According to Doyle, chaperones were assigned to each team. For the Rockford Peaches, managers set the rules. Some chaperones followed them precisely, whereas others showed more leniency. Players were to be in their rooms two hours after a game or no later than 12:30 A.M. The Rockford Peaches traveled on the Illinois Central Railroad until 1946, when the AAGPBL switched to bus travel. Doyle, who considered Dottie Wiltse Collins* of the Ft. Wayne, IN Daisies the toughest pitcher she faced, played for the powerful Phoenix, AZ A-1 Queens in 1951 and 1953, Portland, OR in 1954–1955, and the Orange Linoettes of California from 1956 to 1960.

Doyle married David Doyle in April 1949 and graduated from Long Beach State University in 1958. She taught mathematics and physical education for four years at Compton Unified School District near Los Angeles. She then served as a counselor for 22 years, retiring in 1984. Her second husband died in 1960. The AAGPBL honored her with a display in the National Baseball Hall of Fame in Cooperstown, NY in November 1988.

BIBLIOGRAPHY: Gai Ingham Berlage, *Women in Baseball* (Westport, CT, 1994); Barbara Gregorich, *Women at Play* (San Diego, CA, 1993); Sharon Roepke, *Diamond Gals* (Flint, MI, 1988); Susan Johnson, *When Women Played Hardball* (Seattle, WA, 1994); W. C. Madden, *The Women of the All-American Girls Professional Baseball League* (Jefferson, NC, 1997); James E. Odenkirk, Personal Interview with Dorothy Doyle, Cathedral City, CA, May 10, 1996.

James E. Odenkirk

DOYLE, John Joseph "Dirty Jack" (b. October 25, 1869, Killorglin, Ireland; d. December 31, 1958, Holyoke, MA), player, manager, umpire, and scout, grew up in Holyoke, MA and began his professional baseball career in 1888 as a catcher with Lynn, MA (NEL). In 1889, Doyle signed with Canton, OH (TSL), caught 80 games, hit .280, and stole 81 bases. The 19-year-old backstop made his major league debut with the Columbus, OH Buckeyes (AA) in August 1889. The next season, he appeared in 77 games as a utility player with the Columbus Buckeyes. In 1891 Doyle, who batted and threw right-handed, batted .276 for the Cleveland Spiders (NL). Early in the 1892 season, the Cleveland Spiders sent him to the New York Giants (NL). He appeared in 90 games and raised his batting average to .298. He stayed with New York through the 1895 season, batting a combined .337. In 1894 the 5-foot 9-inch, 155-pound Doyle found a home at first base, batting a robust .367 with 90 runs scored and 100 RBI in 105 games. His performance, along with the stellar hitting of George Davis* and George Van Haltren* and superb pitching of Amos Rusie* and Jouett Meekin,* sparked New York to an 88–44 record and a second-place finish in the 12-team NL.

During the 1896 and 1897 seasons, Doyle held the regular first baseman's job with the Baltimore Orioles (NL). He helped manager Ned Hanlon's* team win the NL championship in 1896 with a 90–39 record and finish runner-up the next season with a 90–40 mark. In 1896, Doyle recorded career highs in both runs scored (116) and RBI (101). For the two seasons combined, he averaged 164 hits and 67 stolen bases and batted .346. Doyle moved from one team to another over the next eight seasons. After Doyle played with the Washington Senators (NL) in 1898, the New York Giants (NL) employed him as the team's starting first sacker in 1899 and 1900. He played first base for the Chicago Orphans (NL) in 1901 and saw action with the New York Giants (NL) and Washington Senators (AL) in 1902. The following season, he played first base for the Brooklyn Superbas, collecting 164 hits and batting .313. The Brooklyn Superbas used him briefly in 1904 before sending him to the Philadelphia Phillies (NL). In 1905 he appeared in one game for the New York Highlanders (AL).

During his 17 seasons spanning 10 different major league clubs, Doyle remained an accomplished hitter with 1,806 hits and a lifetime .299 batting average. Only 20 major leaguers, including Doyle, have played in at least 100 games at four different positions. Some claim that in an 1892 game he was baseball's first pinch hitter, coming off the bench to single for the New

York Giants. After Doyle finished his playing career, he remained active in professional baseball for the rest of his life. He managed Milwaukee, WI (AA) in 1907 and umpired in the EL in 1910 and the NL and NEL in 1911. After scouting for the Cleveland Naps (AL) in 1913, he umpired in the AA in 1915, PCL in 1916, and 3IL in 1919. In 1920, the Chicago Cubs (NL) hired Doyle as the team's New England scout. He proudly held that position until his death. He spent two years as police commissioner of Holyoke, MA.

BIBLIOGRAPHY: *The Baseball Encyclopedia*, 10th ed. (New York, 1996); Chicago (IL) *Daily Tribune*, January 1, 1959, January 2, 1959; Craig Carter, ed., *TSN Daguerreotypes*, 8th ed. (St. Louis, MO, 1990); John Joseph Doyle file, National Baseball Library, Cooperstown, NY; James H. Bready, *Baseball in Baltimore* (Baltimore, MD, 1998); Frederick Ivor-Campbell et al., *Baseball's First Stars* (Cleveland, OH, 1996); James D. Hardy, Jr., *The New York Giants Baseball Club* (Jefferson, NC, 1996); John Thorn et al., eds., *Total Baseball*, 5th ed. (New York, 1997).

Raymond D. Kush

DOYLE, Lawrence Joseph "Larry," "Laughing Larry" (b. July 31, 1886, Caseyville, IL; d. March 1, 1974, Saranac Lake, NY), player, starred for over 12 years for the New York Giants (NL) and captained the team. In 1911, he was named the NL's MVP (Chalmers Award) and led the NL in triples with 25. His best hitting performance came in 1915, when he paced the NL in hits (189), singles (139), doubles (40), and batting average (.320). A lifetime .290 batter, he stole home 17 times, made 1,887 hits, scored 960 runs, knocked in 793 runs, and pilfered 298 bases.

After Doyle began his playing career with Mattoon, IL (KL) in 1906 and Springfield, IL (3IL) in 1907, the New York Giants purchased his contract that June. Nervously anticipating his first appearance at the Polo Grounds, he took the wrong ferry across the Hudson River and arrived late for the game. Although Doyle had played only third base, manager John McGraw* started him that day at second base. In a close game against the World Series champion Chicago Cubs in the ninth inning, Doyle misplayed a fielding chance that led to the winning run. McGraw summoned Doyle to his office the next day. The infielder expected to be released, but McGraw instead delivered encouragement.

The scrappy Doyle calmed down, reassuming the personality that earned him the nickname "Laughing Larry," and helped the Giants win the 1911–1913 NL pennants. During 1911 Doyle commented, "It's great to be young and a Giant." In that World Series, Doyle scored the well-documented "phantom" run on a fall-away slide at home plate to win the fifth game and delay the Philadelphia Athletics' ultimate victory. After the game, umpire Bill Klem* stated that any appeal on the Athletics' part would have resulted in an out call as Doyle had never touched the plate. Doyle shared with Eddie Collins* the record for the most lifetime World Series errors (8). In August 1916 the Giants traded Doyle to the Chicago Cubs (NL). He played in

Chicago through 1917, rejoined the Giants in January 1918, and retired from baseball in 1920.

BIBLIOGRAPHY: Larry Doyle file, National Baseball Library, Cooperstown, NY; Bill Chambers, "Young and a Giant—Laughing Larry Doyle," *TNP* 13 (1993), pp. 43–44; Gene Karst and Martin J. Jones, Jr., *Who's Who in Professional Baseball* (New Rochelle, NY, 1973); Frederick G. Lieb, *Baseball As I Have Known It* (New York, 1977); Noel Hynd, *The Giants of the Polo Grounds* (New York, 1988); Charles C. Alexander, *John McGraw* (New York, 1988); Frank Graham, *The New York Giants* (New York, 1952); Ray Robinson, *Matty: An American Hero* (New York, 1993); *NYT*, March 2, 1974; *The Baseball Encyclopedia*, 10th ed. (New York, 1996).

Alan R. Asnen

DRABEK, Douglas Dean "Doug" (b. July 25, 1962, Victoria, TX), player, graduated from St. Joseph High School in Victoria, TX, where he was selected All-State in baseball, football, and track and field. The 6-foot 1-inch, 185-pound right-handed pitcher attended the University of Houston from 1981 to 1983, winning 27 and losing 11 baseball decisions.

The Chicago White Sox (AL) selected Drabek in the eleventh round of the free agent draft in June 1983. In July 1984, Chicago traded him to the New York Yankees (AL). He appeared in 27 games for the Yankees in 1986 and was traded that November to the Pittsburgh Pirates (NL). The Pittsburgh squad, improving rapidly under manager Jim Leyland,* made Drabek the staff workhorse.

After a horrible 1–8 start in 1987, Drabek won 10 of his next 14 decisions and was named NL Pitcher of the Month for August. In 1988, he won seven consecutive decisions and finished the season with 15 triumphs and seven defeats. He led the 1989 Pirates in victories (14), shutouts (5), and innings pitched (244).

Drabek enjoyed a career year in 1990 with 22 wins and only six losses. He paced the NL in victories and winning percentage (.786), earning the NL Cy Young Award and *TSN* NL Pitcher of the Year honors. He led the Pirates in triumphs, starts (33), complete games (9), innings (231.1), and strikeouts (131).

Drabek appeared in three consecutive NL Championship Series against the Cincinnati Reds in 1990 and the Atlanta Braves in 1991 and 1992. Drabek, victimized by poor Pirates hitting, notched only two victories in seven decisions with a 2.05 ERA.

In December 1992, the Houston Astros (NL) signed Drabek as a free agent. He disappointed Houston in 1993, winning only nine games while losing a NL-leading 18. Drabek rebounded in 1994 with 12 victories and only 6 setbacks. Drabek was named NL Pitcher of the Month that May and made the 1994 All-Star team. In January 1997, he joined the Chicago White Sox as a free agent. The Baltimore Orioles (AL) signed him as a free agent in December 1997. The Orioles released him in October 1998. Through 1998, he had a major league record of 155 victories and 134 defeats with a 3.73 ERA.

Drabek and his wife, Kristy, have three children, Justin, Kyle, and Kelsey, and reside in The Woodlands, TX, where he participates in community relations work.

BIBLIOGRAPHY: *The Baseball Encyclopedia*, 10th ed. (New York, 1996); Doug Drabek file, *TSN*, St. Louis, MO; Doug Drabek file, National Baseball Library, Cooperstown, NY; Bob Smizik, *The Pittsburgh Pirates: An Illustrated History* (New York, 1990); *Houston Astros 1996 Media Guide; Pittsburgh Pirates 1991 Record and Information Guide.*

Frank W. Thackeray

DRESSEN, Charles Walter "Cholly," "Charlie" (b. September 29, 1898, Decatur, IL; d. August 10, 1966, Detroit, MI), baseball and football player, coach, manager, and scout, was orphaned at an early age. The brash, talkative athlete quit school at age 14 to pitch semiprofessional baseball for $7.50 a game. Umpire Beany Johnson told the 5-foot 5-inch, 146-pound right-hander that he lacked the height to be an effective pitcher. Dressen moved to the infield, handling second base for Moline, IL (3IL) in 1919. After hitting .306 in 46 games, Dressen played for Peoria, IL (3IL) in 1920 and 1921. He appeared in 138 games each season, hitting .238 and .301, respectively. He advanced to St. Paul, MN (AA) from 1922 to 1924, hitting .304 the first two campaigns and an outstanding .347 in 1924. The versatile Dressen also played quarterback in 1920 for George Halas's (FB) Decatur, IL Staleys (NFL) and in 1922 and 1923 for the Racine Horlick Legion (NFL) of Chicago, IL.

Dressen played infield for the Cincinnati Reds (NL) from 1925 to 1931 before being demoted to Minneapolis, MN (AA) and Baltimore, MD (IL). He batted .292 and led NL third basemen in fielding with a .967 mark in 1927, but never reached his predicted stardom. Dressen became a player–manager with Fay Murray's Nashville, TN Vols (SA) in 1932. He took the job by pledging his salary if the club did not win half its remaining games that Depression year. The Vols won the last game of the season, finishing with a 39–38 record.

In September 1933, the New York Giants (NL) signed him to replace the injured Johnny Vergez. Dressen hit .222 in 16 games, but did not play against the Washington Senators (AL) in the 1933 World Series. Dressen's advice saved the Giants in a crucial situation in the fourth game. In the 11th inning, the Senators had loaded the bases with just one out and threatened New York's 2–1 lead. Washington slugger Cliff Bolton pinch-hit for pitcher Jack Russell. Dressen sprinted out from the bench to offer some unsolicited advice to Giants manager Bill Terry* and pitcher Carl Hubbell.* Dressen knew that Bolton lacked speed and urged Terry to play back for the double-play. Bolton accommodated and the Giants captured the World Series.

Dressen managed Nashville, TN in early 1934 and was hired by Larry MacPhail* to pilot the Cincinnati Reds (NL) in July 1934. In 1938 Dressen returned to Nashville as manager. The next year, MacPhail selected him as a coach for the Brooklyn Dodgers (NL). Dressen resembled manager Leo Durocher* in temperament and worked well with him. Both expected the Brooklyn Dodgers players to hustle on the field. When Branch Rickey* replaced MacPhail in November 1942, he fired Dressen for gambling on horses. Rickey believed that the Dodgers lacked discipline. Dressen, who had just wed Ruth Sinclair on January 8, 1942, was expendable. The firing of Dressen helped the remaining Dodgers prepare for that season. The following season, Rickey rehired a penitential Dressen at a reduced salary and retained him as coach through the 1946 season.

MacPhail took over the New York Yankees (AL) in 1947 with Dan Topping.* Dressen, adept at stealing opponent's signs, coached for the New York Yankees in 1947 and 1948 and managed the Oakland, CA Oaks (PCL) for the next two seasons. In 1951 Dressen returned to the Brooklyn Dodgers as their manager. Brooklyn saw its mid-August 13½ game lead over the New York Giants (NL) evaporate, necessitating a three-game play-off. Although Bobby Thomson's* HR eliminated Brooklyn that year, Dressen and the Brooklyn Dodgers rebounded to win the next two NL pennants. Brooklyn fell victim to the New York Yankees in both World Series.

At the insistence of his wife, Dressen sought a two-year contract. The Brooklyn Dodgers, however, offered him just a one-year contract. When Dressen refused the offer, Walter Alston* replaced him. Dressen managed Oakland, CA (PCL) again in 1954 and joined the Washington Senators (AL) as pilot in 1955. After being fired from that post following the 1957 season, Dressen coached for the Los Angeles Dodgers (NL) in 1958 and 1959 under Alston. In 1960, he managed the Milwaukee Braves (NL) to a second-place finish. The Braves dropped to third place in 1961, causing Dressen's release. He piloted Toronto, Canada (IL) in 1962 and started the 1963 season as a special scout for the Los Angeles Dodgers. The Detroit Tigers (AL) hired him as manager in June 1963 and retained him until a heart attack claimed his life three years later.

During eight seasons as a player, Dressen appeared in 646 games, batted .272 with 603 hits, made 11 HR, scored 313 runs, and knocked in 221 runs. Pee Wee Reese* called Dressen the "smartest manager I ever played for." Dressen always told his players, "Keep close and I'll think of something." His overall managerial record came to 1,008 wins and 973 losses for a .509 mark.

BIBLIOGRAPHY: Chuck Dressen file, National Baseball Library, Cooperstown, NY; Thomas Aylesworth and Benton Minks, *The Encyclopedia of Baseball Managers* (New York, 1990); Ray Robinson, *The Home Run Heard 'Round the World* (New York, 1991); Lee Allen, *The Giants and Dodgers* (New York, 1964); Donald Honig, *Baseball Between the Lines* (New York, 1976); Peter Golenbock, *Bums* (New York, 1984); Richard Goldstein, *Superstars and Screwballs* (New York, 1991); William F. McNeil, *The Dodg-*

ers Encyclopedia (Champaign, IL, 1997); Roger Kahn, *The Boys of Summer* (New York, 1972); Gene Karst and Martin J. Jones, Jr., *Who's Who in Professional Baseball* (New Rochelle, NY, 1973).

William A. Borst

DREYFUSS, Barney (b. February 23, 1865, Freiburg, Germany; d. February 5, 1932, New York, NY), executive, was one of at least three children of Samuel Dreyfuss, an American of German-Jewish extraction, and Fanny (Goldsmith) Dreyfuss. He was educated at the Karlsruhe Gymnasium in Germany and worked for a year in a Karlsruhe bank. In 1881 he moved to Paducah, KY, reportedly to avoid military conscription. Although initially employed as a laborer by the Bernheim Brothers distillery, he became a company official within six years. At Paducah, Dreyfuss operated a semiprofessional baseball team from 1884 through 1888. He moved to Louisville, KY with the Bernheim company in 1888 and the next year purchased an interest in the Louisville, KY Colonels (NL). After buying out his associates for a reported $50,000 in 1899, he merged his team the following year with the Pittsburgh Pirates and brought Honus Wagner,* Deacon Phillippe,* Fred Clarke,* and other stars with him. With the legal aid of associate Harry Pulliam,* he bought out William Kerr's interest in 1901 and became sole owner.

Dreyfuss' Pittsburgh Pirates won NL pennants in 1901, 1902, 1903, 1909, 1925, and 1927 and world championships in 1909 and 1925. In Dreyfuss' 32 years as team owner, the Pirates finished in the second division only four times. He put his son Samuel in charge of daily operations in 1930, but resumed his active role when the latter died in February 1931. As owner, Dreyfuss was a "benevolent despot." He gave his share of the 1903 World Series receipts to his players, although Pittsburgh had lost to Boston. Dreyfuss remained generous with Wagner and other players providing faithful service, but treated sternly those who crossed him or failed to measure up to his puritanical standards. He reportedly did not acquire Tris Speaker* after seeing the latter smoking a cigarette. After moving the Pirates into new, modern Forbes Field in 1909, he refused to allow advertising on its fences.

Dreyfuss' baseball team remained his principal business, as he guided it successfully through wars with the AL and FL. A major force within organized baseball, he proved instrumental in setting up the World Series and abolishing the three-man commission that ruled baseball until the Chicago "Black Sox" scandal of 1919–1920. After 1902, he chaired the committee coordinating NL and AL schedules. Dreyfuss fought losing battles against the lively ball and the growing use of farm systems. He preferred to scout players personally in independent leagues, keeping detailed records in his famous "dope book." An archetype of the entrepreneurs dominating the game in the first third of the twentieth century, Dreyfuss helped make baseball the national pastime through the teams he fielded, the economic sagacity he displayed in the front office, and the high standards of integrity he helped the game to meet. Dreyfuss, who married Florence Wolf of Louisville on October 16, 1894 and had two children, never lost his German accent. Throughout his career, he remained active in Pittsburgh's community affairs.

BIBLIOGRAPHY: Barney Dreyfuss file, National Baseball Library, Cooperstown, NY; Frederick G. Lieb, *The Pittsburgh Pirates* (New York, 1948); *NCAB* 30 (1943), pp. 271–272; Bob Smizik, *The Pittsburgh Pirates: An Illustrated History* (New York, 1990); Dennis De Valeria and Jeanne Burke De Valeria, *Honus Wagner: A Biography* (New York, 1996); Arthur D. Hittner, *Honus Wagner: The Life of Baseball's 'Flying Dutchman'* (Jefferson, NC, 1996); William Hageman, *Honus: The Life and Times of a Baseball Hero* (Champaign, IL, 1996); Richard L. Burtt, *The Pittsburgh Pirates, A Pictorial History* (Virginia Beach, VA, 1977).

Luther W. Spoehr

DRIESSEN, Daniel "Dan" (b. July 29, 1951, Hilton Head Island, SC), player, is the son of Henry Driessen and Alice (Robinson) Driessen. He was a 5-foot 11-inch, 200-pound first baseman, who batted left-handed and threw right-handed. Driessen attended high school in Hilton Head but did not play on the baseball team. He was not drafted and only participated in baseball on the weekends. The Cincinnati Reds (NL) gave Driessen a tryout and signed him as a free agent in August 1969.

Driessen's first professional baseball assignment came at Tampa, FL (FSL) during the 1970 and 1971 seasons. The following season, he batted .322 for Three Rivers, Canada (EL) and led EL first basemen with a .994 fielding percentage. Driessen began the 1973 season with Indianapolis, IN (AA) before batting a career-high .301 in 102 games for the Cincinnati Reds. The next 10 full seasons from 1974 to 1983 were spent with the Cincinnati Reds. Driessen's best over-all campaign came in 1977, when he posted career highs in base hits (161), RBI (91), and stolen bases (31) while recording a .300 batting average. He in 1979 slugged 18 HR and in 1980 posted career bests in games played (154), runs scored (81), and doubles (36). Driessen also shared the NL lead in walks received (93) and hit by pitches (6). He led all NL first basemen in fielding percentage in 1978 (.996), 1982 (.998), and 1983 (.996).

Driessen split the 1984 season with the Cincinnati Reds and the Montreal Expos (NL), being traded in July for pitcher Andy McGaffigan and Jim Jefferson. Driessen divided the 1985 season with the Montreal Expos and San Francisco Giants (NL). Montreal traded him to San Francisco in August 1985 for pitcher Bill Laskey and first baseman Scot Thompson. After being released by the Giants in May 1986, Driessen signed with the Houston Astros (NL) in June 1986. He appeared in just 17 games for Houston before being sent to Tucson, AZ (PCL) for the remainder of the 1986 season. Houston released him in October 1986. Driessen joined Louisville, KY (AA) in June 1987 and played 58 games there before joining the St. Louis Cardinals (NL). St. Louis released him in November 1987.

Driessen played in the NL Championship Series with Cincinnati in 1973, 1976, and 1979 and St. Louis in 1987, batting .162 in 13 games. Driessen participated on the 1975 and 1976 World Champion Cincinnati Reds and the 1987 NL pennant-winning Cardinals. He appeared in 10 World Series games, batting .276 with eight base hits.

In 15 major league seasons, Driessen scored 746 runs, and made 1,464 base hits in 1,732 games. He batted .267 with 282 doubles, 23 triples, 153 HR, and 763 RBI and recorded 154 stolen bases. Driessen compiled 11,061 putouts, 1,076 assists, and 96 errors with a .992 fielding average.

BIBLIOGRAPHY: Daniel Driessen file, National Baseball Library, Cooperstown, NY; William Leggett, "Red's Rookie Is a Tough Cookie," *SI* 36 (August 27, 1973), pp. 47–48; *TSN Official Baseball Register*, 1988; Donald Honig, *The Cincinnati Reds* (New York, 1992); Greg Rhodes and John Erardi, *Big Red Dynasty* (Cincinnati, OH, 1997); Robert H. Walker, *Cincinnati and the Big Red Machine* (Bloomington, IN, 1988).

John L. Evers

DROPO, Walter "Moose" (b. January 30, 1923, Moosup, CT), player, was signed by the Boston Red Sox (AL) in 1947 upon graduation with a B.S. degree in physical education from the University of Connecticut, where he played baseball, football, and basketball. The 6-foot 5-inch, 220-pound Dropo, a first baseman who batted and threw right-handed, chose baseball over offers to play football for the Chicago Bears (NFL) and basketball for the Providence, RI Steamrollers (BAA). His minor league baseball clubs included Scranton, PA (EL) in 1947, Louisville, KY (AA) and Birmingham, AL (SA) in 1948, and Sacramento, CA (PCL) in 1949.

Dropo joined the Boston Red Sox in 1950 and enjoyed a great season with a .322 batting average, 34 HR, and 144 RBI, one less than the AL rookie record. He shared the AL lead for RBI with teammate Vern Stephens,* making the *TSN* All-Star team and being named AL Rookie of the Year. Dropo, who scored five runs in one game, was traded to the Detroit Tigers (AL) in June 1952 and the Chicago White Sox (AL) in December 1954. Chicago sold him for the waiver price to the Cincinnati Reds (NL) in June 1958. Cincinnati traded Dropo to the Baltimore Orioles (AL) in 1959. He compiled a .270 lifetime batting average with 1,113 hits, 152 HR, and 704 RBI. With the Boston Red Sox in 1952, Dropo batted safely 12 straight times to tie the major league record for consecutive hits. He tied the AL record for most hits in three consecutive games with 13 and in four consecutive games with 15. Dropo, who retired at the end of the 1961 season to enter the family fireworks business, married Elizabeth Ternill Wise in October 1952 and has a son.

BIBLIOGRAPHY: Walter Dropo file, National Baseball Library, Cooperstown, NY; Peter Golenbock, *Fenway* (New York, 1992); Leigh Montville, "Whatever Happened to Walter Dropo?" *SI* 79 (July 19, 1993), pp. 82–83, Jack Lautier, *Fenway Voices* (Camden, ME, 1990); Joseph L. Reichler, ed., *The Great All-Time Baseball Record Book* (New York, 1981); *The Baseball Encyclopedia*, 10th ed. (New York, 1996); Robert Redmount, *The Red Sox Encyclopedia* (Champaign, IL, 1998).

Horace R. Givens

DRYSDALE, Donald Scott "Don," "Big D" (b. July 23, 1936, Van Nuys, CA; d. July 3, 1993, Montreal, Canada), player and sportscaster, was the son of Scott Drysdale and Verna (Ley) Drysdale. His father, a former minor league pitcher, coached him in American Legion baseball and refused to allow him to pitch until age 16. During his senior year, however, he won 10 of 11 pitching decisions for Van Nuys High School. The Brooklyn Dodgers (NL) signed the 6-foot 5-inch, 210-pound right-hander to a $4,000 bonus and assigned him to Bakersfield, CA (CaL) in 1954 and Montreal, Canada (IL) in 1955.

Drysdale occasionally started for the Brooklyn Dodgers in 1956 and defeated the Philadelphia Phillies 6–1 in his first outing. The "Big D" moved with the club in 1958 to Los Angeles, where he experienced four frustrating years pitching in the makeshift Coliseum ballpark. In 1959, however, he registered an NL-leading 242 strikeouts and 4 shutouts, played in both All-Star games, and won MVP honors in one. He topped the NL in strikeouts again in 1960 with 246. Through 1966 he teamed with left-hander Sandy Koufax,* forming one of baseball's most effective pitching combinations.

His finest season came in the new Dodger Stadium in 1962, when his 314 innings pitched, 25 wins, and 232 strikeouts led both leagues. Besides pitching in the All-Star game, he won the Cy Young Award and *TSN* Major League Pitcher of the Year honor. Drysdale, who enjoyed another 20-plus season in 1965 with a 23–12 record, the next year won a one-year $155,000 contract—highest on the Dodgers. He performed in five World Series, pitching a three-hit shutout in 1963 to help the Dodgers sweep the New York Yankees in four games, and made nine All-Star teams. In May and June 1968, he established major league records for most consecutive shutout games (6) and most shutout innings (58), erasing Walter Johnson's* 55-year-old record of 56. His five shutouts in May tied the NL record. A good hitter, the right-hander twice tied the NL record for HR by a pitcher with 7 (1958 and 1965) and finished his career with 29 HR.

The extremely competitive Drysdale threw a sidearm pitch, described as "all spikes, elbows, and fingernails," that intimidated right-handed hitters and tended to knock batters down. Although always a gentleman off the field, he hit a major league record 154 batsmen in 14 seasons. In 1962 he developed a half-way overhand motion, increasing his effectiveness against left-handed batters. He retired from the Dodgers in 1969 with a lifetime record of 3,432 innings pitched, 209 wins, 166 losses, 2,486 strikeouts, 49 shutouts, and a 2.95 ERA and was inducted into the National Baseball Hall of Fame in 1984.

Drysdale directly entered sports broadcasting, announcing games for the Montreal Expos (NL), Texas Rangers (AL), California Angels (AL), and Chicago White Sox (AL). He served as an ABC sports commentator from 1978 to 1987 and announced for the Los Angeles Dodgers from 1988 until his death. He married Ginger Dubberly in September 1958 and had one daughter before their divorce. He married basketball star Ann Meyers (IS) and lived in Pasadena, CA at the time of his death.

BIBLIOGRAPHY: *CB* (1965), pp. 132–134; "Departure of Big D," *Time* 94 (August 22, 1969), pp. 59–60; Don Drysdale file, National Baseball Library, Cooperstown, NY; Don Drysdale and Bob Verdi, *Once a Bum, Always a Dodger* (New York, 1990); Huston Horn, "Ex-Bad Boy's Big Year," *SI* 17 (August 20, 1962), pp. 24–29; Craig Carter, ed., *TSN Daguerreotypes* (St. Louis, MO, 1990); *The Baseball Encyclopedia*, 10th ed. (New York, 1996); *NYT*, July 5, 1993, p. 28; Lowell Reidenbaugh, "Five for the Hall," *TSN* (August 6, 1984), pp. 2–3, 24; Milton J. Shapiro, *The Don Drysdale Story* (New York, 1964); *WWA*, 42nd ed. (1982–1983), p. 880; Robert F. McNeil, *The Dodgers Encyclopedia* (Champaign, IL, 1997); Walter Alston with Si Burick, *Alston and the Dodgers* (New York, 1966); Walter Alston with Jack Tobin, *A Year at a Time* (Waco, TX, 1976).

Gaymon L. Bennett

DUFFY, Hugh (b. November 26, 1866, Cranston, RI; d. October 19, 1954, Boston, MA), player, manager, executive, and owner, married Nora Moore in October 1895 and was inducted into the National Baseball Hall of Fame in 1945. In a 68-year career, longer than that of Connie Mack,* Duffy participated in every aspect of baseball. The last of 29 players active in each of baseball's major leagues, Duffy became the only player batting at least .300 in all four. In 1894, he enjoyed one of the best offensive seasons in baseball history. Duffy led the NL in hits (237), doubles (51), HR (18), RBI (145), and slugging percentage (.694) and established the all-time single-season major league record with a superb .440 batting average. He ended a 17-year playing career in 1906 with a .324 lifetime batting average and 574 stolen bases. In 1,737 games, he made 2,282 hits, 325 doubles, 119 triples, 106 HR, 1,552 runs, 1,302 RBI, and a .449 slugging percentage.

Called by Fred Tenney* the "right-handed Mel Ott*" because of his similar batting stance, Duffy ranked as his era's premier hitter and led the major leagues in HR in the 1890s with 83. As a youth, he worked in Connecticut and Rhode Island cloth factories and played with amateur baseball clubs on weekends. The short, rather stocky Duffy began his professional career as a catcher with Hartford, CT (EL) in 1886 and Springfield, MA (EL) in 1887. That same year, he played outfield for Salem/Lowell, MA (NEL) and was scouted by Adrian "Cap" Anson's* Chicago White Stockings (NL). Although Duffy signed with Chicago in 1888, Anson benched him until July because of his 5-foot 7-inch stature. The single-minded, sharp-tongued Duffy jumped to the PL in 1890 and started in right field for Charles Comiskey's* Chicago Pirates club. He batted a solid .320, stole 78 bases, and led the league in runs, total bases, and hits. After the PL folded, Duffy joined the Boston Reds (AA) in 1891. This team, which included infielders Dan Brouthers* and Charles "Duke" Farrell* and pitchers Charley Buffinton,* "Gentleman" George Haddock, and Clark Griffith,* ranks among the greatest all-time ball clubs.

When the AA disbanded, the NL absorbed four of its franchises and its better players. Duffy joined manager Frank Selee's* championship-bound Boston Beaneaters and experienced his eight most productive seasons there despite his troublesome temper and tongue. Named team captain by Selee in 1896, he earned the wrath of teammates because of his strict discipline. Duffy, who rarely drank or swore and whose actual authority as captain was limited, was criticized by other players for his self-assumed leadership role, standoffish nature, and anti-player sentiments. The undaunted Duffy joined Comiskey, Griffith, and Connie Mack* in forming the AL. Duffy scouted and helped purchase the site where Fenway Park was built and convinced Braves stars Jimmy Collins* and Chick Stahl* to jump to the new Boston Red Sox AL franchise. In 1901 he became Mack's player–manager with the Milwaukee Brewers (AL). After the Brewers folded and became the St. Louis Browns, Duffy managed Milwaukee, WI (WL) in 1902 and 1903 and served as player–manager of the Philadelphia Phillies (NL) from 1904 to 1906.

Duffy managed and owned Providence, RI (EL) from 1907 to 1909 and piloted the Chicago White Sox (AL) in 1910 and 1911 and Milwaukee (AA) in 1912. In 1913, he became manager and president of Portland, ME (NEL). After spending four seasons there, he scouted for the Boston Braves (NL) from 1917 to 1919. He managed Toronto, Canada (IL) in 1920 and the Boston Red Sox (AL) in 1921 and 1922 and scouted for the latter from 1924 until his death. During the 1920s and 1930s, Duffy coached baseball at Harvard University and Boston College. As a major league manager for eight seasons, Duffy compiled a 535–671 mark (.444) and never finished higher than fourth place.

BIBLIOGRAPHY: Frederick Ivor-Campbell et al., eds., *Baseball's First Stars* (Cleveland, OH, 1996); Hugh Duffy file, National Baseball Library, Cooperstown, NY; Gary Caruso, *The Braves Encyclopedia* (Philadelphia, PA, 1995); John Thorn et al., eds., *Total Braves* (New York, 1996); Harold Kaese, *The Boston Braves* (New York, 1948); Gene Karst and Martin J. Jones, Jr., *Who's Who in Professional Baseball* (New Rochelle, NY, 1973); Frederick G. Lieb, *The Boston Red Sox* (New York, 1947); Craig Carter, ed., *TSN Daguerreotypes* (St. Louis, MO, 1990); *NYT*, October 20, 1954; *The Baseball Encyclopedia*, 10th ed. (New York, 1996); Robert Redmount, *The Red Sox Encyclopedia* (Champaign, IL, 1998); *Time* 64 (November 1, 1954), p. 87.

Alan R. Asnen

DUGAN, Joseph Anthony "Jumping Joe" (b. May 12, 1897, Mahanoy City, PA; d. July 7, 1982, Norwood, MA), player and scout, grew up in Torrington, CT. After attending Holy Cross University, Dugan joined the Philadelphia Athletics (AL) for a $500 signing bonus in 1917. He played 14 AL seasons with the Philadelphia Athletics (1917–1921), Boston Red Sox (1922, 1929), New York Yankees (1922–1928), and Detroit Tigers (1931).

During his major league career, the 5-foot 11-inch, 160-pound, right-handed third baseman hit .280 with 277 doubles, 42 HR, and 571 RBI in 1,447 games. He stole 37 bases and compiled a .957 fielding average. In 1923, Dugan led the AL in at-bats with 644. In five World Series (1922–1923, 1926–1928) with the New York Yankees, he batted .267 in 25 games.

Dugan's nickname, "Jumping Joe," was given him by a sportswriter in 1919, when the infielder left the Athletics three times to return to his Massachusetts home because he did not like "the place or the fans." After being traded to the New York Yankees in July 1922, Dugan became a good friend of Babe Ruth* and roomed with him on road trips. Ruth called him "kid" and had him open fan mail. Dugan's productivity and playing time diminished after 1927 when he developed eye and leg problems. He stayed out of the major leagues in 1930 and played in only 8 games in 1931 before retiring.

During the 1930s, Dugan was involved in unsuccessful sporting goods and trucking businesses. Dugan, who married Martha D. Kemmey, worked for the Recreation Department of the Boston Park system in the 1940s and later scouted for the Boston Red Sox. He died of pneumonia and the effects of a stroke and was survived by a son.

BIBLIOGRAPHY: Joseph Dugan file, National Baseball Library, Cooperstown, NY; Boston *Globe*, July 9, 1982; Detroit *News*, March 4, 1956; *NYT*, July 10, 1982; Mike Shatzkin, ed., *The Ballplayers* (New York, 1990); Marshall Smelser, *The Life that Ruth Built* (New York, 1975); *TSN*, January 22, 1942; John Thorn et al., eds., *Total Baseball*, 5th ed. (New York, 1997); *The Baseball Encyclopedia*, 10th ed. (New York, 1996); Mark Gallagher, *The Yankee Encyclopedia*, vol. 3 (New York, 1997); John Mosedale, *The Greatest of All: The 1927 New York Yankees* (New York, 1974); Leo Trachtenberg, *The Wonder Team* (Bowling Green, OH, 1995); Robert Redmount, *The Red Sox Encyclopedia* (Champaign, IL, 1998); Frank Graham, *The New York Yankees* (New York, 1943).

John E. Findling

DUNCAN, Frank, Jr. (b. February 14, 1901, Kansas City, MO; d. December 4, 1973, Kansas City, MO), player and manager, was the son of Frank Duncan, Sr. and starred as a receiver with the Kansas City Monarchs (NNL) during the 1920s and served as their manager (NAL) during the 1940s. He was associated with seven pennant winners, including four as a player, and Negro World Series Champions, including one as a player. The 6-foot, 175 pounder, a hard-nosed, durable receiver with a quick release, possessed one of the best throwing arms in the NAL and was selected to the 1938 East-West All-Star team.

Duncan began his professional baseball career in 1920 with Peters' Union Giants, but jumped to Joe Green's Chicago Giants that season. In 1921, Chicago traded him to the Kansas City Monarchs. Kansas City won three straight NNL pennants from 1923 to 1925 and defeated the Philadelphia, PA Hilldale Daisies in the first Negro World Series in 1924. The Monarchs added a fourth flag in 1929. Duncan also performed with the New York Black Yankees (NNL), Pittsburgh Crawfords (NNL), Homestead, PA Grays (NNL), New York Cuban Stars (NNL), Chicago American Giants (NAL) and the Palmer House Stars, a Chicago-based independent team.

Duncan played five winters in Cuba, including the 1929–1930 season with the champion Cienfuegos (CUWL) team. He also caught in the CWL in 1926–1927 and afterward toured the Orient with the Philadelphia Royal Giants. After being appointed manager of the Monarchs in 1942, Duncan led Kansas City to a NAL pennant and sweep of the Homestead Grays in the Negro World Series. He guided Kansas City to another NAL title in 1946, but lost the World Series to the Newark Eagles. After yielding the managerial reins to Buck O'Neil* in 1948, he later briefly umpired.

Duncan served six months in the U.S. Army during World War II, being discharged as a sergeant to resume his baseball career in 1943. He later operated a tavern and was married to blues singer Julia Lee. Their son, Frank Duncan, III, played briefly in the Negro Leagues.

BIBLIOGRAPHY: *Afro-American*, 1931–1937; Janet Bruce, *Kansas City Monarchs* (Lawrence, KS, 1985); Chicago *Defender*, 1921–1948; Kansas City *Call*, 1921–1948; Robert W. Peterson, *Only the Ball Was White* (Englewood Cliffs, NJ, 1970); Pittsburgh *Courier*, 1931–1937; James A. Riley, *The All-Time All-Stars of Black Baseball* (Cocoa, FL, 1983); James A. Riley, *The Biographical Encyclopedia of the Negro Baseball Leagues* (New York, 1994); James A. Riley, interviews with former Negro League players, James A. Riley Collection, Canton, GA; *The Baseball Encyclopedia*, 10th ed. (New York, 1996).

James A. Riley

DUNLAP, Frederick C. "Sure Shot" (b. May 21, 1859, Philadelphia, PA; d. December 1, 1902, Philadelphia, PA), player and manager, possessed a superb throwing arm and ranked among the best second basemen in early major league baseball. Orphaned at age 10, he was brought up by a middle-aged couple with little regard for his education or welfare. The right-handed Dunlap played club baseball with the Gloucester Club of New Jersey in 1874, Cregar Club of Camden, NJ in 1875, and Kleinz Club of Philadelphia, PA in 1876 and debuted professionally at Auburn, NY in 1876 at age 17. The 5-foot 8-inch, 165-pound infielder also participated in minor league baseball at Hornellsville, NY (IA) and Albany, NY (NA).

His major league debut came with the Cleveland Blues (NL) on May 1,

1880. At Cleveland, he teamed with shortstop "Pebbly Jack" Glasscock* in a famed infield and managed the 1882 squad to a 42–36 win–loss record. The St. Louis Maroons of the short-lived UA signed him in 1884 as field manager and as that era's highest paid player with a $3,400 salary. St. Louis finished first in the UA with a 66–16 mark in 1884. Dunlap continued managing the St. Louis Maroons, which entered the NL in 1885. During the 1886 season, St. Louis sold him to the Detroit Wolverines. After Dunlap helped Detroit win the 1887 NL pennant, the Wolverines sold him to the Pittsburgh Alleghenys (NL) in November 1887. Dunlap held out the next spring, eventually receiving an unprecedented salary and bonus exceeding $6,000.

Dunlap managed the Pittsburgh Alleghenys for 16 games in 1889, but was released in May 1890 because his hitting and fielding skills declined. He began the 1891 season with the Washington Statesmen (AA), but a broken leg ended his career. Dunlap hit .292 in 12 major league seasons, leading the UL in 1884 with a .412 batting average, .448 on-base percentage, .621 slugging percentage, 185 hits, 160 runs scored, and 13 HR. His 160 runs scored set a major league record and ranks 14th best all-time. Despite small hands, he never wore a glove and caught thrown balls with either hand. He frequently led NL second basemen in all fielding categories, pacing his league three times in fielding average. Dunlap, best known for his rifle-accurate throws, demonstrated speedy, aggressive baserunning and good clutch hitting, although not possessing much power. Despite making relatively high earnings, Dunlap died in poverty.

BIBLIOGRAPHY: Fred Dunlap file, National Baseball Library, Cooperstown, NY; Franklin Lewis, *The Cleveland Indians* (New York, 1949); J. Thomas Hetrick, *Chris Von der Ahe and the St. Louis Browns* (Lanham, MD, 1999); *The Baseball Encyclopedia*, 10th ed. (New York, 1996); John Thorn et al., eds., *Total Baseball*, 5th ed. (New York, 1997); Robert L. Tieman and Mark Rucker, eds., *Nineteenth Century Stars* (Kansas City, MO, 1989).

Robert B. Van Atta

DUNN, John Joseph "Jack" (b. October 6, 1872, Meadville, PA; d. October 22, 1928, Towson, MD), player, manager, and owner, "discovered" and later sold Babe Ruth.* Dunn signed Ruth to a $600 annual professional baseball contract out of St. Mary's Catholic School in Baltimore, MD in 1914 and sold him that year to the Boston Red Sox (AL) for $25,000.

When Dunn was a youngster, his family moved to Bayonne, NJ. Dunn began his baseball career with amateur and semiprofessional teams and started playing professionally in the old NYSL in 1895. Dunn played a utility role in the major leagues for the Brooklyn Bridegrooms-Superbas (NL, 1897–1900), Philadelphia Phillies (NL, 1900–1901), Baltimore Orioles (AL, 1901), and New York Giants (NL, 1902–1904). The versatile right-handed hitting Dunn appeared in 143 career games at third base, 98 contests at shortstop, 59 games in the outfield, 35 contests at second base, and 142 games as a pitcher. In 1,622 career at bats, Dunn hit only one HR and compiled a career .245 batting average. In 1897, the 5-foot 9-inch Dunn compiled a respectable 14–9 record as a pitcher for the Bridegrooms.

John McGraw,* the Baltimore manager in 1901, took Dunn with him when he moved to pilot the New York Giants in 1902. After working under McGraw's tutelage, Dunn began his own 24-year minor league managerial career by leading Providence, RI to the EL championship in 1905 as player–manager. After Providence plunged to sixth place in 1906, Dunn managed the Baltimore, MD (IL) minor league franchise from 1907 to 1928 and purchased the Orioles in 1909. With Dunn as manager, Baltimore won the EL championship in 1908. Dunn temporarily transferred the Orioles to Richmond, VA in 1915 for one year to avoid competition with the Baltimore Terrapins (FL). From 1919 through 1925, Dunn led the Orioles to seven straight IL pennants and a superlative .687 winning percentage. In 1921, Baltimore enjoyed an impressive 119–47 record.

The gregarious Dunn had a son, Jack, Jr., a minor league baseball player he trained to take over the team. Tragically, Jack, Jr., died suddenly of pneumonia in 1923 at age 27. Dunn died of a heart attack while astride a horse. His estate, which he left to his widow, Mary, was worth an estimated $500,000 to $1,000,000 and included Oriole Park. After Dunn's death, his widow directed operations of the IL Orioles. Jack Dunn III later owned the IL franchise and served as vice-president of the Baltimore Orioles (AL). The Babe Ruth Birthplace and Orioles Museum in Baltimore has a permanent exhibit of Dunn family memorabilia.

BIBLIOGRAPHY: John Dunn file, National Baseball Library, Cooperstown, NY; AP, Obituary of Jack Dunn III, June 11, 1987; *The Baseball Encyclopedia*, 10th ed. (New York, 1996); Robert C. Creamer, *The Babe* (New York, 1974); Charles J. Foreman, "It Was Will to Win That Killed Jack Dunn," *TSN*, November 1928; Al Kermisch, "A Vote for Dunn's Orioles," *BRJ* 6 (1977), pp. 6–9; James H. Bready, *Baseball in Baltimore* (Baltimore, MD, 1998); Tom Meany, *Baseball's Greatest Teams* (New York, 1949); Paul A. Rickart, "Dunn's Record Most Remarkable in Baseball," *TSN*, December 17, 1925, p. 25; SABR, comp., *Minor League Baseball Stars*, vol. 2 (Cooperstown, NY, 1985); UPI, Obituary of Jack Dunn III, June 11, 1987.

Jack P. Lipton and Susan M. Lipton

DUROCHER, Leo Ernest "The Lip" (b. July 27, 1905, West Springfield, MA; d. October 7, 1991, Palm Springs, CA), player, manager, coach, and sportscaster, was the son of railroad engineer George Durocher and Clara (Provost) Durocher, both of French descent. Durocher attended Main Street and Park Avenue Schools in West Springfield, but left high school to work as a mechanic for the Wico Electric Company, Gilbert and Barker, and the Boston and Albany Railroad and to play for a local semipro team. Durocher's professional career began as a shortstop with the New York Yankees (AL) organization at Hartford, CT (EL) in 1925, Atlanta, GA (SA) in 1926, and

St. Paul, MN (AA) in 1927. Manager Miller Huggins* liked Durocher's heady play with the Yankees in 1928 and 1929, but the latter's antics and weak bat led to his departure when Huggins died.

The remainder of Durocher's 17-year major league career, mostly as a shortstop, came in the NL from 1930 to 1933 with the Cincinnati Reds, from 1933 to 1937 with the St. Louis Cardinals, and from 1938 to 1946 with the Brooklyn Dodgers. The 5-foot 10-inch, 175-pound Durocher, a smart, aggressive player, was recognized by 1934 as the best fielding short-stop in baseball. His hitting, however, proved erratic. Although hitting .333 in two All-Star games (1936 and 1938), he batted only .247 lifetime. In 1,637 major league games, Durocher numbered 1,320 hits, 210 doubles, 575 runs scored, 567 RBI, and 31 stolen bases. His leadership abilities were developed as captain of both the Cardinals "Gashouse Gang" in 1935 and the Dodgers in 1938. In 1939, he became player-manager of the Dodgers and began an NL managing career lasting 24 years.

Durocher, among his era's most successful, controversial managers, fa-vored scrappy players and the running game, played hunches, harassed um-pires, and fought with owners and fans. He piloted the Brooklyn Dodgers (1939–1946), New York Giants (1948–1955), Chicago Cubs (1966–1972), and Houston Astros (1972–1973). He won three NL pennants (1941, 1951, 1954), guided the Giants to a sweep of the favored Cleveland Indians in the 1954 World Series, and quickly molded a last-place Cubs team into a con-tender. In 1939, 1951, and 1954, he was named NL Manager of the Year. With four NL teams, he amassed a 2,008–1,709 won–lost record for a life-time .540 winning percentage. Durocher's private life also proved contro-versial. Fond of gracious living, Durocher made friends in show business. He was married four times (to Ruby Hartles, 1930; Grace Dozier, 1934; actress Laraine Day, 1947; and Lynne Walker Goldblatt) and had two adopted children, Christopher and Michele. In 1947 Commissioner Albert B. "Happy" Chandler* found Durocher's association with gamblers and other activities sufficient grounds for suspending him from baseball for 12 months, the harshest action ever taken against a major league pilot. During the 1955–1966 hiatus from managing, Durocher worked as an NBC televi-sion announcer (1956–1960) and coached third base for the Los Angeles Dodgers (NL, 1961–1964). He lived in Palm Springs, CA and co-authored *Nice Guys Finish Last* (1975). In 1994, the Veterans Committee elected him to the National Baseball Hall of Fame.

BIBLIOGRAPHY: Leo Durocher file, National Baseball Library, Cooperstown, NY; Gerald Astor, "Return of the Lip," *Look* 30 (May 17, 1966), pp. 89–94; *CB* (1940), pp. 266–267, (1950), pp. 128–130, (1953), pp. 150–153; Anthony J. Connor, *Voices from Cooperstown* (New York, 1982); David Craft, *Redbirds Revisited* (Chicago, IL, 1990); John Devaney, "Durocher and His Cubs: How Tensions Can Build a Win-ner," *Sport* 48 (September 1969), pp. 81–87; Leo Durocher et al., *Nice Guys Finish Last* (New York, 1975); Gerald Eskanazi, *The Lip: A Biography of Leo Durocher* (New

York, 1993); Brent P. Kelley, *The Case For: Those Overlooked by the Baseball Hall of Fame* (Jefferson, NC, 1992); Leonard Koppett, *The Man in the Dugout* (New York, 1993); "The Lion Roars a Little," *NYT Biographical Service* 18 (May 1987), pp. 505–506; Eddie Gold and Art Ahrens, *The New Era Cubs, 1941–1985* (Chicago, IL, 1985); Peter Golenbock, *Bums* (New York, 1984); Noel Hynd, *The Giants of the Polo Grounds* (New York, 1988); Roger Kahn, "They Ain't Getting No Maiden," *SEP* 139 (June 18, 1966), pp. 97–101; *NYT*, October 8, 1991, p. D-25; Harold Parrott, *The Lords of Baseball* (New York, 1976); Harold Rosenthal, *Baseball's Best Managers* (New York, 1961).

Douglas D. Martin

DWYER, John Francis "Frank" (b. March 20, 1867, Lee, MA; d. February 4, 1943, Pittsfield, MA), player, coach, manager, umpire, and scout, was the son of John Dwyer, a laborer, and Bridget (Callahan) Dwyer, both Irish immigrants. He attended Hobart College, where he pitched the baseball team to consecutive New York State college championships in 1886 and 1887. After turning professional in 1887, the 5-foot 8-inch, 145-pound right-hander hurled for LaCrosse, WI (NWL). In 1888, he made his major league debut with the Chicago Colts (NL) and posted a 4–1 mark with a 1.07 ERA. After compiling a 16–13 record with the Chicago Colts in 1889, Dwyer posted a 3–6 log for the Chicago Pirates (PL) in 1890.

Following the demise of the PL, Dwyer signed with the Cincinnati Kellys (AA) in 1891. When that club folded, he finished the 1891 season with the Milwaukee Brewers (AA) and compiled an overall 19–23 record. The AA dissolved after the 1891 season, prompting Dwyer's return to the NL. After a brief stint with the St. Louis Browns (NL), he was traded to the Cincinnati Reds (NL). His 20–10 mark with Cincinnati gave him an overall 22–18 record for the 1892 season. During the 1890s, Dwyer became a local favorite in Cincinnati. He successfully adjusted to the extended pitching distance and became a reliable starter for a team that only twice finished as high as third place. Until his final season in 1899, Dwyer compiled a 155–117 NL record. He pitched 2,342 innings, relying more on control than strikeouts and only once posting a losing record.

After suffering five setbacks in 1899, Dwyer ended his 12-year major league career with a 177–151 record, 3.84 ERA, and .229 batting average. Dwyer, who umpired in the AL in 1900 and 1904 and the NL in 1901, managed the Detroit Tigers (AL) in 1902 to a 52–83 record.

Dwyer in 1900 acquired a coal dealership in Geneva, NY, which remained in the family for 62 years. The avid sportsman served on the NYSBC from 1916 to 1923. He served as a pitching coach with the New York Giants (NL) in 1920 and scouted for that team until 1935. The longtime Geneva, NY resident died of a cerebral hemorrhage while visiting relatives in Pittsfield, MA. He was survived by his widow, Margaret (Broderick) Dwyer, and four sons and a daughter.

BIBLIOGRAPHY: John Thorn et al., eds., *Total Baseball*, 5th ed. (New York, 1997); Frank Dwyer file, National Baseball Library, Cooperstown, NY; Thomas Aylesworth and Benton Minks, *The Encyclopedia of Baseball Managers* (New York, 1990); Lee Allen, *The Cincinnati Reds* (New York, 1948); Harry Ellard, *Base Ball in Cincinnati* Cincinnati, OH, 1907); David Nemec, *The Beer and Whisky League* (New York, 1994); David Q. Voigt, *American Baseball*, vol. 1 (University Park, PA, 1983); Richard Gentile, telephone interview, July 1996.

David Q. Voigt

DYER, Edwin Hawley "Eddie" (b. October 11, 1900, Morgan City, LA; d. April 20, 1964, Houston, TX), player, scout, and manager, was of Scotch and Irish descent. He captained the Morgan City High School football team. Dyer served in the U.S. Army infantry in 1918 and entered Rice University in 1924, returning in 1936 to complete a Bachelor of Arts degree and coach freshmen football. The 5-foot 11-inch, 175-pound southpaw signed with the St. Louis Cardinals (NL) in 1922 and shuffled between the St. Louis Cardinals and their farm clubs from 1922 to 1927. After making two relief appearances in 1922, he shutout the Chicago Cubs in his first major league start in 1923. A sore arm caused Dyer to return to the minor leagues and convert to the outfield. In 69 pitching appearances for St. Louis, he won 15 games and lost 15 decisions with a 4.75 ERA. He played 60 games as a pinch hitter and outfielder. Dyer's major league career batting average was .223.

On October 6, 1928, Dyer married Geraldine Jennings. They had one son, Edwin, Jr. After Dyer pitched one inning for the St. Louis Cardinals in 1927, he managed in the St. Louis farm system. From 1927 to 1942, he piloted Springfield, MO (WA), Houston, TX (TL), and Columbus, OH (AA) and won nine minor league championships. In 1942 *TSN* selected Dyer Minor League Manager of the Year for directing Columbus to an AA pennant. He also scouted for the St. Louis Cardinals and signed future star hurler Howard Pollet* in 1938. From 1943 to 1945, Dyer supervised the St. Louis farm system.

When St. Louis Cardinals manager Billy Southworth* left to pilot the Boston Braves, owner Sam Breadon* appointed Dyer. Dyer inherited a St. Louis Cardinals team that had won NL pennants in three of the preceeding four campaigns. Breadon, however, in 1946 sold star catcher Walker Cooper* to the New York Giants in January and first baseman Johnny Hopp* to the Boston Braves in February. A month into the season, pitchers Max Lanier* and Fred Martin and second baseman Lou Klein jumped to the MEL. During 1946, Dyer replaced Klein with a youngster named Red Schoendienst,* Stan Musial* won another batting title, Enos Slaughter* drove in 130 runs, and Pollet won 21 games and led the NL with a 2.10 ERA. The St. Louis Cardinals finished in a first-place tie with Leo Durocher's* Brooklyn Dodgers with a 96–58 record. In the first-ever NL pennant playoff, Pollet bested the Brooklyn Dodgers 4–2 in the opener and Murry

Dickson* finished them off 8–4 in the second game. Dyer's club then defeated the Boston Red Sox in seven games to earn the World Championship.

Dyer's St. Louis Cardinals placed second to the Brooklyn Dodgers in 1947 and second to Southworth's Boston Braves in 1948. Dyer's Cardinals entered the final week of the 1949 season ahead of the Brooklyn Dodgers by two games on the loss side, but dropped four of the last five contests to finish one game behind the Brooklyn Dodgers. St. Louis posted a 78–75 record in 1950. Dyer was offered a one-year contract, but was encouraged to resign by owner Fred Saigh.* His managerial record with the St. Louis Cardinals included 446 wins, 325 losses, and 6 ties for a .578 winning percentage. Dyer returned to Houston, TX and formed Langham, Langston, and Dyer Insurance Counselors. He was joined by his former players Pollet and Jeff Cross in real estate and oil investments.

BIBLIOGRAPHY: Thomas Aylesworth and Benton Minks, *The Encyclopedia of Baseball Managers* (New York, 1990); Bob Broeg, *Redbirds: A Century of Cardinals' Baseball* (St. Louis, MO, 1981); Edwin Dyer file, National Baseball Library, Cooperstown, NY; Joe Garagiola, *Baseball Is a Funny Game* (New York, 1960); Gene Karst and Martin J. Jones, Jr., *Who's Who in Professional Baseball* (New Rochelle, NY, 1973); Stan Musial and Bob Broeg, *Stan Musial: "The Man's" Own Story* (Garden City, NY, 1964); Rob Rains, *The St. Louis Cardinals* (New York, 1992); Bob Broeg and Jerry Vickery, *St. Louis Cardinals Encyclopedia* (Grand Rapids, MI, 1998); Mike Shatzkin, ed., *The Ballplayers* (New York, 1990).

Frank J. Olmsted

DYKES, James Joseph "Jimmy" (b. November 10, 1896, Philadelphia, PA; d. June 15, 1976, Philadelphia, PA), player, coach, and manager, was the son of an engineer at Bryn Mawr College and manager of a local team. Encouraged by his father, he starred on the Philadelphia sandlots and was signed by the Philadelphia Athletics (AL) in 1917. After a year with Gettysburg, PA (BRL), he joined the Athletics. Although a poor hitter, he proved a natural fielder with a strong arm. Under the tutelage of Eddie Collins,* Dykes became a respectable batsman. Dykes married Mary McMonagles in October 1920 and had three children, James, Jr., Charlie, and Mary. During his 14-year tenure with the Athletics, he enjoyed a close father-son relationship with manager Connie Mack.*

The feisty, garrulous Dykes won the admiration of Detroit Tigers star Tyrus Cobb* for his aggressiveness. In 1925 Cobb offered the Athletics $50,000, then a considerable sum, for Dykes, but Mack declined. Dykes became an integral part of the great 1929, 1930, and 1931 Philadelphia championship teams, batting well and playing before immense crowds. Dykes, whose lifetime batting average was .280, made 2,256 hits, 453 doubles, and 108 HR, scored 1,108 runs, and drove in 1,071 runs in 2,282 games. During the Depression, the financially strapped Mack broke up his team. In September 1932 he sold Dykes, Mule Haas, and Al Simmons* to the Chicago

White Sox (AL) for $150,000. Although age 37, Dykes proved the key player in the deal and subsequently enjoyed four solid seasons with the White Sox. He attributed his long career to good conditioning, enhanced by much golf and bowling. The good-natured, nonstop conversationalist enjoyed enormous popularity with the players, press, and fans.

As a manager, however, he did not have championship material and never finished higher than third place. After he completed his managerial tenure with the Chicago White Sox (1934–1946), the New York Yankees (AL) in 1946 and 1948 seriously considered making Dykes their manager. In 1948, Dykes declined an opportunity to manage the Cleveland Indians (AL), a team that won the World Series, and returned to the Athletics as a coach. He became their manager in 1951, but was fired by Earle Mack after three lackluster seasons. Later he managed the Baltimore Orioles (AL, 1954), Cincinnati Reds (NL, 1958), Detroit Tigers (AL, 1959–1960), and Cleveland Indians (AL, 1960–1961). As a manager, he won 1,406 games while losing 1,541 contests. Winning without good players, Dykes contended, was like trying to steal first base. An old-fashioned manager who did not believe in the platoon system, he considered the players of his day more dedicated and skilled than those he managed. Dykes also coached with the Cincinnati Reds (1955–1958), the Pittsburgh Pirates (NL, 1959), Milwaukee Braves (NL, 1962), and Kansas City Athletics (AL, 1963–1964). Dykes retired to Philadelphia in the mid-1960s to enjoy the role of baseball's elder statesman. His autobiography, *You Can't Steal First*, includes charming anecdotes and stories about the stars of the 1920s. After his first wife died in the early 1970s, he married Mildred Boyle.

BIBLIOGRAPHY: Jimmie Dykes file, National Baseball Library, Cooperstown, NY; Jimmie Dykes and Charles O. Dexter, *You Can't Steal First* (New York, 1967); Donald Honig, *The Man in the Dugout* (Lincoln, NE, 1995); Brent P. Kelley, *The Case For: Those Overlooked by the Baseball Hall of Fame* (Jefferson, NC, 1992); Frederick G. Lieb, *Connie Mack* (New York, 1945); Warren Brown, *The Chicago White Sox* (New York, 1952); Connie Mack, *My 66 Years in the Big Leagues* (Philadelphia, PA, 1950); *NYT*, January 16, 1976; "Sox Retain Dykes," *TSN*, July 27, 1944.

Anthony J. Papalas

DYKSTRA, Leonard Kyle "Lenny," "Nails" (b. February 10, 1963, Santa Ana, CA), player, is the grandson of NHL player Pete Leswick and graduated from Garden Grove High School. The New York Mets (NL) selected the 5-foot 10-inch, 188-pound outfielder in the 12th round of the June 1981 draft. Dykstra, who bats and throws left-handed, performed over four minor league seasons with Shelby, TN (SAL) in 1981 and 1982, Lynchburg, VA (CrL) in 1983, Jackson, TX (TL) in 1984, and Tidewater, VA (IL) in 1985.

Dykstra, primarily a singles lead-off hitter, joined the New York Mets in 1985 and homered against the Cincinnati Reds in his first major league at bat. After batting .295 in 1986, he demonstrated unusual power in the NL

Championship Series against the Houston Astros. His dramatic ninth-inning HR won Game 1, while his triple ignited a ninth-inning rally to tie Game 6. Dykstra drove in the winning run in the 16th inning to clinch the NL pennant. He batted .296 with two HR and three RBI, helping the New York Mets capture the World Series against the Boston Red Sox. The Mets won the NL East Division in 1988. Dykstra hit .429 with three doubles, one HR, and three RBI in the NL Championship Series against the Los Angeles Dodgers.

In June 1989, the Mets traded Dykstra to the Philadelphia Phillies (NL). He batted a career-best .325 in 1990, leading the NL with 192 hits and a .420 on-base percentage and starting for the NL All-Star team. In March 1991, commissioner Faye Vincent placed him on one-year probation for losing $78,000 in gambling to card shark Herbert Kelso. An automobile accident in Radnor Township, PA nearly killed him two months later, as he broke a cheekbone, collar bone, and three ribs.

In 1993, Dykstra batted .305 and paced the NL in runs (143), hits (194), and walks (129) to make *TSN* All-Star and Silver Slugger teams. Barry Bonds* edged him in the NL MVP balloting. Dykstra's two solo HR helped Philadelphia upset the Atlanta Braves in the NL Championship Series. He hit .348 with four HR and eight RBI in the World Series loss to the Toronto Blue Jays. Injuries limited his playing time thereafter, although he made the 1994 and 1995 NL All-Star teams. He missed the entire 1997 and 1998 seasons and retired in November 1998.

In 12 major league seasons Dykstra batted .285 with 1,298 hits, 81 HR, 404 RBI, and 285 stolen bases. The tough, aggressive competitor, whose diving, sliding catches made him a fan favorite, slammed into walls and slid head first. He fielded .987 and led the NL in total chances and putouts in 1990 and 1993. The Devon, PA resident married Terri Peel and has two sons, Gavin and Cutter.

BIBLIOGRAPHY: Lenny Dykstra file, National Baseball Library, Cooperstown, NY; Len Dykstra and Marty Noble, *Nails* (New York, 1987); *NYT Biographical Service* 22 (May 1991), pp. 508–509; Charles Pierce, "The Phanatic Phillie," *SI* 76 (May 11, 1992), pp. 62–64, 66, 71; Jayson Stark, "Lenny Dykstra," *Sport* 85 (July 1994), pp. 28–30; I. Thomsen, "Oo-la-la," *SI* 79 (December 6, 1993), pp. 44–47; Rick Weinberg, "The Pepper Martin of the 90s: Len Dykstra," *Sport* 82 (July 1991), pp. 56–57; Rich Westcott and Frank Bilovsky, *The New Phillies Encyclopedia* (Philadelphia, PA, 1993); Steve Wulf, "Off and Running," *SI* 72 (June 4, 1990), pp. 28–30, 33; *TSN Baseball Register*, 1997; *Philadelphia Phillies Media Guide*, 1997.

David L. Porter

E

EASTERLING, Howard (b. November 26, 1911, Mount Olive, MS; d. September 6, 1993, Collins, MS), player, excelled as a versatile, switch-hitting infielder with the Homestead, PA Grays (NNL) from 1940 through 1943 and 1946 to 1947. A complete ballplayer, he could run, throw, field, hit, and hit with power. The 5-foot 10-inch, 175-pounder, a five-time All-Star during his 14-year career in the Negro Leagues, batted .320 in the East-West classics. He was selected to the West squad as a shortstop in 1937 and to the East squad as a third baseman in 1940, 1943, 1946, and 1949.

A consistent hitter, Easterling began his professional baseball career with the Cincinnati, OH Tigers (NAL) with batting averages of .326 in 1936 and .386 in 1937. In 1940, the star infielder joined the Homestead Grays and generated some offense to help compensate for the loss of Josh Gibson* to the MEL.

In Easterling's first four years with the Grays, Homestead won the NNL pennant each year. Easterling contributed batting averages of .358, .307, .226, and .451 those seasons. Easterling, who usually batted either third in front of the power tandem of Gibson and Buck Leonard* or fifth behind the pair of sluggers, also hit the long ball. The star third sacker made six hits in 10 at bats in a crucial doubleheader during the 1941 League Championship Series victory over the New York Cubans. The first World Series between the NAL and the NNL was played in 1942, with Easterling hitting .332 and clouting a HR. The Homestead Grays, however, were swept by the Kansas City, MO Monarchs. In 1943, Easterling's last season before entering the Army in World War II, the Homestead Grays defeated the Birmingham, AL Black Barons in the World Series to reign as champions of black baseball.

After two years of military service, Easterling batted .310 for the Homestead Grays in 1946 and closed out his Negro League career with a .302

average for the New York Cubans in 1949. He extended his playing career with Monterrey, Mexico (MEL), batting .323 in 1951 and .379 in 1953. He also played in the VWL, where he topped the circuit in both HR and doubles.

BIBLIOGRAPHY: *Jet* 84 (October 4, 1993), p. 50; Robert W. Peterson, *Only the Ball Was White* (Englewood Cliffs, NJ, 1970); Pittsburgh (PA) *Courier*, 1936–1948; James A. Riley, *The All-Time All-Stars of Black Baseball* (Cocoa, FL, 1983); James A. Riley, interviews with former Negro League players, James A. Riley Collection, Canton, GA; James A. Riley, *The Biographical Encyclopedia of the Negro Baseball Leagues* (New York, 1994); Mike Shatzkin, ed., *The Ballplayers* (New York, 1990); *The Baseball Encyclopedia*, 10th ed. (New York, 1996).

James A. Riley

EASTMAN, Jean Anna Faut Winsch (b. November 17, 1925, East Greenville, PA), player, ranked among the premier AAGPBL players, hurling two perfect games. The daughter of Robert Faut, an automobile plant worker and park guard, and Eva (Gebert) Faut, she pitched batting practice for the East Greeville High School team and also threw in exhibition games. Unlike most AAGPBL players, she never played softball while growing up. She hurled batting practice for the East Greenville semiprofessional team in the strong EPL, a haven for former major leaguers.

After graduating from East Greenville High School in 1942, Eastman worked in a clothing factory until 1946 and then tried out for the AAGPBL in Pascagoula, MS. The outstanding prospect played from 1946 to 1953 for the South Bend, IN Blue Sox (AAGPBL) as a pitcher, third baseman, and outfielder. She started out as a third baseman because of her strong arm, but began pitching in 1946.

Although an excellent pitcher in her first two years with South Bend, Eastman reached her full potential in 1948. The AAGPBL in 1948 permitted overhand and sidearm pitching and reduced the size of the ball to 10¾ inches in 1948 and to 10 inches in 1949. The smaller ball and overhand delivery made her curve balls more effective.

From 1946 through 1953, Eastman appeared in 235 games as a pitcher and 334 contests as an outfielder or third baseman. She won 140 decisions and lost only 64 with a 1.23 ERA, tossing perfect games on July 21, 1951 against Rockford, IL and September 3, 1953, and recording 12 shutouts in 1949. Eastman led the AAGPBL in ERA with 1.12 in 1950, 0.93 in 1952, and 1.51 in 1953. In eight seasons, she surrendered only 403 runs (243 earned) in 1,780 innings for a 1.23 ERA. Eastman fanned 913 batters and walked 589. She won at least 20 games three times, finishing 24–8 in 1949, 21–9 in 1950, and 20–2 in 1952. Eastman led South Bend to Shaughnessy Playoff Championships in 1951 and 1952. She ranks first in career ERA, second in career victories and led the AAGPBL in wins and strikeouts three times. Her .909 winning percentage led the AAGPBL in 1952.

Eastman batted .243 with 391 hits, 203 RBI, and 180 runs scored. She drew 230 walks and struck out only 100 times. In the final game of the 1952 championship series against the Rockford Peaches, Eastman hurled the victory and hit two triples. She batted .348 for the series. Eastman, the AAGPBL's Player of the Year in 1951 and 1953, made all-star teams in 1949, 1950, 1951, and 1953.

After retiring from baseball, Eastman became a professional bowler. The 5- foot 4-inch, 137-pound right-handed pitcher and hitter, an all-around athlete, starred in field hockey and basketball in high school and excels as a recreational golfer.

Before the 1947 season, Eastman married Karl Winsch from East Greenville. Winsch had pitched in the Philadelphia Phillies (NL) farm system and later managed the South Bend Blue Sox. Her marriage to the South Bend manager caused dissension among players and led to a walkout by six players in 1952. They had two sons, Larry and Kevin, before their 1968 divorce. In 1977 the Rock Hill, SC resident married Charles Eastman. He died in 1993.

BIBLIOGRAPHY: AAGPBL files, Northern Indiana Historical Society, South Bend, IN; Lois Browne, *Girls of Summer in Their Own League* (New York, 1993); Margot F. Galt, *Up to the Plate* (Minneapolis, MN, 1994); Trudy Hammer, *The All-American Girls Professional Baseball League* (New York, 1994); Susan F. Johnson, *When Women Played Hardball* (Seattle, WA, 1994); W. C. Madden, *The Women of the All-American Girls Professional Baseball League* (Jefferson, NC, 1997); Jim Sargent, "Jean Faut: The All American League's Greatest Overhand Pitcher," *RB* 2 (March 1996), pp. 30–32, 34, 36, 38.

Ralph S. Graber

EBBETS, Charles Hercules "Charlie" (b. October 29, 1859, New York, NY; d. April 18, 1925, New York, NY), owner, attended New York public schools and graduated with high honors. A trained draftsman and architect, he designed many New York buildings. He published novels, which he sold door to door, and sold tickets to baseball games with the same entrepreneurial zest. He also served on the Brooklyn City Council for four years and in the state assembly one year.

Ebbets, who epitomized the generation of owner–sportsmen dominating the game at the turn of the century, became a minor stockholder of the Brooklyn Bridegrooms (NL) club in 1890. He soon developed a fondness for marketing the game and making it a family sport. Ebbets assumed control of the club in 1898, although it is not clear when he became the principal owner. By 1902, he fully controlled the club's activities.

Ebbets, who managed Brooklyn to a 38–68 record and a tenth place finish in 1898, made little impact on the game with his field experience. His enterpreneurial outlook made him one of the more imaginative early leaders of American baseball. He is credited with originating the rain check, proposing that the worst teams should draft first, and espousing that World

Series dates should be fixed to a permanent schedule. During World War I, his teams played charity matches for the benefit of widows and orphans. Ebbets also used these games successfully as a device to challenge laws that prohibited Sunday play.

In perhaps his most important contribution, Ebbets in 1912 sold 50 percent of the stock in the Brooklyn Dodgers to build a spacious new park for the team in Flatbush. Ebbets Field symbolized civic pride and community development centered around a sports franchise and became a model emulated thereafter in American sports history.

Ebbets married twice, his first wife being Minnie F. A. Ebbets. They had four children, one son and three daughters, but the marriage ended in divorce around 1920. Ebbets grew attached to Mrs. Grace Slade, who in 1922 became his second wife. His estate, which consisted principally of his ownership of the Dodgers, was valued at $1.25 million when he died of heart failure.

BIBLIOGRAPHY: Charles Ebbets file, National Baseball Library, Cooperstown, NY; Richard C. Crepeau, *Baseball: America's Diamond Mind 1919–1941* (Orlando, FL, 1980); Joseph Durso, *Casey: The Life and Legend of Charles Dillon Stengel* (Englewood Cliffs, NJ, 1967); Richard Goldstein, *Superstars and Screwballs* (New York, 1991); Peter Golenbock, *Bums* (New York, 1984); Frank Graham, *The Brooklyn Dodgers* (New York, 1945); William F. McNeil, *The Dodgers Encyclopedia* (Champaign, IL, 1997); Richard Goldstein, *Spartan Seasons: How Baseball Survived the Second World War* (New York, 1980); Gene Karst and Martin J. Jones, Jr., *Who's Who in Professional Baseball* (New Rochelle, NY, 1973); *NYT*, January 11, May 10, 1922, April 19, 1925.

Charles R. Middleton

ECKERSLEY, Dennis Lee "Eck" (b. October 3, 1954, Oakland, CA), player and sportscaster, one of three children of Wallace Eckersley, a warehouse supervisor, graduated from Washington High School in Fremont, CA, where he excelled in football, basketball, and baseball. The Cleveland Indians (AL) selected the intense, hard-throwing, 6-foot 2-inch, 190-pound right-hander in the third round of the 1972 free agent draft. The affable sidearmer spent the 1972 and 1973 seasons with Reno, NV (CaL) and 1974 with San Antonio, TX (TL).

Eckersley joined the Cleveland Indians (AL) in 1975, compiling an excellent 13–7 record and 2.60 ERA and earning *TSN* Rookie Pitcher of the Year honors. He shut out the World Champion Oakland A's in his initial start and did not surrender his first run until his 29th inning, setting a rookie record. A career-high 200 strikeouts in 199 innings highlighted his 1976 campaign, while two one-hitters and a 1–0 no-hitter against the California Angels on May 30 headlined his 1977 season. His 22.1 consecutive hitless innings that year ranks him second all-time to Cy Young.*

Eckersley was traded to the Boston Red Sox (AL) in March 1978 and enjoyed his best year as a starter with a 20–8 record and a 2.99 ERA. He led the AL in victories with 16 through early August 1979, but then slumped to a 17–10 slate. Eckersley struggled the next few seasons with arm problems and alcohol addiction. In May 1984, the Boston Red Sox traded him to the Chicago Cubs (NL). Chicago captured the NL East Division title in 1984, as Eckersley won 10 of 18 decisions. Eckersley lost Game 3 of the NL Championship Series to the San Diego Padres and soon suffered shoulder tendinitis. In January 1987, he entered a treatment center to help him overcome his alcohol dependency.

The Oakland A's (AL) acquired Eckersley in April 1987 and converted him into a premier relief pitcher. Eckersley combined excellent control, competitive instincts, and an obsession with physical fitness in 1988 to enjoy his best major league season. The Oakland A's captured the AL pennant, as Eckersley compiled a 4–2 record, 2.35 ERA, struck out nearly one batter per inning, and led the AL with 45 regular season saves. He established a major league Championship Series record by saving all four victories in the sweep of the Boston Red Sox, but surrendered the dramatic two-run homer to Kirk Gibson* of the Los Angeles Dodgers in Game 1 of the World Series. Nevertheless, Eckersley was named the 1988 AL Fireman of the Year and finished second in the AL Cy Young Award balloting. Despite injuries, Eckersley in 1989 still saved 33 games, won all four decisions, and compiled a stellar 1.56 ERA. He recorded three saves in the AL Championship Series triumph over the Toronto Blue Jays and saved one game in the World Series sweep over the San Francisco Giants. The 1990 season saw him save 48 games, with a 4–2 record and brilliant 0.61 ERA. Eckersley saved two games in the AL Championship Series sweep of the Boston Red Sox and made two brief World Series appearances against the victorious Cincinnati Reds. He in 1991 became the first AL pitcher to record at least 40 saves three different seasons. He also made the 1977, 1982, 1988, 1990, 1991, and 1992 AL All-Star teams, being the losing pitcher in the 1982 contest and saving the 1990 game.

In 1992, Eckersley compiled a 7–1 record with a 1.91 ERA and led the AL with a career-high 51 saves. He saved one game in three AL Championship Series appearances against the Toronto Blue Jays and won both the BBWAA AL MVP and AL Cy Young awards. Eckersley saved 36 games in 1993 and remained with the Oakland A's through the 1995 season. In February 1996, the Oakland A's traded Eckersley to the St. Louis Cardinals (NL) and reunited him with manager Tony La Russa.* He saved 30 games in 1996 and all three in the NL Division Series against the San Diego Padres. Eckersley combined one victory and one save in the NL Championship Series against the Atlanta Braves. He holds the Championship Series career (11) and single-season (4) records for most saves. The Boston Red Sox (AL) signed him as a free agent in December 1997. Eckersley won four of five decisions as a setup man for Tom Gordon, helping the Boston Red Sox win the Wild Card in 1998. He hurled one inning in the 1998 Division Series against the Cleveland Indians.

Eckersley, who retired in December 1998, compiled 197 wins and 171 losses (.535) in 1,071 regular season games, struck out 2,401 batters in 3,285.2 innings, saved 390 games, and boasted a 3.50 ERA. He holds AL records for most saves (328) and most consecutive errorless games by a pitcher (from May 1, 1987 to May 4, 1995) and Oakland career records for lowest ERA (2.74), most games pitched (525), and most saves (320).

Eckersley married Denise Jacinto on April 11, 1973 and had one daughter, Mandee, before their September 1978 divorce. Eckersley, who resides in Sudbury, MA, wed actress Nancy O'Neil in 1980 and serves as a color analyst for the Oakland A's.

BIBLIOGRAPHY: Dennis Eckersley file, National Baseball Library, Cooperstown, NY; John Benson et al., *Baseball's Top 100* (Wilton, CT, 1997); Ed Lucas and Paul Post, "Ecklersley's Collection Includes Yaz, McGuire," *SCD* 25 (December 25, 1998), pp. 126–127; Mike Bryan, *Baseball Lives* (New York, 1989); Eddie Gold and Art Ahrens, *The New Era Cubs, 1941–1985* (Chicago, IL, 1985); Peter Golenbock, *Fenway* (New York, 1992); Peter Gammons, "One Eck of a Guy," *SI* 69 (December 12, 1988), pp. 50–52, 54, 59; Chuck Greenwood, "The Save Master," *SCD* 25 (April 17, 1998), p. 130; Robert Redmount, *The Red Sox Encyclopedia* (Champaign, IL, 1998); Bob Cairns, *Pen Men* (New York, 1993); John Krich, "Beers With Dennis Eckersley: When Piece Brings the Cheese, It's Iron for the A's," *Sport* 79 (November 1988), pp. 15–17; W. A. Plummer et al., "A Saving Grace," *PW* 38 (October 12, 1992), pp. 137–138; *TSN Official Baseball Register*, 1976–1998; Harry Stein, "Dennis Eckersley's Sweet, Sad Season," *Sport* 68 (March 1979), pp. 34–35, 38–39; Richard Topp letter to David L. Porter, February 8, 1990; Steve Wulf, "The Paintmaster," *SI* 77 (August 24, 1992), pp. 62–66.

David L. Porter

ECKERT, William Dole "Spike" (b. January 20, 1909, Freeport, IL; d. April 16, 1971, Freeport, Grand Bahamas), executive, was the son of Frank Lloyd Eckert and Harriet Julia (Rudy) Eckert. After his graduation from high school in Madison, IN, he attended the U.S. Military Academy at West Point from 1926 to 1930. He married Catherine Douglas Givens on June 15, 1940; they had a son, William, and a daughter, Catherine. He also earned a Master's degree in business administration from the Harvard School of Business in 1940. Eckert enjoyed a distinguished career in the US Army Air Corps, serving as commander of the 452nd Bomber Group in Europe in World War II. He earned several awards, including the Distinguished Flying Cross and Distinguished Service Medal, and retired as Comptroller of the Air Force in 1961.

An organization man with executive ability, Eckert was chosen Commissioner of Baseball on November 15, 1965. His selection surprised the baseball world because he had not sought the position. The 5 foot 8 inch, 160 pound Eckert was an affable man known for his moderation. He proved completely ineffectual as commissioner and became "a striking symbol of baseball's blandness and resistance to change" in the mid-1960s. From the outset, Eckert's real skill as an administrator could not mask his lack of ideas on how to promote the sport.

In 1968, Eckert incurred the ire of the public by not cancelling league games after the assassinations of Robert Kennedy and Martin Luther King. More important, perhaps, he did not deal forcefully with the league presidents and thereby proved that the Commissioner's Office did not control the game. When the threat of a player's strike emerged in early 1969, therefore, the owners acted. Eckert was removed from office on February 3, 1969, although his contract had three years left. Two years later, he died on the tennis court of a heart attack.

BIBLIOGRAPHY: William Eckert file, National Baseball Library, Cooperstown, NY; Jerome Holtzman, *The Commissioners* (New York, 1998); Gene Karst and Martin J. Jones, Jr., *Who's Who in Professional Baseball* (New Rochelle, NY, 1973); "General Who?" *Newsweek* 66 (November 29, 1965), p. 62; "Baseball's Palace Revolt," *Newsweek* 72 (December 16, 1968), pp. 71–72; *NYT*, April 17, 1971; John Underwood, "Progress Report on the Unknown Soldier," *SI* 24 (April 4, 1966), pp. 40–42ff; William Leggett, "Court Martial for a General," 29 (December 16, 1968), pp. 24–25; *WWA*, 35th ed. (1968–1969), p. 655.

Charles R. Middleton

ELBERFELD, Norman Arthur "Kid," "Tabasco Kid" (b. April 13, 1875, Pomeroy, OH; d. January 13, 1944, Chattanooga, TN), player and manager, was considered the most aggressive player in the AL's first decade. Born to German-American parents, Elberfeld grew up in Pomeroy, OH, Mason City, WV, and Cincinnati, OH. He found school boring and quit between grades four and eight.

The 5-foot 7-inch, 138-pound Elberfeld played amateur baseball in Cincinnati, but attracted little attention. He joined a semiprofessional team in Clarksville, TN in 1895, acquiring the nickname "Kid" for his small stature. His pro baseball career blossomed as a third baseman with Richmond, VA (AL), where he batted .335 in 1897. Although having brief trials with the Pittsburgh Pirates (NL) in 1898 and Cincinnati Reds (NL) in 1899, he performed with Detroit (WL) in 1898 and 1899 and the Detroit Tigers (AL) from 1900 to 1903.

Elberfeld batted .308 in 1901 and .301 in 1903, while the little shortstop's scrappy style of play and desire to win earned him a reputation as the John McGraw* of the AL. He admired McGraw, the New York Giants (NL) manager, and wished to play for him. Contemporaries noted his knack of being purposely hit by a pitch and his arguments with umpires and fans.

Elberfeld, however, was traded in June 1903 to the New York Highlanders

(AL). New York sportswriter Sam Crane dubbed him "The Tabasco Kid" because of "the life and ginger he puts into the game." Elberfeld was often ejected from games and argued with his own managers and umpires. The New York Highlanders just missed winning the AL pennant in 1904, but never again came close. "The Kid" injured his knee in a collision with a teammate in 1905 and experienced recurring leg problems thereafter. Injuries limited Elberfeld to 19 games in 1908, the same year he managed New York to a 27–71 record. His major league managerial career ended following the 1908 season. In 1909, his limited range caused his shift to third base and his December 1909 trade to the Washington Nationals (AL).

Elberfeld spent two solid seasons with the Washington Nationals before injuries ended his major league career. During his major league career, he batted .271 with 1,235 hits and 535 RBI in 1,292 games. Washington sold him to Chattanooga, TN (SA) in 1912. He established the Chattanooga area as his home. He and his wife, Emily Grace (Catlow) Elberfeld, who he had married in 1900, brought up five daughters and a son on their Signal Mountain farm. The daughters gained fame in the 1920s for their athletic prowess. *New York Sun* writer Will Wedge rhymed: "A mighty mite, that Elberfeld,/ His boys were mostly girls;/The Kid was father of a team/That swept the field in curls."

Elberfeld continued in baseball for 30 years after leaving Washington. He batted .332 as player–manager for Chattanooga in 1913. The Brooklyn Dodgers (NL) signed him as a player–coach for 1914. Between 1915 and 1938, Elberfeld managed in the minor leagues at Chattanooga (SA), Little Rock, AR (SA), Mobile, AL (SA), Springfield, MO (WA), Gadsden, AL (SEL), and Fulton, KY (KL). In the 1930s, he also conducted baseball clinics for the American Legion and operated his own baseball schools.

BIBLIOGRAPHY: Norman Elberfeld file, National Baseball Library, Cooperstown, NY; Frank Graham, *The New York Yankees* (New York, 1943); Harry "Steamboat" Johnson, *Standing the Gaff* (Lincoln, NE, 1995); Frederick G. Lieb, *The Detroit Tigers* (New York, 1946); Bill O'Neal, *The Southern League: Baseball in Dixie, 1885–1994* (Austin, TX, 1994); Lawrence S. Ritter, *The Glory of Their Times* (New York, 1966); Fred Smith, *995 Tigers* (Detroit, MI, 1981); Mark Gallagher, *The Yankee Encyclopedia*, vol. 3 (Champaign, IL, 1997); William M. Anderson, *The Detroit Tigers* (South Bend, IN, 1996); Shirley Povich, *The Washington Senators* (New York, 1954).

                                                                    William E. Akin

ELLIOTT, Robert Irving "Bob," "Mr. Team" (b. November 26, 1916, San Francisco, CA; d. May 4, 1966, San Diego, CA), player and manager, grew up in El Centro, CA. The son of a plaster plant superintendent, Elliott attended Harding Grammar School, Wilson Junior High, Union High School, and El Centro JC before signing with the Pittsburgh Pirates (NL). In March 1938 he married Iva Reah Skipper, whom he had known since junior high school days; they had two daughters. After outstanding minor league seasons at Savannah, GA (SAL), Knoxville, TN (SA), Louisville, KY (AA), and Toronto, Canada (IL), the 6-foot, 185-pound, right-handed Elliott played with the Pittsburgh Pirates from 1939 through 1946. He participated in the 1941, 1942, 1944, and 1948 All-Star games. An outstanding clutch hitter, Elliott drove in over 100 runs from 1943 through 1945. He moved from the outfield to third base to help his team and developed into a wide-ranging fielder. From 1942 through 1944, he led NL third basemen in assists and errors.

After being traded to the Boston Braves (NL) in September 1946, Elliott batted .317, slugged 22 HR, made 113 RBI, and led the NL in fielding. He became the first third baseman ever chosen the NL MVP. In 1948, Elliott helped lead the Braves' drive to the NL pennant. Nicknamed "Mr. Team," Elliott paced the Braves in RBI (100), runs scored (99), HR (23), and walks (an NL-leading 131), and struck out only 57 times. Although the Braves lost the World Series, Elliott batted .333 and hit two consecutive HR against Bob Feller* of the Cleveland Indians in the fifth game.

On September 4, 1949, Elliott belted three HR in one game. He left the Braves after the 1951 campaign and played the next two seasons with the New York Giants (NL), St. Louis Browns (AL), and Chicago White Sox (AL). From 1939 through 1953, he made 2,061 major league hits, knocked in 1,195 runs, slugged 382 doubles and 170 HR, and compiled a career .289 batting average. Elliott managed San Diego, CA (PCL) and Sacramento, CA (PCL) from 1955 through 1959, piloted the last place Kansas City Athletics (AL) in 1960, and coached for the Los Angeles Angels (AL) in 1961. He later worked for a beer distributor and died of a ruptured vein in his windpipe.

BIBLIOGRAPHY: Bob Elliott file, National Baseball Library, Cooperstown, NY; Gary Caruso, *The Braves Encyclopedia* (Philadelphia, PA, 1995); Richard L. Burtt, *The Pittsburgh Pirates, A Pictorial History* (Virginia Beach, VA, 1977); Bob Smizik, *The Pittsburgh Pirates: An Illustrated History* (New York, 1990); Frederick G. Lieb, *The Pittsburgh Pirates* (New York, 1948); Harold Kaese, *The Boston Braves* (New York, 1948); *The Baseball Encyclopedia*, 10th ed. (New York, 1996); John Thorn et al., eds., *Total Braves* (New York, 1996); Frank Waldman, *Famous American Athletes of Today*, 11th series (Boston, MA, 1949).

Sheldon L. Appleton

ENGLISH, Elwood George "Woody" (b. March 2, 1907, Fredonia, OH; d. September 26, 1997, Newark, OH), player, was the son of Wilbur English and Gladys (Carpenter) English. He developed an early interest in baseball from his father, who sponsored a local grocery store team. English began his baseball career in 1923, when he joined an amateur team of a local rubber company in Newark, OH. After playing in a Sunday league in nearby Zanesville, OH the following year, he signed his first professional baseball contract with Toledo, OH (AA). In his first season as the Mud Hens' shortstop in

1925, English hit only .220 and sparkled defensively. With the help of Toledo pilot Casey Stengel,* English raised his batting average the next year to .301 in 162 games. The Chicago Cubs (NL), at the urging of manager Joe McCarthy,* signed English in 1926 to a contract reportedly exceeding $30,000.

English, who batted and threw right-handed, made his major-league debut as the Chicago Cubs' shortstop in 1927. He batted a respectable .290 in 87 games that season and improved to a .299 mark in 1928. English combined in 1929 with newly acquired second baseman Rogers Hornsby* to give the Chicago Cubs a solid double-play combination, batting .276 and scoring 131 runs for the NL pennant-bound Cubs. But he batted only .190 in the World Series, as the Chicago Cubs lost to the Philadelphia Athletics in five games. English enjoyed his best season offensively in 1930, when he batted .335, scored 152 runs, and collected 214 hits, including 36 doubles, 17 triples, and 14 HR. Hornsby, the Cubs manager, made English team captain in 1931. English responded with a .319 batting average, 202 hits, and 117 runs scored.

In 1932, English moved to third base to make room for shortstop Billy Jurges* and helped the Chicago Cubs capture the NL flag. In the World Series, however, the New York Yankees swept Chicago in four games, and English hit just .176. When rookie Stan Hack* started at third base in 1934, English was relegated to a utility role. In December 1936, Chicago traded him to the Brooklyn Dodgers (NL). As the Dodgers' regular shortstop the next season, English batted .238. Brooklyn sold him in July 1938 to the Cincinnati Reds (NL), but he refused to report. After an unsuccessful comeback attempt with the Chicago Cubs in 1939, English remained there. He operated a saloon there and managed a local Bloomer Girls ball club.

In 10 seasons with the Chicago Cubs, the popular 5-foot 10-inch, 155-pound leadoff batter batted a composite .290. The Cubs finished lower than third place only once during that span. English, who led NL shortstops in putouts (322) in 1931 and NL third basemen in fielding percentage (.973) in 1933, played in the first All-Star Game, held at Comiskey Park in Chicago in 1933. During 12 major league seasons, he batted .286 with 1,356 hits and 422 RBI.

English, who married Helen Alice Golan in 1930 and Isodene Schaf in July 1938, resided in Newark, OH. His uncle, Paul Carpenter, pitched five games for the Pittsburgh Pirates (NL) in 1916.

BIBLIOGRAPHY: Elwood G. English file, National Baseball Library, Cooperstown, NY; "Former All-Star Infielder Woody English," *SCD* 24 (October 24, 1997), p. 10; Eddie Gold and Art Ahrens, *The Golden Era Cubs, 1876–1940* (Chicago, IL, 1985); Norman Macht, "Woody English Insists—The Babe Didn't Point," *BRJ* 20 (1991), pp. 67–68; Charles C. Alexander, *Rogers Hornsby: A Biography* (New York, 1995); Warren Brown, *The Chicago Cubs* (New York, 1946); Warren Wilbert and William Hageman, *Chicago Cubs: Seasons at the Summit* (Champaign, IL, 1997); Jim Enright,

Chicago Cubs (New York, 1975); John Thorn et al., eds., *Total Baseball*, 5th ed. (New York, 1997).

Raymond D. Kush

ENGLISH, Madeline Catherine "Maddy" (b. February 22, 1925, Everett, MA), player, is the daughter of Ambrose Tobias English, a pipe-fitter and longtime Everett city official, and Anna (Henneberry) English. She attended parochial grammar schools and graduated from Everett High School. Although there were no organized girls interscholastic sports, English began participating in pickup softball games at age ten on Boston area playgrounds. Her older brother, Edward, a high school star third baseman, saw his major league aspirations dashed by lengthy war service. English, likewise a third baseman, possessed a strong throwing arm and an aggressive style. In 1939 she made a Massachusetts 14-year-old softball team, which competed against opponents from Connecticut and New York in summer exhibitions. English and her Bay State teammates, coached by Boston Bruins (NHL) hockey players, played their home games on the concrete floor of the Boston Garden.

English's strong play in the 1939 exhibitions and a high school friend's recommendation impressed Chicago Cubs (NL) scout Ralph Wheeler, who invited her to try out for the AAGPBL. Cubs owner Philip Wrigley* had founded the AAGPBL in 1943. Upon surviving the tryout at Wrigley Field in Chicago, the 5-foot 4-inch, 130-pound English, who batted and threw right-handed, joined the Racine, WI Belles, one of four original AAGPBL teams. Batting second in the order and anchoring third base for eight years from 1943 to 1950, English helped the Belles win three pennants and AAGPBL championships in 1943 and 1946 and was selected an All-Star in 1946 and 1948. The highly regarded fielder and baserunner tied an AAGPBL record by stealing seven bases in a 1947 game, but also chipped in with her share of clutch hits as a batter. Her double drove in the winning run in the 14th inning of the first game of a best-of-five playoff series with the South Bend, IN Blue Sox in 1946. Racine defeated South Bend, three games to one, and then topped the Rockford, IL Peaches for the AAGPBL title. The excellent fielding third baseman was noted primarily for her defense, with an .896 fielding percentage, 1,439 putouts, 2,255 assists, and 106 double plays. English, who batted .171 lifetime, enjoyed her best offensive season in 1948 with 95 hits, including five HR, eight triples, 16 doubles, and a .231 batting average. When the Racine franchise moved to Battle Creek, MI in 1950, she played in another women's league in Chicago for two seasons. After returning to Massachusetts and waiting the required two years to regain her amateur status, she served as player–manager of an all-star softball team in Lynn, MA for five years.

English worked as a recreation leader in Everett, MA and attended Boston

University evenings and Saturdays during the off-season. She earned her B.S. degree in education in 1957 and a Masters degree in 1962. After spending 10 years as a classroom and physical education teacher and 17 years as a guidance counselor at Parlin Junior High School in Everett, English retired in 1984. She resides in Everett and regularly attends the biennial reunions of the AAGPBL players.

BIBLIOGRAPHY: Richard Gentile, Telephone interviews with Maddy English, July 2, 8, 1996; W. C. Madden, *The Women of the All-American Girls Professional Baseball League* (Jefferson, NC, 1997); Gai Berlage, *Women in Baseball* (Westport, CT, 1994); Barbara Gregorich, *Women At Play* (San Diego, CA, 1993); Lois Browne, *Girls of Summer* (New York, 1993); Jack Fincher, "The 'Belles of the Ball Game' Were a Hit with Their Fans," *Smithsonian* 20 (July 1989), pp. 88–97.

Richard H. Gentile

ENNIS, Delmer "Del" (b. June 8, 1925, Philadelphia, PA; d. February 8, 1996, Huntingdon Valley, PA), player, grew up in the Olney section of Philadelphia. His father worked for the famous John B. Stetson Hat Company of Philadelphia. After graduation from Olney High School in 1943, Ennis signed with the Philadelphia Phillies (NL) and played with Trenton, NJ (ISL). He enjoyed a superb season there, hitting .346 with 18 HR and 93 RBI. In the U.S. Navy (1944–1945), he honed his baseball skills playing against Billy Herman,* Johnny Vander Meer,* and other major leaguers. In April 1946, he was discharged from the Navy and joined the Phillies roster. Although expecting assignment to the minor leagues again, he played outfield in 141 games for Philadelphia and won *TSN* Rookie of the Year Award. The 6-foot, 195-pound right-hander batted .313 with 17 HR, the latter a club rookie record for 18 years.

After a sluggish sophomore year, Ennis in 1948 belted 30 HR, batted .290, and knocked in 95 runs. From 1948 to 1950, he ranked among the top NL sluggers and as the best Phillies power hitter since Chuck Klein.* During that stretch, Ennis averaged 29 HR and 111 RBI and hit over .300. In 1950, he helped Philadelphia win the NL pennant and became the first Phillie since Klein to lead the NL in RBI with 126, a total no club member matched until Greg Luzinski* drove in 130 runs in 1977. Ennis set another Phillies record that year in August by driving in 41 runs in one month. After an off season in 1951, he enjoyed five straight excellent power years and again averaged over 25 HR and drove in over 100 runs per season. On the Phillies all-time list, Ennis ranks high in HR, RBI, extra-base hits, total bases, and doubles. His career 259 HR remained a club mark until broken by Mike Schmidt* in 1980. The remarkably durable Ennis missed only 64 games in 11 years with Philadelphia.

In November 1956 Ennis was traded to the St. Louis Cardinals (NL) for Rip Repulski and Bobby Morgan. After driving in 105 runs in 1957, he faded rapidly, was traded to the Cincinnati Reds (NL) in October 1958, and finished his career briefly with the Chicago White Sox (AL) in 1959. An average defensive left fielder, he compiled a .284 lifetime batting average, 358 doubles, 288 HR, and 1,284 RBI.

Ennis married Lenore Clear in February 1947. He lived in suburban Philadelphia with his second wife, Elizabeth, and had six grown children. For around three decades, he owned and managed a popular bowling alley, Del Ennis Lanes, in Huntingdon Valley, PA. He died of complications from diabetes.

BIBLIOGRAPHY: Del Ennis file, National Baseball Library, Cooperstown, NY; Frederick G. Lieb and Stan Baumgartner, *The Philadelphia Phillies* (New York, 1953); Rich Westcott and Frank Bilovsky, *The New Phillies Encyclopedia* (Philadelphia, PA, 1993); *NYT Biographical Service* 27 (February 1996), p. 289; Rich Westcott, *Diamond Greats* (Westport, CT, 1988); Bob Broeg and Jerry Vickery, *St. Louis Cardinals Encyclopedia* (Grand Rapids, MI, 1998); Robin Roberts and C. Paul Rogers III, *The Whiz Kids and the 1950 Pennant* (Philadelphia, PA, 1996); Harry Paxton, *The Whiz Kids* (New York, 1950).

John P. Rossi

ERSKINE, Carl Daniel "Oisk" (b. December 13, 1926, Anderson, IN), player, became a mainstay of the Brooklyn Dodgers (NL) and Los Angeles Dodgers (NL) pitching staffs. The star Anderson High School pitcher was drafted into the U.S. Navy in 1945. While Erskine still was in the Navy into 1946, general manager Branch Rickey* of the Brooklyn Dodgers signed him for a $3,500 bonus. Baseball Commissioner A. B. Chandler* declared Erskine a free agent because the Brooklyn Dodgers had violated the rule forbidding signing players while still in the armed forces. The Dodgers, though, were permitted to rebid for Erskine's services and signed him again for a $5,000 bonus.

Brooklyn assigned Erskine to Danville, IL (3IL) for a few 1946 games and the entire 1947 campaign. Erskine moved up to Fort Worth, TX (TL) in 1948 and in July was promoted to the Brooklyn Dodgers. In 1949, he again pitched for both Fort Worth and Brooklyn. His 8–1 mark, mostly in relief, helped the Brooklyn Dodgers win the 1949 NL pennant. Erskine began the 1950 season with Montreal, Canada (IL), but rejoined the Brooklyn Dodgers permanently later that year.

Erskine played an important role for Brooklyn's "Boys of Summer," who won five NL pennants and one World Series. Despite hurting his shoulder in his initial 1948 start, he endured the recurring pain. Erskine tossed no-hit games on June 19, 1952 against the Chicago Cubs and on May 12, 1956 against the New York Giants. A first inning walk denied him a perfect game against Chicago. On October 2, 1953, he broke the existing World Series games strikeout record by fanning 14 New York Yankees. The mark remained until Sandy Koufax* broke it with 16 in 1963. The Dodgers moved to Los Angeles in 1958. In 1959, Erskine retired after only 10 games.

Although only 5-feet 10-inches, the 165-pound right-hander possessed a great overhand curve. In 1,718.2 innings, he compiled a 122–78 record with 14 shutouts and a 4.00 ERA. Erskine fanned 981 batters while walking only 646. In 1953, he led the NL in winning percentage (.769) with a 20–6 record. Erskine pitched 41.2 innings in 11 World Series games with a 2–2 record. In his record-setting World Series game against the Yankees, he struck out slugger Mickey Mantle* all four times.

Erskine, who married Betsy Palmer on October 5, 1947 and has four children, Gary, Danny, Susan, and Jimmy, retired to his hometown to become a partner in an insurance firm and attended Anderson College. He served as a vice-president and director of the First National Bank of Anderson. Known for his courtesy, compassion, and clean living, Erskine was nicknamed "The Gentleman from Indiana" by Roscoe McGowen, *NYT* sportswriter.

BIBLIOGRAPHY: Carl Erskine file, National Baseball Library, Cooperstown, NY; T. S. O'Connell, "Oisk Recalls Dem Bums of Brooklyn," *SCD* 18 (May 24, 1991), pp. 100–102; Paul Green, *Forgotten Fields* (Waupaca, WI, 1984); Roger Kahn, *The Boys of Summer* (New York, 1971); Rich Marazzi, "1955: The 'Boys of Summer' Have Their October," *SCD* 22 (May 12, 1995), pp. 140–142; Paul Post, "Gone Fishing," *SCD* 24 (May 16, 1997), pp. 110–112; William F. McNeil, *The Dodgers Encyclopedia* (Champaign, IL, 1997); Peter Golenbock, *Bums* (New York, 1984); Richard Goldstein, *Superstars and Screwballs* (New York, 1991); Bill Madden, *The Hoosiers of Summer* (Indianapolis, IN, 1994); Dave Sabaini, "Indiana's Boy of Summer," *SCD* 15 (December 16, 1988), pp. 82–84; *TSN Baseball Register*, 1959.

Ralph S. Graber

EVANS, Darrell Wayne (b. May 26, 1947, Pasadena, CA), player, coach, and manager, grew up in a baseball environment. His father, Dick Evans, played semiprofessional baseball. His mother, Eleanor (Salazar) Evans, and an aunt starred in professional softball. His brother, Bob, grandfather, Dale Salazar, and an uncle all played minor league baseball. Evans starred in baseball and basketball both at Muir High School and Pasadena JC, leading the latter teams to junior college titles in both sports. He also attended California State University at Los Angeles for one year. On June 15, 1968, he married Sondra Jean Wigman, with whom he had a son, Derek. After their divorce, he married LaDonna Martin. They had three children, Stacy, Nicholas, and Chad.

The 6-foot 2-inch, 200-pound, left-handed–hitting, right-handed–throwing Evans is of Welsh, Spanish, and Mexican descent. After being signed by scout Bob Zuk for the Kansas City Athletics (AL), Evans began his professional baseball career in 1967 at third base with Peninsula, VA (CrL) and was named Player of the Year for Bradenton, FL (GCL). Subsequent stops included Leesburg, FL (FSL), Birmingham, AL (SL), Richmond, VA (IL), and Shreveport, LA (TL). He appeared briefly for the Atlanta Braves (NL) in 1969 and 1970 and became a regular in 1971.

In a 21-year major league career, his lifetime batting average ended at only .248. However, he drew 1,605 walks (leading the NL in 1973 and 1974), belted 414 HR, drove in 1,354 runs, and hit into only one double play per 66 at-bats. He probably ranked as the premier NL defensive third baseman during the mid-1970s, leading the NL in chances taken five times and setting an NL record for double plays by a third baseman (45 in 1974). His best year came in 1973, when he, Davey Johnson,* and Henry Aaron* each hit 40 or more HR for a fifth-place Braves team. The same year, he batted .281, drew 124 walks, slugged 41 HR, scored 114 runs, drove in 104 tallies, and played in the All-Star game. The Atlanta Braves traded Evans in June 1976 to the San Francisco Giants (NL), where he played through the 1983 season.

The Detroit Tigers (AL) signed Evans as a free agent in December 1983. He played first base and served as DH on their 1984 world championship team. He hit .300 in the AL Championship Series against the Kansas City Royals, but batted only .067 against the San Diego Padres in the World Series. In 1985, 38-year-old Evans topped the AL with 40 HR to become the first player to hit 40 HR in both leagues. Two years later, he became the oldest player to belt at least 34 HR in a season. Evans won the hearts of Detroit Tigers fans as a team leader of the 1987 Eastern Division champions. The Tigers released him in December 1988. Evans returned to the Atlanta Braves (NL) in 1989 for a last hurrah. He coached for the New York Yankees (AL) from 1990 through 1993, taught hitting at an instructional school in the Pasadena, CA area in 1994, served as a minor league hitting instructor for the New York Yankees in 1996, and managed Wilmington, NC (CrL) in 1998 and Huntsville, AL (SL) in 1999.

BIBLIOGRAPHY: William M. Anderson, *The Detroit Tigers* (South Bend, IN, 1996); Sparky Anderson and Dan Ewald, *Sparky* (New York, 1990); Richard Bak, *A Place for Summer* (Detroit, MI, 1998); *The Baseball Encyclopedia*, 10th ed. (New York, 1996); Darrell Evans file, National Baseball Library, Cooperstown, NY; Ron Fimrite, "A Specialist in Flying Objects," *SI* 64 (June 2, 1986), pp. 52ff; Ross Forman, "Darrell Evans: Patient at the Plate and as an Instructor," *SCD* 21 (December 2, 1994), p. 136; John Thorn et al., eds., *Total Baseball*, 5th ed. (New York, 1997).

Sheldon L. Appleton

EVANS, Dwight Michael "Dewey" (b. November 3, 1951, Santa Monica, CA), player and coach, is the son of Duff L. Evans and Maria A. (Baldwin) Evans and graduated from Chatsworth, CA, High School in 1969. The 6-foot 3-inch, 208-pound right-handed outfielder was selected by the Boston Red Sox (AL) in the fifth round of the 1969 free-agent draft and performed for Jamestown, NY (NYPL) in 1969, Greenville, SC (WCL) in 1970, and Winston-Salem, NC (CrL) in 1971. The IL selected Evans as its MVP with Louisville, KY (IL) in 1972.

Evans played mostly right field with the Boston Red Sox (AL) from September 1972 through 1990. During the 1970s, the injury-prone Evans struggled offensively and fielded superbly. Defensively, Evans possessed a very strong, accurate, throwing arm and often threw out runners trying to score or reach third base. The .987 lifetime fielder recorded an impressive 228 career assists and led AL outfielders in fielding percentage (.994) in 1976 and double plays (8) in 1975 and (7) 1980. *TSN* awarded Evans eight Gold Gloves (1976, 1978–1979, 1981–1985).

During the 1980s, Evans blossomed as a hitter under coach Walt Hrniak. In the strike-shortened 1981 season, he led the AL in both walks (85) and total bases (215) and shared the AL lead in HR (22). Between 1980 and 1984, Evans led the star-studded Red Sox four times in extra base hits and walks, three times in runs scored, doubles, triples, and slugging percentage, and twice in HR and RBI. In 1984 he belted 37 doubles and 32 HR, made a career-high 186 hits, led the AL in runs scored (121), and knocked in 104 runs. Jim Rice* and Tony Armas* joined Evans that year in becoming the first outfield trio since 1929 to drive in more than 100 runs each. He enjoyed his best offensive season in 1987 with a career-best .305 batting average, 123 RBI, and 34 HR, tied his career-high 37 doubles, and shared the AL lead in walks (106). In December 1990, the Baltimore Orioles (AL) signed him as a free agent for his final major league season.

His numerous honors include being named to the *TSN* AL All-Star Team three times (1982, 1984, 1987) and *TSN* Silver Slugger Team twice (1981, 1987). He batted a superlative .600 in the 1978, 1981, and 1987 All-Star Games and appeared in the AL Championship Series against the Oakland A's in 1975, 1988, and 1990 and against the California Angels in 1986. Evans batted .300 with 15 hits, 3 HR, and 14 RBI in seven game World Series against the Cincinnati Reds in 1975 and New York Mets in 1986. In 1975, he made a sensational catch to rob Cincinnati's Joe Morgan* of a two-run HR in Game 6.

In 20 major league seasons, Evans batted .272 with 2,446 hits, 483 doubles, 73 triples, 385 HR, and 1,384 RBI. He coached for the Colorado Rockies (NL) in 1994. The Lynnfield, MA, resident married Susan Ann Severson on September 12, 1970 and has three children, Timmy, Kirstin, and Justin. Timmy and Justin both made dramatic recoveries from serious illnesses.

BIBLIOGRAPHY: Dwight Evans file, National Baseball Library, Cooperstown, NY; Robert Redmount, *The Red Sox Encyclopedia* (Champaign, IL, 1998); Peter Golenbock, *Fenway* (New York, 1992); Peter Gammons, "Out of Right Field," *Sport* 72 (September 1981), pp. 66–68, 70–71; E. M. Swift, "Back on the Right Track," *SI* 62 (May 6, 1985), pp. 36–40; Richard Topp, letter to David L. Porter, February 8, 1990; *TSN Official Baseball Register*, 1973–1992.

David L. Porter

EVANS, William George "Billy" (b. February 10, 1884, Chicago, IL; d. January 23, 1956, Miami, FL), baseball umpire and executive, football executive, and sportswriter, spent his childhood in Youngstown, OH and attended Cornell University to study law in 1901. Upon his father's death in 1902, he left school to write for the Youngstown *Vindicator*. A year later, Evans substituted as the umpire at a local game he was covering. He spent two years as sports editor of the *Vindicator* and as part-time arbitrator and then became an umpire in the Class C OPL. In 1906 22-year-old Evans joined the AL umpire crew, thus becoming the youngest major league arbiter and the only one promoted directly from Class C ball. As an AL umpire, he worked six World Series and encouraged using four arbiters for fall classic games. On-field fights frequently occurred then, but Evans substituted diplomacy for belligerency. An impeccable dresser, he was lauded for fairness and high integrity and provided an excellent model for future umpires. Besides being an AL umpire from 1906 to 1927, Evans continued his writing career. He contributed articles to *Collier's* and *TSN*, helped compile *Knotty Problems of Baseball*, authored *Umpiring from the Inside*, served as sports editor for the NEA, and wrote the widely syndicated "Billy Evans Says" column.

Upon retiring as an umpire, Evans became general manager of the Cleveland Indians (AL) in 1927. During Evans' nine-year tenure, the Indians signed stars Bob Feller,* Tommy Henrich,* Wes Ferrell,* and Hal Trosky* and improved in the standings. From 1936 to 1940, he served as farm director for the Boston Red Sox (AL). Evans persuaded Boston to purchase the Louisville, KY (AA) franchise to obtain shortstop Pee Wee Reese,* but resigned when the Red Sox sold Reese to the Brooklyn Dodgers (NL). In 1941, he served as general manager of the Cleveland Rams (NFL) football club. As president of the Class AA SA from 1942 to 1946, he increased baseball attendance from 700,000 to over 2 million spectators per year. Evans, general manager of the Detroit Tigers (AL) from 1947 to 1951, was elected in 1973 to the National Baseball Hall of Fame.

BIBLIOGRAPHY: Billy Evans file, National Baseball Library, Cooperstown, NY; Martin Appel and Burt Goldblatt, *Baseball's Best: The Hall of Fame Gallery* (New York, 1977); Peter Golenbock, *Fenway* (New York, 1992); Franklin Lewis, *The Cleveland Indians* (New York, 1949); John Thorn et al., eds., *Total Indians* (New York, 1996); Frederick G. Lieb, *The Boston Red Sox* (New York, 1947); Robert Redmount, *The Red Sox Encyclopedia* (Champaign, IL, 1998); James M. Kahn, *The Umpire Story* (New York, 1953); Lowell Reidenbaugh, *Baseball's Hall of Fame-Cooperstown* (New York, 1993).

                                                                         Dan E. Krueckeberg

EVERS, John Joseph "Johnny," "The Trojan," "The Crab" (b. July 21, 1881, Troy, NY; d. March 28, 1947, Albany, NY), player, coach, manager, and scout, was the son of Troy government clerk John J. Evers and Ellen (Keating) Evers and graduated in 1898 from St. Joseph's Christian Brothers Teachers School. Evers married Helen Fitzgibbons and had two children, Helen and John, Jr. Evers, who threw right-handed and batted left-handed, began playing professional baseball in 1902 with Troy, NY (NYSL) and joined the Chicago Cubs (NL) that same season. He played second base for the Cubs through 1913 and helped lead them to four NL pennants (1906–1908, 1910) and two world championships (1907–1908). Evers paced the Cubs with a .300 batting average in 1908 and finished fourth among NL hitters in 1912 with a .341 batting average and led the NL with a .431 on-base percentage. The speedy Evers stole 324 career bases and ranks fourth on the all-time list with 21 thefts of home. In 20 World Series games, he made 24 hits and compiled a .316 batting average.

Evers, although small of stature, proved a smart, aggressive, driving, scrappy, trigger-tongued, determined player. With Joe Tinker* and Frank Chance,* he was the pivot man in baseball's most celebrated double-play combination. A participant in the famous play making the 1908 pennant race a tie, Evers observed that Fred Merkle* had not touched second base on a game-winning hit. He called for the ball and forced Merkle out at second. In a replay to decide the NL pennant, the Cubs defeated the New York Giants.

After joining the Boston Braves (NL) in 1914, Evers participated on the "miracle team" which rose from the cellar in July to a world championship in October. At Boston, he teamed with "Rabbit" Maranville* to take the World Series from the powerful Philadelphia Athletics in four games. After batting .438 in the World Series, Evers was voted the NL's MVP. In 1917, he completed his 18-year playing career. In 1,784 major league games, he made 1,659 hits, scored 919 runs, walked 778 times, and batted .270.

Evers managed the Chicago Cubs in 1913 and 1921 and piloted the Chicago White Sox (AL) in 1924, guiding his teams to 180 victories in 375 games. He also served as a major league coach (NL, New York Giants, 1920; AL, Chicago White Sox, 1922–1923); assistant manager (NL, Boston Braves, 1929–1932); and scout (NL, Boston Braves, 1933–1934). Evers managed Albany, NY (IL) in 1935 and served as vice-president and general manager of Albany, NY (EL) in 1939. Subsequently, Evers operated a sporting goods store and was superintendent of Bleeker Stadium, a municipal sports complex in Albany. The co-author of *Touching Second*, he was elected to the National Baseball Hall of Fame in 1946.

BIBLIOGRAPHY: Thomas Aylesworth and Benton Minks, *The Encyclopedia of Baseball Managers* (New York, 1990); John Evers file, National Baseball Library, Cooperstown, NY; Eddie Gold and Art Ahrens, *The Golden Era Cubs, 1876–1940* (Chicago, IL, 1985); Warren Brown, *The Chicago Cubs* (New York, 1946); Jim Enright, *Chicago Cubs* (New York, 1975); G. F. Fleming, *The Unforgettable Season* (New York, 1982); Craig Carter, ed., *TSN Daguerreotypes*, 8th ed. (St. Louis, MO, 1990); Frank Keetz, "Johnny Evers: The Find of the Season," *BRJ* 12 (1983), pp. 132–136; Lowell Reidenbaugh, *Baseball's Hall of Fame-Cooperstown* (New York, 1993); Warren Wilbert and William Hageman, *Chicago Cubs: Seasons at the Summit* (Champaign, IL, 1997); Harold Kaese, *The Boston Braves* (New York, 1948); John Thorn et al., eds., *Total*

Braves (New York, 1996); Gary Caruso, *The Braves Encyclopedia* (Philadelphia, PA, 1995).

John L. Evers

EVERS, Walter Arthur "Hoot" (b. February 8, 1921, St. Louis, MO; d. January 25, 1991, Houston, TX), player and executive, was of German descent and attended high school in suburban Collinsville, IL. The 6-foot 2-inch, 185-pound right-hander combined speed with some power and was nicknamed after the Western screen hero "Hoot" Gibson. Evers starred in baseball at the University of Illinois and also performed in track and field and on the basketball squad there. As a junior, Evers led the BTC in runs scored, RBI, HR, and triples and was signed by the Detroit Tigers (AL).

Evers debuted professionally at Winston-Salem, NC (PiL) in 1941, appearing briefly with Beaumont, TX (TL) and the Detroit Tigers. In 1942, he excelled defensively for Beaumont and hit .322 with 10 HR and 92 RBI. After spending three years in the Army Air Forces, Evers in 1946 claimed the center field post for a Detroit Tigers team that was seeking to replace several aging prewar stars. He missed half the season with a broken ankle, but played center field in 1947 and 1948. He moved to left field in 1949 to make room for rookie Johnny Groth.

From 1948 through 1950, Evers batted over .300 each year and twice knocked in over 100 runs. He made the AL All-Star team twice and in 1950 led AL outfielders with a .997 fielding percentage. The Tigers finished second to the New York Yankees in 1950, but declined quickly thereafter and made sweeping personnel changes. Evers, third baseman George Kell,* and others were sent to the Boston Red Sox (AL) in a June 1952 blockbuster deal. The Red Sox wanted him as a replacement for Ted Williams,* who had been recalled to active military duty in the Korean War. A broken finger, however, hampered Evers' effectiveness at the plate. He never approached his earlier offensive success and was released in May 1954. He subsequently performed with the New York Giants (NL), Baltimore Orioles (AL), and Cleveland Indians (AL), concluding his major league career with Baltimore in 1956. In 12 major league seasons, he batted .278 with 98 HR, 1,055 hits, and 565 RBI.

Evers held several front-office jobs, including farm director with the Cleveland Indians, director of player development with the Detroit Tigers, and special assignment scout with the Houston Astros (NL). He married Nancy Maude Kalbfleisch on Christmas Day 1941 and had two daughters, Nancy and Kay.

BIBLIOGRAPHY: Walter Evers file, National Baseball Library, Cooperstown, NY; *WWIB, 1951*; Rich Marazzi and Len Fiorito, *Aaron to Zuverink* (New York, 1981); *NYT*, January 30, 1991, p. D-20; *Who's Who in the Big Leagues, 1955*; Robert Redmount, *The Red Sox Encyclopedia* (Champaign, IL, 1998); Peter Golenbock, *Fenway* (New York, 1992); William M. Anderson, *The Detroit Tigers* (South Bend, IN, 1996);

Fred Smith, *995 Tigers* (Detroit, MI, 1981); Joe Falls, *Detroit Tigers* (New York, 1975); Richard Bak, *A Place for Summer* (Detroit, MI, 1998).

Lloyd J. Graybar

EWING, William "Buck" (b. October 17, 1859, Hoagland, OH; d. October 20, 1906, Cincinnati, OH), player and manager, was one of the finest all-around athletic performers of his day. Although basically a catcher, the 5-foot 10-inch, 188-pound Ewing played many games at all other positions. Ewing was credited by some historians as the first catcher to crouch behind the plate. Ewing, who batted and threw right-handed, began his baseball career at age 19 with the Mohawk Browns and Buckeyes (1878–1880), independent teams in Cincinnati, OH. After joining Rochester, NY (NA), Ewing in 1880 signed with Troy, NY (NL) and remained there until 1883. In 1883, he became a charter member of the New York Gothams (NL) and stayed with the Gothams Giants through 1889. Ewing hit at least .300 in 11 of his 18 major league seasons and compiled a .303 career batting average. He owned a remarkable arm, enabling him to throw out runners without rising from his squat position behind the plate. A brilliant field leader, Ewing stole 53 bases once and seven times exceeded the 30 mark. He led the NL in HR (1883), triples (1884), and putouts and assists (1889) and in nine different seasons recorded 100 or more base hits. The captain of the New York Giants, the first NL champions (1888 and 1889), Ewing participated in 15 post-season games against the St. Louis Browns and Brooklyn Bridegrooms (AA), collecting 18 hits and a .290 batting average.

Ewing in 1890 joined many others in moving to the newly formed PL as player–manager of the New York Giants. When the PL collapsed after one season, Ewing returned to the NL Giants for two seasons. In 1893, he was traded to the Cleveland Spiders (NL) for George Davis.* Following his release in 1894, he signed as player–manager of the Cincinnati Red Stockings (NL, 1895–1897). He managed through 1899 and piloted the Giants part of the 1900 season. His clubs won 489 games, lost 395, finished third three times, and placed fourth once, sixth once, and eighth twice. In 1,315 major league games, Ewing collected 1,625 hits, 250 doubles, 178 triples, 71 HR, and 883 RBI. Upon retiring from baseball, Ewing was considered wealthy because of his land holdings in the West. He managed several amateur teams, including the Miami Military Institute of Germantown, OH. He married Anna Lawson McCaig on December 12, 1889 and had two children. The Cincinnati resident, who died of diabetes and Bright's disease, was elected to the National Baseball Hall of Fame in 1939.

BIBLIOGRAPHY: Buck Ewing file, National Baseball Library, Cooperstown, NY; Noel Hynd, *The Giants of the Polo Grounds* (New York, 1988); Frederick Ivor-Campbell et al., eds., *Baseball's First Stars* (Cleveland, OH, 1996); James D. Hardy, Jr., *The New York Giants Baseball Club* (Jefferson, NC, 1996); Lee Allen, *The Cincinnati Reds* (New York, 1948); John Phillips, *The Spiders—Who Was Who* (Cabin John, MD, 1991);

National Baseball Hall of Fame and Museum Brochure (Cooperstown, NY, 1974); Lowell Reidenbaugh, *Baseball's Hall of Fame-Cooperstown* (New York, 1993); Craig Carter, ed., *TSN Daguerreotypes*, 8th ed. (St. Louis, MO, 1990); Bob Rathgeber, *Cincinnati Reds Scrapbook* (Virginia Beach, VA, 1982).

John L. Evers

F

FABER, Urban Charles "Red" (b. September 6, 1888, Cascade, IA; d. September 25, 1976, Chicago, IL), player, was the son of Nicholas Faber, a hotel manager, and Margaret (Greif) Faber and grew up in Cascade. Nicknamed "Red," he attended Sacred Heart boarding school and spent two years at St. Joseph's College in Dubuque, IA. A fine college pitcher, he was signed by the Pittsburgh Pirates (NL) and assigned to Dubuque, IA (3IL) for the 1910 season. Faber, who began experimenting with the spitball, worked 334 innings, struck out 200, and pitched a perfect game. He played the next year at Minneapolis, MN (AA) and Pueblo CO (WL) and then two at Des Moines, IA where he led the WL in strikeouts.

Following the 1913 season, the Chicago White Sox (AL) purchased him for $35,000 and took him on the world tour against the New York Giants. To replace the absent Christy Mathewson,* the Giants "borrowed" Faber. Faber won his first "major league" game in Hong Kong and defeated his own team three more times before losing in London, England. John McGraw* tried to purchase Faber, but the White Sox refused the offer. From 1914 to 1933, Faber hurled for the White Sox.

The 6-foot 2-inch, 185-pound Faber possessed a good fastball, but increasingly used his spitball to force batters to drive the ball into the ground. Faber once threw only 67 pitches in an entire game and three times retired the side on three pitches. The right-hander compiled a career record of 254 wins and 213 losses, completed 273 games in 483 starts, and had a 3.15 ERA. Four times, he won at least 20 games in one season.

In 1915 Faber compiled 24 victories, second only to Walter Johnson,* and recorded a 2.55 ERA. In 1921, he led the AL with 32 complete games in 39 starts and recorded 25 victories. When the White Sox defeated the New York Giants in the 1917 World Series, Faber took three of four decisions. An unfortunate injury prevented him from playing in the 1919 World Series.

In the midst of the Black Sox scandal of that series, Faber remained one of the "clean" players. The spitball was outlawed in 1920, but Faber and a few others were permitted to continue to use it. The last legal AL spitball hurler, he was elected in 1964 to the National Baseball Hall of Fame and in 1951 to the Iowa Sports Hall of Fame. After the 1933 season, Faber operated a bowling alley in Greys Lake, IL, from 1933 until 1946, coached for the White Sox for three seasons (1946–1948), and worked as a surveyor for the Cook County Highway Department from 1948 to 1965. Faber married Frances Knudtzon in 1947 after his first wife died and had one son, Urban II.

BIBLIOGRAPHY: Urban Faber file, National Baseball Library, Cooperstown, NY; Lee Allen, *The American League Story* (New York, 1962); Martin Appel and Burt Gold-blatt, *Baseball's Best: The Hall of Fame Gallery* (New York, 1977); Warren Brown, *The Chicago White Sox* (New York, 1952); Jerry E. Clark, *Anson to Zuber: Iowa Boys in the Major Leagues* (Omaha, NE, 1992); Frank Graham, *McGraw of the Giants* (New York, 1944); Richard Lindberg, *Who's on Third?* (South Bend, IN, 1983); John J. McGraw, *My Thirty Years in Baseball* (repr. New York, 1974); George S. May, "Major League Baseball Players from Iowa," *The Palimpsest* 36 (April 1955), pp. 133–164; *NYT*, 1913–1934, February 18, 1934; Lowell Reidenbaugh, *Baseball's Hall of Fame-Cooperstown* (New York, 1993).

                                                                                      Thomas L. Karnes

FACE, Elroy Leon "Roy," "The Baron of the Bullpen" (b. February 20, 1928, Stephentown, NY), player, is the second of four children of Joe Face, a woodchopper, carpenter, farmer, and millhand, and Bessie Face. As a youth, he survived rickets and five bouts with pneumonia and suffered a weakened heart from excessive sulfa treatments for strep throat. He attended Averill Park High School in Averill Park, NY for two years and played baseball there before serving in the U.S. Army from February 1946 to July 1947. After signing with the Philadelphia Phillies (NL), Face pitched for Bradford, PA (PoL) in 1949–1950. The Brooklyn Dodgers (NL) drafted him, after which he hurled for Pueblo, CO (WL) and Fort Worth (TL). He was drafted by the Pittsburgh Pirates (NL) in 1952 and spent the 1953 season with the Pirates.

Face mastered the forkball in 1954 with New Orleans, LA (SA) and returned to the Pirates in 1955. Between May 30, 1958 and September 11, 1959, he pitched in 98 games without a defeat. He won five straight contests at the end of 1958 and captured 17 consecutive games in 1959, finishing the year at 18–1 and leading the NL with a .947 winning percentage. In Pittsburgh's 1960 World Series victory over the New York Yankees, he recorded three saves. His 802 appearances with Pittsburgh tied Walter Johnson's* record for pitching appearances with one team. He was traded to the Detroit Tigers (AL) in August 1968 and the next year joined the Montreal Expos (NL), who released him on August 15, 1969.

The 5 foot 8 inch, 145 pound right-hander, wrote Myron Cope, was "fearless . . . with a build like Frank Sinatra's and the impassive features of Buster Keaton." He won 104 major league games and lost 95, with 877 strikeouts, 193 saves, and a 3.48 ERA. His .947 winning percentage in 1958 remains a major league record. He led the NL in pitching appearances in 1956 and 1960, in saves in 1958, 1961, and 1962, and in losses by a relief pitcher in 1956, 1961, and 1963. His 848 total appearances rank twelfth and 96 relief wins sixth in major league history.

After leaving baseball, he pursued carpentry work full-time at Mayview State Hospital and served on the State of Pennsylvania Civil Service Commission. He married Jeanne Kuran Face on July 15, 1953, has three children, and resides in North Versailles, PA. The "Baron of the Bullpen," he became premier reliever in the late 1950s and early 1960s and was a forkballing prototype for future split-fingered relief specialists.

BIBLIOGRAPHY: Elroy Face file, National Baseball Library, Cooperstown, NY; John Benson et al., *Baseball's Top 100* (Wilton, CT, 1997); Myron Cope, "The Luck of Roy Face," *Sport* 29 (April 1960), pp. 34–35, 85–87; Dick Groat and Bill Surface, *The World Champion Pittsburgh Pirates* (New York, 1961); Lee Heiman et al., *When the Cheering Stops* (New York, 1990); Bob Smizik, *The Pittsburgh Pirates: An Illustrated History* (New York, 1990); Richard L. Burtt, *The Pittsburgh Pirates, A Pictorial History* (Virginia Beach, VA, 1977); John T. Bird, *Twin Killing: The Bill Mazeroski Story* (Birmingham, AL, 1995); Bob Cairns, *Pen Men* (New York, 1993); Jim O'Brien, *Maz and the 1960 Bucs* (Pittsburgh, PA, 1994); Abby Mendelson, "Face to Face with Elroy," *BQ* (Winter 1977), pp. 23–27.

Luther W. Spoehr

FAIN, Ferris Roy "Burrhead" (b. March 29, 1921, San Antonio, TX), player and coach, was a left-handed first baseman, who led the AL in batting average with .344 in 1951 and .327 in 1952. Fain, who grew up in Oakland, CA with parents of German-English background, graduated from Roosevelt High School. His father, Oscar, one of the nation's premier thoroughbred jockeys in the early 1900s, later engaged in prize fighting. The chunky, 5-foot 11-inch, 180-pound Fain signed with the San Francisco, CA Seals (PCL) in June 1939. To ensure Fain's physical well-being, the San Francisco club paid him $200 a month in high school to skip football. He appeared in just 12 games for the Seals in 1939, but played full seasons there from 1940 to 1942 and in 1946. His batting averages included .310 in 1941 and .301 in 1946. Although having fine fielding ability, the aggressive Fain led PCL first basemen in errors each year. Fain, whom Seals teammate Win Ballou nicknamed "Burrhead" because of his kinky hair, spent from 1943 to 1945 as a Staff Sergeant in the U.S. Army Air Corps and saw World War II action on Guam and New Guinea.

After the 1946 season, the Philadelphia Athletics (AL) drafted Fain. He played with the Athletics through the 1952 campaign and won two batting titles there. In 1952, he led the AL with 43 doubles and a .438 on-base percentage. Fain's defensive skills resembled early 20th-century star Hal Chase,* although he led AL first basemen in errors from 1947 to 1950 and in 1952. Fain charged bunts aggressively, often fielding them on the third base side of the pitcher's mound. He participated in 6 double plays in one 1947 game and in 194 double plays during the 1949 campaign. Fain spent the 1953 and 1954 seasons with the Chicago White Sox (AL) and split the 1955 campaign with the Detroit Tigers (AL) and Cleveland Indians (AL). A career .290 batting average, 1,139 hits, and 904 walks highlighted his nine year major league career. He was named to five All-Star games and compiled a phenomenal .425 on-base percentage.

Fain was selected *TSN* AL Player of the Year in 1951 and served as a player–coach for Sacramento, CA (PCL) from 1956 to 1959. Fain, who married Jacquelin Turner in 1941 and has three children, worked as a building contractor for 20 years. He was arrested in 1985 and 1988 for growing marijuana plants in Eldorado County, CA, where he lives with his second wife, Norma. He has fought leukemia, diabetes, and other health problems.

BIBLIOGRAPHY: *The Baseball Encyclopedia*, 10th ed. (New York, 1996); Mary Bonner, *Baseball Rookies Who Made Good* (New York, 1954); Jimmie Dykes and Charles O. Dexter, *You Can't Steal First* (New York, 1967); Ferris Fain file, National Baseball Library, Cooperstown, NY; Gene Karst and Martin J. Jones, Jr., *Who's Who in Professional Baseball* (New Rochelle, NY, 1973); Ted Kent, "The Story of Ferris Fain," *BM* 88 (April 1952), pp. 22–24; Rich Marazzi, "Two-Time Batting Champion Ferris Fain was Part of a Legendary DP Combination," *SCD* 24 (August 22, 1997), pp. 110–112; Rich Marazzi, "Slick Fielding Ferris Fain Was a Bright Light in a Moribund Philly Franchise," *SCD* 24 (August 29, 1997), pp. 70–71; John Thom, *Champion Batsman of the 20th Century* (Los Angeles, CA, 1992); Fred Smith, *995 Tigers* (Detroit, MI, 1981); Connie Mack, *My 66 Years in the Big Leagues* (Philadelphia, PA, 1950); Al Stump, "Fearless Ferris Fain," *Sport* 15 (July 1953), pp. 28–31; Bob Vanderberg, *Sox: From Lane and Fain to Zisk and Fisk* (Chicago, IL, 1982); Richard Lindberg, *Who's On Third?* (South Bend, IN, 1983); Edgar Williams, "The Angry Champion," *BD* 12 (March 1953), pp. 49–54.

James K. Skipper, Jr.

FAIRLY, Ronald Ray "Ron," "Mr. Clutch" (b. July 12, 1938, Macon, GA), player, coach, and sportscaster, is the son of Carl Fairly, a minor league infielder, and attended David Starr Jordan High School in Long Beach, CA. In 1958, the Los Angeles Dodgers (NL) signed him out of the University of Southern California for a $60,000 bonus. He married Mary Sinclair in February 1963 and has three sons, Steven, Michael, and Patrick.

After hitting well and with some power in 69 games at Des Moines, IA (WL) and St. Paul, MN (AA), the 5-foot 10-inch, 175-pound outfielder joined the Los Angeles Dodgers for the final month of the 1958 season and experienced a modest rookie year in 1959. A horrible start in 1960 found him being optioned to Spokane, WA (PCL). Fairly made the most of the demotion, blasting 27 HR with 100 walks and 100 RBI and a .303 batting average. In 1961, Fairly cemented a position with Los Angeles by batting .322 in 111 games. He proved excellent defensively, leading NL first basemen with a .995 fielding average in 1963. He appeared in four World Series with the Dodgers, reaching safely in all seven games with 2 HR against the Minnesota Twins in 1965.

When the left-handed-hitting Fairly struggled at the plate in early 1969, the Dodgers sent him that June to the Montreal Expos (NL) for Maury Wills* and Manny Mota.* Fairly provided stability, leadership, and steady offense for the expansion Expos. After trading Joe Torre* to the New York Mets (NL) in October 1974, the St. Louis Cardinals (NL) acquired Fairly two months later to platoon with rookie Keith Hernandez* at first base. Fairly responded with his first .300 season in 14 years. He was traded to the Oakland Athletics (AL) in September 1976 and Toronto Blue Jays (AL) in February 1977. In 1977, Fairly attained a career-high 19 HR as a 39-year-old Blue Jay and became the first player to appear as an All Star for both Canadian major league teams, his other appearance having come in 1974 with the Montreal Expos.

After spending the 1978 season with the California Angels (AL), Fairly retired with 1,913 hits, 215 HR, 1,044 RBI, and a .266 batting average in 2,442 games. The first baseman and outfielder joined Stan Musial* and Ernie Banks* as the only players to participate in 1,000 games at two positions. Fairly served as a Los Angeles, CA television sportscaster and announcer, hitting instructor for the California Angels, and handled color radio-television commentary for the San Francisco Giants (NL). He has worked as radio-television color analyst for the Seattle Mariners (AL) since 1994.

BIBLIOGRAPHY: Ronald Fairly file, National Baseball Library, Cooperstown, NY; Gene Karst and Martin J. Jones, Jr., *Who's Who in Professional Baseball* (New Rochelle, NY, 1973); William F. McNeil, *The Dodgers Encyclopedia* (Champaign, IL, 1997); Richard Whittingham, *The Los Angeles Dodgers: An Illustrated History* (New York, 1982); Walter Alston, *A Year at a Time* (Waco, TX, 1976); Walter Alston with Si Burick, *Alston and the Dodgers* (New York, 1966); Dick Miller, "Fans Big Losers as 'Lucky' Fairly Goes to Pasture," *TSN*, March 24, 1979, p. 44; Neal Russo, "Card Businessman Fairly Refuses to Act His Age," *TSN*, August 16, 1975, p. 5; Neal Russo, "Labeled Redbirds' Backup, Fairly Seeks More Action," *TSN*, December 21, 1974, p. 41.

Frank J. Olmsted

FALK, Bibb August "Jockey" (b. January 27, 1899, Austin, TX; d. June 8, 1989, Austin, TX), player, coach, manager, and scout, starred as a University of Texas athlete whose pitching and hitting in an exhibition game against the Chicago White Sox (AL) in 1920 earned him a major league contract. The lean, well-muscled, 6-foot, 175 pounder excelled as an All-SWC football tackle, an undefeated southpaw hurler in three varsity seasons, and a near-.400 hitter as a pitcher, first baseman, and outfielder. In 1919, he struck out 30 batters in 16 innings for the Donna, TX town team and produced the winning hit in a 2–1 victory.

Falk became a Chicago White Sox regular in 1921, moving into left field after the superlative Joe Jackson* was banished from baseball. Falk's batting average exceeded .300 in eight of his 12 major league seasons. His career .314 batting average included a high mark of .352 in 1924, surpassed that year only by Babe Ruth* and Charlie Jamieson.* Although a capable fielder, he also probably benefited from having Johnny Mostil* in center field. Falk used his excellent throwing arm to record 26 assists from his left-field position in 1924. Falk batted .345 in 1926 and led the AL with a .992 fielding percentage.

In February 1929, Chicago traded Falk to the Cleveland Indians (AL) for journeyman catcher Martin "Chick" Autry. Cleveland shifted Falk to right field to accompany outfielders Jamieson and Earl Averill.* Falk gave Cleveland three consecutive .300 years at the plate and ranked among the AL's premier pinch hitters in 1930–1931 with a two-year .351 batting average. After managing the Toledo, OH Mud Hens (AA) to a fourth-place finish in 1932, he returned to the Cleveland Indians a year later as a coach. He coached for the Boston Red Sox (AL) in 1934. The Red Sox employed him as a scout from 1935 to 1939.

From 1940 to 1967, he coached baseball at the University of Texas. Appropriately nicknamed "Jockey," he spurred generations of Longhorn players with his aggressiveness and sharp-tongued wit. His teams responded with a 468–176 record for a .727 winning percentage, winning or sharing 20 SWC titles and taking the 1949–1950 NCAA championships. Falk ranks thirteenth among NCAA-Division I coaches in winning percentage. Texas finished third both in the first NCAA playoffs in 1947 and in 1953. Many of Falk's players advanced to the major leagues, including third basemen Grady Hatton and Randy Jackson and pitchers "Tex" Hughson and Howie Reed.

Falk, who never married, joined the U.S. Naval Reserves in World War I and served as a U.S. Air Force sergeant for three years during World War II. His younger brother, southpaw Chet "Spot" Falk, pitched for the St. Louis Browns (AL) from 1925 to 1927 and won five of nine decisions.

BIBLIOGRAPHY: *The Baseball Encyclopedia*, 10th ed. (New York, 1996); Warren Brown, *The Chicago White Sox* (New York, 1952); Franklin Lewis, *The Cleveland Indians* (New York, 1949); Bibb Falk file, National Baseball Library, Cooperstown, NY; *NYT*, June 10, 1989, p. 12; Mike Shatzkin, ed., *The Ballplayers* (New York, 1990); *TSN*, June 19, 1989, p. 73.

A. D. Suehsdorf

FARRELL, Charles Andrew "Duke" (b. August 31, 1866, Oakdale, MA; d. February 15, 1925, Boston, MA), player, coach, and scout, grew up in Marlborough, MA, where he caught for a strong town team and met his future wife, Julia Bradley. Chicago White Stockings (NL) manager Cap Anson* discovered Farrell in 1887, when he was playing for Salem, MA (NEL). The

6-foot 1-inch, 208-pound, right-handed, switch-hitting Farrell began an 18-year major league career the following season with the Chicago White Stockings. In 1890, he jumped to the Chicago Pirates (PL). When the PL folded after one season, he signed with the Boston Reds (AA). Farrell played the majority of his games at third base, helping lead the Boston Reds to an AA pennant with the finest offensive season of his major league career. His 12 HR led the AA, while his 110 RBI shared first and his .474 slugging average ranked third. These marked career highs for Farrell, as did his 108 runs scored.

When the AA was absorbed into the NL after the 1891 season and the Boston Reds dissolved, Farrell was assigned to the Pittsburgh Pirates (NL). In 1892, he batted a career-low .215. For the only season of his career, he caught no games and played primarily at third base. For the remainder of his career, he principally caught. After a season with the Washington Senators (NL) in 1893, he played over 3 years for the New York Giants (NL). Farrell then returned to the Washington Senators for over 2 seasons, achieving career highs in batting average with .322 in 1897 and .314 in 1898.

The Washington Senators sent Farrell in early 1899 to the Brooklyn Superbas (NL), where he remained through 1902. Blood poisoning from a spike wound in 1901 and illness in 1902 limited his playing time, causing Farrell to gain weight and lose much agility. When the Brooklyn Superbas dropped him after 1902, he signed with the Boston Beaneaters (NL) and lost some excess weight. A broken leg, however, limited Farrell to just 17 games. After a substandard season in 1904, he concluded his major league career with seven games for the Boston Beaneaters in 1905. He worked as a federal marshall and served as battery coach for the New York Highlanders (AL) in 1909, 1911, and 1915–1917. He scouted and coached two years for the Boston Braves (NL) until his death six weeks after surgery for abdominal trouble. He was survived by a daughter, Grace, and two sisters.

During his major league career, Farrell batted .275 and averaged around one hit per game. His 1,564 hits included 211 doubles, 123 triples, and 51 HR. He drove in 912 runs, more than half between 1889 and 1894, when he averaged 81 RBI per year. His offense ranked about average for catchers of his era, but he excelled defensively. Among major league catchers with 1,000 or more games, Farrell's 1.42 assists per game place second only to Bill Bergen's 1.54, while his 93 fielding runs (a modern measure of a player's overall defensive contribution) rank him eighth on the all-time catchers list. Farrell recorded two of the top 10 seasons behind the plate, his 30 fielding runs in 1894 finishing third and his 24 fielding runs in 1890 placing tenth. In three World Series (1894, 1900, 1903), he batted .360 with nine hits and four RBI in six games.

BIBLIOGRAPHY: Charles Farrell file, National Baseball Library, Cooperstown, NY; James D. Hardy, Jr., *The New York Giants Baseball Club* (Jefferson, NC, 1996); Shirley Povich, *The Washington Senators* (New York, 1954); Mike Shatzkin, ed., *The Ball-*

players (New York, 1990); John Thorn et al., eds., *Total Baseball*, 5th ed. (New York, 1997); Robert L. Tiemann and Mark Rucker, eds., *Nineteenth Century Stars* (Kansas City, MO, 1989).

Frederick Ivor-Campbell

FAUT, Jean. *See* Jean Faut Winsch Eastman.

FEENEY, Charles S. "Chub" (b. August 31, 1921, Orange, NJ; d. January 10, 1994, San Francisco, CA), executive and administrator, is the son of Thaddeus Feeney and Mary (Stoneham) Feeney and nephew of Horace Stoneham.* He graduated from Dartmouth College and Fordham Law School. He has five children, Katy, Charles, Jr., John, Will, and Mary, from a marriage that ended in divorce. Katy serves as NL Public Relations Director. After spending three years in the US Navy, Feeney was admitted in 1949 to the New York Bar Association. After joining the New York Giants (NL) front office staff at the end of World War II, Feeney was elected vice-president of the franchise in 1946 and became general manager after the team moved to San Francisco in 1958.

With the forced retirement of General William Eckert* in 1969, Feeney became a leading candidate for major league baseball's commissioner after John McHale* withdrew from consideration. The Cleveland Indians ownership, however, allegedly held some animosity toward Feeney because of a feared predisposition against its manager, Alvin Dark.* Feeney actually had interceded previously on Dark's behalf at the end of the 1964 season, keeping the stormy manager from being fired by the Giants' owner Stoneham. Team owners became deadlocked between Feeney and New York Yankees executive Mike Burke. This impasse produced the nomination and ultimate selection of Bowie Kuhn* as commissioner.

NL owners, meanwhile, selected Feeney as their president in 1970 when Warren Giles* retired. Like his baseball mentors, the Stonehams, Feeney kept an extraordinarily low profile as league president. His face appeared before the cameras only during post-season play, while his name appeared in the papers only in conjunction with the assessment of fines and union negotiations. He opposed the DH rule and encouraged the NL to split into two divisions. Feeney retired as NL president following the 1986 season. He succeeded Ballard Smith as president of the San Diego Padres (NL) in June 1987 and served one year. He and his second wife, Margaret Ann, resided in San Francisco.

BIBLIOGRAPHY: Charles Feeney file, National Baseball Library, Cooperstown, NY; Alan R. Asnen, correspondence with Katy Feeney, September 6, 1984, Alan R. Ansen Collection, Columbia, SC; Charles Einstein, *Willie Mays* (New York, 1963); Alvin Dark and John Underwood, *When in Doubt, Fire the Manager* (New York, 1980); Frank Graham, *The New York Giants* (New York, 1952); Noel Hynd, *The Giants of the Polo Grounds* (New York, 1988); Charles Einstein, *Willie's Time* (New York, 1979);

Gene Karst and Martin J. Jones, Jr., *Who's Who in Professional Baseball* (New Rochelle, NY, 1973); *NYT*, January 11, 1994, p. 87.

Alan R. Asnen

FEHR, Donald Martin (b. July 18, 1948, Marion, IN), executive, is the son of Louis Alvin Fehr and Irene Sylvia (Gullo) Fehr and moved to Prairie Village, MO, where he graduated from Shawnee Mission East High School. Fehr graduated from Indiana University in 1970 with a B.A. degree in history and government and three years later with distinction from the University of Missouri Law School. Married in 1971, Fehr and his wife, Stephanie, have four children and reside in Ryebrook, NY.

As a law school student, Fehr worked for George McGovern's 1972 Democratic Party presidential campaign. Deeply committed to civil rights, the young law student was imbued with "a healthy respect for the individual and skepticism over the nature of big business and monopolies." As a fledgling lawyer, Fehr clerked for two years with U.S. District Court judge Elmo Hunter in Kansas City, MO and then joined a Kansas City firm that specialized in labor law.

Fehr's involvement with major league baseball began in 1976, when the major league club owners chose the U.S. District Court in Kansas City as the forum for appealing arbitrator Peter Seitz's decision granting pitcher Andy Messersmith's* free agency. The MLPA hired Fehr as their local counsel in the case. Fehr persuaded the court to uphold the Seitz decision.

Fehr's adroit handling of this case prompted MLPA executive director Marvin Miller* in 1977 to name him the MLPA's general counsel to replace Dick Moss. In Miller's judgment, Fehr proved to be "a skillful, bright, hard working lawyer who was totally compatible with the players." As Miller's chief lieutenant, Fehr successfully represented the MLPA during the 50-day players' strike of 1981. The following year, Miller retired as executive director of the MLPA. The players fired Miller's successor, Ken Moffett, in November 1983 and named the 35-year-old Fehr its interim director.

As interim executive director, Fehr successfully negotiated a four-year Basic Agreement in 1985. The players retained most of their previous gains while conceding only to raise the time for a player to become eligible for free agency from two to three years.

Fehr contemplated returning to private law practice in 1985 when the players' executive committee offered him a long-term contract as executive director of the MLPA. As director, Fehr continued to consult with Miller, his friend and mentor. Fehr's successful use of arbitration during his first five years won the players an estimated $330 million settlement from the club owners, who were found guilty of collusion against free agent players between 1985 and 1988. In another arbitration action, Fehr blunted the owners' attempt to impose mandatory drug testing on players.

In 1990, an impasse in negotiations prompted the owners to lock out the players from the spring training camps. Fehr, nevertheless, held firm. The resulting Basic Agreement, negotiated by Fehr, fended off owner attempts to impose salary caps and place limits on salary arbitration procedures.

By 1993 the hard-working Fehr's tough-minded approach in labor negotiations had won the respect of major league players and *TSN*, whose editors ranked him fifth among the 100 most powerful people in professional sports. Fehr's reputation was further enhanced by the gains scored by organized players under his leadership. Since 1985, players had received 40 percent of the industry's $600 million annual revenues. Player salaries averaged above $1 million a year as of 1993, while the MLPA's annual revenues from licensing amounted to $70 million a year. Under Fehr, the MLPA's bargaining strength extended to such issues as deciding on league expansion, league realignment, rule changes, television contracts, and minor league player development. These issues, along with salaries and pension rights, remained on the bargaining table in 1993, when Fehr and the owners met to hammer out a new Basic Agreement. Since an agreement could not be reached, the major league players walked out on August 12, 1994. The owners insisted upon establishing a salary cap, a concept the players rejected. The strike lasted until April 1995, when owners accepted a players' offer to return to work without a new collective bargaining agreement. The season opened April 25 with a revised 144-game schedule.

BIBLIOGRAPHY: Michael Knisley, "The TSN 100," *TSN*, January 4, 1993; Lee Lowenfish and Tony Lupien, *The Imperfect Diamond* (New York, 1991); John Thorn et al., eds., *Total Baseball*, 5th ed. (New York, 1997); Marvin Miller, *A Whole Different Ball Game* (New York, 1991); *NYT Biographical Service* 25 (August 1994), pp. 1206–1207; E. M. Swift, "The Perfect Square," *SI* 79 (March 8, 1993), pp. 32–35.

David Q. Voigt

FELLER, Robert William Andrew "Bob," "Rapid Robert" (b. November 3, 1918, Van Meter, IA), player, is of German-French descent and grew up on a farm west of Des Moines. By performing farm chores, Feller developed strong muscles and broad shoulders. The 6-foot, 190 pounder graduated in 1937 from Van Meter High School. Feller developed a very close relationship with his father, William, who trained him to be a pitcher from his preteen years. By the time Feller pitched high school and local amateur baseball, he already had earned a regional reputation with his blinding fastball. In early 1936, he pitched five no-hitters for Van Meter High School.

Feller, who exhibited rare ability, won games for the Cleveland Indians (AL) in 1936 before finishing high school. His experience illustrated how breaking the rules in professional sports paid rich dividends. Feller's discovery usually is credited to Indians general manager Cy Slapnicka and Iowa scout John McMahon. Feller, however, exhibited such natural talent that many scouts perceived his potential. In order to enlist him, Cleveland violated the prevailing regulations forbidding the signing of pre-college amateurs. The Indians "covered up" Feller for a few months via bookkeeping legerdemain, unveiling him as a pitcher in July 1936. Commissioner Kenesaw Mountain Landis* could have made Feller a free agent for this offense, but his parents insisted that he wanted to pitch for Cleveland. The Fellers, grateful to the Indians for their solicitude when Bob briefly experienced a sore arm, declined a free agent fortune.

Feller enjoyed a spectacular career despite losing almost four peak years to World War II military service. As Navy chief specialist on the great battleship *Alabama*, Feller won five campaign ribbons and eight battle stars in Pacific theater combat. He married Virginia Winther in January 1943 and had three sons, Steve, Marty, and Bruce, before their 1971 divorce.

Feller combined a phenomenal fastball with a great curve. Before World War II especially, he fanned numerous batters when strikeouts were more difficult to achieve. Feller reached his one-game peak on October 6, 1938 by striking out 18 Detroit Tigers. In 1946 he fanned 348 batters, a near season record then and still the sixth highest total. Feller still ranks among the first 20 in career strikeouts. At Washington, DC, soon after World War II, his fastball was measured at 98.6 miles per hour.

Feller's pitching feats remain indelible. Despite military service, he led the AL in various pitching categories 31 times. Six times he won 20 or more games and paced in victories each time. His career high in victories came in 1940. Feller led the AL thrice in total games pitched and complete games, five times in innings pitched, four times in shutouts, seven times in strikeouts, and once in winning percentage. He pitched three no-hit games, exceeded only by Nolan Ryan's* seven and Sandy Koufax's* four, and a record twelve one-hitters. Feller, however, never won a World Series game. In the 1948 World Series, he lost two games to the Boston Braves. His controversial 1–0 loss resulted partly from an umpire's dubious call on an attempted pickoff play. In the 1954 fall classic, Feller did not pitch in Cleveland's four consecutive losses to the New York Giants.

Feller's career ended in 1956 with 266 wins, 162 losses, 2,581 strikeouts, and a sparkling .621 winning percentage. In 1962, he was elected to the National Baseball Hall of Fame. If World War II had not intervened, Feller probably would have ranked among the very greatest pitchers with perhaps 100 more victories and another 1,000 strikeouts. Feller enjoyed touring minor league ballparks and visiting sports memorabilia shows and was employed in insurance after his retirement. He also works for the Indians Speaker's Bureau and co-authored *Now Pitching Bob Feller* with Bill Gilbert in 1990. Feller married Anne Gilliland in October 1974 and resides in Gates Mills, OH. He opened a Bob Feller Hometown Exhibit in Van Meter, IA in June 1995 and has a life-size bronze statue in pitching motion at Jacobs Field.

BIBLIOGRAPHY: Bob Feller file, National Baseball Library, Cooperstown, NY; John Benson et al., *Baseball's Top 100* (Wilton, CT, 1997); Anthony J. Connor, *Baseball for the Love of It* (New York, 1982); Bob Feller with Bill Gilbert, *Bob Feller Now Pitching* (New York, 1990); Donald Honig, *Baseball When the Grass Was Real* (New York, 1975); John Thorn et al., eds., *Total Indians* (New York, 1996); Russell Schneider, *The Boys of Summer of '48* (Champaign, IL, 1998); John Phillips, *Winners* (Cabin John, MD, 1987); Bob Feller, *Strikeout Story* (New York, 1947); Jerry E. Clark, *Anson to Zuber: Iowa Boys in the Major Leagues* (Omaha, NE, 1992); Lowell Reidenbaugh, *Baseball's Hall of Fame-Cooperstown* (New York, 1993); Ed Linn, ed., "Trouble with the Hall of Fame," *SEP* 165 (January 27, 1962), pp. 49–52; *TSN*, December 15, 1954, May 16, 1983; Rich Westcott, *Diamond Greats* (Westport, CT, 1988).

                                                                    Lowell L. Blaisdell

FELSCH, Oscar Emil "Happy" (b. August 22, 1891, Milwaukee, WI; d. August 17, 1964, Milwaukee, WI), player, was one of 12 children of Charles Felsch, a labor union official and skilled amateur first baseman, and was educated only through the sixth grade. Felsch began his organized baseball career with Fond du Lac, WI (WIL) in 1913 and, after batting .319, joined Milwaukee, WI (AA) near the end of the season. In 1914, he hit .304 with 19 HR at Milwaukee and was purchased for $12,000 by the Chicago White Sox (AL). His major league career spanned six years from 1915 to 1920 before his suspension, resulting from the Black Sox scandal, abruptly ended it.

During his major league career, the 5-foot 11-inch, 170-pound Felsch batted .293 with 38 HR and 446 RBI in 749 games. Ironically, his best campaign by far came in his last season, when he hit .338 and slammed 14 HR. The speedy center fielder stole 88 career bases and set or shared several defensive records. He also possessed an exceptionally strong throwing arm and tied a major league mark with four assists in a nine inning game on August 14, 1919. Felsch tied an AL single game record on June 23, 1919 with 11 putouts and set a major league mark in 1919 for outfielders with 15 double plays. His .981 fielding average led the AL in 1916.

Felsch gained notoriety for his involvement in the 1919 Black Sox scandal. Although not one of the Black Sox leaders, he was centrally involved with his subpar performance in the 1919 World Series. His .192 batting average and two errors in 26 chances may be evidence of his involvement. His dropped catch of an Edd Roush* fly in Game 5 led to a four run inning, breaking open a tight game. Felsch later told sportswriters that he received $5,000 from the gamblers, but never had the opportunity to contribute deliberately to a White Sox loss. After his suspension, he joined summer "barnstorming" tours with other Black Sox in the Pacific Northwest and Canada and played semiprofessional baseball in Milwaukee for over 10 years. Felsch eventually worked as a crane operator and managed a tavern and a grocery store. He also bowled well for many years. In 1925, Felsch won $1,166 from the White Sox in a lawsuit claiming that he had not been paid all the salary due him. He died of a liver ailment and was survived by his wife, Marie, two daughters, and a son.

BIBLIOGRAPHY: Eliot Asinof, *Eight Men Out* (New York, 1963); Warren Brown, *The Chicago White Sox* (New York, 1952); Harvey Frommer, *Shoeless Joe and Ragtime Baseball* (Dallas, TX, 1992); Milwaukee *Journal*, August 18, 1964; *NYT*, August 18, 1964; Mike Shatzkin, ed., *The Ballplayers* (New York, 1990); *TSN*, August 29, 1964; John Thorn et al., eds., *Total Baseball*, 5th ed. (New York, 1997); *The Baseball Encyclopedia*, 10th ed. (New York, 1996); Dan Gutman, *Baseball Babylon* (New York, 1992); Daniel E. Ginsberg, *The Fix Is In* (Jefferson, NC, 1995).

John E. Findling

FERGUSON, Charles J. "Charlie" (b. April 17, 1863, Charlottesville, VA; d. April 29, 1888, Philadelphia, PA), player, was the son of George M. Ferguson, a baker, and grew up in Charlottesville. Ferguson pitched for the 1882 University of Virginia team, although not a registered student. In 1883, he batted .283 as a pitcher–catcher for the independent Virginia Club of Richmond, and drew attention by holding the Boston Beaneaters (NL) to one run and four hits during a late-season exhibition game. George Reach, therefore, signed Ferguson to hurl for the Philadelphia Phillies (NL) in 1884. Appeals from the Virginia Club, now a charter EL member, that Ferguson previously had committed himself to the Virginians were rejected.

The 6-foot, 165-pound right-hander won the season opener in Philadelphia, 13–2, hitting two singles and a triple. Despite a month's absence due to an injury suffered running bases, he finished 21–25 for the sixth-place, weak-hitting Philadelphia Phillies. Ferguson combined blazing fast balls, effective curves, control, and judgement. He hurled brilliantly for three more seasons, posting 26–20, 30–9, and 22–10 records. Ferguson also excelled at center field and second base, batting .306, .253, and .337 (the latter officially .412 if counting bases on balls as hits). In 1887, he remarkably drove in 85 runs, made 89 hits, and scored 67 runs in only 72 games. A switch hitter, Ferguson sometimes upset pitchers by stepping across the plate during windups. Frequently he complained of being too ill to play, but then competed with his normal skill and vigor. Teammates never decided whether the ailments were real or imagined.

Clearly his club's best pitcher, hitter, fielder, and base runner and arguably the NL's best all-around player, Ferguson seemed destined for greatness. In April 1888, however, he contracted typhoid fever. His condition worsened, causing his death three weeks later at age 25. He was survived by the daughter of Lewis H. Smith, of Richmond, who he had married in 1885. They had one daughter, who died in infancy. During his brief NL career, Ferguson compiled a 99–64 won–lost record with a 2.67 ERA. He pitched a no-hitter on August 29, 1885 and batted .288 in 257 games.

BIBLIOGRAPHY: *The Baseball Encyclopedia*, 10th ed. (New York, 1996); Rich Westcott and Frank Bilovsky, *The New Phillies Encyclopedia* (Philadelphia, PA, 1993); Richmond

(VA) *Dispatch*, May 1, 1888, p. 1; Philadelphia *Press*, April 30, 1888, May 1, 1888; *SL*, January 2, February 6, March 5, 1884; John Thorn et al., eds., *Total Baseball*, 5th ed. (New York, 1997); Robert L. Tiemann and Mark Rucker, eds., *Nineteenth Century Stars* (Kansas City, MO, 1989); Frederick G. Lieb and Stan Baumgartner, *The Philadelphia Phillies* (New York, 1953).

Frank V. Phelps

FERGUSON, Robert Vavasour "Bob," "Death to Flying Things" (b. January 31, 1845, Brooklyn, NY; d. May 3, 1894, Brooklyn, NY), player, executive, captain, manager, and umpire, began his baseball career in 1864, graduating to the Enterprise Club of Brooklyn in 1865 and the famous Atlantic Club of Brooklyn in 1866. One of the game's best all-round players, he specialized as a defensive wizard. His nickname came from his great range on fly balls. He became the game's premier third baseman, but played every position during his 20-year professional career. At 5-feet 9½-inches and 149 pounds, he threw right-handed and was baseball's first switch-hitter. He ranked among the first catchers to position himself close behind the batter.

Ferguson, an established leader, developed distinguished traits. He either captained or managed every team he played on beginning in 1869 and served four years as president of the NA, baseball's first professional league. Terms like *competitive*, *absolutely honest*, *straightforward*, *quick-tempered*, *rule-wise*, and *sterling character* have been used to describe Ferguson. With his byline being integrity, he did more than anyone else in the fight for honest baseball and was a constant opponent of gambling.

Ferguson played with the Brooklyn Atlantics (NA) until 1874 with the exception of spending 1871 with the New York Mutuals (NA). Ferguson first gained national acclaim in 1870, when his Brooklyn Atlantics handed the Cincinnati Red Stockings their first loss in two years. In perhaps the first instance of switch-hitting, he drove in the tying run and later scored the winning tally.

Ferguson played for and captained-managed the Hartford, CT Dark Blues (NA, NL), 1875 to 1877; Chicago White Stockings (NL), 1878; Springfield, MA (NA), 1879; Troy, NY Trojans (NL), 1879 to 1882; Philadelphia Quakers (NL), 1883; and Baltimore, MD (EL) and Pittsburgh Alleghenys (AA), 1884. He also managed the New York Metropolitans (AA) in 1886 and 1887, being an outstanding judge and developer of talent.

Ferguson also umpired in the NA from 1871 to 1875, in the NL in 1885, in the AA from 1887 to 1889 and 1891, and in the PL in 1890. As an arbiter, he proved first-class, dictatorial, and impeccably honest. His understanding and interpretation of the game remained so basic and logical that many of his decisions influenced rules.

Ferguson suffered from partial paralysis that may have been caused by excessive smoking and died as a result of an attack of apoplexy. He proved wise in financial investments and was well-off at his death. Ferguson was involved in our national game for 28 straight seasons, usually serving in several capacities at once. The much-respected, very prominent baseball personality wielded a major influence on how the game developed.

BIBLIOGRAPHY: Robert V. Ferguson file, National Baseball Library, Cooperstown, NY; Sam Crane, *NYJ*, December 23, 1911; David Pietrusza, *Major Leagues* (Jefferson, NC, 1991); William I. Ryczek, *Blackguards and Red Stockings* (Jefferson, NC, 1992); David Nemec, *The Beer and Whisky League* (New York, 1994); Mike Shatzkin, ed., *The Ballplayers* (New York, 1990); *SpL*, May 12, 1894; John Thorn et al., eds., *Total Baseball*, 5th ed. (New York, 1997); Robert L. Tiemann and Mark Rucker, eds., *Nineteenth Century Stars* (Kansas City, MO, 1989).

John R. Husman

FERNANDEZ, Octavio Antonio Fernando (Castro) "Tony" (b. June 30, 1962, San Pedro de Macorís, DR), player, attended Gasto Fernando de Ligne High School. His parents, José Fernandez and Andrea Fernandez, supported 11 children by sugar cane fieldwork. He and his wife, Clara, have three sons, Joel, Jonathan, and Abraham. Fernandez signed at age 16 with the Toronto Blue Jays (AL) in 1980. He began with Kinston, NC (CrL), making the CrL All-Star team at shortstop in 1981. He moved up to the Syracuse, NY Chiefs (IL), making the IL All-Star team and being selected the Chiefs' MVP in 1982 and 1983.

Fernandez became the Toronto Blue Jays' starting shortstop in 1985. His fielding achievements include having 65 consecutive errorless games in 1988; fielding .992 in 1989, a major league shortstop record until Cal Ripken, Jr.* broke it in 1990; and earning four Gold Gloves from 1986 to 1989. The 6 foot, 2 inch, 175 pounder exhibited exceptional range, a powerful and accurate arm, and tremendous anticipation. Solid switch-hitting performances of .310 in 1986 and .322 in 1987 gained him selection to AL All-Star teams each year, *TSN* and UPI AL All-Star teams in 1986, and the AP All-Major League team in 1986. Subsequent injuries prevented him from returning to these fielding and hitting levels, but he was chosen an AL All Star in 1989 and 1999 and an NL All Star in 1992.

Following the 1990 season, the Toronto Blue Jays traded Fernandez and Fred McGriff* to the San Diego Padres (NL) for Joe Carter* and Roberto Alomar.* San Diego traded him to the New York Mets (NL) in December 1992. In June 1993, New York sent him to Toronto. His nine RBI in the 1992 Toronto World Series victory over the Atlanta Braves led all players. He spent 1994 with the Cincinnati Reds (NL) and joined the New York Yankees (AL) in 1995, hitting for the cycle against the Oakland A's. After Fernandez spent the 1996 season on the disabled list, the Cleveland Indians (AL) signed him as a free agent in December 1996. He batted .286 to help the Indians win the 1997 AL Central Division and knocked in 4 runs in the AL Division Series against the New York Yankees. He batted .357 with two

RBI in the 1997 AL Championship Series against the Baltimore Orioles. His dramatic 11th inning HR clinched the AL pennant in Game 6. Fernandez hit .471 with four RBI in the 1997 World Series against the Florida Marlins, but made a crucial error on Craig Counsell's ground ball in the 11th inning, 3–2 loss in decisive Game 7. In December 1997, the Toronto Blue Jays signed the humble Fernandez as a free agent. He led the Toronto Blue Jays with a .321 batting average in 1998, recording 36 doubles and 72 RBI. He batted .329 with 41 doubles and 75 RBI in 1999.

Fernandez holds the major league career shortstop fielding record with a .980 average. His career totals include a .288 batting average, 2,240 hits, 92 triples, and 245 stolen bases. He hit .364 in 34 League Championship Series and World Series games.

BIBLIOGRAPHY: Tony Fernandez file, National Baseball Library, Cooperstown, NY; Paul Hoynes, "Tony Fernandez: Another Slick Glove at Short for the Blue Jays," *BD* 44 (December 1985), pp. 59–61; http://www.yankees.com/html/teamcenter/roster/players/fernandez.t.html., May 1996; Craig L. Miller, "A Second Look: Tony Fernandez," *BBM* 7 (June 1990), pp. 73–74; David Moriah, "Steady Personality Keeps Fernandez in the Game," *SCD* 26 (January 15, 1999), p. 108; Joe Sexton, "From Poverty to Pushcart to Pros," *NYT*, December 6, 1992, VIII, p. 6.

John T. English

FERRELL, Richard Benjamin "Rick" (b. October 12, 1905, Durham, NC; d. July 27, 1995, Bloomfield Hills, MI), player, coach, scout, and executive, grew up on a farm at Guilford, NC. He was one of six sons of Rufus Benjamin Ferrell, a Southern Railway locomotive engineer who raised dairy cattle, and Alice (Carpenter) Ferrell. His brother, Wesley,* played in the major leagues, while brother, Marvin, pitched in the minors and George played the outfield for 20 minor league seasons. Ferrell graduated from Guilford High School and attended Guilford College for three years (1924–1926). After rejecting an offer from the St. Louis Cardinals (NL), Ferrell signed with the Detroit Tigers (AL) and played at Kinston, NC (VL) in 1926 and at Columbus, OH (AA) from 1926 through 1928. In 1928, he was selected as AA All-Star catcher. He complained to Judge Kenesaw Mountain Landis* when his name was omitted from draft lists that fall. Upholding the complaint, the judge declared him a free agent. He signed with the St. Louis Browns (AL) for a $25,000 bonus, bypassing a similar offer from the New York Giants (NL).

The cool, even-tempered Ferrell stayed with the Browns until May 1933, when he was traded to the Boston Red Sox (AL). During May 1934, Boston acquired his brother Wes. For several years, Rick caught whenever Wes pitched. Both were traded to the Washington Senators (AL) in June 1937, Rick remaining there until being dealt back to the Browns in May 1941. A March 1944 trade returned Rick to the Senators, where he finished his catching career in 1947 as a player–coach. He continued coaching with Washington through 1949 and coached the Detroit Tigers from 1950 through 1953.

For Detroit, he scouted from 1954 through 1958 and served as general manager in 1960 and 1961, as vice-president from 1962 through 1975, and as a consultant thereafter.

In 18 AL seasons, the 5-foot 10-inch, 160-pound, right-handed Ferrell batted .281 (above average for a catcher) with 734 RBI spanning 1,884 games. Ferrell's 1,692 hits included 324 doubles and 28 HR. He struck out only 277 times in over 6,000 times at bat. Behind the plate, the fair-skinned North Carolinian set an AL record for most games caught (1,805). Carlton Fisk* broke that record in 1988. For nine consecutive years (1930–1938), he caught over 100 games per season. The smart, excellent receiver and expert handler of pitchers was elected to six consecutive AL All-Star teams from 1933 through 1938. He caught all nine innings of the first All-Star game in 1938. In his youth, he proved a good lightweight boxer before entering professional baseball. Ferrell married Ruthe Virginia Wilson of Greenville, TN in January 1941. She predeceased him in 1968. They had two daughters and two sons. In 1984, Ferrell was elected to the National Baseball Hall of Fame.

BIBLIOGRAPHY: Richard Ferrell file, National Baseball Library, Cooperstown, NY; Bob Broeg, "Ferrell's a Blue-Ribbon Battery," *TSN*, January 29, 1977; Paul Green, *Forgotten Fields* (Waupaca, WI, 1984); Harold (Speed) Johnson, *Who's Who in Major League Base Ball* (Chicago, IL, 1933); Frederick G. Lieb, *The Boston Red Sox* (New York, 1949); Robert Redmount, *The Red Sox Encyclopedia* (Champaign, IL, 1998); Shirley Povich, *The Washington Senators* (New York, 1954); *NYT Biographical Service* 26 (July 1995), p. 1094; Craig Carter, ed., *TSN Daguerreotypes*, 8th ed. (St. Louis, MO, 1990); *The Baseball Encyclopedia*, 10th ed. (New York, 1990); *TSN Baseball Register*, 1950; *TSN*, December 12, 1951, July 23, 1952, March 18, 1968; Lowell Reidenbaugh, *Baseball's Hall of Fame-Cooperstown* (New York, 1993); Bill Borst, ed., *Ables to Zoldak*, vol. 1 (St. Louis, MO, 1988); Bill Borst, *Still Last in the American League* (West Bloomfield, MI, 1992).

Frank V. Phelps

FERRELL, Wesley Cheek "Wes" (b. February 2, 1908, Greensboro, NC; d. December 9, 1976, Sarasota, FL), player and manager, grew up on a 150 acre dairy farm at Guilford, NC. He was the son of railroad locomotive engineer Rufus Benjamin Ferrell and Alice (Carpenter) Ferrell, graduated from Guilford High School, and attended a military school in Oak Ridge, TN. Rick Ferrell,* an older brother, also played major league baseball. During 1927, Ferrell pitched briefly for a semipro team at East Douglas, MA. After signing with the Cleveland Indians (AL), he pitched one inning there in 1927. Ferrell won 20 games and lost 8 for Terre Haute, IN (3IL) in 1928 before finishing 0–2 with Cleveland. During his first four full seasons (1929–1932) with the Indians, the handsome, blond, 6-foot 2-inch, 195-pound right-hander uniquely won over 20 games each year. His other impressive marks included a 13-game winning streak in 1931 and a no-hit game against the St. Louis Browns on April 29, 1931. In 1933, he hurt his pitching arm and compiled a mediocre 11–12 record. After holding out the next spring, he was traded in May 1934 to the Boston Red Sox (AL).

Although his blazing fastball had disappeared, Ferrell regained effectiveness as a curve and "junk stuff" hurler. With brother, Rick, as catcher, he achieved 14–5, 25–14, and 20–15 records from 1934 through 1936. After the Ferrells were traded to the Washington Senators (AL) in June 1937, he finished 14–19 and was released in August 1938. He signed with the New York Yankees (AL) and registered a composite 15–10 mark for the 1938 season. He pitched briefly for the Yankees in 1939 and toiled for the Brooklyn Dodgers (NL) in 1940 and Boston Braves (NL) in 1941. His 15-year major league totals included 193 wins, 128 losses, and a 4.04 ERA. Ferrell led the AL four times in complete games, three times in innings pitched and hits surrendered, twice in games started, and once in wins and walks. From 1941 through 1949, he was a manager–outfielder for southeastern minor league teams: Leaksville, VA (BSL) in 1941, Lynchburg, VA (VL) in 1942, Greensboro, NC (CrL) in 1945, Lynchburg, VA (PiL) in 1946, Marion, NC (WCL) in 1948, and Greensboro again and Tampa, FL (FIL) in 1949. Out of organized baseball for 14 years, he returned to manage Rock Hill, SC (WCL) in 1963 and Shelby, NC (WCL) in 1965.

The great major league hitting pitcher batted .280, slugged .446, and set HR by pitcher records: 38 career HR and nine for a single season (1931). He pinch-hit frequently and played 13 games in the 1933 Cleveland outfield. He also won batting championships in the VL with .361 (31 HR) in 1942 and in the WCL with .425 (.767 slugging percentage and 24 HR) at age 40 in 1948.

A fierce competitor, Ferrell often stormed and raged when he lost. He engaged in frequent salary disputes and periodic hot controversies with baseball authorities. In 1932, Cleveland manager Roger Peckinpaugh* fined him $1,500 for refusing to leave the mound. Four years later, Boston manager Joe Cronin* fined him $1,000 for taking himself off the mound. In the minor leagues, he drew a one-year suspension for punching an umpire and a 60-day suspension for taking his team off the field. Ferrell married Lois Johnston in 1940 and had one son, Wesley Cheek, Jr., and one daughter, Mrs. Gwenlo F. Williard. In his later years, Ferrell became a gentleman farmer.

BIBLIOGRAPHY: Franklin Lewis, *The Cleveland Indians* (New York, 1949); Frederick G. Lieb, *The Boston Red Sox* (New York, 1947); Robert Redmount, *The Red Sox Encyclopedia* (Champaign, IL, 1998); Shirley Povich, *The Washington Senators* (New York, 1954); Bob Broeg, "Ferrell Was a Blue-Chip Redneck," *TSN*, January 22, 1977; Wes Ferrell file, National Baseball Library, Cooperstown, NY; Peter Golenbock, *Fenway* (New York, 1992); Donald Honig, *Baseball When the Grass Was Real* (New York, 1975); Paul MacFarlane, ed., *TSN Daguerreotypes of Great Stars of Baseball* (St. Louis, MO, 1981); *The Baseball Encyclopedia*, 10th ed. (New York, 1996); *TSN*, November 12, 1942, December 14, 1944, July 23, 1952, December 25, 1976.

Frank V. Phelps

FIELDER, Cecil Grant "The Big Man" (b. September 21, 1963, Los Angeles, CA), player, dazzled Detroit Tigers (AL) and AL fans with his HR slugging in the early 1990s. He is the son of Tina Fielder, a business manager, and graduated from Nogales High School in La Puenta, CA, where he made All-State in baseball, football, and basketball. Although basketball was his best sport, he attended the University of Nevada at Las Vegas on a baseball scholarship. The Baltimore Orioles (AL) drafted him in the 31st round in June 1981, but the Kansas City Royals (AL) took him in the fourth round of the 1982 secondary draft and traded the right-handed batting and throw-ing first baseman to the Toronto Blue Jays (AL) in February 1983. The 6-foot 3-inch, 250-pound Fielder made it to the major leagues by 1985, but never exceeded 175 at bats with the Toronto Blue Jays through 1988. In December 1988, the Toronto Blue Jays sold Fielder to the Hanshin, Japan Tigers (JCL). He ranked among the JCL leaders in most offensive categories in 1989 with a .302 batting average, 38 HR, and 81 RBI in 106 games.

The Detroit Tigers in January 1990 signed Fielder, who set Motown agog by clubbing a major league–leading 51 HR—including a 520-foot tape mea-sure blast—and leading the major leagues with 132 RBI. His final two HR came dramatically at Yankee Stadium on October 3, the last day of the 1990 season, against the New York Yankees. Fielder also led the AL in total bases (339), slugging average (.592), and strikeouts (182). In 1991, his 44 HR tied for the AL lead, while his 133 RBI topped the major leagues again. A major league–leading 124 RBI in 1992 made Fielder the first slugger since Babe Ruth* to lead the major leagues in RBI three consecutive years. Fielder made the AL All-Star team in 1990, 1991, and 1993 and finished runner-up in the AL MVP voting in 1990 and 1991. A 1990 *USA Today* survey of AL players revealed Fielder to be the overwhelming choice for MVP among his peers. He was named *TSN* AL Player of the Year in 1990 and *TSN* All-Star team member and *TSN* Silver Slugger member in 1990 and 1991. In his first four years with the Detroit Tigers, Fielder averaged over 125 RBI per season. Fielder clouted 28 HR with 90 RBI in the strike-shortened 1994 season and 31 HR with 82 RBI in 1995. In July 1996, the New York Yankees acquired Fielder in a trade. He supplied 39 HR with 117 RBI in 1996, as New York won the AL East. His .364 batting average, one HR, and four RBI in the Division Series against the Texas Rangers and two HR with eight RBI in the AL Championship Series against the Baltimore Orioles helped the Yan-kees capture the AL pennant. The New York Yankees defeated the Atlanta Braves in the 1996 World Series, in which Fielder batted .391 with two RBI. In December 1997, the Anaheim Angels (AL) signed him as a free agent. He joined the Cleveland Indians (AL) in August 1998, but spent just one month there. He tried out with the Toronto Blue Jays in 1999.

In 14 major league seasons through 1998, Fielder batted .255 with 319 HR, 1,008 RBI, 1,316 strikeouts, and only two stolen bases, both in 1995. He belted 11 career grand-slam HR and clouted three HR in games on May

6, 1990, June 6, 1990, and April 16, 1996, tying major league records for most times with at least three HR in a game and in one season. Fielder, who proved particularly effective in night games and against left-handed pitching, became one of the few players to homer over the roof in Tiger Stadium and the first to power a fair ball out of Milwaukee's County Stadium.

Fielder is admired for his prodigious slugging, affability, modesty, and devotion to his family. He is married to Stacey (Granger) and has one son, Prince, his costar in a widely seen TV commercial, and a daughter, Cecilyn.

BIBLIOGRAPHY: Cecil Fielder file, National Baseball Library, Cooperstown, NY; Barbara Carlisle Bigelow, *Contemporary Black Biography*, vol. 2 (Detroit, MI, 1992), pp. 75–78; N. Cohen, "A 50–50 Chance," *Sport* 82 (June 1991), pp. 81–85; P. De-Jonge, "The Slugger Nobody Wanted," *NYT Magazine* (April 5, 1992), pp. 20–23; *Detroit Tiger Yearbooks*, 1991–1994; "Cecil Fielder," *BT* 2 (September 1993), pp. 64–70; Gary Gillette, *The Great American Baseball Statbook* (New York, 1993); Richard Hoffer, "Big Daddy," *SI* 75 (September 30, 1991), pp. 36–40; Steven Rushin, "Flirting with 50," *SI* 73 (September 24, 1990), pp. 68–70; William M. Anderson, *The Detroit Tigers* (South Bend, IN, 1996); *NYT Biographical Service* 23 (April 1992), pp. 402–408; *TSN Official Baseball Register*, 1998; *WWA*, 48th ed. (1994), p. 1087.

Sheldon L. Appleton

FINGERS, Roland Glen "Rollie" (b. August 25, 1946, Steubenville, OH), player, is the son of George Fingers and Edna (Stafford) Fingers. Fingers, whose father and brother, Gordon, played minor league baseball, attended Chaffey JC in California. He signed with the Kansas City Athletics (AL) on Christmas Eve 1964, and pitched for Leesburg, FL (FSL) in 1965, Modesto, CA (CaL) in 1966, and Birmingham, AL (SL) in 1967 and 1968.

From 1969 to 1976, the 6-foot 4-inch, 190-pound right-hander pitched for the Oakland A's (AL) and teamed with Mudcat Grant,* Blue Moon Odom, Catfish Hunter,* and Vida Blue.* He learned much from reliever Grant and developed into a dependable relief pitcher. Besides consistently ranking among leaders in saves, he also led the AL in total games with 76 in 1974 and 75 in 1975 and finished 59 games in relief the latter season. With the A's, Fingers pitched in five AL Championship Series and established an AL record for the most series saves. He compiled a 2–2 mark in three World Series and made 6 saves in 16 appearances (both league bests) for a 1.35 ERA. Fingers, whose performance in 1974 won him the World Series MVP Award, was named to seven All-Star teams—twice from Oakland.

Fingers joined the San Diego Padres (NL) in December 1976 and led the NL with 78 appearances, 69 games finished in relief, and 35 saves in 1977. He was named both Rolaids Relief Man of the Year and *TSN* Fireman of the Year. In 1978, he tied the then NL record for most saves with 37 and again collected the top relief awards. After being traded to the Milwaukee Brewers (AL) in December 1980, Fingers propelled the Brewers to the AL playoff in 1981 with a 6–3 record, a league-leading 28 saves, and a 1.04

ERA. With an incredible strikeout-to-walk ratio of almost 5 to 1, he won or saved 55 percent of the Brewers' wins and received both the AL MVP and Cy Young awards. He earned his $750,000 salary in 1982 by pitching well for the Brewers until September, when an arm problem kept him out of the playoffs and World Series. Although missing the 1983 season, he returned in 1984 with his trademark handlebar mustache to record 23 saves and a 1.96 ERA on a team that won only 67 games. The Milwaukee Brewers released Fingers in November 1985. In 944 games, he compiled a 114–118 mark, surrendered 1,474 hits in 1,701 innings, saved 341 games, and recorded a 2.90 ERA.

By throwing 80 percent of his pitches where he wants them, Fingers compiled 1,299 strikeouts compared to only 492 bases on balls. His remarkable control and durability helped him establish baseball's all-time record for saves plus wins (455). Fingers and his former wife, Jill, have three children and resided in San Diego. In 1992, he became the second reliever elected to the National Baseball Hall of Fame.

BIBLIOGRAPHY: Rollie Fingers file, National Baseball Library, Cooperstown, NY; Bruce Markusen, *Baseball's Last Dynasty* (New York, 1998); Dave Anderson, "Rollie Fingers Is Trying to Pitch," *NYT Biographical Service* 14 (March 13, 1983), pp. 300–301; Melissa Ludtke Lincoln, "Rollie's Rolling Again," *SI* 49 (September 11, 1978), pp. 81–82; Lawrence Linderman, "Sport Interview: Rollie Fingers," *Sport* 73 (May 1982), pp. 16–21; Barry Mednick, "Cy of Relief: Rollie Fingers," *BRJ* 21 (1992), pp. 105–106; *The Baseball Encyclopedia*, 10th ed. (New York, 1996); *TSN Official Baseball Register*, 1986; *TSN*, October 15, 1984, p. 38; *WWA*, 42nd ed. (1982–1983), p. 1041.

Gaymon L. Bennett

FINLEY, Charles Edward "Chuck" (b. November 26, 1962, Monroe, LA), player, is the only son of Charles Ellis Finley, a tree nurseryman and landscaper, and Sue Finley and graduated in 1980 from West Monroe, LA High School. He attended Louisiana Tech University in 1980–1981, pitching for the baseball team. Although exhibiting a blazing fast ball, he walked 33 batters and threw eight wild pitches in just 26.2 innings. After working the next year in his family business, he attended Northern Louisiana State College from 1982 through 1985 and compiled a mediocre baseball record.

The California Angels (AL) selected the 6-foot 6-inch, 214-pound Finley, who bats and throws left-handed, in the secondary phase of the January 1985 draft. He pitched just 41 minor league innings with Salem, OR (NWL) in 1985 and Davenport, IA–based Quad Cities (ML) in 1986 before joining the California Angels. In 1986, he finished 3–1 with a 3.30 ERA for California and appeared briefly in the AL Championship Series against the Boston Red Sox.

Finley, who has spent his entire major league career with the California Angels, struggled his first two full major league seasons until developing a devastating fork ball. He enjoyed his two finest major league seasons in 1989 and 1990, making the AL All-Star and *TSN* All-Star teams both years. Finley compiled a 16–9 mark and 2.57 ERA, second best in the AL, in 1989, hurling a 5–0 one-hitter against the Boston Red Sox on May 26 and fanning 15 Baltimore Orioles on June 24. His best major league season came in 1990, when he finished 18–9 with a 2.40 ERA and trailed only Roger Clemens* in ERA. He failed to win 20 games because the Angels scored just three runs in his final three starts.

After another 18–9 campaign in 1991, Finley enjoyed less success. In 1993, he won 16 games, shared the AL lead with 13 complete games, and toiled over 250 innings for the only time in his career. Finley won 15 games in both 1995 and 1996, making the AL All-Star team both times. He struck out 15 New York Yankees on May 23, 1995 and fanned a career-high 215 batters in 238 innings in 1996, but led the AL with 17 wild pitches. He anchored the Anaheim Angels (AL) with an 11–9 record and 3.39 ERA in 1998. In 1999, Finley won 12 games and ranked second in strikeouts (200). The Cleveland Indians acquired him in December 1999.

In 14 major league seasons through 1999, Finley has 165 wins, 140 losses, a 3.72 ERA, 14 shutouts and 2,151 strikeouts in 2,675 innings. For a time, he ranked as the best southpaw in major league baseball. The Newport Beach, CA resident married Julie Kitaen in November 1997 and has one daughter, Wynter.

BIBLIOGRAPHY: Charles E. Finley file, National Baseball Library, Cooperstown, NY; *TSN Baseball Register*, 1998; Steve Rushin, "Chuckin' " *SI* 75 (July 1, 1991), pp. 34–36, 38, 43; Tom Singer, "The Week of Pitching Excellently," *Sport* 82 (March 1991), pp. 62–64, 66–67.

David L. Porter

FINLEY, Charles O. "Charley" (b. February 22, 1918, Ensley, AL; d. February 19, 1996, Chicago, IL), owner, was the son of Burmah and Oscar Finley, a Birmingham, AL steel worker. He attended Emerson High School and graduated from Horace Mann High School in Gary, IN in 1936. After attending Gary JC and Indiana University, he married Shirley McCartney in May, 1941. They had seven children. The enterprising Finley worked numerous odd jobs to augment his working-class family's meager savings, but still maintained an active interest in sports. Before moving north during the Depression, he had served as batboy for the 1931 Birmingham, AL Barons (SL). As a high school student, he played baseball and boxed in the Gary Golden Gloves tournament. In college, he worked nights at the U.S. Steel plant and spent days and weekends playing first base in several semipro leagues in Indiana. After World War II, Finley became a salesman for the Travelers Insurance Company and earned a fortune from his commission on the sale of a group insurance policy for the American College of Surgeons in 1952.

With his combined insurance, manufacturing, and real estate interests, Finley pursued his lifelong dream of owning a major league baseball franchise. During the 1950s, he attempted to purchase the Detroit Tigers (AL), the Chicago White Sox (AL), and the faltering Philadelphia Athletics (AL) and sought to create an expansion franchise in Los Angeles prior to the Brooklyn Dodgers' move west. He purchased 52 percent of the Kansas City Athletics (AL) stock in 1960 and acquired the remainder the next two years. Finley, primarily a businessman regardless of his love for baseball, saw his losing team's dwindling profit margin. After abortive attempts to shift his club to Louisville, KY and Dallas, TX, he moved the franchise to Oakland, CA in 1968. The team encountered immediate success on the field and at the box office, finishing above .500 that first season in Oakland. Finley's Athletics ultimately earned profits in 19 of 20 seasons.

Finley assembled key young players who formed the first genuine baseball dynasty since the decline of the New York Yankees earlier in the 1960s. The very popular team was embroiled in turmoil, achieving notoriety because of constant feuding between Finley and his players and managers and because of the attention paid by the media to the owner's headline-making stunts and personality. Oakland finished second in the first two years of divisional play (1969, 1970), won its first divisional title in 1971, and captured its first AL pennant in 1972. The A's won AL pennants in 1973 and 1974 and a division title in 1975, but succumbed to Finley's refusal to coexist with free agency and declined considerably by the end of the decade. Finley hired ten managers, two of them twice, in 14 seasons. Billy Martin,* the last mentor, brought the team in 1980 from seventh to second place. In 1979, the team drew sparse crowds (often under 1,000 paid customers) and had the worst attendance and win-loss records in baseball. Martin's demeanor and baseball knowledge brought renewed team success and rejuvenated popular interest in the Athletics. After being rumored to sell the franchise to interested parties in Denver, CO, Memphis, TN, and New Orleans, LA, Finley sold the team to a local group headed by Walter J. Haas in 1981 and left baseball gracefully. After attempting to acquire the Chicago Cubs in 1981, he drew up plans the next year with Bill Veeck* for an international league with teams from U.S. minor league cities, Latin America, and Japan.

Finley also owned the California Golden Seals (NHL) hockey club and the Memphis Pros/Tams (ABA) basketball club. During 20 stormy years filled with interviews, press conferences, and the most media coverage ever devoted to one sports team owner, Finley changed the structure and nature of the baseball business almost single-handedly. He expedited general free agency for players with his firings of Ken Harrelson and Mike Andrews and engaged in contract disputes with Jim "Catfish" Hunter* and other star players. Volatile relationships with his players and managers led to much fan dissent and constant disputes with Commissioner Bowie Kuhn,* who often levied substantial fines on Finley. His players, protesting Finley's personal conservatism and reflecting the temper of the times, popularized facial hair in American baseball. Besides his persistent publicity stunts to increase ticket sales, Finley was partly responsible for initiating night World Series and All-

Star games, brightly colored player uniforms, the DH rule, and the increased use of special promotional dates and gifts. Several ideas not adopted at the time by professional baseball included the use of yellow or orange baseballs, designated runner, interleague play, regional reorganization of the leagues, and early entry into the National Baseball Hall of Fame. After leaving baseball, Finley still operated his insurance business, Charles O. Finley Corporation, and served as president of a Canadian firm, Century Energy Corporation.

BIBLIOGRAPHY: Charles O. Finley file, National Baseball Library, Cooperstown, NY; Tom Clark, *Champagne and Baloney* (New York, 1976); Alvin Dark and John Underwood, *When in Doubt, Fire the Manager* (New York, 1980); Glenn Dickey, *The History of American League Baseball* (New York, 1980); Jim Hawkins, "Finley Was Pompous, Persuasive, and Powerful," *SCD* 23 (March 22, 1996), p. 40; Brad Herzog, *The Sports 100* (New York, 1995); R. O'Brien, "Another Bright Idea," *SI* 71 (October 23, 1989), p. 30; Bruce Markusen, *Baseball's Last Dynasty* (New York, 1998); *TSN*, May 28, 1984.
                                                                    Alan R. Asnen

FISK, Carlton Ernest "Pudge" (b. December 26, 1947, Bellows Falls, VT), player, probably is best remembered for his game-winning HR with the Boston Red Sox (AL) at Fenway Park in the twelfth inning of the sixth game in the 1975 World Series against the Cincinnati Reds. Fisk, who attended the University of New Hampshire on a basketball scholarship, caught for Waterloo, IA (ML), Pittsfield, MA, Pawtucket, RI (EL), and Louisville, KY (IL) during his minor league career in the Red Sox farm system. After brief trials with the Red Sox in 1969 and 1971, Fisk became the regular Boston catcher in 1972 and won the AL's Rookie of the Year Award. Fisk also led the AL in triples (9) his rookie season. He appeared in 10 All-Star games (1972–1973, 1976–1978, 1980–1982, 1985, 1991) for the AL and batted .240 in the 1975 World Series.

Fisk remained with Boston through the 1980 season before joining the Chicago White Sox (AL) in March 1981 through the free agency route. In 1984 a season-long groin injury hampered Fisk's effectiveness, causing his batting average to drop nearly 60 points to .231 and his RBI to plummet to one-half (43) of those of 1983. Due to a winter-long weight training program, however, Fisk in 1985 hit a career-high 37 HR to set a single-season record for AL catchers, placed second in the AL in HR, and knocked in a career-high 107 runs. No AL catcher had clouted as many HR in a single season. Fisk's successful career has featured his leadership and ability to handle pitchers. He led AL catchers with a .993 fielding percentage in 1989 and remained with the White Sox until released during the 1993 season. Fisk thought he could still play and remained upset with the White Sox for several years. Chicago retired his uniform number 72.

In 24 major league seasons, Fisk batted .269 with 2,356 hits, including 421 doubles, 47 triples, and 376 HR, knocked in 1,330 runs, and stole 128 bases. He holds major league records for most games by a catcher (2,226) and most HR by a catcher (351) and AL career catching records for most seasons (24), putouts (11,369), and chances accepted (12,417). He was elected to the National Baseball Hall of Fame in 2000 and resides in Lockport, IL.

BIBLIOGRAPHY: Carlton Fisk file, National Baseball Library, Cooperstown, NY; D. Hall, "Carlton Fisk, Won't You Please Come Home," *Yankee* 56 (September 1992), pp. 78–83; Peter Gammons, "Sharp as Ever," *SI* 72 (February 26, 1990), pp. 62–66; Peter Golenbock, *Fenway* (New York, 1992); Robert Redmount, *The Red Sox Encyclopedia* (Champaign, IL, 1998); Dan Shaughnessy, *The Curse of the Bambino* (New York, 1990); Bob Vanderberg, *Sox: From Lane and Fain to Fisk and Zisk* (Chicago, IL, 1982); Richard Lindberg, *Who's on Third?* (South Bend, IN, 1983); Gene Karst and Martin J. Jones, Jr., *Who's Who in Professional Baseball* (New Rochelle, NY, 1973); Robert Grayson, "The Class of '99," *SCD* 25 (December 25, 1998), pp. 80–81; G. Richard McKelvey, *Fisk's Homer, Willie's Catch and the Shot Heard Round the World* (Jefferson, NC, 1998); Robert E. Kelly, *Baseball's Best* (Jefferson, NC, 1988); P. Korn, "Old Catchers Never Die," *Sport* 80 (July 1989), pp. 44–49; Leigh Montville, "Bitter Ending," *SI* 78 (May 31, 1993), pp. 36–38; Dan Valenti, *Clout: The Top Home Runs in Baseball History* (Lexington, MA, 1989); George Vecsey, "Commanding Fisk Is a Red Sox Bastion," *NYT Biographical Service*, May 1980, pp. 677–678.

William J. Serow

FITZSIMMONS, Frederick Landis "Freddie," "Fat Freddie" (b. July 28, 1901, Mishawaka, IN; d. November 18, 1979, Yucca Valley, CA), player, manager, and executive, pitched for the New York Giants (1925–1937) and Brooklyn Dodgers (1937–1943) of the NL. During his 19-year career, the 5-foot 11-inch, right-handed Fitzsimmons compiled a 217–146 won–lost record with a 3.51 ERA and 29 shutouts. The control pitcher struck out 870 and walked 846 batters in 3,223.2 innings. Fitzsimmons' best year occurred in 1928, when he posted a 20–9 mark and hurled four relief victories. He led the NL in winning percentage (.889) in 1940 with a 16–2 record. From 1928 to 1937, Fitzsimmons and Carl Hubbell* combined for 325 victories and provided the Giants with a potent right-lefty duo. Fitzsimmons, who played in three World Series, was shutout, 4–0, by the Washington Senators in Game 2 of the 1933 classic. He suffered two defeats, including a four-hit, 2–1, hard luck loss in Game 3, to the New York Yankees in the 1936 World Series. In the 1941 World Series, Fitzsimmons pitched for the Dodgers against the Yankees. After holding the Yankees scoreless for seven innings, he was hit in the knee by a line drive and forced to leave the game. The Yankees eventually won both the game and the World Series, while Fitzsimmons never fully recovered. After the 1941 World Series, he won only three more games the next two seasons and retired.

Fitzsimmons, who curiously never appeared in an All-Star game, batted a respectable .200 lifetime and hit 14 career HR. On May 10, 1931, he hit a grand-slam HR off Chicago Cubs pitcher Pat Malone.* Fitzsimmons managed the Philadelphia Phillies (NL) three years (1943–1945), guiding them to a 105–181 record, one seventh place and two last place finishes. He also served as coach for the Boston Braves (NL, 1942), New York Giants (1949–1955), Chicago Cubs (NL, 1957–1959, 1966), Kansas City Athletics (AL, 1960), and Salt Lake City, UT (PCL), and as general manager of the Brooklyn Dodgers (NFL).

Of Irish ancestry, Fitzsimmons married Helen Burger, in 1925 in Indianapolis, IN as a minor league player there. He had one daughter, Helen. Fitzsimmons' wife described him as having "bright blue eyes and a smile that warms you all over." Fitzsimmons regarded "mental discipline—the willingness to bear down and go all-out on every play" as a good ballplayer's chief asset.

BIBLIOGRAPHY: Fred Fitzsimmons file, National Baseball Library, Cooperstown, NY; Thomas Aylesworth and Benton Minks, *The Encyclopedia of Baseball Managers* (New York, 1990); Craig Carter, ed., *TSN Official World Series Records* (St. Louis, MO, 1983); Freddie Fitzsimmons, "Did the Best Teams Get in the Series?" *SEP* 228 (October 1, 1955), pp. 25, 110–112; Mrs. Freddie Fitzsimmons, "I Married Baseball," *Coronet* 38 (September 1955), pp. 96–100; Tot Holmes, *Dodgers Blue Book* (Los Angeles, CA, 1983); Noel Hynd, *The Giants of the Polo Grounds* (New York, 1988); Fred Stein, *Under Coogan's Bluff* (Glenshaw, PA, 1978); Peter Golenbock, *Bums* (New York, 1984); Richard Goldstein, *Superstars and Screwballs* (New York, 1991); Peter Williams, *When the Giants Were Giants* (Chapel Hill, NC, 1994); William F. McNeil, *The Dodgers Encyclopedia* (Champaign, IL, 1997); *The Baseball Encyclopedia*, 10th ed. (New York, 1996); *TSN Official Baseball Guide, 1980*.

Jack P. Lipton

FLANAGAN, Michael Kendall "Mike," "Flanny" (b. December 16, 1951, Manchester, NH), player, coach, and sportscaster, is the son of Edward Flanagan, a cabinetmaker, and Lorraine Flanagan, a hospital dietician and part-time newspaper columnist. After starring in high school baseball and basketball, Flanagan was drafted in 1971 by the Houston Astros (NL). He attended the University of Massachusetts, where the left-handed pitcher finished 12–1 in two seasons and started at guard on the 18–1 basketball team in 1972–1973.

The Baltimore Orioles (AL) drafted Flanagan in June 1973, with scout John Stokoe signing him. During his 18-year major league career, the 6-foot, 200 pounder considered putting on a major league uniform for the first time as his biggest thrill. His father, Edward, and grandfather had pitched in the Boston Red Sox (AL) minor league organization without making it to the major leagues. After achieving a 13–4 mark with Rochester, NY (IL) in 1975, Flanagan made his debut for the Baltimore Orioles against the New York Yankees on September 5.

Flanagan, who considered the Orioles' Ray Miller his best pitching coach, ranked among the last generation of starting pitchers expecting to hurl a complete game. He started more games and toiled more innings than any other AL pitcher from 1977 to 1984, recording 17 complete games in 1978. Overall, he finished 25 percent of his career 404 starts.

Flanagan's other personal highlights included winning the AL Cy Young Award with a 23–9 record in 1979 for his only 20-victory season. He led AL hurlers in victories and shutouts (5). He made his first World Series start, a 5–4 win over the Pittsburgh Pirates in the 1979 opening game. He lost Game 5 of the 1979 World Series and started Game 3 of the 1983 World Series against the Philadelphia Phillies without being involved in the decision. He finished 2–1 in the 1979, 1983, and 1989 AL Championship Series. Although selected for the 1978 All-Star team, he did not appear in the game.

The Baltimore Orioles traded Flanagan to the Toronto Blue Jays (AL) in August 1987 for pitchers Jose Mesa and Oswaldo Peraza. Flanagan worked 211 innings while producing a 13–13 record in 1988. Arm problems sidelined him in May 1990 and caused the Blue Jays to release him after that season. The Orioles invited Flanagan to 1991 spring training without a contract. He won a job as a middle reliever, appearing in 64 games with a 2.36 ERA. The popular Flanagan pitched the last two-thirds of an inning in the final game at Baltimore's Memorial Stadium on October 6, 1991. His major league playing career ended in 1992. Flanagan's major league career record included 167 wins, 153 losses, and a 3.90 ERA. His 141 victories in a Baltimore uniform rank fourth highest in Orioles history.

Flanagan's witticisms kept his teammates loose. He created imaginative nicknames for many teammates and opponents, and adeptly handled both quick quips and throws to first base, making only nine errors in 18 seasons.

Flanagan spent 1995 with the Baltimore Orioles as a pitching coach, characterizing the season as both frustrating and rewarding. He was released with most of the coaching staff when rookie manager Phil Regan was fired. Flanagan has served as a radio-television analyst for the Baltimore Orioles since 1997.

Flanagan, who contemplated becoming a forest ranger, lives in Cockeysville, MD with his wife, Alex, and their three children, Kerry, Kathryn, and Kendall.

BIBLIOGRAPHY: Mike Flanagan file, National Baseball Library, Cooperstown, NY; *Baltimore Orioles Media Guides*, 1992, 1995; Rex Barney, *Rex Barney's Orioles Memories* (Woodbury, CT, 1994); Norman Macht, interview with Mike Flanagan, September 29, 1995; Ted Patterson, *The Baltimore Orioles* (Dallas, TX, 1995); James H. Bready, *Baseball in Baltimore* (Baltimore, MD, 1998).

Norman L. Macht

FLETCHER, Arthur "Art" (b. January 5, 1885, Collinsville, IL; d. February 6, 1950, Los Angeles, CA), player, coach, and manager, batted and threw right-handed. He was 5 feet 10½ inches and weighed 170 pounds. Fletcher held what he considered to be "The best job in baseball" from 1927 through

1945, serving as third base coach for some of the New York Yankees' (AL) greatest teams.

Fletcher began his professional baseball career as an infielder with Dallas, TX (TL) in 1907. New York Giants manager John McGraw* saw him play several preseason games and took an option on him. In 1909, McGraw exercised the option and promoted Fletcher to the New York Giants. Fletcher's erratic fielding limited his appearances for two years, but he began playing several infield positions regularly in 1911 before settling down at shortstop. A tough, competitive shortstop in the McGraw mold, he helped the Giants win NL pennants from 1911 through 1913 and in 1917. His best personal season came in 1911, when he hit .319. He led NL shortstops in fielding in 1917 and 1918. In June 1920, the Giants traded him to the Philadelphia Phillies (NL). The deaths of his father and brother caused Fletcher to retire voluntarily from baseball in 1921. During his 13-year major league career, Fletcher batted .277, made 1,534 hits, knocked in 675 runs, and struck out only 348 times. After an unsuccessful comeback as player in 1922, he managed the Philadelphia Phillies to a lackluster 231–378 record from 1923 through 1926. The serious family man found managerial responsibilities more time-consuming than he wanted. In 1927, he accepted an offer from manager Miller Huggins* to join the New York Yankees as coach. Fletcher declined managerial offers from the Chicago White Sox (AL), Detroit Tigers (AL), and St. Louis Browns (AL). After Huggins died in September 1929, Fletcher piloted the Yankees to a 6–5 record at the end of the regular season. This marked his final stint at the helm of a major league team. Although offered the New York managerial job, he remained as coach. During Fletcher's tenure, the Yankees won 10 AL pennants and 9 World Series. Fletcher married Blanche Dieu in November 1910 and had two daughters, Jeanne and Betty.

BIBLIOGRAPHY: Thomas Aylesworth and Benton Minks, *The Encyclopedia of Baseball Managers* (New York, 1990); Mark Gallagher, *The Yankee Encyclopedia*, vol. 3 (Champaign, IL, 1997); Noel Hynd, *The Giants of the Polo Grounds* (New York, 1988); Frank Graham, *The New York Giants* (New York, 1952); Charles C. Alexander, *John McGraw* (New York, 1988); *The Baseball Encyclopedia*, 10th ed. (New York, 1996); Arthur Fletcher file, National Baseball Library, Cooperstown, NY; Gene Karst and Martin J. Jones, Jr., *Who's Who in Professional Baseball* (New Rochelle, NY, 1973); Joseph L. Reichler, *The Great All-Time Baseball Record Book* (New York, 1981); Rich Westcott and Frank Bilovsky, *The New Phillies Encyclopedia* (Philadelphia, PA, 1993); Frederick G. Lieb and Stan Baumgartner, *The Philadelphia Phillies* (New York, 1953).

Horace R. Givens

FLETCHER, Elburt Preston "Elbie" (b. March 18, 1916, Milton, MA; d. March 9, 1994, Milton, MA), player, was the son of Elmer P. Fletcher, a salesman, and Elizabeth (McLory) Fletcher and grew up in comfortable circumstances in the Boston suburb of Milton, where he played baseball, football, ice hockey, and basketball. His baseball skills attracted the attention of Boston Braves (NL) manager Bill McKechnie.* The Braves signed the 17 year old to a contract in 1934 and used him in eight games that season.

The 6-foot, 175-pound, left-handed first baseman shuffled between Boston and the minor leagues until remaining with the Braves the entire 1937 season. In June 1939, the Boston Braves traded him to the Pittsburgh Pirates (NL). Fletcher enjoyed his best years with the Pirates, hitting .273 with 16 HR, in 1940. His 104 RBI ranked fourth highest in the NL. In 1940 and 1941, he led the NL in walks.

Fletcher, once billed as the "future George Sisler,"* frequently was slowed by leg injuries. Nevertheless, the slick-fielding first baseman made the 1943 All-Star team. In 1944 and 1945, he served in the U.S. Navy during World War II. Fletcher returned to the Pittsburgh Pirates in 1946, but was sold to the Cleveland Indians (AL) in December 1947. Injuries struck again, however, causing the Indians to release him.

In 1948, Fletcher joined the New York Giants (NL) farm club at Minneapolis, MN (AA). In May 1949, the Boston Braves purchased him from the Giants' Jersey City, NJ (IL) farm team. Fletcher played in 122 games for the Braves, but was released after the 1949 season. During his 12-year major league career, Fletcher hit .271 with 1,323 hits, 79 HR and 616 RBI.

Fletcher worked in radio and television and served as recreation director for Melrose, MA from 1958 until 1981. He married Martha Hanson in November 1938 and had two sons, Robert and Steven. Fletcher recalled, "Baseball to me was great fun. Perhaps if I had been more serious I might have been a better ballplayer. However, that was my style and I never changed."

BIBLIOGRAPHY: *The Baseball Encyclopedia*, 10th ed. (New York, 1996); *Boston Globe*, March 1, 1994; Elbie Fletcher file, PPAA, Pittsburgh, PA; Elbie Fletcher file, *TSN*, St. Louis, MO; Donald Honig, *Baseball When the Grass Was Real* (New York, 1975); Harold Kaese, *The Boston Braves* (New York, 1948); Gary Caruso, *The Braves Encyclopedia* (Philadelphia, PA, 1995); Frederick G. Lieb, *The Pittsburgh Pirates* (New York, 1948); Richard L. Burtt, *The Pittsburgh Pirates, A Pictoricial History* (Virginia Beach, VA, 1977); Brent P. Kelley, *The Early Stars* (Jefferson, NC, 1997).

Frank W. Thackeray

FLICK, Elmer Harrison (b. January 11, 1876, Bedford, OH; d. January 9, 1971, Bedford, OH), player, was the son of Zachary Taylor Flick and Mary (Caine) Flick. His father, a farmer, also conducted a threshing business. Flick attended Bedford High School, where he starred as a catcher on the baseball team. He married Mary Ella Gates in 1900 and had five daughters. Flick's introduction to semi-pro baseball was worthy of fiction, coming when he was at the station to give the Bedford team a send-off. Since the train was about to leave and only eight players were present, someone asked 15-year-old Flick to join. Flick jumped at the opportunity, even though he was barefoot.

Flick entered organized baseball as an outfielder with Youngstown, OH

(ISL) in 1896 and spent the next season with Dayton, OH (ISL). In the spring of 1898, he reported to the Philadelphia Phillies (NL) with a bat that had been fashioned on a lathe. One writer described him as "one of the most promising youngsters the Phillies had ever had." Philadelphia boasted a veteran outfield, but Flick replaced the injured Sam Thompson* on April 26. He made two hits that day and remained a major leaguer for the next 13 years. In four full years with Philadelphia, he averaged .345 at the plate and hit a career-high .367 in 1900. On May 11, 1902, he was sold to the Cleveland Blues of the fledgling AL. The speedster led the AL in stolen bases in 1904 and 1906 and in triples three years (1905–1907). In 1905 he topped the AL with a .308 batting average, the lowest leading mark up to then. His 13-year career batting average stood nine points higher at .315. After physical problems restricted his play the last three years at Cleveland (1908–1910), he closed out his career with Toledo, OH (AA) in 1911 and 1912. In 1,483 major league games, Flick made 1,752 hits, 268 doubles, and 164 triples, scored 950 runs, and stole 330 bases.

Some of the best trades are those not made. Flick became involved in one such trade. After the 1907 season, the Detroit Tigers offered Ty Cobb* for Flick. Despite Cobb's three great years, Detroit feared that his aggressive base running would shorten his career. Cleveland rejected the offer! Cobb played 21 more seasons in the major leagues, set numerous career records, and entered the National Baseball Hall of Fame with the first five players named in 1936. Flick lasted only three more years and 99 games in the major leagues.

When his baseball days ended, Flick became a builder in northern Ohio. Always an outdoorsman and horse fancier, he owned and ran trotters. A summer high school league and Bedford's ball park are named for Flick, who never lost interest in young people and baseball. In 1963, the Veterans Committee voted Flick into the National Baseball Hall of Fame.

BIBLIOGRAPHY: Elmer Flick file, National Baseball Library, Cooperstown, NY; John Thorn et al., eds., *Total Indians* (New York, 1996); Lee Allen and Tom Meany, *Kings of the Diamond* (New York, 1956); Martin Appel and Burt Goldblatt, *Baseball's Best: The Hall of Fame Gallery* (New York, 1977); Scott Longert, "Elmer Flick," *TNP* 15 (1995), pp. 32–33; Lowell Reidenbaugh, *Baseball's Hall of Fame-Cooperstown* (New York, 1993); Frederick G. Lieb and Stan Baumgartner, *The Philadelphia Phillies* (New York, 1953); Rich Westcott and Frank Bilovsky, *The New Phillies Encyclopedia* (Philadelphia, PA, 1993); Franklin Lewis, *The Cleveland Indians* (New York, 1949); Paul MacFarlane, ed., *TSN Hall of Fame Fact Book* (St. Louis, MO 1983); Daniel Okrent and Harris Lewine, eds., *The Ultimate Baseball Book* (Boston, MA, 1979).

Emil H. Rothe

FLOOD, Curtis Charles "Curt" (b. January 18, 1938, Houston, TX; d. January 20, 1997, Los Angeles, CA), player and sportscaster, is the youngest child of hospital menials Herman Flood and Laura Flood. The Floods moved with their six children to Oakland, CA in 1940 in search of work. Flood experienced a typical, bleak ghetto upbringing in a world where sports offered one of the few ways out. The exceptionally fast Flood was developed by Oakland talent guru George Powels, whose list of young athletes included Frank Robinson,* Billy Martin,* and Vada Pinson* in baseball and Ollie Matson (FB), John Brodie (FB), and Bill Russell (IS) in other sports. A superior center fielder and versatile hitter, Flood starred at McClymonds and Oakland Technical high schools and was signed by the Cincinnati Reds (NL) upon graduation in 1956. The young ballplayer spent two years on southern minor league teams, Thomasville, NC (CrL) in 1956 and Savannah, GA (SAL) in 1957, before being traded to the St. Louis Cardinals (NL) in December 1957.

The 5-foot 9-inch 165-pound Flood emerged as one of baseball's stars during the 1960s. From 1961 through 1969, he averaged .302, finished fourth in batting average in 1967, placed fifth in batting average in 1968, and tied for the NL lead in hits (211) in 1964. Flood also replaced Willie Mays* in the minds of many as the game's premier defensive center fielder. He earned consecutive Gold Gloves from 1963 through 1969 and set major league records for consecutive chances and games by an outfielder without an error. A 1968 *SI* cover story proclaimed Flood "baseball's best centerfielder." His skills helped the Cardinals capture NL pennants in 1964, 1967, and 1968 and world championships in 1964 and 1967, when he served as team co-captain.

Flood made baseball and legal history in 1969 by declining a trade from St. Louis to the Philadelphia Phillies (NL). On December 24, 1969, he wrote Commissioner Bowie Kuhn,* "I do not feel I am a piece of property to be bought and sold irrespective of my wishes." Forsaking a $100,000 contract for 1970, he secured the moral and financial support of Marvin Miller* and the MLPA and the legal counsel of former U.S. Supreme Court Justice Arthur Goldberg to challenge baseball's reserve clause in the federal courts. The U.S. Supreme Court rejected his plea in Flood v. Kuhn on June 18, 1972 in a 5–3 decision, but its ruling was narrowly construed and hinted that legislation or the collective bargaining process between owners and players could overturn the reserve system. Moreover, Flood's suit probably influenced the owners to agree to an arbitration system, which eventually terminated the reserve clause in December 1972. Flood attempted a comeback with the Washington Senators (AL) in 1971, but advancing age and the pressure of off-the-field battles had eroded his skills. He retired at the end of the 1971 season and became a portrait painter and bar owner on the island of Minorca. In 1,759 career games, he batted .293 with 1,861 hits, 271 doubles, 44 triples, 85 HR, 851 runs scored, 636 RBI, and 88 stolen bases.

Flood's autobiography, *The Way It Is*, written with the assistance of journalist Richard Carter, occupies a major position in baseball literature. Flood confirmed stories of player insecurity and tight-fisted owners. But his book, above all, portrayed the residue of racism encountered at all levels of professional play. Besides its inside look at the game, *The Way It Is* frankly revealed a sensitive, introspective athlete whose public accomplishments and trials overshadowed a troubled personal life. Flood's February 1959 marriage to Beverly Collins ended in divorce, with his wife assuming guardianship of the four children. The murder of a close friend and the tragic imprisonment of his talented elder brother, Carl, further marred Flood's private life. *The Way It Is* depicted the story of a man seeking his own identity as it chronicled the life of a famous athlete.

During the late 1970s and in the 1980s, Flood appeared often in "where are they now pieces" that noted his pioneering role in the advent of free agency and observed that he had failed to profit from his fight. He secured a few commercial endorsements and found employment in the Oakland area as a broadcaster for Charles Finley's* A's, as a painter, and as head of the Oakland Little League. He was selected to serve as commissioner of a rival major league and died of throat cancer.

BIBLIOGRAPHY: Curt Flood file, National Baseball Library, Cooperstown, NY; "Baseball's Forgotten Man," *Newsweek* 93 (April 2, 1979), p. 18; George Will, *Bunts* (New York, 1998); David Craft, *Redbirds Revisited* (Chicago, IL, 1990); Curt Flood (with Richard Carter), *The Way It Is* (New York, 1970); Brad Herzog, *The Sports 100* (New York, 1995); William Leggett, "Not Just a Flood, but a Deluge," *SI* 29 (August 19, 1968), pp. 18–21; Lee Lowenfish and Tony Lupien, *The Imperfect Diamond* (New York, 1980); Bob Broeg and Jerry Vickery, *St. Louis Cardinals Encyclopedia* (Grand Rapids, MI, 1998); Rob Rains, *The St. Louis Cardinals* (New York, 1992); Larry Moffi and Jonathan Kronstadt, *Crossing the Line* (Jefferson, NC, 1994); David L. Porter, ed., *African-American Sports Greats* (Westport, CT, 1995); Richard Reeves, "The Last Angry Man," *Esquire* 89 (March 1, 1978), pp. 41–48; Jules Tygiel, *Baseball's Great Experiment* (New York, 1983); David Quentin Voigt, *American Baseball*, vol. 3 (University Park, PA, 1983); "What Ever Happened to Curt Flood?" *Ebony* 36 (March 1981), pp. 55–56; *NYT Biographical Service* 28 (January 1997), p. 113; John McCallum et al., "Obituary," *SI* 86 (January 27, 1997), pp. 19–20; D. Whitford, "Curt Flood," *Sport* 77 (December 1986), pp. 102–103ff.

James W. Harper

FLORREICH, Kathleen Lois "Flash" (b. April 29, 1927, Webster Grove, MO; d. September 11, 1991, Mexico), player, starred as an AAGPBL pitcher. The 5-foot 5-inch, 140-pound Florreich played eight seasons in the AAGPBL with the South Bend, IN Blue Sox (1943–1945), Kenosha, WI Comets (1945–1946), and Rockford, IL Peaches (1947–1950). Although originally an outfielder with South Bend, she switched to third base with Kenosha in 1945. She became a pitcher in 1946 when the delivery method changed from underhand to overhand. Florreich, who batted and threw right-handed, won 20 or more games for the Rockford Peaches in 1948, 1949, and 1950. In 1948, she compiled a 22–10 record. Rockford won AAGPBL championships in 1948 and 1950. In 1949, her .759 winning percentage, based on a 22–7 mark, and 0.67 ERA led the AAGPBL. Her ERA set an all-time single-season record. She also threw the most innings (269) in 1949. The 1950 squad, with Amy "Lefty" Applegren, Dorothy Doyle,* Nickie Fox,* Rosie Gacioch, and Dorothy Kamenshek,* ranks among the best teams in AAGPBL history. Florreich, a 20–8 All-Star pitcher with a league-best 171 strikeouts, during the 1950 regular season, was injured for the championship series against the Fort Wayne, IN Daisies, but the Peaches still won in seven games. She batted .192 with 139 career RBI, stealing 251 bases (including 113 in 1944) in 504 games.

For her pitching career, Florreich finished 86–60 with 774 strikeouts in 1,304 innings, a 1.40 ERA, and a .589 winning percentage. She was nicknamed "Flash" because of her fastball and her base-stealing ability. Her 171 strikeouts in 1950 surpassed the next AAGPBL pitcher by 53. In one game, she struck out 22 batters. Florreich intimidated batters due to her speed and occasional lack of control. An All-Star pitcher from 1948 to 1950, she considered pitching a no hitter and one hitter in consecutive starts as her greatest accomplishment. Florreich batted .204 with 251 stolen bases.

Florreich, who never married, owned and operated The Sonic Wire Company in Los Angeles, CA, until 1968. She also operated a mobile home park in northern Idaho and a RV Park and resort in Spokane, WA before retiring to the Sea of Cortez in Mexico. She loved to travel, fish, and be outdoors.

BIBLIOGRAPHY: AAGPBL files, Northern Indiana Historical Society, South Bend, IN; Barbara Gregorich, *Women at Play* (San Diego, CA, 1993); Susan E. Johnson, *When Women Played Hardball* (Seattle, WA, 1994); W. C. Madden, *The Women of the All-American Girls Professional Baseball League* (Jefferson, NC, 1997).

Dennis S. Clark

FONSECA, Lewis Albert "Lew" (b. January 21, 1899, Oakland, CA; d. November 26, 1989, Ely, IA), player, coach, and manager, enjoyed a solid major league career and produced baseball films for instructional and promotional use. He was married twice and had two children, Lewis Jr. and Carolyn.

Before playing baseball full-time, Fonseca studied for 18 months at San Francisco's College of the Sacred Heart and sang regularly in vaudeville and music hall theater. After having an excellent 1920 season with an "outlaw" independent baseball club in Smithfield, UT, the 5-foot 10½-inch, 180-pound right-hander moved directly to the major leagues with the Cincinnati Reds (NL). He played with the Cincinnati Reds from 1921 to 1924 and with the Philadelphia Phillies (NL) in 1925, batting .319. Fonseca agreed to spend 1926 with Newark, NJ (IL) when he was offered a major league salary plus a share of his sale price to a new team. His superb play at Newark earned him a promotion in 1927 to the Cleveland Indians (AL), where he enjoyed great success and led the AL with a .369 batting average in 1929. The Cleveland Indians traded Fonseca in May 1931 to the Chicago White Sox (AL).

He retired as a player after the 1932 season with a .316 career batting average, 1,075 hits, 31 HR, and 485 RBI for 12 major league seasons. His appearances mostly came at first base and second base, but he also played third base, shortstop, and in the outfield and pitched one scoreless inning.

In 1932, Fonseca was named player–manager of the woeful Chicago White Sox. He was the first manager to use film analysis to enhance player performance. Chicago fired him during the 1934 season after he compiled a 120–196 record for a .380 winning percentage. Fonseca began a new career producing baseball films. He and several other players had appeared in the MGM 1927 silent film version of "Slide Kelly Slide." He used slow motion to analyze players' form, prepared instructional sequences, and pioneered the filming of the World Series and All-Star Games. He convinced the AL and NL front offices that baseball films could stimulate fan interest in major league baseball and served as promotional director for both leagues. During World War II, an estimated ten million servicemen saw his films worldwide. Subsequently, Fonseca continued to produce promotional films for the major league Motion Picture Division. After spending until 1967 behind the camera, he became a hitting instructor for the Chicago Cubs (NL) and Cincinnati Reds and served as a consultant for several other teams until 1981.

BIBLIOGRAPHY: Lew Fonseca file, National Baseball Library, Cooperstown, NY; Richard Miller, "Lew Fonseca Was a Major League Video Pioneer," *SCD* 21 (December 23, 1994), p. 190; John Thom, *Champion Batsman of the 20th Century* (Los Angeles, CA, 1992); Thomas Aylesworth and Benton Minks, *The Encyclopedia of Baseball Managers* (New York, 1990); Warren Brown, *The Chicago White Sox* (New York, 1952); Franklin Lewis, *The Cleveland Indians* (New York, 1949); Edgar Munzel, "Bucketfoot Al Started Fonseca to Filmland," *TSN*, March 6, 1965, pp. 7–8; John Thorn et al., eds., *Total Baseball*, 5th ed. (New York, 1997).

Allen E. Hye

FORD, Edward Charles "Whitey," "The Chairman of the Board" (b. October 21, 1928, New York, NY), player, coach, scout, and sportscaster, is the son of James Ford and Edith Ford and graduated from Manhattan High School of Aviation in New York City. His father was employed as a bartender and meat market worker, while his mother worked at a grocery store and as a bookkeeper. After playing high school baseball, Ford performed as a pitcher and first baseman for the Thirty-Fourth Avenue Boys amateur club in the Queens-Nassau League. A New York Yankees (AL) scout urged Ford to concentrate on pitching and signed him in October 1946 to a Yankees contract and $7,000 bonus, outbidding both the Boston Red Sox (AL) and Brooklyn Dodgers (NL). The left-handed pitcher began his minor league career by posting a 13–4 record at Butler, PA (MAL) in 1947. After compiling a 16–8 mark at Norfolk, VA (PiL) in 1948, he boasted a 16–5 slate and a league-leading 1.61 ERA at Binghamton, NY (EL) the following year.

Ford opened the 1950 season at Kansas City, MO (AA) with an impressive 6–3 record before joining the New York Yankees.

As an AL rookie, he triumphed in nine consecutive games and assembled a 9–1 record and a 2.81 ERA to help propel the Yankees to the 1950 AL pennant. He won the World Series clincher 5–2 against the Philadelphia Phillies. The U.S. Army then drafted Ford and assigned him the next two years to the Signal Corps at Fort Monmouth, NJ. Ford returned to the Yankee lineup in 1953 and posted an impressive 18–6 record in another AL pennant-winning season. By 1955, the 5-foot 10-inch, 178 pounder was considered the Yankees' premier starter and consummate "money pitcher" by winning the most important games. In 1964, the Yankees named him the first active pitcher–coach in major league history. He retired in May 1967 because of a circulatory problem in his left arm and a bone spur in his elbow. Thereafter, he remained with the Yankees as a scout and minor league pitching coach (1967), first base coach (1968), television commentator for Yankees home games (1969), and full-time pitching coach in 1974 and 1975. Since then, Ford has pursued various business interests and maintained his visibility as one of the Yankees' all-time great pitchers.

Ford's 16-year major league career with the Yankees featured numerous records and remarkable achievements. In 498 games, he compiled a 236–106 mark and a major league record for the second best lifetime percentage (.690) by a pitcher with 200 or more decisions. He struck out 1,956 batters in 3,170.1 innings while recording a 2.75 ERA, the second best lifetime ERA by a left-handed hurler with at least 200 victories. He hurled consecutive one-hitters in September 1955 and struck out 6 batters in a row twice. In a 14-inning game on April 22, 1959, Ford defeated the Washington Senators, 1–0, and struck out 15 Senators. Two years later, he won the Cy Young* Award as best pitcher and triumphed in 14 consecutive games, including 8 during June.

Ford led the AL in winning percentage with 19–6 (.760) in 1956, 25–4 (.862) in 1961, and 24–7 (.774) in 1963. He paced the AL in victories in 1955 (18), 1961 (25), and 1963 (24), in ERA in 1956 (2.47) and 1958 (2.01), in innings pitched in 1961 (283) and 1963 (269.1), and in games started in 1961 (39) and 1963 (37). Besides having 45 career shutouts, he paced the AL in that category in 1958 (7) and shared the lead in 1960 (4). Ford's pitching prowess was reflected in his being named to the AL All-Star team from 1954 through 1956, 1958 through 1961, and in 1964. World Series records are replete with Ford's pitching accomplishments. He holds the fall classic records for most series (11), games pitched (22), games started (22), opening games started (8), innings pitched (146), victories (10), losses (8), strikeouts (94), bases on balls (34), and consecutive scoreless innings (33.2). His World Series performances include a .556 winning percentage, 2.71 ERA, and three shutouts. Ford's brilliant career resulted in his induction into the National Baseball Hall of Fame in 1974. The Lake Success, NY resident married Joan Foran on April 14, 1951 and has three children, Sally Ann, Edward, and Thomas.

BIBLIOGRAPHY: John Benson et al., *Baseball's Top 100* (Wilton, CT, 1997); Jim Brosnan, *Great Baseball Pitchers* (New York, 1965); Whitey Ford, Mickey Mantle, and Joseph Durso, *Whitey and Mickey* (New York, 1977); Whitey Ford file, National Baseball Library, Cooperstown, NY; Whitey Ford and Phil Pepe, *Slick* (New York, 1987); Mark Gallagher, *Fifty Years of Yankee All Stars* (New York, 1984); Joseph Gies and Robert H. Shoemaker, *Stars of the Series* (New York, 1965); Al Hirshberg, *The Greatest American Leaguers* (New York, 1970); Craig Carter, ed., *TSN Daguerreotypes*, 8th ed. (St. Louis, MO, 1990); *The Baseball Encyclopedia*, 10th ed. (New York, 1996); Tony Kubek and Terry Pluto, *Sixty-One* (New York, 1987); Mark Gallagher, *The Yankee Encyclopedia*, vol. 3 (Champaign, IL, 1997); Milton J. Shapiro, *Baseball's Greatest Pitchers* (New York, 1969); Milton J. Shapiro, *The Whitey Ford Story* (New York, 1962); Ken Young, *Cy Young Award Winners* (New York, 1994).

Louis J. Andolino

FORD, Russell William "Russ" (b. April 25, 1883, Brandon, Canada; d. January 24, 1960, Rockingham, NC), player, was credited with inventing the "emery ball," a delivery that allowed him to rank among the best major league pitchers in 1910 and 1911. His father, a native of Scotland who farmed and played cricket, encouraged his sons to play baseball. The elder Ford moved his family from Nova Scotia to Manitoba the year before Russell's birth and by 1900 to Minneapolis, MN.

Two of Ford's brothers played professionally. Eugene, the eldest, played briefly with the Detroit Tigers (AL) in 1905. Ford's successful pitching for semiprofessional teams in Enderline, ND and Lisbon, SD led Minneapolis, MN (AA) to sign him to his first professional contract in 1904. After failing to make an impression that year, Ford pitched for Cedar Rapids, IA (3IL) in 1905 and 1906. In the latter year, Ford's 22 victories led Cedar Rapids to the 3IL pennant and earned him a promotion to Atlanta, GA (SA). He enjoyed two solid years there with 18 and 16 wins. The New York Highlanders (AL) drafted Ford, but quickly sold him to Jersey City, NJ (EL).

A misshapen thumb and a crushed third finger on his right hand enabled Ford to develop unusual movement on his pitches. With Atlanta, he added the spitball to his repertoire. At Jersey City, he discovered that a ball scuffed with emery paper moved in unusual ways and sewed pieces of emery paper to his glove. After Ford's 13 wins at Jersey City in 1909, the New York Highlanders reacquired him.

Ford's trick pitches made him almost unhittable his first two seasons in the major leagues. In 1910 he won 26 games, the second highest in the AL, while losing only six decisions, compiling a 1.65 ERA, and allowing only 5.8 hits per nine innings. In 1911, Ford posted his second straight 20-win season with a 21–11 mark. In 1912, the New York Highlanders plummeted to last place, with Ford's record reflecting the fortune of the team. His 13 wins in

1912 and 12 victories in 1913 led the club (renamed the Yankees), but his 21 losses topped all AL pitchers in 1912.

When the FL began operation in 1914, the Buffalo Buffeds inked Ford to a $24,000 four-year contract. In its inaugural season, Ford led the FL in ERA and win–loss percentage with a 20–6 record. For the 1915 season, however, the FL banned the emery ball. With his main pitch no longer legal, Ford slipped to a dismal 4–16 record for the renamed Buffalo Blues with a 4.52 ERA. His major league career ended with the demise of the FL. He won 99 major league games against 71 losses, with a lifetime 2.59 ERA. Ford pitched effectively (16–9) for Denver, CO (WL) in 1916 and ineffectively (1–2) for Toledo, OH (AA) in 1917.

After his baseball career, Ford was employed as a structural engineer for the Submarine Boat Corporation in Newark, NJ. In 1922, he moved with his two daughters, Mary and Jean, and his wife, Mary Hunter (Bethel) Ford, to Mary's hometown in Rockingham, NC and became a bank cashier. The Depression saw the Fords move north, where Russell worked as a draftsman in New York City. After his wife's death in 1957, he returned to Rockingham, NC to live with a daughter and died there of a heart attack.

BIBLIOGRAPHY: Russ Ford file, National Baseball Library, Cooperstown, NY; Mark Gallagher and Neill Gallagher, *Baseball's Great Dynasties: The Yankees* (New York, 1990); Mark Gallagher, *The Yankee Encyclopedia*, vol. 3 (Champaign, IL, 1997); Dan Gutman, *It Ain't Cheatin' If You Don't Get Caught* (New York, 1990); Frank Graham, *The New York Yankees* (New York, 1943); Tommy Holmes, "Baseball's Inventive Ford," *BD* 4 (September 1945), pp. 37–39; Frederick G. Lieb, "Russell Ford," *BM* 7 (August 1911), pp. 36–42; Marc Okkonen, *The Federal League of 1914–1915* (Garrett Park, MD, 1989).

William E. Akin

FORSCH, Robert Herbert "Bob," "Forschie" (b. January 13, 1950, Sacramento, CA), player, is the son of Herbert Forsch, a semiprofessional baseball player in the San Joaquin Valley, CA League during the 1940s and owner of an electric motor repair shop, and the brother of Ken Forsch, a pitcher for 16 years with the Houston Astros (NL) and California Angels (AL). The St. Louis Cardinals (NL) selected Forsch in the 38th round of the 1968 free agent draft from Sacramento City College as a third baseman.

Forsch struggled for four years with St. Louis Cardinals farm clubs before converting to a pitcher at Cedar Rapids, IA (ML) in 1971. There, the 6-foot 3-inch, 212-pound right-hander met and married Mollie Kneen. They have two daughters, Amy Lynn and Kristin Rae. Forsch pitched no-hitters for Little Rock–based Arkansas (TL) in 1972 and Tulsa, OK (AA) in 1973 before joining the St. Louis Cardinals during the 1974 season and fashioning a 7–4 win–loss record with a 2.97 ERA. From 1975 to 1988, he led St. Louis Cardinals pitchers in victories six times and enjoyed his best season in 1977 with a 20–7 mark.

Forsch hurled a 5–0 no-hitter against the Philadelphia Phillies on April 16, 1978 and became the only St. Louis Cardinals pitcher in history to toss more than one no-hitter when he silenced Montreal Expo bats, 3–0, September 26, 1983. Bob and Ken Forsch remain the only brothers in major league history to pitch no-hitters. Forsch began as a power pitcher, but developed pinpoint control. The fine fielder and fierce competitor was an outstanding hitting pitcher. He batted .308 in 1975 and won *TSN* Silver Slugger awards in 1980 and 1987. On August 10, 1986, Forsch smashed a grand-slam HR off the Pittsburgh Pirates' Mike Bielecki.

On August 31, 1988, the St. Louis Cardinals traded the popular Forsch to the Houston Astros (NL) for infielder Denny Walling. Although Forsch never was named to an All-Star team, the Cardinals honored him at Busch Stadium in St. Louis on May 29, 1989. Only National Baseball Hall of Famers Bob Gibson* and Jesse Haines* pitched more innings and won more games for the St. Louis Cardinals than Forsch. Forsch's career totals included 2,794.2 innings pitched, 168 wins, 136 losses, 1,133 strikeouts, and a 3.76 ERA in 498 games. He pitched in the 1982, 1985, and 1987 World Series for St. Louis, winning one of four decisions.

Forsch declined offers to come to spring training or coach in 1990, opting to spend time with his family and build a new home in Chesterfield, MO. He enjoys golf and bass fishing.

BIBLIOGRAPHY: Bob Broeg and Jerry Vickery, *St. Louis Cardinals Encyclopedia* (Grand Rapids, MI, 1998); Robert Forsch file, National Baseball Library, Cooperstown, NY; Kevin Horrigan, "Forsch Adrift after 15 Years of Cards Stability," St. Louis (MO) *Post-Dispatch*, September 2, 1988, pp. F1–F2; Rich Hummel, "Forsch Locks Self Out for Summer," St. Louis (MO) *Post-Dispatch*, March 5, 1990, p. C5; Rob Rains, *The St. Louis Cardinals* (New York, 1992); John Sonderegger, "Finesse: Variety Adds Spice to Forsch Deliveries," St. Louis (MO) *Post-Dispatch*, August 10, 1986, pp. F1, F15; John Sonderegger, "Forsch-ful," St. Louis (MO) *Post-Dispatch*, August 11, 1986, pp. 1–2; Marybeth Sullivan, ed., *The Scouting Report: 1986* (New York, 1986); Tom Wheatley, "Complete Game: Bob Forsch Enjoys Retirement with No Regrets," St. Louis (MO) *Post-Dispatch*, August 23, 1990, pp. C1, C4; Tom Wheatley, "Forsches Wisely Heeded Pa's Pitch," St. Louis (MO) *Post-Dispatch*, July 7, 1987, pp. C1, C4.
Frank J. Olmsted

FOSS, Betty Weaver (b. May 10, 1929, Metropolis, IL; d. February 8, 1998, Metropolis, IL), player, starred for the Fort Wayne, IN Daisies (AAGPBL) from 1950 to 1954 as a switch-hitting outfielder, first baseman, and third baseman, best known for her hitting and speed. She was the oldest of three sisters who played for Magnavox before joining Fort Wayne.

Foss won the batting title and MVP honors in 1950, hitting .346 with 61 RBI. In 1952, Foss also received the highest honor when she was named the AAGPBL Player of the Year. She led the AAGPBL with 81 runs, 137 hits, 26 doubles, 17 triples, and 74 RBI that year while hitting .331 in 106 games.

Her best offensive season, however, came in 1951, when she led the AAGPBL with 34 doubles, a .368 batting average, and 176 total bases. Besides batting .321 in 1953, she led the AAGPBL with 99 runs, 144 hits, and 80 stolen bases. In 1954 Weaver hit .352, but lost the batting crown to her sister Joanne.* Her sister batted over .400 that same season.

During her five-year career with Fort Wayne, Foss compiled a .342 batting average in 498 games. Only her sister Joanne compiled a higher career batting average. Besides having 649 hits, she scored 401 runs and knocked in another 312 runs. Although only hitting 32 HR, Foss stole 294 bases and led the AAGPBL three times in doubles. She holds the single-season records for hits, doubles, and triples and the career record for doubles (117). Her career .963 fielding average would have been higher except for her rookie season at third base, where she committed 47 errors in 374 chances. Her fielding average at first base and in the outfield never dropped below .964. Foss' playing accomplishments helped her club win three straight AAGPBL pennants beginning in 1952.

After the AAGPBL folded, Foss played for the Bill Allington All-American travelling team from 1954 to 1957. She returned to Fort Wayne to work for Wangs Pumps until retiring in 1995 and died after a lengthy battle with Lou Gehrig's disease.

BIBLIOGRAPHY: W. C. Madden, *The Women of the All-American Girls Professional Baseball League* (Jefferson, NC, 1997); Gai Berlage, *Women in Baseball* (Westport, CT, 1994); Sharon Roepke, *Diamond Gals* (Flint, MI, 1986); AAGPBL files, National Baseball Library, Cooperstown, NY; Merrie Fidler, "The Development and Decline of the All-American Girls Baseball League, 1943–54," MA Thesis, Amherst, MA, University of Massachusetts, 1976.

Leslie Heaphy

FOSTER, Andrew "Rube" (b. September 17, 1879, Calvert, TX; d. December 9, 1930, Kankakee IL), player, manager, and executive, was "the Father of Black Baseball." The son of Sarah Foster and minister Andrew Foster, he attended the Negro school in Calvert through the eighth grade and began pitching for the Fort Worth, TX Yellow Jackets by 1897. In 1902 Foster joined Frank Leland's Giants in Chicago, but jumped later that year to the Otsego, MI white semipro team and then to E. B. Lamar's Philadelphia Cuban X-Giants. The next year, the X-Giants played the Philadelphia Giants for the "colored championship of the world," as Foster pitched four of the five X-Giant victories. In 1904 he joined the Philadelphia Giants team he had defeated, leading them to the pennant and defeating the X-Giants in the playoff.

Foster rejoined the Leland Giants in 1907 after a salary dispute, but left again in 1910 and took the entire team with him. The next year he entered a partnership with John Schorling, a white tavern owner and son-in-law of Charles Comiskey.* Schorling had leased the old White Sox grounds, erected a new grandstand, and wanted Foster to provide a black team to play there. They agreed to split the profits evenly and closed the deal with a handshake, thus forming the Chicago American Giants.

Foster's American Giants became the "most consistently superior" team in Negro baseball between 1911 and 1915 and remained a power into the 1920s. Foster attracted black stars, including Christobel Torrienti,* John Beckwith,* and Bingo De Moss.* Foster's playing days had ended except for an occasional stint at first base, but he employed his vast knowledge as the Giants' manager. He also dominated Chicago baseball, controlling the bookings of many white semi-pro teams and the American Giants.

Faced with declining attendance and feuding with East Coast baseball magnate Nat Strong, Foster began agitating in 1919 in the Chicago *Defender* for the creation of a Negro Association modeled after the white major leagues. On February 13, 1920, six Midwestern owners met with Foster in the Kansas City, MO YMCA to arrange details. Foster was elected temporary president, upon which he presented the gathering with a league charter already written and incorporated in six states. A constitution was drawn up literally overnight, after which Foster was formally elected president and treasurer of the new NNL. Foster cited many reasons for the new league. The NNL would "create a profession that would equal the earning capacity of any other profession" for black players. Economic advantages for the owners included pennant races, a possible Negro World Series, and an end to player raids. Detractors claimed that Foster extended his own power over black baseball and became a virtual dictator, but the formation of the NNL saved the Negro game.

Besides administering the NNL, Foster continued operating the American Giants as manager and owner. His work day often began at 8:30 A.M. and stretched through midnight. He drew no salary for his NNL work and kept 5 percent of the gate of every NNL game, but contributed part of that to NNL expenses and often to players and clubs in financial straits. Foster's American Giants won the first three NNL pennants from 1920 through 1922. In 1925 other owners grumbled about the extent of Foster's influence, but gave him a unanimous vote of confidence when he offered to resign. In 1926, perhaps because of his grueling schedule, Foster suffered a nervous breakdown and was committed to the state asylum at Kankakee, IL. After his death four years later, crowds lined up for three days to view his casket in an unparalleled outpouring of grief. Foster's wife, Sara, whom he had married in 1908, survived him. Due to the lack of a written contract, however, neither she nor her two children collected any money from the American Giants. In 1981 Foster was elected to the National Baseball Hall of Fame.

Foster dominated black baseball before Jackie Robinson.* One of the great right-handed pitchers of the black era, he survived on wiles and raw skill. As a manager, he believed that games were won or lost in an inning or two and that every opportunity must be seized upon. Foster expected his players to bunt proficiently and execute the hit-and-run on command. His teams dominated games although opponents frequently batted for much higher averages. The stern disciplinarian called games when on the bench, pitching, and hitting. Foster's players became the best paid in Negro baseball. With the advent of the NNL, player salaries throughout the league rose to an average of $2,000 per year. In 1923 Foster's lowest paid player earned $175 a month, a fine wage then. His teams resembled white major leaguers by traveling on Pullman coach and received regular bonuses, often as high as $3,000. He had planned to make further innovations, including playing big league teams on their off-days in Chicago and adding a white player to the American Giants' roster.

Foster's main contribution remained his belief in black baseball. "Foster had a chance to leave Negro baseball," Dave Malarcher* recalls, "and go into white semipro baseball . . . when he was pitching. . . . He refused because he knew that all we had to do was to keep on developing Negro baseball, keep it up to the high standards and the time would come when the white leagues would have to admit us."

BIBLIOGRAPHY: Rube Foster file, National Baseball Library, Cooperstown, NY; William Brashler, *Josh Gibson* (New York, 1978); Janet Bruce, *The Kansas City Monarchs* (Lawrence, KS, 1985); Chicago *American*, July 24, 1955; Chicago *Defender*, November 29, December 13, December 20, 1919, December 13, December 20, December 27, 1930; Chicago *Tribune*, July 4, 1955; John Preston Davis, *The American Negro Reference Book* (Englewood Cliffs, NJ, 1966); John Holway, *Rube Foster* (Alexandria, VA, 1981); John Holway, *Voices from the Great Black Baseball Leagues* (New York, 1975); John B. Holway, *Blackball Stars* (Westport, CT, 1988); Rayford W. Logan and Michael R. Winston, *Dictionary of American Negro Biography* (New York, 1982); Robert W. Peterson, *Only the Ball Was White* (Englewood Cliffs, NJ, 1970); David L. Porter, ed., *African-American Sports Greats* (Westport, CT, 1995); James A. Riley, *The All-Time All-Stars of Black Baseball* (Cocoa, FL, 1983); James A. Riley, *The Biographical Encyclopedia of the Negro Baseball Leagues* (New York, 1994); Donn Rogosin, *Invisible Men: Life in Baseball's Negro Leagues* (New York, 1983); A. S. Young, *Great Negro Baseball Stars* (Chicago, IL, 1953).

Gerald E. Brennan

FOSTER, George Arthur "The Destroyer" (b. December 1, 1948, Tuscaloosa, AL), player, was a teammate of Dave Kingman* in Little League and graduated with scholastic honors from Leuzinger High School in Lawndale, CA, where he lettered in football, basketball, and baseball. After a lengthy bachelorhood, Foster married and has one daughter. Foster signed with the San Francisco Giants (NL) in 1968 and made the All-Star teams at Medford, OR (NWL) and Fresno, CA (CaL). He joined the Giants in late 1969, was sent down to Phoenix, AZ (PCL) in 1970, and had another brief trial with the parent club. After being traded to the Cincinnati Reds (NL) in May 1971, he experienced two mediocre seasons there and was shipped to their Indianapolis, IN (AA) farm team in 1973.

Foster remained with the Reds in 1974 as a part-time player and then reached stardom in 1975, slugging 23 HR with a .300 batting average. In 1976 his .306 batting average, 29 HR, and league-leading 121 RBI placed him second to teammate Joe Morgan* in the NL MVP voting. *TSN*, however, named Foster its NL Player of the Year. In the 1976 World Series against the New York Yankees, he hit .167 with four RBI in four games and set a fall classic record for most putouts (8) by a left fielder in one game. Nicknamed "The Destroyer," Foster in 1977 became only the tenth player in major league history to hit 50 or more HR in a single season. Foster, whose 52 HR included three in one game, on August 3 slugged one HR that an engineer estimated might have traveled 720 feet had it not struck the stands. He set a major league record that year for most HR by a right-handed hitter on the road with 31. His 52 HR, 149 RBI, and 388 total bases that season established Cincinnati club records. He was named the NL's MVP that year and repeated as *TSN* NL Player of the Year. In 1978, he tied a major league record by winning the NL's RBI title for the third straight season and belted 40 HR to again lead the NL. After Riverfront Stadium opened in 1970, Foster hit three of the eight balls slugged into the upper deck in the first decade.

In February 1982, Foster was traded to the New York Mets (NL) and signed a multiyear, multimillion dollar contract, giving him the then highest single salary in major league baseball history. His five seasons as a Met, however, produced disappointing results. Despite missing very few games, Foster averaged only 20 HR a year and batted .257. After slumping to a .227 batting average in 1986, he was released by the Mets in August. He batted .216 for the Chicago White Sox (AL) before retiring in September 1986. Foster batted .274 lifetime, made 1,925 hits, slugged 348 HR, scored 986 runs, and knocked in 1,239 tallies. A very quiet, honest individual with dry wit, Foster holds deep religious convictions and makes his Bible a constant companion.

BIBLIOGRAPHY: George Foster file, National Baseball Library, Cooperstown, NY; Donald Honig, *The Cincinnati Reds* (New York, 1992); Malka Drucker with George Foster, *The George Foster Story* (New York, 1979); Joe Jares, "Shouting over a Quiet Man," *SI* 45 (July 19, 1976), pp. 74ff; *NYT Biographical Service* 19 (July 1988), pp. 785–786; Bob Rathgeber, *Cincinnati Reds Scrapbook* (Virginia Beach, VA, 1982); Greg Rhodes and John Erardi, *Big Red Dynasty* (Cincinnati, OH, 1997); Robert H. Walker, *Cincinnati and the Big Red Machine* (Bloomington, IN, 1988); Robert Obojski, "Former Mets Prove Popular Signers at NYC Area Shows," *SCD* 25 (December 18, 1998), pp. 126–127.

John E. DiMeglio

FOSTER, Willie "Bill" (b. June 12, 1904, Calvert, TX; d. September 16, 1978, Lorman, MS), player and manager, was the half-brother of Rube Foster* and moved with his mother, Sarah, to Mississippi when he was still an infant. He grew up with his maternal grandparents after Sarah's death around 1908 and attended the elementary school at Alcorn College. Around 1918, he journeyed to Chicago to work in the stockyards and approach half-brother Rube about playing for the American Giants. When Rube refused, Willie returned to Mississippi. In 1923, the tall left-hander signed as a pitcher with the Memphis, TN Red Sox. Rube, however, reacted furiously and ordered Memphis owner Bubbles Lewis to send Willie to the Chicago American Giants (NNL). This action poisoned the relationship of the two brothers permanently. Pitcher Willie deliberately resisted Rube's coaching until the latter's nervous breakdown forced him off the bench. Then Foster began applying everything his half-brother had taught him. In 1926 he won 29 games, including 26 in a row. For the next ten years, Foster ranked as the top left-hander in the Negro Leagues and may have surpassed even Satchel Paige.* As a young pitcher, Foster relied mainly on his blinding speed. Upon maturing, he added a fast-breaking curve, a change-up, and an early version of the slider to his repertoire and delivered all his pitches with the same motion. At the end of the 1926 season, the American Giants needed to win the final two games to edge the Kansas City, MO Monarchs for the NNL pennant. Foster pitched both ends of a doubleheader and won both games. He completed three contests during the ensuing Negro World Series against the Atlantic City, NJ Bacharach Giants (ECL), winning two decisions and compiling a 1.27 ERA. He repeated in 1927 with two more complete game victories and a 3.00 ERA. A participant in Negro All-Star games in 1933 and 1934, he played with the American Giants except for short stints with the Kansas City Monarchs and the Homestead, PA Grays in 1931. He served as player–manager of the American Giants in 1931, but resigned as pilot, believing that he could not perform both roles simultaneously. In 1933, he pitched the American Giants to another NNL pennant and hurled a complete game for a victory against the East All Stars. Foster, whose baseball career ended with the Yakima, WA Browns in 1938, became Dean of Men and baseball coach at Alcorn College (Mississippi) in 1960 and held the latter position until shortly before his death. In 1996, he was elected to the National Baseball Hall of Fame.

BIBLIOGRAPHY: Willie Foster file, National Baseball Library, Cooperstown, NY; John Holway, *Rube Foster* (Alexandria, VA, 1981); John Holway, *Voices from the Great Black Baseball Leagues* (New York, 1975); Robert W. Peterson, *Only the Ball Was White* (Englewood Cliffs, NJ, 1970); James A. Riley, *The All-Time All-Stars of Black Baseball* (Cocoa, FL, 1983); James A. Riley, *Biographical Encyclopedia of the Negro Baseball Leagues* (New York, 1994); Donn Rogosin, *Invisible Men: Life in Baseball's Negro Leagues* (New York, 1983).

Gerald E. Brennan

FOTHERGILL, Robert Roy "Bob," "Fats," "The People's Choice" (b. August 16, 1897, Massillon, OH; d. March 20, 1938, Detroit, MI), player and coach, was the son of William Fothergill and Anna (Featheringham) Fothergill.

After playing semiprofessional baseball in Massillon, OH, he entered professional baseball in 1920 with Bloomington, IL (3IL) and led the 3IL with a .332 batting average. The Detroit Tigers (AL) purchased Fothergill and assigned him to Rochester, NY (IL), where the 5-foot 10½-inch, 190-pound outfielder batted .338 in 1921. After hitting .322 in 42 contests with the Detroit Tigers in early 1922, he finished the season with Rochester and led the IL with a .383 batting average. Fothergill batted .315 his first full season with Detroit in 1923, followed by .301 in 1924 and .353 in 1925. The line-drive-hitter enjoyed his best season in 1926 with a .367 mark. His 1927 season yielded a .359 batting average and career high 93 runs scored and 114 RBI.

Although hitting .317 in 1928 and .354 in 1929 and considered an outfielder with fine range, Fothergill possessed a lusty appetite and consequently developed a weight problem. Threats of suspension and fines did not help. The Chicago White Sox (AL) acquired him on waivers in July 1930, but his batting average fell below .300 for the first time. Although Fothergill hit a respectable .282 in 1931 and .295 in 1932, the Chicago White Sox traded him with Johnny Hodapp, Greg Mulleavy and Bob Seeds to the Boston Red Sox (AL) for Ed Durham and Hal Rhyne in December 1932. He batted .344 in 28 games with the Red Sox in 1933 and was optioned to Minneapolis, MN (AA), retiring after the season. In a 12-year major league career spanning 1,106 games, the popular, non-power hitting Fothergill made 1,064 hits, scored 453 runs, recorded 582 RBI, and compiled a .325 batting average and .961 fielding average. His .337 career batting average with Detroit trails only National Baseball Hall-of-Famers Ty Cobb* and Harry Heilmann.* He holds the Tigers mark for all-single-season pinch-hits with 19 in 1929, then an AL record.

Fothergill played sandlot baseball in Detroit and worked as a guard at the Ford Motor Company. He began coaching baseball at Lawrence Institute of Technology in Highland Park, MI in January 1938, but succumbed to a stroke in March. He married Marie Barth on February 21, 1922. They had no children.

BIBLIOGRAPHY: *The Baseball Encyclopedia*, 10th ed. (New York, 1996); Robert Fothergill file, National Baseball Library, Cooperstown, NY; David Nemec and Pete Palmer, *1001 Fascinating Baseball Facts* (Stamford, CT, 1993); John Thorn et al., eds., *Total Baseball*, 5th ed. (New York, 1997); Fred Smith, *995 Tigers* (Detroit, MI, 1981); Frederick G. Lieb, *The Detroit Tigers* (New York, 1946); William M. Anderson, *The Detroit Tigers* (South Bend, IN, 1996); Richard Bak, *Ty Cobb: His Tumultuous Life and Times* (Dallas, TX, 1994).

Jack C. Braun

FOURNIER, John Frank "Jack," "Jacques" (b. September 28, 1892, Au Sable, MI; d. September 5, 1973, Tacoma, WA), player, manager, coach, and scout, attended Aberdeen, WA High School for two years. A good boxer and wrestler as a youngster, he grew into a 6-foot, 195 pounder, batted left-handed and threw right-handed. Although beginning his baseball career as a catcher for Aberdeen-Seattle, WA (NWL) in 1908, he switched to first base in 1910. With Moose Jaw, Canada in 1911, he led the WCaL in batting average (.377), runs, hits, doubles, and triples. He started 1912 with the Chicago White Sox (AL), but finished the season with Montreal, Canada (IL).

From 1913 to 1917, he played first base for the Chicago White Sox, and he led the AL with a .491 slugging percentage in 1915. After being replaced by Chick Gandil* in 1917, Fournier played the next two seasons for Los Angeles, CA (PCL). During the war-shortened 1918 season, he briefly replaced the New York Yankees' (AL) Wally Pipp.* Fournier batted .350 in 27 games before the National Commission ruled that his contract belonged to the White Sox. Chicago returned him to Los Angeles, where he stayed until the St. Louis Cardinals (NL) bought his contract in 1920. He performed well in his three years with the Cardinals, batting .317 and slugging .472. After Jim Bottomley* joined the Cardinals in 1922, Branch Rickey* traded Fournier to the Brooklyn Robins (NL) in February 1923.

On June 19, 1923, Fournier made six hits in six at bats for Brooklyn. Manager Wilbert Robinson,* record holder with seven for seven, ordered an unsuccessful steal with Fournier at the plate to end the game. In 1924, Fournier led the NL in HR (27) and assists by a first baseman and finished second in RBI (116) and walks. Although batting .350 in 1925, Fournier publicly complained about the foul language Brooklyn fans directed at him. He belted three HR in one game in 1926, but was replaced by Floyd Herman.* Fournier, a top-notch bench jockey and spring training absentee, finished his major league career in 1927 with the Boston Braves (NL). In 15 seasons, he played 1,530 games, batted .313, made 1,631 hits, 252 doubles, 113 triples, and 136 HR, scored 822 runs, knocked in 859 runs, and slugged .483. He managed Johnstown, PA (MAL) in 1937 and Toledo, OH (AA) in 1943 and coached at the University of California, Los Angeles from 1934 to 1938. Fournier scouted for the St. Louis Browns (AL, 1938–1942, 1944–1947), Chicago Cubs (NL, 1950–1957), Detroit Tigers (AL, 1960), and Cincinnati Reds (NL, 1961–1962). He married Helen L. Commings on November 27, 1913.

BIBLIOGRAPHY: Jack Fournier file, National Baseball Library, Cooperstown, NY; *The Baseball Encyclopedia*, 10th ed. (New York, 1996); Frank Graham, *The Brooklyn Dodgers* (New York, 1945); Brent P. Kelley, *The Case For: Those Overlooked by the Baseball Hall of Fame* (Jefferson, NC, 1992); Warren Brown, *The Chicago White Sox* (New York, 1952); William F. McNeil, *The Dodgers Encyclopedia* (Champaign, IL, 1997); Richard Goldstein, *Superstars and Screwballs* (New York, 1991). *TSN Official Baseball Guide, 1974*; Ira Smith, *Baseball's Famous First Basemen* (New York, 1956).

Steven P. Savage

FOUTZ, David Luther "Dave," "Scissors," "Hunkidori Boy" (b. September 7, 1856, Carroll County, MD; d. March 5, 1897, Waverly, MD), player and manager, was the son of Solomon and Miriam Foutz. He married Minnie Glocke. Leadville, CO knew Foutz as the "Hunkidori Boy," while NL fans nicknamed him "Scissors." Foutz compiled the highest winning percentage (.690) of any major league pitcher, winning 147 and losing only 66 decisions. He started 216 games and finished 202 (also appearing in 35 as a relief pitcher) with a 2.84 ERA. According to an 1887 reporter, Foutz made an "enviable reputation in the baseball world." Besides pitching, he played 915 games at first base and in the outfield and one game at shortstop. During his career, he hit .276 for the St. Louis Browns (AA), the Brooklyn Bridegrooms (AA), and the Brooklyn Bridegrooms (NL). From 1893 to 1896, Foutz served as player, captain, and manager for the Brooklyn Bridegrooms.

The 6-foot 2-inch, 167-pound "gentlemanly, earnest" Foutz traveled frequently before reaching the major leagues. He played for Baltimore in 1877, but found no openings as a pitcher and journeyed to America's best-known silver mining town, Leadville, CO. Foutz gained his first fame there by starring in 1882 for the champion Leadville Blues. Since the Leadville club succeeded beyond expectations, Foutz became the toast of the city and state. At Bay City, MI, he became one of the NWL's best pitchers.

In July 1884, the owner of the St. Louis Browns (AA) purchased the entire Bay City franchise just to secure him, commenting that he "is a bewilder and make no mistake." The right-hander responded brilliantly by winning 99 games and helping to pitch St. Louis to three consecutive championships from 1885 to 1887. In 1886 his 41–16 record led the AA, while his 504 innings pitched and 11 shutouts marked career highs. A solid team player, Foutz appeared in 45 other games and batted .280. Although winning only 25 games the next year, he batted a spectacular .357 in 102 games.

The premier St. Louis Browns (AA) club, meanwhile, possessed several high-salaried stars. Owner Christian Von der Ahe* converted some of that fame to cash. To the astonishment of the baseball world, Foutz and star pitcher Robert Caruthers* were sold in November 1887 to the Brooklyn Bridegrooms (AA) for $13,500. The *NYT* predicted that these acquisitions would "add greatly to the playing strength of Brooklyn." The prediction proved accurate because a championship nine soon graced Brooklyn, NY.

Although pitching only occasionally and playing primarily first base, Foutz was an important factor in Brooklyn's win in 1889, driving in 113 runs and averaging .275 for the NL champions the following season. Foutz, renowned for pitching and hitting, proved a good right fielder and first baseman and stole 280 bases during his career. A power hitter, he slugged 186 doubles, 91 triples, and 31 HR among his 1,253 career hits.

As manager, he never succeeded in piloting his team to the first division. Commenting on the 1896 season, *Spalding's Base Ball Guide* noted that the record was the poorest of the past ten years, and "no club disappointed its patrons as much as the Brooklyns." Ill health forced Foutz to retire at the end of the 1896 season. He applied for an umpiring position, but died before the next season started.

BIBLIOGRAPHY: David L. Foutz file, National Baseball Library, Cooperstown, NY; Bill Borst, *Last in the American League* (St. Louis, MO, 1976); Bill Borst, ed., *From Ables to Zoldak*, vol. 1 (St. Louis, MO, 1988); J. Thomas Hetrick, *Christian Von der Ahe and the St. Louis Browns* (Lanham, MD, 1999); Leadville (CO) *Daily Herald*, 1882, July 27, 29, 1884; David Nemec, *The Beer and Whisky League* (New York, 1994); *NYT*, November 30, 1887, March 6, 1897; *The Baseball Encyclopedia*, 10th ed. (New York, 1996); Harold Seymour, *Baseball: The Early Years* (New York, 1960); Duane A. Smith, "Baseball Champions of Colorado," *JSH* 4 (Spring 1977), pp. 51–71; *Spalding's Base Ball Guide*, 1883–1897; *The Sun* (Baltimore), March 6, 1897; Robert L. Tiemann and Mark Rucker, eds., *Nineteenth Century Stars* (Kansas City, MO, 1989); Richard Goldstein, *Superstars and Screwballs* (New York, 1991); David Quentin Voigt, *American Baseball* (Norman, OK, 1966).

Duane A. Smith

FOWLER, John W. "Bud" (b. John W. Jackson, March 16, 1858, Fort Plain, NY; d. February 26, 1913, Frankfort, NY), player, was the first black professional baseball player and the son of barber John Jackson and Mary (Lansing) Jackson. He grew up in Cooperstown, NY and first played professionally on a white team in New Castle, PA in the early 1870s. He played all positions like most players of his era, but excelled as a second baseman. Over a 30 year span, Fowler played in virtually every section of the United States, including eastern cities, midwestern crossroads towns, pioneer villages, western settlements, and southern communities during several winters. Near the end of his career, Fowler claimed to have performed on teams in 22 states and Guelph, Canada.

Between 1878 and 1895, he played in white organized leagues with Lynn, MA (IA), Binghamton, NY (IA), Keokuk, IA (WL), Topeka, KS (WL), Pueblo, CO (CdL), Montpelier, VT (NEL), Crawfordsville, IN (CIL), Terre Haute, IN (CIL), Galesburg, IL (CIL), Greenville, MI (MISL), Adrian, MI (MISL), Lansing, MI (MISL), Sterling, IL (3IL), Galesburg, IL (3IL), Burlington, IA (3IL), Lincoln, NE (NeSL), and Kearney, NE (NeSL). Fowler also played with the Cuban Giants, the era's best all-black team, and formed black barnstorming clubs. In 1895, the Page Fence Giants of Adrian, MI, the best-known of these barnstormers, traveled in their own railroad car and paraded to the ballpark on bicycles. His most colorful barnstorming team, the All-American Black Tourists, formed in 1903, also traveled by rail and offered to play ball in full-dress suits, opera hats, and silk umbrellas.

At his peak, Fowler consistently batted over .300, pitched, and was ranked among the best second basemen. The color line, however, barred him from the major leagues. During the off-season, he sometimes worked as a barber. Fowler, who never married, died of pernicious anemia at the home of a sister following a long illness.

BIBLIOGRAPHY: Robert W. Peterson, correspondence with Ocania Chalk, Merl Kleinknecht, Jerry Malloy, and Raymond J. Nemec, Robert W. Peterson Collection, Ramsey, NJ; Robert W. Peterson, *Only the Ball Was White* (Englewood Cliffs, NJ, 1970); James A. Riley, *The Biographical Encyclopedia of the Negro Baseball Leagues* (New York, 1994); Robert L. Tiemann and Mark Rucker, eds., *Nineteenth Century Baseball Stars* (Kansas City, MO, 1989); Sol White, *History of Colored Base Ball* (Philadelphia, PA, 1970).

Robert W. Peterson

FOX, Ervin "Pete" "Rabbit" (b. March 8, 1909, Evansville, IN; d. July 5, 1966, Detroit, MI), player, was the Detroit Tigers' (AL) solid right fielder from 1933 to 1939. The fourth of six sons born to Henry Fox, a fire captain, and Beana (Morgen) Fox, he worked in a furniture factory and pitched for a sandlot team before signing professionally with Evansville, IN (3IL) in 1930. Fox developed into a solid hitter and a dependable, strong-armed outfielder. At Beaumont, TX in 1932, his .357 batting average led the TL. His nickname evolved from "Rabbit," bestowed by Beaumont fans for his speed, into "Peter Rabbit" and, finally, "Pete."

In 1933, the Detroit Tigers made Fox their right fielder. Fox played on three AL pennant-winners, setting a record in 1934 for the most doubles (6) in a seven-game World Series against the St. Louis Cardinals. In 1935, he batted a World Series–high .385 in the Tigers' triumph over the Chicago Cubs. His best season came in 1937, when he hit .331. Teammates like Hank Greenberg,* Charlie Gehringer,* Goose Goslin,* Schoolboy Rowe,* and Tommy Bridges* often overshadowed the reliable Fox. In 1938, he led AL outfielders with a .994 fielding percentage.

In December 1940, the Boston Red Sox (AL) acquired Fox. When Boston lost outfielders Ted Williams* and Dom DiMaggio* to military service in 1943, he started again. In 1944, Fox made his first All-Star team and contended for the batting title with a .315 average. The 5-foot 11-inch, 165-pound right-handed hitter retired after the 1945 season with a .298 career batting average, 314 doubles, 65 HR, 694 RBI, and 158 stolen bases in 1,461 games.

Fox married Betty Stuteville in September 1927 and had two sons, Don, a minor league pitcher, and James. After serving several years as a minor league manager and scout, he worked as a manufacturer's representative. He was stricken with cancer in 1964.

BIBLIOGRAPHY: Ervin Fox file, National Baseball Library, Cooperstown, NY; *The Baseball Encyclopedia*, 10th ed. (New York, 1996); Peter J. Cava, Indiana-born Major League Player files, Peter J. Cava Collection, Indianapolis, IN; Pete Fox file, National Baseball Library, Cooperstown, NY; Joe Falls, *Detroit Tigers* (New York, 1975); Bill Madden, *The Hoosiers of Summer* (Indianapolis, IN, 1994); Fred Smith, *995 Tigers* (Detroit, MI, 1981); Frederick G. Lieb, *The Detroit Tigers* (New York, 1946); William M. Anderson, *The Detroit Tigers* (South Bend, IN, 1996); Richard Bak, *A Place for*

Summer (Detroit, MI, 1998); Frederick G. Lieb, *The Boston Red Sox* (New York, 1947); Robert Redmount, *The Red Sox Encyclopedia* (Champaign, IL, 1998); John Thorn et al., *Total Baseball*, 5th ed. (New York, 1997); *TSN Baseball Register, 1940.*

Peter J. Cava

FOX, Jacob Nelson "Nellie" (b. December 25, 1927, St. Thomas, PA; d. December 1, 1975, Baltimore, MD), player and coach, was the son of carpenter Jacob Fox and Mae Fox. Nicknamed "Nellie," he enjoyed soccer and baseball as a youth. After leaving school at age 16, Fox signed a professional contract with manager Connie Mack* of the Philadelphia Athletics (AL) in 1944. He married Joanne Statler in June 1947 and had two daughters, Bonnie and Tracy. Fox spent the 1944–1948 seasons in the minor leagues at Lancaster, PA (ISL), Jamestown, NY (PoL), and Lincoln, NE (WL), appearing briefly with Philadelphia in 1947 and 1948 and making the Athletics roster in 1949. After being traded to the Chicago White Sox (AL) in October 1949, Fox became the premier AL second baseman. He played there from 1950 through 1963 and spent his final two seasons with the Houston Astros (NL).

The 5-foot 10-inch, 160-pound Fox used a short, thick bat, controlled swing, and sharp batting eye to set major league records for most years leading the league in singles (8) and having fewest strikeouts (11). In 1958, he played 98 consecutive games without striking out. He led the AL in hits four times (1952, 1954, 1957–1958), batted over .300 six seasons, proved a good bunter, and compiled a .288 career batting average. In 2,367 games, he made 2,663 hits, scored 1,279 runs, and struck out only 216 times. Despite his size and the physical dangers of second base play, Fox played in 798 consecutive games (1955–1960) to set the record for second basemen. Only Eddie Collins,* Joe Morgan,* and Lou Whitaker* surpassed Fox' 2,295 games at second base.

As a fielder, Fox holds major league records for most years leading second basemen in putouts (10) and total chances (9) as well as AL records for career double plays (1,619) and years leading in double plays (5). He paced the AL in fielding percentage six times and won four Gold Glove awards. Fox was selected for 15 All-Star games, batting .368 and making an AL record 14 hits. His hits won the 1954 and first 1959 games. The heart of the "Go-Go" White Sox teams of the 1950s, Fox led Chicago to the 1959 AL pennant and was chosen AL MVP. He hit .375 against the Los Angeles Dodgers in his only World Series appearance. Fox' trademarks included his bottle bat, large chaw of tobacco, and energetic, enthusiastic play. His buoyant personality made him extremely popular in Chicago, with his uniform number (2) being one of only eight retired by the White Sox. He served as coach for the Houston Astros (NL) in 1966 and 1967 and for the Washington Senators (AL) in 1968 and owned a bowling alley in Pennsylvania after his playing career. He died of lymph cancer in 1975. In 1997, the Veterans Committee elected him to the National Baseball Hall of Fame.

BIBLIOGRAPHY: Nelson Fox file, National Baseball Library, Cooperstown, NY; John Benson et al., *Baseball's Top 100* (Wilton, CT, 1997); David Condon, *The Go-Go Chicago White Sox* (Chicago, IL, 1960); William B. Furlong, "He Ain't Big But He's All Fire," *SEP* 227 (May 14, 1955), pp. 30, 139, 142; David Gough, "Nellie Fox," *BRJ* 26 (1997), pp. 110–113; Roger Kahn, "Little Nellie's a Man Now," *Sport* 25 (April 1958), pp. 52–61; Rich Lindberg, *Who's on Third?* (South Bend, IN, 1983); Brent P. Kelley, *The Case For: Those Overlooked by the Baseball Hall of Fame* (Jefferson, NC, 1992); Bob Vanderberg, *Sox: From Lane and Fain to Fisk and Zisk* (Chicago, IL, 1982); Edgar Munzel, "Fiery Fox," *TSN* (September 2, 1959), pp. 1, 6; *NYT*, December 2, 1975.

Phillip P. Erwin

FOX, Helen Nicol "Nicky" (b. May 9, 1920, Ardley, Canada), player, is the daughter of Alexander Nicol and Elizabeth (Gray) Dunn of Scottish heritage and attended Western Canada High School in Calgary. Fox played in the Calgary Senior Ladies Softball League at age 13 and in ice hockey, excelling on several championship teams in the late 1930s. She skated for the champion Calgary Chinooks at the Banff, Canada Winter Games in 1938 and 1939. In 1940 Fox competed in the Banff Winter Games as a speed skater, placing first in the 220 meter and 800 meter races and second in the 440 meter race. She claimed three Western Canadian speed skating titles.

Fox, an original recruit for the AAGPBL for $85 a week, joined the Kenosha, WI Comets in 1943. The 5-foot 3-inch, 130-pound right-handed pitcher compiled an impressive record during her 10-year stint in the AAGPBL. Her effective, unique wristball, a rarely seen delivery, exhibited considerable velocity. The adept competitor, the only AAGPBL pitcher to compete for 10 consecutive seasons, spent her last six campaigns with the Rockford, IL Peaches, retiring in 1952. Fox compiled a record of 31 victories and eight losses with 348 innings pitched in 1943, recording the most complete games (33) and a 1.81 ERA. Her ERA, .795 winning percentage, 220 strikeouts, 47 games pitched, and innings pitched paced the league. She garnered Pitcher of the Year and All-Star honors. She also won 13 consecutive games in 1943 and continued her supremacy in 1944 with a 0.93 ERA and in 1945 with a 1.34 ERA. In 1944, she retained Pitcher of the Year honors with a 17–11 mark and a no-hitter. In 1946, she finished 24–19 with a 1.34 ERA. She posted winning records from 1949 through 1951, helping Rockford win three consecutive titles. Fox recorded 15 or more victories in six of her 10 AAGPBL seasons, ending her career with 163 victories, 118 defeats, an outstanding 1.89 ERA, and two no-hitters. No AAGPBL pitcher won more career games. Her other league career records include 1,076 strikeouts, 313 games pitched, 2,302 innings pitched, 1,579 hits allowed, 118 losses, and 499 earned runs allowed.

When the AAGPBL moved the pitching mound to 60 feet in 1950, Fox won 14 of 26 games. She set many career records and pitched in all three styles. Fox's outstanding record easily qualified her for entry into the women's wing of the National Baseball Hall of Fame at Cooperstown, NY. The Arizona resident also was inducted into the Canadian Sports Hall of Fame and the Alberta Sports Hall of Fame and Museum in 1996. The truly outstanding athlete earned her niche in the annals of U.S. and Canadian sporting history. Her marriage to Gordon on Fox lasted just over a year. She worked for Illinois Gas and Electric Company in Rockford from 1952 through 1959, American Motors in Kenosha from 1960 to 1972, and Motorola Company until 1982.

BIBLIOGRAPHY: Gai Ingham Berlage, *Women in Baseball* (Westport, CT, 1994); Barbara Gregorich, *Women at Play* (San Diego, CA, 1993); Sharon Roepke, *Diamond Gals* (Flint, MI, 1988); Susan Johnson, *When Women Played Hardball* (Seattle, WA, 1994); W. C. Madden, *The Women of the All-American Girls Professional Baseball League* (Jefferson, NC, 1997); James E. Odenkirk, personal interview with Helen Fox, Scottsdale, AZ, April 15, 1996.

James E. Odenkirk

FOXX, James Emory "Jimmie," "Double X," "The Beast" (b. October 22, 1907, Sudlersville, MD; d. July 21, 1967, Miami, FL), player, coach, and manager, was the son of farmer Samuel Dell Foxx and Margaret (Smith) Foxx and exhibited right-hand batting power at Sudlersville High School and in semipro games. Frank "Home Run" Baker,* then managing Easton, MD (ESL), discovered Foxx in 1924, converted him from an infielder to a catcher, and sold him to the Philadelphia Athletics (AL) for 1925 spring delivery. After the 16-year-old batted .296 in 76 games for Easton, however, Philadelphia manager Connie Mack* brought him up to sit on the Athletics bench for the balance of 1924. Foxx was inserted in 10 games in early 1925 and then optioned to Providence, RI (IL), where he hit .327. Mack used him sparingly at first and increasingly through 1926 and 1927. Foxx started in 1928 and batted .327 in 118 games as a first baseman, third baseman, and catcher. For the rest of his career, he performed at first base with average ability and occasionally played other positions.

For seven more seasons and three World Series (1929–1931), Foxx starred for the Athletics and averaged 41 HR per season with his straddle stance. His 58 HR in 1932 fell two short of Babe Ruth's* then record 60. During that season, he attained .364 batting and .749 slugging percentages and paced the AL with 151 runs, 169 RBI, and 100 extra-base hits. The financially strapped Mack traded the strongboy to the Boston Red Sox (AL) for cash and players in December 1935. Taking advantage of Fenway Park's short left field wall, Foxx averaged 36 HR per year from 1936 through 1941. In 1938 he hit 50 HR, scored 139 runs, and drove in 175 tallies. He led the AL in batting with .356 in 1933 and .349 in 1938.

By 1942 excess alcohol, too many late nights, and a sinus affliction caused his deterioration. In June, he was waived to the Chicago Cubs (NL) and hit only .205 in 70 games. After doing war work in 1943, he returned to the Cubs the next season as a coach and fringe player and finished the season managing Portsmouth, VA (PiL). In 1945, he batted .268 in 89 games and pitched 9 contests for the Philadelphia Phillies (NL). Subsequently, he managed St. Petersburg, FL (FIL) in 1947 and Bridgeport, CT (CtL) in 1949.

The easygoing Foxx then failed at several business ventures and could not hold jobs for sustained periods. A public admission of his destitute condition caused the Boston (AL) organization to enlist him as coach with the Minneapolis, MN (AA) club during 1958. He continued drifting, holding intermittent jobs at different places. He suffered from heart disease, and choked to death at his brother Sam's house when a piece of meat lodged in his throat.

Nicknamed "Double X," he terrorized pitchers, particularly left-handers, and belted some of the longest, hardest hit HR ever seen in AL ballparks. Exceptionally strong with broad shoulders, bulging biceps, moon face, and square jaw, the well-liked, good-natured Foxx was affectionately called "The Beast" by his peers. The truly great slugger was elected to the National Baseball Hall of Fame in 1951. In 20 major league seasons, he batted .325, slugged .609, hit 458 doubles, 125 triples, and 534 HR, drove in 1,922 runs, walked 1,452 times, and struck out 1,311 times in 2,317 games. He won the AL MVP Award in 1932, 1933, and 1938 and was selected as first baseman on *TSN* Major League All-Star team five times. Foxx led the AL in strikeouts (seven times), slugging average (five times), HR (four times), RBI (three times), walks and batting average (twice), and runs (once) and batted .344 in three World Series.

Foxx, who married Helen Heite in December 1928 and later divorced, wed Dorothy Anderson Yard in 1943. He had two children, James Emory, Jr., and William Kenneth, by his first marriage and two children, John and Nancy (Mrs. Canaday), by his second.

BIBLIOGRAPHY: Martin Appel and Burt Goldblatt, *Baseball's Best: The Hall of Fame Gallery* (New York, 1977); Bob Broeg, *Super Stars of Baseball* (St. Louis, MO, 1971); Jimmy Burns, "Foxx Takes Post as Miller Coach; Many Offer Help," *TSN*, January 29, 1958; W. Harrison Daniel, *Jimmie Foxx* (Jefferson, NC, 1996); Frederick G. Lieb, *Connie Mack* (New York, 1945); Connie Mack, *My 66 Years in the Big Leagues* (Philadelphia, PA, 1950); Frederick G. Lieb, *The Boston Red Sox* (New York, 1947); Robert Redmount, *The Red Sox Encyclopedia* (Champaign, IL, 1998); James Foxx file, National Baseball Library, Cooperstown, NY; Peter Golenbock, *Fenway* (New York, 1992); Bob Gorman, *Double X* (Kent, CT, 1990); Donald Honig, *The Power Hitters* (St. Louis, MO, 1989); Frederick G. Lieb, "Foxx, No. 3 on All-Time Homer List, Dead," *TSN*, August 5, 1967; Tom Meany, *Baseball's Greatest Hitters* (New York, 1950); *NYT*, July 22, 1967; Mark R. Milliken, *Jimmie Foxx* (Lanham, MD, 1998); *The Baseball Encyclopedia*, 10th ed. (New York, 1996); *TSN*, February 4, June 10, 1943, February 7, 1951; Frank Yeutter, "Art of Home-Run Hitting Dying, Declares Foxx," *TSN*, February 14, 1951.

Frank V. Phelps

FRANCO, John Anthony (b. September 17, 1960, Brooklyn, NY), player, is the son of James Franco and Mary (Starace) Franco and is a 5-foot 10-inch, 185-pound pitcher who throws and bats left-handed. He graduated in 1978 from Lafayette High School in Brooklyn, which produced former major leaguers Sandy Koufax* and Ken Aspromonte, and played baseball at St. John's University (NY). He and his wife, Rose, have one daughter, Nicole, and one son, John James.

The Los Angeles Dodgers (NL) selected Franco in the fifth round of the June 1981 free-agent draft. His first professional assignment came at Vero Beach, FL (FSL). Franco hurled in 1982 for Albuquerque, NM (PCL) and San Antonio, TX (TL), where he compiled a 10–5 won–lost record. He started the next season at Albuquerque and in May 1983 was traded to the Cincinnati Reds (NL). He was optioned to Indianapolis, IN (AA), where he finished 6–10. Franco began the 1984 season with Wichita, KS (AA) and joined the Reds in April, debuting on April 24th. He recorded his first save on April 29th and posted his first victory two days later. The reliever hurled for Cincinnati between 1984 and 1989, compiling a 42–30 record and posting an all-time club record 148 saves. Franco led all major league relievers with a career-best 12 victories in 1985 and paced the NL with a career-high 39 saves in 1988.

The Cincinnati Reds traded Franco in December 1989 to the New York Mets (NL), where he relieved for 10 seasons since 1990. Hc has compiled a 37–38 won–lost record and 249 saves, an all-time club record, with the Mets. Franco led the NL with 33 saves in 1990 and 30 saves in 1994. Despite having arm surgery in 1992 and several injuries in 1993, he has enjoyed nine seasons with 20 or more saves. Franco picked up his 300th career save in 1996, becoming the first lefthanded pitcher in major league history to accomplish this feat. His 416 saves rank him second on the all-time list. Other honors received by Franco include being named *TSN* NL Fireman of the Year in 1988, 1990, and 1994, winning the NL Rolaids Relief title in 1988 and 1990, and being voted the Top Lefthanded Relief Pitcher in the major leagues in the last 20 years. He made five All-Star teams, appearing in two games and pitching in 1.3 perfect innings. Franco in 1991 received the Thurman Munson Award for his charitable work. His 19 saves helped New York reach the playoffs in 1999. He won one game in the NL Division Series and made two appearances in the NL Championship Series.

In 14 major league seasons through 1999, Franco has compiled a 77–70 won–lost record with a 2.64 ERA. He has appeared in 878 games, recording 416 saves. Franco has allowed 961 hits and 404 walks in 1,041.1 innings pitched while striking out 801 batters.

BIBLIOGRAPHY: John Franco file, National Baseball Library, Cooperstown, NY; Hank Hersch, "A Hometown Hero," *SI* 70 (May 15, 1989), pp. 48–50ff; M. Moran, "Franco Basks as All-Star," *NYT Biographical Service* 17 (July 1986), pp. 890–891; Donald Honig, *The Cincinnati Reds* (New York, 1992); Bob Cairns, *Pen Men* (New York, 1993); *New York Mets Information Guide*, 1998; *TSN Official Baseball Register*, 1998.

John L. Evers

FRANCO, Julio Cesar Robles (b. August 23, 1961, Hato Mayor, DR), player, attended Divine Providence High School in San Pedro de Macoris and was signed as a free agent by the Philadelphia Phillies (NL) in June 1978. His minor league stops included Butte, MT (PrL) that season, Central Oregon (NWL) in 1979, and Peninsula, VA (CrL) 1980. He played with Reading, PA (EL) in 1981 and with Oklahoma City, OK (AA) and the Philadelphia Phillies (NL) in 1982, batting .276 in 16 games with the latter. In five minor league seasons, Franco batted .300 or better every campaign. He hit 53 HR, including 21 in 1982. His highest RBI season came in 1980 with 99 for Peninsula.

The 6-foot 1-inch, 190-pound second baseman–shortstop bats and throws right-handed. The Philadelphia Phillies traded Franco in December 1982 to the Cleveland Indians (AL), for whom he played six seasons and batted over .300 the last three seasons. In his first season with the Cleveland Indians, Franco played shortstop and hit .273 with 80 RBI. He played at shortstop in 1984, hitting .286 with 79 RBI. He split duties between second base and shortstop from 1985 to 1987 and played second base from 1988 to 1991. In 1985 he batted .288 with 90 RBI. He hit .306 in 1986, providing 74 RBI. In 1987, he batted .319 with 52 RBI. His final year with Cleveland featured him batting .303 and attaining 54 RBI.

In December 1988, the Cleveland Indians traded Franco to the Texas Rangers (AL). During his first season with the Texas Rangers in 1989, he batted .316 with 92 RBI. The next season, he hit .296 with 69 RBI. In 1991 he led the NL in hitting with a career-high .341 and produced 201 hits and 78 RBI. Injuries in 1992 limited Franco to only 35 games at second base and outfield. His batting average fell to .234 with only eight RBI. Franco rebounded the following season to bat .289 and knock in 84 runs. During the strike-shortened 1994 season, he batted .319 with 20 HR and 98 RBI for the Chicago White Sox (AL). In December 1994, the Chiba Lotte, Japan Marines (JCL) signed Franco to a $3.5 million, one-year contract. After spending 1995 with the Chiba Lotte Marines, he batted .322 with 76 RBI for the Cleveland Indians (AL) in 1996 and struggled in the AL Division Series against the Baltimore Orioles. In August 1997, the Milwaukee Brewers (AL) signed him as a free agent. Franco signed a minor league contract with the Tampa Bay Devil Rays (AL) in February 1999.

Franco was selected on the AL All-Star team from 1989 through 1991, hitting .333 in the first two games. He was named CrL MVP in 1980, second baseman on the *TSN* AL Silver Slugger team in 1988 and 1991, and second baseman on the *TSN* AL All-Star team from 1989 to 1991. Through 1999, he batted .301 with 2,177 hits, 141 HR, 981 RBI, and 260 stolen bases.

Franco and his wife, Rose Trueba Franco, have one son, Joshua.

BIBLIOGRAPHY: E. Pooley, "Sports," *NY* 23 (September 10, 1990), pp. 122–123; Julio Franco file, National Baseball Library, Cooperstown, NY; Rick Weinberg, "Texas Terror," *Sport* 83 (May 1992), pp. 38–40; Jack Torry, *Endless Summers* (South Bend, IN, 1995); *Texas Ranger Media Guide*, 1994; *TSN Official Baseball Register*, 1998.

Stan W. Carlson

FRANCONA, John Patsy "Tito" (b. November 4, 1933, Aliquippa, PA), player, is the son of Carmon Francona, a Protestant minister of Italian ancestry, and Josephine Francona. Francona starred as a football running back and baseball player at New Brighton, PA High School, where he also worked in the steel mills.

In 1952 the muscular 5-foot 11-inch, 185-pound Francona signed a professional baseball contract with the St. Louis Browns (AL). The left-hander hit .226 that year for York, PA (PiL) and .325 the next season at Aberdeen, SD (NoL). After spending two years in the U.S. Army, Francona made his major league debut with the Baltimore Orioles (AL) in 1956. The fast-ball hitting first baseman–outfielder batted .258 with 16 doubles and nine HR in 139 games.

Following disappointing seasons with the Baltimore Orioles, Chicago White Sox (AL), and Detroit Tigers (AL), Francona excelled with the Cleveland Indians (AL). Cleveland traded Larry Doby* to obtain him in March 1959. He became the Indians' regular center fielder in early June after learning to hit slow pitches. Francona stroked the ball to all fields with occasional power. He batted .363 with 17 doubles, 20 HR, and 79 RBI in 399 at bats, just 78 plate appearances shy of winning the 1959 batting title. Still, Cleveland baseball writers selected him the Indians' Man of the Year. He batted .292, .301, and .272 the next three seasons, while scoring at least 82 runs, driving in at least 70 runs, and hitting at least 28 doubles and 14 HR each season. His .228 batting average in 1963 relegated him to part-time play in 1964. Cleveland sold him to the World Champion St. Louis Cardinals (NL) in December 1964.

Never again did Francona remain a regular player for an entire season, as he drifted to the Philadelphia Phillies (NL) in 1967, Atlanta Braves (NL) from 1967 to 1969, Oakland A's (AL) in 1969 and 1970, and Milwaukee Brewers (AL) in 1970. He batted .286 in 1968 and .295 in 1969 for Atlanta and .341 for Oakland in 1969. He led the AL in doubles with 36 in 1960 and was selected for the 1961 All-Star game. In 1,719 games spanning 15 major league seasons, Francona batted .272 with 1,395 hits, 125 HR, 224 doubles, 650 runs scored, and 656 RBI.

Francona married Roberta Jackson on October 2, 1956. They have a son, Terry, a former major league player and now manager, and a daughter, Amy. Francona served as recreation and parks director in Beaver Park, PA and worked at the ice arena in New Brighton.

BIBLIOGRAPHY: Tito Francona file, National Baseball Library, Cooperstown, NY; Tito Francona, letter to James N. Giglio, March 25, 1996; *TSN*, March 28, 1956, August 8, 1956, July 22, 1959, November 18, 1959, January 25, 1964, January 2, 1965,

August 10, 1968, May 17, 1969; Larry Moffi, *This Side of Cooperstown* (Iowa City, IA, 1996); Gary Caruso, *The Braves Encyclopedia* (Philadelphia, PA, 1995); Terry Pluto, *The Curse of Rocky Colavito* (New York, 1994); John Thorn et al., eds., *Total Baseball*, 5th ed. (New York, 1997); Jack Torry, *Endless Summers* (South Bend, IN, 1995).

James N. Giglio

FRANKS, Herman Louis (b. January 4, 1914, Price, UT), player, scout, coach, and manager, is the son of Italian immigrants. His father, a professional photographer, bore the last name of Franchi before coming to America. After attending the University of Utah, Franks played, scouted, coached, and managed for 40 years in professional baseball. Franks, the quintessential journeyman catcher, began his professional baseball career with the Hollywood, CA Stars (PCL) in 1932 and spent several seasons in the minor leagues before breaking into the major leagues with the St. Louis Cardinals (NL) in 1939. He played for the Brooklyn Dodgers (NL) in 1940 and 1941. After serving in World War II, Franks joined the Philadelphia Athletics (AL) for the 1947 and 1948 campaigns and ended his major league playing career briefly with the New York Giants (NL) in 1949. His lifetime .199 batting average spanned 188 games.

The 5-foot 11-inch, 200-pound Franks, who became better known following his playing career, coached for the New York Giants from 1949 to 1955 and San Francisco Giants (NL) in 1958 and 1964, and scouted for the Giants in 1957 and in 1959 and 1960. From 1965 to 1968, he managed the San Francisco Giants to four second place finishes and a 367–280–2 composite record. Under Franks, the Giants boasted powerful hitters Willie Mays,* Willie McCovey,* and Orlando Cepeda,* and dominant pitcher Juan Marichal.* Nevertheless, the Los Angeles Dodgers or the St. Louis Cardinals finished ahead of the Giants for the NL pennant. Tired of the franchise serving as annual bridesmaids, the Giants fired Franks after the 1968 season. Franks coached the Chicago Cubs (NL) part of 1970 and managed them from 1977 to 1979, finishing fourth, third, and fifth in the NL's Eastern Division. Altogether, his clubs compiled a 605–521–2 mark in seven major league seasons. Franks, who married Amneris Lorenzon in September 1948, lives in Salt Lake City, UT.

BIBLIOGRAPHY: Herman Franks file, National Baseball Library, Cooperstown, NY; Thomas Aylesworth and Benton Minks, *The Encyclopedia of Baseball Managers* (New York, 1990); Eddie Gold and Art Ahrens, *The New Era Cubs, 1940–1985* (Chicago, IL, 1985); Mike Mandell, *San Francisco Giants* (San Francisco, CA, 1979); David Nemec, *The History of Baseball in the San Francisco Bay Area* (San Francisco, CA, 1985); John E. Spalding, *Sacramento Senators and Solons: Baseball in California's Capital, 1886 to 1976* (Manhattan, KS, 1995); John Thorn et al., eds., *Total Baseball*, 5th ed. (New York, 1997).

Joel S. Franks

FRASER, Ronald George "Ron" (b. June 25, 1936, Nutley, NJ), coach, is the son of William Alexander Fraser, a professional boxer and public service worker, and Mary (Smith) Fraser. Upon Rod Dedeaux's* retirement from the University of Southern California in 1986, Fraser assumed the mantle as the dean of college baseball coaches. At the University of Miami, FL, Fraser coached 30 years from 1963 through 1992. His teams won 1,271 games, lost 438 contests, and tied nine for a .742 winning percentage. Miami captured NCAA Championships in 1982 and 1985. Fraser ranks third all-time in career victories and eleventh in winning percentage. Fraser was named Coach of the Year three times in Europe for leading the Dutch team to the European title, once by the NCAA, twice by *TSN*, and once by the IBA, becoming the first American to win that award.

A great promoter and tactician, Fraser revived the popularity of college baseball in Southern Florida. His various activities included creative promotions, raising funds for a beautiful stadium, convincing the University of Miami to provide its first baseball grants-in-aid, and pioneering an "All-in-the Family" ticket plan. Fraser's ideas, along with his winning baseball program, catapulted Miami among the leaders in college baseball attendance for the 1980s. Miami led the nation in baseball attendance five times, setting the NCAA record in 1981 with 163,261 spectators.

Fraser, the single individual most responsible for the national exposure of college baseball on ESPN, personally lobbied the all-sports network on behalf of the exciting college game. Fraser arranged an ESPN series in 1981 with the University of Southern California, matching two baseball dynasties and dynamic coaches. Fraser coached the U.S. baseball team at the 1992 Barcelona, Spain Summer Olympic Games.

Fraser combined his splendid tactics, great wit, and a little larceny in an international game in the 1960s. His team was playing a night game against a Columbian team in their homeland when the lights went out. Steve Greenberg, a star player at Yale University and son of National Baseball Hall-of-Famer Hank Greenberg,* was a runner on first base. Fraser instructed Greenberg to steal second before restoration of the electricity. Greenberg followed instructions and lasted three or four pitches after the lights returned before the Columbians realized what had happened. Nearly the entire Columbian team ran out onto the field to begin a huge rhubarb, while coach Fraser turned away from the field and stayed out of the fray. Greenberg, a former assistant to Baseball Commissioner Fay Vincent,* still chides Fraser about the incident.

BIBLIOGRAPHY: *Official NCAA Baseball Records*, 1964–1993; *University of Miami Baseball Media Guide*, 1983–1993; *The 1999 ESPN Information Please Sports Almanac*; Steve Wulf, "Last Hurrah!," *SI* 77 (July 22, 1992), pp. 150–152.

Cappy Gagnon

FREEDMAN, Andrew (b. September 1, 1860, New York, NY; d. December 4, 1915, New York, NY), executive, was the son of grocer Joseph Freedman and Elizabeth (Davies) Freedman, both German Jews. He attended public schools, graduated from City College of New York with a law degree, and entered the real estate business. He joined Tammany Hall at age 21 and became an intimate of future machine boss Richard Croker. Although never holding public office, he exercised enormous political influence through his association with Croker as a member of Tammany's Finance Committee and as national Democratic party treasurer in 1897. Freedman used his political ties to make many choice real estate and government bonding deals through the Maryland Fidelity and Guarantee Company, which he founded in 1898. His most important project comprised the bonding for the construction of the New York City subway.

Freedman first became involved in sports in the 1890s as the receiver of Manhattan Field, where the New York Giants (NL) played in 1889 and where Big Three college football teams subsequently performed. In January 1895, Freedman purchased the controlling interest in the Giants for $48,000 from local Republican politicians. An extremely unpopular owner, he was criticized for operating his franchise like a Tammany fiefdom. The irascible, quick-tempered Freedman hired 12 managers in eight years and repeatedly fired pilots for no cause. He encouraged rowdyism on the field and fought with the anti-Semitic "Ducky" Holmes and other players. Freedman, a penurious owner, fined star hurler Amos Rusie* $200 in 1895 after the latter had won 24 games, causing him to sit out the next season. Journalists who chastised the Giants owner were barred from the ballpark, while Freedman used his political clout to bully fellow team owners. He sought to establish a national baseball trust to operate the sport on sound business principles, including exercising tight control over wages and shifting franchises to the most profitable sites. His scheme to pool profits ultimately was defeated in 1901.

Freedman's presence in New York proved a major stumbling block for the AL, which wanted to establish a franchise there. His political influence and his position in the real estate market enabled him to control most potential park sites. AL president Ban Johnson* also feared that Freedman could order streets built through any field the junior circuit might find.

In 1902 Freedman sold the Giants because the club did not make the anticipated profits and had caused him aggravation; he concentrated instead on the forthcoming subway construction. John T. Brush,* who bought most of Freedman's stock for $200,000, just had sold his Cincinnati Reds (NL) to Freedman's friend, Mayor Julius Fleischmann, and other members of that city's Republican machine. Freedman assisted the new Giants owner by keeping Manhattan free of interlopers and using his influence as a director of the IRT to block the subway from subsidizing an AL team, scheduled to begin play in New York the following season. The AL was forced to find investors with personal political clout in Tammany Hall capable of overcoming Freedman's opposition and breaking into the potentially lucrative New York market.

Freedman, a lifelong bachelor who had accumulated an estimated $7 million fortune at his death, lived at Sherry's on Fifth Avenue and owned an estate at Red Bank, NJ. He belonged to 14 clubs and admired fast horses and yachts. The bulk of his estate was used to construct a home for the aged in the Bronx.

BIBLIOGRAPHY: Andrew Freedman file, National Baseball Library, Cooperstown, NY; James D. Hardy, Jr., *The New York Giants Baseball Club* (Jefferson, NC, 1996); Pat Edith Aynes, *The Andrew Freedman Story* (New York, 1976); "Andrew Freedman," *DAB* 7 (New York, 1931), p. 8; *NYT*, December 5, 1915; Noel Hynd, *The Giants of the Polo Grounds* (New York, 1988); Steven A. Riess, *Touching Base* (Westport, CT, 1980); Harold Seymour, *Baseball: The Early Years* (New York, 1960).

Steven A. Riess

FREEHAN, William Ashley "Bill" (b. November 21, 1941, Detroit, MI), player and coach, was one of the finest athletes ever at Bishop Barry High School in St. Petersburg, FL. By age 15, he already had attracted the attention of Detroit Tigers (AL) scout Louis D'Annunzio. At the University of Michigan, he starred in both football and baseball and broke Bill Skowron's* BTC record by batting .485 as a sophomore in 1961. Freehan completed his bachelor's degree several years after beginning his professional baseball career. Freehan had signed with the Detroit Tigers for a $100,000 bonus in 1961.

The oldest of four children of Ashley James Freehan, a sales representative, and Helen (Morris) Freehan, and reportedly of Cherokee ancestry, the 6-foot 3-inch, 200-pound, right-handed hitting catcher enjoyed one of the most distinguished careers in Detroit Tigers history from 1963 to 1976. Earlier minor league stints had included Duluth, MN–Superior, WI (NoL), Knoxville, TN (SAL), and Denver, CO (AA) in 1961 and 1962. Despite serious back problems and other injuries, Freehan ranks among the top ten in team history in games played (1,774), hits (1,591), HR (200), and total bases (2,502). An 11-time AL All-Star (1964–1973, 1975) and five-time Gold Glove catcher (1965–1969), he compiled a .412 lifetime slugging average and a .993 fielding average to set the AL career record for catchers. He led AL catchers in fielding percentage in 1966, 1970, and 1973. In the Tigers' 1968 world championship season, his slugging average soared to .454 with 25 HR, 84 RBI, and 73 assists as a catcher. Freehan grounded into only nine double plays and finished second in the MVP voting to teammate Dennis McLain.* Freehan, however, hit only .083 in the World Series against the St. Louis Cardinals. He wrote a memoir of that season, *Behind the Mask*, which was published in 1970. Freehan played a key role on the Tigers' 1972 Eastern Division championship team and was inducted into the Michigan Sports Hall of Fame in 1982.

On February 23, 1963, Freehan married high school classmate Patricia Ann O'Brien. They have three daughters, Corey, Kelley, and Cathy, all of whom graduated from college. After retiring from baseball, Freehan established a successful second career as an auto parts representative and handled color commentary on cable for the Tigers and the Seattle Mariners (AL). In August 1989, the University of Michigan named him head baseball coach. Under Freehan, Michigan compiled a 166–167 win–loss record from 1990 through 1995 and finished with a season best of 34–23 in 1991.

BIBLIOGRAPHY: Detroit Tigers, *The Press Guide, 1989*; William Freehan file, National Baseball Library, Cooperstown, NY; William Freehan, letter to Sheldon L. Appleton, 1989; William Freehan, *Behind the Mask* (Cleveland, OH, 1970); Bill James, *The Bill James Historical Abstract* (New York, 1985); Gene Karst and Martin J. Jones, Jr., *Who's Who in Professional Baseball* (New Rochelle, NY, 1973); Joe Falls, *Detroit Tigers* (New York, 1975); Brent P. Kelley, *The Case For: Those Overlooked by the Baseball Hall of Fame* (Jefferson, NC, 1992); William M. Anderson, *The Detroit Tigers* (South Bend, IN, 1996); Fred Smith, *995 Tigers* (Detroit, MI, 1981); Richard Bak, *A Place for Summer* (Detroit, MI, 1998); John Thorn et al., eds., *Total Baseball*, 5th ed. (New York, 1997).

Sheldon L. Appleton

FREEMAN, John Frank "Buck," "Bucky" (b. October 30, 1871, Catasauqua, PA; d. June 25, 1949, Wilkes-Barre, PA), player, manager, umpire, and scout, made his major league debut on June 27, 1891 with the Washington Statesmen (AA) as a pitcher. He compiled a 3–2 win–loss record with a 3.89 ERA and batted .222 in five games. The 5-foot 9-inch, 160 pounder, who threw and batted left-handed, spent the next six seasons in the minor leagues and was converted to the outfield. In 1894 for Haverhill, MA (NEL), he hit .390 with 31 HR, 27 doubles, and 29 stolen bases. During one game on July 5, he accumulated 20 total bases on four HR and a double in five at bats. Freeman joined the Washington Senators (NL) in 1898 and the next year knocked in a career-high 122 runs. He belted 25 HR to establish the major league record, which stood until Babe Ruth's* 29 in 1919.

The Boston Beaneaters (NL) purchased Freeman in 1900, but he jumped to the Boston Pilgrims when the AL was formed in 1901. He ranked second in the AL in HR (12) in 1901 and led the AL in RBI (121) in 1902, again finishing second in HR (11). He paced the AL in both RBI (104) and HR (13) in 1903, becoming the first batter to lead both the NL and AL in HR. Sluggers Sam Crawford* and Mark McGwire* are the only other players to achieve that feat. The Boston Pilgrims captured the first AL pennant in 1903. Freeman hit three triples, helping Boston defeat the Pittsburgh Pirates, 5–3, in the first World Series. The Boston Pilgrims won the AL pennant the following season, but did not play a postseason series because New York Giants manager John McGraw* refused to meet the AL champions.

Freeman led the AL with 19 triples in 1904 and remained a popular player with Boston fans, but the cost-cutting owners released him early in the 1907 season. He joined Minneapolis, MN (AA), finishing the season with a .335 batting average and leading all minor leaguers with 18 HR. He completed his playing career in the minor leagues, serving his final season with Scranton, PA (NYSL) in 1912 as player–manager. He owned a popular pool hall in Wilkes-Barre, PA and remained active in baseball, umpiring in the minor leagues from 1913 to 1925, scouting for the St. Louis Browns (AL) from 1926 to 1933, and managing Bloomsburg, PA in 1934 and 1935.

In his 11-year major league career, Freeman batted .293 with 199 doubles, 131 triples, 82 HR, and 92 stolen bases. As an outfielder, he possessed speed and a strong arm. Several attempts have been made, most notably in 1958 and 1976, to influence the National Baseball Hall of Fame Committee on Veterans to induct the first "Home Run King." Freeman died after a brief illness, being survived by four sons and a sister. He was preceded in death by his wife, Annie (Kane) Freeman.

BIBLIOGRAPHY: Morris Bealle, *The Washington Senators* (Washington, DC, 1947); *The Baseball Encyclopedia*, 10th ed. (New York, 1996); John Freeman file, National Baseball Library, Cooperstown, NY; Gene Karst and Martin J. Jones, Jr., eds., *Who's Who in Professional Baseball* (New Rochelle, NY, 1973); Frederick G. Lieb, *The Boston Red Sox* (New York, 1947); Shirley Povich, *The Washington Senators* (New York, 1954); Richard Scheinin, *Field of Screams* (New York, 1994); Robert Redmount, *The Red Sox Encyclopedia* (Champaign, IL, 1998); Mike Shatzkin, ed., *The Ballplayers* (New York, 1990); John Thorn et al., eds., *Total Baseball*, 5th ed. (New York, 1997).

Gaymon L. Bennett

FREGOSI, James Louis "Jim" (b. April 4, 1942, San Francisco, CA), player, manager, sportscaster, and executive, was signed by the Boston Red Sox (AL) in 1960 while attending Menlo College in California. Later that year, the young shortstop was acquired by the Los Angeles Angels (AL) in the expansion draft. After playing with Dallas–Fort Worth, TX (AA), Fregosi joined the Los Angeles Angels late in 1961. For the next 11 seasons, he started at shortstop for the team that became the Anaheim-based California Angels in 1965. This favorite of the fans and of owner Gene Autry was voted the Angels' greatest player in 1969.

A durable player, Fregosi showed versatility in his batting and fielding. He played on six All-Star teams and received MVP votes for eight successive seasons from 1963 through 1970 with the Angels. The 6-foot 1-inch, 190-pound Fregosi won a Gold Glove award in 1967 and led AL shortstops in double plays (125) in 1966. Offensively, Fregosi paced the AL with 13 triples in 1968 and batted .265 lifetime with 151 HR and 706 RBI in 18 major league seasons. At the peak of Fregosi's playing career, California traded him in December 1971 to the New York Mets (NL) for formidable pitcher Nolan Ryan* and three other players. Ryan achieved legendary pitching feats, but Fregosi batted only .232 for the 1972 Mets and was dealt to the Texas Rangers (AL) in July 1973. With the Rangers, Fregosi hit slightly over .260 from 1973 to 1975. A slump in 1976 caused Texas to trade him in June 1977 to the Pittsburgh Pirates (NL).

In June 1978, Fregosi was released by the Pirates and became the manager of the California Angels. Fregosi's team won a Western Division title in 1979, but lost the AL Championship Series to the Baltimore Orioles. After the Angels struggled in 1980 and 1981, Gene Mauch* replaced Fregosi as manager. From 1982 to 1986, Fregosi piloted the Louisville, KY Redbirds (AA) to three playoff berths and two AA championships. He was named AA Manager of the Year in 1983 and 1985.

In June 1986, Fregosi replaced Tony La Russa* as manager of the Chicago White Sox (AL). Fregosi's three years at the helm of the White Sox, however, produced a disappointing 193–226 win–loss record. In October 1988, the White Sox fired him for "philosophical differences" with the team's general manager. He served as a minor league pitching instructor for the Philadelphia Phillies (NL) from May 1989 to April 1991 and worked as an analyst for Sports Channel in April 1991. After struggling to a 4–9 start, the Phillies selected Fregosi to replace Nick Leyva as manager. Fregosi guided Philadelphia to a third place tie in the Eastern Division. In 1993, he guided Philadelphia to first place in the NL East with a 97–65 record and to a NL Championship Series upset of the Atlanta Braves in six games. The Toronto Blue Jays defeated the Phillies, 4–2 in the 1993 World Series. Philadelphia struggled to losing records thereafter, leading to Fregosi's dismissal following the 1996 season. His managerial record spanning 13 major league seasons featured 945 wins and 1,016 losses for a .482 winning percentage. In 1998, he served as special assistant to the general manager of the San Francisco Giants (NL). In March 1999, Fregosi replaced Tim Johnson as manager of the Toronto Blue Jays (AL). Toronto finished 84–78 in 1999.

BIBLIOGRAPHY: Thomas Aylesworth and Benton Minks, *The Encyclopedia of Baseball Managers* (New York, 1990); Jim Fregosi file, National Baseball Library, Cooperstown, NY; *NYT*, May 29, 1981; St. Louis (MO) *Post-Dispatch*, March 9, 1985; John Thorn et al., eds., *Total Baseball* 5th ed. (New York, 1997); *TSN*, July 28, 1973, May 30, 1981; *TSN Baseball Register, 1996*.

David Q. Voigt

FREITAS, Antonio, Jr. "Tony" (b. May 5, 1908, Mill Valley, CA; d. March 13, 1994, Orangevale, CA), player and manager, remains the winningest left-handed pitcher and fourth winningest hurler in minor league history. One of four children born to farmer/street superintendent Antonio Freitas and Maria (Fonseca) Freitas, he spent his youth in Mill Valley. He attended Tamalpais High School, delivered groceries, and pitched for the town team. Freitas's professional debut came with Phoenix, AZ (ArSL) in 1928 and Globe, AZ (ArSL) in 1929. He was promoted to Sacramento, CA (PCL) that year and spent 15 seasons there. After hurling consecutive 19-victory efforts in 1930 and 1931 and pitching a no-hit game on his birthday in 1932, Freitas joined Connie Mack's* Philadelphia Athletics (AL) in 1932. Mickey Cochrane* caught the 5-foot 7-inch, 155 pounder, who enjoyed his finest major league campaign with a 12–5 record, 10 complete games, and a shutout in 1932. The following season, the Athletics and Freitas both started slowly. Philadelphia sent him to Portland, OR (PCL). Freitas enjoyed success at St. Paul, MN (AA) in 1934 and pitched for the Cincinnati Reds (NL) from 1934 through 1936. Despite a sparkling 1.29 ERA in seven innings for the struggling 1936 Reds, the 0–2 Freitas was demoted to Columbus, OH (AA). Freitas's major league service ended with a 25–33 record, reflecting weak Cincinnati support and the challenge of finesse pitching in baseball's "hitters' era."

Freitas returned in 1937 to Sacramento, his off-season home, with his wife, Lillian (Armstrong), and stepson Jack. His string of six consecutive 20-win campaigns for the Sacramento Solons (included a 24–11 mark in 1938) was ended only by service in the U.S. Army Air Corps during the 1943–1945 seasons. He pitched in the CaL, winning 85 games in four years for Modesto, CA (1950–1951) and Stockton, CA (1952–1953). The Stockton fans honored the 45-year-old Freitas, whose career had spanned 26 seasons, with a new car in 1953. A grateful Freitas responded with a shutout. His 22–9 record that year brought his minor league career totals to 342 wins, 238 losses, a record nine 20-win seasons, 2,324 strikeouts and a 3.11 ERA. He managed with modest success at Modesto in 1951, Stockton in 1952, and Sacramento in 1955. Freitas later worked as a mechanic and enjoyed hunting, fishing, and playing the accordian. He treasured the thrill of "just putting on a professional uniform and getting paid for the game I loved to play for fun."

BIBLIOGRAPHY: Antonio Freitas, Jr., file, National Baseball Library, Cooperstown, NY; Lee Allen, *The Cincinnati Reds* (New York, 1948); John Thorn et al., eds., *Total Baseball*, 5th ed. (New York, 1997); SABR, *Minor League Baseball Stars* (Cooperstown, NY, 1978).

James D. Smith III

FRENCH, Lawrence Herbert "Larry" (b. November 1, 1907, Visalia, CA; d. February 9, 1987, San Diego, CA), player, married Thelma Grace Olmstead on June 2, 1928, and attended the University of California at Berkeley for one year. The 6-foot 1-inch, 195-pound left-hander of English-Scotch descent entered professional baseball in 1926 with Portland, OR (PCL) and Ogden, UT (UIL) and spent the 1927 and 1928 seasons with Portland. French broke into the major leagues in 1929 with the Pittsburgh Pirates (NL). His 7–5 record that year was followed by a 17–18 mark, leading the NL in losses. During the early 1930s, however, French became the workhorse of the Pirates staff and twice won 18 games.

In November 1934 French was traded to the Chicago Cubs (NL). The trade gave Chicago a needed left-hander and paid immediate dividends with an NL pennant, as French contributed 17 wins and 2 saves. The amiable southpaw enjoyed some of his best years with the Cubs, hurling 20 shutouts (twice tying for the NL lead) and producing a 95–84 record in a little over six seasons. His 18–9 and 15–8 1936 and 1939 seasons were his finest campaigns there, while his 10–19 mark in 1938 proved his worst. In two World Series, he recorded a good 3.21 ERA. French compiled two losses and no wins in five appearances, as Chicago lost both World Series.

French fit in well with the strong Cubs teams of the 1930s. A "go-getter" with business acumen, he advised many of his teammates on business transactions and dabbled in real estate. After suffering an injured thumb and a miserable 5–14 start in 1941, French was sent to the Brooklyn Dodgers for the waiver price in August 1941. He hurled one inning in the World Series for the Dodgers without any decision. In 1942, French rebounded brilliantly with his knuckleball to lead the NL in winning percentage (.789) with a 15–4 mark. He joined the U.S. Navy in World War II and became a career officer, retiring in 1969. Never a robust hitter, he enjoyed his finest season in 1942 with a .300 batting average. During his 14-year major league career, French won 197 games and lost 171, struck out 1,187 batters in 3,152 innings, hurled 40 shutouts, and compiled a 3.44 ERA.

BIBLIOGRAPHY: Warren Brown, *The Chicago Cubs* (New York, 1946); Larry French file, National Baseball Library, Cooperstown, NY; Eddie Gold and Art Ahrens, *The Golden Era Cubs, 1876–1940* (Chicago, IL, 1985); Frank Graham, *The Brooklyn Dodgers* (New York, 1945); Peter Golenbock, *Bums* (New York, 1984); William F. McNeil, *The Dodgers Encyclopedia* (Champaign, IL, 1997); Richard Goldstein, *Spartan Seasons* (New York, 1980); *The Baseball Encyclopedia*, 10th ed. (New York, 1996).

Duane A. Smith

FREY, James Gottfried "Jimmy" (b. May 26, 1931, Cleveland, OH), player, coach, scout, manager, sportscaster, and executive, is the son of John Bauer Frey and Rose (Schafer) Frey and attended Ohio State University. The 5-foot 9-inch, 170-pound Frey played outfield for 14 minor league seasons, compiling a .302 career batting average. His best season came with Tulsa, OK (TL) in 1957, when he batted .336 and was selected MVP.

Frey started his managerial career in 1964–1965 with Bluefield, WV (ApL) and scouted for the Baltimore Orioles (AL) from 1966 to 1969. After coaching with Baltimore from 1970 to 1979, he became manager of the Kansas City Royals (AL) in 1980. His first year produced outstanding results, as he guided Kansas City to the AL pennant and defeated the New York Yankees in the AL Championship Series. The Royals lost the 1980 World Series to the Philadelphia Phillies in six games. The strike-dominated 1981 season found Frey's team struggling. Kansas City replaced him as manager on August 31. He joined the New York Mets (NL) the next season as a coach.

In October 1983, the Chicago Cubs (NL) named Frey manager. Chicago won the NL Eastern Division in 1984 with a 96–65 mark, the first time the club had won anything since 1945. Despite winning the first two playoff games, the Cubs lost the NL Championship Series to the San Diego Padres. Frey earned NL Manager of the Year honors. Injuries killed Chicago's chances the next season and dashed fans' hopes for reaching the World Series. Frey managed the Cubs until June 1986, leaving with a 196–182 record. He served as a radio broadcaster for the Chicago Cubs in 1987 and as Executive Vice President of Baseball Operations from 1988 to November 1991. Frey married Joan Miller in March 1952 and has four children, Jim, Cindy, Mary, and Jennifer.

BIBLIOGRAPHY: Jim Frey file, National Baseball Library, Cooperstown, NY; Thomas Aylesworth and Benton Minks, *The Encyclopedia of Baseball Managers* (New York, 1990); *Chicago Cubs Media Guide* 1985, 1988, 1992; *The Baseball Encyclopedia*, 10th ed. (New York, 1996); Eddie Gold and Art Ahrens, *The New Era Cubs, 1941–1985* (Chicago, IL, 1985).

Duane A. Smith

FREY, Linus Reinhard "Lonny," "Junior" (b. August 23, 1910, St. Louis, MO), player, is the son of Frank B. Frey, a salesman, and Louise (Scherer) Frey and grew up in St. Louis, where he worked in a factory after graduating from grammar school. An amateur baseball player, he pursued the sport professionally after losing a factory job in St. Louis in 1931. He played for Montgomery, AL (SEL) and York, PA (NYPL) in 1932 and for Nashville, TN (SL) in 1933. The Brooklyn Dodgers (NL) promoted Frey in August 1933 because of injuries to their infielders. Frey made his major league debut at shortstop on August 29, 1933. He started at shortstop for the Brooklyn Dodgers from 1934 to 1936 and was dealt to the Chicago Cubs (NL) in December 1936 for Roy Henshaw and Elwood "Woody" English.* After Frey played one season with the Cubs, Chicago sent him to the Cincinnati Reds (NL) for cash in February 1938. Frey played six seasons at second base for the Cincinnati Reds before joining the U.S. Army in late 1943. After his discharge, he played for the Cincinnati Reds in 1946 and split the 1947 season between the Chicago Cubs and the New York Yankees (AL).

Frey, a rather ordinary hitter, compiled a career .269 batting average with just 61 HR. He possessed some speed, leading the NL in stolen bases with 22 in 1940. His best year came in 1939, when he batted .291, scored 95 runs, and hit a career-high 11 HR. Defensively, he played significantly better at second base than shortstop. He led all shortstops in errors in 1935 and 1936, making a remarkable 62 miscues in 131 games in 1936. But he led NL second basemen in fielding in 1941 and 1943, putouts and assists in 1940, and double plays from 1940 to 1943.

Frey, voted the starting second baseman on the 1939 NL All-Star team, also made the 1941 and 1943 teams and batted .333 in All-Star action. He also played in the 1939 and 1940 World Series with the Cincinnati Reds and the 1947 World Series with the New York Yankees, but made no hits in 20 trips to the plate. A broken toe limited him to pinch-hitting duty in the 1940 World Series.

Frey married Mary Albrecht in October 1935 and had three children. Contemporaries described him as a "good, fast, smart" ballplayer, known for his "tricky and spectacular hook slide" and his ability to tag runners trying to reach second base. Following his retirement from baseball, he and his family lived quietly in Snohomish, WA and then Hayden, ID.

BIBLIOGRAPHY: Lonny Frey file, National Baseball Library, Cooperstown, NY; Lonny Frey file, *TSN*, St. Louis, MO; Frank Graham, *The Brooklyn Dodgers* (New York, 1945); Eddie Gold and Art Ahrens, *The Golden Era Cubs, 1876–1940* (Chicago, IL, 1985); Lee Allen, *The Cincinnati Reds* (New York, 1948); Donald Honig, *The Cincinnati Reds* (New York, 1992); *NYT*, August 27, 1933, October 1, 1940, October 2, 1940, December 12, 1943; Mike Shatzkin, ed., *The Ballplayers* (New York, 1990); John Thorn et al., eds., *Total Baseball*, 5th ed. (New York, 1997); *The Baseball Encyclopedia*, 10th ed. (New York, 1996).

John E. Findling

FRICK, Ford Christopher (b. December 19, 1894, Wawaka, IN; d. April 8, 1978, Bronxville, NY), sportswriter and baseball executive, was the son of Jacob Frick and Emma Frick and grew up in northern Indiana farming communities. After graduating from DePauw University in 1915, Frick spent six years as a teacher and journalist in Colorado. He married Eleanor Cowing in 1916 and had one son, Frederick. In Colorado, Frick taught high school and college, briefly played for an industrial league baseball team, wrote for a newspaper, and in 1918–1919 supervised rehabilitation for World War I veterans. His stories about a devastating flood for the Colorado Springs, CO *Telegraph* after the war won national recognition.

Frick, who moved to New York City in 1922, became a sportswriter with the New York *Journal* and covered the New York Yankees (AL) from 1923 to 1934. His career blossomed when he agreed to ghostwrite newspaper articles for Babe Ruth* and subsequently wrote *Babe Ruth's Own Book of Baseball*. Between 1930 and 1934, Frick combined newspaper work with radio announcing and shared in the first radio broadcast of Brooklyn Dodgers (NL) games in 1931.

Frick left journalism in 1934 to become director of the NL Service Bureau, a publicity office, and began his climb to the top of baseball's hierarchy. Nine months later, he was elected NL president to replace John A. Heydler.* Heydler resigned after a dispute with a team owner, but officially cited health reasons for his departure. Between 1934 and 1951, NL president Frick avoided conflict with club owners and concentrated on routine administrative matters. He stabilized NL affairs, found new capital for financially weak teams, and promoted the addition of a Hall of Fame to the baseball museum that opened at Cooperstown, NY in 1939. Although apparently content with the major league's exclusion of black players, Frick accepted Jackie Robinson's* appearance for the Brooklyn Dodgers (NL) in 1947. Acting through the team owner, he warned St. Louis Cardinals (NL) players threatening not to play the Dodgers that they would be "barred from baseball even though it means the disruption of a club or a whole league."

Baseball Commissioner Albert B. Chandler,* who had upset team owners, resigned in 1951, opening the way for Frick's election as the game's third commissioner and first from within baseball's ranks. He served two seven-year terms, retiring in 1965, and was voted into the National Baseball Hall of Fame in 1970. Baseball faced serious challenges during his tenure as commissioner: franchise shifts, major league expansion, player demands, congressional hearings into the business side of baseball, survival of the minor leagues, the impact of television, and competition from other professional sports. Frick treated most challenges as "league matters" beyond his control. Frick deferred to the most powerful owners and, critics said, primarily to Walter O'Malley,* who moved his Dodgers from Brooklyn to Los Angeles in 1957. During Frick's administration, five teams relocated, the AL added teams in Los Angeles and Minnesota in 1961, and the NL established franchises in New York and Houston in 1962. In a controversial 1961 decision, Frick ruled that official records show that Yankee Roger Maris* surpassed Babe Ruth's* season mark of 60 HR in 161 rather than 154 games.

In bland, sentimental memoirs, Frick praised baseball owners and defended his own record of executive restraint. An alternative view came from maverick owner Bill Veeck,* who complained that the succession of commissioners from Judge Kenesaw Mountain Landis* to Frick should appear as a perpendicular line on a chart. Instead, Frick may have embodied the dominance of club owners in the period and baseball's own smug certainty about the future.

BIBLIOGRAPHY: Ford Frick file, National Baseball Library, Cooperstown, NY; Jerome Holtzman, *The Commissioners* (New York, 1998); Lee Allen, *The National League Story* (New York, 1961); Ford C. Frick, *Games, Asterisks, and People* (New York, 1973); Lee Lowenfish and Tony Lupien, *The Imperfect Diamond* (Briarcliff Manor, NY, 1980); Paul MacFarlane, ed., *Hall of Fame Fact Book* (St. Louis, MO 1982); *NYT*, April 9, 1978; Bill Veeck and Ed Linn, *Veeck—as in Wreck* (New York, 1972); David Quentin Voigt, *American Baseball*, vol. 3 (University Park, PA, 1983); Lowell Reidenbaugh, *Baseball's Hall of Fame-Cooperstown* (New York, 1993).

Joseph E. King

FRIEND, Robert Bartmess "Bob," "Warrior" (b. November 24, 1930, West Lafayette, IN), player, was a 16-year major league veteran. He spent 15 seasons with the Pittsburgh Pirates (NL) as one of the hardest throwing right-handers and most durable NL starters during the 1950s. A high school football star in West Lafayette, IN, Friend rejected football scholarships from Purdue University and several West Coast schools to sign with the Pittsburgh Pirates in 1948.

Debuting in 1951, Friend spent most of his major league career with Pittsburgh on a Pirates ballclub that finished either seventh or eighth his first seven major league seasons. A hurler on five last-place teams in that decade, the strapping 6-foot, 190-pound right-hander became the only pitcher in major league history to lose more than 200 games (230) while winning fewer than that number (197). He compiled a lifetime 3.58 ERA, hurled 36 shutouts, and struck out 1,734 batters in 3,611 innings. Twice he paced NL hurlers in hits allowed and 19 defeats (in 1959, 1961). During the Pirates' remarkable 1960 championship season, the unlucky Friend lost both Game 2 and Game 6 of the dramatic World Series against the New York Yankees.

Despite numerous defeats, hits, and runs allowed, and having double-digit losses in 15 of his 16 major league campaigns, the workhorse hurler also boasted stellar accomplishments. In 1955, he achieved a first by leading the NL in ERA (2.83) for a last-place club. Friend tied Warren Spahn* for the NL lead in victories with 22 in 1958, led senior circuit pitchers in starts for three consecutive seasons (1956–1958), and also paced the NL in innings pitched in 1956 and 1957. He still shares the NL record with two All-Star Game victories (1956 and 1960), but was assessed the loss in the 1958 mid-summer classic. In December 1965, Pittsburgh sold Friend to the New York Yankees (AL). Friend's final season was split between the New York Yankees and New York Mets (NL) in 1966, after which he earned a bachelor's degree from Purdue University.

Friend settled in Fox Chapel, PA and pursued a successful career in investment and finance in Pittsburgh. As an active player, Friend served as both Pittsburgh Pirates and NL player representative. He defeated the New York Giants in the final game ever played in the Polo Grounds in 1957. He barely missed joining Bobo Newsom* and Jack Powell* as the only hurlers ever to win over 200 games and yet lose an even larger amount. He married Patricia Koval on September 30, 1957 and has a son, Bob, who golfs professionally.

BIBLIOGRAPHY: Martin Appel, *Yesterday's Heroes* (New York, 1988); Bob Friend file, National Baseball Library, Cooperstown, NY; John T. Bird, *Twin Killing: The Bill Mazeroski Story* (Birmingham, AL, 1960); Jim O'Brien, *Mac and the 1960 Bucs* (Pittsburgh, PA, 1994); Dick Groat and Bill Surface, *The World Champion Pittsburgh Pirates* (New York, 1961); Richard L. Burtt, *The Pittsburgh Pirates, A Pictorial History* (Virginia Beach, VA, 1977); Bob Smizik, *The Pittsburgh Pirates: An Illustrated History* (New York, 1990); Lester J. Biederman, "The Pirates Find a Friend," *BD* 15 (April 1956), pp. 51–53; Myron Cope, "Bob Friend, Symbol of the New Ballplayer," *Sport* 32 (September 1961), pp. 72–107; Rich Marazzi and Len Fiorito, *Aaron to Zuverink* (New York, 1982); Mike Shatzkin, ed., *The Ballplayers* (New York, 1990).

Peter C. Bjarkman

FRISCH, Frank Francis "Frankie," "The Fordham Flash" (b. September 9, 1898, New York, NY; d. March 12, 1973, Wilmington, DE), all-around athlete, baseball player, manager, and sportscaster, was the son of immigrant Franz Frisch, a wealthy lace linen manufacturer, and Katherine (Stahl) Frisch. He attended Fordham Prep School and graduated from Fordham University in 1919. Besides being a sprinter on the track and field team, he played catcher on the baseball squad. Frisch captained Fordham's baseball, basketball, and football squads and was named as halfback on Walter Camp's (FB) mythical All-American football second team in 1918.

Frisch signed with the New York Giants (NL) baseball club in 1919 and never played in the minor leagues. He married Ada E. Lucy in November 1922; they had no children. Although using an unorthodox cross-handed batting style in college, Frisch corrected his stance with the Giants to become one of baseball's finest switch-hitters. With the Giants, he played second base and third base. From 1921 to 1924, Frisch's batting and fielding helped the Giants to four consecutive NL pennants and two world championships. Manager John McGraw* admired Frisch's ability and named him captain, but later clashed with him in 1926 when the Giants dropped into the second division. On December 20, 1926, Frisch and pitcher Jimmy Ring were traded to the St. Louis Cardinals (NL) for stellar player–manager Rogers Hornsby.* Although the Cardinals had just won the world championship, Hornsby had wrangled with owner Sam Breadon* over salary and other issues.

Frisch, who faced hostile St. Louis fans upset at losing the popular Hornsby, responded in 1927 with a brilliant season by fielding spectacularly, batting .337, and leading the league with 48 stolen bases. The second baseman led the NL in fielding and assists and set a major league record for total chances accepted. He struck out only 10 times in 153 games, setting a major league record for fewest strikeouts in a season by a switch-hitter. Frisch helped the Cardinals win NL pennants in 1928, 1930, and 1931, when he was selected as the NL's MVP. He was named player–manager of the Cardinals on July 24, 1933 and led his team to another pennant in his first full season (1934) as pilot. In 1931 and 1934, the Cardinals won world championships. Frisch, who retired as a player in 1937, was released as Cardinals manager on September 10, 1938. Frisch piloted the Pittsburgh Pirates (NL) from 1940 through 1946 and the Chicago Cubs (NL) from June 10, 1949 through July 21, 1951. In 16 major league seasons as manager, Frisch saw his clubs win 1,138 of 2,246 games for a .514 percentage. He announced over radio for the Boston Braves (NL) in 1939 and from 1947 through 1949 for the New York Giants.

As a player, Frisch appeared in 2,311 games, made 2,880 hits, slugged 466 doubles, knocked in 1,244 runs, stole 419 bases, and batted .316. Besides leading the NL in stolen bases in 1921 (49), 1927 (48), and 1931 (28), Frisch set numerous fielding records for NL second basemen and various batting and fielding marks in his 50 World Series games. In 1947, he was elected to the National Baseball Hall of Fame.

BIBLIOGRAPHY: Rob Rains, *The St. Louis Cardinals* (New York, 1992); Bob Broeg and Jerry Vickery, *St. Louis Cardinals Encyclopedia* (Grand Rapids, MI, 1998); Frank Frisch file, National Baseball Library, Cooperstown, NY; Thomas Aylesworth and Benton Minks, *The Encyclopedia of Baseball Managers* (New York, 1990); John Benson et al., *Baseball's Top 100* (Wilton, CT, 1997); Bob Broeg, *Super Stars of Baseball* (St. Louis, MO, 1971); Arnold Hano, *Greatest Giants of Them All* (New York, 1967); Robert E. Hood, *The Gashouse Gang* (New York, 1978); Frederick G. Lieb, *The St. Louis Cardinals* (New York, 1945); Eddie Gold and Art Ahrens, *The New Era Cubs, 1941–1985* (Chicago, IL, 1985); Noel Hynd, *The Giants of the Polo Grounds* (New York, 1988); Gene Karst and Martin J. Jones, Jr., *Who's Who in Professional Baseball* (New Rochelle, NY, 1973); Leonard Koppett, *The Man in the Dugout* (New York, 1993); *TSN*, March 24, 1973; Frank Frisch and Roy Stockton, *Frank Frisch: The Fordham Flash* (Garden City, NY, 1962); Joseph J. Vecchione, ed., *The New York Times Book of Sports Legends* (New York, 1991); Frank Graham, *The New York Giants* (New York, 1952); Charles C. Alexander, *John McGraw* (New York, 1988).

Gene Karst

FURILLO, Carl Anthony "Skoonj," "Little Flower," "Reading Rifle" (b. March 8, 1922, Stony Creek Mills, PA; d. January 21, 1989, Stony Creek Mills, PA), player was the sixth child of Michael Furillo and Philomena (Petiucci) Furillo, both Italian immigrants. Nicknamed "Skoonj" (Italian for "snail"), he grew up in the extreme poverty of the Depression and dropped out of school in the eighth grade to work in the apple orchards.

Furillo began his professional baseball career at Pocamoke City, MD (ESL) and Reading, PA (ISL) in 1940. After the 1940 season, the Brooklyn Dodgers (NL) purchased the Reading club from the Philadelphia Phillies (NL) for $5,000. Of the 18 players and the team bus, the Dodgers most coveted Furillo. Furillo started the 1942 season at Montreal, Canada (IL). Furillo was called the "Little Flower" because of his resemblance to New York City's mayor Fiorello LaGuardia. His U.S. Army military service included 18 months on the Pacific front. Furillo played with the Brooklyn Dodgers in 1946, replacing Pete Reiser* in center field. Furillo earned $3,750, batting .284 in 117 games.

Furillo became a regular outfielder in one of the most potent lineups in major league baseball history. The 6 foot, 190 pound Furillo led the NL in hitting in 1953 with a .344 average and became a vital cog for the "Boys of Summer." That season, Furillo was named the Comeback Player of the Year and engaged in his celebrated fight with New York Giants (NL) manager Leo Durocher.* Someone stepped on his hand, breaking his finger. He played the concave wall at Ebbets Field as if he had designed it. Nicknamed the "Reading Rifle" for his strong arm, Furillo once threw out Cincinnati Reds pitcher Mel Queen at first base on an apparent hit to right field. He held the Brooklyn Dodgers franchise season records for most games (158) and most at-bats (667), both set in 1951.

During his 15-year career with the Brooklyn-Los Angeles Dodgers, Furillo drove in 90 runs or more six times. Altogether, Furillo played in 1,806 games, with a lifetime .299 batting mark, 1,910 hits, 324 doubles, 56 triples, 192 HR, 1,058 RBI, and 48 stolen bases. He performed in seven World Series, hitting .266, scoring 13 runs, and knocking in 13 tallies in 40 games. His 34 safeties included 9 doubles and 2 HR. The always dependable Furillo made the NL All-Star team in 1952 and 1953.

His baseball career ended on a sour note following his contract dispute with the Los Angeles Dodgers. Known as the "hardhat who sued baseball," he won a breach of contract suit from the Dodgers. Los Angeles had released him without pay because of a leg injury, which was suffered while running out a grounder on the lumpy Los Angeles Coliseum turf in 1960. Furillo contended that baseball blacklisted him after his dispute. He was awarded $21,000 as a settlement.

An embittered Furillo worked at several different jobs. He worked as a factory worker installing Otis elevators at the World Trade Center, as a prison guard, and as a delicatessen operator. He and his wife, Fern (Reichart), had married in 1948 and had two sons. Furillo's anger ebbed over the years as declining health and several different jobs occupied his time and energies. His older brother, Nicholas, played in the St. Louis Cardinals (NL) organization.

BIBLIOGRAPHY: Carl Furillo file, National Baseball Library, Cooperstown, NY; Bill Borst, *A Fan's Memoir: The Brooklyn Dodgers, 1953–57* (St. Louis, MO, 1982); Roger Kahn, *The Boys of Summer* (New York, 1973); Gene Karst and Martin J. Jones, Jr., *Who's Who in Professional Baseball* (New Rochelle, NY, 1973); Richard Goldstein, *Superstars and Screwballs* (New York, 1991); Peter Golenbock, *Bums* (New York, 1984); Rich Marazzi, "1955: The Boys of Summer Have Their October," *SCD* 22 (May 5, 1995), pp. 160–162; *NYT*, January 23, 1989, p. D-11; Rich Westcott, *Diamond Greats* (Westport, CT, 1988); William F. McNeil, *The Dodgers Encyclopedia* (Champaign, IL, 1997).

William A. Borst